EDWARD IRVING'S WRITINGS

SERMONS AND LECTURES

BY THE

REV. EDWARD IRVING

EDITED BY HIS NEPHEW
THE REV. G. CARLYLE, M.A

WIPF & STOCK · Eugene, Oregon

Wipf and Stock Publishers
199 W 8th Ave, Suite 3
Eugene, OR 97401

Sermons and Lectures
By Irving, Edward and Carlyle, G., M. A.
ISBN 13: 987-1-61097-236-9
Publication date 2/7/2011
Previously published by Alexander Strahan, 1864

CONTENTS.

JOHN THE BAPTIST.

LECTURE I.
LUKE III. 1, 2, ... PAGE 3

LECTURE II.
LUKE III. 3, ... 16

LECTURE III.
LUKE III. 7, 10, ... 29

LECTURE IV.
LUKE III. 10, ... 40

LECTURE V.
LUKE III., ... 56

LECTURE VI.
LUKE III. 15-18, ... 69

LECTURE VII.
LUKE III. 16-18, ... 81

LECTURE VIII.
MATT. III. 13; LUKE III., ... 95

CONTENTS.

LECTURE IX.
JOHN I. 19–28, ... 105

LECTURE X.
JOHN III. 23, ... 113

LECTURE XI.
JOHN III., ... 127

LECTURE XII.
LUKE III., ... 136

LECTURE XIII.
LUKE III. ; MATT. XIV., ... 148

LECTURE XIV.
LUKE III. ; MATT. XIV. ; MARK VI., ... 161

LECTURE XV.
LUKE III. ; MATT. XIV. ; MARK VI., ... 174

THE TEMPTATION.

LECTURE I.
LUKE IV., ... 191

LECTURE II.
LUKE IV., ... 207

LECTURE III.
LUKE IV., ... 216

LECTURE IV.
LUKE IV., ... 231

LECTURE V.
LUKE IV., ... 240

CONTENTS.

HOMILIES ON BAPTISM.

	PAGE
DEDICATION,	247

HOMILY I.
THE SIGNIFICATION OF THIS ORDINANCE, ... 249

HOMILY II.
THE SEALING VIRTUE OF BAPTISM, ... 270

HOMILY III.
THE DOCTRINE TAUGHT IN BAPTISM, ... 289

HOMILY IV.
THE NEW STANDING INTO WHICH BAPTISM BRINGETH THE CHURCH, AND THE ENGAGING PARENT OR SPONSOR, TOWARDS THE CHILD, ... 306

HOMILY V.
THE DUTIES OF THE CHURCH AND THE ENGAGING PARENT OR SPONSOR, ... 321

HOMILY VI.
THE STANDING OF THE BAPTIZED IN THE CHURCH, . . 343

HOMILY VII.
THE STANDING OF THE BAPTIZED WITH RESPECT TO THE LORD'S SUPPER, ... 358

HOMILY VIII.
CONCLUSIONS OF DOCTRINE FLOWING FROM BAPTISM, . . 375

HOMILY IX.
PRACTICAL CONCLUSIONS FLOWING FROM BAPTISM, . . 395

HOMILY X.
JUSTIFICATION AND RECAPITULATION OF THE WHOLE DOCTRINE CONTAINED IN THE ABOVE HOMILIES, . . 414

HOMILIES ON THE LORD'S SUPPER.

HOMILY I.

	PAGE
ON SELF-EXAMINATION,	435

HOMILY II.

THE THING WHICH IS SIGNIFIED IN THE LORD'S SUPPER, . 482

HOMILY III.

THE INVITATION, ADMONITION, AND ARGUMENT FOR ALL BAPTIZED PERSONS TO COME UNTO THE TABLE OF THE LORD, ... 502

HOMILY IV.

THE INVISIBLE GRACE SIGNIFIED AND CONVEYED TO THE FAITHFUL IN THE RECEIVING OF THE BREAD, . . . 526

HOMILY V.

THE RECEIVING OF THE CUP, ... 552

HOMILY VI.

THE INVISIBLE GRACE SIGNIFIED AND CONVEYED TO THE FAITHFUL IN THE RECEIVING OF THE CUP, . . . 578

HOMILY VII.

THE LORD'S SUPPER AS A COMMEMORATIVE ACT, . . . 589

HOMILY VIII.

THE SUBSTANCE OF THE DOCTRINE CONTAINED IN THE LORD'S SUPPER, ... 605

JOHN THE BAPTIST.

JOHN THE BAPTIST.

LECTURE I.

Luke III. 1, 2.

THESE verses are to the narrative which follows, of precisely the same import as the date is to a letter or any official document, ascertaining the precise time, place, and circumstances, under which the wonderful events that follow began their course; and, therefore, instead of being slightly passed over as an uninteresting enumeration of names with which the mind refuses to be burdened, they should be used by the expounder of the record, for that very purpose for which they were set down by the writer, as affording a clue by which to ascertain the veracity of the narrator, and the certainty of the things narrated. Therefore, though it may not be so agreeable to many ears to discourse of historical fact and evidence, as of orthodoxy, doctrine, and religious experience, yet, seeing the thing must sometimes be done for the conviction of the gainsayer and the knowledge of all, I hesitate not to treat of that of which the evangelist has written; of the circumstances of place and time; and the evidence thence to be derived of the character of the narrator and the things narrated.

The verses draw our attention to the state of Judæa at the time when the word of the Lord came to John, the son of Zacharias, in the wilderness. To understand the civil or political state of Judæa at this time, it is necessary to go back nearly two hundred years, when the connexion between the Jews and the Romans commenced. You will see it all recorded in the first book of the Maccabees, which, for a beautiful narrative of heroic and pious deeds, is not to be surpassed by any poetical or true history that was ever written.

A little more than three hundred years before the birth of Christ, Alexander the Great had the empire of all the East given into his hands, according to the prophecies of Daniel. He infringed in nothing the religious worship or civil immunities of the Jews, but treated them with the highest regard; while upon Thebes, and Tyre, and Gaza, and other cities around, he wreaked his utmost wrath. He left no heir to his unbounded empire, which at his death fell into the utmost troubles. Still Jerusalem was preserved from contamination by the mercy of God, and enjoyed the government of her own high-priests and laws for more than one hundred and fifty years of these troubled times. By degrees, however, she fell away from the statutes of the Lord, and profaned His holy temple. The high-priesthood was bought for money of the kings of Syria, to whom Palestine fell after the death of Alexander, and Jason the high-priest introduced heathen rites into Jerusalem, and sent offerings to Hercules, the god of Tyre. He also brought thither the customs of the Greeks, establishing games and gymnasiums, and other profanations, to which the priests and the people were speedily given up. Therefore it pleased the Lord to bring up against them the armies of Antiochus, king of Syria, who twice plundered the city, and spoiled the temple, and wrought all the abominations, with the account of which the book of the Maccabees opens. But, lest the whole land should fall away, and the promises of the Lord should fail, He raised up His servants of the house of Maccabeus, and especially Judas, one of the bravest and most heroical men that ever arose in the day of a country's need. He struggled long and sore with the armies of the oppressor, and by strength of the arm of God he did redeem the land and give it rest. But, perceiving the host gathering upon its borders like the locusts of the East, he was directed to crave the help of the Roman republic, which was beginning about this time to grapple with the strength of established thrones. And the Romans, who, in their better days, never refused to listen to the voice of the distressed, struck a league, offensive and defensive, with the Jewish people. This was not well completed till the host of the tyrant king of Syria burst upon the land of Judah once more. Judas threw himself in their way with a handful of men, and, after the most pious devotedness and valour, was cut off, with the greater part of his host. After him his brothers rose up in his stead, and kept the heart of resistance within the land, till about one hundred and forty years before the birth of Christ.

From this time, for one complete century, the high-priests assumed the state of kings; and having fallen into many quarrels amongst themselves, at length referred their disputes to the Roman consul, whose decision dissatisfied the injured party. Civil wars broke out afresh, with much confusion, and continued until forty years before Christ, when Herod, by the authority of the Romans, was settled upon the throne. Between Judas Maccabeus and Herod there intervened but one century, during which the political and persevering Romans had possessed themselves of the arbitration of the Jewish state, which shews how sore a remedy for the disturbance of any land it is to invite or permit foreign interference. This Herod, who was but the tool of Augustus Cæsar, emperor of Rome, was guilty of many cruelties, cutting off his wife and children, and addicting himself to enormous crimes. He still reigned when our Saviour was born; which event being intimated to him by the wise men from the East, brought about the murder of the innocents of Bethlehem; after which, God, unable to endure him any longer, smote him unto the death with one of the most shocking and monstrous diseases of which there is any record. Upon his death the kingdom was divided amongst his three sons, of whom two, Herod and Philip, are mentioned in the verse before us. This division took place about thirty years before the time mentioned in our text. Two of his sons still reigned over their portions at the time John came forth in the wilderness, preaching repentance for the remission of sins. The third brother, who was the oldest, had received for his share Judah and Jerusalem, over which, at the Baptist's coming forth, Pontius Pilate, a Roman, governed. The name of this brother was Archelaus, and he is made mention of by Matthew as reigning in Jerusalem when Joseph and the virgin returned out of Egypt, which deterred them from going up to Jerusalem, and made them turn aside for concealment to the despised town of Nazareth. This Archelaus having given offence to the Romans by some plots which he was making against their power, was by them removed, and his government taken into their own hands that very year our Lord appeared in the temple, and claimed it as His Father's house. The three parts, therefore, of Herod's kingdom are stated to have been in these hands at the coming forth of John—Judæa and Samaria, in the south, under Pontius Pilate, having been forfeited by Archelaus; Galilee and its coasts, in the centre, by Herod, the son of Herod; Ituræa, and the region of Trachonitis, in the west, by Philip, also the son of Herod. There is a fourth region mentioned by name, Abilene, under the administration of Lysanias, a Roman, of whom little is known. This country, Abilene, which in the Gospels is more frequently named the region about Decapolis, was a part of the ancient inheritance of Israel lying beyond the Jordan, and pertaining to half the tribe of Manasseh. It was not included in the kingdom of Herod, and it fell not to any of his sons, but was under Roman administration.

These three sons of Herod who succeeded him came each one to a dishonourable end—Archelaus dying in banishment, as did also another of them, and the third escaped by a timeous death the punishment of his crimes. This did not take place till after the death of our Lord, which was seven years from the time of the Baptist's appearance, here so circumstantially defined. During all this time, Pontius Pilate was governor of Judæa, and Herod tetrarch of Galilee; and these two became friends upon the condemnation of Christ. This is the same Herod that had John the Baptist beheaded, and the same Philip whose wife he had adopted into his house, and the Herodias whom he had adopted was his own father's daughter; and indeed the crimes of this family are not once to be named, they are so enormous. When they had died off from the earth which they had polluted, Herod Agrippa, the grandson of that Herod who sought Christ and murdered the innocents, was promoted to be their successor; and in the reign of the Emperor Claudius had also Judæa and Samaria bestowed upon him: so that under him all these four provinces mentioned in the text came to be united into one, and for three years Jerusalem again had a king. Hence, in the 12th chapter of the Acts, it is written, "Herod the king stretched forth his hands to vex certain of the church, and he killed James the brother of John with the sword. And because he saw it pleased the Jews, he proceeded further to take Peter also." After this enormity, he was not permitted long to abide upon the earth; but having gone down to Cæsarea upon a heathenish errand, he harangued the deputies of Tyre and Sidon from his throne, and was applauded as a god, at which his heart being elated with vanity, God could endure him no longer, but smote him with the most humiliating of all diseases, making him while living the food of worms. The grandsire smote the babes, the grandson smote the saints, and the vilest of creeping things smote them in their turn. We cannot dismiss this brief account of that bloodthirsty and blasphemous crew without pronouncing the old truth, that there is a God who reigneth over the realms of the earth, and bridleth their impotent rage—a God who, though He may bear with minor offences till the day of judgment, yet if any man, great or small, dare to transact enormities in His creation, He will descend at once, and smite him into pieces like a potsherd; and it will nothing avail to protect him, though, like these ancient offenders, his habitation be the munition of rocks, and his seat a well-established throne, and his speech persuasive as the voice of a god. Judgment shall reach him, and scorch him, and consume him, as easily as the fire of heaven doth pierce, and scorch, and consume the most secret and interior parts of our dwellings.

To return to our delineation of Jewish affairs at the time the Baptist came, which was the fifteenth year of the reign of Tiberius Cæsar; that is, fifteen years from the time that Augustus had taken him into a share of the government, or the twenty-sixth of our era; but it is necessary to be remembered, as we mentioned on a former occasion, that, our era not having been fixed till five hundred years after the birth of Christ, has been found by more accurate chronology to be fixed four years too late; so that, though we say it is 1822 years from the birth of Christ, it is actually 1826. Our Saviour, therefore, was in His thirty-first year, and John the Baptist some months older, when he appeared on his commission to prepare Messiah's way. From the twelfth year of Christ, when, as hath been said, the sceptre departed from Judah, and a lawgiver from between her feet, up to this His thirty-first year, during this period of nineteen years, of which we have no account in the evangelists, we know from Roman and Jewish history that Jerusalem and the land of Judah were sorely vexed with the Roman yoke. The power of life and death were taken from them, and placed in a Roman governor; their strongholds were garrisoned by Roman soldiers; justice was administered by the Roman laws; the means and property of the people were registered, and exactions taken thereon; and every other badge of a conquered province was laid upon them. Only in matters of religion, of which the Romans were always very tolerant, were they left in possession of their proper customs. They retained their sanhedrim or national assembly, and their high-priest, and their feasts, and the service of their temple; and a certain respect also, when it could be done, was given to their national laws and customs.

Now it could not otherwise be expected than that the Jews, the most ancient and high-minded of nations, so often preserved by special interpositions of Jehovah, should groan under such a bondage. They were expressly commanded in the book of the law, "One from among thy brethren shalt thou set king over thee: thou mayest not set a stranger over thee, which is not thy brother." The people were fain to submit, and to pay tribute to Cæsar; but they held the principle that it was not right, and came upon our Saviour with that most popular question, Whether it was lawful to pay tribute to him? thinking to disgust the people with Him, if He answered, Yea; and if He answered, Nay, to embroil Him with the ruling powers. Hence also publicans, who were such as farmed the imposts from the Romans, were held in great hatred as a sacrilegious race, who lent themselves to the violation of the nation's heaven-derived rights, and were placed under the ban of excommunication, so that no one would eat with them; and it was brought as a chief accusation against our Saviour, that He did eat with publicans and sinners. One small relic of independency they still possessed in their high-priest. Of this Luke has not been unmindful, in fixing the time and circumstance at which the event he hath recorded took place—Annas and Caiaphas being the high-priests. This seems to bear against that law of the Jews which appointed there should be but one high-priest at a time. But though, properly speaking, there was never but one high-priest, he had always a substitute to officiate in his stead, in case of any accident or ritual uncleanness disqualifying him from his duties. This personage is denominated in the last chapter of Jeremiah the second priest. In the eleventh of John's Gospel they are joined together by the appellation of the chief priests. The most probable solution of the difficulty that two are named in the passage before us is this, that Annas was the chief priest, and Caiaphas his son-in-law was associated with him in office. The appointing of the high-priest was at this time usurped by the Romans, and there were changes in it almost every year. Hence the expression in John, "Caiaphas was high-priest that same year." Hence also this Annas, who was superseded during our Lord's ministry by Caiaphas, we find again at the head of affairs after the day of Pentecost, when they hauled Peter before him to answer for his preaching. The probability is, that whether in office or out of office, Annas, whose experience had been great, having been high-priest fifteen years before this time, took the sway over Caiaphas, his son-in-law, who had never before held this most responsible office. It is also worthy of remark that the most approved reading of the passage is not "high-priests," but "high-priest:" "Annas being the high-priest, and Caiaphas," a form of expression which manifestly throws Caiaphas into the secondary place mentioned above.

Such, then, was the state of civil and ecclesiastical affairs when John the Baptist came forth from the recesses of the wilderness, in which he had grown in serene and solitary devotion apart from the haunts of men; visited, doubtless, as was Elias, with special messengers from on high, to occupy his time and thoughts with the high commission on which he was about to appear. The time and condition of things are narrated with the same exactness with which the prophecies of the Old Testament are opened, and with the same form of expression—"The word of the Lord came to him in the wilderness." There he was reserved, his body communing with the inclemency of earth and heaven, annealing itself to severe encounters, his soul turned inward upon itself, and upward to God, uninfluenced by compliances, untamed by customs, filled with meditation and the Spirit of God. He waited the appointed time when God should call him; and, when called, he issued fearlessly upon his office, which the wickedness of Herod and Herod's adulterous wife permitted him only three years and a half to occupy. Then Jesus stepped forth at large into the room of His precursor, and for the same space of three years and a half was permitted to occupy His office of salvation, completing between them the one week of the prophet Daniel, during which the covenant was to be confirmed with many; for a week in the prophetic language is seven years.

It is not necessary with intelligent men, who seek the good of knowledge, and the satisfaction of doubt, and the clearing up of difficulty, no less than the establishment of doctrinal discourse, to make any apology for the above information, which has been collected from the most authentic sources. But I should not have been at the pains of collecting it, had it not been of the utmost importance, not only to the doctrinal understanding of the whole narrative that is to follow, but especially to the verification of the facts attendant upon John's appearance. These facts are of the highest consequence to the ascertaining of our Saviour's commission; for this was the occasion upon which he came among the rest to be baptized. John publicly refused, but being commanded, obeyed, upon which a voice from heaven proclaimed, and a dove from heaven pointed out, the One whom God honoured by the name of beloved Son, and announced as the sin-offering of the world. This, Christ made the foundation of His claim; this, His disciples appealed to; and it is of the utmost importance that this should be well authenticated to all coming ages. Now, we shall shew that the vouchers which authenticate it lie all in the appendage of the date; and had it not been for the most minute way in which it is dated, had these two verses on which we lecture been awanting, I hesitate not to say that it would have been difficult, perhaps impossible, to deal with an adversary. As it is, I shall build upon it an argument on which I am willing, in any similar case that might now occur, to stake not only faith, but fortune and life.

First, then, it is to be observed that this gospel or history of Christ, containing, amongst other things, this narrative of John's preaching and Christ's baptism and divine separation in presence of all, must have been in circulation within thirty years after these events. For the author of this treatise wrote another subsequently to this, the Acts of the Apostles, in which he speaks of himself as having been an actor; so that this Gospel was written in the lifetime of one who bore a part in the actions which immediately ensued. Now, his second treatise, the Acts, brings down matters to sixty years after Christ's birth, or thirty years after the date mentioned in our text; so that this Gospel being finished before the Acts were begun, and sent to Theophilus, must, at the very latest calculation, have come into circulation within thirty years after the events here recorded, when a great part of the multitude baptized by John must have been still alive, and many who were eye-witnesses and ear-witnesses to the separation of Christ must have been living, to contradict the thing if it was not so. I take for granted that the treatise of Luke, so soon as it was written, was spread abroad, and not confined to a corner. Of this we have far more evidence than could have been expected at such a distance of time, not only of the circulation of Luke's Gospel, but also of the other three. In a century they had, by their superior worth, thrust out of notice the various other narratives which had been drawn up and circulated of the gospel history. Before that time they are quoted from by Christian writers as if universally acknowledged. Nay, in little more than a century, a book was actually composed, by name, a harmony of the four. Now, this could not otherwise have happened in times when there was no art of printing, but by the most rapid and free diffusion of the books, and the most eager desire to transcribe them.

It is, therefore, beyond a doubt, that, however much earlier, certainly within thirty years from the date of John's baptism, this narrative was circulating upon the spot where the very events narrated took place, and where the memory of events so singular must have been as fresh as the memory of the French Revolution is amongst us at this day. Now, do but conceive how strong a test this is to the truth of everything narrated. Suppose a similar case. Say that a book were published and circulated in London by a set of men as the foundation of their claims to belief—by the followers, say, of Johanna Southcot; and that this their public document commenced by saying that, at the beginning of this century, in the fortieth year of George III., when such a man was mayor of London, and such another high sheriff of the county, and such another lord bishop of the diocese. At that time, dated after the manner of our text, there came a man out of some neighbouring forest, say Epping Forest, to the banks of the Thames. That he was dressed in the most uncouth and savage attire, and fed on the roots of the earth, refusing all the comforts, and despising all the forms of civilised life. That he lifted up his voice day by day, sparing no rank nor description of men, and night by night retiring into the gloomy and savage wilderness, from whence he issued again only to take up his woeful burden against the universal declension of the land; until the whole of the city was moved to its centre, and went forth with one consent to hear the savage and severe denouncer of their conditions. That, in our hearing, he pronounced our priests hypocrites, our rulers extortioners, our soldiers spoilers, and all men gone astray and needing repentance; and having done his terrible office day by day, he returned night by night to the wilds of nature, and harboured with the savage tenants there. Let us be told, moreover, that the man was no raving fool, but of such terrible energy of eloquence that the common herd quailed before him, and every rank, stooping its particular pride, craved of him what he wished them to do—the priests, the governors, the soldiers; that the general inhabitants flocked to him, and rank after rank submitted to be schooled by him. Upon which he requires of every man the unseemly and inconvenient rule of allowing himself to be taken and by him dipped in the river, with certain solemn promises of repentance and reformation. Let us be told, moreover, that thirty years ago, while all this was going on, and multitudes were submitting soul and body to the terrible reformer, there came from the assembled thousands one youth, at the sight of whom the haughty preacher stood humbled and abashed; that the preacher refused to do the duty for him alone of all, declaring himself to need his ablution, and that he was not able to tie the latchet of his shoe. Let us be told, moreover, that in our sight and hearing the modest stranger declined the honour, and insisted upon submitting to the ritual, that upon his coming up out of the water, there descended, cleaving the clear blue heavens, a dove, which lighted and sat upon his head in the midst of the assembly, all-forgetful of its timorous nature, whereupon the hollow vault was filled with a voice like the voice of thunder, and from the empyrean descended these solemn words, "This is my beloved son, in whom I am well pleased."

I say, let the followers of any religious sect that started into being thirty years ago, ay, I may say fifty years ago, or one hundred or two hundred years ago, set forth such a story as this now related as the ground of their claim to divine origin, and insist thereon that we should break up our whole establishment of church and state, and model ourselves upon their outlandish and novel doctrines. Would people, building upon so extraordinary a tale, so lately happened, so much in our power to remember, or so much in our fathers' power, or in our fathers' fathers, would they obtain one single convert? The very publicity of the thing, the extraordinary nature of it, would at once expose its untruth if so be it happened not. Any one who should set up his face for it, would be hooted as an idiot, or silenced as a terrible liar; and if he had ultimate views, he would be put out of the way as a most unblushing and horrible knave. He and his infamous trash would be spouted forth with the highest indignation and the most sovereign disgust from the ear and faith of every man but a bedlamite or a fool. But such was not the case with this narrative, though beginning with precisely such a tale; it was received, and believed in, and made converts, thousands in a day, who sacrificed all their wealth for it, and many of them their lives also. That, I say again, is to my mind the most indubitable proof that the whole affair actually happened as it is narrated; unless the people of Jerusalem were with one consent resolved to be duped, and for the sake of being duped, which men hate as they hate death, for this were resolved to sacrifice all possessions, life present, and hope of the life to come.

Now, all the weight of evidence rests mainly upon the narrative being dated. Say such a narrative of events by the river Thames had come forth without being dated, like the story of Whittington, or the tale of Nigel's fortunes, then it might have got into circulation for the pleasant moral or the great talent of it, or some other recommendation, and no one might have taken the pains to expiscate the truth. Then after lying dormant a season, it might be brought to light, and set forth as having been once received, and therefore entitled to credit, and so slip into currency without having even received the necessary sifting. But not so when it hath a date, and that date within the memory of living men, or men lately departed. That is a challenge of every man's veracity. Each one is pitched against it; and each one, if it be worth his while, will expose it, so that it can never creep into circulation through the remissness or neglect of the people.

Of so much consequence to the whole ensuing narrative are these two verses, which the modern taste of discoursing would pass by as utterly unprofitable, for some matter of a more latent and popular kind. But conceiving the religion of a country to rest upon many pillars, which are founded all upon the Word of God, and that we Christians are set by the state to uphold it each in his proper sphere, I confess I cannot in conscience permit any opportunity to pass of bringing any illustration or strength to the Divine record on which our whole faith is pillared.

Let me urge every one to the serious consideration, not of the evidence only, but of the matter which John came to preach—repentance for the remission of sins. This is the beginning of a spiritual life, the foundation of religion—repentance, with a view to the remission of sins through the blood of Christ.

LECTURE II.

LUKE III. 3.

HEROD the Great and Archelaus, his son, who ruled Judah and Jerusalem for more than fifty years previous to Christ's first appearance in the temple, were placed upon the throne by the influence of Rome, and held it only upon their good and respectful behaviour to the emperor. Their policy was therefore not Jewish but Roman, and bore directly against the national feeling, which burst out from time to time among the priests and the people. Every patriotic man was cut off from appointments in church or state; creatures of the reigning power were introduced into office; and all things adverse to the independence and freedom of the nation were promoted. When Archelaus was deposed, the sceptre departed from Judah and a lawgiver from between her feet, and she became in appearance, as well as in truth, a conquered, subjugated province. In this state she had continued now for eighteen years, having been fleeced by four successive governors, who, so much as is known of them, had a bad reputation even in that Augustan age of rapacious governors; and Pontius Pilate, who now held the reins under Tiberius, was noted for a flagitious and unprincipled man.

For any high-minded nation to be ruled for fifty years by foreign influence, and for eighteen more to be galled by a foreign yoke—for an imperial city, which for twelve centuries had reared its head in imperial greatness, to be overawed by the presence of outlandish soldiers, spoiled by the exactions of rapacious governors, and treated after the forms and fashions of foreign laws, hath always been considered by men as the sorest tribulation under which they can groan, and as calling for the sacrifice of their dearest blood in order to shake it off. But for Judah and Jerusalem to be so enslaved—the tribe and city of

David, the seat of God's temple and of His holy presence, whose walls had been built in troublous times and defended by the Lord of hosts in the face of all nations—must have been tenfold misery. Their law to be discarded, which had been given at Mount Sinai; their sceptre to be beaten in pieces, which had been promised to be everlasting; their holy hill to be made the citadel of an uncircumcised soldiery; and their streets, which had echoed to the minstrelsy of David and his sacred choir, to be invaded with the ensigns and march and music of a Gentile nation, hardly known to them longer than a century—this must have been insufferable to the noble feelings and ancient spirit of the people, no less than the actual imposts were oppressive to their worldly comfort and prosperity. And to crown all, they had Moses and the prophets read to them daily in their synagogues—Moses, who reminded them of God's selection and nurse-like watchfulness of their infant nation, and His condescending to become their Lawgiver and King; the prophets, who were wont to deal the woes of God upon the nations round about, and to comfort Israel with the tidings of a great deliverance. Those prophets to whom the fates had been revealed were now no more. For five centuries no seer had arisen in Israel to foretell the end of her calamities. These had thickened around her until the enemy had entered into her city, over which many years revolved with no vestiges of hope or better fortune in reserve.

This was the sad condition of the holy city upon which Isaiah cast his prophetic eye; and seeing in the depths of the gloomy darkness which overspread her hopes, the harbinger of a great deliverance appearing, he lifted up his voice, as if he had been one of the people who were suffering the misery of forlorn fortunes and departed hopes, and cried, "Comfort ye, comfort ye my people, saith your God. Speak ye comfortably unto Jerusalem, and cry unto her that her warfare is accomplished and her iniquity is pardoned, for she hath received of the Lord's hand double for all her sins. The voice of him that crieth in the wilderness, Prepare ye the way of the Lord, make straight in the desert a highway for our God. Every valley shall be exalted, and every mountain and hill shall be made low; and the crooked shall be made straight, and the rough places made plain; and the glory of the Lord shall be revealed, and all flesh shall see it, for the mouth of the Lord hath spoken it." This which Isaiah saw with his prophetic eye, and spoke in figurative disguise six hundred years before, the Lord now prepared His hand to fulfil by the ministry of His servant John, whom He had brought into the world and educated for that single intent. But to understand the fulfilment, you must understand the language in which the prophecy is written, for it is all an emblem of the moral condition of men. The wilderness from the midst of which John was to cry, and the desert over which a pathway for the Lord was to be prepared, is that same wilderness and solitary place which, in another place, he saith was to become glad—that same desert which was to rejoice and blossom like a rose; and the glory of the Lord which was to be revealed, and which all flesh should behold, is the pacification of the warring inhabitants and elements of the earth, which in that same place he describeth, when there shall be " nothing to hurt or to destroy in all my holy mountain; for the earth shall be full of the knowledge of the Lord as the waters cover the sea."

John was to pioneer the way for this grand proclamation of peace and goodwill on earth. He was first to face the rugged wastes of moral nature, and lift up his voice through all its desolation, commanding the valleys to be filled, and the high places to be abased, and the crooked places to be made straight, and the rough places to be made plain: that is, he was to summon every obstruction to Messiah the Prince to give way and surrender; he was to rebuke the proud elevations of human life which might resist Him; he was to raise and comfort the depressed conditions of life which had cast away hopes of Him; he was to rebuke the uneven and crooked policies of men, which would eye Him askance, and wilfully mistake Him; and the rough severities and unpeaceful tempers of life which would tear the Saviour's dove-like affections, he was to tame and smooth for His coming. For the moral world was then a wilderness, whereon grew at pleasure every rank and noxious weed, and wherein raged every excessive passion and brutal lust. There was a hot warfare of every interest—people struggling with princes, and princes with each other;

knowledge making for itself a place, and obliged thereto to shut itself up in the strong tower of stoical apathy. But especially had the daughters of impurity possessed the people; and liberty lived no longer upon the world, save amongst the recesses of the north and east, where it lived by the strength of the desolation which frowned around it. The world was a waste howling wilderness, in which no repose of peace, nor voice of happiness was heard, and speculation wearied out, and hope sickened to death, had fled the breasts of all, save a few who were persecuted out of life.

It was no easy ministry to enter unbefriended into this hot warfare of lust and pride and passion, and meet it in the face, and struggle with it single-handed and alone. To rebuke the soldier in his fiercest moods, to discover the priest in his most hidden and secret hypocrisies, to bridle kings in the race of their powerful wickedness, and in the breasts of oppressed and degraded people to kindle the spark of hope and feeling anew, —such was the Baptist's office in that wilderness, into which, for five hundred years, no pruning, reforming hand had been sent by Heaven. It was the sublimest and the most terrible position into which a frail man could be put by the Almighty, and I much question whether another mortal hath ever occupied a similar position. Christ afterwards sent out twelve, then seventy, in bands of two, to cultivate the ground the Baptist had broken up; but the Baptist was alone upon the ground. Elias, whom the Baptist much resembled, was left alone among the prophets; but Elias was the remnant of many whose example he had before him. John was the beginning of a new race. Elias fled from the face of the persecutor; John fled not, but bearded power in its very palace. Elias had a miraculous Hand to sustain his words with signs; John did no miracle, but had to stand in his own defenceless humanity. He was to attack the universal customs and likings of men, and all his armoury was his voice. Samson the Nazarite had a work to work, and the strength to perform it was placed in his hair. John had a greater work to work, and the power to perform it was his voice. "What art thou?" said the Pharisees. "I am the voice of one crying in the wilderness," replied the Baptist.

To educate him for this terrible office, (for the Lord doth not despise the education of His ministers, as do many modern upstart sects,) he was subjected to the rite of the Nazarite, by which no razor could come upon his head, and no strong drink pass his lips, and no luxury soften the severity of his holy office. Such should ever be the ritual of a true reformer and missionary. And he who cannot keep his body under, and put it, when need is, upon the shortest, hardest allowance, is not worthy to talk to others of restraining and restricting their present indulgences of power and pleasure within narrow bounds. And the Baptist had his habitation in the wilderness; he fared upon locusts and the wild honey, and he girdled his loins with the hair of the camel. "The child grew, and waxed strong in spirit, and was in the desert till the day of his shewing unto Israel:" that is, till his thirtieth year. What he communed with, or how he spent his time, God hath not informed us; but, as hath been said, it was a noble training for the rebuker and reprover of a world, for a greatly endowed and virtuously disposed mind hath nothing to fear from solitude. Our Saxon Alfred came forth from his shepherd concealment recruited by meditation with his own soul, with nature, and with nature's God, and refreshed for the deliverance of England. Gustavus Vasa of Sweden came forth from his concealment amongst the miners of Dalicarlia, and overthrew, in the strength of severe virtue, the oppression of the Dane. ·Hoffer, whose name is holy in the bosom of oppressed ones over the face of Europe, before he made his demonstration for the Tyrolese, retired to the loneliest mountain of the Alps, and dwelt many days apart from men, feeding upon the milk of a goat, his only companion, and then came forth purified from all sinister intention by communion with his Maker, to whom, unlike our home-bred patriots and reformers, he did devote his whole soul; and he ceased not from the work to which he had girded up his soul until the earth beneath his scaffold drank the blood which no bribes of the usurper could corrupt. And so also of religion it hath been found; for religion and freedom are twin-sisters, which may never be parted without risk to both. Christ, after His baptism and setting apart, we have no account of for three years, during which He doubtless counted the cost of His undertaking. Paul being called, retired three years no one knows whither, and came forth to shatter the theology and customs of Judæa, Greece, and Rome. Luther came forth from his temporary concealment, like a lion from his den, to roar in the teeth of all his foes. Knox meditated with his noble soul his pious work of reformation while he was lashed to the oar like a convict upon the rivers of France, and from his place of banishment he blew the first blast of his trumpet; after which he returned, like a flame of pure fire, to set his country in a blaze of religious ardour, and, like a pillar of fire, to guide them in their most glorious work. And what is there good that cometh not out of suffering? and what is there great that cometh not out of self-denial? what is there new in knowledge or in virtue that cometh not out of solitary thought? and what is there noble and lasting in purpose that cometh not out of long nursing and strengthening in the secret chambers of the mind?

Now John, as hath been said, had given unto him the most terrible office of attacking everything in society's customs which might impede the progress and success of Him that was to follow after. It was needful, therefore, that he should be armed at every point to meet opposition, that he should have nothing to love but his life, and nothing that he cared for but the end and object of his mission. Therefore he was taught to brave life's hated extremities; abstemiousness was his highest feast, and I doubt not hunger and thirst and nakedness were his familiar friends. And looking upon the wild beasts of the desert, he would not fear the face of an infuriated man or a blood-thirsty woman. What to him was a scowling Pharisee, or a mocking Sadducee, or a fawning publican, or a rough soldier, or a riotous mob?—these were jocund, cheerful sights to one who had roamed amongst the roaming denizens of the desert, and in the midst of them laid his head down under no canopy and with no defence but the canopy and defence of the providence of the Most High. And what lessons of Providence he would learn during these trials and troubles of his forlorn estate! For without many such interferences, he must have perished utterly. And what time for conning the Word of God, and holding communion with Him that was with His people forty years in the wilderness! And what a nursery for schooling the young Nazarite into contempt of those stately forms and cunning disguises in which sin doth prank herself, the vanities, the affectations, the pomp and circumstance, and painted decorations, under which wickedness hides her shocking head and vile deformed person! What a school for the severe and terrible moods of the Spirit which he was called to utter; what a rough training for a rough prophet! He was to weep with no lamentation, like Jeremiah; he was not to ride in the chariot of the sublime, like Isaiah; or clothe himself with the cloudy mysteriousness of Ezekiel, nor flee like Jonah; but he was to strike home at every thrust the point blank of his rebuke, was to shake and shiver and demolish the retreats of self-esteem. He was to lay every man a wreck upon the waves, and disappoint him thoroughly of all his bravery, and bring all to one common confessional, and make them passive under the same rebuke, and submit them to the same humiliating rite of washing and cleansing. He was to spare no living wight; the portals of the palace were not to be sacred against the spiritual leveller, nor beautiful women to be sacred from his uncivil tongue. If such a preacher was to appear again even here in this Christian island, leaving rule aside, and striking into the bosom of every corruption the land groaneth under, why, the religious would disown him, saying that he was no preacher of the peaceful Jesus, and the irreligious would wag their heads at him in scorn, and power would libel him, and a prison or worse would be his certain doom.

Foreordained in the ancient prophecies to such an office, given of God to childless parents for such an office, educated for it, and now, after thirty years' most special education, called to it, what topic was meet for him to preach,—what single word could express his many-toned exhortations and his much-varied rebukes,—what single word express the soul and intention of his office,—what word but this single one, repentance, change of mind, and change of life? The word of the Lord came unto him in the wilderness, and he came into all the region about Jordan, preaching the baptism of repentance unto the remission of sin. His business, as hath been said, was to level and reform the sinful exuberances of his countrymen, and bring them under a common sentiment of unworthiness, that they might welcome him who came in the name of the Lord to save. Therefore he preached repentance and a change of life. His brief exhortation was—" Repent and be baptized, confessing your sins."

There must have been in the tongue of this wayfarer of the desert some terrible fire of conviction, some wonderful unction of holiness, that with such a brief in his hand he should have found any audience or verdict in his favour. To come criminating men with one general accusation of wickedness, remorselessly cutting through all decent disguises into the naked breast of their character,—without any insinuation of manner or soft forms of language,—without smiles, apologies, or any indulgence, to cut up the whole form of life, and with ruthless denunciation devote it like chaff to the whirling fire of hell; all unaided, unbefriended, a savage man to do this, and in no strength but the intrinsical beauty of holiness and odiousness of sin, to carry his point with all classes of the community, is one of the noblest triumphs of the truth; and it ought to encourage for ever the lonely possessor of any truth to give it forth to the world, in the assured hope that the Father of truth will sooner or later find for it acceptance. John's success is not a matter of speculation, but is recorded in this very chapter. His method of discourse is also upon record, and no matter of speculation. Such a severe and heart-piercing style of ministering religious truth may, by the blessing of God, do good in this lame age of the Church; and we shall therefore do our utmost to give it breadth of exposition in our future discourses.

But our object at present, after contemplating the sublime position of the Baptist as the great forerunner of Messiah, is to study the method which he took in executing his office. They are wont to tell you upon all hands that the way to herald the good news of the gospel of peace is to droop the wing, and glide softly and gently into the hearts of the people; and every other method they decry as improper and unpropitious to the gospel of peace. But they know not what they talk about, neither do they know the history of the propagation of the gospel. Here is John, the first herald of salvation; his was a withering blast. There is Christ, the very Teacher: what a stern upbraider was He of worldly customs! Few are the honeyed words of His speech. There was Stephen after Him, who cut the people to the heart, so that they gnashed on him with their teeth. There was Paul, that uncourtly apostle, who had the presumption to speak to kings of temperance in their pleasures, of righteousness in their power, and of judgment to come, to bridle their haughty dealings. There were all the prophets before the inauguration of the gospel; there have been all the reformers since. Were they sleek and silken men? No; they were terrible men. Were they prudential men? No; they were men who bore their lives in their hand, and wore their wealth in thin rags of clothing, and had all their preferment in heaven. Well then, I ask, whence cometh this universal call for soft, prudential, complimentary discourse? Who hath commanded it? When did it reform the Church, or propagate the faith, or purify morals, or put Satan and his power to flight? Out upon it; it is a taste, an ephemeral taste, that hath no sanction in any age of the Church. 'Tis an upstart of the worldly wisdom that hath now the helm of presidency, a product of that soft enjoyment to which all men, religious and irreligious, would devote themselves.

What an ungracious orator was this John the Baptist—a very firebrand, a most unguarded man. He joined himself to no party; he entered into no paction with any one; he sought no backing; he trusted to the truth he had in commission to make its own way. His was to give it voice, God's to give it success. And behold how successful he was withal! He excited a sensation, and, as is usual, roused the jealousy of the vested interests. They sent to know what or who he was, and in what right he spoke. He answered that he was a voice, and no more; that his speech was all he was good for, and all he wished to stand by. To that he referred them, leaving them to digest its severe sentences as best they might.

Now it seemeth to me that the Baptist is the type of every herald of salvation. We have to do with the same overgrown wilderness of moral life. There are the same towers of pride and mountains of vanity to be brought low; the same hollow hopelessness and deep despair to be filled with consolation and assurance; the same rough asperities of character to be shorn smooth; the same crooked and intriguing policies to be made straight, that the gospel of Christ may have free course and be glorified; there is the same gate upon the heart to be lifted up; the same bolted, barred gates have to lift up their heads, that the King of glory may enter in. I do therefore consider the Baptist as our pattern and permission to take strong weapons of argument, and terrible denunciation, wherewithal to clear away these obstructions, and make a highway for the descent of our Lord. Christ came not until the Baptist had come. The gospel of salvation cometh not until the fear of condemnation and ruin hath seized us. The Baptist rested his lever upon the instant coming of Christ, and from that fulcrum took his purchase upon the present. The preparation took its character from that which was to be prepared for. The usher and forerunner made his address and approach as beseemed the character of Him who was to follow. From which I conclude that this previous debate, this work of the pioneer before the main battle, should by the preacher have a Christian bearing and intention. Though he discourses bitterly and terribly against all forms and conditions of the world which repulse the progress of Christ, and without remorse demolishes them, he is to do so only to open up the way of Christ, not out of natural violence of temper, not out of the sourness of disgust, not out of satirical taste, not out of conscious power, not out of ambitious levellings of dignities, nor cruel anatomy of characters—these are mean advantages taken of this dignified place, unholy weapons which God blesseth not; and they are to be exploded for ever from this divine service. Not the less is severity of manner and strength of argument, and dissection of character, and every other method of demolition to be employed, but employed with the view and intent of opening an easier passage for Christ the Saviour, who cannot come until the towers of carnal security have been shaken, and the refuges of lies destroyed. Such weapons of our warfare are not only legitimate, but they are commanded to be used. John the Baptist is the great type and emblem of this preliminary discoursing, and he is not a well instructed scribe, nor a wise disciple, who doth not so employ the preliminary pioneering of the way as well as the main battle.

Therefore, in the free exercise of my vocation, I command all to repent, every one of his peculiar transgressions, and to flee from the wrath to come. "Turn ye, turn ye, why will ye die, ye that work iniquity." There cometh One who shall lay the axe to the root of the tree and consign every unfruitful one to fire unquenchable. He shall separate the wheat from the chaff, preserving the one in His garner, consuming the other with fire. A few years, and the voice of the preacher will be heard no more. A few years, and the overtures of salvation will be unclasped no more. A few years, and your ear will listen only to the shrieks of horror and the throes of despair. And a drop of water to cool your tongue will not be able to be commanded by the soul which now refuseth all the treasures which heaven contains.

And, will ye then die with the voice of salvation in your ear, and the pledge of salvation in your hand? Why will you do so? What gain ye by such a course? What? What? Some miserable pittance of world's wealth and enjoyment for a transient season. Say it were a coronet, what then?—say it were a throne, what then?—say it were the wide world, "what is a man profited though he should gain the whole world and lose his own soul?"

Turn, then, each one from your sins, that your immortal soul, against which a world is no equivalent, perish not; turn unto God confessing your sins, for "He is faithful and just to forgive us our sins," and "the blood of Christ cleanseth from all sin." The end of all things seen and temporal is at hand. The beginning of all things spiritual and eternal is at hand. "There is no device in the grave, whither we hasten." And at the judgment-seat, nothing but a changed life hath any hearing, and from the judgment-seat there is no appeal, and in hell there is no repentance nor city of refuge.

Therefore, now, while the light of heaven gleameth in your eye, and the soul stayeth in her insecure and fragile tabernacle, even now, ere death's finger hath stopped your ear from all hearing of salvation, and your soul from all tender touch of remorse,—now while God lingereth, yea, lingereth at the solicitation of the Vine-dresser, ere He cut you down as cumberers of the ground,—turn even now at the voice of this remonstrance that His Spirit hath sent on purpose to quicken and resuscitate decayed and irresolute souls,—now, now, come confessing your sins, and seeking of the Holy Ghost what you shall do to inherit eternal life.

And, ye generation of godless rebels, that refuse and will not come to any terms, however gracious, but hold out in perfect contempt of God, the sands of your life are fast ebbing, and the last particle shall soon fall, and you shall sink speechless into the waste places of spirits reprobate; when desolation's blast shall come over your well-being, as the whirlwind cometh over the deep; and changeless, pitiless, iron-clasped destiny shall engirdle you for ever.

Therefore let the vicious man break his vicious engagements, and the blasphemous dismiss his oaths, and the unjust man restore fourfold of his ill-gotten gains, and the impure man cleanse himself, and the proud man humble himself to a praying mood, and the vain man clothe his vanity in self-abasement, and all put on bowels of charity, and robes of holiness. For He cometh, He cometh, " and every eye shall see Him, and they that pierced Him shall mourn and weep, and they that trampled Him under foot shall call upon the hills to cover them from His terrible vengeance." But He shall come, not in human guise a simple peasant youth, as He came to the baptizing of John, He shall come in the clouds of heaven, with the archangel and the trump of God; and His enemies shall flee howling from His terrible presence and consuming wrath.

The children of Israel repented at the preaching of John the Baptist, and were baptized in the waters of Jordan, confessing their sins. They went forth from Jerusalem, hardened in wickedness and guilt—they came home humbled in spirit, dressed like modest virgins to meet the Bridegroom when He might arrive. But ye, shall I say ye all repent, and resolve in the strength of God to change the tenor of your ways? Then God speed ye, and advance ye in holiness, that ye may be ready to meet the great Bridegroom when He cometh, and enter with Him into the marriage-feast, and for ever live in the mansions which He hath prepared for you, with the banner of His love over your heads, and the praise of His love on your lips, and the sense of His love ruling in your hearts.

LECTURE III.

LUKE III. 7, 10.

IN our last discourse we considered John, the precursor of Christ, as an emblem of that precursive work which must always precede the reception of Christ, and the desert in which he lifted up his voice, commanding it to be levelled and dressed for the approach of One that was coming, we did regard as an emblem of that moral wilderness of pride, cruelty, cunning, and lust, upon which the gospel, according as it advanceth, worketh a pruning, repressing, and purifying influence; and we took to the pastoral office an equal liberty to pull down and demolish, to rebuke, to condemn, to pour and utter wrath and indignation upon every evil thing that exalteth itself against the coming of Christ. And if any challenge us for following such a course, or ask at us our authority for such a daring invasion upon the pleasant places of their fond affections, it is our part to answer them as the Baptist did, "that we are the voice of one crying in the wilderness," and that not we, but God, is responsible for the fearful tidings which we bring. For it seems to me, that though the ministers of religion be not called to any catholic renouncement of home and its soft affections, nor of the world and its active intercourse, but rather to set forth therein before the common eye the wisdom and discipline of Christ, they should be on their guard lest by these or other tender attachments, by the fear of the world's power or lofty patronage, they be led to attemper the severe and terrible truth to the feelings of a soft and luxurious age.

In which expostulation with the temper of the times and the shackled state of the prophetic office, we doubt not that many whose ears have been accustomed to the soft and slender tones of peace wherewith the land abounded, and spoiled for the audience of anything resolute and terrible, did think we were of a cruel and biting temper, unkind and unevangelical, in which they are indeed deceived; for we only sought, against the stomach of our own feeling, to catch the spirit of the unabashed Nazarite of the desert, conceiving that this city before which we testify hath much need of the same weeding and pruning and gracious reformation; and therefore we shall not shrink from continuing that which we have begun, and pursuing the Baptist's short-lived and shortly-recorded ministry in the same spirit in which it was uttered by the Baptist and is recorded by our evangelist.

The Baptist came forth in rough and hairy garments from his rough and desert abode, and the multitude assembled from Jerusalem and the country around Jordan, to the skirts of the desert, to hear the sublime and solitary man; but rougher far than hairy raiment or rocky wild was that ungentle voice which he rung among the thousands of Israel. Such a salutation as he opened with never perhaps smote the pride of any assembly, "O generation of vipers!" It was bitterly, it was uncourtly, but oh, it was truly said. They were the offspring of vipers: for often had their fathers stung to the death the benefactors, the saviours, sent from heaven to save the nation, and soon were the children to shew themselves born in the likeness of their sires, by stinging with persecution and death him before whose voice of judgment they now stood abashed, and that greater One whose shoe-latchet he was not worthy to unloose. And to this biting salutation he adds the cold, sarcastic question, "Who hath warned you to flee from the wrath to come?"—no congratulation that they had taken flight, no cheerful welcome, no encouragement to persevere—nothing but the taunting question, "Who hath warned you?" It was no wish for information that moved the interrogation, for he knew well who and what had moved them; but it was to upbraid them with all the calls and messages their worthless nation had spurned, to express wonder that any warning should have virtue to bestir them, and to set their spirits on the search whether motives of curiosity, of censure, or of malice did not bring them together. Out of one form of speech into another he casts the burning indignation of his spirit, composing altogether a very masterpiece of the indignant and scornful style so frequent in the prophets, and always the best suited to a declining age. His next stroke is a summons—an unwelcome summons—at their cold, formal, and lifeless hearts, " Bring forth the fruits meet for repentance." Well they knew whereat this blow was aimed, at their ritual and ceremonial fervour, upon which they built their assurance of salvation—"I thank Thee, O God, that I am not as other men are—extortioners, unjust, adulterers, or even as this publican. I fast twice in the week. I give tithes of all that I possess ;"—and well they knew how ungracious were these fruits of repentance—humility towards God, and love towards men, defence of the widow and the injured, protection to the stranger and the cripple, and justice towards all. All this they had learnt, or might have learnt, from their prophets, and especially from Isaiah, the opening expostulation of whose prophecy is the best commentary upon this address of the Baptist. But the last is the unkindest cut of all, " And go not to say, We have Abraham for our father." This was the very palladium of the nation, to which they confided when driven from every other hope. How they used to recoil upon our Saviour, "We be Abraham's seed, and were never in bondage unto any man." "Abraham is our father:" " art Thou greater than our father Abraham?" This John touches with sacrilegious hand, and tells them in his iron-hearted tone, "I say unto you that God is able of these stones to raise up children unto Abraham." Take no credit, then, for circumcision and pure descent; dismiss all your confidence in the promise made to your father: for the stones you tread upon might have been entitled to as much. If upon these stones—I fancy the Baptist casting his eye around the rocky waste— the Spirit of the Lord should breathe, as upon the dry bones in Ezekiel's valley of vision, and they should receive the breath of life, and arise full of thought and feeling, what would you, O generation of vipers, think if the thoughtless, ungrateful creatures, new started into conscious being, should employ their first faculty of thought and speech in casting contempt upon the rock from which they were hewn, and the hole of the pit from which they were dug—in boasting themselves before their Maker of their newly-derived honour, and challenging Him, as He had now endued them with animation, 'twere monstrous cruelty and high injustice not to lift them higher still, even to the very highest, and bestow upon them the nearest or equal honour to Himself? And you, ye ungodly race, will go to boast of your high original in the ears of God's deputies, and claim right upon the head of special favour; and because God hath favoured you most of nations, ye will therefore expect to continue most favoured still; nay, ye will take His heaven by storm, ye will have it over the head of your ingratitude and all your viperous cruelty. Then, know to your discomfiture, that now the axe is laid to the root of the trees, and every tree which bringeth not forth good fruit is cast into the fire.

Here concluded the Baptist's stern deliverance of his message, and here concludeth our comment upon it. For, being entrusted with the same office, we would rather disburden our mind for the salvation of the age in which we live, and to the people before whom we minister, than comment upon any passage, however expressive. Be the Baptist, therefore, our warrant for what we now advance.

It doth not become me, who have been educated in the softness of civilised life, to affect the rough and scornful language so becoming in the son of Zacharias. And though this country has been disgraced by martyrdoms of the Lord's servants no less than Israel was, still, as by the singular providence of God upon the liberties of the land, we are not likely again to be troubled with such inhuman spectacles, I shall not use the reproachful language of the Baptist, and salute ye a generation of vipers; but I will not fear to salute ye a cold-hearted generation, who are not moved as ye should be by the overtures of God. Else, why this standing upon the porch of salvation, and never entering in? why feel conviction, but never obey? why admire saintliness, and not seek it? why weary of the world, and not rise unto the world to come? why apprehend death, and not think of it? why foresee judgment, and not prepare for it? why shudder at doom, and not flee from the wrath to come? Oh, flee from

JOHN THE BAPTIST.

the wrath to come, for you are often warned. Already the axe is laid to the root of the trees, and they are falling fruitless into the fire unquenchable. Here is another emblem of the terrible effects of hell, and it is an impressive one. While those that have the fruits meet for repentance shall stand in their gracefulness, refreshing the eye of every beholder with the odour of their presence, and shall be transplanted into paradise, there to flourish with embowering shade in Eden's first bloom; the others, rudely smitten in their unfruitfulness by the axe of death, shall fall from their stock, though proud thereof as were Abraham's seed, hewed down as cumberers of the ground, and all their strength and beauty resolved into a few handfuls of idle dust. But ah, how this, like every other emblem, falleth short of the very truth! The tree is an unfeeling lump; but man is pregnant with feeling. Briefly is the tree resolved into its original elements, but man never resolveth again into the dust of the ground. Oh, it goes against nature to look into this terrible abyss and shipwreck of humanity. But it behoveth us, the watchmen of the people, to look with a steady eye upon the roughest wave, and warn the crew to stand to their posts, lest it whelm them in its bosom. Oh, be warned then of that fearful dismantling which those unhappy foredoomed men amongst us, who are fruitless of good works, must undergo. The tender shoots of worldly affection, which are woven over the beautiful and sociable world, as the vessels are ramified over the tree, shall all be nipped up, and leave their solitary unbefriended hearts cold and naked, and unsightly as the stunted trunk bereft of all its honours. All love, esteem, patronage, and veneration, however pure their origin, their duration will be brief. Though you hold in the embrace of your affections the choicest of the race, set off with all elegance and art, their jewels of the present life, like fairy gold, will become leaves and sand, when they are swept from their place, and their remembrance will remain within our breast the source and origin of a thousand lamentable regrets. But there will take place at that great consumption of all our glory, an erasure finer still than this erasure of the outward affections of the mind. I doubt not the mind will fall into jarring contention with itself, and destroy its own intrinsic fabric; for, even though you cut us off from all the tender objects of our regard, the soul hath the divine faculty of pleasing and gladdening itself in the solitude which surrounds it, and it can dress a feast of recollections sweeter than the realities, and open up regions of hope brighter than any regions of enjoyment; and not only delight itself therewith, but give them force and utterance, and acquire power over other spirits from its solitary dwelling-place. All which noble functions and privileges of manhood must depart, as the pure organisation of the tree disappears before the consuming fire, and is not seen in the dusky dross.

But I must go further in this disclosure. It is not the cutting off of outward objects, and the erasing of the mind's inward capacities of enjoyment, but something infinitely worse. Did annihilation come—annihilation were joyous to that which it is my painful duty to portray. Being thus stripped of her joyful and pleasant powers, she is left to be invaded and possessed by the spirits of those bad passions and appetites which vexed her in life. For I reckon that every evil affection of the world and the flesh hath a patron demon, who useth them in life to cheat poor souls whom he enthrals through eternity, having established a right over them in time. All strong appetites, all impetuous passions, all malignant affections, will fire the soul, and sting her into madness, yea, torture her, as the demons did the maniacs in our Lord's day and generation. Reason reigneth not, providence restraineth not, grace quickeneth not, repentance availeth not—there is free scope for the demon of every unsubdued passion to reign and domineer, and run on tilting against each other within the field of the all-enduring soul. And I doubt not, as it happeneth generally in the prison-house of criminals, it will happen in this prison-house of souls. If criminals be not kept apart, and good men do not enter to hold their evil passions in check, nor heart-softening visits of kinsmen, nor hope of reprieve or conclusion, then that house of criminal confinement becomes worse than a den of savages, or an asylum where reason is dethroned. Now yonder come no soft intercessions, nor earnest entreaties, nor blithe hopes, nor solicitous friends, nor better subjects, to impregnate the hellish mixture of spirits reprobate. Things must wax worse and worse, for there is no element of amendment. When I talked of obliteration coming over the fair parts of damned spirits, I talked mercifully. For, say that your benevolent men took thither your benevolence, and had nought to give, or none but ingrates to bestow it on; say that you who had taste did take it to a formless pit, and you who had feeling, to a herd of men worse than banditti or a press-gang; and you who had fancy, to have your brain seared with ceaseless images of woe, whereof these words convey hardly a pale reflection;—oh, my friends, avoid it all—though there was nothing to be gained, take the Baptist's advice, and avoid the worm that dieth not, and the fire that is not quenched, the lake that burneth, the outer darkness, where is weeping, and wailing, and gnashing of teeth — avoid all this, seeing it is in your power, by bringing forth the fruits meet for repentance. The Baptist preached repentance for the remission of sins, preaching at the same time Him through whom that repentance was rendered available. We preach repentance to the remission of sins, through the blood of Christ, to every one who heareth us, praying them to "turn unto the Lord, and He will have mercy, and unto our God, and He will abundantly pardon." Now, seeing that there turneth upon this repentance such a grace and such a salvation, it behoves us, like wise men, to study whether we have the fruits of it or not;—if we have them, to rejoice in Christ, who hath given us the victory; if not, to seek them forthwith through the Holy Spirit, which worketh in the children of disobedience. Our delineation of the terrible issue to the impenitent was meant to stir and move attention to that which we are now to set forth; and therefore we crave your ear to the things of your peace, ere they be for ever hid from your eyes. It behoves us to be very guarded, lest we confound that repentance which is through Christ to the remission of sins, with those temporary regrets and remorses which are produced by the changes of temper or the reverses of life. That repentance which bringeth remission of sins and deliverance from the wrath to come, is not a fit of anguish brought on by some outrageous commission, though that anguish should be so intolerable as to draw tears from our eyes, and scare sleep from our pillow, and give our spirits over for a season to thoughtful moods, and agonising fears, and direful compunction. This may be the mere revolting of nature—the recoil of the better parts of nature from some act of the worse parts; the natural contention which there is in every breast between the good and the evil. But we do not say that it may not be the beginning of a good and godly work of repentance. It proved so in David; there is no evidence that it proved so in Cain. In the generality of cases, we fear, from want of the knowledge of Christ and Him crucified, it proves like the morning cloud and the early dew, which soon passeth away. Mark the end. Do such visitations of regret die away by remedy of time and worldly intercourse, and come to life again only upon similar gross delinquencies? If so, then put it down as no salutary symptom of eternal health, but as the fits and paroxysms of a fatal disease, which will wax fainter and fainter as life ebbs away, until all commotion be sealed up in death.

There may not only be many compunctions of conscience which produce no abiding reformation of life, but there may be many reformations, fair and comely in the world's eye, which are no pledge nor evidence of a remission of sins. A rake reformed into a good member of society; a headstrong youth tempered down into a sober man; or a vain coxcomb changed into a grave office-bearing citizen; or an avaricious merchant satiated with success till he become a munificent benefactor or a dispenser of God's ordinances, brought into the reverence of seating himself at the table of the Lord;— these and a thousand other reformations, seemly in the world's sight, and for which the world is properly content to forget former delinquencies, may none of them go deep enough to bring in their train the forgiveness of sins, because not one of them may have any reference to God, or originate in any consciousness of sin against His holiness, or bring us to seek salvation through the great propitiation for the sins of the world.

Nay, more, a man may get entirely disgusted with his

former ways through the experience and necessity of a new discipline and the pursuit of a new object. The keen and well-disciplined soldier gets often disgusted with voluptuousness, the careworn statesman with all sorts of gay dissipations, and the disappointed statesman with all sorts of manœuvre and intrigue; nay, it is endless enumerating to what sudden veerings the human character is liable according to the object of desire which allures our pursuit. So that in the midst of these manifold strains of compunctious feeling, and their manifold alterations of character, we have the more need with precision to define and with distinctness to feel that repentance which is for the remission of sins. By these marks you shall never be at a loss to distinguish it:—

First, By a sense of guilt in the sight of God present in the conscience, springing, not from any consequence of our sins, though that may well enough originate it, but living in our minds through an apprehension of God's extreme holiness, and our entire worthlessness in his sight. In a natural state, men never once imagine themselves to be under the divine law, but form a rough estimate of themselves by comparison with others. Now, this average of character which we take for a standard, this comparing of ourselves by ourselves, is the most blinding of all things, and while it abides, never can admit a comparison of ourselves with the law of God. There are others who carry an appeal to the law of God, but upon principles which defeat all the good that might accrue. They see how it overreaches their performances, but they think that if they do their best their delinquency will be overlooked. I say not that any one can do more than his best, or that God will require more. But to live under this rule of judgment is to take upon us the judgment of ourselves, and to hinder any divine feelings from springing up in our minds of humility, of dependence upon Christ for forgiveness, or upon the Spirit for help. If we are always cogitating whether we have done our best, we are judging ourselves, whom the law of God should judge; and all affections for ourselves are brought into active operation, so that no self-condemnation may be expected; and thus there is no self-condemnation, no self-conviction, nor self-humiliation, nor confidence in the cross of Christ, nor spiritual feeling of any kind. It is the vainest of all things to have a law, and judge by the culprit's own ideas of his own ability. And if this principle, so commonly applied to divine judgment, were acted upon at human tribunals, you might as well burn the statute-book at once, and shut the door of every court. Do I say that God will punish any one who has done his best, or that He requires of us to do more than we are able? No; but He is to be judge of that, not we ourselves. That question, whether we have done our best, is the very count upon which we are to be indicted at the last tribunal, and fairly tried out and out by impartial justice. But do not imagine that God will bow Himself on that day from His lofty judgment-seat, and sist all procedure upon a reference to ourselves whether we had done our best—that, in short, He will allow every criminal to do the office of a grand jury to himself, and if he ignore the bill, pass him untried and uncondemned. But to stop all mouths, say I were to put that question this moment, Hast thou done thy best? couldst thou answer, Thou hast? Then thy conscience never reproved thee; then thou hast never known regret or remorse, never thought what thou durst not speak, nor spoken what thou would have fain recalled, nor done what thou heartily repented; and thou hast whiled away no time, and shut thine ear to no wholesome counsel, and shut thy conscience on no light of conviction, and indulged thy mind in no prejudice. Now, if thou thinkest so, ask thy neighbour if he thinketh so; ask the wife of thy bosom, who certainly were not willing to divulge thy faults. All these subterfuges, springing from pride, and vanity, and fondness of sin, must be scattered; we must bring ourselves *bonâ fide* to the measure of the law, and distinctly perceive our deficiency; and we must not blink the consequences of unrepented guilt, nor shut out of view the terrible punishment of sinners through any sentimental disrelish of horrid things. Nay, it is the meditation of these awful issues, and the imagination of that crisis, when this law, which now speaketh in a still, small voice, will speak in thunder as it did from Sinai, whence it came—when the array of the last assize shall display itself, and every fleet minister of execution shall stand ready harnessed at his post,—the mustering of thoughts like these, make the unrelenting soul of man quake for his sin like the timid child. And such thoughts, we think, are generally the beginning of repentance; and it was by such thundering denunciations that the Baptist brought the people to the waters of repentance.

But here it endeth not. There must be moreover a confession of our sins, which were vain unless we knew the humble confession of them would find an audience on high. But this we are assured it will, through the blood of Christ. "If we confess our sins, God is righteous and just to forgive us our sins, and the blood of Christ cleanseth from all iniquity."

LECTURE IV.

LUKE III. 10.

THIS is the first baptismal service upon record. And if anything were needed as a commentary upon the sacrament of baptism, we should refer to the stern and severe welcome to the fount, upon which we have already discoursed, and to those imperious commandments to all who came. But there needeth no commentary upon either of the Christian sacraments; whereof the one before us signifies by its very emblems an ablution and purification from former uncleanness—the other, a divine nourishment in a new life, and a sacred union to the body of Christ;—the two taken together presenting to our eye the two great principles of our dispensation—repentance towards God, and faith towards the Lord Jesus Christ. Therefore it doth at all times become the ministers of this ordinance, at its celebration, to discourse to the people present upon their sinfulness by nature, and the necessity of repentance and regeneration, and a life of holiness; as at the celebration of the other, it becomes them to discourse of the union with Christ, and the privileges and enjoyments and duties of His members. Of the former of these, the Baptist hath set us the example in the exhortation to all ranks to amend their ways; and in the latter, our Lord hath set us the example in that divine discourse recorded in the Gospel of John. Of these two models of discoursing over the two sacraments of the Church of Christ, it now falleth to our lot to expound and apply the former.

The uncivil epithets, and harsh upbraidings, and gloomy forebodings of the Baptist had the effect, not of alienating and disaffecting the people, but of making them gentle and docile, because they perceived in him the spirit of the ancient prophets. The dulness and monotony of forms, and the wearisome traditions and customs, had not so degraded the voice of nature within the breast of the people, that she should not know and acknowledge the force of truth. In the views and doctrines of one who had studied in the desert, and perused nature in her severest mood, and derived his theology fresh from the Word and Spirit of God, there must have been an originality and freshness of divine unction highly relishable to one who had been led with the stale and unspiritual traditions of men. In the inward principle of repentance, a change of feeling, a change of soul, as well as a change of life, there is something infinitely nobler than in the eternal drudgery of outward observances. The spirit becomes her own master. The streams flow from an inward fountain. The life and the heart are in union, and there is no master between them, save the invisible mastery of God. Nature speaks for this self-government, she desires to be set right inwardly by divine teaching and reformation, that she may be outwardly right. She hateth, by blind prescription of any man, or any positive rules, to be watched and constrained into the proper course. The Baptist's style of preaching, though severe, commends itself to nature's highest and noblest moods; and when we add to this the Baptist's personal accompaniments, we shall not wonder at the sway which he wielded over every class of men, the most hardened and the most fierce. Around a man who can despise accommodations and conveniences, and deal with nature in ancient simplicity and independence, and move amongst her social and religious institutions, like a traveller from another world, free to judge, and censure, and approve, as having himself nothing at stake,—around such a man there is a moral grandeur and authority to which none but the narrowest and most bigoted minds will refuse a certain awe and reverence. And when such a personage assumeth to himself divine commission, and publisheth new truth with divine authority, and rebuketh all wickedness, and scorneth all consequences, he taketh by the natural right of the wiser, the bolder, and the better man, a high place above those who feel themselves enslaved and shackled by customs which they despise.

Therefore, not without sufficient cause, it came to pass

that people of all descriptions, and also of various nations, Jews and Gentiles, excommunicated publicans and soldiers of old Rome, levied from every quarter of the earth, overawed and tamed, came to this wayfarer of the desert, asking him with humility and simplicity what they ought to do. "What shall we do then?" Oh, it is a noble triumph which this forerunner of Christ achieved, to lay prostrate before the edge of truth the distinctions of society, and the pride of the heart and the pride of life, and every other thing which exalteth itself against Christ— raising the valleys, levelling the mountains, straightening the crookedness, and smoothing the roughness of the people! For here they are of every class beseeching to know what it behoved them to do against that terrible coming whereof he spake. First came the people, by which you are to understand the mixed and indiscriminate assemblage; after them came the publicans, who were a hated and excommunicated tribe, because they ministered to the rapaciousness of the conqueror; after them the soldiers, who were the conquerors themselves. These three classes came in turns, according to their moral rank—first, the people who were living under the law, and whose, by right of many promises, was the Messiah whose advent was proclaimed; then the publicans, who, though of the nation, were held as traitors to the heaven-bestowed law and constitution of the country; finally, the soldiers, who had brought the country into subjection, and might fear the severest treatment from such a union. They came humbly praying to be informed what it became them to do. And the Baptist, who yesterday was a solitary dweller in the desert, and to-day is a counsellor of multitudes, dispenseth to each rank and class of men that advice, and openeth up that walk of repentance and reformation, which became their several vocations in the community.

In commenting upon these three several injunctions to the people, the publicans, and the soldiers, it would be altogether unsuitable to the style of modern life to make an express discourse to the people generally, a second to those in public vocations, and a third to military men, expounding to each that line of duty which becometh them as persons baptized

JOHN THE BAPTIST.

into the faith of Christ. This would not be convenient, because it would require a congregation of each sort of men to listen to the exhortation. But there is a way of treating the subject which, while it alters the form, will still retain the spirit of the original. In our modern state of society each man doth, as it were, contain within himself a part in union with each of these three divisions of the Baptist's audience. The people who first came before him represent that part of our character which is brought into play by the interests of private and social life, and the Baptist's exhortation to them containeth a lesson of the spirit in which we should fulfil our duties to each other; his lesson to the publicans teacheth us how we should fulfil our duties to the state, which every one hath to discharge in a lesser or greater degree; and his lesson to the soldiers may be considered as an address to our more fierce and intractable moods, teaching us how to use the power we possess over others, and the weapons which we are entrusted with by the Most High. These three strains of exhortation to these three conditions of our nature we shall open up apart, and apply to you who have been baptized into the Church of Christ, and are therefore called on for the repentance and reformation set forth in this the first baptismal service which the world ever witnessed.

To the people the Baptist said, "He that hath two coats, let him impart to him that hath none; and he that hath meat, let him do likewise." It is the privilege and prerogative of every brief proverb or maxim to be interpreted in the same large and liberal sense in which it was uttered, as it is the right of every detailed and argumentative discourse to be tried and balanced in all its parts. A proverb is the compressed spirit of wisdom, and requires much prudence in expanding it into detailed conduct. And this proverb of the Baptist's, which we shall shew before we close to be full of the greatest wisdom as well as benignity, might easily be strained to a latitude of application which would burst the whole framework of well-tempered society. If we were to follow it without discrimination, then would each needy person, who chose to claim our superfluities, have a divine right therein, whatever may have been his previous character, and whatever may be his present habits. So that the honestly-acquired and well-preserved substance of the worthy would become the store at which every thriftless prodigal had a right to supply himself, until he made it bare and impoverished. A general subjection of industry to wastery would be the fatal consequence, if every one, so soon as he became unprovided, could draw upon the bank and storehouse of the rest; and the terrors would be overthrown which wait on poverty and abject fortunes to stimulate industry and deter from dissipated courses. This is all true, and shews the danger of interpreting the proverb rashly. But, upon the other hand, it is well known how the superfluities of fortune are wont to be expended unprofitably upon the pampering of our appetites, which doth lay the seeds of disease in our mortal frame, and expose our immortal souls to a thousand soft temptations and gay delusions; how they are expended viciously upon the pursuit and purchase of forbidden pleasures, which drown the soul in fleshly lusts; expended vainly in splendid decorations of our persons and our houses, which generally involve us in the slavery of a thousand worldly fashions; expended ambitiously in reaching place, title, and preferment, for no end save that of figuring in the annals of the day. All which customary methods of expending superfluities are the strength of the enemy's position against the soul, being in truth various idolatries in which he holds us, and which must be burst asunder before we can be baptized with the baptism of repentance. I know that a defence is made for these extravagances, upon the score of the many artizans who are thereby honestly supported. But I would not have any one to benefit others at the expense of ruining his own soul; for "what is a man profited though he should gain the whole world and lose his own soul?" Nor is it my intention to rebuke a noble, dignified, and splendid way of life. It is the part of Christians to occupy their stations, high or low, with a divine dignity. I only speak of the sacrifices which are made to vice, to vanity, and to worldly ambition, in which no one may indulge himself for any gain that may thence accrue to others.

Now the Baptist, knowing well how much the selfish did prevail over the generous adaptation of our superfluous means;

perceiving how the former leads to every species of degradation, the latter to divine dignity and honours, and foreseeing little chance of men passing the bounds of prudence and becoming prodigal of their gifts; and also knowing how law seemeth to every man his own, and hindereth any claim which a wild fanatic might make from religion upon his brother's property,—the Baptist perceiving these strong provisions of nature and society against the too generous interpretation of his maxim, did, in laying down the law upon the subject of superfluities, express it as it is in the text, "He that hath two coats, let him give unto him that hath none; and he that hath meat, let him do likewise." The maxim is a good maxim, and it is one of the children of the wisdom that cometh from above. There is no danger of our forgetting our own interest, and reducing ourselves to nakedness or want for another's sake. There is great danger of our forgetting the naked and the destitute in the deep sea of occupation, and the incessant noise of business in which our own concerns do involve us. If we need, therefore, to be admonished upon any side, it is that upon which the Baptist hath touched; and if we can bear an extreme admonition, it is there where we are extremely forgetful.

We have been at pains to defend the maxim by guarding it against the abuses to which its brevity and generality make it liable, and shewing that it was neither intended as a harbour for squanderers, nor as an encouragement to injudicious lavishness and profusion, but simply as a guide to the direction in which a Christian's superfluities should go—meant to instruct us in the will of God concerning the overflowings of our cup, and the superabundance of our portion. But in carrying the precept into effect, there is required of us as much exercise of judgment and prudence, as if we were laying out the same amount upon a speculation of merchandise, or a scheme of enjoyment. The Almighty doth but indicate His will, He leaves it to our heart and soul and thought and mind to perform His will. And he who giveth not both the feelings of his heart, and the faculties of his mind to his charities, is a meagre servant of God, withholding from Him the allegiance of His noblest endowments, and spreading amongst His creatures temptations which are the most powerful against integrity and holiness. For charities are to the poor the same snare which the merchandise of silver and gold is to the rich, engendering the same aspirations after the temporal good, awakening the same covetousness, and setting them upon the same ignoble shifts. And therefore, unless wisdom and caution be employed, we are responsible, I think, to God, as great tempters and workers of evil through heedlessness, rather than as great redressers of evil and workers of good. I do allow that the weight of the crime lieth with the poor, who thus take advantage of our openness of heart and hand; but we are not guiltless, if by due consideration we could have saved our brother from offending.

Therefore I would be at pains to caution you against the mastery and profusion of the precious means of well-doing which God hath put within your power. Not that I think too much is given by us, but that with a little more thought it might turn to more profit both to ourselves and those upon whom we confer it. Our charities, like our devotions, or our acts of faith, should be personal things as much as possible, and public things as little as possible—offerings to need which we have taken pains to ascertain to be free from all imposture, tributes to our merciful Saviour who died for miserable sinners, and acknowledgments to God who hath made our basket and our store to superabound. And to this end time is demanded of us, and personal knowledge, which must always precede hearty feeling, and visitation to the distressed such as our Saviour paid, and consolation such as He bestowed, in order that our heart may be made better by the vision of mercy, and our gratitude quickened to the Most High, and our dependence upon Him bound more closely, and all our Christian graces revived and refreshed;—in order, on the other hand, that the poor may be cheered with a counsellor for Heaven, and improved in the hour of their temptation, and led to God by the presence and bounty of His servants, and instructed in the providence of God, and the riches of a gracious Saviour;—in order, also, that the rich and poor may meet together, and their mutual dislikes be removed, and the gospel may have free course and be glorified over all ranks of the people.

But, whereas it is one thing to know a duty and another thing to do it, and no Christian precept hath been expounded until the strength hath been displayed in which it is to be carried into effect, we now hold ourselves to give out sufficient inducement to move every Christian to walk in the footsteps of his blessed Saviour.

Therefore, if ye would imitate the example of your blessed Saviour and be to the downcast and miserable what He was to the sons of men when they were low and lost, be at charges to humble yourselves to those of poor estate; and for that end divest yourselves of all the attributes of place and rank, as our Lord divested Himself of His divine attributes. Take under your superintendence certain portions of oppressed and miserable men, as He took under His superintendence the whole fallen race of Adam; humble yourselves as He humbled Himself; engage yourselves with all your affections as He did, and the blessing of God will rest upon you, and the little ye bestow will be amply refunded. And the feelings of Christian affection, which you gratify within your breast, will build up your own sanctification, and ye shall obtain evidence of your calling and election; and the bread cast upon the waters of the present afflicted state, shall return unto you through eternity, after this troublesome season is past.

If anything should bind these duties upon you, beyond the command of the Baptist, it is the example of your Saviour. And ye are baptized; therefore it is your proper vocation, and truly it is the vocation of every Christian, the royal law of love, the new commandment of love, the only true test of discipleship, without which, as Paul hath said, all gifts of utterance, all gifts of faith, all power of miracles are utterly vain. Therefore look to it; for though we may seem to this critical age to have been touching only as it were a side of Christian discipline, we have been touching its heart; and according as men do respond in their feelings and answer in their conduct to this suggestion of the Baptist, they may consider themselves sound at the heart or hollow at the heart.

So may the Lord enable you, that when you come to judgment ye may be found with all your other works to have possessed this the only qualification which will pass the bar of judgment, and introduce us to life eternal. I know no one that is to do this greatest charity for the needy but the charitable, the truly charitable. This is the first duty. It is like delivering a man out of the spoiler's hand before you feed him. It is like breaking the fetters of a slave before you advance him. Nay, it is delivering a whole race, which we have always with us, and our Lord says are to have always with us, delivering them from the oppression of the oppressor before we proceed to take further cognisance of how their state may be improved. Therefore the man that shieldeth himself from charity on this score is a sophist—a sophist to his own heart, for it is only another argument for charity. It is charity moving to a deed of justice. It is justice and charity combined, which is the noblest pair that can meet in a human breast.

Do you ask me how this just office is to be done for the sake of charity. I would not legislate to you, but I would advise. First, for the conviction of those who come forth out of doors to solicit, I commend to you the support of the Mendicity Society, which undertakes on a large scale the inquisition of those characters whom no private inspection could wind through all their deceptive haunts. Their tickets will relieve your charitable feelings when they are excited by street-petition; their inspection will take care that your charitable feelings are not cast away upon the undeserving But it is not street-solicitors, but misery in its thousand retiring forms of shame, poverty struggling hard to keep its head above the wave, worth pining in neglect, iniquity trampled over by necessity, shame waiting for forgiveness, heart-sick vice longing for virtue's paths, dishonour too severely punished, virtue too severely tried, health prostrated through over-exertion of body and over-anxiety of mind, disease preying upon famished frames, the wants of nature unsupplied, souls unevangelised, children uneducated, wives and families deserted or borne down by graceless husbands and unaffectionate fathers. These, and a thousand other forms of misery, which harbour unseen, and cry to Heaven for redress; and Heaven crieth to men in this holy book, but men hear not, and the abject miserables perish for evermore. Ohon! ohon! a fancy cometh upon my brain which I dare hardly utter, lest it overwhelm the feeling of this assembly, and unman myself into unbecoming weeping. I fancy in some sad abode of this city, upon some unvisited pallet of straw, a man, a Christian man, pining, perishing, without an attendant, looking his last upon nakedness and misery, feeling his last in the pangs of hunger and thirst. The righteous spirit of the man being disembodied, I fancy to myself arising to heaven, encircled by an attendance of celestial spirits, daughters of mercy, who waited upon his soul when mankind deserted his body—this attended spirit I fancy rising up to the habitation of God, and reporting in the righteous ear of the Governor of the earth how it fared with him amidst all the extravagance and outlay of this city. And saith the indignant Governor of men, "They had not a morsel of bread nor a drop of water to bestow upon My saint. Who of My angels will go for Me where I shall send? Go, thou angel of famine; break the growing ear with thy wing, and let mildew feed upon their meal. Go, thou angel of the plague, and shake thy wings once more over the devoted city. Go, thou angel of fire, and consume all the neighbourhood where My saint suffered unheeded and unpitied. Burn it; and let its flame not quench till their pavilions are a heap of smouldering ashes."

It is my intention to dilate upon the history of God's judgments in the hearing of this city, after the manner of an ancient prophet, and with none of the soft lullabies of modern speculation, that the city may be warned, and turn unto righteousness, otherwise, like Nineveh, it shall be destroyed.

But at present, to guard your several homes and neighbourhoods, I exhort each man to set on the vigilance of a Christian watchfulness, and to take heed unto the people, to go in and out before them, and make a place in their affections, that they may haply be won over to the Lord our God. I ask each one that hears me to do a little, to give a little money, more words, many prayers, and as much time as he thinketh

God entitled to out of the twenty-four hours, to some such hallowed vocation. Stand like guardian angels between men and perdition. Heave off from them necessity's fangs—the ravenous tooth of want. Keep their bodies from an untimely grave, that their blood be not on the land. Keep their souls what in you lies from wickedness, that their sins may not smell rank to Heaven, and draw down the thunderbolt.

Say not, we give to this charity so much and to that charity so much more. God wants not money alone—the silver and gold are His; but He wants your heart, your feelings, your time, your anxiety. He curseth these mere money charities, making them engender poverty in far greater abundance than they annihilate it, and scourging them with the means of those who grudgingly bestow it. The mere mammon works mammon's work; divine charity worketh God's work. A Christian may as well give over his faith into the hands of a public body, and believe what they appoint to be believed, and think that he thereby satisfieth God, as cast his charity over to a public body, yea, or to a private individual, and think that he thereby satisfieth God. Our right hand is not to know what our left hand doeth. It is with the heart, and soul, and strength, and might, that He is to be worshipped and served.

Therefore, take heed to the Baptist's exhortation to baptized people, for ye are baptized. He does not command you to subsidise indolence, or support extravagance, but with your excess and superfluity in hand, to make a pilgrimage in miserable places, and do your endeavour to relieve their misery, to save human nature from intolerable grievance, to supplement what is lacking in the providence of God, to lend your substance over to God's purpose, that it may be repaid manifold, that the blessing of him that is ready to perish may come upon you, and that you may become, in God's room, fathers to the fatherless, and friends to the friendless, the stranger's shield, the orphan's help, the refuge of the destitute, and the salvation of many sinful souls, and shine like the stars in the firmament for ever and ever.

The general sense in which the proverb should be interpreted, as it bears upon superfluities, is therefore this, that we should prefer the claims which come from without upon our humanity, our charity, our benevolence, to those which come from within upon our personal, social, or anti-social gratifications; that we should be as willing to contribute to the enjoyment of another as to contribute to our own, because it is more blessed to give than to receive. That instead of hunting the shops and bazaars for refinement of ornamental dress and furniture, or buying from foreign collectors objects of *virtu* and antiques, and ranging the round globe for its idle and exquisite singularities, we should seek the alleys and lanes of this city, where the abject and miserable dwell, and the melancholy prisons into which the wretched are cast out of sight and out of help; seek there to refit shipwrecked fortunes, and right disabled and diseased frames, and comfort sore affliction, and pour the oil of consolation into wounded spirits, and give the oil of joy for mourning and the garment of praise for the spirit of heaviness. Often, very often, I could weep amidst the emblems of smiling fortune, enshrined in chambers and antechambers and lofty saloons. Like old Diogenes, I could leap and trample upon silken couches and massy tables, in no cynical pride, but in Christian indignation, when from out the windows of these chambers I look upon the unpitied, unattended, unbefriended habitations of the wretched poor. Out upon the votaries of state and equipage and fashion! They care for nothing but self-indulgence and vanity, and have no pity of their kind, but would turn pale and wax sick of sentiment to behold that misery which flesh and blood as good as theirs is fain to endure in its feverish veins and filthy habitations. Away, away with such unsubstantial men and women — their hollow hearts let fumes of vanity fill, their silly heads let intoxication of excess continue to sicken; their vain routine of life let vanity continue to drive in his airy chariot; let age plant its wrinkles upon their dissembling faces, and *ennui* consume the years of their old age; and let there be no mourning over their death, nor tears dropped in their grave, nor broken-hearted mourners to visit it in the shadowy twilight; but instead, let cold marble entomb their colder hearts, and unfeeling stone be the bearer of their memory. Away with them; they are good for nothing, except to flutter in the train of some greater personage than themselves, or themselves to lead out the train of splendid triflers. God convert them with some voice as terrible as the voice of him that cried in the wilderness.

I speak to other men, to honest men, to men in whom nature is not shipwrecked, and in whom, happily, a better nature hath come to birth or maturity. To you I speak, my Christian flock, over whom the Lord hath appointed unto me the oversight. I guard you, young men, whose guide for life and eternity I am honoured to be; and to you, domestic men, who are the strength of this flock; and to you, elderly men, who are its counsellors. I warn you against the invasion of the pomp and circumstance of human life. I warn you against the parade and retinue of state. I warn you against luxurious meals and splendid fêtes. I warn you against the wine-cup when it sparkles, and against beauty when it wreathes itself in the witchery and enchantment of its smiles I warn you against the many inventions of luxury and convenience, which are the links of a chain that girdles the mightiest of the earth in ignoble bondage—the fuel of a fire that consumes the world's myrrh and frankincense before the shrine of Belial, and in the end catches and consumes the very heart that ministers at his altar. And I counsel you to expend your thoughts upon the nobler offices of humanity, to be a father to the fatherless and a husband to the widow, and the orphan's help and the stranger's friend. As God pours into your coffers, return Him part back upon the poor and the needy and the destitute, who are His special care. Make visits to the abject; speak comfort to the downcast. Be a blessing to your neighbourhood, and make the hearts of the destitute to sing for joy. Then shall the eye bless you, and the ear shall taste the sweetness of your worthy praise, and your heart shall be filled brimful of enjoyment, and merrily shall your life pass under the eye of the great Spirit of joy, who shall at length remove you to the habitations of His righteousness.

I am not ignorant of the difficulty of carrying into effect in this unprincipled city these exhortations, for I have felt that difficulty; every day of my life I feel it. There are locusts that prey upon the generous, and grub up all that they can catch from Christian benevolence, idlers, deceivers, wretched spendthrifts, and contemptible souls, who steel one against giving, and draw down upon one the character of a mere novice in London life. But, if to be an adept in London life is to shut one's purse to charity, and open it to gaudy shows, then Heaven keep all my flock in a constant noviciate. For, after all, let the greatest novice yesterday imported from the most innocent and unpolluted simplicity of rural life, gratify all the freshness of a Christian and benevolent heart for one year, and, when the year is over, cast a reckoning, and, after deducting from his whole expenditure the necessaries, examine what part of the residue went to liberality, what part to please the world's fashions, which in his heart he doth nauseate and despise, and I mistake if he shall not find a result turn out which shall silence into shame any talk about being duped into over-liberal giving. But as I said at the beginning, it is not my part to recommend a clothing of all the backs of the thriftless, and a feeding of all the mouths of the dissolute. I know that too much clothing, systematic clothing, charity-school clothing, is carried to excess in those parts, which makes men of a northern training blush for the paltry meanness of those who receive, and the thoughtless squandering of those who bestow. If the Baptist did support or command this, then I would argue against his position upon a thousand grounds. For, connected as it is with schooling, it doth almost more harm to the little creatures than their education doeth good; and upon the parents and the population generally it worketh the basest effects, which I do not speculate upon, but know from much study and observation and converse with the lower classes in this city. First of all, it lowers their ideas of schooling or learning, which they think worth nothing of itself, but needing the bribe of clothing to make it worth the having. Then it separates the child from the family, who now think him provided for; or it makes the little degraded thing in his charity-living a little idol upon holidays to the family, to corrupt the fine old homely independence of this ancient land. Then, being dissevered from his parents, it casts the little nursling into the lap of some lady's favour, where he remains until he can have a place obtained for him. Now, if there be good in educating men, it is to teach them to act for themselves, not to act as another's puppet. If there be any good in educating one of a family, it is to cast him back into the bosom of that family that he may raise the honest pride of his father's house; and if there be any good in educating the people, (which I am sorry to see men calling themselves Christian, and at the head of our most self-magnifying Christians, begin in this realm to doubt,) if there be any good in educating the people, which was wont to be the watchword and is now the bugbear of Christian leaders, it consisteth in raising the tone of the people's mind, in fermenting and inspiriting and ennobling the populace, and delivering them from vulgar, sensual, and brutal vices. All which good effects this system of drafting out from the midst of them a sort of pigmy militia of school-boys and school-girls, all dressed and marshalled in uniform, doth completely hinder; for instead of casting them back upon the mass from which they came to improve and soften its character, it doth make them despise their birth-place, forget their lineage, and oft, very often, despise the parents who gave them birth.

Therefore to such a system I do not ask your help, except it were to open its blinded eyes and introduce into it the heart of better feeling; but nevertheless I ask your rags of clothing for the naked, your crumbs of meat for the hungry. It is no excuse to tell me that there are impostors. That is no argument against what I say, but it is an argument for another duty which I shall shortly explain. There are impostors, I allow, but there are necessitous cases, you must allow me in return. Well, between these two descriptions of persons, how are we to proceed?

I am well aware, that in a city like this, or any other city or country, by blindly following the rule of the Baptist you would foster idleness and reward deception, and do much more injury to the community than you would do good. You say truly it is borne in upon your conviction, when beholding an object of want, that it is a case of importance, and between your doubts and your feelings you are sorely distracted what to do. Now, it is not difficult to tell you what it behoves you to do. Consider what an impostor is, one who invadeth the sacred domain, the sanctified domain, of poverty and want, in order to pilfer it of its heaven-derived right upon humane and Christian hearts. Now, say you saw a man slinking out of a poor cottage, which you knew for the moment to be deserted of its inhabitants, and suspected he had been upon no good errand there, what would be your duty?—to keep your eye upon the skulking knave, and watch his hiding-place; and if aught is amissing, hand him over to justice. And where, I ask you, is the houseless stranger's cottage? is it not in the heart of charitable men? And where is the naked man's wardrobe? is it not in the heart of charitable men? And where is his meal of meat? is it not from the crumbs of the table of generous men? And what is he who takes his stand in the way of generous men, or solicits at their gate with false appearances, to win that remnant which is holy to the children of poverty and want? Is he not a pilferer upon their undefended habitation? is he not a filcher of their poor, uncertain pittance? is he not a vilifier of their whole order, yea, a murderer of their pitiful existence? And who is to right the state of abject poverty from these its stout and daring plunderers? Can poverty right itself?—poverty which lives by grace and favour, can she exalt her voice and talk of right? Can she who bends in suppliancy and asketh aid to her feebleness take arms into her withered hands, and exile from her domain these marauders and these vilifiers of her poor, abject condition? Who, then, shall right her wronged estate? Who is to right the man stricken of God's providence out of his means, and out of his hopes, and out of his confidence; and by being rendered dependent, rendered likewise bashful and timorous, and incapable of making siege on such? Who is to right this claimant of God's from the hands of the ruffian, mighty in artifice and guile, stored with all pitiful tales, and pertinacious in all bold solicitations?

LECTURE V.

LUKE III.

WE had intended, as we stated in a former lecture, to apply the Baptist's exhortation of the publicans to that part of our character and conduct which concerns the public, and his exhortation of the soldiers to that part of our character and conduct which concerns our own defence, and the power we hold over others; but, upon second thoughts, we have abandoned this purpose, conceiving it to be too minute for the nature of the lecture, which should follow strictly the current of the text, diverging as seldom as possible into any adjacent topic, however useful. We shall therefore continue to follow forth the train of the Baptist's discourse.

In the exposition of this discourse, whose unity we have endeavoured to restore, we had advanced to the point at which the publicans came forward, asking what it behoved them to do. These publicans were the collectors of the revenue in the interest of the Romans. At Rome, where everything was saleable, to the very city itself, according to the saying of the Numidian prince, the revenues of the provinces were set up to sale by the Senate, and were generally rented or farmed by men of the equestrian or second rank. But these Roman knights would have thought themselves degraded by personally collecting the dues, and were wont to employ some of the conquered people—to one, farming the toll of a bridge; to another, the impost of a particular commodity; and so forth through all the articles of excise and custom. These were the publicans, who made their living by gathering the taxes for the conqueror. It was their interest to be extortioners, for all beyond the rent they paid to the Romans was their own. It was the nature of their office to press upon the sorest feelings of the people. They were the tools of the conqueror to fleece the conquered, and made their living out of their country's degradation: all which made it an office for unfeeling and ignoble spirits to undertake. Its tendency was to extortion and to false accusation, as we see by the declaration of Zaccheus, a chief man among the publicans: "If I have taken anything from any man by false accusation, I restore him fourfold." On these accounts, this class was excommunicated from the very privileges of Jews, and ranked upon the same file with the heathen, as we learn from that expression of our Lord, "Let him be unto thee as a heathen man and a publican." It was disgraceful to eat with them, and in this respect they ranked with heinous and hardened sinners, as we learn from that railing of the Pharisees, "He eateth with publicans and sinners." The sense of this degradation had eaten into the heart of these people, and they stood aloof like men infected with disease; they came not to John with the rest of the people, but in a body by themselves. In the parable, the publican durst not draw near, he stood afar off; he dared not lift up his eyes, but looked upon the ground; he smote upon his breast under the agitation of strong remorse for crimes, and cried, in the agony of his heart, "Lord have mercy upon me a miserable sinner." All this is necessary to be understood in order to perceive the force of the Baptist's exhortation, which struck home to the heart of their besetting iniquity. The publicans came to be baptized, and said unto him, "Master, what shall we do?" And he said unto them, "Exact no more than that which is appointed you." In which reply the Baptist shewed as much discretion as he shewed faithfulness. He did not blame them for occupying a place which must be filled by some one, and without which no government can uphold itself for a single day; he did not involve his ministerial character with political questions, and rebuke them for lending themselves to the conqueror, knowing that conquest and subjection are dispensations of God for good, however bitterly they may taste, and however evil they may work: and yet, while he kept clear of these questions foreign to his vocation, he did not fail to strike a sure and decisive blow for the sake of righteousness, —admonishing them upon the weakest part of their character, and commanding them to guard against it. "Levy," says he, "the dues of Cæsar, but go not beyond. Raise no false accusations in order to obtain confiscations of property. Push not to extremities. Guard against extortion and unjust exaction; and if you cannot bear mercy, bear justice before you, and faithfully perform your part between the conqueror and the conquered—between the exactor and the object of his exactions." This might be an example to every preacher of righteousness: how it behoveth him, in the first place, to guard against tides and currents of popular feeling, and to be moved by the interests of righteousness alone; and, in the next place, being so moved, to be fearless and strike home at every blow. Here, before the Baptist, were the extortioners of a people, and the people they ground with their extortions were standing by; here were the scorn and byword of a nation, and the nation which scorned them were standing by: yet the Baptist catches none of the nation's scorn and fury, neither identifies himself with any popular feeling; but remembering that he is a man set for God, not for a party, he takes God's part, and not the nation's part, and admonishes the tribe of their offences against God, not against the national spirit or national feeling. Now my experience of the pastoral office in both the extremities of this island hath taught me a sore lesson upon this head. How dangerous to one's reputation, and unwelcome to the people professing Christ, it is to stand aloof from their approved strains and party feelings, upon the rock of your pastoral liberty! If you will not cry up what they cry up, and cry down what they cry down, you are held at naught, talked against, and wickedly misrepresented both by pastors and by people: which experience giveth me much pain and anguish of soul, because of the worldly spirit of confederation and party which it shews still harbouring among the disciples of Christ. But ye, the people of the flock, will justify me for upholding the interests of righteousness among them, though I see no duty in banding and confederating with any sect, however popular; and ye are my defence against these misrepresentations of Christians which grieve my heart. And while John struck for no party, you will observe how fearlessly he struck for God. He feared not the frown of any class, and he sought not their favour; he consulted not their station, for he was minister of high as well as low; he aimed to turn all to the Lord by repentance, and therefore he pointed out the sins of all. And so it will always be with the faithful minister of Christ. If he become popular, it will be, not because he humoureth the people's opinions, or tastes, or failings, but because he teacheth the people truth, and openeth up to them the whole counsel of God; not because he can be pronounced Calvinistic, or because he can be pronounced Arminian; not because he preacheth for the Established Church, nor because he preacheth against the Established Church; not because he chimeth with the party of the state in power, or with the party out of power; not because he affecteth a low and vulgar manner of discoursing, nor because he affecteth a high and refined,—all which strains of popular feeling are beside his office, and beneath his dignity: but he wisheth to be beloved of his people, and of all men, from the beggar to the prince, because he is the faithful shepherd of their souls—who prays for them all, and preaches for them all, and deals plainly between God and the souls of them all, doing what in him lies to deliver their souls from death, and their feet from falling. He will be a censor, but he will not be censorious; he will be satirical, but he will not be a satirist; he will be a denouncer, but he will denounce for salvation's sake. What saith the Scriptures? "All scripture is given by inspiration of God, and is profitable for doctrine, for reproof, for correction, for instruction in righteousness." Even such various profit should the preacher of righteousness bring to those who listen to his voice.

Now, I have no hesitation in declaring that the liberty of prophesying is fallen into bondage, and needeth to be enlarged. You must shape your discourse by the rule of the schools either of Geneva or of Holland. You must deal in generalities of doctrine which hath nothing but dogmatism; or if you speak of practice, it must be wide of the conscience. If you come home and sift the secrecies of the heart, and lay bare the errors of the time, and burst the sores of the several ranks of men, paying the tribute of your counsel to rich as well as poor—to religious as well as irreligious—to nobles, to statesmen, to princes, to kings, as well as to mechanics, to tradesmen, and to merchants,—you are suspected for some dangerous one, some leveller of distinctions, some radical disseminator of sedition. But, in the name of the free gospel, is it come to this, that when we address a class of men, we should be thought to do them an injury? Are our counsels evil things, that they should be valued by their fewness? Are our rebukes invasions, that they should be watched, not welcomed? I for one conceive more highly of my office. I regard it as a favour done to a man to tell him of his sins; and the oftener I do it, the more love do I manifest for him. I dare omit no man, nor rank of men, because it is my office to love them all, and preach repentance and forgiveness to all; which certainly were in vain, and simply commonplace, unless I might preach previously the courses to be repented of and the sins to be forgiven. When I look to Paul, and see him commencing a high philosophical discourse before the Areopagus of Athens,—when I see the same Paul before a bench of kings, preaching to them of righteousness in their government of the people, and of temperance in their pleasures, and of judgment to come, when their judgments were to be reviewed, and themselves judged,—when I see the same Paul melting with a farewell discourse upon the desolate shore the Ephesian elders into outbursting lamentation, and pleading for his life before tribunals, and in popular assemblies,—it seemeth to me —and I cannot but express it—that of the ancient arts which are lost, the art of apostolical preaching is one.

Last came the soldiers, crying, "What shall we do?" and he said unto them, "Do violence to no man, neither accuse any falsely: and be content with your wages." That these were Roman and not Jewish soldiers is rendered probable— first, by everything elsewhere mentioned in the Gospels and the Acts concerning soldiers; and, secondly, by the well-known policy of the Romans to quarter in every province soldiers raised in other parts of the empire, and to send the soldiers raised in that particular province away to a distance from their homes. Therefore it is to be inferred that none of these soldiers were educated in Jewish customs, or versed in the prophecies which testified of John, or of Messiah which was to come. They were rough sons of pillage, congregated from all heathenish lands, adhering to a godless and fearless craft, and perhaps never before addressed in the name of God. Yet before the Baptist—such was his authority,—before the man of the wilderness, naked of all human ornaments or graceful commendations, clothed with no orders or robes ecclesiastical, but with camel's hair and a leathern girdle, supported by no civil insignia or authorities,—before this man (such is the awfulness of naked truth) these legionary bands laid aside their fierceness and forgot the mockeries of their profession, and at once became transported into the feelings of simple peasantry, and came forward like the rest praying for advice and admonition from the mouth of this inspired youth; and, though an unarmed youth, he gave it to those steel-clad warriors with the plainness and fidelity of a father. "Do violence to no man, neither accuse any falsely: and be content with your wages." We of this age can hardly judge of the licence of military life in the days of old. What would be thought of the soldiers who, in these times, should scourge and deride and crown with thorns the man they were leading to execution, and in the midst of his agonies should mock his sufferings by offering for his refreshment vinegar and gall, and after death insult his lifeless body by piercing it with a spear? To do violence, to plunder, to sack and despoil, and if the briefest way of possessing cannot be used, to come with false accusations of disloyalty, of insolence, and of secreting enemies, and anything, in short, which may give the victim to execution and his goods to confiscation, was the character of the Roman soldiery when on service; and some century and a half ago it was the character of British soldiery, when they were let loose like wolves and tigers upon the unoffending Church to which we have the honour to belong; and during the times of peace it was the character of that same Roman soldiery to turn their fierceness against their superiors, and to cry out for increase of pay and extravagant largesses, to mutiny, to enthrone emperors and dethrone them at their pleasure, and to hasten into all riot and excess. The Baptist, though reared in the wilderness, was no stranger to the camp; and now that an opportunity is offered of exhorting them, he doth it like a fearless servant of the living God. " Do violence to no one, neither accuse any falsely: and be content with your wages."

My spirit is recreated and refreshed by such manliness. It is like inspiration from on high to know the customs of the primitive ministry, to behold these heralds of the skies—these messengers of heaven, to read and see their dealings with the sons of men. John was nowise afraid of inquiring the cause as now-a-days we are. He knew his cause was like an adamant, and would not break by the roughest treatment—the stone cut out with hands which was to become a mountain, and fill the whole earth. He feared not to hurt his usefulness, as they constantly talk of, as if the disciples of Christ were all changed into disciples of utility. He thought not of prudence, which now is thought to be the chief furniture of a Christian minister. No! here he was a vessel fraught with truth, launched by God to every inhabitant of the earth, disloading at every man's door that commodity of truth which Heaven hath charged him with for his particular use. And he hesitates not to bear up against the stream of man's prejudices, or to face man's strong embattlements of error, well knowing that while the Lord is pleased, he should continue his bountiful voyage, and can by no power be restrained; and when the Lord is pleased to remove him, He will send others in his stead; and so he is content to be removed from the service by the blows of those he would benefit, or any other instrument whatsoever.

Now, do you ask what serves such strictures upon the Baptist's style of serving his commission? I answer, for my encouragement in these times to do the same, were it not for these everlasting memorials of the Church's priesthood, I should strike sail, and lay myself up in some little harbour of thought; but, by the grace of God and the example of the Baptist, I will venture forth amongst your several avocations, and speak a word of admonition for the living God. You may say this is not preaching Christ. I answer, This was the Baptist's way of preaching Christ, and he was the first preacher of Christ. But it is idle talking with the bigotry and narrow-mindedness of the age, which taketh pleasure in being fettered and benighted. This method of the Baptist's will continue to the end of the world the best method of preparing a sinner for the welcoming of the Saviour. Could any power at this moment break open the hidden solitudes of angelic and heavenly life, and give this world's incurious gaze a sight and feeling of its order and blessedness, they would return disgusted with the trifling, the hypocrisy, and the misery of these terrestrial scenes, and long to be home among those things whereof they have had a foretaste. Such a glimpse of glory, and such a disgust with this pitiful existence, would do more for the cause of Christ than to plead a thousand times the round of all popular doctrines. John the Baptist aimed to produce the effects of such a transfiguration of the soul. He sought to spread doubt and dismay where formerly confidence and complacency were felt. He sought to school every class out of their long-cherished habits, and to disgust them with their present enjoyments, and create a craving after something nobler and better. Then having brought them by his glimpses of better things into disgust with the old, he opened up to their levying spirits the gain and blessedness of the new, which, without such management, they would neither have had the disposition to relish or room to contain.

Now, we crave upon this example the liberty of our office to summon forth the people of every class, and to dismiss them with an admonition of what becomes them as a people baptized into Christ.

The poor we exhort to be poor in spirit, rich in faith, and heirs of the kingdom; to trust to the Lord's providence, which clothes the lily of the field and feeds the raven's brood; to be industrious and frugal, and live by honest arts, not by dependence upon, or flattering of, those above them; not to be envious of superiors, or to delight in railing against those that have the rule over them, but to be sober-minded, and to hope unto the end for the glorious coming of Christ, who shall exalt those that fear Him to high and noble estate. The industrious tradesman we exhort to guard against dishonest and fraudulent dealings; to keep his heart from the love of accumulating wealth and from sensual enjoyments; to make the house of God, not the verdant fields, his Sabbath recreation; to make his fireside, not the tap-room, his evening joy; to trust in God for promotion in his craft and in the affairs of the corporation; to receive his gifts with gratitude, and to enjoy them with a merry heart, as an heir of the grace of God. To the speculative merchant, I say serve God rather than Mammon, lest the cares and anxieties of this world eat out the desire of the world to come; in all your getting, get understanding, whereof the merchandise is more precious than the merchandise of silver and gold; lay up treasures in heaven, where neither moth nor rust corrupt, and where thieves break not through and steal; oh, guard against a worldly mind; set your affections upon the things above, and hold commune with the skies, otherwise your ever-occupied activity will consume your soul with earthly cares; above all things, avoid the love of money, which is the root of all evil, and which, some having coveted after, have pierced themselves through with many sorrows; keep also from intemperance and luxurious meals, and let the exquisiteness of your meat and drink never be your boast, but give thanks to God, who hath made your cup to run over, and goodness and mercy to follow you all the days of your life. To those retired from affairs and at liberty to enjoy their ease, I say—in your present plenty and prosperity forget not your former scantiness, and remember the poor neighbourhood with which your villas may chance to be surrounded; feed the hungry and clothe the naked, and turn not the beggar from your gate; in your present rest and refreshment, forget not the many who are still plunging in the sea of this troublous world, and give them succour and sustenance according to your wisdom and ability; exalt not yourselves proudly, but condescend to those of mean estate, remembering that the Lord can bring you low; for the sake of power prostrate not your sense of sacred truth and honest principle, but stand by your country's welfare and honour in your various spheres; in your prosperity forget not God in your hearts, remember Him in your enjoyments and recreations, then will He remember you when you are in sickness and are brought down to the chambers of the grave. To those who are occupied in the world of fashion and of gaiety, I speak with admonition equally kind and instructive, for they are not outcasts from God, as they are generally regarded, but have a station of great trust and great peril committed to their watchful intendancy. You are the wardens of the forms and fashions of high life, which soon disseminate themselves through the community. Therefore, yours is no common post. Into your parties and assemblies, admit those only, men as well as women, whose reputation is unblemished by any public crime. Keep others at a distance, until by penitence and reformation they have made atonement to offended virtue, and, even then, admit them with a mark of observation. Let those parties and assemblies be graced by truth, and ornamented with cheerfulness and joy. Dismiss the vain and empty youth, who careth only for his attire; and the aged person who affects the levities and gay colours of youth, likewise dismiss. Flatterers, dismiss, and censurers, and foolish jestings, and unsober fancies. Upstart wits, who make merry with grave and serious things, dismiss. Idlers and lookers on, and paraders and flippant fools, and all the varied tribe which flutter around beauty, and bow the knee to greatness, and track the heels of influence, away with them to schools of wisdom, that they may learn to fill their empty heads with knowledge, and their more empty hearts with feeling. Sunday sports follow at your peril. Give your servants rest, and shew them an example of holiness. Take your whole household to the house of God, and, like your godly ancestors, seat yourselves at their head. Follow such customs, make such customs fashionable, and God will reward and ennoble you for evermore.

To servants, I do, in the Baptist's room, give exhortation, that they serve their masters not only with fidelity, but with affection, and contract a love for the family in which they dwell, taking an interest in its prosperity, and endeavouring to promote the same; that they guard themselves against evil company, and keep at home; that they devote their Sabbaths to the recreation of their soul, as well as their body; that they serve God, who is above all, and adorn themselves with the robes of righteousness as with a vesture, and make faithfulness the girdle of their loins. Masters, I exhort to take a charge of their household, and watch over its moral and spiritual concerns; to read the Scriptures to their assembled domestics, and to pray with them and for them; to have an eye to every chamber of the house that it be undefiled, and to allow no evil communication to pass beneath their roof, in order that the blessing of God may descend upon them from above, and their dwelling-place may become a house of God and a gate of heaven. Children, I exhort to love their parents, and honour them in the Lord ; to defend the honour of their parents by a wise and becoming behaviour at home and abroad; to second the care of their parents by giving diligent heed to their instructors, and serving their masters with faithfulness; not to forget their parents in old age, but to be around them a wall of affection and loving-kindness, that their gray hairs may come down with honour to the grave. Parents, I exhort to tend their children as a shepherd doth his sheep, and as God doth the sons of men; to teach them the fear of God, which is the beginning of wisdom, and to shun evil, which is understanding ; to train them up in the nurture and admonition of the Lord when they are young, that when they are old they may not depart from it.

Husbands, I exhort to love their wives, and wives to love their husbands, and give them honour. Young men, to guard against youthful lusts, which war against the soul, and to turn their youthful strength to the subjugation of the evil one, and the service of the living God, who will reward them with an old age of honour and an eternity of glory. Young women, to clothe themselves with modesty, not with vain apparel; to love home, and practise household virtues ; to adorn their minds with tender affections and with pious sentiments, that their very presence may wear a vestal severity, and banish far from them the idle, flippant creatures who use them for their amusement, or watch for their ruin.

Men of letters, who write for the behoof of the public, I exhort to study truth, and to set it forth with honest and intrepid zeal; to deliver themselves from prejudice, that they may set the world free from prejudice; to remember they hold the pen for God, and that God, who hath given them talents, calleth for an account of the talents which He hath given. Readers, I exhort to be of a severe and manly taste, and to discriminate between virtue and vice that is decked in virtue's guise; between noble principle and self-interest which weareth the mask of principle; between idle romance and solid truth, between amusement and edification; and, above all, to make God's own Book the standard whereunto to refer all the writings of this and other ages.

Governors, and senators, and judges, and magistrates, and all trustees of the commonweal, I exhort to hold their offices with a patriotic and a pious soul, to abjure bribery and corruption, to forget personal promotion, yea, even to forget their own interest in the higher interest of the many whose happiness dependeth in a certain manner upon their administration. Ye are God's representatives, the sacred depositaries of His power, ye wear the sacred sword of justice, ye are the hands and instruments of His providence to the nation. Therefore, remember your high estate and dignity, do faithfully by the high trusts committed to your charge; and it will come to pass that the nation's heart will beat at the mention of your names, and the nation's tongue will sing to your praise, and ye will have your tomb in the nation's remembrance, and your monument in the annals of the nation.

And the governed, the subjects, I exhort not passively to obey, but to obey out of an enlightened loyalty to the state and to the magistrate who standeth at its helm, and to turn a deaf ear to the clamours of sedition, and the speculations of political sophists. To look to the character of men, and with high disdain spout forth every renegado from honest and virtuous life, and every assassin of high and noble reputation. Nevertheless, as the good plebeians of this free realm, I exhort you to take an interest in the administration of affairs, and watch and ward the ancient liberties of the land, and keep power in check, and make corruption, as ashamed, to hide its face.

And, finally, all good Christians who have been baptized in the name of Christ, I exhort to keep their head above the world, and dwell in heaven before the time, and mortify their members which are upon the earth, and walk before the Lord in love and unity, and keep themselves unspotted from the world. I exhort you to love your Lord and Saviour, who came to seek and save you, and devote yourselves to His service, who died for you and rose again, knowing that you thereby secure to yourselves a crown of glory, which He in His time will shew who is the King immortal and invisible, the only Potentate, the King of kings and the Lord of lords. Finally, brethren, be strong in the Lord and in the power of His might, keeping truth, and doing righteously, sanctifying the Lord God in your hearts, and working the good pleasure of His will. And may the God of peace that brought from the dead our Lord Jesus, that great Shepherd of the sheep, through the blood of the everlasting covenant, make you perfect in every good work to do His will, working in you that which is well-pleasing in His sight, through Jesus Christ, to whom be glory for ever and ever. Amen.

LECTURE VI.

LUKE III. 15-18.

BEFORE proceeding, we think it necessary to make a critical remark in order to restore the unity of the discourse, which in our version is broken, as if its parts had been delivered on two separate occasions. This is caused by the version of the 15th verse, where the subject changes from the exhortation of the several classes to the announcement of Christ. It runs thus in our version, "And as the people were in expectation, and all men mused in their hearts of John, whether he were the Christ or not, John answered, saying." This has altogether the air of the beginning of a new discourse, occasioned by a new state of things, the musing and meditation of the people. It carries us from the congregation whom he had baptized and exhorted to the general public, by the expression, "All men musing in their hearts," leading us to imagine that after a season the leaven of John's preaching began to foment through the mass of the nation, upon which he took up the new strain, advertising them of Christ's speedy arrival. Now, if this break of place and time, which our translation leadeth us naturally to imagine, were actually so, we would have the unseemly and improbable spectacle of a congregation baptized and addressed by the forerunner of Christ without one hint of Him whose way his voice was consecrated to prepare. For you will take notice that in no part of the discourse which we have handled has there been one allusion to Him that was to follow, the quotation from Isaiah being by the evangelist, and not by the Baptist. Now, upon turning to the original, you that are learned will find that at the beginning of the 15th verse the very opposite of a new topic is suggested, the two parts of the discourse being linked and bound together by the most powerful conjunction of the Greek tongue. You may remember in many of our Saviour's discourses to the Pharisees and to His disciples such expressions as these,—"The Pharisees therefore said within themselves," "His disciples thereupon reasoning within themselves," which are thrown in to state the effect produced by what He said upon the minds of His audience, which effect induced Him to follow it up by something appropriate. Such expressions, instead of disjoining, do actually conjoin the two parts of the discourse, which might seem diverse the one from the other, were it not for the interjection of such a clause to signify the occasion of the new drift which it took. Now, exactly the same in the conjunctive words and in the form of grammatical construction is the clause rendered, "And as the people were in expectation, and all men mused in their hearts concerning John;" the word rendered "expectation" implies merely a casting in the mind, and that rendered "all men" is merely all. So that it runneth by the original thus, "Thereupon the people musing, and all casting in their thoughts of John whether he were the Christ or not, John answered, and said unto them all, I indeed baptize you with water, but One mightier than I cometh, the latchet of whose shoe I am not worthy to unloose; He shall baptize you with the Holy Ghost and with fire." The new rite of baptism, unknown under the Mosaic dispensation, the authoritative manner of the Baptist, and his prophetic announcement of the opening of a new era, led the people to imagine that He who was promised had now arrived; and within their hearts they meditated and mused upon this, the great national expectation. This was the very state of mind into which John had aimed to bring the congregation; he seizes it therefore, and strikes at once into the great purpose of his commission, the first advent of Christ. The two parts of the discourse, therefore, are not to be disjoined; they were addressed to the same people at the same time; the one part ushered the way for the other, and the latter took advantage of the impression which the former had made. To confirm this, we refer you at your leisure to the Gospel by Matthew, which contains the counterpart of this discourse wrought into one, without any interruption whatever.

This second part of John's discourse with the people depends then with the strongest and closest connexion upon that which went before, and is not to be separated to a different time, and place, and audience, as our version of the 15th verse disposeth one to imagine. In truth, it is the substance of his message, the end of his appearance, for which all that he had said and done was skilfully intended to prepare the way. To excite the more notice of his person, and give the more weight to his severe exhortations, he came forth from the desert in the most uncivilised garb; and having gathered the people, he took them to task in the most stern and fearful mood. He spoke as if he had held the commission of the Eternal to calumniate, and denounce, and sentence the world, proclaiming the instant commencement of a new age of judgment, and division, and wrath. Then, to cleanse the people, and wash away their pollutions, and fit them for this great investigation of men, he brings them to the stream of Jordon, so holy from the first of times, and purifies them with the baptism of repentance unto the remission of sins. Then he rises in his tone, and with notes of terror names them all; he schools them like children into a new discipline, and subdues their fierce and fiery natures by the unquenchable power of truth and holiness. All the while the people are passing through his hand, and sitting under his biting and instructive tongue, he speaketh no word in explanation of what or who he was, or in whose authority he did these terrible and unheard of things. Over this he preserveth an impenetrable silence, until the curiosity of the people arose to the highest pitch, and they began to cast within their breasts whether he might not be Messiah himself, unto whose coming they looked for deliverance from all their tribulation and thraldom. Now was the time for the skilful messenger of Heaven, for the voice crying in the wilderness, to do the office to which it had been anointed by the Most High. The people are now excited: the Messiah is present in their thoughts; they are delivered from their misconception of a high temporal prince; they think they see Him in a poor wayfaring man; they are disabused of their prejudices; and recovered to the simple conceptions of Messiah as the sent of Heaven for the world's redemption; they can be content to imagine this simple, unadorned son of holiness to be "the Wonderful, the Counsellor, the mighty God, the everlasting Father, the Prince of peace." Such power is there in wise and skilful speaking to move the minds of men, and such art is it allowable, nay, dutiful, for the messenger of Heaven to employ in his great and good office of heralding Messiah. John waited; he broke not the matter abruptly to the people full of a thousand misconceptions. But he veered about the point. He smote the consciences of the people, and shook their courage, and made them apprehensive of Divine wrath. Their nature called for protection, and they flocked to baptism, the symbol of protection; and their hearts drew to him who administered it, and they thought such a one might be Messiah, their Prince. Then he broke his mysterious, well-preserved silence, and answered to the eager, longing anxiety of the people,—" No, I am not Messiah, your Prince; I am but the forerunner of His glory, and the messenger of His coming. I am not worthy to untie the latchet of His shoe. He cometh, and is hard at hand, who is mightier than I; and when He cometh I shall wax and wane, and be forgotten. And when He baptizeth, He shall not anoint your body with water, but your soul He shall anoint with the Holy Spirit of God, and your hearts enkindle with that coal from off the altar of God with which the angel anointed the lips of the prophet. Therefore, prepare. He cometh, and every eye shall behold Him. He goeth abroad upon the earth, and divideth the sons of men in twain with the sword of division. The earth shall be before Him as the threshing-floor before the husbandman; and the people upon the earth shall be under His hand like the chaff and the corn in the hand of him that winnoweth the thrashing-floor. And the wheat He shall convey clean away to His sacred storehouse of redeemed spirits; the chaff He shall drive upon the blast of His indignation to the fire that is never to be quenched."

I cannot help remembering, before entering upon this the last prediction of Messiah, that it is the last, and that herewith the prophecy is ended, and the testimony of Christ is sealed. These verses complete the great roll of the prophecies and preparations with which God brought His only-begotten Son into the world. It had its beginning from the mouth of

God in paradise, and here it hath its close from the mouth of a wanderer in the wilderness. Strange contrast! the mouth of the Almighty, and the mouth of a houseless wanderer—the paradise of Eden, and the wilderness beyond Jordan! Yet, without being superstitious or mystical, it doth seem to me an alteration of place and person emblematical of the woeful change which four thousand years had brought upon our race. That same divine truth, the hope and ensign of a world's salvation, which flowed at first from the lips of God, as the refuge and hiding-place of our first parents from His deserved wrath, and which in the earlier ages had such credit upon the earth as to have its heralds among kings, and high priests, and princes—Enoch, and Noah, and Abraham; and Melchisedek, prince of peace; and David, the most devout, and Solomon, the most wise of kings—being spoken in temples, and palaces, and high-places: that same truth, I say, hath, in the lapse of this world's degeneracy, so fallen out of reputation with the sons of men as to find its heralds only among captives, and herdsmen, and outcasts, who, if they ventured with it into august presences, were stoned, or cast into pits and dens of the earth, or fiery furnaces and fatal prisons. Truly the time for deliverance was fully come, when the world had waxed so wicked that for a man to have a message from God was like the sealing of his warrant of death. For even this same John, who now got an audience from the mixed people, paid the price of his head for venturing it in palaces. And Christ himself was crucified, and Stephen was stoned, and eleven of the twelve apostles were put to death; and so was Paul, and thousands who, in the first ages, witnessed the good confession of Jesus Christ, the Son of the living God. This contrast of the first and last scenes and speakers of this great prophecy of a coming Saviour is not less instructive of the world's gradual removal from God and the message of God, than is the contrast of the spirit in which the beginning and ending of it are breathed. Its beginning breathes consolation and hope, its ending breathes threatening and terror. The first, which was given in these words, "The seed of the woman shall bruise the head of the serpent," was a sweet assurance that the enemy who had so rifled them of their innocency and their immortality should yet pay dearly to One of the woman's seed the price of his malice; while the last, now before us, is a stern warning of an approaching Judge, who, with rigid judgment and more rigid execution, was to make strict inquest into the characters of men. So true is it that the Almighty suits and tempers the nature of His communications to the character of the people to whom He sends them;—to the humble shewing Himself humble, to the froward shewing Himself froward; to every wicked man making Himself known according to his unrighteousness, to every good man making Himself known according to his righteousness, that men might stand in awe of His mighty power and purest holiness.

But to return to the proper subject of lecture. The people being by the skilful management of John's discourse removed from the universal misconceptions of Messiah, and doubting in their minds whether this outcast friendless person might not be He, John broke the silence of their musings, and declared, "I indeed baptize you with water; but One mightier than I cometh, the latchet of whose shoe I am not worthy to unloose: He will baptize you with the Holy Ghost and with fire." The whole subject of John's baptism as distinguished from Christ's, we separate for the subject of some future theological lecture, when we shall have brought John's ministry to an end; and therefore we say nothing of it at present. Our object is rather to catch the spirit of the Baptist, and engender in your hearts that same most dignified estimation of Christ which the Baptist expresseth. And assuredly He must have been transcendently great, and by some singular attributes elevated above the rest of men, to whom the Baptist would pay the tribute of such self-humiliation. He had rebuked every class of men in his presence, and trampled all their pride and glory in the dust, upbraiding them as a viperous generation, rebuking them as heirs of wrath, and commanding them to flee out of the tabernacle of pride, vanity, and self-conceit, and take refuge in the baptism of repentance for the remission of sins. This same stern and haughty censor of public manners, stopped not at the assembled people, but carried his searching spirit into the private recesses of individual character, advancing far and wide his humiliating and holy discipline, until he reached the very palace; and there he stayed not, but so prevailed with Herod, as to work high respect in the breast of the tyrant, not certainly by fawning flattery, but by plain and truthful dealing. He dealt with the conscience of the king as Paul did after him, and as all worthy ministers of Christ will not fail, when occasion serveth, to do to king or subject, who before God's judgment are alike; yea, he rebuked the king in his palace, the morals of which he commanded him to reform. And being cast into prison, he bore his confinement with patience, until the Lord by the cruelty of a woman saw meet to remove His faithful messenger. Such was John, so faithful to his office, and so fitted for his office, so unquenchable in his zeal for holiness, and so unabashed before the state and dignity of man. All which is necessary to be had in mind, in order rightly to appreciate the value of his testimony to Christ, that he was not worthy to untie the latchet of His shoe. The man who with his last breath levelled all distinctions, now stands abashed before one that was not present, stands self-confessed as a worthless unserviceable creature, not fit for the most menial office about His person. What an idea he must have had of the Saviour's dignity! He was himself no mean one; we have high testimony that of the sons of women, there was never a greater than John the Baptist How infinitely exalted, then, above the sons of women must He have been, of whom the sternest, the severest, and the greatest of the sons of women uttered that declaration, "He cometh after me, the latchet of whose shoe I am not worthy to unloose!" If truly Jesus be no more than what these modern heretics make Him, a prophet, an anointed prophet and no more, a son of Mary and Joseph, then John must have been strangely beside his proper character, must have forgot himself, or spoken to deceive the people, when he declared that he was not worthy to unloose the latchet of His shoe.

John truly entertained other notions of Christ when he pronounced this panegyric upon His dignity. He saw in Him the expectation of all ages, the heir of all the prophets, and the object of all the types and ceremonies of the law. He saw in Him the Judge of all the earth, who was to make division between the good and the wicked, and in whose hands were the destinies of the world. He perceived in Him the Redeemer promised to the fathers, whose name is "Wonderful, Counsellor, the everlasting Father, and the Prince of peace." He in whose distant day Abraham rejoiced, whom Moses desired the people to expect and to hear, whom David adored as his Lord, whom Solomon celebrated in his adoration of eternal wisdom, of whose sufferings and glory Isaiah wrote at large, of whose new reign Jeremiah and Ezekiel gave glorious predictions, whose arrival Daniel dated and defined, whose triumphant entrance into Jerusalem Zechariah foretold, and of whom Moses, and the Psalms, and all the Prophets bear the amplest testimony,—before all this weight of divine testimony to Christ, John felt abashed. He felt himself as nothing before Him. He abased all the high temper of his mind, and humbled himself as infinitely beneath His regard. But though a greater prophet than John never arose in Israel, yet the least in the kingdom of heaven is greater than he; that is, the least of us who live under the dispensation of Christ, know more than the Baptist knew with respect to the person of Christ. We know more than Christ himself was able to reveal to Jewish minds, we know the higher things which the Spirit taught to the apostles, and which they have taught unto us—that Jesus was the Son of God, above all powers, and dominions, and thrones, and principalities, and every name that is named in heaven; the brightness of the Father's glory and the express image of His person, who upholdeth all things by the word of His power, by whom also He made the worlds; that He is the Alpha and the Omega, the first and the last, who was, and is, and is to come—our Saviour, and our Redeemer, who hath reconciled us to God by His death, and justified us by His resurrection from the dead, who is the resurrection and the life, and in whom if a man believe he shall never die. Now if John, who saw these things dimly as through a glass, gave such high testimony to Christ, how much more ought we who live under the dispensation of the very blessings which he dimly foresaw! And in demonstrating that high reverence of our Redeemer which we feel, the Baptist also may set us the example. His rapid transition from the contempt and rebuke of other things to the adoration of his coming Lord, should not only set us the example, but shew us the proper way, of testifying our reverence to Christ.

That fine and rapid transition of John's from condemning all the painted forms and artificial vanities of human life to profound veneration of Christ, is, it seems to me, very instructive, not only to the heralds, but to all the followers, of the Saviour. Jesus Christ should be our standard of admiration, and whoever possesseth the resemblance of Christ should have our profound regard. To be a Christian is to resemble Jesus, and to feel like a Christian is to love whatsoever resembles Him. All accomplishments of body and mind ought to be viewed only as the modes and manners of the soul, which alter with time and place; and beyond these we should look for something, before yielding our homage. It is well to pay due respect to dignities; learning, also, should have its value in our eyes, and taste, and politeness, and whatever other rules the world hath adopted for preserving its welfare; but these are not ultimate things for a Christian to love or admire; they are mere conventional things for him to understand and use at the proper season. And whenever he finds them stealing upon him as ultimate goods, let him beware; whenever he finds others regarding them as such, let him pity their delusion, but by no means encourage it. Therefore, these various idols which occupy the souls of men, the fashions, the manners, the state and equipage of life, we should outface in their effrontery, and not allow them to carry it over the solid and substantial excellencies of a Christian spirit. In order to cast all these into the shade, our Lord appeared in the humblest guise, destitute of them all, without a house, without a home, without a place to lay His head. And in declaring ourselves the disciples of our Lord, we do in a manner signify that we are heedless of all these things, by attaching ourselves to One that did without them all. Now, believe me that reverence for Christ is shewn in this very thing which I now set before you. It is not merely in our glorifying Him as God by our prayers and confessions, though that should not be withheld; it is not in our upholding the value of His redemption for the sins of men, though that also should not be withheld; it is not in protesting, as we have done in this discourse, against those who underrate His nature, though that also should not be withheld; but the true exaltation of Christ consists in that which John the Baptist so well exhibited,—in despising everything by men most admired, when laid in the balance with the least upon which Christ hath set the seal of His approbation. Is not this taught in the account of the last judgment, where the prisoner, the stranger, the hungered, the naked of His house are pitched upon, not only as the most honourable characters upon the earth, but as admitting to heaven those who consulted for their welfare? The things despised, the things that are accounted nothing of the world, by these God saveth the world. Now, ye who are called by the name of Christ, I ask you if ye have the Saviour in such exaltation as to regard with high honour every virtue, every quality, which holdeth of Him, however remote it may be from the world's estimation? Do you love peace more than victory? do you covet meekness more than power? do you rejoice in the good rather than in the evil? Do you seek out those who honour their Saviour, that ye may honour them? And in short, have ye abjured the vain and pompous qualities of the world for the lowly and despised qualities of Christ?

Ah! it is an easy matter to praise the Lord and His Christ with the lips, and it is an easy matter to thunder anathemas against all who do Them dishonour; but something is required besides. Had Christ been content with expressing His sympathies for fallen man, or had He thundered His vengeance against His enemies, and cut them off from Him for ever, or used His riches and dignity only for the sake of those rich and dignified places where He dwelt from eternity, then where should this poor and desolate earth have been dwelling still but in the midst of darkness and sin and sorrow? But no, this dignified Personage, whose shoe-latchet the first of men would not have presumed to loose, made Himself of no reputation, and was content with the meanest attendance, or rather Himself became the servant of the meanest when He could do them good. He cared for no state of rank or royalty or numerous attendance; He performed for His followers the most servile office of washing their feet; He complained not of scanty meals and houseless wanderings; He complained not of misusage, and when railed upon by the lowest of the people, He railed not again, but committed Himself unto Him that judgeth righteously; He never exhibited a heart swollen with the sense of His insulted dignity, nor did He abandon wretched places over which His heart was swollen almost to bursting with sympathy, and suffering, and sorrow. Why did He so? In order to bring out to us in perfect relief a pattern of the mild, and benevolent, and patient, and persevering parts of human character, and affix our love thereto, that it might be detached from the gaudy and ceremonious, and proud, and ambitious aspects of this world.

Therefore, as many of you as the Lord our God hath called, I do entreat to take example from the Baptist's ministry, and while you look severely and with rebuke upon the idle and ostentatious displays of the world, to cultivate within yourselves admiration of the lowly graces of your Lord and Saviour, who, "though rich, for our sakes became poor, that we through His poverty might become rich." Shew forth your admiration and adoration of Him by admiring and adoring everything which apperteineth to Him. Go about and seek those who reverence Him in their hearts, and do them acts of grace. Go about among the poor, and the prisoners, and the hungry, and the naked, and be unto them as angels of mercy. Let the world roll its own way, regard it not, envy it not, and when occasion serveth, rebuke it; but be your walk in the footsteps of your Master, undervaluing gay assemblies for poor and abject places, refusing high invitations for charitable suggestions, watching over the wants of your neighbourhood, and blessing it with the tender sympathies of a disciple of Christ. In this way testify your love and estimation of Christ, and His Spirit will dwell within you. Oh, if I chose to be severe on the professing members of Christ, I could read against them sore rebukes of their paltry affectations of the world's opinions, and the world's costly and unprofitable fashions, to the injury and danger of their own souls; but I rather choose to pray you, for the sake of Christ, to be entreated to walk in His footsteps, and attach yourselves to works of charity and love, that you may bring honour to your great Head and Lord, and live in the light of His countenance all the days of your life, and after death be received unto His rest. "Blessed are the dead who die in the Lord. They rest from their labours, and their works do follow them." "Those that honour Me I will honour, and I will raise them up at the last day." "Therefore, follow after righteousness, holiness, faith, temperance. Be rich in good works, ready to distribute, willing to communicate, laying up in store for yourselves a good foundation against the time to come, that you may lay hold on eternal life." In this way testify your regard for Him who hath brought you out of darkness into His marvellous light. In the spirit of your minds do Him honour, in all your acts do Him honour; then your lips shall testify to Him of their own accord, and without a voice you shall rebuke those that undervalue Him, and by the blessing of God convert them to the knowledge of the same truth in which you stand. Which offices of Christian love may the God of all grace, the Father of our Lord and Saviour Jesus Christ, enable you to perform, to the glory of His own great name, to the manifestation of His blessed Son our Saviour, and to the salvation of your own immortal souls!

LECTURE VII.

LUKE III. 16-18.

LEAVING for separate discourse the theological question of John's baptism, what it was, and how connected with and distinguished from the baptism of Christ, we enter, not without solemn and painful feelings, upon the topic of the 17th verse, wherein is set forth the discernment and severation which the coming of Christ was to make between the wheat and the chaff, into which the sons of men are metaphorically divided by the Baptist. This effect of the preached gospel, at once to create a chasm in society, and set men apart to the right and to the left with a kind of preparatory judgment, was revealed so conspicuously upon Christ's arrival, which brought a sword upon the earth; and hath so uniformly attended the progress of His religion since, in this country and in all countries of the world; and is so much prophesied of in the Revelation, in the contest between Michael and Satan, to terminate in the great battle of Armageddon, that it may be pronounced not a casual, but a necessary, not an initiatory, but a constant attribute of the faith; and therefore it doth become a great question of Christian economy, upon which inquiry should be held, and for which the servants of Christ should be prepared. Now, this discernment and severation which Christ and His doctrines make, by their presence, between the good and the evil, cometh to pass not out of any uncharitableness or malice which they bear to men, whom they are commanded to love as they do themselves; but out of a natural disunion and disagreement which there is between Christ and the world, such as there is between light and darkness. For, while the members of Christ's body do cultivate the graces and virtues for which the Head of the Church was distinguished, it will come to pass that the world will hate them, even as it hated Him, according to His own premonition of His disciples,—" If ye were of the world, the world would love its own: but because ye are not of the world, but I have chosen you out of the world, therefore the world hateth you." Into the causes and present form of this difference between the Church of Christ and the world I shall now enter at large, according to the grace given to me, and endeavour to graft thereon such admonitions to both parties as may, by the blessing of God, be profitable unto both.

If any man will look into his own heart, and institute a comparison between its dispositions and the dispositions of the Word of God, he will find the source, the everlasting source and perennial fountain, of the discord which I have undertaken, in God's strength, to disclose. Each man must here be judge for himself; and let each man severally judge whether what I am to say be according to the truth of his own experienced feelings. First of all, there is a forgetfulness of God, a not caring to have Him in our remembrance, which is an eclipse of the soul's natural light, an eclipse, however, not like those in nature, unfrequent and incomplete, and soon passing away, but constant and ever-enduring, being under the active agency of the powers of evil, who seek to devour him with darkness, even as the savage tribes suppose of the natural eclipses of the heavenly bodies. In this absence of God's illumination, which fallen nature is born into from age to age, the soul, not seeing nor feeling God, not rejoicing in Him, nor prompted by His Spirit in righteous paths, betakes herself to the things which solicit her natural desires, and rejoice her natural inclinations, and minister to her present happiness—to things of sense, to things of science, to things of present gain. What else can she do in her prison-house, in her dark prison-house, but make the best of it? There shooteth a ray of conscience from heaven, through the grate-work of her cell; but the light from the world or the glare of hell consumeth it up, and it falls unnoticed, and exciteth to no heavenward ambitions. We become, in this absence of the divine light, in this degradation of our noble industry, like the old hoary man, who, being set free from the Bastile of France, begged for Heaven's sake to be taken back into that prison, which had unfitted him for the enjoyment of the liberal air of heaven. I know that these similitudes fall upon the ears of men like visions and dreams. They say, "What talk you of a prison-house? This earth is a spacious theatre of blooming beauty and rich enjoyment, and no prison-house or wilderness, such as your theologians do prattle of. And this natural understanding, which ye liken to darkness, is the glorious receptacle of all knowledge and all truth, the fountain of all ideas which are written in books, or established in the works of men." Even so I allow the earth doth seem, and the understanding doth feel itself to be. And by this communion with the lovely and beautiful things which are seen, this glory in the many truths which are known to nature, the soul is filled full of her own self and her own abode, and hath little or no room for the tidings which the eternal Word of God revealeth of higher intelligence, dark to nature, and of a better world—to nature unknown. The soul confineth herself to things seen and temporal, and will not be enlarged to things unseen and eternal. It will not have a wider scope, it will not be winged for heaven, it will not commune with the Father of universal truth; it is content with its present limitations, it is sophisticated by its present ideas, it loveth its present drudgery: and therefore I say again, it is naturally an imprisoned slave. What boots it to talk of enjoyment! the slaves of the West Indies have enjoyments; and what boots it to talk of liberal movements! the slaves of the West Indies have no walls about them, and yet they are pitiful, wretched slaves; they have privileges also, they have affections also, they have reason also, yet they are such slaves as no prisoner within the walls and grates of the Fleet would exchange conditions withal. And what do you talk of the spacious earth and the capacious reason! the earth is as spacious and the reason is as capacious to the Italian or the Greek; and who of you would call them free? Freedom lives in the manly mind which hath no superior but the superior of reasonable and legal government, and cannot be constrained by the will and pleasure of any other mind. And I return to my first position, and say that men are naturally wretched and imprisoned slaves. They obey not reason, with which their conduct varieth; they obey not conscience, which is the admonition of high reason; they obey not even the conceptions of their understanding, or the rules of prudence, or the receipts of experience; but they jolt from side to side, and run in all directions, they retrograde, they advance, they are stationary, they are inconsistent and incoherent, and always at war with their own selves. Repentance, remorse, new resolutions, reformations, relapses, crimes against good feeling, pains and penalties and acts of penance done before the mind's consciousness,—these are the history of every man's conduct. Who, then, is the man that will talk of his being free, in the only good and noble meaning of the term? But with the bondage of this ignoble life men have got so enamoured, entangled, and debased, that, taken as a body, they have no more heart for the enlargement which Christ bringeth to their ears, than the prize-fighters, taken as a class, have for doctrines of humility and peace; or the gipsies, taken as a class, have for the doctrines of regular settled life; or the paupers, taken as a class, have for doctrines of severe economy and noble independence; or ale-house politicians, taken as a class, have for the Saturday night of the pious cottager. The human race, taken as a whole, are in the same predicament towards Christ, and maintain against Him the same front of opposition which these several classes would maintain against any one who would go amongst them and preach redemption and deliverance from their several degradations, by which each is so degraded as to conceive it his most noble privilege and immunity.

How may such a world be expected to treat Christ, who cometh into it, teaching its fallen condition, disreputing all its glory, and stripping bare all its self-conceit, telling its good men that they are not good, its wise men that they are not wise, its kings that they should rule in righteousness, its people that they should live in peace and love. Oh, what can He expect who cometh forbidding revenge, condemning quarrel, strife, and bloodshed, that sweet game of kings and people; who cometh prohibiting intemperance and bridling lust, and stripping vanity of all her gaudy train, and striking pride low, and placing humility on high; who cometh blessing poverty of spirit, mourning, meekness, love of righteousness, mercy, peace-making, and persecuted men, and denouncing woe upon those that are rich, and those that are full, and those that laugh, and those that are well-spoken of by all mankind;—what, I say, can He expect but that those ancient masters of mankind,—those princes of the heart and rulers of the life of men,—shall rise and combine against Him, and slay His precious life, and cut off the memory of such unsparing doctrine from the face of the earth! And yet it was a wondrous pity, for truly this was like the insurrection of his countrymen against the man Moses, who would have delivered them—like the world's rejection of Noah, who could have saved them—or as if Nineveh had rejected the message of Jonas. But what can be expected of benighted men but that in their darkness they should do things of which they should be ashamed? or of enraged, infuriated men but that they should strike the mediator who would make peace between them? The men of Athens poisoned Socrates, their wisest man, because he told them truth; they also poisoned Phocion because he flinched not from the truth. And Plato was sold for a slave, and the apostles were put to violent deaths, and the reformers were either slain or ran hairbreadth escapes; and, in later times, Wesley and his followers, in this land of freedom, had often the severest encounters from the natural passions of men. Why be surprised that the world should arm against Christ? The world were not the world, if it could do anything else. If a man arise to tell them unwelcome truth, I have shewn you how the people smite him. Need I tell you how power muzzles him, and how spies watch and entrap him? It maketh no matter in what land a man maketh advances upon his age. Galileo they imprisoned. They dug up the bones of old Wickliffe, and sent them, as of old the bacchanalian rout did the limbs of Orpheus, down the stream to the mighty deep. They imprisoned Bunyan; upon Locke's head they set a price; and the patient Penn they restricted of liberty. And, in short, the world is so restful, so error and prejudice-bound, and the powers of evil do so restrain and hinder her advancement, they do so cut and maim and destroy every one who would unbind her and help her forward, that verily I declare it again, to me the wonder would have been if men could have spared Jesus Christ, the prince of truth, in whom are hid all the treasures of wisdom and knowledge, the captive earth's redeemer, heaven's champion, truth's arch-advocate, error's arch-enemy, death's destroyer, the grave's conqueror, and the bruiser of Satan's head. Oh, had the world, the devil, and the flesh done anything less than scorn and mock Him, and crown Him with thorns, and spit on Him, and crucify Him, and smite His cold and lifeless clay, then I should have hesitated whether He was the Messiah, the messenger of the living God!

And His followers must fare the same for ever, until God hath put all things under His feet. If they be bone of His bone, and flesh of His flesh, as the spouse of Christ should be; if they partake of His body as their bread, and of His blood as their living water, and bear fruit in Him as the branches do in the vine, and work concurrent with Him, as the members of the body do with the head of them, how can they otherwise fare than as He fared? "The disciple is not greater than his master, nor the servant than his lord. If they hate me, they will also hate you; if they persecute me, they will persecute you also." Whoso looketh for the love of the world and the love of Christ must be deceived, for Belial hath no communion with God, nor light with darkness, and the friendship of the world is at enmity with God. The world may alter the nature of its hostility, and even disguise it with feigned patronage; but it is not in the nature of things that they should cease to persecute this way until they wholly embrace it with their souls. Perhaps there never was an age or country in which religion had more friendly treatment than this in which our lives have been happily cast. For which it behoveth us to thank God without ceasing. But though it be an invidious task, it is not difficult to point out the enmity even of this age to Christ and the followers of Christ. There is no open persecution in person and property, which I hope is done away with for evermore. But there is a persecution of all that distinguishes the faith of Christ. Do not I call modern Unitarianism a persecution of Christ in all His most essential characters? They have robbed Him of His divinity, they have robbed Him of His offices, leaving Him only the condition of a prophet. Why, if He had claimed no more than this, the Jews would never have quarrelled with Him. The Jews persecuted not the son of Mary, but the Son of God. Had He claimed no more than a commission from on high, He would have got no worse treatment than an ordinary prophet. Into this late-sprung sect every hater of Christ at heart edgeth himself, and striketh the old favourite blow of the world under the sanction of a divine name; and they boast at heart that half the kingdom are with them, which I willingly allow, because they refuse no one to their brotherhood, and are content to admit any one who will rail upon Christ's divinity. They crucify Him, they put Him to an open shame; they strip Him of all His glory; they clothe Him in imperfect manhood, and bandy words and arguments with "the Word which was in the beginning, which was with God, and which was God." Under this banner rally all kindreds and denominations of men; your witty scoffer, your excommunicated believer, your semi-infidel, your liberal, your thin-witted speculator, and your arrogant disputer,—all under this banner launch their animosity and dislike against the true, essential, only valuable traits of Christ's character. And need I say how they stigmatise the believers in the old orthodox doctrines of His divinity and atonement,—doctrines upon which the Romish Church and both the Churches of this island, and every Church since the first foundation of our religion, have been rooted and grounded; how they stigmatise us as enthusiasts and fanatics, and men who have made shipwreck of reason, and can give no account of the hope that is in them? This, I reckon, is the most covert but most effectual head which in these times the world maketh against Christ. Next to this is the dislike of the higher ranks of fashion. If you talk to them of the humility of a Christian, of his being in the Spirit all the day long, of his denying himself to all untruth and ungodliness; if you set religion in array against their hollowness of heart, their vain pretences, their time and life-consuming gaieties, their squanderings and dissipations—they make brief work of it, and call you mad. You are bit as with an infection, and lost to all good. So that to be a Christian in their atmosphere, you must be in a great degree an outcast, or you must take up the cross against father and mother, and brother and sister, and friend. Next to this I place in order the persecution of men of business, whether professional or mercantile. Your medical men are too knowing, and your lawyers are too busy in their chambers, and merchants too intent on drudgery and luxury, and the lower classes so set upon recreation-potions to steep weary labour in oblivion, that, if all these classes have any idea about heartfelt godliness and living faith in Christ, it is to scoff at it, and to decry it as cant or weakness. Truly it is not my wish to exaggerate, but when to this coldness, and scoffing, and hatred I add the discountenance of sober-minded, zealous pastors, by those who have the power, the decrying of Calvinism, which this age mistaketh for necessity and fatalism, and the adoption of meagre, unsubstantial Arminianism, the discountenance and discontinuance of the strong, manly, spiritual discourse of our fathers, and the patronage of empty essays of morals or rhapsodies of enthusiasm,—when I take these things into account, it seemeth to me that there is at bottom as successful an opposition maintained to vital religion in this day as in former times, and that the world is as full of animosity as ever it hath been to the cause of our blessed Saviour.

When I reflect upon what hath been said, and cast an eye upon the mass of popular opinions and feelings, to observe whether I have spoken according to the truth, the conviction is borne in upon my mind that I am not up to the true mark of this age's mistreatment of Christ. The best index of the esteem in which the world holdeth any set of opinions will be found in the printed and popular books. These are, as it were, the voice of the time, the record of the common mind. Now, if you compare the thought at present expended in the service of Christ with what was wont to be expended in former times, you shall find it infinitely decreased both in quality and in quantity. There are no such men now as there were wont to be, girded about with the girdle of the truth, and engaging for Christ in the front ranks of the great contest of thought. If you want a powerful demonstration against the infidel, or a strenuous wrestling with the world, or a heart-searching appeal to your own personal condition, any divine contemplation, any quintessence of thought, or unction of godliness, you have to go back several ages to draw it forth from the great men of old, who, though dead, still speak by their works. The men of Christ are dismayed, driven back, and heartless; they make no onset, they muster not, they gather not, they burst not upon the enemy, they are content to be unmolested, they allow the science, the literature, the poetry, the policy of the age to depart from God; they give them bad names, they curse them, and then they are contented. They wait in expectation of some second Pentecost to do the marvellous and hopeless work of recovering this nation; they pray for the outpouring of the Spirit, they form societies, and do little else. But verily they ought to think, they ought to reason, they ought to rouse their manhood, and awake these gifts, and be brave and expeditious in the warfare of the soul, and so serve Christ with the very utmost, noblest capacities which He hath bestowed. Not only do the books printed in behalf of Christ manifest by universal consent a waning strength, but the other books against Him have gotten a strength inestimable. Books of science and philosophy have in general waxed so contemptuous as to think the subject beneath mention, or worthy only of an equivoque or a sneer. Books of imagination, how insolent they generally are towards vital godliness, I say not, because it needeth not to be said. And your circulating literature, which I suppose composeth two-thirds of this nation's reading, is a most unweeded garden of envious and hostile feeling, of sectarian and partisan passions. The Church, the catholic and universal Church, the mystical body of Christ, is totally forgótten in the midst of party contentions and worldly interests. It is all about right and establishment, emolument, power, and such like adventitious attributes of religion. On these they are very eloquent, very indignant, very bold; but upon the verity itself, upon the hindrances and opposition to Christ, upon the currents of power setting against Him, say but a word, and they will devour you. Such defenders of the faith! such advocates of truth! And will any man who taketh all these things into account, and many more, of which it is not convenient to speak at this time, say that this world hath dropped its hostility towards the Church, or that the same discrepancy and discordance which hath existed from the beginning existeth not still, ay, and will exist till the world end, or the Church hath annihilated the world by converting it and taking it to its bosom?

Seeing, then, that the presence of Christ and His discipline doth continue down to the present time to make division upon the earth, and rouse up all the evil passions and interests of man into an active hostility against His peaceful, unoffending Church, and that the thing threatened by the Baptist doth exist amongst us, and that our people are divided into two portions, the fruitful friends and barren enemies of Christ, who are lying confused and intermingled like wheat and chaff upon the unwinnowed threshing-floor, it now falleth to my office to lift up my voice amongst you and strike the warning of the great Husbandman's arrival, who will thoroughly purge His floor, and will gather the wheat into His garner, and burn the chaff with fire unquenchable. And think not that I love this office of fearful admonition. I love it not, but I hate it not, and I will not flee from it when our evangelist presents a proper occasion. I would make my lecture as broad as my text, and so discourse as widely as the inspired document. And this, the age having neglected, hath run itself into narrows and creeks in the great ocean of religious thought, instead of keeping the open and illimitable ocean, and trafficking to all the regions of human interest and knowledge.

Let the enemies of Christ be therefore warned—those who, under various forms, have been mentioned above: His enemies under guise and name of friends, who, under covert of the name of the Most High, put to shame His only-begotten Son, and think they serve God by depreciating the brightness of His glory and the express image of His person; next, His enemies for the world's sake, who, from their several spheres of power, and pride, and fashion, and knowledge, and riches, frown indignation upon His humble, faithful followers; next, His enemies who revile Him in the standing monuments of books, who, by their wit serve discord, folly, and wickedness, and renounce the faith, and sell themselves to some adverse interest within the land: all these, and every other class or individual man who hath not the love of Christ in his heart, and bridleth not his tongue by His wisdom, nor directeth his life by His commandments, but maketh his religion a matter of form, or a matter of gain, but not a matter of all-directing principle,—all, I say, to whom religion in their mind stands by the side of morality and of policy and of worldly wisdom, as a book in a library standeth by the side of other books, whereas it should be to them what intelligence is to all the books, the very thing which maketh them profitable,—all such religious (that is, self-named religious) or irreligious, public or private, avowed or secret enemies of Christ in this Christian land, must take warning that their destruction will come and will not tarry, that they shall be accounted of only as the chaff which the wind driveth to and fro, and used as the chaff is used, to be consumed in the fire unquenchable. They are but the husks of men, the outward slough, and no more; they shroud within their body or their mind no divine generative principle. They can propagate their kind upon the earth, but in the soil of heaven they root not, they spring not, they flourish not. What availeth it to mince the matter and shipwreck souls? If ye cannot hear, ye cannot; if ye will not, ye will not. But that mattereth not. It is certain as that the Lord liveth that ye shall be consumed if you abide and continue in your animosity to the most merciful and forgiving Son of the most high God. Here twice, nay, thrice, in one brief discourse hath the Baptist rung your peal, "Who hath warned you to flee from the wrath to come?" Every tree which bringeth not forth good fruit is cast into the fire and is burned; the chaff He shall consume with fire unquenchable. And the Lord himself hath read unto you the same most awful fate—" If a man abide not in me, he is cast forth as a branch, and is withered; and men gather them, and cast them into the fire, and they are burned." The tares are at the great harvest gathered together and cast into the fire that never shall be quenched. What say ye then, fellow-men, who bear an evil heart to Christ? This is the end and issue of your enmity. It came not of man's wit, and cursed is the man who hideth it from his fellow-men. We are but the organ of the word, the voice that crieth in the wilderness.

Ours is not to provoke you, but to announce the will of God concerning you, which is this, that if you drop not the weapons of your warfare against Christ, be they riot, or wickedness, or wilfulness, or lust, or pride, or avarice, or vanity, or cruelty, or any form of abused power,—if ye lay them not down, and repent of your past rebellion, and humble yourselves in dust and ashes, and accept His overtures of forgiveness, and strike with Him an everlasting covenant of peace and amity, and keep in His cause till the end of your days—this way, this only way of salvation, if you refuse, then verily there remaineth for you only the way of destruction which you now tread, which leadeth down to the chambers of the grave, with the fearful looking for of judgment and of fiery indignation to consume you quick. Call me not cruel, my fellow-men, for so stating the truth; then Christ was cruel who died for the world, and every prophet who warned the world, and every apostle who compassed the world with the ministry of salvation; and every father is cruel who sets the ruin that waits on evil courses before his child; and every friend is cruel who holds back his friend and points to ruin in his path; and every physician who prognosticates the fatal issues of disease to his patients, or to hinder those issues, cuts and lacerates his tender frame. Call it not cruelty that I thus from time to time make known the fatal issues and conclusion of an unchristian life; but call it kindness: for therein I do for your sakes disguise and discompose my own proper nature, which is to preach the tender mercy of Christ to all to whom, consistently with the truth of Christ, it may be preached. And, accordingly, all friends of the persecuted Saviour, who love Him in their heart, and with their heart believe unto righteousness, I hail with all my affections to the inheritance of the promise which accompanies the threatening in the text; and my only grudge is, that this welcome doth not embrace the whole world. But there is this consolation, that every one hearing me it doth, if they choose, embrace; and if it embrace them not, their own obstinacy, and that alone, is to be blamed. They will not come unto Jesus that they may have life. Those, therefore, who have within them the everlasting seed of the word, which liveth and abideth for ever, shall soon be removed from this the winter of their growth. Whatever be their unsightliness or their lowliness in the eyes of the world, however despised and underrated—if they sanctify the Lord God in their hearts, and have within them the germ and principle of the divine life, they shall be removed in the midst of all their depression, and admitted to the mansions which Christ hath prepared for those that love Him. It rejoiceth my heart to think what bed-ridden, infirm, heart-broken sufferers, what humble cottagers, what reviled and persecuted worthies, what imprisoned and tortured martyrs, what men of truth whose reproofs society could not endure, what men of divine schemes whose bosoms laboured with desires of good, which philosophy contemned and power held back, shall be brought, each from his unnoticed abode, and his unbefriended employment, and translated by the Lord to uphold the concerns of heaven.

O brethren! Christian brethren! if ye be persecuted by the world for Christ's sake, rejoice and be exceeding glad, for great is your reward in heaven. "Ye shall rest from your labours, and your works shall follow you." And let not your imperfections trouble you, and Christ will present you to God pure and blameless, without spot or wrinkle, or any such thing. And the husbandman valueth not more the precious wheat, the reward of his labour, and the hope of future harvests, than Christ valueth you, who are the reward of the much travail or His soul, and whom He hath purchased with His precious blood out of all kindreds, and nations, and tongues. And the husbandman doth not, when he hath parted the wheat from the chaff, store it with more care in his garners, and there defend it from every risk, than will your Saviour, when He hath by judgment once parted you from the wicked, remove you from the reach of all that now trouble your peace, and place you in as much safety as was he who was removed from the rich man's gate and carried to Abraham's bosom.

Now, when I take this thing to thought—this thing which is commonly spoken of, but seldom thought of—that a creature should be trained for heaven in the school of this sinful world, in a place where sin is reigning on all hands, for a place where sin is not, it doth seem to my mind the most amazing of all things, and one of the highest exercises of Almighty grace; in a place where all is dust and corruption, for a place where all is pure essence and immortality; in a place where all God's works are marred with sin, where men verge in their baseness to the very edge of brutality, where our notions are vulgar, our intercourse impure, our words deceitful, our books ungodly; the whole shape and form of life—the painted sepulchre or the adorned coffin of purity and godliness, which it containeth not, but hideth and burieth,—that such a place as earth should become a nursery for such a place as heaven, is, we declare the most marvellous of all things; and in proportion as it is marvellous, the more devoutly to be admired and praised. And that this should be compassed upon the heirs of glory, without altering one law of temptation, or culling one agent of sin, but permitting to them as varied arms and as fair a field as before, compassed by the love and watchfulness of the great Bishop of our souls, is the most wonderful display of Divine power, and wisdom, and grace, whereof we have any record.

The more do ye require, who feel within your souls the growing meetness for heavenly places. "It is the doing of the Lord, and wondrous in our eyes." Be of good cheer under the enmity of men. Greater is He that is for us than all who can be against us. Take not the maltreatment of the world amiss; for thereunto ye are called, that ye might inherit a blessing. For Christ also suffered for us, the just for the unjust, that we should follow His steps. If ye suffer for righteousness, happy are ye, and be not afraid of their terror, neither be troubled. But sanctify the Lord God in your hearts, and be ready always to give an answer to every man that asketh you a reason of the hope that is in you with meekness and with fear.

LECTURE VIII.

MATT. III. 13; LUKE III.

TO this baptism of John, at Bethabara beyond Jordan, came Jesus the son of Mary, from Nazareth, in which place He had lived since the death of Herod, subject to His parents, increasing in wisdom and in stature, and in favour with God and men—being about thirty years of age, the time at which the Levites under the law were wont to be anointed and set apart to the priestly office. He came on purpose to be baptized of John, in the river Jordan, along with the rest. John, though he knew Him not, as he himself declareth, knew that upon this occasion He was to be made manifest unto Israel; therefore, says he, am I come baptizing with water. So that the Almighty, by this general assembly of the people, and solemnising of their minds and purifying of them in Jordan, intended to put things into a condition sufficiently dignified for that event which we are now to discourse of. He wished to manifest His Son by a voice and a sign from heaven, and to that end it was necessary to assemble a multitude of the people, which multitude being assembled, it was necessary to bring into a reverend and attentive frame, that the effect might not be transient, but abide. From this assembly, His Son was to draw the most faithful of His adherents, His first witnesses and apostles. Therefore the Lord sent forth His servant whom He had prepared in the wilderness to rebuke and chasten the minds of the people out of levity and sinfulness, and induce upon them all a frame of penitence and apprehension of wrath, and desire of the Saviour's appearance; which end being accomplished by the act of baptism and the discourse ye have listened to, all was mature and ready for the great demonstration now about to be given of the Son of God.

Jesus came forward and offered Himself for baptism, but not until all the people had been baptized before Him. John, by what sign we know not, recognised His person, and forbade Him, saying, "I have need to be baptized of thee, and comest thou to be baptized of me? But Jesus answering said unto him, Suffer it to be so now; for thus it becometh us to fulfil all righteousness. And he suffered him." The baptism being a baptism of repentance for the remission of sins, John perceived it to be out of place for One who had done no sin, neither was guile found in His lips, and would have hindered Christ from being subjected to a rite which had in it a confession of sin of which He was guiltless. With that humility and self-abasement, therefore, before higher gifts, which is not only consistent with, but always attendant upon, a hatred and free rebuke of meanness and iniquity, John wished to receive the rite at the hands of Jesus, as being conscious of much imperfection and wickedness. "I have need to be baptized of thee, and comest thou to me?" So ought every minister of the Lord to feel in the presence of his Saviour, that he is but a servant; and though it be his duty in that office to rebuke the various frailties and errors of men, to feel that he himself standeth in the same necessity, and would do well to submit to the same ritual at his Master's hand; for the best are unprofitable servants, and come short of the glory of God. The Saviour, who was better acquainted with the nature both of His own and the Baptist's commission, answered and said unto him, "Suffer it to be so now, for thus it becometh us to fulfil all righteousness. Then he suffered him." In which answer you will observe the Saviour payeth respect to John's scruple, and asks it not upon right but upon sufferance; thereby admitting that the true purport of the ordinance appertained not to Him, but that it behoved or became Him to fulfil all righteousness. To understand this expression, I crave your attention to the following explanation :—This baptism was an ordinance of God, whereby the gospel dispensation was to be introduced. It was part of the Divine appointments, and it became Christ as the end and fulfilment of the law, to submit Himself thereto. "Forasmuch as the children were partakers of flesh and blood, he also

Himself took part of the same;" and taking part of the same, He must submit to all the conditions flesh and blood are heir to. Therefore He was born of a woman; therefore He was submitted to the rite of circumcision, and presented before the Lord in the temple; and went up to the passover, and attended in the synagogue, and observed all the law, which He came not to destroy but to fulfil; and not only so with respect to the institution of Moses, but also with respect to the institution which He Himself was to set up. He partook of the supper which He instituted, and humbled Himself to wash the disciples' feet. He bore His own cross, which we are commanded to take up and follow Him. He was crucified in the flesh, which we have also to submit to; and He was quickened by the Spirit, by which same Spirit that raised Him from the dead, we also are raised to newness of life; and in everything He set us the example of our Christian calling, that we might follow His steps. Whether, therefore, this baptism of John be understood as holding of the old dispensation or of the new, it was incumbent upon Christ, who submitted to every institution of both, to fulfil it. It was a part of righteousness, that is, it was a part of God's holy commandments, which Christ came into the world to shew us the example of fulfilling, both in the letter and the spirit; and therefore, though He had no wickedness to repent of, nor sins to be forgiven, it became Him to be immersed in the water of baptism, that the apostle might afterwards be able to say, "Being buried with Him in baptism."

To fulfil all righteousness, I understand therefore to mean, to observe every institution appointed or sanctified by God. For the word in the original is not "holiness," but justice, —not "spiritual purity," but clearness from condemnation, and innocency before the law; and the word "to fulfil" is not to perfect, but to implement. "It behoveth us, it is necessary, or a part of my office, to implement the demands of the divine law, though they apply not to My proper and everlasting nature. I am come forth from the Eternal for this very end of submitting to the laws, moral or ceremonial, which God imposeth on man; to brave all the ills and natural maladies which sin hath brought upon the world; to be tempted by the alternate powers of the devil, the world, and the flesh, to finish transgression and make an end of sin, and with My dying breath to testify in the face of heaven, 'It is finished:' the work which Thou gavest me to do, that I have performed; the cup which Thou gavest me to drink, I have drained it to the very dregs." The Captain of our salvation, saith the apostle, was made perfect through suffering,—not that in His proper nature He was ever affected with imperfection, but that, in order to be the Captain and Leader of men out of thraldom, it behoved Him to be brought in contact with their sympathies, to obtain their confidence; and it behoved Him to come down into the shaded forest-chamber of this suffering world, to sound the depths of sorrow, and become acquainted with the extreme passages of grief, and thence to ascend, bearing all and braving all, with all the whips and scourges of misery upon Him, and all the arrows of the enemy sticking round about Him, to ascend through the very article of death and jaws of the grave, through the rent veil of His flesh,—to ascend, conquering and to conquer, into that glory to which, as the Captain, He would lead all the captive suffering children of men. This is the spirit of His incarnation, one great end and meaning of His manifestation in sinful flesh, to teach humanity how there resideth with the Spirit of God a power to fortify humanity, and make it victorious over all trials and temptations,—a power to reconstruct the fallen ruins of humanity into a temple of holiness, wherein the service of God shall proceed more purely than it did in the tabernacle of Moses, or in the temple of Solomon, or any other emblem of the heart of man, which is the only temple of the most high God. This courage and confidence in his power of being regenerated could never, never have been imparted to sinful human nature but by an instance, an experiment made into the world of human nature of very flesh and blood, being preyed upon at all points, and standing fast in its integrity through the mighty operation of that Spirit, which is freely offered to perform the same office in all who will take up His cross and follow His footsteps. Therefore He said unto John, "Suffer it to be so now, for thus it is My office to fulfil every righteous appointment of God's, and in the end to stand acquitted before the law of Moses, and before My own better law of having fulfilled to the very uttermost all their obligations." And John suffered Him,—that is, he acquiesced in His higher wisdom and better judgment, acting in the spirit of his declaration just uttered to the people, "There cometh One, the latchet of whose shoes I am not worthy to unloose." So also the centurion was humbled with a sense of unworthiness before the Lord, and thereby grew in His favour, and drew forth His admiration. So also the woman who washed His feet with tears in Simon the Pharisee's house, drew down the forgiveness of her many sins by her silent abasement before His holiness. So also the woman who shewed that last attainment of faith and humility by touching the hem of His garment, as He went on His way to heal the daughter of Jairus, the ruler of the synagogue. Which instances do all testify that there is a timorous unwillingness, proceeding from a sense of insufficiency—a misgiving before the thought of Christ's holiness or holy law, which is to Him a great commendation, and draweth from Him encouragement and a supply of the needful grace and strength; even as Paul, under that strong self-conviction, three times besought to be delivered from any longer contention with his infirmity, had that most gracious inspiration bestowed on him, "My grace is sufficient for thee, and My strength is perfected in weakness." Wherefore, holy brethren, partakers of the heavenly calling, humble yourselves and ye shall be exalted; when you are weak, then are you strong; when you feel your insufficiency, and cry with strong prayer and intercession unto God, then your help cometh from His sanctuary, where reside the chariots and horses of the Most High.

When John had yielded to the will of his Lord and Master, and done the office of baptizing Him, He straightway came up out of the water, and being absorbed in prayer, the heavens were rent, and the Holy Ghost descended in a bodily shape like a dove upon Him, and a voice came from heaven, which said, "This is my beloved Son, in whom I am well pleased." Every outward ordinance of God's appointment is intended as the vehicle or instrument for conveying divine grace from on high. Of these ordinances, that of the written Word is the first and noblest, which is the great vehicle of immortal truth; and being used as a vehicle for the spirit of man to come into audience of the Spirit of God, it never faileth to bring down the light of divine intelligence into the soul. Creation also is a vehicle of divine wisdom; and being contemplated with devout regard, will yield no small knowledge of His eternal power and godhead, which are clearly seen in the things that are made. So also is providence a medium of communing with the invisible things of God, and the richest and most constant food to prayer. So also of the ordinance of baptism, which some are apt to regard as a mere ceremony, and which others misinterpret into complete regeneration. But it is an instrument of grace to every child who is admitted thereto, a constant presentation to the opening mind, that, as it opens and feels the darkening of its sinful nature, there is also coeval therewith the opening of a dawn, whereof by baptism the portals were disclosed, and from which it may expect a fountain of light, able to struggle with and overcome the darkness of nature. On which account I regard infant baptism as a question of high importance in the Church of Christ. And, in like manner, there is a grace which accompanieth the communion of the body and blood of Christ, and which is present in those symbols to all who with devout souls come to seek it,—as much present as nourishment is present in the bread and wine to the body of man. Therefore, when the body submitteth to the ceremony, the soul should expect and seek the grace therein contained; and as prayer is the action of an expecting and seeking soul, prayer, inward prayer of the soul, should always go in concert with the action of the body, whether that action be in reading the Word, in beholding creation, in studying providence, in administering baptism, or in receiving the communion of the supper. Agreeably to this principle of all divine institutions, our Lord having submitted to baptism, was wrapt in prayer or communion with His Father's throne; just as any of us ought to be when waiting upon the Lord in His ordinances. For, brethren, you ought always to remember, in meditating the actions of Christ's life, that He was very man; that He was liable to human reason, as well as to human sense and human suffering; that He was on earth towards God, seeking His face, and following His counsel, and meditating His nature, even as men are upon the earth; not an angel, but an embodied spirit, and that the spirit which was embodied was the spirit of man. I consider Him waxing from youth to manhood, according to the growth of human nature, struggling with its infirmities, tried with its trials, living in the same twilight of divine knowledge, and needing the same aids of a written Word, of prayer, and of communion, which man doth need. And, therefore, when He ascended out of the water, He waited in expectation of grace to be given to Him from on high; and He besought it with the humility of a supplicant.

Nor did He wait nor beseech in vain. God in heaven prepared to make the great and glorious demonstration of His incarnate Son. He had concerted all this assembly, all these ceremonies for this very end; and now the conjunction was come, and the time was fulfilled. The moment the ceremony had been performed upon Jesus of Nazareth, and He ascended out of the water praying in His heart, and the universal Eye being bent upon Him as the last of the baptized; then the heaven was rent and divided asunder, and the blue vault disclosed the empty space within the ethereal curtain, and the winged messenger of peace, which, in Noah's time, brought tidings of God's mercy returned to the earth, came forth, and sought the head of Jesus as He came unto the dry land. And when the people stood beholding the miracle of God, stunned into the mutest silence, the awful silence of the people was broken by the voice of Jehovah as of thunder, and in the ears of all the people it pronounced these words:—"This is my beloved Son, in whom I am well pleased."

Now was fulfilled the ancient prophecy of Moses—"A Prophet shall the Lord your God send like unto me, hear Him." Now was fulfilled the prophecy of Isaiah—"There shall come forth a rod out of the stem of Jesse, and a Branch shall grow out of his roots; and the spirit of the Lord shall rest upon

Him, the spirit of wisdom and understanding, the spirit of counsel and might, the spirit of knowledge and the fear of the Lord." Now He was consecrated with the oil of joy above His fellows, and now was declared the decree of the Lord— "Thou art my Son, this day have I begotten Thee; ask of me and I shall give Thee the heathen for an inheritance, and the uttermost parts of the earth for Thy possession." To this event St Peter, looking back, says on this wise—" The word was published throughout all Judæa, and began from Galilee, after the baptism which John preached; how God anointed Jesus of Nazareth with the Holy Ghost and with power: who went about doing good, and healing all that were oppressed of the devil; for God was with Him." To this Paul maketh reference in the same manner in his discourse to the men of Antioch, referring the beginning of his ministry to this same event—" Of David's seed hath God, according to His promise, raised unto Israel a Saviour, Jesus: when John had preached before His coming the baptism of repentance unto all the people of Israel."

When God called Moses to be His messenger unto Israel, it was by the back of Horeb, over against the wilderness; when He called Samuel to be a prophet in Israel, it was in the dead of night in the temple of the Lord; and when He, by the hand of Samuel, anointed Saul to be king over Israel, it was between themselves two; and when He anointed David, it was in the midst of his brethren, in his father's house; and Ezekiel was visited among the captives by the river of Chebar; and it came to Amos among the herdman of Tekoa; and unto the Baptist it came in the lonely wilderness; and unto Saul, the persecutor, as he travelled onward to Damascus; and unto John, the apostle, in the solitude of Patmos. Not one of these, the anointed ones of God, His angels and messengers unto the sons of men, had any congregation of the people assembled, any general diet of Israel before whom to bring him forth with honour, no herald to foreshew his coming, no baptism to purify the bodies, no Baptist's discourse to purify the hearts of the people, no opening of the vault of heaven, no formal messenger from on high, or visible presentation of the Spirit of God, no voice of the Eternal, no words of loving kindness from the tongue of the Most High, nor fatherly benediction, nor celestial commendation unto all the sons of men, "This is my beloved Son, in whom I am well pleased."

This was an honour reserved for Him whom prophet, priest, and king prefigured; in whom Israel was to be glad and Judah to rejoice; who was to manifest His glory to the Gentiles, and of whose fulness all the nations were to partake.

This testimony, which God gave at Bethabara to the children of Israel, is not less given to us, men and brethren, upon whom the ends of the earth have fallen. It was not given in that miraculous way in order to astound their ears or terrify their hearts into acquiescence, but it was given in that way in order to overcome the strong prejudices in which that people, and in which all people, are bound towards the messages of Heaven. The daily routine of life, and the sensible, visible laws of nature so fix the attention of mankind, and carry them away from stale contemplations upon the nature of God and the obligations of duty, that, in order to deliver them, the Almighty had to break the laws of nature, and thereby dissolve the confidence in visible things, which, as it were, charmed the people away from hearing His voice. Nature, visible nature, in some shape or other, is the idol of all men. The Almighty had to enter the temple of this idol, and, as it were, set its ritual aside, in order to shew how weak the idol is.

The miraculous part of the testimony is, therefore, a small part of it, only accessory, and rendered so by the stupid devotion of men to sensible things. The true and substantial part of the message is the information that Jesus of Nazareth, the man Jesus, was the Son of God, in whom He is well pleased, and whom we are commanded to hear. God singled Him out from myriads of men, as the one to whom they were to give ear, as the one whom He loved and honoured as His Son. Now, this Son of God, so approved of Heaven, hath left His words on record, and brought them into your hands. And God requireth of us attention to the same. He will question us why we listened to every teacher and perused every author's book, but heeded not that which He licensed and stamped with His own hand—"None of those masters of taste or science, in whom you take pleasure, have any authority, yet you hear them; Him only you do not hear whom I proclaimed from My holy place."

I trust, my Christian brethren, this accusation applieth not to you, that you give to the Saviour the reverence to which this signal distinction entitles Him. He cometh as your Brother, seeking your love; He cometh as your Friend, seeking your friendship. He will introduce you to His Father, and His Father will dwell with you, and you will have the marvellous honour of being called the sons of God; and when He who is our life shall appear, we shall be like Him, for we shall see Him as He is.

Such honour doth Christ present to you. In order to bring this within your power, He loved you from eternity. And to make it known, He became flesh, and submitted to the various appointments of the law, and to this ceremony of which we have discoursed. Therefore, I pray you to be stirred up and magnify the Son of God, who died for us, and rose again.

LECTURE IX.

JOHN I. 19-28.

FROM this passage of Scripture we learn that besides the people, and publicans, and soldiers mentioned by Luke, there came a deputation from Jerusalem to wait upon the Baptist, and discover from his own lips what was his character and intentions. The Jews sent priests and Levites from Jerusalem to ask him "Who art thou?" Out of some political motive, some reason of state, or some vile apprehension of their place and nation, they dispatched these subtle and crafty men to put the question to the Baptist. And the Baptist met their subtlety and craft with truth and simplicity—the proper and always successful antagonist of duplicity. He confessed, and denied not, and said plainly, "I am not the Christ." And they asked him, "What, then, art thou Elias?" building upon the last words of the Old Testament, "Behold I will send you Elijah the prophet before the coming of the great and fearful day of the Lord." Now, John truly was the object of this prediction; as our Saviour declareth, "All the prophets and the law prophesied unto John, and if ye will receive it, this is that Elias which was to come." The prophet gave John the name of Elias, as denoting best the character he was to be of; but the Jews misinterpreted it into the notion that Elias was to come again, and at the passover were wont to put it in the form of a question to their children. And in this sense the scribes and Pharisees asked the Baptist if he was Elias returned; to which John replied that he was not. Then they put it to him, "Art thou that prophet?"—meaning, it is likely, the prophet foretold by Moses before his death, "A Prophet shall the Lord your God raise up among your brethren like unto me, Him shall ye hear in all things." To this also he answered, "No." Then said they, "Who art thou, that we may give answer to them that sent us? What sayest thou of thyself?" He answered, "I am the voice of one crying in the wilderness, Make straight the way of the Lord." Then they questioned him of the authority of his baptism, to which he replied, announcing the better baptism which was to follow. Such was the record that John gave concerning Christ to the official people that waited upon him from Jerusalem—simple, and full of truth, self-denying and glorifying the Master before whose face he came to prepare His way. Of this witness the Saviour Himself maketh honourable mention in the defence of His divinity before the Jewish people:—"There is another that beareth witness of me; and I know that the witness which he witnesseth of me is true. Ye sent unto John, and he bare witness unto the truth. But I receive not testimony from man: but these things I say, that ye might be saved. He was a burning and a shining light: and ye were willing for a season to rejoice in his light. But I have greater witness than that of John: for the works which the Father hath given me to finish, the same works that I do, bear witness of me, that the Father hath sent me." Notwithstanding of all this honest self-denial, and faithful witness to Messiah, we are told in another place these deputies believed not, neither were impressed by the man who prevailed over the ignorance of the people, and the hard-heartedness of the publicans, and the ferocity of the soldiers; which shews that, of all the strongholds of Satan, pride is the strongest, which truly is more than ordinary error, being the boast and bravery of error. A proud man is not only hardened like the rest of this world, but he is annealed. He hath added to the hardness of the iron the temper of the steel; and when others are bruised he will not yield, but will fly to pieces sooner. Also we are taught by this example, that of all the forms of pride, the pride of knowledge is the most insuperable; the pride of riches in the publicans yielded, as also the pride of chivalry in the soldiers, when the pride of knowledge in the scribes and Levites did only gather fresh importance. Of which also the reason is most obvious, because knowledge is the eye of the mind, which, being blinded by error, leaves all passage impervious; and when pride comes to the aid of such knowledge, it employeth our hands and all our faculties in withstanding any kind friend who would remove the veil, so that we are in darkness, and vain of our darkness, and barricaded in it till One stronger than ourselves do set us free. These spies having done the duty of spies, went home to their masters more hardened than they came, and reported things, I doubt not, with the usual exaggeration of spies. But however this was, their masters believed as little as the deputies, insomuch that we have not the slightest hint that one of them listened with any favour to the Baptist; but, on the other hand, we have reason to believe they utterly rejected him and his doctrine. For the Saviour, when they put Him to the torture of dangerous questions, retorted upon them with that which silenced them at once. "John the Baptist's ministry, was it from God?" They durst not say from God, for then the question followed, "Why believed ye him not?" They durst not say of men, for then they feared the people, who all believed John to be a prophet. This is a most instructive lesson to us upon the subject of religious prejudice, which perhaps of all other forms of prejudice is the most difficult to be convinced. For religion, when it hath taken a seat in any heart, is the most sacred and the most valuable of its possessions; and anything which threatens it is regarded as a most deadly enemy. And truly, if it threaten the strongholds of religion, a most deadly enemy it is. But not only the strongholds, but everything connected with it comes to take equal importance; the forms, the ceremonies, the abstractions and subtleties of faith acquire as much, yea, often more sanctity than the tempers, and graces, and godly habits which are the end of the revelation. And any one who sides not with us in these, the devices of man, and the accommodation of particular times and ages, we reject from our charities, of whatever report he may be in the attainments of the divine life. This pharisaical spirit, this love of outward and traditional things, hath afflicted every age, and afflicteth this present age in no small degree; and I question whether, in this state, we shall ever have it extinguished. For there is an opinionativeness which seems almost inseparable from faith, and which yet is not of the essence of faith. If indeed our faith cometh from hearing of men, or from tradition, or from any other source than the fruits of the Spirit wrought in our heart and life, this dogmatism will continue to attend it; but if it spring from the proof of the thing, from the inbred conviction of its holy fruits, from the growth of heavenly temper, then that charity riseth up within the breast which thinketh no evil, is the death of all divisions and of all evil-speakings, and the true form of Christ's discipleship is manifested within us. In looking upon the outward, visible Church, it hath always appeared to me divided into two classes—one which held Christ in all charitableness, and another which held Him in all uncharitableness; the former lying open to light, and trying every spirit with a kind experiment, and hoping the best, and hard to be convinced of evil—the latter, doubting and distrusting every one, weighing his every word with a critical exactness, and with all their ears listening to the report of evil; the former intelligible, by their simplicity and singleness of heart—the latter most confused and unapproachable, by reason of their bigotry to their church and favourite pastors, and their forms and other credentials; the former most soft and touching, by their tender pity of your frailties, and their kind counsels of your waywardness—the latter most repulsive by their firm and constrained fellowship, into which you can enter as a party only through the needle's eye of their prejudices. In the one class you will find the school of Christ, in the other the school of the Pharisees; and I do exhort those who listen to my unworthy exhortations to become of the former, Christians in heart, not churchmen, nor sectarians, making no difference among the spiritual servants of Christ, and trampling under foot the little distinctions of outward form. For if you do not watch over this with diligence, if you allow yourselves to be all of this or of that sort, saying, "I am of Paul, and I of Apollos, and I of Cephas;" then you place a fence around your liberty, and become the dupes of your favourites; if they be designing, the partisans of their fallibility, the reflection of their imperfect light, and, in short, anything within the limits of positive idolatry, if it go not ofttimes to that very extreme. Into these remarks I am led by the melancholy spectacle of all believing on John but the religious Pharisees, who had become the slaves of traditional faith, the idolaters of the elders rather than the servants of the living and true God.

But to continue our exposition of the Baptist's ministry, so far as it is recorded in the other evangelists. It is further stated by St John, that the next day after this on which Jesus was baptized, John seeth Jesus coming unto him and saith, "Behold the Lamb of God, which taketh away the sin of the world!" And the next day again—for it appears that this congregation at Bethabara was for several days—John stood again with two of his disciples, and beheld Jesus walking by, and said, "Behold the Lamb of God!" This testimony I quote, and dwell upon with delight, because it not only manifests the rapture which the Baptist had in contemplating his Lord, and how he burst forth with expressions of fondness and admiration, but because it testifies the object and end of Christ's coming, to take away the sins of the world. There are many this day who give in to the doctrine of His being the sent of God, the true Messiah promised to the fathers, but refuse to acknowledge the purpose for which He came—to take away the sins of the world; which to our eyes is a most marvellous blindness, seeing the end marked out through all the prophecies of the Old Testament where His coming as foretold is "to finish transgression and make an end of sin, and bring in an everlasting righteousness." "To bear our sins and carry our sorrow." I know not what blindness of sight should hinder men from recognising this as the whole spirit of the Christian dispensation; still less do I know what hardness of heart should hinder them from hailing it as the only hope of their salvation. If there was a man who had no sin whereof to accuse himself, no deep-seated spring of iniquity for ever overflowing his heart and life, that man might well object to a Saviour from sin; but there being no man unconscious of sin, or unwilling to confess it to himself or others, how we should reject the mediation of Christ I cannot understand: it is one of those devices of Satan, one of those perversities of human nature of which no account can be rendered. But however much we may start in these times from the preaching of Christ as the great atonement of our sins, it was the first idea which arose in the Baptist's mind as he looked upon Him walking by the banks of Jordan. His ejaculation, "Behold the Lamb of God, which taketh away the sin of the world," may be well supposed to have reference to the scape-goat which bore with it into the wilderness the sins of all the people. The ordinance of the scape-goat is recounted in the book of Leviticus after this wise :—" And Aaron shall put both his hands upon the head of the live goat, and confess over him all the iniquities of the children of Israel, and all their trespasses, and all their sins, putting them upon the head of the goat, and shall send him away (by the hand of a man appointed) into the wilderness. So the goat shall bear upon him all their iniquities into the land that is not inhabited, and he shall let that goat go into the wilderness. And he that carried forth the goat called the scape-goat shall wash his clothes, and wash his flesh in water, and after that shall come into the host." With a view to this ordinance, it seemeth to me not unlikely that the Baptist used the expression, " Taketh away the sin of the world." The transgressions of men were laid upon the head of Christ, and He bore them away into the land of God's forgetfulness. And though I know sufficiently the theological disputations upon the question of Christ's sacrifice, for whom it is offered up, such abstract disputations must be kept as the exercises of the learned. Our office here is freely, as did the Baptist and the Saviour and the apostles, to present Him as the propitiation for your sins ; and not yours only, but the sins of the whole world; in which, if you put your trust, and, putting your trust in it, follow after the walk and conversation of those who believe, then shall you be justified from all things from which you could not be justified by the law of Moses. If you say you have no sin, then you are liars, and the truth is not in you. If you have sin, then no one can redeem the soul of his brother from death, and there remaineth nothing but a fearful looking for of judgment. Therefore, draw near unto Christ and confess your sins over the head of this Lamb of God, and He shall bear them away from the sight of God for ever. But it is not only as the Holy One, who bore our sins and carried our sorrows, that Christ is presented by the

Baptist to the congregation of the people, it is also as the deliverer from the power and bondage of sinfulness, which cheateth men out of their New Testament right as the sanctified and preserved people of God, and bringeth them under double condemnation, as those who have preferred the bond of Satan to the redemption of Christ, and loved darkness rather than light, their deeds being evil.

Now, here is a nobler aspect of the Saviour than the former. He not only will bear away the guilt of your sins upon His own head, but He will by the mighty working of His Spirit bring you out of the darkness of error and the bands of ignoble vice into the clear vision of light and the noble liberty of the sons of God. And who is he that hath known the thraldom of sin, and wisheth not to escape from it, its blindfolding of the noble and virtuous perceptions of man, yea, its shearing of the very locks wherein lie all his moral strength and gracefulness, its base captivation and binding of him, and ultimate demands for drudgery or sport,—where is the ignoble soul that would not thence escape into the liberty of serving God in holiness and fear all the days of his life? And who that hath known the weepings and wailings of this sore captivity of sin, its mean concealments, its dreaded exposure, with all its burning shame, and doth not long to be at ease from its inward torments of the soul and its castigation of the conscience with everlasting scourges? But it availeth not for nature to wrestle with the universal contagion, it cleaves to her closer than clenched fetters, it burneth in the blood, and is warped with the strings of the heart, and it looketh forth from the lurking eye, and it speaketh in the imprinted features of passion and pride, and the heart within is deluged with the floods of iniquity, its guiles and deceptions and desperate wickedness surpass the knowledge and the power of man. From this thraldom and sorrow, and from the cleaving curse of this foul disease, behold the Lamb of God will deliver you. He will take away your sin, and thoroughly cleanse you from your iniquity. He will wash you as with hyssop, and make you whiter than the snow. Behold, then, the Lamb of God which taketh away the sin of the world; come unto Him that ye may be made partakers of His grace and saved from the wrath to come. Ye have been baptized into His name, ye need further to be baptized with the Holy Ghost and with fire. The great emblem of this deliverance of the soul from fear and bondage ye have in the pouring out of the Spirit upon the Church at Pentecost. This is the baptism with the Holy Ghost and with fire, with which the servants of Christ having been baptized, became enlightened and emboldened and manifested new powers and energies upon every occacasion; and if ye feel still oppressed with the sense of your sinfulness, and still fearful toward God, and under the potent dominion of the prince of this world, ye will be delivered and enlarged by that same Spirit which delivered and enlarged the Church of Christ. Your Saviour died for your sins, and straightway the Spirit was poured out on the Church; so if you die to sin, straightway the Spirit will be poured out on you, and work the same deliverance and emancipation of your souls. But if ye set spies upon the Saviour, as the Pharisees did, mistrusting Him, or if ye seek to depreciate Him, as do many in this day, and strip His character of all its glories, then hardness of heart and continuance in sin will be the fatal issue. Come, therefore, my beloved brethren, come unto Him and seek the forgiveness of all your sins, that they may be blotted out and days of refreshing may come from the Most High.

LECTURE X.

JOHN III. 23.

TO go about to examine the traits of the Baptist's character, and his performance of the high part appointed him of God, would be presumptuous, were it undertaken in the spirit of criticism, whose chief occupation is to discover faults; but, being undertaken in the spirit of reverend contemplation, to observe the characteristics of a Christian herald and witness, and hold them up to your imitation and our own, it is not a presumptuous, but a dutiful office, and hath in it that desire to be taught of God, and to profit from His works, which He never faileth to bless with instruction and improvement. For if we do not scruple, in the works of nature, to study the wise contrivance and curious adaptation of every creature, the means and the final ends of things created; nor to submit the works of Providence to exact account and profitable study in history, natural and civil, and in the biography of private men, —no more ought we to hesitate in submitting to examination those men whom He hath chosen for the purpose of instructing the earth, and thereto endowed them with His gifts and graces. And in the same proportion as the regenerated soul and devout life of a messenger of God is nobler than the history of any inferior creature, or the character of any natural man, however virtuous, may we expect the lessons thence derived to be more exalted, and the blessing remaining with ourselves more enlarged, than from contemplating any other of the works of God. Therefore we shall continue to consider the life and character of the Baptist with the same devout contemplation and study with which we would survey any wonderful work of God's hands, or any singular revolution of His providence, in order to get insight into the mind and will of God concerning human nature, and derive illumination upon that path in which He wisheth us to go.

You will understand us, therefore, not as exalting ourselves into judges of the Lord's approved messenger, but as students and interpreters of the same, while we proceed to exhibit some features of his character which have not yet come before us in the course of our meditations.

From the opening of the Baptist's ministry at Bethabara, beyond Jordan, to this his baptism at Ænon, near to Salem, there is an interval of three years and a half, concerning which we have no record either of the Baptist or of Christ. The reason of this silence as to Christ we stated, when we discoursed of the thirty unrecorded years of His youth, to be this, that these documents called the Gospels are not intended for a biography, nor yet (St John's, perhaps, excepted) as a record of doctrine, but simply as a witness or testimony unto the world that Jesus is the Christ, the sent of God, the Messiah promised unto the fathers. There is every reason to believe that the Jews had amongst them a book, into which were collected all the prophecies that regarded the great hope of the nation, in which His place of birth, the time and signs of His coming, His works and character were described, that no usurper might insinuate himself into the confidence of the nation. Hence Herod sent to inquire of the chief priests where Messiah should be born. The apostles being Jews, and deeply imbued with the common expectation, and conversant with the common ideas respecting Messiah, out of which they were most hard to be delivered, drew up those grounds upon which their own conviction rested, and pre-. sented them to their countrymen in the form of these Gospels —Matthew and Mark first; Luke afterwards, and with more universality and enlargement, as addressing himself to people less exclusively Jewish; John, not till twenty or thirty years afterwards, and chiefly to refute certain mistakes concerning the person of Christ, which were already beginning to shew themselves. The first three Gospels being therefore of the nature of testimony, pleaded at the bar of the Jewish nation, and of the world then interested in the question, and to all succeeding ages, must needs confine themselves to matters of notorious publicity, which could be contradicted if they had not been so; and they must hold as much as possible to the course and train of the digest of ancient prophecy, by which the Jews defined the person of Messiah, and which was engraven upon the common mind of the nation. Hence Peter, in his speeches to the people after Pentecost, pleads always some prophecy, which he took for granted not only that his audience knew, but that they were wont to apply to Messiah the Prince. Consulting for this end of public conviction, Matthew, Mark, and Luke made no account of those three years and a half which intervened from our Saviour's baptism to His entering on His ministry, and which, it is reasonable to suppose, He spent in solitude, until the Baptist should have ripened things for His appearance. John, His forerunner, during these three years and a half,—the first half of the week during which Daniel prophesied that Messiah should confirm the covenant with many,—did doubtless continue to tread in the course which he began with such heroic boldness and fidelity; and though nothing is said of his encounters or success, we shall, in this and future discourses, have to exhibit the storm of envy and malice which was gathering in the temple and the palace against the messenger of God, soon to burst upon his devoted head. We may grudge this silence over the acts of so noble a personage, the most poetical, perhaps, in history, and whom certainly poetry, if she had not lost her high faculty of selection, would choose for her subject; but that envious silence which we grudge is another testimony amongst many to the high aims with which the evangelists wrote. Poetry and pathos, or justice to the best of men, or recording the memory of deeds better recorded in the book of God's remembrance, all that which prompts historian, biographer, or man of genius, was second-rate or out of the question with men who were travailing as in birth with a world's salvation; who beheld a world lying in wickedness, and shot across from land to land to save them; and committed to scattered leaves of Epistles words of healing and saving virtue—every word precious as a soul—and sent them forth to seek their fortune amongst the disbelieving part of men. What had they to do with taste, criticism, finish, and such puny accomplishments, when life, life eternal, immortal, was breathing in their sentences? Oh that we had such men again; men who coined truth, and made it current in its first mintage, striking spirit with the first impression of spirit, and taking men with the pure virgin tints of nature and truth,—spirit-stirred, enrapt with the high themes of salvation, and who left behind them in their glorious course literary, sectarian, and clerical distinctions, as the trifles of the present world with which the enemy entraps the souls of the unwary. The evangelists, so girt to their high object of preaching Jesus to an ignorant world, and proving Him Messiah before a prejudiced people, looked upon John as the secondary person which he regarded himself to be, and brought him forward only as the attendant and witness of the Son of the Highest. Therefore they record the transactions of that celebrated day when by his hand He was baptized with water, and by the Holy Spirit with power from on high. And they notice him no further until another incident occurred which brought him again into connexion with Christ.

The Pharisees, who sought at the beginning to question him into some betrayal of his trust, and reaped the reward which God hath appointed to duplicity, viz., greater conviction in error, and in the end shame and confusion of face,—these disciples of tradition, not of Moses, finding the Baptist going counter to some of their favourite religious nostrums about purifyings, took it greatly to heart, and entered into disputation with his disciples. "There arose a question between some of John's disciples and the Jews about purifying." Some have thought that this question was honestly stated by those Jews who wished well to John, and that the purifying of which they disputed was the purifying of baptism, and that the question was of the relative importance of the Baptist's and the Messiah's baptism. At first sight this notion seems congenial with the spirit of the context, for the whole passage is introduced by the information that Jesus came into Judæa, and His disciples began to baptize, and goes on to state that John was also baptizing in the neighbourhood at Ænon, and then the dispute arose between the Jews and John's disciples concerning purifying. But, upon more mature consideration, it is manifest that the Jews who entertained this dispute were not friendly to John, and that the dispute was not concerning the two baptisms, or concerning baptism at all. The Jews who entertained the dispute were not of John's believers, because it was with John's disciples they disputed. By John's disciples we must understand his adherents, and those who disputed with his adherents must have been not of his adherents, otherwise it would have been written, "John's disciples disputed amongst themselves." But further, the form of these interrogations is invidious, and evidently seeks to stir up envy and strife between him and Christ, and the whole strain of his answer bears the character of a rebuke to them, a defence of his ingenuousness, a still more powerful testimony to Christ, a blessing also upon those who believed, and a threatening upon those who disbelieved Him. That it was not a dispute concerning their relative baptisms I judge from this, that the word is "purifying," not baptism. Now, the word for purifying is never applied either to the baptism of John or of Christ's disciples, or of Christ's apostles, or of the Holy Ghost, or any other baptism. The word "baptism" is in one place applied to purifying, as the baptism of cups, pots, and tables, (and once in the Hebrews, where it is rendered "the doctrine of baptisms," I think it much better to translate the baptisms of doctrine, or the purifying influences of doctrine.) But the word "purifying" is never, on the other hand, used for baptism, and on that account cannot be so taken in this place without violence to every rule of just translation.

The incident I understand, interpreting the words literally, and taking the whole spirit of the context, to have been this: —The disciples of John, taking their views of doctrine from John himself, who took his from Moses and the prophets, were not found so wise as the disciples of the Pharisees in the smaller matters of the law. Like our Saviour, they ate without having previously washed their hands, and paid no respect to the traditions of the elders. This could not pass unnoticed, being under the daily observation of men. It was like neglecting in Catholic countries to kneel before the passing host, or to cross and pray at the sound of the *Ave Maria* bell. It could not escape notice even in our Saviour, as Mark informs us, in these words, which cast light both upon the customs of the time and the character of the people, (chap. vii.) :—" Then came together unto him the Pharisees, and certain of the scribes, which came from Jerusalem. And when they saw some of his disciples eat bread with defiled, that is to say, with unwashen hands, they found fault : for the Pharisees, and all the Jews, except they wash their hands oft, eat not, holding the tradition of the elders. And when they come from the market, except they wash, they eat not. And many other things there be, which they have received to hold, as the washings of cups, and pots, brazen vessels, and of tables. Then the Pharisees and scribes asked him, Why wash not thy disciples according to the tradition of the elders, but eat bread with unwashen hands ?" Such an incident and dispute as this I suppose to have happened between the Jews and John's disciples, and not once to have occurred, but to have been constantly maintained. It was in truth the great point of difference between them and the Jews, just as between us and the Catholics ; the great point of difference is, whether the traditions of the Church, the mummery of mass, and processions, and images, and relics, and beads, and indulgences, shall be conformed to with as much exactness as the graces, and virtues, and works of the Christian life. This source of constant soreness to the Pharisees, whose power, like that of Catholic priests, lay entrenched behind the habitual reverence of their outward bulwarks, was doubtless the cause of their disbelieving John and persecuting him as they did. They could not part with their power over an ignorant people. They knew where lay the strength of their spell, and whoso revered not that cabala was an enemy, and not worthy to live. Now, when Christ appeared with His disciples, baptizing on His own account, and the fame was spread abroad that a great Prophet had risen up amongst them, and that God had visited His people, the Pharisees, enemies of both, thought this a fine occasion for bringing their malice to bear upon them both. Thinking that the Messiah and the Baptist were of the same make and mould with their own double-minded selves, and that the same love of power and jealousy of a rival, and envy of a superior, had a dwelling-place in the bosoms of Heaven's messengers, as in the bosoms of the devil's messengers,—they thought now was the appointed time for dissolving the confederacy of Heaven, and retaining their sovereignty of the ignorant and abused people. And so with the dispute about purifyings in their minds; they came to the Baptist, and tried him with this cunning bait, "Rabbi, He that was with thee beyond Jordan, to whom thou barest witness, behold the same baptizeth, and all come to him!" Rabbi being a term of reverence which Christ forbade His disciples to covet, as being too lofty and consequential, they meant to insinuate themselves into the favour of the Baptist, as if the rough son of Zacharias was to be cajoled, like a courtly, pompous Pharisee, with a smooth and sounding word. In like manner, they came to Christ with their courtesies when they were thirsting for His blood— " Master, we know that thou art a teacher sent from God; is it lawful to give tribute to Cæsar, or no?" "Rabbi, He that was with thee beyond Jordan, to whom thou barest witness." To the flattery of a name they add a soothing speech—He to whom thou barest witness, who owes His dignity to thy testimony—not to God's, as was the truth—He that was with thee beyond Jordan, that is, one of thy great company, one of thy attendants, behold, the same baptizeth; behold, mark His presumption, He hath taken up thine own high vocation; He usurpeth upon His master—upon him to whom He owes His distinction; and all come to Him: thou art no more anything; thou art deserted; the whole world flock to His standard; and He hath fairly cast down thee the instrument whereby He himself arose. Now, that this was a well-concerted bait for human nature, any one who knows human nature will at once allow. It hit every malignant feeling. It began by speaking his self-consequence, for it carried memory back to the great day of his shewing unto Israel; it referred Christ's distinction to his doing; and thus, having endeavoured to exalt his pride, it aimed a blow at it, by insinuating Christ's ingratitude, by magnifying His success, by wondering at it, and wickedly pitying the Baptist's greatness come to an end. I know how difficult these things are to stand. They are the chief arts of hell, the arch-mocks of the fiend. He puts them into the mouth of affected friends; they smooth them down to your affections; they carry their intrigues cautiously on; they work and wind your writhing spirit, and seek to fill it with all the contents of envy and malignity. The world is full of such weak or wicked persons, who are the first to pity your departed glory, to tell you of another's success, to tarnish all your well-won honours with the breath of their spitefulness. And they call it teaching you humility; they wag the head, and call themselves your guardians; they applaud not, they approve not, because they are prudent, and would not blow the fire of your vanity. Wretched, uncharitable men, they perceive not that they are all the while taking your vanity for granted: they accuse you of vanity, they are acting upon their accusation, all before you have been tried. Which doth reveal only this, what vain creatures they would be in your condition, and how uncharitable they are to him whom they call their friend. Now, all such, and all who are infested with such, and all men who would learn a lesson of wisdom and gentleness and true-hearted friendship, I crave to attend to the divine reply which this servant of God gave to these servants of the evil one.

John answered and said, "A man can receive" (assume) "nothing, except it be given him from heaven. Ye yourselves bear me witness that I said, I am not the Christ, but that I am sent before him. He that hath the bride is the bridegroom; but the friend of the bridegroom, which standeth and heareth him, rejoiceth greatly because of the bridegroom's voice: this my joy therefore is fulfilled. He must increase, but I must decrease."

The piety, the humility, the beauty, the tenderness of affection, and the noble self-abasement which are contained in this reply to one of the most vile and insidious questions that ever was propounded, bespeak for the Baptist another character than that rough, warlike, and intrepid front of opposition in which we have heretofore seen him entrenched. It opens with a pious ascription to God of all power which he himself, or He they wished to oppose to him might possess. "A man can assume nothing except it be given him from Heaven." He strips himself of all self-begotten or self-continued power, and at once undeceives these dissemblers by bowing himself before the throne of God. "I am nothing," saith he, "therefore trouble not yourselves about my reputation, whether it rises or declines. I am the depositary of so much of Heaven's strength while Heaven pleaseth, therefore care not for me. God will not withdraw it till He seeth it to be consistent with His good and holy purposes. And then most gladly will I resign to Him that which I was unworthy to have ever possessed." Thus, then, doth piety, with one of her simple words, unveil deception, outwit sophistry, unriddle enigmas, and cheat the envious wretches who would ensnare her steps. Thus God giveth His servants words in the time of their need, according to His promise; that is, He keepeth their bosoms so confident and untroubled, and supplies the springs of righteous and pious feeling, that it ever occurreth to them to speak the truth; and their eye being single, their whole body is full of light. If I were surrounded with ten thousand enemies, I should ask no other armour. If I were set upon by a thousand sophists, I should ask no other wisdom. And if the tongues of all the envious men in this wide world were raised at me, I should ask no more eloquent defence than this, which prevailed over all the enemies of the Baptist. The reply doth embosom in it so much piety, and such complete defence against the assaults of envy and malignity, that I cannot help opening it up for the encouragement and consolation of every one here present who hath to meet such attacks of the enemy.

Envy, and jealousy, and malignity, have their origin in the same evil principle which moves the thief to possess himself of our property, or the fraudulent to outwit us in our dealings. It is a stealing of reputation and of good name. It springs from the consciousness of inferiority, and it is a confession of that inferiority. It hides a discontented mind; and yet it cannot hide it, but divulges it. The envious are not only thieves, but they tell upon themselves. Every one who hears their envious tale is their confessor, and would do well to give them pity, but not absolution. They deserve no absolution till they have the grace to perceive how much they need it. The thing, when looked upon nakedly, is the meanest, worst of knaveries; and therefore it becomes necessary cunningly to hide it under various disguises. The most common is, an interest in our welfare. They profess to know how rich we are in the commodity they would deprive us of, and then they would sicken our enjoyment of it by shewing how full of snares it is, and therein they do well act one part of friends, if they bear up the other part, which good men delight in more, of rejoicing with us in our joy, and bearing up our hearts against the envies of others, as well as bearing it down with their fears. If they shew confidence in our good parts, as well as distrust of our evil, then it is excellent friendship, and the more to be admired that it hath in it counsel and warning, as well as congratulation. But, if this be the eternal cant—" I am no flatterer, I am plain with my friends, I love you too well to flatter you, beware of vanity, beware of pride, beware of the world"—then I say, Down with it; it is rank envy, and proceeds from absence of kindness; it is the satyr disguised and cloaked with friendship, and will cast the mask the moment you are found tripping; it will bear you down with calumny, instead of aiding you with counsel. Call they this Christ's discipline, call they this charity, which rejoiceth in the good, not in the evil, which is the minister of hope, not of suspicion, the inspirer of joy, not of cold distrust? Away with it from our communion. Let friends rejoice with friends, speak tenderness, love with pure hearts fervently, and reserve suspicion, keep it far back, unwillingly advance it, never display it; but weep over it secretly, and talk of it alone in prayer to God, that it may prove unfounded. Another way envy hath of shewing itself is by criticism, or a regard for truth. There is a noble love of truth, and a fearlessness of uttering it before friend and foe, which one of the most truth-loving of English philosophers pronounced to be the seed-bed of every other virtue. This liberty of speaking truth one who means to take its full scope from the chair of truth should be the last to blame. Let truth be said, come what will. But this noble virtue is one of the commonest cloaks of envy in these times. They stab through this veil private character, domestic charities, public virtues: whosoever hath any elevation, there are a thousand ready to assail and pull down. They take an error in a word to be the sign of a malignant heart, and a gesture of the body to speak the darkest, deepest hypocrisy. It is painful to witness the many of this land who feed and fatten upon scandal, who lacerate and suck the blood of the worthiest men, giving full scope to their villanous weapons, for no end I can see, but because, being themselves in the sink of all vice and iniquity, cowardly and behind a screen, they would drag down to the same abominable vileness the fair reputation and honourable purposes of the most unblemished men and women. They play a game between truth and falsehood, between sincerity and sport; they make no difference between things good and evil, calling bitter sweet and sweet bitter; and, being themselves divested of virtue, of religion, of honour, broken in name, which therefore they dare not avow, ruined in prospects, they do wreak the malignity which the devil hath stocked them withal, in reward for their souls sold over to his service, upon all who have not the interests of their master, his hellish interests of strife and malignity, at heart.

Many other are the disguises, besides personal affection and love of truth, which malignity and envy do assume in order to gratify their wicked purposes. And I do exhort the people of my flock to be on their guard against their own hearts, lest they indulge under these or other forms this most wretched passion against the fair name and good fortune of others. Probe deep, and put yourselves to severe and painful inspection, lest this arch deceit may be lurking in your hearts; for where it is present, the devil hath a friend sure and steadfast, and the Saviour hath an enemy the most difficult to be cast out. And as all men of fair reputations and good success have this stealth and plunder to expect, I pray you to take the Baptist's way of meeting and defeating it. Do not give them the advantage by losing your temper; for, being thrown off your guard, you may chance to do or say something of which they will make a handle to abuse you. But are we patiently to stand by and hear our good report blasted and blasphemed? There is the mistake. They cannot blast or blaspheme your good report—which is good only while it stands with the good and with God, the author of all goodness. To stand well with the scum of men is no standing whatever; to be well spoken of by all men is one of the four woes which Christ pronounced, "Woe unto you when all men speak well of you. Blessed are ye who are persecuted for righteousness' sake. If ye suffer for righteousness sake, happy are ye. This is your calling, to suffer for the sake of Christ." Take it well, therefore; take it all joy when ye fall into divers persecutions; for so persecuted they the prophets that were before you. The creatures are a sort of reptile which adhereth to the stem of noble plants, and hath its food from that which their bark and leaves can well enough spare. But the noble plant riseth not against the reptile that feedeth on it. No more do ye.

But this lesson is more easily taught than practised. And the reason why it is of such difficult practice is, that we do not sufficiently remember from whom our various gifts of good name or good deeds proceed. We consider our distinction as our own, whereas it is God that maketh us to differ; and having this touched, we feel as if our own were invaded, and make an effort to defend ourselves. Now, though I blame not self-defence, but consider it as a Christian privilege, yet that you may be guarded in the true defensive armour of the Baptist, I pray you to remember that God is your defence, and will bring you safety. Remember that if God were to take away His restraining Spirit, ye would soon sink into all the evil conditions into which your enemies would fain bring you. Therefore separate not your confidence from Him who sustaineth you, but remember, in the extreme assaults of the enemy, that He is for you who is greater than all that can be against you. Therefore, when they revile you, revile not again, but commit yourselves unto Him that judgeth righteously. Let their calumnies be your incitements to prayer and watchfulness. Let their far-blown words and vanities, greedily devoured by the world, teach you what a bubble worldly reputation is, and induce you less and less to consider it in your conduct, and to transfer more and more of your allegiance unto the living God. So shall you convert these ministers of Satan into ministers of God, these enemies into friends. And ye will feel what a wise man once said, "Oh that we knew the value of an enemy! we would purchase

JOHN THE BAPTIST.

him with purest gold." Were there not thieves of our property, we would never become acquainted with the wisdom of laws, and the defences of government, and the securities of home, and the severer virtues of citizens. In like manner, were there no thieves of reputation, we should never become acquainted with the value of a good conscience and a trust in Heaven, nor have known half so well the lessons of forgiveness, and meekness, and long-suffering, and mercy. The most precious part of our Saviour's life is His mistreatment and crucifixion; the most precious part of the lives of the worthies is their imprisonment and martyrdom. And at this day, depend upon it, the most precious part of every Christian's experience is the reviling of the wicked, in public and in private.

But while we thus counsel you to be armed in pacific and enduring graces, we exhort you to give the enemy no cause to blaspheme. Exercise Christian prudence and Christian courtesy towards all; becoming all things to all men, as far as consisteth with sincerity and singleness of heart. Have about you the wisdom of the serpent; for he is a serpent with whom ye have to contend. And when they do break out and discharge the artillery of their spitefulness and scorn, present to it a soft and yielding defence; so shall it injure you the less. But oh! forget not to pity them, forget not to pray for them. "They know not what they do." "Whosoever offendeth the least of these little ones, better for him that a millstone were hung about his neck, and he were cast into the depths of the sea." "Forgive your enemies, love them which hate you, and pray for them which despitefully use you, and persecute you." Think of their pitiable and miserable condition. It is a sore thing for them to live on spleen; it is a sad thing for them to become friendless through their spitefulness. Think on the viperous stings which they have within them, and the venom which they breed in their inward parts. If the thing they utter be loathsome, how much more loathsome the heart from which it came! And think of the poor wretches who bear such hearts in their bosom continually: it is as a consuming fire within them. Their breast is a habitation of demons, an unclean lurking-place of evil spirits. And think of their debaucheries and dissipation by night and day, of their ruined characters, of their heart without a friend, of their soul without a refuge, of the tyranny of their master,—think of these things, and pity them from the bottom of your heart, and pray for them, and do them good, that peradventure they may be won upon by your kindness, and seek forgiveness of the Lord for the persecution of His people, and be saved from the wrath to come, "when the Lord Jesus shall be revealed from heaven with his mighty angels, in flaming fire taking vengeance on them that know not God, and that obey not the gospel of our Lord Jesus Christ: who shall be punished with everlasting destruction from the presence of the Lord, and from the glory of his power; when he shall come to be glorified of his saints, and to be admired of those that believe."

LECTURE XI.

JOHN III.

NOT to feel envious of another's exaltation, but to rejoice in it, even when it interferes with our own place and brings with it our downfall, is so rare yet so necessary an attainment of Christian life, and is so strikingly exemplified in these words of the Baptist, that we have thought it good to make it the subject of another discourse. For this world is the theatre of so much rivalry, and men, forgetting the interests of everlasting truth and universal love, do so attach themselves to their own personal advantage, as to account every one an enemy who trespasseth thereon, and cry, "Away with him," without any regard to the humility of his conduct or the righteousness of his intention; and, on the other hand, there is so much emulation and endeavour to outstrip our fellows, so much ambition of high places, that, with a savage gladness, they delight to invade the good and established rights of those who have obtained the lead; so that, between the resolution of those above to dispute, and, if possible, keep down the pretensions of others, and the resolution of those beneath to pull down those above and rise into their places, must discord, and bad feeling, and evil-speaking arise to trouble the happiness of life. First, feelings of jealousy, and envy, and rivalry are bred within the breast, and soon give birth to acts of wickedness, and malice, and malignity, out of which come strifes, and quarrels, and dissensions of various kinds, which occasions those agonising scenes and shocking crimes of which the world is full. These bitter and malevolent passions are the foes of faith, virtue, patience, temperance, brotherly-kindness, and charity, and everything else which belongs to the discipline of Christ, and they are veils upon the understanding, and keep out the light of truth. A man under the influence of malignant passions is at the opposite pole from truth, and is in darkness, and, if he be brought to believe, his faith is like that of the devils, and maketh him to tremble but not to obey.

All this cometh of too much devotion to our own selfish passions and interests, and too little regard to the feelings and interests of others; and the only cure for it is to bring the latter more prominently forward, and to cast the former into the shade. By dwelling upon our sensations, and consulting for our own gratification, and keeping an eye to our own interests, we forget the rights and feelings of others; and, on the other hand, according as we attend to the well-being of others we lose interest in our own. A bad temper is nothing but a succession of selfish feelings and selfish actions in small matters; when it ascends to higher, it is called a bad heart and a bad life. And tyranny of rulers is another form of the same evil. They use the sacred power consigned to them by God and their country for their own private and peculiar gratification. And even the best parts of human nature may become tyrannical. An hospitable man may be a tyrant by his hospitality, and a generous man by his generosity, and one who loves you may, by the excess of his love, make you his slave. And this often occurs in human life, that the most selfish men, when unobserved, can do the most generous actions, and delight in their secrecy, as a miser delighteth in his wealthy store, and will not bear even the acknowledgments of the party whom they have obliged; so that this intense regard to one's self corrupts even those parts of human nature which God hath implanted for the welfare of our neighbour, and converts acts of kindness into inflictions of self-willedness, and takes from them the power of propagating kindness in return. And this also I have found, that the spirit of this selfishness hath insinuated itself into things admired amongst men—into friendship, for example, which they value by its poverty, and esteem most highly when it is bestowed upon one alone; in love likewise, which they hold can exist in truth only between two hearts; in clanship, which is thought more valuable by the strength of its antipathies; in patriotism also, which they shew forth very often by their hatred and declamations against other lands. Which are all but refinements of that selfishness, jealousy, and rivalry, whereof we have undertaken to exhibit the remedy in these words of John the Baptist; who, in his person, exhibited the most notable instance of pure and perfect freedom from all such evil dispositions. But that you may sufficiently apprehend the extent of this evil whereof I discourse, and the value of the remedy which I have to propose, I crave of you to follow me while I point out the ineffectual endeavours which society makes by her own wisdom and strength to overcome the mischief.

First there is the institution of marriage and of families, which may draw out the feelings of selfishness from the breast, and disperse them over the whole house; and society, discerning the advantage of such a diffusion of a man's interests, hath merely done its utmost to bind him to his household, and bind him from deserting it to indulge any other varying or wandering of affection. Perceiving the advantage of extending our interests further, it hath joined us in townships and corporations, and other local jurisdictions, whose interests it expects us to superintend; and finally cometh nations, in whose common interests we are expected to embark a portion of our private interest; and after all comes confederations of nations, and alliances of peoples, for the defence of some common right or the attainment of some common good. And over each of these, law extendeth a shield and canopy of defence, endeavouring to join all in a common sentiment of equity and justice; and what law cannot do, well-regulated society endeavours to discharge, which, careful of the weak and jealous of the strong, establisheth a rule of common politeness and civility, which doth take a man's personality and power out of his hand, and oblige him for the while either to be good and gracious, or to play the part of a hypocrite by seeming to be so. Now, while these several spheres of sympathy continue to be filled, the family sphere, the neighbourly, the political, and the social, society goes on prosperous and happy. And society dissolves by the breaking up of these honest and dutiful relations, and the introduction in their stead of vanity, ambition, pleasure, self-aggrandisement, and other affections which centre in ourselves. But these excellent institutions of the community do but call a truce, or strike up an armistice, or fence off a space, and define a time within which there is to be peace, and all beyond it leaves as irreclaimable; and truly it is irreclaimable, by any hands save those of our Maker and ourselves. Within the rules of society and of law, decent trust and confidence is reposed; but beyond them, all is activity for our own interests and jealousy of the encroachments of others. For while we regard the world, as philosophers of the selfish school do regard it, as a collection of beings intent each upon his own aggrandisement by all means which society allows, we feel it necessary to battle it for ourselves, to make what ground we can, and keep it how we can. And while we regard ourselves as the fabricators of our own lot, good or bad, keeping out of sight the government of God, we must regard every other man in the same light, and so come to be jealous of each other's power. And so truly it is, almost always, when a sense of God and of religion is absent.

What society hath done its utmost to promote, the Almighty, by the revelation of the everlasting gospel, hath sought entirely to secure, by teaching us that great lesson with which His apostle opened his discourse before the judges of learned and polished Greece: "God hath made of one blood all nations of men for to dwell on all the face of the earth, and hath determined the times before appointed, and the bounds of their habitation." Or as John delivers it to the Jews who tried him with their wiles: "A man can receive nothing except it be given him from heaven." In which sentences are disclosed the great doctrine of God's government over all, which bruiseth the serpent head of selfishness and malice. By this doctrine, taught through all Scripture, of God's overruling all things by the word of His power, we are instructed that however active we may be in securing our welfare and averting evil, it is God that directeth the whole action, and bringeth out the issue; that no one can prevail against us beyond His permission, and that in permitting it He hath ends the very best in view; and that if we will but put ourselves under the authority of His laws, He will keep us by His providence, enrich us with His grace, and bless us with the copious streams of His salvation; and that seeming evil shall be substantial good, and trials become our deliverances, and adversities benefits, and afflictions blessings in disguise, and all things shall work together for our good.

Now, exactly in proportion as this lesson is learned and acted on, we get delivered out of the power of selfishness, with all its anxieties, cares, jealousies, and malignant actions, into the power of faith and trust, with all their fruits of peace, joy, long-suffering, gentleness, meekness, patience, temperance; and being now in confidence and communion with the Father of spirits, whose sceptre is a sceptre of righteousness, we are not afraid of what man can do against us, neither are we afraid that the power of the wicked can prevail against the progress of the truth. "For He maketh the wrath of man to praise Him, and the remainder of his wrath He doth restrain." There ensueth a divine contentment with our lot, a resignation to the evil, a temperate enjoyment of the good, and a thankfulness for all. The limitations of our faculties give us no distress. We are as God made us, and we shall be answerable for that only which He hath given us. And the higher gifts and offices of another do not grieve us. "To his God he standeth or falleth." We rejoice in what is true and worthy and righteous, wherever it is found. Every device of goodness we promote and hasten forward; and we love those who love it, and we help those who strive for it. Truth and righteousness are to us the voice and footsteps of God, and we revere them for His sake who first manifested them in the person of His dear Son. And if we can promote good works in others, we delight to do so, and we delight to have good promoted by others in ourselves. We become absorbed in God's commonwealth: our citizenship is in heaven, and we do the works of our Father who is in heaven. For evil-doers we fret not ourselves; and though they be high in power and spread like the green bay-tree, we only pity the more their speedy overthrow. We are not restless, timorous, or dismayed, because we know the Lord's hand is over them to restrain the excesses of their wrath. We scorn them not by day, we plot not against them by night. Our sweetness is not soured by their corruption, because our confidence is in God, who dasheth the wicked in pieces like the potter's vessel. Our vocation is not to labour against them, but to labour for God; not to hunt them through their labyrinths of error, but to push forward the interests of truth; not to grieve ourselves with all the abominations of the earth, but to do justly, to love mercy, and to walk humbly with our God. Thus the good that there is or hath been rejoiceth us, and the evil that there is or hath been doth not alarm or vex us. The one is the food of our joy, the other of our faith; both of our steadiness and perseverance. A constancy of purpose, a tranquillity of speech, a steadiness of execution, mark us to be the children of the God of order and of truth, around whom, though there may be clouds and darkness, yet righteousness and judgment are the habitation of His throne. Where is envy, rivalry, and jealousy? They have died of their own accord. Where is malice, cruelty, revenge? They cannot live upon the soil of such devotion. We are become like the children of God, merciful and kind, to our enemies forgiving, because they are only our enemies according as they are His, and even upon His enemies He maketh His sun to arise, and His rain to drop fatness down.

The true and proper antagonist, therefore, of the selfish feelings is not the social feelings, which are limited or confined within the range and application of social institutions, and which at the ultimate make but a republic of men, each watched by his fellow, but the religious feeling, which at once destroys our own individuality, by making us a subject of the Most High, and subordinates our wishes and our interests to the revealed will and purpose of God. And not in proportion to the refinements of society is selfishness subdued, but in proportion to the progress of religion. And a country is civilised and happy according to the regard which it hath for the authority of God, not according to the subjection which it hath to the laws of men. The one eradicates, the other only opposes—the one removes, the other only restrains, the selfish and malignant passions of the heart. A man may be intensely selfish and malignant, yet a good subject and a reputable member of society. A man cannot be a Christian in the least, without being in the same degree delivered out of his own will into the will of God. And whatever of our own free-will we surrender, is surrendered into the hands of One who is wiser to guide, and more able to promote. And if we surrender all our will and personal interests into His hand, then indeed we become a part of His family, His children, the brethren of Jesus Christ, His disciples and servants, and the active ministers of His Holy Spirit. We are nothing, He is everything. We love Him, and He loveth us, and He dwelleth with us: He in us, and we in Him.

This is the secret of the Baptist's disinterestedness and self-forgetfulness, that he was dedicated and devoted unto God, and had no object but to do His will; and whosoever was engaged in the same work, was a fellow-worker of the household of saints. And when the Pharisees tried him with their artful and insinuating words, he told them that a man can receive nothing except it be given him of God. In like manner, when another's wealth or another's power or worth or reputation are presented to us by the Evil One as the incitements of our envy, we ought to remember that God hath been pleased to bestow it upon them, and that they have it not of themselves; and that what God hath seen it meet to permit, it becometh not us to grudge or to oppose. If he seem to us to use his powers or privileges ill, then let us in our province stand against the mischief and oppose it. Let us look to our own liberty in Christ, and not have it invaded by him or any one; but let us beware of stepping beyond our own responsibility and intermeddling in another's matters, which God judgeth. This mild way of beholding the evil which we cannot hinder is not inconsistent with remonstrance and friendly counsel, and free declamation upon the evils which will ensue from such wickedness. For our Saviour and the Baptist and Paul, though they launched not their denunciations upon the wicked governors and avaricious people with whom they were surrounded, yet, when called upon in the way of their own duty, did not flinch from facing iniquity and rebuking it; which brought them all three to an untimely end. There is a nice balance which a Christian should maintain between a trust in the overruling providence of God, and his own desire of seeing righteousness triumph. What he wisheth, prayeth for, and doth his utmost to accomplish, he should still leave in the hands of God, who in His good time will bring it to pass. If such be our duty when we see the wicked wax in power, how much more when we see the righteous growing up before the Lord! Then indeed we should rejoice with all our hearts, as John doth in the passage before us. For though we possess not the blessing, he is our friend who possesseth it, and we will rejoice because of his happiness. There is one interest between us; we are members of the same household, and labour under the same Master, whose service is easy and whose burden is light. It would be to nourish secret rebellion did we not rejoice when His friends rejoice, and grieve when they grieve. Nay, though the rise of any of Christ's servants should be attended with our downfall, it is the pleasure of our Lord, and we will not be afraid. He sees him to be better fitted for bearing the burden of His house, or more worthy to be honoured with its preferments. Let us not repine because of the preference, but be glad to keep a door in His house; yea, count it joy to suffer for His sake. Let us have that notion of our own undeserving which shall make us say with the prodigal, We are unworthy to be called thy sons; make us thy hired servants.

In such a way we ought to rejoice in each other's prosperity, and not to grieve; we should assist each other's progress, and bear each other's burdens, and count ourselves honoured in giving a cup of cold water to a disciple in the name of a disciple. What though we have no money to bestow, we have our prayers, our wishes, our welcomes, and all our Christian charities. Of these we need not be scanty; they grow by use, they increase by dispersion; and, like the sun, they fling heat and light around on every side and for ever, yet is not their light and heat diminished. And for envies, grudgings, and evil-speakings, let them not once be named amongst you, as becometh saints. Live in peace with one another, loving each other; and if any one have a fault against his neighbour, forgive him, as Christ also forgave you. And let this example of the Baptist, the first servant of Christ, be an example to His disciples unto the end of the world, to sink themselves and their interests in the interests of their Lord, to become nothing, and to make Him all in all. Then, by the diffusion of His Spirit, and by His presence in every heart, we shall live as becometh saints, and enter at length into the joy of our Lord.

LECTURE XII.

LUKE III.

THE Baptist came forth from the wilderness unknown and unbefriended of any one save Him to whom he was devoted from the womb. And though he did no miracle, and certainly studied no popular arts, he wrought his way among the thousands of Israel until he reached the court and palace of Herod, the king of Galilee. This man is the Herod whom our Saviour characterises with the name of fox, when the Pharisees endeavoured to put Him to silence: "Go ye, and tell that fox, Behold, I cast out devils to-day, and to-morrow, and the third day I shall be perfected." To his cunning this prince added adultery and lust, for he lived with his brother Philip's wife. And to his cunning and incestuous lust he added contempt and mockery of the Son of God; for when Pontius Pilate, more honourable than he, liked not the work of condemning an innocent person, and gladly handed him over to Herod, the curiosity of the tyrant was whetted—he had long desired to see Him, and expected that He would do some miracle to please him. Which tyrannical moods when Jesus refused to indulge, or to answer his impertinent questions, Herod, with his men of war, set Him at nought, and mocked Him, and arrayed Him in a gorgeous robe, and sent Him again to Pilate. And the same day Pilate and Herod were made friends together, for before they had been at enmity between themselves. Such was the man to whose court and palace the Baptist, after three years and a half preaching amongst the people, found his way.

Now, let us gather our thoughts together for an observation and experiment, to witness and consider this meeting of two men from the opposite extremes of life, of the most opposite character, and in the most opposite conditions. The one brought forth in silken luxury—the other cradled in nature's roughest couch; the one bred in the midst of plenty, and pleasure, and power—the other in the midst of hoary deserts and savage creatures, and fed upon the locusts and the wild honey, and within whose lips no luxury had ever passed; the one clothed in incorruptible truth, stripped of every ornament and grace—the other adorned with every ornament and grace of life, divested of sincerity and truth. The Baptist, when he set his foot within the threshold of the palace, was encircled with every temptation within a tyrant's grasp, in the midst of flatterers, with no memorial of God, no fear of Him around. Beauty, festivity, and folly, luxury, falsehood, and wickedness; but no fear of God, nor regard of man.

How is he to behave himself in such a scene? Will he be overawed into silence, allow himself in indulgence, favour the customs, as they say, "Be at Rome like the people of Rome," and pass unnoticed what is worthy of rebuke? or will he bend to circumstances, and play the courtier for a while till he have made his footing good? Will he encircle himself with wary prudence? or will he be brave and resolute, firm and unmovable, and discourse to Herod as he would to another sinner? This is a wise experiment, and well worthy the attention of all, especially of the ministers of Christ. Christ's first ambassador in a court and palace, and preaching to a lustful and tyrannical king—that is the observation we have to make, and how honourable the result! His spirit quaileth not; he riseth sublime above the temptations of the place; his eye discerneth the truth amidst all its gaudy concealments, and his tongue fears not and falters not to utter it. Like Nathan, he tells the monarch his fault, and makes no concealment of his shame. He speaks the unvarnished truth in ears which had perhaps never before listened to it. The minister of God, the servant of truth, prevails over the fears of man, and all the civility and politeness of a court. He said, "It is not lawful for thee to have thy brother's wife."

Now, upon the cautious and prudential principles which are now applied to the pastoral office, it were not difficult to raise a very powerful argument against the rashness of the Baptist.

What ado had he with the affairs of courts and palaces? A minister of Christ is a man of peace, not of strife. The gospel is preached to the poor. Ambitious meddling man! to embroil himself with state affairs. He had scope enough amongst the people, with whom he was such a favourite; and in turning them from the evil of their ways, might have spent a long and profitable life. Was there not enough of hypocrisy and irreligion to be detected nearer home, that he should travel to the palace to find it? How admirably to the Baptist would apply the reproaches which are brought against our Scottish Reformer for speaking so rudely to a beautiful queen! Uncourteous it was, ungallant it was, so to speak of the beautiful Herodias and her accomplished daughter. And when he did preach to this royal assembly, what tempted him, like St Paul, another of these imprudent ministers, to speak upon royal vices? Could he not have preached before a king as if he had been another man? Are not all men equal in the house of God? It is not to amuse myself that I make these strictures on the Baptist's conduct, but to set strikingly forth the notions which prevail of wise ministration of the Word of Christ. These are the very speeches, to the letter, which they hold against Knox, and the few men who have had the courage to walk in the footsteps of Nathan the Prophet, John the Baptist, and Paul the Apostle. They give praise and they take praise for preaching to people of station as to ordinary Christians—that is, if they abstain from flattery, it contenteth their notion of duty. Ah, it is fortunate that constancy, and truth, and heroical boldness have their appeals to the oracles of truth, and the practice of primitive times, from the changing maxims and current sophistry of the times;—very fortunate that, in the North, we have the noble example alluded to above; and that, in the South, you have the discourses which were preached by your Latimers, and your Cranmers, and your Gilpins before the court of the godly Edward, and the correspondence held by your Grindal and others with the stern and mighty Elizabeth.

Now, the answer to all this is plain, and is indeed in their own words, which contain the true principle, but overlook its true application. It is just for this very reason—that all men before a pastor are alike and equal, that a king is as a subject, and a noble as a peasant—for this reason it is, that, when he hath a noble or a royal audience, the pastor should take their way of life to task, and expose its blemishes as if they were common men. The minister knows no rank, and he knows the fear of no rank, and the formality of no rank. He is a man of God, set for instructing, for reproving, for correcting, and for teaching men, and for making them meet for the kingdom of heaven. Their royal place, their noble station, doth not acquit them of responsibility unto God, but addeth more; and therefore it were cruel, it were sporting with their souls' eternal salvation, for the minister of God not to advertise them beforehand of the judgment of God. Therefore Paul preached to them of judgment to come. Seldom is it they have an opportunity of hearing truth. They are cradled in falsehood, and fed with flattery. Self-willedness, pride, and passion are nursed in them, and the ministry of every evil is around them. A man of truth is to them like a stranger from a far country, whose visits are short and far between. Should that precious moment be lost of warning their souls—the souls of those in whose hands is the welfare of thousands? A minister should pray for such an occasion of serving his country; and, having gotten it from the Lord, he should use it by casting away smooth and flattering words, and speaking like the very minister of doom.

John the Baptist, therefore, was trustworthy; he was more than a prudent man, he was a man worthy the trust of God, and to be sent on perilous errands. Prudence dwelleth in earthly courts; truth is the badge of heaven's court. Prudence teacheth not what duty is, but how duty may be best discharged. Conscience and the Word and Spirit of God teach what duty is. The voice of duty speaketh from within and from above, not from the world around. And he that would find it hath no need to seek here or to seek there, to consult this oracle or that counsellor, but to ask counsel of his soul. Let him bring things to a state of rest within his breast, put down clamorous passions, disinherit evil interests, and reject the solicitations of a thousand customs; silence vanity, the world's opinion, gain, and fashion; and when their stormy waves, restless as the ocean, have been calmed, he will hear a still, small voice,—that is the voice of duty ; and, if he will obey it, it will wax louder and louder, until it be distinct as the notes of a trumpet, and sweeter than the voice of love. Now prudence cometh into play, but not till now. When the sacred three—conscience, the Word of God, and the Spirit of God—have given forth their fiat, then let wisdom and prudence come in to determine what is the best method of carrying their fiat into effect. This is the true philosophy and the true divinity of the matter.

Now is the time for Christian courtesies of manner, for graces of behaviour, for gainliness of speech, for meekness, gentleness, and all the arts of pacification. Now is the time for argument, eloquence, and fearless urgency. Take now unto yourself all calculations of foresight, strengthen yourself with all friendly advice and aid, and even of your fears take friendly counsel. Afterthoughts and calculations of consequences are not for determining the thing to be done, but the way to do it most effectually—therefore not the inward counsellors and advisers of the mind, but the outward ministers and servants who execute her counsels. It may do well enough for a Jesuit or an ambitious courtier, but it is not for a Christian, who has line upon line, and precept upon precept, to run a calculation of chances, and out of the future, more uncertain in its issues than the public lottery, to draw forth a very doubtful probability, and make of it a rule to influence, if not to counteract, the unerring rules of God's revelation. And where is faith, if thus we are to travel by sight ? This prudence is the death of faith ; it leaves it nothing to do whatever ; for when all is seen and calculated to a certainty, where is there any more trust in God ? A Christian's life— a Christian minister's life—is one great series of imprudences. It courts not the world's favour; then it is imprudent. It standeth not for its rights, but forgets and forgives, and comes by loss ; then it is imprudent. It careth not anxiously for to-morrow—it hoardeth not—it is open-handed—it speaks truth which is despised. Imprudence! It is unpolite often, and often offensive. In short, it is a life of loss and resignation; and just in proportion as it is so, it is a life of faith, which looketh at the things unseen and eternal. Ay, I mistake; it doth calculate, but it calculates for the whole scope of existence, not for the period merely that is on this side the grave. It taketh in all the future consequences, and not a few only—therein it is prudent; but in respect to the world, it is little better than a long list of imprudences.

Think not that I cut off prudence, wisdom, and discretion from the life of a Christian as of another man—I do but assign to them their secondary place. There are these three —conscience, wisdom, and faith—which do each preside over a separate province of Christian life; or rather, to every Christian action they contribute each a part. Conscience I consider as the eye and voice of the soul, which, being guided by the Word and Spirit of God, beholds and tells the thing that is good and wise to be done. This prime minister of the inward man works best alone. If you bring to his side considerations of usefulness, of practicability, or of outward seemliness, you confuse his judgment, or tamper with his faithfulness; and according as you silence advocates from without, and make stillness within the breast, to hear the suggestions of reason—God's gift—and of reason's two helps —the Word and Spirit of God—you are the surer of an honest and upright judgment. The purpose being resolved within the heaven-determined conscience, it then comes to action; and now, as hath been said, is the time for prudence, discretion, and wisdom, which are handmaidens for executing the counsels of reason and of God. These are not to bring down the lofty decision of the soul, to divest it of heaven's plumage, and make it creep by the earth. Nay, though it should not only be unwise but foolish, if it be heaven-suggested, "the foolishness of God is wiser than the wisdom of man." Though it should not only be foolish but dangerous— not only dangerous, but fatal to be carried into effect—still, being counselled as above, it must not be forsaken. What is to keep our courage up, then? What is to recompense us? What is to divide us from foolhardy and violent men? Faith is that which is to keep our courage up, and recompense us, and distinguish us from foolhardy and violent men — high trust that what God hath counselled, God will prosper and finally reward. Faith stands in stead of present utility. The world to come brings out its glories to countervail present losses; and the more that, for the sake of faith, is resigned of renown, reputation, and advantage, the more is that faith perfected, and the more is conscience cheered in her divine dictatorship. The doctrines of faith and of present utility are the antipodes of each other. Where all is done for utility there is no faith. Now, prudence is the philosophy of present advantage. "Faith is the substance of things hoped for, the evidence of things not seen." Is wisdom then excluded? No; but a Divine wisdom cometh instead of a human wisdom. The conscience is guided by the oracles and Spirit of God. Now the Word of God is surely wiser than all books, and the Spirit of God wiser than all men. So that the fountainhead of wisdom poureth itself into the springs of action. Conscience is to the stream of life like what the ancients fabled of their rivers, that each river had a guardian god who resided in the solitude and caverns of its fountains, guided the useful course of every streamlet, and presided over the majestic flow of their united waters, and entered on its majestic wave into the full court of the ocean god, where he had a seat of dignity in proportion to the tribute which he brought to Neptune's watery domain. So conscience sits and reigns supreme at the fountainheads of action, and holdeth counsel of the Lord, and directeth her various courses according to Divine admonition, and, gathering force, rideth upon the full stream of a Christian life, which is not lost among the shifting sands of human policy, but is borne, a noble testimonial, into the ocean of eternal good, to contribute its part to the great and good ends of the Almighty counsels; and the good conscience, which presided so well over its appointed trust, is in very truth received into the court of God, with honour in proportion to the tribute which it hath brought to the universal good, over which God appointeth every man a guardian, and to which He honoureth every man to be in some sort a contributor.

On these principles the Baptist is to be justified from the accusation of rashness and imprudence which would be brought against such conduct in times like the present, when usefulness hath gone well-nigh to supplant, certainly greatly to straiten, the liberty of conscience, and the strong sustenance of faith. The Baptist brought his useful ministry to a speedy end by this act. I doubt not that he knew his fate, and saw his death in all its horrors, and perceived that his usefulness was to be extinguished by a ghastly death, yet he flinched not at the suggestion of any earthly counsel. Oh, I allow it is a frightful and a painful thing, and well worthy to be shunned, that the venerable man should yield up the ghost under the cloud of night in a gloomy cell—that the eye which gleamed with heaven's light, and shot heaven's own fire through all impediments into the vulnerable consciences of men, was to be glazed in death by the minister of a tyrant; and those lips upon whose breath the thousands of Israel hung ravished, and which overmastered the hardest and most flinty resolutions of man, were to grow pale under the knife or bow-string of a haggard headsman; and that the ruler of the land, who should have feed such a minister of righteousness as John the Baptist with half his domains, should make a gazing-stock to revellers and flatterers of that reverend head whose desires were all for the salvation of men, and quench that voice which spoke only for righteousness, as if it had been blowing poisoned pestilence over the land; and, most painful thought of all, that with this preacher of repentance were now spilt the lives of many souls, and their eternal salvation shipwrecked for ever. It was a most unsightly crime and a most sad calamity. And all this the Baptist could have avoided, if he had kept his foot from the palace, or, being in the palace, had refrained from one uncourtly word. But he would not take that prudent step, he would not flinch from his commission of truth. He unburdened himself before royalty, and was content to forfeit first his liberty of preaching and then his life.

These measures he never would have taken had he listened to the universal outcry there is now raised of usefulness. But he consulted with God and his conscience, and bore himself as you see. And he murdered his usefulness—at least so they would be apt to say in these times. But no, he was more useful in his death than he could have been by a thousand lives, even such lives as he lived. He died for truth, which is more noble than to live for truth—by how much death is more painful than life, and the deprivation of all things more trying to human nature than the possession of all things. I say he died for truth, the noblest fate which a human being is permitted to have, amply recompensed in heaven and on earth; the brightest ensign that can be raised for the hopes of a dark and benighted world.

To die by the visitation of God,—that is, to wait until we have no longer time allowed us,—is to yield to necessity's law; and we cannot expect any praise or admiration. To forestall our time by willingly running into hazards may be very noble or very base, according to the occasion which moves us. But to die for daring to utter God's truth when others have not the heart to speak it, is at all times a godly death. It is godly, because the consciousness of truth for which we die is from God; it is celestial, because it prefers truth, the offspring of heaven, to all the blessings of home and all the possessions of the world; it is a kind of immortality in death, because that same truth for which we have died is immortal. Therefore I have a kind of veneration for ancient heathens who died for the sake of truth,—a veneration not diminished but increased by the circumstance that they perceived it but dimly. And for all men who have died for their principles, even though they should afterwards turn out false, I feel the same respect, especially if I perceive them to be virtuous men, who were not moved by rage, desperation, and stoical pride, but by a calm preference of death to dissimulation and falsehood. Oh, of how much more honour are they worthy who, being called of God on high to be His ministers abroad unto the sons of men, and thereto furnished with a portion of the Divine Spirit, Divine sons of wisdom purified from all selfishness, sanctified from all duplicity and malice, are troubled, imprisoned, and put to death because they will not betray their sacred trust! Such are entitled to a Divine honour, if any imperfect mortals are. They were taken up by God and preferred to His special confidence, whereof they proved themselves to be worthy. They came by loss in His service, the loss of father and mother, and brother and sister, and life itself; and having resigned all for God, they have received all which a glorified saint is capable of receiving. They walk clothed in white, they have palms of victory in their hands, and sing the song of Jehovah and the Lamb. In the New Jerusalem they are honoured, in God's sight they are honoured, above the rest of His saints. And much more upon the earth, for whose sake they suffered and poured forth their precious blood,—much more upon the earth, which hath few that it can with justice honour, ought these the honourable ones of heaven to be magnified above all sons of the mighty.

And in the eye of thoughtful and righteous people it doth but magnify the honour of such worthy deaths, when they are done at the bidding of the basest and most brutal passions. A show of justice, a trial and a sentence, and a mockery of righteous execution, do somewhat cover over the foulness of the deeds; and a battle arrayed against such men in the field, and the gallantry and chivalry of a war against the saints, doth cast a glare over the wretchedness of the persecution; and the forms of inquisition and antic dresses are able to blind virtuous and manly natures to the shocking principles and barbarous cruelty of persecuting deeds. But when, as in the case before us, riot and jollity prepare the way, and wiles and wantonness bring up the attack, and lust moves the measure forward, and pride will not allow the cruel purpose to recede, and the order is given for the murder in cool blood, and in the very giving is declared to be against justice; ay, and in the teeth of the highest estimation and regard—not against innocency alone, but against a life worth half a kingdom: and, being thus declared horrid cruelty by the very tongue that gave it, when it is carried into effect in the inward dungeons of a prison, without an eye to witness the shedding of sacred blood, or a heart to condole, or one ear into the cell of whose most tenacious memory the cry of vengeance might arise; and, being performed in such dark disguise, and in such an untimely way, when the reverend head, elected by God, and by God anointed with wisdom above its fellows, is for mockery's sake served up in a lordly dish, as if it were a dainty thing, served up to a woman—a beautiful and admired woman—to glut the raven of her eyes, and compose the vengeance that rankleth in her heart;—so hellish a martyrdom, a sacrifice so decked by the spirit of every lust, whereon every demon of the pit hath a feast,—such a piece of glory in hell hath doubtless in heaven a high renown. The murdered man is tenfold murdered, and hath tenfold honour in heaven and in earth. He is murdered in spite, in sport, in jollity, and jest—he who deserved a crown. And a crown noble in proportion to his hardest fate he hath received in heaven. He is one of those who have not defiled themselves with untruth, nor known the blemish of hypocrisy—who have washed their robes and made them white in the blood of the Lamb, and walk on high with triumphant palms in their hands, clothed in the raiment of unsullied purity.

And on earth such a death is the life of thousands. It begetteth its like in distant ages; and in benighted lands it kindleth spirits to preach repentance as fearlessly as the Baptist did. When courts put forth their artifice, and kings their power, it teacheth men of God how to behave themselves fearlessly. And when the painted beauty and artificial loveliness of woman would wean them from their course, it shews them how to behave themselves. The cause of truth never received such an exaltation over courtiership, gallantry, and shamefacedness, as in this example of the first Christian herald. And wherever it is told over the world, it shall breed men of the Baptist's heavenly function, to brave the wickedness of courts and the wiles of seducing women, and speak the truth at the hazard of their lives. What names shall stand like those of Knox and Luther in the forefront of the annals of nations, the Christian heroes thereof, begetting another progeny, each in their proper realm! So that such a death for the Almighty's sake is the generation of a thousand spirits; its fruits are countless, and its value not to be reckoned up.

Therefore the Baptist did well to go fearlessly forth upon the field of his destruction, and speak his message to the man who held his life in his hand. Learn you, brethren, to do likewise—to speak the truth in your several places, and to those into whose company Providence brings you. We have no commission from God to preach repentance to a land, as had the Baptist; but each one of you in his province is bound to speak the truth as fearlessly as he. Now, if ye will search into this matter as hath been said, with conscience, the Word, and the Spirit of God for your guides, you will discover how much of the truth is sacrificed for courtesy and custom's sake. If you speak the truth, your friends will take offence; but speak it for the pleasing of God. Your counsellors will call it imprudent, but speak it, relying upon faith for your reward. Whatever you speak, let it be the truth, spoken gently, softly, and with a persuasive tongue, but still in truth, so as not to be mistaken. One day of such discipline shall reveal more falsehoods to be in you than you could well believe. One day of such discipline will convince you more of the wickedness of the heart than a thousand sermons. One day of such discipline will teach you the necessity of divine grace and the unction of the Spirit of truth, better than all that I or any minister can ever persuade.

LECTURE XIII.

LUKE III.; MATT. XIV.

WHEN the conscience of truth so prevails within the bosom as to set at naught the courtesies of life, and the distinctions of rank, and the fear of death itself, then the messenger of truth hath a sacredness in his person, and his words take a weight which overawes the most wilful, and for a while melts the most hardened mind. From the perilous extremes in which it is spoken, it is divested of all suspicion, and takes the stamp of sincerity; and a speech which can make its sincerity good, hath secured almost every point of conviction. The reason that we disregard each other's counsels is, that we distrust each other's motives; referring their speeches to the study of self-interest, to the influence of custom, to the commonplace of the times, to the love of power, to a fault-finding temper, to self-conceit, and a thousand other obliquities, to which, being liable ourselves in giving counsel, we think it reasonable that others should be likewise liable. Truth is so masked up and disguised, and made to play so many parts, that falsehood, borrowing her dresses, passeth herself off for truth. But when truth casts away these disguises, and appears in naked simplicity, she is not to be mistaken. Woe to the man that yieldeth her not reverence and welcome; for she hath within his bosom a friend that will punish him for his mistreatment, and in his tender part he will be wounded, and stricken, and seek for rest in vain. To reject truth when she cometh undisguised is a kind of suicide upon our conscience; it is a suicide upon our happiness, either in time or in eternity—most frequently in both.

Of all which we are to lay before you now a notable example; not singular, but very remarkable, as being exhibited upon one of the most hardened and wicked of men. That Nathan should have prevailed upon King David is not so wonderful as that he should have failed; for his speech was witty, his parable a finely-laid snare for an erring conscience, and he to whom he spoke was a generous and noble-hearted prince, overtaken in a fault, and seeking to veil from the public eye what the most of kings in those barbarous times would have gloried in. That Paul should have made Felix to tremble, and almost persuaded King Agrippa to be a Christian, we are prepared to expect, from the specimens of his irresistible discourse which we have recorded. But that John the Baptist should have been able to work conviction upon the crooked mind of Herod, to outwit those policies which made our Saviour designate him "fox," and check the arbitrary wilfulness and pride of his character, of which we are soon to have a melancholy instance, and awaken a heart that seemed to be drowned in luxury and vice, and allay his thirst of revenge when he was attacked in one of his strongest affections,—this is a triumph of truth whereof I do not remember a parallel in ancient or in modern times, in history sacred or profane. And yet that Herod was so affected we are informed in the most positive terms by the inspired historian.

Herodias had a quarrel with John, and would have killed him, but she could not; "for Herod feared John, knowing that he was a just man and a holy, and observed him," (or, as it is in the margin, kept him or saved him,) "and when he heard him, he did many things, and heard him gladly." Also, when Herodias sought his death, "the king was exceeding sorry," and consented only because his royal word was pledged before the high estates of the nation. And the remembrance of him whom he had beheaded he could never erase; for when the rumour of Jesus went abroad, he said, "It is John whom I beheaded: he is risen from the dead, and therefore mighty works do shew forth themselves in him."

"Herod feared John, knowing that he was a just man and a holy." What a triumph to justice and holiness these words record, that they should be able to strike fear into the heart of Herod! In the original it is literally fear or dread, not reverence. Herod had a fear of him. Whether this proceeded from the Baptist's reputation with the people, as Matthew would lead us to suppose when he saith of Herod, "that he would have put him to death, but he feared the multitude, because they counted John as a prophet," or from the immediate influence of a just and holy character upon his own mind, is of little account; as in either case it is a testimony to the power of those high qualities in the most unpropitious places, and over the most abandoned men. The character of the Baptist could reach a man whom hardly anything else could reach, and hold in the chains of fear one who made many to tremble. Herod, though in his palace, surrounded with his royal guards, feared him. He knew the Baptist was stronger than he; for truth is mighty, and mightily prevaileth. And being already conscious of his offendings, and having enough to do to keep down the voices of crime and transgression within him, he feared this righteous man, whose words gave such edge to his self-accusations, such point to his remorse. Unarmed, the Baptist daunted him more than an army of men, an embattled city, or a fenced tower, or any other source of physical and outward force. It reminds me of the saying of the first James, when Knox's daughter came to petition for her husband Welsh's pardon. The monarch asked her who she was; she replied, "The daughter of John Knox." "Knox and Welsh," said he, "that is a fearful junction of bloods. And had your father any sons?" "No, only three daughters." "Had his three daughters been three sons," said the conscience-struck monarch, "I would ill have bruiked my three kingdoms in peace. He may return if he will consent never to preach again." "Sooner than he should consent to that," said the godly and heroic woman, "I would kep [that is, I would receive] his bloody head here," stretching out the matronal apron in which she was attired. Such was the saying of a man who, having declared the Church of his native country the most perfect under heaven, a few years afterwards sought to overthrow it, and had banished into perpetual exile its most faithful pastors, and, among others, this same Welsh, whose wife had with him that instructive dialogue. Might hath an instinctive dread of right, and dare not face it. Conscience makes cowards of the wicked, by the same influence by which she maketh heroes and martyrs of the righteous; and there never upon the earth occurs a more unequal strife than when a man with a clear conscience comes to contend with a man whose conscience is defiled; no numbers can make up the odds; no power, no armour, no subtlety of eloquence. As to subtlety of eloquence, see how simple truth in Paul's lips overthrew the state orator Tertullus; as to power, see in the instance before us how John's justice unmanned and made of a king a timorous man; and as to numbers, contemplate Luther alone before the imperial diet of Germany, how he outwitted all the Italian arts of nuncios and ambassadors, and, after three days' debate, stood up before them all and said, "I can do no more, God be my help," and they were discomfited before him. O brethren, I would let you know what strong men ye would every one become if you would disband the artifices and addresses of life whereby truth is strangled, and adopt these counsels; allowing no human policy to colour the fountain-head of action, but listening to the voice of conscience and of God, and bringing truth from a heart possessed with the spirit of truth. John did not more prevail against Herod, nor the Reformer's daughter against the backsliding king, nor the father of the Reformation against the assembled courtiers and false priests of Christendom, than ye would prevail in your various circles of life by observing at all times the sacred counsels of truth. Even the world hath discovered the might of truth in that most noble maxim, that honesty is the best policy; and we have heard of an English statesman who went into some subtle court—I think of France—and outwitted all their intrigues by speaking nothing but the truth. So that the world knows the usefulness of this doctrine in the long run; but unfortunately the world hath not the means of bearing up under the present and pressing evils to which it may dare to expose one—the sour looks, the uncivil words, the temporary alienation of those who cannot hear truth, and the mistakes and slanders of the world; so that it is rare to find one natural man who shall, before all companies and in all conditions, have resolution to speak the plain unvarnished truth. He fears the offended, he dreads consequences: or if he can look hard upon hard issues, then his affections, his tender affections, fear to wound the affections of another, and he softens the matter down till it hath in it no sting of offence, and then it hath generally no sting of truth. So that the old cynical Athenian who, with a lighted lantern in his hand, peered about the streets of Athens seeking for an honest man, and finding none, might haply meet with no better success in the present age among such as have not been anointed with the spirit of truth from on high. But I should hope he would find many in the Church of Christ who is the way, the truth, and the life; for it is the nature of their discipline to lay their account with the displeasure of the world, and not to be afraid with its terrors, nor with its judgments to be amazed, but to commit themselves unto God, that judgeth righteously. They are lights—certain, steadfast lights—upon the uncertain navigation of life, unto which the rest may take heed. And if they be careful against the spread of jesuitry, whereof, I think, a small infusion threateneth, if it be not already present, in the religious spirit of these times,—if the Church, I say, clothe herself in the white raiment of truth, and every disciple of the Holy Catholic Church stanchly standeth by righteousness and truth, then, sure as the first Christian missionary carried terror to the heart of the proudest and subtlest tyrant of the times, will the Church carry terror to the breast of the deceitful and malignant world, and in the end prevail against it, and destroy it, and bring in a universal righteousness, a universal reign of truth.

Herod being held in check by the justice and holiness of the prophet, is said to have observed him, or kept him, or saved him. The word in the original means diligently to keep or preserve anything that it come by no harm; and the drift of the context favoureth, then, the radical meaning of the word, for it is said in the preceding verse that Herodias would have killed him, but she could not, for Herod feared John, knowing that he was a just man and a holy, and carefully watched or preserved him. Now, if it were that he watched him lest he should do any harm, then there is no reason in it why Herodias could not kill him; but if it means that he watched him lest he should come by any harm, then both the spirit of the context is saved, and the radical sense of the word perceived. Not that we fancy Herod had any dear affection for the Baptist, which led him to place him out of the reach of the snares of the revengeful adulteress,—for I do not give him the credit of any such honourable feeling; but he had a mingled feeling, partly fear, partly policy,—fear to lift his hand against so holy a man, and so revered of all that knew him,—policy lest if any unadvised mischief were perpetrated against him, the blame of it might rest with his tyrannical measures; therefore he thought it best to put him beyond the reach of danger in a place of safety. It is observable how God makes the wickedness of men to praise Him, so that His saints escape by the jarrings of the wicked. Paul was preserved by the contention between Sadducees and Pharisees before the council held by Claudius Lysias, the governor of Jerusalem. So Luther was preserved in a place of safety by the Elector of Saxony, and made way for his doctrines through the divisions which then agitated the empire, being protected by the one party against the violence of the other. And here John is for a while preserved by Herod against the prompted passion of his queen Herodias. Upon which I cannot refrain from making one remark—how prompt, saucy, and revengeful is the indignation of women. It taketh no time for deliberation, and hath no coolness to weigh the matter, but hasteth and hurrieth onward to the execution of its purpose. And herein the wisdom of God is to be noted in appointing unto man the head and rule of his house, that he may let and restrain these humours by command and power, until reason and reflection have time and opportunity to come in and determine. God having gifted man with a greater faculty of reason, and woman with a greater faculty of feeling, and reason being needed to preside over feeling, He gave to man the presidency of the house. That Herod confined John, not for the purpose of putting his tongue to silence, but for the ends of his safe keeping, is manifested further by the other particulars given by the evangelist of the regard in which he held him. He did many things, and heard him gladly, or sweetly, as the original signifies. He did many things at the suggestion and bidding of the Baptist. What these were in point of fact, we have no account; what they were in spirit, we have no need of any account. The Baptist was not the man to suggest anything of an ambiguous or dubious kind. His lessons were all of one character—repentance towards God, and preparation for Christ that was to come. And from the aptness of his reproofs and exhortations to publicans and priests, and people and soldiers, whereof we formerly discoursed, we may form some idea how faithful, how uncompromising would be his dealings with the king. They would be of a piece with that only note of the royal lecture which is given, that Herod should not have Herodias, his brother Philip's wife. Doubtless they would concern the function of royalty and respect the means of government. He would command him to set faithful men around his throne, who loved God, and hated covetousness. He would command him to purify his court, and begin with the example of purifying his own chamber. He would command him to submit himself to God, and publish edicts throughout his realm enjoining the fear of God; and the heathenish customs which had crept in, of games and contests, of amphitheatres and gymnasiums, of the arena and the palestra, he would order him to put down, as having no concert with the service of the living God; and many right judgments he would command him to execute, and not to oppress the poor, or to grind the people with exactions, or to surfeit himself with luxury, or to please himself with flattery, or to exalt himself with pride, or to forget the living God, or to do aught else unworthy of the prince and ruler of the people. It is impossible that the Baptist could speak within the portals of Herod's court, and not speak of those things which were everywhere submitted to his eye. If he bearded the lion in his den, he would not crouch before him in the way, or fear to encounter him in his ravagings. If he touched him in his private and peculiar affections, he would not fear to touch him in his court and public acts of government. And many of those recommendations of the Baptist he followed. The force of truth and righteousness thus far prevailed against the pride and force of custom. What a noble triumph again of unarmed righteousness! What an encouragement, in these milder times, to speak everywhere the sincere and simple truth, to exhort, to rebuke, to instruct in righteousness, to be bold, to lift up the voice like a trumpet, to tell the people their sins, and the leaders of the people their transgressions! It cannot be that men are now more deaf to truth than they were then, or less ready to reform what they are convinced is amiss. If they shut their ears to counsel, it is because they suspect the by-ends and intents which suggest it. Therefore let every one who giveth counsel purify himself from all selfishness, and all self-seeking, from all evil temper and fault-finding, and bring out his truthfulness like the day, and his righteousness like the noon-day. And he shall certainly prevail to work some improvement upon the most stubborn men. I know how our pride bridles up and starts back at the mention of our misdoings, and sets ingenuity to work to detect some evil or ambiguous motive in him that gives it. But I likewise know that if the counsel touch a real flaw in our character, or an error in our conduct, or a wilful act of wickedness, it is not lost; it sinks down into the mind, but it is not lost. Conscience takes it in keeping, and is troubled, and many days, perhaps many years after, confession giveth testimony that it hath not been in vain. Therefore continue patiently to sow the seeds of truth, and in due time your friend shall reap if you fail not. Be not offended that he is at pains to detect some unworthy motive inducing you. If you love the cause of truth, you should be willing to endure a little sifting and a little severe handling. Nor be dismayed though your friend should call you officious, meddling, and hypocritical, but continue faithfully to assure him of your honest intentions; and though he should cut you off from his friendly trust, and debar you from his home and his haunts, never despair. These are far better symptoms than if he heard you as though he heard you not, or turned aside your counsel with some commonplace remark upon our common failures, or some slight sally upon your being so good and so honest and so full of advice. I would rather have a tough encounter for the cause of truth, than have it slip out of hand through these smooth railleries, which content the soul of the receiver, and too often content the soul of the giver, whereas it contenteth nothing but the vanity of both. Hold to your friend, if so be that he allow the truth of what you say. Well then, say to him, but if it is true, why not follow after it? And allow not yourself to be smiled out of your object, but hold to it, keeping a steady and serene aspect. Do not frown down, but sober down the gay and sprightly air of confession with which your counsel is received. This mood of the mind will never do for the entertainment of sober truth. Therefore put it to flight with a steady, unmoved countenance, which will not smile in accordance with their sweet, strict, and reviling tone of confession. Confession is no confession which is not made with shamefacedness and downcast magdalene looks, and soft and sorrowful tones, and feelings and signs of sadness. Therefore, I say again, stand it out, until the gay and courtly humour is gone, and the mind is come into a mood for entertaining truth. Now it is, but not till now, that the contest begins—the preceding was but a gay avoiding of the contest. And now will pride arise, and summon up its advocates, and a vigorous self-defence will be commenced; and now is your time to put forth manly and divine power in behalf of truth, and prepare yourself for retorts—first courteous, then discourteous. And now be upon the watch how to defend yourself: if with pride, then pride encountering pride is like flint encountering flint; and fiery contention, and high words, and strife, and separation, perhaps blows and blood, may be the result. And in such a case you have betrayed the truth; it hath been wounded in the house of its friends, and between you hath it been slain. But if you make your defence with meekness and humility, and sorrowful confession in the slight things with which they upbraid you, and receive their hard words upon the soft and downy defences of Christian grace and charity, then your defence is worth a thousand attacks, and, like the Scythian, you wound your enemy in his onset, you wound him by submitting. He catches in his arms, not his foe, but his friend—he presses to his bosom one whom he meant to kill, but whose meek and merciful touch melts and overcomes him. Such urgent constancy for truth's sake, such yielding for interest's sake, almost no one can withstand. In the personal question they find you yield, and acknowledge all your imperfections; this is such a rebuke to those who in a greater matter are fighting for personal interest against the truth, that it generally breaketh the bone. And here it is the advocates of truth are to wait and expect their victory —when the battle is turned against themselves, and they endure so much and confess so willingly.

All this mockery of pride on the part of Herod, John doubtless encountered in the outset; for, as we see by the sequel, Herod was one of the proudest of men. And all this he withstood. He had the advantage of being feared as a just and a holy man. There could be no accusation of ambition or of advantage brought against one who bore all his wealth on his person, and held all his influence in his voice— who made no head for himself but for Another who was afterwards to arise. One so disinterested, one so advanced upon the vantage-ground of his disinterestedness, never appeared upon the earth, as John the Baptist. And to this he owed no small part of his success in every quarter. And if we priests in the latter day would compel men by the awful voice of truth, not hunt them out by the soft words of policy, we must take our stand upon the same vantage-ground, and care for nought that is valued, that is told and talked of under the sun. The earth, and all it holds, must be to us as nothing—our food the plainest, our raiment the simplest, and everything awarded to an earth-despising mind. I do not say positively that we should be reduced to houseless wanderers, but we should have a spirit in us ready for it. We should suffer, yes, I say we should suffer the dignities, the honours, the splendour, the very conveniences and comforts of life; we should suffer them for the sake of the times and the feelings of our friends, and for their usefulness' sake, (if I may use that most unclerical word, never used in the New Testament to a pastor, though now the only one that is used;) but we should be ready to resign our all when we are staked against a point of conscience, and to go forth upon the wide and wild world, like the two thousand non-conforming priests of England, and the six hundred covenanting priests of Scotland, at the era called *glorious era* of the Restoration.

Herod heard him gladly or sweetly. The eloquence of the Baptist, nursed in deserts, the wild costume of his language, his oration like an old prophet's woe-denouncing burden, or like an Indian orator's song of lamentation and revenge, the harmony of gesture, and the desert-like array of his person, —all this was, as a spectacle, one of the most fresh and racy things which could pass the threshold of a court. And I figure to myself the gay gallants of the place making merry with the rude bearing of the wanderer, and the silver-tongued courtiers inwardly shaking their sides at the bold truthfulness of this man, and the false women trembling for some unmannered exposure, and the heartless enviers hoping for the exposure of all but themselves. It was, doubtless, no small pleasure to them all to hear the Baptist preach and talk— the novelty and freshness of the whole exhibition, and the great entertainment which there was in it.

But the Baptist was of other metal than to stop short at these impressions. His discourse was not a spectacle; his doctrine would not turn a joke; his rebukes would not be repaid with a smile; nor his services with salutations or applause. These are current coinage for vain ostentatious performers at a theatre; but such newspaper, pamphlet, and courtly applause or censure hath no nourishment for a man of God. It toucheth, it moveth him not, except to shew him that he hath not yet reached his mark. Thereupon he setteth his arrow on his bow again; he wingeth it anew, and sendeth it with a double strain, that it may strike through these courtly coverings and trappings of vanity into the inner man of the heart. He stands to his post; he spies out the vulnerable parts of the van host; he lieth in wait for them; he findeth his occasion, and sendeth his bolt into the quick.

So did the Baptist to Herod, who, with all his faults—and they were many—was a proud and resolute man, far beyond the sphere of vanity and ostentation; a self-determining man, who knew to value manly qualities in another, and valued them in the Baptist; a clear-headed man, who knew truth when he heard it even against himself; and a man of counsel, who could discern that the Baptist's way of it was the best, though bearing against his own throughout. And I doubt not he listened to the Baptist with honest conviction, and purposed to listen to him longer, and either to yield to him or to make the Baptist yield. And fain, fain would I have seen the issue of the contest; but an incident occurred, which we shall hereafter consider, to mar it in the midst of its operation. Yet Herod heard him sweetly, and was exceeding sorrowful to put him to death, and never afterwards could wipe the memory of him from his conscience.

"It is the Baptist risen from the dead." It haunted him, and would not give him rest. When Christ's fame arose, he sought to see him, that he might be satisfied it was not the Baptist. Such way had this servant of God made upon this arch-servant of the devil, that he had not only sway in life, but in death domineered over him. From his ashes he spoke to the tyrant. His blood spoke loud from the inmost dungeon of the palace into the ears of the prince; it planted thorns upon his unholy court; it slew his enjoyment with his mistress, and rankled like poison in his breast; and he said, when he heard of any extraordinary person, "This is John the Baptist: he is risen from the dead." "John have I beheaded, but who is this?"

Such is the influence which a man of God, with truth upon his lips, may gain over a man of Belial, cunning as the fox, proud as Lucifer, and blood-thirsty as the tiger. I have opened it up for your encouragement to follow the same course of speaking truth in the love of it; and hereafter I shall shew you the resistance in the tyrant's mind, that ye may be upon your guard. This discourse hath been to encourage you to speak the truth; the next shall be to discourage you from resisting truth.

Now, I have not been unmindful, all the way, of shewing you the only fountain of truth, the Lord Jesus Christ; one lesson of whose discipline I have been teaching you. And yet I cannot close without informing you that the strength to speak, the purpose to speak, and the words of truth to be spoken, come all from above; and that while pride, vanity, courtesy, or any other worldly custom, holds dominion over you, you are under the power of him who, from the beginning, was a liar and a murderer, and who is the father of liars.

Therefore, if there be any truth in what hath now been delivered—any nobility, any persuasion, or any counsel—it amounts to this, that ye turn unto Christ, who is the truth, and submit yourself to His Spirit, which is the Spirit of truth, and walk in His statutes, which are right, rejoicing the heart. (Ps. xix.)

LECTURE XIV.

LUKE III.; MATT. XIV.; MARK VI.

THIS notable instance of the first preacher of Christ we have dwelt upon the more, because in him is presented to us a model of a Christian preacher and a Christian disciple, in those sterner and severer aspects which are now either held in no account or treated with disrepute. When the preaching of the gospel is conceived of as all grace and mercy, and no motive hath any sanction but that of love, and masculine truth hath learned to lisp in accents of courtesy, and to seek her way by prudence and address, we have thought, by holding up for a while the Baptist's unsavoury diction, and the Baptist's uncivil demeanour, we might find a good apology for infringing the soft custom of the time, and speaking with force and determination, as they were wont to do in the times of old. For you will observe how the Saviour sent from His tongue words like edged swords, and made havoc amongst the most heart-cherished idols of His hearers:—at one time, in the house of Simon the Pharisee, who entertained Him courteously, preferring to all the pomp and preparation of his supper-table, the simple, devoted act of a despised and unfortunate woman; at another time, in a large assembled party, telling them to ask the halt and lame, the blind and beggarly, to their feasts, that it might be the hospitality of the heart, and not a trade and barter in splendid entertainments; again, preferring the mite of a widow to the costly offerings of the rich; at all times stinging every hypocrite to the quick through all his veils; denouncing whole orders of men—Pharisees, Sadducees, scribes, and lawyers, the highest ranks in Jerusalem—for their abuse of their place, and devoting them to the wrath and indignation of God. And when He sent forth the seventy on their errand of preaching, He not only gave them a message of peace, but a burden of woe:—" Into whatever city ye enter, and they receive you not, go your ways out into the streets of the same, and say, Even the very dust of your city, which cleaveth on us, we do wipe off against you;" thereby teaching us that there are two sides of the commission-roll whereby we preach Christ—one fair and hopeful as the morning, the other dark and gloomy as the setting of midnight. And Paul, I am sure by many examples, walked in the same footsteps:—at one time braving the magistrates of Philippi in their duty, and scorning their insufficient apologies; at another, daring the Roman governor to lay a lash on him; at a third, appealing to Cæsar like a free man; and through all his Epistles conducting himself like a magnanimous man, and a devoted saint, and the very opposite of a timorous devotee. And the Reformers did the same; and the missionaries, before they prosper, will have to do the same; and at home, Christian preachers, to make a lodgment in strong and stubborn hearts, must do the same. The great and awful attributes of God must shine forth; His sword of justice must be unsheathed in the heavens over a wicked world. Then truth must go before Him, and tell that One is coming after with the axe of discrimination in His hand, to hew the profitless cumberers of the ground from their place. And there must be a shaking of the high towers of the heart, which are riches, pride, and glory; and there must be a quaking of the soul for its very existence, and a loud cry of "Repent, or perish; repent, or in a few years ye shall, like Nineveh, be destroyed." This rough beginning of it must still be made in every soul, and in the general world; and the harsh discourse which is to make this rough beginning of it must be held—it must be a part of every discourse. A summons to surrender must precede every overture of mercy, and the direful alternative of death and destruction must close this overture, otherwise it will never come to pass that the people will take alarm, be moved, and shaken, and cry out for mercy to the living God, and accept His offered mercy in Christ, and come unto Him that they may be healed and their souls may live. Do the whole seek the physician? No; but the sick. Therefore, sicken the people at the heart, and afflict their soul with fear, that they may flee unto the Chief Physician. Do the honest men cry you mercy, or heed your offer of mercy? No; they turn it aside with high disdain: but the poor criminal, who groaneth his soul out in bondage, heareth it most gladly. Convict the people, then; sist them at judgment, and fairly convict them against all their subterfuges, and hand them over to execution; and then they will listen to the slightest suggestion of mercy, and hunt the avenues of it out, and seek its ministers, and sue them, and catch their words with more delight than ever did felon catch the words of his reprieve, or prisoners the merry news of a general gaol-delivery. The Baptist's office is gone much into disuse—so much so, that had I not a flock to feed and edify in holiness, as well as an audience to convert, I would willingly forego the preaching of mercy, address myself to topics of warning, expostulation, and denouncement, and leave the people to their chance of peace and comfort, which, it seemeth to me, they could not miss, go whither their feet might carry them to the house of God. Mercy is too soft for this hard and flinty world to have been sent from heaven alone. They would have pierced her ample bosom, and nailed her outstretched arms to an accursed tree, and otherwise entreated her vilely. Therefore the Lord sent in her company the terrible form of Justice, with his arm revealed; and hand in hand they go over the populous earth, from city to city. And Mercy begins the parley, saying, "Peace be unto this city, good-will to the children thereof from God on high; salvation to the sons of men, through the cross of Christ, from the punishment of all their sins." Justice standeth by her side, but she shieldeth his blows with her radiant form. They hear, and they are saved; they hear not, and Justice prepareth himself to act. He girdeth himself for death and slaughter like a man of war; but Mercy intercedeth, and haply prevaileth. But if obdurate the people of any city remain, then she gathereth up her raiment, and from its purity she shaketh off the polluted dust of that city, devoted to destruction from the arm of the justice of Almighty God.

Now, the idea having got possession of my mind that the preaching of the everlasting gospel, whereby we are saved from the wrath to come, hath lost the accompaniment of the law, of the stern and spiritual law, which was the only thing that brought the apostle's self-confidence to the ground, wherein lieth the strength of sin, and without which the strongholds of sin shall never be discovered; being convinced, on the one hand, that the orthodox and evangelical adhere to grace and mercy, and other topics of consolation, too pertinaciously for the conviction and conversion of the unregenerate world, and that the Socinian and heterodox do, on the other hand, take from Mercy her olive-branch, and from Justice his sword, and send them forth like two conquerors from the schools, to ply the head with words, but seldom make the heart to quail within its natural holds, or melt before the love and attachment of its Maker; being convinced that by the one Mercy is sent to the work with too slight an attendance for this sin-armed and Satan-defended world, and that by the other the self-deceived world is not solicited either by heaven-professing Mercy, or shaken by hell-denouncing Justice,—I thought it might be profitable to the place and time, and encouraging to our own purpose of upholding the ancient custom, thus to hold up, as I have done at great length, this ministry of the Baptist and forerunner of Christ, which now hastens to a close.

In treating this last act of the Baptist's tragical life, these views directed our method, and we began by what might be thought very singular,—a defence or justification of his boldness in chastising the crimes of a monarch,—and thereafter we examined what success he had in that perilous ministry; in both which topics of discourse we had an eye mainly to your improvement in the difficult duty of speaking truth, and nicely acting on behalf of truth. In doing which office for your spiritual welfare, we took occasion to lay down the true doctrine of duty, which consists, first, in listening to the voice of conscience, guided by the Word and Spirit of God; then in taking human wisdom and prudence to execute the inward counsel, and to perform it in the face of disadvantage and disapprobation, through the help of that faith which is the gift of God. This course the Baptist followed. He had begun with the common people who came out to him from the regions round about Jerusalem; he wrought his way amongst the higher orders, setting his face steadfastly against unrighteousness; and at length he arrived at the sacred seat of power, the throne of the king, and went to work after his ancient fashion of preaching repentance, because the kingdom of heaven was at hand, and he followed up his preaching by challenging whatever he saw amiss: for he had received his commission from Heaven to forewarn men, and advertise them beforehand of a Saviour. And the tetrarch was a man, and no more than a man, before the living God. And his soul was precious in the Lord's sight, all wicked as it was. And the Lord, though He saw what counsel the tyrant would take against His servant, was too merciful even to Herod to let him go down to the pit without a warning. Though his father had persecuted the infant Saviour, and slain the innocents, whose mangled limbs and harmless blood cried to Him for vengeance; though he himself had been guilty of many a crime, and lived in open contempt of Heaven's decrees,—yet the Lord, who is rich in mercy, sent him a note of warning. And the Baptist being commissioned to all men, went in unto him, and shunned not to declare unto him the counsel of God. But the Baptist being resolved in the point of duty, took to himself, I doubt not, all the arts of speech which did not compromise the truth. He did his utmost before the king, and was not unmindful of respect and reverence to his elevated station, and cleansed his breast of plebeian spitefulness—if ever it harboured in his breast—and guarded himself against rudeness, pride, and vanity; and, I doubt not, reasoned with the king, and besought him, and earnestly entreated him, if he saw any gentle mood coming over his mind; or if he saw in him noble moods, I doubt not he addressed himself to these, and shewed his royal virtues and sovereign graces of character, and taught him the majesty of justice and honour. I doubt not the sincere yet wise messenger of God took all the measures which were likely to insure success, and did not assail the weak parts of the monarch, mock him, or harrow up his soul with fear, but spoke to him as a messenger of God should speak to one whom God hath appointed the ruler of the people. For had not the Baptist so entrenched himself in truth and uprightness, and graced his speech with all the ornaments which are proper to truth, and poured into it the affection and love which, in his most terrible moods, the messenger of Heaven maintains, it is not conceivable that he should have gained the monarch so far as to become his protector, his scholar, his servant—for in many things he took his instructions, and obeyed them—that he should have overawed him, or secured so deep a place in his heart, as that when he did him wrong he could never afterwards be at peace. How far the Baptist prevailed with the monarch we set forth at large in our last discourse; and we now proceed to follow the tragical history onwards to its close.

Though the Baptist bore hardest against the affections of the monarch, the king had too much regard for him to sacrifice him to wounded affection. He did not imprison him, we shewed, out of revenge for his faithful admonition in respect of his brother Philip's wife, but to protect him from her vengeance. Now, here I take another distinction between men and women. There are stronger parts in man than his affections; in woman there are none so strong. Herod bore John's assault upon his affections, and heard him gladly notwithstanding; but Herodias could not. Herod did many things at the Baptist's suggestion; and Herodias feared he might also, at his suggestion, put her away, and therefore hastened to precipitate his death. In which difference in the constitution of man and woman, I pray you to observe the wisdom of the Creator again. The woman being destined for the part of a nurse and a mother to the world, and the man for the father and governor of the world, the Almighty made affection strongest in the breast of the one; in the breast of the other, He made authority and command prevail over affection, when it so happens that they cannot be sweetly accorded. Woman was intended for the solacement of man, and to that end was bestowed upon him in Paradise at first; and when she led him astray, her share in the sentence was, that her desire should be to her husband, and that he should rule over her. But to man the bitterest half of the curse did fall—that he should labour the ground, and win his bread with the sweat of his face. So that man was made the slave of labour, the tiller of the ground, the owner of the ground, the governor of the earth; and woman was made the comfort of man in the midst of his many toilsome labours, and of his heartless supremacy. Therefore, affection was made the strongest in the one, and in the other, understanding, rule, and strength—understanding to direct, rule to undertake, and strength to carry into effect, the management of this niggard earth, which the Lord yielded to his sovereignty. Now, in making these remarks, I am so far from dividing, that I do, in truth, unite the bond between man and woman, by pointing out the proper domain of each; for upon the proper regulation of this rudimental relation of all society, its prosperity, in a great measure, dependeth. For example, in old Rome, when women nobly did the part of wives and mothers, what noble men were reared, patriotic, affectionate at home, and terrible abroad; and in this country, where these domestic virtues are equally prized, what a seed of pious and heroic men we have to boast of. But when the ordinances of society go in this respect against the ordinances of God, to what unseemly conditions it leads. Amongst the American Indians, you have women in bondage to the men; they bear the burdens, they work the work, they do everything but hunt and carry on war; and being thus abstracted from their natural office of soothing and softening the man, it hath come to pass that the men are of an indomitable pride, —strength of will, cunning, and revenge being their chief characteristics. They have rejected the alliance of woman's heart, and see to what they have been brought! In ancient Egypt, again, the opposite experiment was made. The woman had, by the marriage contract, the supremacy; and see what effects it produced upon the people! They became quiet, peaceable, lovers of justice and order—and so far it was well; but they became soft and effeminate, and submissive to tyranny and misrule; their understanding became debased, and their very senses fell from their proper use, when they arrived at and became subservient to soft affection—the most miserable pass of meanness. They worshipped every timid creature, and paid them divine honours; even cruel creatures they worshipped, for possessing that boldness which they wanted—loving the one, fearing the other. And all the idolatry which elsewhere had been rendered to the ideas of things, or to forms which represented these ideas, or to noble and useful men, was by them rendered to living creatures, whose brutal proneness of nature they beheld by outward sense. Much more might be said upon this subject, with regard to which, instances crowd upon our remembrance; but we pass on to the drift of our discourse, and observe, that the affections being wounded in Herodias, set the whole course of her nature in arms; Herod bore the wound, being controlled by higher faculties, which we are now to discover.

It was on his birth-day, always an auspicious day for pride and vanity, when religious men are wont to look back upon their past life, and confess its worthlessness unto the Lord, and recount the mercies of their God, and their own wondrous preservation,—when they humbly make prayers for their forgiveness, and meekly set about better purposes and resolutions;—on his birth-day, which pride regards as the noblest in the calendar, and vanity magnifies with ostentation and display;—on this day Herod, unlike troubled and patient Job, who prayed that it might not be joined to the days of the year, nor come into the number of the month, that it might be solitary, and no joyful voice be heard therein;—on his birth-day Herod assembled the pride of his kingdom, his lords, high captains, and chief estates of Galilee; and having feasted them well, the daughter of Herodias came in, and danced and pleased Herod and them that sat with him. It was an auspicious moment for pride. The monarch on his throne, with all his peers around him; the monarch holding the celebration of his birth-day; the monarch's heart delighted with the performance of his daughter, and all his peers sharing in his delight; the heat of wine, added to the inflammation of pride and power and vanity,—you will allow it was an auspicious moment for pride; and he who was the first to conceive pride, and to bring it forth, to the disturbance of heaven, and who hath ever since watched over his child, was at hand to join the tyrant in his proudest mood; and having no enemy on the earth whom he dreaded more than the Baptist, he now seized his opportunity to revenge on him all the lessons of penitence and humility which he had taught mankind. See ye not it was Satan again arrayed against God—as formerly he was in the person of Job, so now in the person of the Baptist? If he contended with the archangel Michael for the body of Moses, so now he contended for the life of the Baptist, who was born to humble pride in the penitence of sackcloth and ashes; and the enemy chose his fittest instrument, the proud king of Galilee, and took him in his most heroic mood, and plied him with wine and wassail, and fed him with the adulation of his nobles; and thus having intoxicated him, sent in his beautiful daughter to display her graces before them all. It would have been more becoming her, like Vashti, the high-minded queen of Ahasuerus, to have refused such a summons to exhibit her beauty and gracefulness before a company of revellers. But whether with invitation or without it, she presented herself, and thus to the assemblage of evil passions within the breast of Herod, added the intoxication of joy at that for which a father or a kinsman should have blushed. The king, swollen with vain delight, said that whatever she should ask he would grant her, to the half of his kingdom; and, like a headstrong fool driven to some foul catastrophe, he confirmed his large promise with an oath in the presence of all his court. Pride, vanity, and immodesty having done their office, revenge came next to complete the transaction. Herodias went to her mother, in whose thoughts the Baptist was always first, who, combining the coolness of a man with the fury of a woman, bade her ask the head of John the Baptist in a charger. The girl, whose youth should have shuddered at the thought of blood, was of too bloodthirsty a stock, and too well fleshed in blood, with which the scutcheon of her father was stained over, to hesitate a moment; and forth she sallied from the chamber of the woman, with the fate of the first of men upon her lips.

Ah, this is a cruel tragedy, and pity it is that woman's tender nature should have been the chief actor herein. But let no flattery or praise of poets put tender-hearted woman off her guard; and let no gallant speeches of men obscure in them the truth, that they are of the same mould, and liable to the same frailties, and in some directions to greater frailties, than men; even as in other directions man is liable to greater frailties than woman. Against all prejudices of the affections, let woman be on her guard—jealousy, disappointment, and revenge. Also, let her be on her guard in identifying herself with the ambition and crimes of her husband, which she ought to hold against. And oh! most especially, against cruelty of every kind let her be watchful; for woman was made to be a mother to the needy and a nurse to the weak, and a personification of God's providence here below. But while out of this instance of woman's wickedness I bring forth these admonitions for the sake of woman, let me justify the honour of womanhood by stating, that though the forerunner of Christ was so entreated of them, Christ himself had His chief care and consolation from women. He owned no parent but a woman; a woman watched over His youth; and women waited on Him in all His wanderings; and He wept for the sorrows of a woman; and a woman anointed Him for His burial; and when all forsook Him in the hour of His need, the women watched at His cross; and a heathen woman warned her husband to have nothing to do in the fate of so good a man; and women were the first to visit His tomb, and had the first revelation of His resurrection; and in every age they have been ready to lay down their lives for His sake.

Had the daughter of Herodias been of such a stock, she would have shuddered at her mother's request, and rather than have sought such a suit she would have consented to be herself the victim to pacify her mother's thirst of blood. But she hastened to fulfil it. She came in straightway with haste unto the king, and said, "I will that thou give me by and by," or forthwith, out of hand, "in a charger the head of John the Baptist." Now began the struggle in Herod's breast. He was exceeding sorry; yet, for his oath's sake, and their sakes that sat with him, he would not reject her. It was not, as hath been said, out of affection to his wife, nor yet to her daughter, but for his oath's sake, and those that sat at meat with him, that he consented to the heinous act; by which he proves himself, as we observed in our former discourse, to have been a man who joined stern pride to all his policy and wickedness. But mark, his passions gave way, his policy also gave way, but his pride would not give way. That which is called "the last infirmity of noble minds" should have been called the strongest and most irreducible bulwark of the mind. A wanton man, a wily man, a vain man, a worldly man, you will far sooner master than a proud man, who despises those things upon which the others build themselves, regarding the approbation of his own breast, and deriding the vain man who striveth for human approbation. If he be a slave of the senses, he despiseth himself for being so; if he laugh with the merry throng, he scorns his own smile; and you will see scorn looking through the light of his smile as the storm lowereth over the blink of sunshine, and hasteneth to swallow it up. The proud man is the true Stoic. Pride is the highest form of unregenerate nature, being strong within itself, even as Satan, the father of pride, was the highest and strongest angel that fell from heaven. No wonder, therefore, that the pride of his oath, and of his consistency, should withstand in Herod what his passion and policy had not been able to resist. It withstood his fear of the Baptist's influence with the people, his reverence of his holiness and integrity, and he sent the executioner to behead him in the prison, and so his precious life was sacrificed on the altar of pride. The preacher of humility and the messenger of Christ yielded his life to the minister of Satan, and once more the blood of the righteous cried from the earth to heaven for vengeance.

Oh, it was a horrid crime for that magistrate, into whose hands God had committed the sword of justice, to be a terror to evil-doers and a praise unto them that do well, to proceed against the life of an innocent man without charge or accusation, and to murder him out of hand, as if he were a vicious and venomous creature! A fine conclusion to a royal banquet this, to immolate the prophet of the Lord—a grand consummation to the joy of a royal birth-day to extinguish the light and glory of the nation! And these were fine lords, captains, and chief estates of Galilee, who sat patiently by, and sanctioned the massacre of the most honoured of the lieges! Ah, brethren, learn the blessings of our times, when neither king, nor lords, nor captains, nor chief estates, nor all conjoined, durst put to death, without fullest and fairest trial, the greatest felon in the land. Value them above price. Let them not be wrested from you by any power on earth; and transmit them to shield the heads of your children, as they now shield our own, permitting us to sit every one under his own vine and his own fig-tree, without any to make us afraid. These blessings are due unto the grace of our God, who thought our fathers worthy of His special mercy, but for which we might have been in a condition as prostrate as they are in other lands. Therefore to God let the praise of them be rendered, for to Him alone is it due. And let us not forget that religion is the mother of law—our Protestant religion, the religion of the Scriptures, open to every man; which if you once fall from, then superstitious dependence upon your priests, misrule of every kind, such as now afflict our sister island, will be the fatal issue.

When ye behold this example of arbitrary power, and of submissive statesmen, oh render thanks unto the Lord that power in these lands hath been bridled by law, and that wholesome law is sustained by free religion; and when you read unto your children how this first of Christian martyrs fell within the dungeon of a prison, under no eye but that of Heaven, tell them of their invaluable privileges, and turn their thoughts to God who bestowed them, and likewise tell them to be ready to go equal lengths for sacred truth. So shall this martyrdom of the Baptist beget within many breasts a heroic love of truth, a hatred of arbitrary government, gratitude to God, and devotedness to the Lord Jesus Christ;—by which means the Baptist's death, as hath been said, will be a thousand times more profitable than his life, and the ends of God's providence will be served.

Pride, brethren, is that which defendeth the prerogatives of self, and beware lest in any of your breasts it cast out the doctrine which the Baptist came to teach. He had but one life to lose, but the doctrine which he taught is many times murdered, and in most cases it is murdered by pride. The Baptist may be regarded as an allegorical personage, representing the rough and unwelcome nature of repentance, which must ever go before the grace of the gospel. Now that penitence which he represents is often besought of you, and you will find your pride steadfastly resist it, for pride is the antagonist of humility, and rises in arms at the very mention of its name. Therefore beware lest ye silence the voice of repentance, as Herod did the voice of the Baptist—that you put it to a distance, and mure it up in procrastination. Beware, lest in your high and joyous moods ye murder humility, and for ever after be haunted of remorse as Herod was. And though Herod saw the face of Christ, he found no room for forgiveness. So you may often hear the voice of the gospel, but find no room for repentance. Therefore, I pray you be upon your guard that you act not in the breast this tragedy which Herod acted in the face of day.

LECTURE XV.

LUKE III.; MATT. XIV.; MARK VI.

THE Almighty is not prodigal of the blood of His saints, whose death is precious in His sight, and whose souls He redeemeth from deceit and violence. And as He sacrificed His own dear Son for no smaller object than the redemption of the soul, which nothing in the world nor all the world could purchase; so the blood of His Son's members, which are His saints, He never permitted to be shed save for some good not otherwise to be purchased. And yet, though He hath over them a tender watchfulness, they must not shrink from desperate trials, nor desire to be without them; for being formed unto Christ by a living faith, they are no longer their own, but bought with a price; and being of Christ's purchased inheritance, they are no more at their own disposal, but set apart from a profane to a holy use—from the dominion of a depraved will and an evil spirit to the dominion of the divine will and the Holy Spirit; by which adoption into the household of faith and among the children of God they are brought into new conditions, consulting no longer for convenience, or pleasure, or honour, or wealth, but following after righteousness, godliness, faith, love, patience, meekness—fighting the good fight, laying hold on eternal life;—in which new pursuits they are to look for suffering, whereby the Captain of their salvation was perfected, and whereunto St Peter says we are all appointed, and for the fellowship of which St Paul mightily prays; with patience they are to take the loss of all things, to reckon it joy when they fall into divers temptations, and when they are counted worthy to suffer for their Redeemer's sake.

Therefore when we behold, as in this instance of the Baptist, that the Lord sendeth His servants on perilous errands, and by the impulse of truth forceth them into conditions out of which there is no escape, save by the bloody path of martyrdom which Christ also trod, we should not be satisfied with paying the deserved tribute of lamentation upon the martyr's tomb, or holding up to execration the bloody men who persecuted him to the death, but advance into the inward counsel of the transaction, and endeavour to discover what good purposes upon earth the Almighty intended thereby to accomplish. This is the office which still remains to be performed over the memory of this sainted man; and we enter upon it with humble prayer to Almighty God that He would open our minds to understand the high purpose of His providence, and that He would cause our discourse to strengthen the faith of many.

The post to which the Baptist was called was one of peril, being the farthest advanced post of the Christian army, for he was the forerunner of Him whom we are all called to follow; and the commission with which he was intrusted was full of danger and of fear, being no less than a summons of unconditional surrender to all the sons of men, whom he accused of rebellion, and commanded to lay down the arms of their warfare, and to bow the lofty heads of their pride, and prepare themselves for One coming in the name of the Lord mighty to save. Four centuries had elapsed since a prophet had appeared with tidings from on high, during which interval the nation had been crushed and bruised with oppression, and wearied out with exterminating wars; and now for more than half a century the bloodiest family of that bloody age had held tyrannical sway over it, created in the bowels of society various factions, corrupted the patriotism and the sacred feeling of the people, and made the face of society a waste and howling wilderness. And if in the best times the prophets of the Lord had a rough reception, and generally met with an untimely end, it was not otherwise to be expected of the Baptist coming upon an errand far more perilous than Jonah's, and to a royal race more bloodthirsty than was that of Ahab and Jezebel.

Light cometh into the world, but the darkness of the world comprehendeth it not. And this is their condemnation, that they love darkness rather than light, their deeds being evil.

The prophets of the Lord come unto their own, but their own acknowledge them not. Their brethren rise up against them, their familiar friends and those of their own household prove their foes. Oh, how many, since the days that righteous Abel fell a sacrifice to his brother's wickedness, have poured out their souls unto death, for the sake of a stiff-necked and rebellious generation! St Paul, himself a noble martyr, had made a catalogue of the triumphs of faith in the death and suffering of the saints before the time of Christ; and a much larger and blacker catalogue might be made of those who, since that time, have given testimony to His name before the bloody persecutors of the churches. And the Baptist's case is only one among ten thousand, and the dispensation of God to the Baptist is the dispensation with which He hath visited myriads of His people. But let not the righteous be dismayed.

This is one of the ordinances of the Most High, that the souls of men should be perfected through suffering, and come to great honour through manifold tribulation. He bereaveth them of their earthly treasures, that they may lay up all their treasure in heaven; He cutteth off their earthly days, that they may put their trust in the rod and staff of His strength; and all refuge faileth them, that they may betake themselves to the covert of His wings. Their manifold distresses are so many craving appetites, which nothing but faith can satisfy; and according to the number and greatness of them, so is their faith. The resignation of present emolument and advantage for the sake of principle, the resignation of reputation and worldly favour, and the putting up with contumely and scorn, for the sake of the profession of Christ, is the only evidence of our faith. Indeed, I have no idea of faith without sacrifice on account of it. If faith be a divine trust in God, what strength hath it, if for its sake we make no earthly surrender? There can be no faith without some surrender of will, of affection, of interest, of pleasure, of reputation; and the more of will, affection, interest, pleasure, and reputation we surrender, the more is our faith strengthened. And the more our trust or faith in God is confirmed, the more is every divine affection, hope, and enjoyment enlarged. For faith is the root of all spiritual life, and the channel through which spiritual influences are diffused over the several paths of our inward and outward existence.

Therefore, when many things adverse to pleasure and interest, and abhorrent to flesh and blood, befall any of the servants of God, they should regard themselves as more highly favoured than others, and as destined to more high advancement in the divine life upon earth, and in the glorious life of just men made perfect. There are so many blows dealt by the providence of God against the worldly and fleshly nature, that the spiritual nature may breathe and flourish through the chinks and ruins thereof, and finally crumble it into dust. For the divine life, in its birth, is like the kingdom of heaven, to be compared to a grain of mustard seed which shoots through a rocky soil, and the bereaving trials of life are like the fire of heaven which splits and shivers the rock, and allows the roots and stem of the slender plant to work their way, until they acquire such vegetative power, as by their own strength to cut and crumble the impenetrable stone which hinders its enlargement. And what is death to this plant but the envious axe of the woodman, which comes with cruel intent to hew the hardy plant to the earth? But while he doth so, it sheds a seed upon fertile and nutritious ground, by the living nature whereof its roots shall always be fed, and its leaf shall never fail.

John the Baptist, therefore, and all the sore-tried martyrs of the Lord, who to our eyes are suffering life's sorest mishaps and sternest adventures, are, before God and their own conscience, training up to a high seat in the heavenly places in Christ. . They are mortified in the body, but quickened in the spirit. They are evil entreated of men, but of God their spirits are enlarged and comforted. And hence it comes to pass that when others grieve, they rejoice—when others curse their persecutors, they bless and curse not. When the noble indignation of bystanders, with convulsive grasp of hand, and tread of foot, and holding in of breath, sends the blood back upon the heart as the axe descendeth, the godly sufferer relaxes every muscle, and lays him down as upon a pillowed couch to take his everlasting rest. For why? Because his soul is visited—he feels a present Lord—he feels a faith bursting into vision—a hope breaking into enjoyment—a suffering, painful life, departing like night before the dawn of an untroubled and joyful morn.

So much is it the nature of suffering to perfect holiness, that in the ages which followed those of martyrdom, when men were not called to it in the ordinary providence of God, they made an artificial set of sufferings, and went into a voluntary exile from all the comforts and conveniences of life. This, if I may so speak, is the weakest side of Christianity, or that upon which Christians are most apt to act—will-worship, a voluntary humility and neglection of the body, as the apostle calleth it. Our dispensation having been sown in suffering, and indeed founded on death, the death of the Lamb of God, and ever since the blood of the martyrs having proved the seed of the Church, and our most noble characters having come out of persecution's school, and the whole of our dispensation breathing of self-denial and hard endurance, of mortification and crucifixion of the old man, it is always ready to be corrupted into a system of asceticism or of voluntary self-denial and suffering. Such expressions as these occurring—"That he who hath suffered in the flesh hath ceased from sin;" "Count it all joy, brethren, when ye fall into divers temptations;" "I count all things but loss that I may know the fellowship of His sufferings;" "He who suffers with Him shall also reign with Him"—it comes to pass that Christians are always falling into error upon the head of self-inflicted mortification. Amongst the Catholics it is one of the sacraments, and everywhere there is a yoke of observance, less or more, upon the necks of the disciples, which they submit to under the idea that they thereby do God service. Now, the only preservative from this, which I call the weak side of Christianity, —not that it is weak on any side, but that human nature hath shewn itself most disposed to err and mistake it on that side;—against this voluntary humility the only preservative is spiritual knowledge and understanding, with the progress of which formality decays and spirituality grows apace. As the inward man becomes enlightened, he perceives that there is no need to make artificial suffering, and go into voluntary exile from enjoyment. As he is able to read his own thoughts, and estimate the many moods of his mind by the Word of God, he perceives that there is a discipline of the spirit which will bring with it enough of trial and endurance to occupy the resolution of his mind; and as he proceeds to set his spirit in order, he will soon find that his sayings, and his manners, and his actions, must work against the stream of the world, and meet with strife, struggle, and desperate encounters. And nature will always go with the world, and friendship also, and the habits perhaps of his own home, so that he will find a combination against the Lord and His anointed which will hold his graces and his instruments of spiritual warfare in constant use. But to persevere and feel this requires spiritual discernment. A man's conscience must be alive to have this kind of precaution. It cannot have place in a formalist, or in a priest-guided mind, or in a darkened understanding; and hence, just as ignorance and blindness of the mind prevail, will this superstitious prostration and voluntary humility come to life; and to its destruction nothing is necessary but to have a priesthood who address the conscience of the people, and summon up their thoughts, and give them not "ipse-dixits" of their own, or traditions and customs of the Church, by which to shape their obedience.

Nevertheless, though there be enough of trial inwardly and outwardly in all ages to keep the soul in active life, and holy discipline, and progressive sanctification, yet when the Almighty thereto adds sore trials of His providence—bereavements, losses, crosses, persecution, perils, and sword—we are to regard them as so many fostering and nutritious measures to hasten ourselves into premature perfection, and raise us to a preternatural purity; and those who endure such afflictions patiently are to account themselves highly favoured of the Lord, and to reckon that His grace and His providence are working together for their good.

Take this, therefore, as the first intention of Providence in bringing the Baptist to so hard and untimely an end. The Baptist had done the Almighty good service—he had not turned back on any occasion from his perilous duty—he had kept his Nazarite ritual both in body and in spirit, sustaining the one upon the simplest meat, and the other upon the hardest conditions. The Almighty heard the voice which he spoke always for His well-beloved Son; He saw that he spoke truth, and held his integrity steadfast unto the end. And perceiving in His servant such noble and excellent qualities, He resolved to perfect him for a high place in heaven, and so directed his footsteps to the fiery furnace of a court, that the temper of his truth and piety might be purified manifold. And in the fiery furnace He walked with His servant, so that his spirit was not harmed; and having thus annealed his nature to the utmost which this earth could do, He took him hastily away and placed him among the glorified in heaven.

But, besides the spiritual advantage, both in time and through eternity, which this dispensation served to himself, there are others served to the Church of Christ, concerning which we now come to treat so long as time shall permit us. It was intended by God that the gospel should go round the various classes of the community and knock at every door, because within every door there are souls which have to do with God, and to whom He hath a message to deliver. Hence the Saviour, upon sending forth the seventy, gave them no commission to any one class rather than to another; but generally, "Into whatsoever city ye enter, and into whatever house in that city, say, Peace be in this house." And in the New Testament there is an equal sympathy for the souls of all; and though it be said that few great men after this world, few noble men, and few wise men are called, that seems to me only the stronger reason for warning them of the aggravated darkness and danger which surround them. Now the Baptist being the forerunner of the gospel, who bore the tidings of its speedy arrival, needed to leave a summons with every class, and accordingly was brought by the providence of the Lord from the lowest even to the highest, throughout them all. The experiment was tried upon all, that the Christian Church might be premonished by his fortunes where lay the sands and whirlpools and sunken rocks of the voyage. He was set forth that we who were to come after might take knowledge of him, and be on our guard. He is truly an allegorical person, if ever there was one; and had his mission not been recorded in the holy gospel, we should have believed him an imagination of the brain, rather than a real person who had lived and moved, with human passions and affections. And truly he was a creature of the imagination—imagined by God for a specific end, and to that end trained by God's own discipline. Therefore his person was unattended and unadorned, his wants were slender, his dealing with all conditions alike. At all times faithful to others, never careful of himself; he was a voice, and besides his voice he was nothing. But that voice was truth—truth of the sternest, roughest kind, yet sterling truth. And the meaning of the whole mystery of the forerunner of Christ is to teach us what is the strength of truth, and how far, being unmingled with selfishness, it will prevail over the prejudices and errors in which we lie benighted. The Baptist is the ideal of the reformer and the missionary, the first planter and the restorer of religion; and the example of Brainerd, who, like the Baptist, fared after the scanty fashion of the Indians—of Schwartz, who domesticated himself, not with Europeans, but with the natives—of the Moravians in every quarter—and, in general, of all successful missionaries, proves that the Baptist's manner of propagating truth is the only successful one. The same also of the Reformers, who only half accomplished the work while they kept themselves within the constraint of plan, and wrought by means of authority, and succeeded best when they cast themselves among the people, and wrought from the foundation of society upwards to its high places. And in later times, the examples of Whitfield and Wesley are illustrative of the same great truth in the divine economy, that to make truth prosper we must cast ourselves entirely upon its sustenance, throw other considerations to the winds, and, like the Baptist, rest all our strength upon the weighty matters of our lips;—to the simplicity and sincerity of which, if the simplicity and sincerity of our own lives be conformed, and we yield to no fear of consequences, nor truckle to prejudice of time, or place, or power, but cast ourselves upon the everlasting strength of truth, then, surely, we shall prevail as the Baptist prevailed.

Now, while the Baptist's life and progress teach high confidence in the power of truth, his violent death teacheth for what truth should hold herself in readiness, and what she is likely in the end, from one quarter or another, to expect. The world judgeth so much of success by visible prosperity, that when a messenger of truth comes under a cloud of persecution all forsake him, and consult for themselves, and leave him alone, like Paul the prisoner of the Lord. And the messenger of truth, thus left to pine alone in cold desertion, might think that he had taken the improper course, and lose confidence in the cause. The Lord, to guard against this fatal dejection of the mind, and the alteration of measures consequent thereon, set forth this divine personage as an emblem to all succeeding messengers of what they were to look for in the propagation of His revealed will: not to despair though their mouth was muzzled, their persons mured up, and the whole progress of their ministry stopped—not to regard this as an evil omen, or a token of the Almighty's displeasure, but as the best evidence that they had been walking in the straight and forward path. Samson, the Nazarite of the old dispensation, did more detriment to his enemies by his death than he did in all his lifetime; and what influence John's death had among the people to sanctify and confirm what he said, we may have some idea from the circumstance that the Pharisees, who hated him, durst not, for fear of being stoned by the people, deny his heavenly commission.

In truth, without his death John would have been nothing. A stern man is a rude, uncivil man if he shrinks when he is put to proof. His boldness is accounted forwardness; his plainness, harshness; and all his reforming doctrines, upstart ambitious notions and levelling doctrines, if he stand not the searching proof of adversity and death. I do not say that death verifies what in his lifetime a man has declared, or that truth needs any such verification; but this I say, that if a man make free with the customs and concerns of his fellow-men, and set forth a searching and purifying discipline, and shrink from suffering when he is calling upon all to lay down their enjoyments, and murmurs at sacrifice when he is calling for sacrifice from all his brethren—then there may be shrewd suspicion that he is either a weak man himself, and not worthy to be followed, or that he is a deceiver, and worthy of all rejection.

So the Almighty instructs us, that he who calls upon his brethren for reformation, and preacheth among them the humbling doctrines of repentance, will himself be called upon, in the providence of God, for evidence of his disinterestedness; and in perilous times and places may be summoned to pass the ordeal of death, to which he should make up his mind, ere he set out upon the high and perilous emprise of propagating truth over the face of a truth-hating world.

Moreover, He manifesteth, by the instance of the Baptist, from what quarters the storm of trial is likely to arise against the messenger of truth,—from the corrupt priests of religion, and the hand of arbitrary power, from superstition and from tyranny; and from these quarters the Church hath experienced all her persecution. There never, that I remember, was a persecution of the ministers of truth from the common people, save under the leading of priestcraft or tyranny; in general the people have given them shelter. But if I were called upon to decide whether more martyrs had been made to civil or to ecclesiastical rage, I should be at a loss to determine; for against the ten persecutions of the Roman Emperors we have to set the persecutions of the Albigenses and the Waldenses, and the Hussites and the Lollards, and the Huguenots and the Covenanters, the Sicilian Vespers and Bartholomew's Eve, and the Inquisition's horrid murders, most numerous of all, and Alva's massacres in the Low Countries, and much more which it were tedious to enumerate. From these two quarters the Baptist's example teacheth us to expect the storm—from corrupt religionists and arbitrary governors; and therefore, if any man hath truth in his heart, the more he steers wide of these, the safer and the longer will he hold his course. But this same fruitful example teacheth that it behoveth him to obey the summons of these powers when they take offence at his truthfulness, and to appear with the voice of truth against them—to carry his lamp into their nest, and expose its pollution in the sight of all the people; not daringly to encounter them for the sake of his speeding well, nor to shrink from the encounter either, also for the sake of his speeding well, but to be always ready to stand to his post and speak the truth.

And should they lay hands on him, and separate him to a sad and gloomy cell, let him be of good cheer. From bonds Paul wrote the chief of those epistles, which he would not otherwise, it is probable, have had time to compose; so that by his bonds he hath edified and converted more than by his liberty. From prison in Patmos those Revelations which are the day-star of the Church's hopes were sent forth upon the world. Luther from his prison poured forth his arguments upon the Roman Catholic Church. Knox, while his arm was lashed to the oar upon the rivers of France, conceived the scheme of his country's deliverance. Your chief men made themselves exiles in foreign lands during the reign of the popish Mary, and kept up the heart of the people by their writings. Therefore the messenger of truth should be undismayed by cells and prison gloom, but use his opportunities well, and the Lord will bless him there no less than elsewhere.

I knew a man, some three years ago, who was put in prison by the hard dealings of a creditor; and being offered liberty of escape, refused to accept it, being willing, like old Socrates, rather to die in prison than to escape against the spirit of truth. And to a narrow cell in the prison he was conveyed by the hand of justice, and to, what was worse, the company of wicked, outcast men. Hither he was followed by a friend, dear to his heart, and was found occupying his hand, unaccustomed to labour, in cleaning away the filth and impurity of his narrow abode. That friend visited him every Sabbath evening, in order to dispense to him the ordinances of religion, of which he was now hindered; and there, at first, they themselves two spent, like Paul and Silas, the time in praise and prayer. One week passed, and brought another Sabbath-evening's exercise; but meanwhile his grave and decent demeanour had won a point of conviction upon one of his fellow-prisoners, who solicited to be present at the worship of God, and another, and another, until that whole quarter of the prison where he dwelt was solicitous to join. And oaths were no longer heard, and the appearance of decent, orderly men, and the happiness of intelligent, well-ordered society, was restored to those who were lately outcast and abandoned—all by the influence of this devout man, whom the adverse providence of God cast into bonds.

But if the worst should come to the worst, and the minister and messenger of truth be subjected like a culprit to the lash of punishment and the infliction of death, then this example of the Baptist teacheth him not to be cast down or dismayed, as if some extraordinary thing had happened, but to gird up the loins of his mind, and prepare for martyrdom. That honour of England, and first of English parish priests, Bernard Gilpin, commonly called the Reformer of the North, after preaching before the courtiers and councillors of Edward VI., sent such a withering blast of truth concerning the corruptions of the Church, as in these times would almost dispossess any priest, and unchurch him; afterwards he refused double livings and bishoprics under Elizabeth, and did, under the bloody Mary, prepare himself for martyrdom. He had the white robe prepared; and knowing the hot malice of his enemies, and perceiving their hastening plots, he regularly dressed himself in it for a space of every day, and sat alone preparing his soul for the utmost of human trials. And when the order of the Council came down, he told the messenger he was ready; he saddled his beast, like Abraham, for an act of faith like Abraham's—to offer up, not his son, but himself; and as the Angel of the Lord interfered for Abraham, so also He interfered for His aged servant, by sending him an accident on the way, during the time of his recovery from which the bloody Mary died. So ought every messenger of truth daily to gird himself for the severest encounters; for in proportion as he adhereth to truth will his trials and his sufferings be many,—yes, even in this day be many. Every kind of accusation it will expose him to; every kind of mistreatment, to every extent but the spoiling of his goods and the taking away of life, from which the good laws of Old England have now delivered us; but which extreme sacraments for truth every messenger of truth may still elsewhere be called upon to take.

Upon the whole, let this great first messenger of Christian truth prepare all succeeding Christian messengers or upholders of the same to be ready for every sort of suffering and loss; to make up their minds to it,—not to imprisonment of person, but to exile from the place which they deserve in the hearts of men,—not to martyrdom of body, but to martyrdom of reputation,—to scoffs, contempts, and all kinds of personal abuse. Let them prepare for misunderstanding, misrepresentation, and opprobrious abuse, in all possible ways, by private tongues, in public assemblies, in periodical writings, and everywhere. To this let them make their minds up; for it will come, just in proportion as they drop the frivolous, false, and hypocritical styles of the world, and address themselves to the methods and manners and expressions of openhearted and open-handed truth.

But what of that? Thereby your faith is profited; thereby the world is crucified to you, and you crucified to the world; thereby the desires of the earth are put under, and the desires of heaven brought to light; thereby Satan's chains are struck off, and Christ's deliverance achieved; thereby you die daily to that which is seen and temporal, and arise daily to things spiritual and eternal.

And think you not, brethren, in proportion as you make sacrifices for your God and His Christ, that you will not love Them more, and They love you more, for the dangers you have run, and the sufferings you have undergone? Think you not that faith so shaken will not root itself the more deeply, until it so enwrap you with the foundation of faith which cannot be shaken, that it shall become your only hold, your rock, your tower, your horn, your buckler, and your strong tower? You shall be more and more rooted and grounded in the faith, and you shall grow up to the glory of God.

And for you the habitations of the righteous shine afar; even for you who are followers of them that by faith and patience inherit the promises. Therefore be of good cheer, and prepare your soul for every encounter. You know the cloud of noble witnesses with whom you are surrounded. They are written in the oracles of God; they are written in the chronicles of both these lands. These men were the founders of everything we hold dear. They wrought out by their blood the liberty of conscience which we enjoy, the toleration of spiritual men which we can demand. If you would go still further into the bowels of the body of darkness and iniquity which still oppresseth the land, and work out, not the toleration of the goods and the lives of spiritual men; if you would deliver them clear from all opprobrious gibes, from all exhibitions, and shame the poor deluded, deceived world, overawe it into shame and confusion of face,—then you have only to exhibit yourselves in the pure light of truth, and stand a little buffeting of wit and ridicule, and other harmless blows,—perhaps some harmful ones, as loss of reputation, sacrifice of place and favour and promotion. Prepare yourself to brave it. Lend yourself to it, like the old martyr. And it will come to pass yet that the name of saint, which now savoureth ill in the land, will, in the days of your children and your children's children, be the most honoured name; and that the good cause will grow and flourish to the ends of the world and the utmost ages of time.

THE TEMPTATION.

LECTURE I.

LUKE IV.

WE are now delivered from all the preliminaries of our Saviour's ministry,—His miraculous conception, the glorious auguries of His birth, His honourable welcome to the temple by prophet and prophetess while yet a babe, His appearance there in the strength of youthful wisdom to take possession of it as His Father's house, His opening manhood spent in the favour of God and man, and in full obedience to His earthly parents; until at length, when the fulness of time is come, He is presented by the Baptist to the assembled people, sealed with the testimony and proclaimed by the voice of Heaven, and anointed by the Holy Ghost to prepare Him for the duties of that high office to which, by this glorious succession of signs and wonders, He hath been set apart. All these things our evangelist hath set forth in order, redeeming the promise which he made to his friend in the dedication of his treatise; and having paused a moment to give the authentic document of His descent from the first man, through all the fathers out of whose loins it was promised that He should spring, he now enters upon the succinct and orderly narrative of the ministry itself, for which all those signs and wonders, and the Baptist's preaching, prepared the way;—a narrative which well demands the deepest cogitation, containing, within the compass of a small tract, all, or almost all, the recorded transactions of a life whose perfect story, St John says, would have filled the world with books, and all, or almost all, the recorded sayings of a wisdom which hath wrought more amelioration upon the world than all the books which it contains. What a depth of meaning must be in every sentence of a tract which hath subdued the outward aspect of society, and the inward character of myriads of men; what a breadth of exposition they must bear; and over how large a surface (if I may so speak) of human feeling and action will each one of them extend! What a power and gracefulness in a life which hath approved itself in the sight of almost all men, and against which, with a few singular exceptions, hardly any, even of His enemies, have lifted up their voice! The whole narrative of the redemption of the world is now to come under our review,*—the foundation of the Christian Church, the nature of its government, the power of its ministers, the privileges of its members, and, in short, everything which, as men and as Christians, can interest us most deeply; —to expound all which we have undertaken in the strength of the Lord, to shew forth the light which it may please His Spirit to impart to our own soul, and to utter the deep things of God for the edification of the members of Christ. We have likewise to defend the faith from the attacks of its avowed enemies, and to find for it entrance into the hearts of those who have not yet professed themselves its friends. For all which undertaking we are utterly unable in ourselves, and go forward in the strength of the Lord, through the ministry of your prayers, which we beseech for ourselves, that we may be found faithful to the gospel of Christ, and be strengthened to speak the whole counsel of God.

That Christ, from the moment He was baptized with water and anointed with the Holy Ghost sent down from heaven, was set apart from His former occupation as a tradesman in Nazareth, to the divine mission of redeeming a lost and abject world, from the obedience of His earthly parents to the obedience of His Father in heaven, and entered forthwith upon the work which was given Him to do, is manifested by the language in which the evangelist ushers in the mysterious scene of the trial or temptation in the wilderness. In the subject of lecture it is said, "And Jesus being full of the Holy Ghost returned from Jordan, and was led by the Spirit into the wilderness." St Matthew says, " He was led up of the Spirit into the wilderness to be tempted of the devil." St Mark, " Immediately the Spirit

---

* These lectures, delivered in 1823, formed part of an intended series on the Gospel of St Luke; the plan of which was, however, only partially carried out.

THE TEMPTATION.

driveth Him into the wilderness," and He was then in the wilderness forty days tempted of Satan. According to each of these three, He is taken, as it were, out of His own hands, under the guidance of that supernatural power which came upon Him in the form of a dove, in order that it might be manifest to the people. The mysterious addition that was then made to His being, possessed Him with powers which He had not hitherto proved, which filled Him, which moved Him, which drave Him away from the haunts of men into desolate regions wherein to abide, unsustained by earthly succour, a dread combat with the prince of darkness, and the adversary of God and man. That I am not rash or self-guided in saying that Christ received, by the sign of the dove, and the voice from heaven, His commission and power to go forth, is manifest from various parts in the Acts of the Apostles, which always date the beginning of His ministry from this time, and the power to carry it on, as thus derived, " How God anointed Jesus of Nazareth with the Holy Ghost and with power, who went about doing good, and healing all that were oppressed of the devil." With regard to the conditions of His Being before this era of His life, I speculate, and have speculated no further than the record bears, that He was an obedient son, advancing in the favour of God and man, and possessed with the spirit of wisdom. Much was fabled by the prurient fancies of the early ages concerning His infancy and youth, which was rejected by the Church almost as soon as produced. His youth up to the date of His consecration, from all authentic documents which we have seen, passed without anything worthy of record, and not till then commenced aught miraculous in His works, aught authoritative and dictatorial in His sayings, aught intended for a pattern to the world in His life. But from this time forth He becomes the Messenger of the everlasting covenant, the Messiah promised unto the fathers. Now His prophetic and priestly offices have commenced. The Spirit is descended upon Him from above, He is filled with the Holy Spirit, and He must testify to the truth of Him that sent Him. From the something additional that is now bestowed upon Him, it is vain to argue that heretofore He must have been inferior to what He now is, and inferior to His Father by whom those things were bestowed. Surely He was inferior before His baptism to what He now is after His baptism, and inferior to His Father from whom those things were bestowed; but that has no relation to His everlasting equality with His Father. For in order to prepare for the mediatorial office which He had undertaken, He needed to divest Himself of His celestial state, to lay down His supercelestial glory, to make Himself of no reputation, to take upon Himself the form of a servant, and to be found in fashion as a man; and that power which He resigned, He, not in appearance but in truth, resigned. So that He was a child, and grew in the grace and faculties of His nature like another child into mature manhood, struggling with the temptations, and spoiling the tempters of each stage of life, until He stood at thirty years before His Father, ready to undertake for the salvation of men whatever His Father might be pleased to require. And His Father bestowed upon Him for that same undertaking whatever powers were necessary for its manifestation; He added to the manhood in which He stood arrayed whatever powers of the Spirit were necessary for the work. And having received His Father's pleasure to perform, and His Father's supply of strength to perform it withal, the obedient Son addressed Him to the undertaking which from all eternity He had yielded Himself to work out. So that it is the weakest of all things for the opposers of His divinity to build their arguments hereupon. I, for one, who hold His divinity, will grant His inferiority while He was travailing in the greatness of His strength through the wine-press of sorrow. But who made Him inferior? He himself humbled Himself and became obedient. Why became He inferior? That as a man, and the son of man, He might grow perfect through sufferings, and by death destroy him that had the power of death, which is the devil. And when will He cease to be inferior? When He hath finished the work which was given Him to do, and hath given up the kingdom into the hands of His Father. Then will He resume the place which He had from the beginning of years, and which, till the end of days, He shall maintain, as the everlasting Word of God; unless in the lapse of ages and the compass of the universe of God, He should, for some other fallen world, bow Himself again to the work of salvation, and once more abdicate the right hand of power to make another demonstration of love and obedience, in order to bring another glorious family of sons unto God. There were various stages in the Redeemer's work, and different aspects which in these various stages He assumed. In the Old Testament dispensation, He was the Angel of the Covenant that spake the word of God unto our first parents, unto Abraham, and Isaac, and Jacob, and Moses; He was the Spirit of praise and prophecy in the psalmist, the Spirit of wisdom in Solomon, and the Spirit of revelation in all the prophets; then, in the fulness of time, He became flesh, and grew by the natural growth of the body and mind of man; now He stands equipped in manhood's prime, and the Lord bestows upon Him the Spirit of power and wisdom and love; then He lays down His body in death, that by death He might triumph over death; then He resumes His body from the jaws of the grave, and ascendeth up on high. His incarnation being complete, He then enters upon another state, the state of His exaltation, and takes the character of Intercessor and King, and for this new condition of His mediatorial office He receives new powers from His Father. Hence He says to the eleven, "All power is given unto me in heaven and in earth." With these powers He now maketh way over the earth, subduing all things unto Himself, and also in the heavens He prepareth mansions for the souls of glorified saints, and receiveth them to their everlasting rest. And last shall come the fulness of all, when He shall deliver up the kingdom to His Father, after the great work of redemption is complete. In passing through these various stages and conditions of His mediatorial office, various degrees of power and dignity were necessary, which could come from no one but His Father, unto whom He had surrendered all; and the account of their bestowal, instead of being construed into a sign of His inferiority, ought to be accounted of as a sign of the humility to which He had reduced Himself, of the perfect obedience which He learned, even as of a son unto a father, and of the perfect satisfaction of the Father with the successive portions of the mighty work which He achieved.

These things are necessary to be noticed, that the enemies of His divinity may have no occasion to triumph in these the signs and expressions of that humiliation unto which He had reduced Himself, and from which He returned to glory through successive stages of elevation, at each of which new conditions of existence were necessary, and new powers for fulfilling the same. We are therefore to conceive Him now as arrayed in His heavenly armour, and furnished forth for the mighty work.

Now He hath planted Himself in the breach, and hell and earth have leave to pour out their fires against Him. And His heavenly Father withdraws to behold the achievement of His self-devoted Son, and all the host of heaven look on. And again there hangs upon one man, as aforetime hung upon one man, the whole hope of the earth. The second Adam hath taken His human form, and standeth for the sake of all His children, their federal Head, in whom they rise again, or are for ever fallen. The world hath now a second chance for its well-being. Upon this one man, Jesus of Nazareth, its fate again depends. And now all is to be lost or won for ever. Ages on ages of sorrow had rolled over its dejected condition. Darkness and gross darkness had settled down upon the habitations of men, and the throne of God was compassed about with clouds and thick darkness. The world lay wasted; the princes of the world had it all in hand; the devils from the pit were its masters, who ruled it with a rod of iron. Chains of tyranny had just been forged by the ambitious Cæsar for the free people who had conquered the world; and all things boded a long reign of that misery and wretchedness which the instability of the first Adam had brought to pass. The caldron of its misery was seething on, and sin, which is the fuel of it, was raging still, and the judgments of the Lord from on high were descending upon the sorrowful nations. And all things wore the signs of perplexity and distress, when a new leader stood forth in the person of this despised Nazarene, who was to turn the tide of misery at its height, and roll back its waves of affliction from the sorrowful earth. A Captain of salvation hath appeared on our behalf; He is proclaimed from heaven; He is prepared with powers to stand for the fallen world; and the sinful masters of the fallen world are to stand another contest for their long-possessed empire.

And it is not long before these two rival powers, the Prince of light and the prince of darkness, the Friend and the enemy of men, do meet together, in strong contention for the mastery of the world. Forthwith Jesus is hurried to the wilderness to be tempted of the devil; and for forty days in the solitary wilderness He withstood unaided all the powers of darkness. The first Adam stood the trial in the garden of Eden, with all the tokens and provisions of his Maker's goodness; the second Adam had to stand the trial in the naked wilderness, with no companion but the wild beasts which prowled around. The first Adam had all things that were convenient for his well-being; the second had nothing wherewith to comfort or sustain His existence—but, far from those for whom He was enduring the spiritual contention, and with no spiritual host to assist Him, He had turned loose upon Him the prince of the host of hell. It lasted forty days, which are a blank in the history of Christ's ministry, concerning which nothing is revealed, and nothing can be discovered. For, you will observe, it was not till the end of these forty days that the three human trials commenced—the trial of appetite, the trial of ambition, and the trial of spiritual pride. The recorded instances must therefore be considered apart from the forty days' temptation. This sore and long-continued assault of Satan, which was sustained in the wild wilderness, not upon the exceeding high mountain, or upon the pinnacle of the temple, is that which we have first to consider. The supernatural part is now before us, in which the temptations arising from the world had no influence. The natural part, derived from the world, under the three forms of appetite, power, and spiritual pride, we have afterwards to consider—in this lay the stress and struggle of the contest.

The intercourse of spirit with spirit, with which we have at present to do, is that of which we have and can have little understanding, save through the means of things visible and sensual. But that such an intercourse of spirit with spirit exists, altogether apart from, and independent of, a bodily medium, we cannot for a moment doubt. The evidence of it hath been manifested upon Christ in the last passage, by the descent of the dove. The dove was no medium of communication; it was but the visible sign of it to the people, and somewhat of its emblem, yet at that moment doubtless His soul drank in powers vastly superior to those which He possessed before. The apostles at Pentecost are an evidence of the same, when there was a visible sign and emblem, but no material cause. Christ's presence, which rebuked and dismayed the demons that possessed the bodies of men, is another evidence of the same immediate power of spirit over spirit. And the Holy Spirit, who worketh in the souls of believers, is a standing monument to all ages of the same mighty operation. No man knoweth how, no man knoweth why, but certain it is the truth—that which once told death unto his soul now telleth life, that which once slew now maketh alive. Such is the power of spirit over spirit, that the Holy Spirit maketh the whole visible universe, which once spoke only falsehood and ungodliness to the spirit of man, to speak truth and godliness, to reveal Him whom it formerly beclouded, and to argue for Him whom it formerly argued against. It hath pleased God to marry the soul of man to a sensitive body, and through the senses of that body to address the feelings of the soul; therefore He worketh the wheels of the universe so as to turn up unto every one lots and fortunes which may strike into his soul, and His own nature He hath pictured forth in symbols, and then in written words, for the sake of human understanding. But this intervention of matter, with its causes and effects, He hath not made to be vital. The atheist makes it a god instead of Himself: but He can set it to a side; He can strike through it whenever it seemeth good unto Him so to do.

In like manner, there can be no doubt that the arch-enemy of God and man hath powers appertaining to him by right of the fall, which he useth within his limited province against the sons of men, in which God permitteth him, as appeareth from the history of patient Job.. He goeth about like a roaring lion, seeking whom he may devour. He is the father of lies. He is the father of murders. Pride is the livery of his servants, and vanity is the snare with which he catcheth them. He is the prince of this world, whose judgment took place at the crucifixion of Christ; whose chief strength, death and the grave, were then conquered; and whose bereavement is now proceeding apace, until he shall be cast into the bottomless pit, and Christ shall reign with all His saints. He is the prince of the power of the air, the spirit which now worketh in the children of disobedience. He is the most knowing, the most proud, the most artful, the most powerful, of earthly potentates. He hath got the customs and course of the world on his side. He hath buried under heaps of adversity the spirits of men, from whose thraldom naught availeth to deliver them but the Spirit of the living God. Now this master spirit, this omnipotence of evil,—for over all the dominions of evil he is omnipotent,—and not absolutely omnipotent, only because truth is greater than evil, and the high and holy King of truth greater than the prince of evil,—this master spirit, perceiving the second Adam, who had been pledged against him from the beginning, and whom he had sought by Herod, his royal servant, to cut off in His earliest youth, perceiving Him now entered on the arena of conflict, prepareth to give Him battle, spirit with spirit; and that there might be no inroad or interruption, they meet upon the waste wilderness, far remote from the haunts of men. And for forty days it is contested between them.

There were no seven flourishing sons, nor three beautiful daughters, as in the case of righteous Job, upon whom to put forth his murderous hand; there were no flocks, nor herds, nor flourishing household of domestic servants, in the havoc of whom to make hellish sport; nor great substance, upon the four corners of which to lay his withering hand. He condescended not to try the body of Christ, and to smite Him with sore boils, and humble Him among the ashes, and make Him abhor Himself, and scrape Him with a potsherd, until His friends, when they beheld Him, should sit in mute amazement for seven days and seven nights. But it was something of a more terrible kind than this which he dealt upon the Prince of peace. He who had conquered all the common soldiers and subalterns of the Lord's host, and been flushed with a thousand triumphs, was not, when he came to cope with the Captain of the salvation of men, to be content with such humble efforts. And doubtless the Lord Almighty, who had given up His Son to utmost trial, was not like to interfere, but allow the enemy to put forth his utmost power. Now or never he was to be humbled. Now or never his conquests were to be turned back, and the acceptable year of the Lord to be proclaimed.

The great and venerable master of English song hath, in the sixth book of his "Paradise Lost," endeavoured to depict the war of spirits, in dubious battle on the fields of heaven; but, according to universal criticism, he hath failed to impress the mind with the terrible or the awful, but rather with the incoherent or the ridiculous, although to that part of his work he seems to have brought the whole muster of his unrivalled powers. So also hath the venerable father of Greek poetry, when he mingled his gods and demigods with physical strife, failed to render them noble, but demeaned them from their proper place. Our evangelist attempted no such undertaking, and we are not about to depart from the wise silence which he observes. But I imagine that when spirit rusheth upon spirit in strong contention, or spirit worketh against spirit in wily contention, they must be most awful shocks which are sustained; for body hampereth spirit, and time wearieth it with its slowness. A sword is not sufficient for its vengeance, nor single men harvest enough for its strokes: the spirit of revenge would sweep up whole kindreds by the roots; it would root out the name and remembrance of men; it would subvert whole cities, plough up the foundations thereof, and sow them with salt, that they might be no more heard of for ever. Oh, when I think of the true, leal, and hearty servants of the devil,—your Herods, who sacrificed the innocency of sucking children; your Neros, who for sport would set in flames the whole quarter of a metropolitan city; your Attilas, who brushed whole nations with the besom of destruction;—when I remember the rage of envious hosts, how they massacre man, woman, and child, and strike their shafts, and balls, and weapons of war into the smoking, half-consumed timbers of houses without inhabitants; and remember that Satan is the father of all, and hath within himself all the cruelty, ferocity, and horrid perfidy which have manifested themselves in this world, and will for ever be manifested in hell, and that at this moment he brought the whole of his forces to the attack against the man Christ Jesus, this seed of the woman, for whose arrival he had been preparing his artillery for four thousand years,—that not for one instant, in which he made Job a wreck, nor by one insinuating speech, by which he overthrew Eve, and brought wreck and ruin upon a world, but for forty days he came up to the attack, and for forty days was met and foiled;—when I remember all these the circumstances of this trial, it stands before my imagination as the most terrible thing to which the earth or the heavens above have ever been witness.

I venture not to depict it, because no mind can conceive of purely spiritual strife; but I view it as the crisis upon which the history of the world turned—the stern strife which decided who should be victor over the world, God or the devil; not the completion of the warfare—for it is not yet nearly complete—but the turning of the tide of battle, the stemming of the victor in his pride, the heat of the conflict by which the work of victory was set on foot, the assurance of prophetic hope realised, and humanity once more bestirred to cope with its oppressor, and taught how he might be foiled. Hence, by our poet already referred to, this temptation has been considered under the title of "Paradise Regained." In which title he beautifully expresseth at once the character of Christ as the second Adam; the end of the strife for what was lost by the fall; the opposite party in the strife, he by whose arts paradise was made shipwreck of; and the success of the exploit, the foiling of the tempter, and the teaching him how in human shape he had still one superior. But in that most instructive and finished poem, the great author hath not regarded the trial of the forty days as distinct from these three several forms of trial which followed after.

If any one regard these views of Christ's previous strife with the master of spirits in his own spiritual domain as fanciful, he doth betray his ignorance of one main part of the history of Christ's ministry, and the effects of His redemption. Christ's ministry was not a warfare against the devilish passions of men alone, but against the devils themselves, who had power given them over the bodies of men. To cast out devils was one great end of His ministry; and by the testimony of devils His high character and commission as the Son of God was proclaimed abroad. They trembled before Him, they cried out at His presence, and prayed Him to begone; they craved His mercy, and besought mild terms from Him as a conquered race. And after His death He descended into hell to preach unto the spirits in prison. And it is said that the devils believe in Him and tremble. And throughout all Scripture, the devil is held forth as the great antagonist power to the Saviour. And in the Revelation of St John, the devil and his angels have a warfare with Christ and His angels, and are cast into the bottomless pit. So that there is a part of the Christian economy from beginning to ending which hath reference to the invisible world. Into these mysteries we pry not, but we will not allow them to be swept from our revelation by the cold hand of their philosophy which dreameth not of many things that are in heaven and earth. Now, if these spiritual agents had won a portion in the earth, and grown unruly thereupon, and broke their bound of hell, to roam far and wide over the wide world, and wield its infernal influences to and fro—if the fall, besides working downfall here below, had wrought, moreover, in the foul pit a courage, a boldness, a larger scope of daring against the creation of God, which, when they had overrun this world, might league them against some other, and so create elsewhere that distress which here they have created—if all this new animosity, new activity, new region of the demons grew out of the fall, as well as the discord which they have here occasioned, in us a loss of the Divine image, in them a deeper stamping of their satanic image—then, I say, was it not the part of the Redeemer, the great Restorer, the second Adam, not only to bring recovery to the earth, and restoration of the Divine image to man, but to cool that new cheer in hell, and to blast their pride of success and hopes of future triumph, to defeat them, to spoil them, to cover them with blank confusion, and restrain their rovings, to bound them within the limits of their infernal pit, and leave them to gnarl in their infernal fury, and to be doubly damned—first, by the loss of heaven, next, by the loss of this verdant earth, which they had fondly hoped was theirs for ever, by right of the subtle triumph of their chief over the mother of mankind? And how was this double damnation, this second restraint of these infernal spirits, to be compassed, but by meeting their chief and encountering all his array, and teaching him that at length the seed of the woman had arrived who should bruise his head? Such I conceive to be the mysterious uses of this great adventure in the history of human redemption. But besides its bearing upon the world's redemption from the thraldom of Satan, it was a fit beginning to our Redeemer's trying life, which, I pray you, to hear me open up a little. All His life long, Christ endured certain unseen, unknown encounters with the powers of darkness, and the visible part of His endurance is not worthy to be compared with that which no eye hath seen, nor ear heard, nor heart of man conceived. It is not the suffering which appears, the houseless and homeless wanderings, the despisings of His offered mercy, the waylaying of His life on every side, nor His death the bitter consummation of a bitter life, that made up the bitter cup which He had given Him to drink. How much of suffering there was beyond this palpable fact, no man is able to determine; but that the far greater part was beyond it, no man who readeth the history of Christ can doubt. Else to what purpose served those frequent retirements from the society of men, the nights He spent alone upon the mount of Olives, the scene of communion and consolation upon the mount of transfiguration, the audible encouragements from the mouth of Heaven, and the ministration of angels and the spirits of holy men, the three successive retirements in the garden of Gethsemane, with the agony and the bloody sweat, and the utterance of blank desertion upon the accursed tree? Why these reinforcements of mind? why these sequestered communions with angels and the spirits of holy men, and with the voice of God himself?

why this misgiving of His spirit when alone, this dreading of sorrow, if it were that He had no trials to bear, but such as were visible to human sympathy? One should think that He would have been fiercest put to it when the press of His enemies was most upon Him. Yet with what unruffled meekness He bears Himself in His hardest trials! He parries the intellectual thrust of His Pharisaical and priestly enemies, as if He had been dealing with witless children. And how He brooks the mistreatment of Pilate and His judges, yea, and the menials, too, of that disorderly court, as if that part of Him which they could torture and try, gave Him no care and cost Him no trouble! Men's mistreatments He seems to have received, and forgiven without an effort. These, then, did not compose the load which lay so heavy upon His breast, and which He taketh every occasion to unburthen, shewing as if it could not be expressed to men, nor by men be understood, and needed other counsellors and other comforters, which were to be found in these ministering spirits, of which whole legions were always at His command.

Put the case, brethren, that any man amongst ourselves who bore him meekly in the commonplaces of life, and when rudely handled by misfortune or mistreatment evinced only the greater self-possession and repose, until it seemed that nothing which man could inflict, or Providence dispense, had any power to chafe the serenity of his mind. Suppose this man retiring whole nights from his family, and passing them in gloomy solitude—suppose him to have been wretched, and found struggling with the severest agonies, and summoning to his aid other power than mortal—would you not pronounce at once that some secret grief was pressing him, which did not derive its origin from the persons or things around him, but from some haunting recollection, or some foreboding fear? So also reckon it with Jesus, that the enterprise of our salvation had in it scenes and distresses to which no human spirit was conscious, and of which they could no more have borne even the external accompaniments, than Peter and John could bear the bright light and pure vestures of the transfiguration; and if not the external accompaniments, how much less the intercourse and the contention of spirits, which at those awful seasons was carried on!

That same Spirit which hurried Christ into the wilderness, and strengthened Him to overcome these arts of the tempter, will work effectually in each one of His children, to enable them to overcome the smaller temptations with which their life may be assailed. Adam's posterity after the fall did not more surely yield to the various forms of sin, than Christ's spiritual posterity, from the day of this great victory, will triumph over the various forms of sin. Therefore it is said by St John that His children cannot commit sin—that is, the part of us which is born of God sinneth not. It is the old man which sinneth; the new man sinneth not. Therefore, brethren, if ye would overcome, be born of God, children of the second Adam, and the second death shall not have any power over you. Except ye be born again, ye cannot inherit the kingdom of heaven.

This transaction in the wilderness is, therefore, the birth of righteousness, as that in Eden was the birth of sin; and to this we should look with gladness, as we look to the other with sorrow. Here let our hearts be lightened, let us now rejoice in the victory of our great Redeemer. Let us be glad that He hath led captivity captive, and received gifts for men. He is our Captain, He is our King; He will save us—He who encountered the mighty, and turned not back from the battle of the strong, but triumphed alone against the great father of evil. In Him we will set up our banner, and exalt our horn on high. Rejoice, therefore, and be glad, O daughter of Zion, in your King; rejoice, and be glad, O ye seed of the righteous; for the arch-enemy of men will be spoiled, he hath been put to flight, and his host is scattered. His throne is overturned in the hearts of men, and the Prince of peace hath begun His reign. Therefore, be of good cheer, my brethren, and contend stoutly against your adversaries for the salvation of your souls. That Spirit which came down as a dove upon Jesus, and as cloven tongues upon the apostles, is spread abroad upon the earth, and bestowed upon every one who asketh. "What man is there of you, of whom if his son ask bread, will he give him a stone? Or if he ask a fish, will he give him a serpent?"

Therefore, ask for the Spirit, and it shall be given unto you. God sendeth you not in this warfare on your own charges, but is present with every soldier who calleth upon His name. Go forth, therefore, and contend with Satan in your various places, taking strength and courage from the scene of triumph that hath now been discoursed of. "Putting on the whole armour of God, that ye may be able to stand against the wiles of the devil. For we wrestle not against flesh and blood, but against principalities, against powers, against the rulers of the darkness of this world, against spiritual wickedness in high places. Wherefore take unto you the whole armour of God, that ye may be able to withstand in the evil day, and having done all, to stand. Stand therefore, having your loins girt about with truth, and having on the breastplate of righteousness; and your feet shod with the preparation of the gospel of peace; above all, taking the shield of faith, whereby ye shall be able to quench all the fiery darts of the wicked. And take the helmet of salvation, and the sword of the Spirit, which is the word of God: praying always with all prayer and supplication in the Spirit, and watching thereunto with all perseverance and supplication for all saints."

LECTURE II.

Luke iv.

THE fall of our first parents was not due to the natural working of their own spirits, like the fall of the reprobate angels. In the beginning, while yet the angels kept their first estate, there was no outward solicitation to evil in any part of the creation of God; and the cause of it must, therefore, have been bred within their own breasts—how, we know not; but this, I think, we know, that the leader of that revolt, inasmuch as he is called the father of lies and the prince of evil, had the wicked distinction, and hath the terrible responsibility of giving birth to sin, that most hateful and miserable of things. It did not seem good unto the Almighty to annihilate this new-sprung faction, and the horrid thing to which they had given birth, but to appoint unto both a habitation and a name in the existing universe;—its habitation, hell; its name, sin; and the name of those that hatched it, Satan and his angels. Why the Almighty should rather remove the turbulent to miserable quarters of their own than annihilate them at once and for ever, and remove the eye-sore and the heart-sore of hell from the happy universe—of this, I think, it is not impossible to perceive the reasonableness and the wisdom. For if Satan, that angel of light, and son of the morning, and the angels of light whom he drew along with him into misery and ruin, were not hindered by the laws of their being from revolting against God, then it is to be concluded that other angels and archangels, thrones and dominions, are no more hindered in like manner from falling. If in one instance it was possible for the angelic host to forget the goodness and love of their Creator, and rise against His most just and blessed government, then I see not why, in another instance, it might not likewise be possible. If any one ask me how it is possible at all, I answer, that is not the present question. But the question is, Having once taken place, what reason is there that it might not take place again? Out of this event, therefore, which had taken place in the history of angels, it was wise and good in the Almighty to provide that it might not take place again. The cause of it lay in aspiring to be higher, in hoping something better from disobeying God than from obeying Him. To prevent this fatal ambition from possessing, and, in like manner, ruining those who still stood in their allegiance, the Almighty allowed the rebels to prove and experience the disappointment of their bad ambition and their fallacious hope. He allowed them to take the consequences, and the consequences they have taken, and continue to partake. Thus, out of this sad event was made to issue stability to those who had not fallen. The fate of the other was their continuance. For as knowledge is taught by contrasts, they now knew what it was to rebel against God; whereas formerly they did not know, and did but imagine. Had Satan known, as Michael and Gabriel now know, haply Satan would not have ventured; but Satan, only imagining, did venture for his own imaginations against God's constitution, and so came into that misery from which we have no tidings that he shall be delivered.

With regard to that previous question, so much agitated in the schools, concerning the origin of evil, and how it should be possible for the creature of a God in whom no evil is, to conceive evil within himself, and to bring it forth—concerning the possibility of this thing, it is not material for us to speculate, who have the revelation of the fact; and I have always avoided such speculation upon the great possibility of things, as being beyond the scope of my faculties, if they be at all within the scope of the faculties of any man. But if I were called to give an account of this matter, I would say thus, that unchangeableness of nature is a condition only of the Creator; and that if it were impossible for a creature not to change, that creature would have conveyed to it one of the attributes of God. Creatures indeed there are which cannot change their nature—the lowest creatures of all,—the plants and inorganic matters of the earth, the agents with which the physical and chemical philosophers are conversant; the law of whose nature is their very existence, and without which they are nothing, and by which they become the servants of intelligence, which taketh advantage of this their necessity to work and wind them at its will. But the higher creatures, upon whom intelligence, and judgment, and recollection, and forethought are bestowed, such as men and angels, are not placed in such low conditions; but there are opened up to them on every side the avenues of enjoyment, which are capable of being known by the right exercise of those higher faculties; and being known, of being obtained; and thus their well-being consists in an active occupation of those their faculties subservient to the will, and in reaping the happy fruits of such activity. Hinder the possibility of evil, and you at once hinder the activity of those powers by which that higher being is distinguished, and you reduce him into the condition of the inferior parts of creation. Besides, our obedience of God, if it doth not proceed from choice and preference, is naught but the obedience of the sun and moon and stars in their courses; it doth not become of any dignity or worth, save by its being maintained in the possibility of disobedience; so that it seems to me, to be able to sin and fall is the very condition of created existence. With regard to the heinousness of the offence, that depends upon the constitution of the creature, and the condition in which it is placed, and the barriers which it hath to overleap in its wilfulness before it can bring itself to offend against a holy God. And, therefore, in order to understand that much-disputed question of the admeasurement of the punishment to the offence, it were necessary to understand the good and happy conditions in which the creature was placed, and against the sweetness of which he revolted and rebelled and fell into condemnation.

But without insisting further upon that previous question of the origin of evil, we observe, again, that being once introduced, God turned it in His wisdom to the most account, when, instead of annihilating the rebels and the hateful thing which they had begotten, He cast them headlong into hell, and allowed them to know those consequences of revolt, which, not knowing, they had dared, and which having dared, they could not find fault if they should experience. In which He did no injustice to them; He gave demonstration to all heaven of those fates which lay upon the side of disobedience, and secured by another tie continued obedience and continued blessedness. With regard to annihilation, or extinguishing a spirit that hath been once brought into existence by the Spirit of God, which was the only other contingent possibility, I do not know the soundness even of the idea, whether or not it is not inconsistent with itself, and have not time to spend upon a subject so metaphysical; but granting it were possible, although it might have eased the fallen of their pains, it would have removed the standing proof from the unfallen, and instead of keeping before them both sides, would have kept before them only one, which had not been sufficient to preserve their allegiance, otherwise Satan and his followers had never fallen.

But being fallen and removed from their place, I pray you to observe, that evil hath thereby gotten a head, a habitation, and a name. No doubt it hath limitations.

With this remark, which we introduce that your faith be not shaken, we now proceed to open up further views of the forty days' temptation of the devil, which preceded the three attempts of which the particulars are recorded.

When the man Adam was formed of the dust of the ground, and God had breathed into him the spirit of lives, and he became a living soul, his Creator prepared for him the blessed paradise of Eden, and took him, and placed him there, that he might undergo a trial of his obedience. And having surrounded him with every precious thing, and subjected to him every living creature, and honoured him with His own society —that is, the society of His everlasting Word, through whom the Godhead holdeth communion with men,—He interdicted from him one thing alone of all that was seen, handled, and enjoyed, and prohibited it by a heavy curse. There was the fulness of enjoyment, with only the possibility of loss. The good was the greatest possible—the evil was the least possible. And in what proportion the taste of an apple was to the full beatitude of Eden, in that same proportion the temptation to disobey was to the inducement to obey. No one can complain that the trial was severe. In this trial of his fidelity, man, having failed by the cunning and lies of the prince of evil, became an exile from that spiritual beatitude of which the garden of Eden was the emblem, and fell into that spiritual misery and moral barrenness of which the wilderness and the solitary place are the emblem. Into the wilderness, therefore, was the Saviour transported to undergo the trial of His strength and fidelity, because the wilderness represented the condition from which He had condescended to remove the sons of men. He had undertaken to make the solitary place become glad, and the desert to rejoice and blossom like the rose. Therefore, upon the ultimate stage of this world's unredeemed wildness He planted Himself, in order to bring back the world's unredeemed wildness. The savage beasts were around Him, which are emblems of men's untamed passions: the tiger, of his fury,—the lion, of his pride,—the fox, of his cunning,—the hungry wolf, of his rapacity,—the serpent, of his grovelling lusts,—and the eagle, pouncing from his pride of place upon the lowly creatures, an emblem of that tyrannical power with which man loveth to oppress all inferior men. Thus the Saviour stood in the hoary wastes, with all these forms and emblems of man's fallen nature around Him, in order to undo the evil which Adam, by eating the forbidden fruit, had done unto his race. And whereas the tempter had been the prime mover and instigator of that huge crime, and ever since had flown abroad in the princely rule of the air, and roamed abroad in his princely mastery of the world, it was needful, nay, it was natural, and impossible that it should be otherwise, that he, who is no coward, though cunning, having braved the Omnipotent in arms, should come up against the second Adam, who stood amidst these miserable conditions to give him battle for his long-possessed reign. The strong man of the house must first be bound by a stronger than he, otherwise it is idle to think of casting him out. If Satan yieldeth not, the world cannot be redeemed. If Satan is made to yield, then redemption is possible, and may take its course. Therefore, it was necessary that He who was mighty to save should begin His career of conquering and to conquer, as He is here stated to have begun it, by single combat with the prince of darkness.

But, moreover, the Almighty intended by His Son a double blow, not only at sin upon the earth, but at sin in hell. Sin He purposed clean to purge out of the earth, and bring the millennial reign about, which is, as it were, Eden in the distant future, into which the great Husbandman is turning the wilderness whereon He waged this strife for the world's salvation. But likewise He purposed to drive into their own throats the bravadoes of hell, their boasts, their blasphemies; and to unclasp their iron yoke from the sons of men, into whose souls they made its iron bands to pierce; to send them back howling to their den, and shut them there for evermore; and not only defeat their ravaging of this fair earth, but to punish them for their temporary subjection of it; to root the serpent race out of their new quarters, whence they had conceived a spark of hope, and got a taste of power, the ambition of which hurled them from heaven. Thus, I say, did the Almighty purpose to make the iron, which the Chief Physician extracted from the soul of man, to enter into their own hearts; and visit upon their guiltiness, first, the loss of heaven, and next, the loss of earth; and coop them up for ever within that sulphurous pit which is alone fit scenery for their hellish nature. For the wretched warring spirits, when they get abroad into any dominion of God, do work desolation therein, and waste its beauty with fire and sword. They breathe pestilence, they sow discord, they water it with blood, they cause it to be reaped with tears; the lamentations of widows and children are their music, the groans of broken hearts their ecstacies of delight, the pangs of death their shouts of victory, death their triumph, and the corruption of the grave their fruit. Such creators of all discord, heart-sickness, and desolation, the Creator of all good purposed to restrain for ever within their own infernal quarters, and He by whom and for whom all things were created, was to be the performer of the mighty work. All heaven were the spectators. The security of heaven from any second insurrection was the great ultimate good, and the redemption of man was the immediate cause.

What less was this second enterprise of Christ, but a second driving in of the power of those demons whom He had once defeated? Heretofore, He had cleansed heaven of their adulterous rebellion against God. He rose in His might, with ten thousand of His angels; strong in His might, He cast them headlong from the glory of heaven to the condemnation of hell. But God did not thoroughly reduce them. He did not altogether crush them, but gave them a little scope; for Satan even presented himself with the sons of the morning in the presence of God. Through this incompleted vengeance, this relic of mercy, even to the rebellious angels, they did in the lapse of time, and the devices of their maliciousness, come roaming forth, and obtain a hold of this earth, which they have brought into this abject condition. Therefore they needed to be dispossessed of earth, as aforetime they were dispossessed of heaven, and hunted back, baffled, into their horrid habitations, and then bound for ever and ever. But to make this second head against them, Christ summoned not the host of heaven, He called not upon the legions which evermore attend Him unseen, but came forth a naked child, and grew an untitled man, with His body His only earthly possession. He took no power but as God measured it out to Him; and having received it, He commenced, here in the wilderness, the great enterprise, not of baffling Satan merely, but of dispossessing all His angels of their power over the souls and bodies of men.

Now, mark how God put things into a condition for revealing this subjection of the nether world by His own dear Son. To those spirits which possess the souls of men, and lead them into error and various idolatry, and torment them with the pains and agonies of sin,—to those very spirits which now work in the children of lust, mammon, Belial, pride, and revenge,—to those spirits within the breast which are commonly silent, and make no manifestation of their presence, in this age and in this country, when His Son appeared, He gave a voice, so that they spoke from the breasts of those whom they possessed. He made them testify to their presence in the bosom of man, also to their mischief-making powers therein. The whole race of demoniacs which existed in this age, I conceive to have been a phenomenon permitted by God, in order to make this triumph of His Son over the spirit of evil manifest. The angels of heaven might have known it without any such demonstration to the sense; because spirit can discern spirit, and perceive their distant habitations, and know their condition, whether exalted or humiliated. But not so with man while in the body; he needeth to have demonstration of the sense; therefore, the Almighty allowed those evil spirits which are still present in the breast to manifest their presence in those days, in order that Christ, in His goings to and fro, might cast them out; in order that they might manifest their fear of Him, their dread of His very name, their supplication of His mercy, their obedience to His command, and every other mark of a subjugated and deposed race; by which men might be taught no longer to fear the arts of the old serpent who prevailed against Eve, or the arts of his messengers who plant the tares among the good seed of God's planting; by which they might take heart, and trust in the Captain of their salvation, and His power to cast them forth.

Thus, if I may so speak, there was a double incarnation: first, an incarnation of the Word of God in the Son of man, and of His Spirit in the apostles at the day of Pentecost; and, secondly, an incarnation of the devil and his angels in the breasts of demoniac men; in order that in flesh the battle might be fought and won, which formerly in flesh had been lost, and in flesh the triumph over death and the grave might be gained, which formerly had power to lay all flesh prostrate, and consume it like the grass. Therefore, a life which was intended to beat back these froward devils from the soul of man which they had usurped, and to manifest unto all that should believe in Christ that, trusting in His strength, and in the operation of the Spirit which wrought in Him effectually, they had nothing whatever to fear from the hellish confederacy which had borne down the spirit of man, and continueth, in all who believe not Christ, still to bear it down,—I say, a life which was destined not only to do this very thing, but to give demonstration that it was done, needed to be begun, as Christ is here reputed to have begun. The chief of these legions, attended with all his host, must be defeated. In silence they are defeated. The strife must be at the first with the strongest, who being foiled, all the weaker are likewise foiled, and the work goes on, without interruption, of banishing the wicked powers from the spirits of men.

So Christ came into the power of the devil, that He might defeat the devil, as He came into the power of death, that He might defeat him that hath the power of death, which is the devil; He came into the grave, that He might rise from the grave, and deprive it of its victory; He came into the power of malice, that He might triumph over it. He descended into hell, that He might preach to them in prison, and teach them to believe and tremble. He took upon Him the form of a servant, that He might teach His followers obedience; and, in short, came into all possible conditions, that He might shew Himself triumphant over all, and put all things under His feet.

But, besides this view of the temptation, as holding, with respect to our redemption and recovery, exactly the same place which the temptation of our first parents held in respect of our fall and captivity,—the one the first of a long career of triumphs over Satan, the other the first of a long career of conquests by Satan,—there is another view of it, of which I shall treat in the next lecture.

LECTURE III.

Luke iv.

THE views which we have given in our two former lectures, arising out of the forty days' temptation, were sufficient to shew the relation which this great incident in the life of Christ had to the work of the world's redemption, and to the defeating of Satan and his angels, and driving of them back discomfited within the limits of their ancient reign. We are now to open up our views of this as it bore upon our Lord himself, and upon the work of His ministry.

We stated in a former discourse, that though Jesus of Nazareth was the incarnation of the everlasting Word of God, who created the worlds, and for whose pleasure they are and were created, He is to be conceived, while He tabernacled amongst men, as being really that which He seemed—a man, and the son of man. "Forasmuch as the children are partakers of flesh and blood, he also himself likewise took part of the same. In that he himself hath suffered, being tempted, he is able to succour them that are tempted." In all the sensations of flesh and blood He partook,—He was liable to hunger and thirst, to heat and cold; His appetite longed with all desires natural to man, and His heart had pleasure in the savours and relishes of the things which are created and made. The comforts and accommodations of life He knew the pleasure of, and lamented the want of, in that pathetic appeal, "The foxes have holes, and the birds of the air have nests, but the Son of man hath not where to lay his head." He felt both the pain and indignity of a blow, and rebuked the menial who smote Him. In all these bodily attributes, therefore, was He very man. Again, in respect to what is called the mind of man, and those feelings which the world produces in us, He was also as one of the children. He rejoiced with those that did innocently rejoice, and He wept with those that wept. He was indignant at hypocrisy, and with wickedness He was wroth. He reasoned as a man reasoneth. His disciples approached Him as a man is approached; and the multitude consulted Him as a wise and holy man is consulted. If He had not been congenial with other men in the affections and operations of His mind, other men would not have been able to hold with Him any conference. Therefore we conclude, that as man is acted upon by man, in the same manner was Christ acted upon. In other words, He had a reasonable soul, without which, the body of a man would no more have made him man, than the dress of a man would make an inferior creature man; for the body is but the dress by which the inward man hath intercourse with the inward man of another, and with the outward world of matter. Further, the outward world affected the Saviour as it affects every human being; its fruits nourished Him, its evil afflicted Him, and its good pleased Him. And I doubt not, from the tastefulness of all His images, that its beauty pleased Him, its sublimity affected Him, its twilight shades awakened meditation, and its gloomy shades helped Him to hold commune with His griefs. I understand not that tremulousness of mind with which I say these things, but Isaiah and the psalmist have spoken prophetically of His pains of body and anguish of mind, and the evangelists have recounted them in the most simple narratives, and the apostles constantly refer to them and argue upon them as our example patiently to endure. Now, if Christ had not really and truly undergone those trials with which His followers are tried; if His flesh had been intangible by torture, and His spirit impassive to painful feeling, as the stoics would have persuaded themselves to be; if the world had in all its vanity passed before Him as a phantasmagorical representation, affecting only the sight of the eye, but touching not the sympathies and antipathies of the heart, then what use would His life have served as an example? or how could we now quote it as the only painful and sinless life upon record? If so be that He did not feel, He had no need of fortitude, firmness, patience, wisdom, skill, and every other means of standing against trial; and what availeth His triumph, if so be that He felt not a tendency the other way, which, by these means, He counteracted? Thus to bestow upon Christ the power of being acted upon by temptation, and liability to err in all ways in which we are liable, we do not take from His divinity, we do but make good His humanity, which is an attribute of His being no less important than the other. The question of His divinity rests upon other grounds, and is to be gathered from the declarations of the prophets, the evangelists, and the apostles, and from His own lips. But whatever way that question be taken, it must not affect His humanity, whereof I now treat.

This human being, then, was to be sent forth upon the most perilous exploit which had ever been appointed to human nature. He had to pass through every suffering and trial which it is possible for man to encounter. He was to meet with the blackest ingratitude, the highest perfidy, the utmost scorn, the basest mistreatment. He was to perform constant services to humanity, and by humanity to be as constantly abused; He was to utter constant wisdom in the ears of men, and in almost all His attempts to find an answer in their hearts He was to be defeated. They were to gather about Him, and raise Him to majestic height with hosannas, and anon disperse like the tide when it hath left the ship which it bore upon its breast, a wreck broken to pieces by its unstable violence. Many good works was He to do, and for these good works they were to take up stones to stone Him. Many attempts He was to make to gather Jerusalem, as a hen gathereth her chickens under her wings; and through the obstinacy of the ill-fated people, He was at length to sit down and weep over her, ineffectual tears. Ah me! what He must have suffered, who had within Him such stores of truth to unbosom, and could find no one prepared to hear Him; whose breast travailed with a world's salvation, and could hardly find in all the world one faithful adherent; whose voice could command every element of destruction, and add thereto legions of invisible spirits, and yet had to bear the contumely of every worthless menial, who could sharpen his tongue or lift up his heel against Him!—and this abused man a Being of perfect virtue, a Being of sovereign power, a Messenger of God, the only Son of God, the Redeemer of the world! The father of heathen philosophy imagined that if a perfect man should appear upon the earth, the sons of men would arise and crucify him. And therein he shewed almost prophetic insight into the fate which truth might expect. And the prophets who foresaw this event were struck with terror at what passed before their view, and cried out, "Who is this that cometh from Edom, with dyed garments from Bozrah? Wherefore art thou red in thine apparel, and thy garments like him that treadeth in the wine-fat?" Another thus describeth it: "Trouble is near; for there is none to help. Many bulls have compassed me: strong bulls of Bashan have beset me round. They gaped upon me with their mouths, as a ravening and a roaring lion. I am poured out like water, and all my bones are out of joint: my heart is like wax; it is melted in the midst of my bowels. My strength is dried up like a potsherd; and my tongue cleaveth to my jaws; and thou hast brought me into the dust of death. For dogs have compassed me: the assembly of the wicked have inclosed me: they pierced my hands and feet. I may tell all my bones: they look and stare upon me. They part my garments among them, and cast lots upon my vesture." Another prophet hath said—" His countenance was marred more than any man, his form more than the sons of men. He is despised and rejected of men; a man of sorrows, and acquainted with grief: and we hid as it were our faces from him; he was despised, and we esteemed him not." And another—" Awake, O-sword, against my shepherd, against the man that is my fellow, saith the Lord of hosts: smite the shepherd." And our Lord himself, when reflecting upon His sufferings, was in an agony, and sweat great drops like drops of blood falling down upon the ground.

All this was to be endured without once swerving from the path of blameless rectitude. His spirit, all human though it was, and able to be wounded, and to feel the smart of every wound, was to bear without any retort. When reviled, He was not to revile again; when threatened, He was not to threaten. He was human as to its suffering, and had the severest cast of suffering which hath been allotted to any son of man; but He was to have no recourse to the refuges of suffering humanity. No stoical pride to wrap Himself in, no silent contempt of superior wisdom to support him, no triumph of argument to indulge, nor successful argument to follow up; no lifting of the hand, no inciting of the multitude by an eloquent manifestation of his wrongs, no partizanship nor personality, no temper nor strife was He to bring to his aid. He was to meet all, to bear all, without any of the arms offensive with which men express the passion that is awakened within them—to be the model of that long-suffering endurance, and forgiveness of enemies, of that all-blessing charity which He was the first to hail—to be led as a lamb to the slaughter, and as a sheep before his shearers is dumb, so was He never to open His mouth.

I believe that in the minds of many the edge of this mighty trial is taken off by a certain vague apprehension that He was helped to bear it by the new power which He had received from heaven: but this is a notion against which we protest, as totally unsupported by Scripture, and defeating one chief end of His coming in the flesh, which was to conquer every form of wickedness and trial that could come against Him from the cradle to the grave, and to set us an example that we might follow His steps. If His humanity bore not His human encounter, but needed the aid of His superior faculties, then how serveth it as an encouragement or an example to us who are mere men, and have no such divinity to bear us up? His humanity sustained Him against all earthly encounters; and whatever His divinity served Him, it served not to lighten the load which lay heavy upon His shoulders.

I speak not now of the mere inward struggles which He had to maintain as the surety of mankind, which many sound divines have thought could not be of less amount than all the sufferings which all that believe in Him are saved from through all eternity. Neither do I speak of those unrecorded temptations of the powers of darkness which He had to sustain throughout His life, and of which we have a shrewd intimation in the expression with which this recorded temptation concludes, "The devil departed from Him for a season;" nor of the hidings of His Father's countenance, nor of anything save the outward visible sufferings with which men can sympathise. It may be said many of His followers have endured as much; but hath any one endured it without sin? To endure is nothing. The tortured Indian endures many crucifixions. Bed-rid patients endure whole years of torture, of which single nights have in them the materials of many a tragedy. Nature must endure what the hand of God layeth on, however great it be. But doth she endure without murmuring, even what she cannot avoid enduring? And what is laid upon her by every wicked son of Belial, doth she endure without the resentment of a man? But here is a man, a very man, by distinction the Son of man, enduring heaps of trouble and affliction from every outward and inward quarter, and carrying Himself under it, not like a man, but like a God. It is Adam, sent not into paradise, but into hell, for the trial of His faithfulness, and enduring all the tortures of hell with no defalcation of His faithfulness. This was the trial, not that He should bear, but that He should bear as one who bore not; not that He should endure in a sinful world, but that without sin He should endure; that for all His cruel condition He should be able to challenge the severest inspection of that host of enemies He was surrounded with, and who had risen up against Him; that He should bear the knowledge of Him who searcheth the heart and trieth the reins of the children of men, and receive the testimony that He had done no violence, neither was any deceit in His mouth. Such was the heavy work which Christ undertook, and such the happy issue to which He had to bring it.

Having before Him this yet unattempted work of conquering in flesh and blood all the enemies of flesh and blood, both on earth and in hell, of preserving Himself immaculate though a man, perfect and sinless though a sorely tempted man, it was very desirable that He should have at the outset of such a perilous voyage some trial of His strength to endure its hardships. Having a human soul full of anticipation and feeling, as we see through all His life, especially in the garden of Gethsemane, He could not look upon the trial before Him without misgivings. If, after having proved His strength in this wilderness, and through all the scenes of His ministry, such horrors overtook Him on entering the last scene of it, what anxieties and fears must have pressed Him at its outset, when, from being a private man, He undertook so high a task! Think not I take from His dignity thus to behold Him accessible to those troubles of the spirit. It doth but prove the more the tenderness of His humanity, and encourage that fellow-feeling with Him which is the most genuine mark of His disciples. But take from your idea of His dignity or not, it is the truth that He had such misgivings, and prayed His Father in His agony to let the cup pass from Him. We have been so much agitated with disputes about His divinity that we dare hardly trust ourselves to conceive of His humanity, lest we should trespass upon the integrity of the former. But this nervous delicacy must not be indulged either by you or by me; we must look upon His true humanity, and speak of it as the evangelists and the apostles likewise spoke of it. And when need is, we must do the same of His divinity. These misgivings of the human soul of Christ, it was the purpose of this temptation to chase away;—to give Him, in the very outset and beginning of His undertaking, a proof that He was equal to its utmost perils; that He might take courage and enter upon it with boldness; that in all His difficult passages memory might have a spot to flee to, whereat He encountered this, and more than this. This temptation I consider to be one of three remarkable passages of the same kind, which are recorded in His life. The other two are the transfiguration and the agony. In the transfiguration, Moses and Elias came to Him, and conversed with Him of the death that He was to accomplish at Jerusalem. In the agony, there appeared an angel unto Him from heaven strengthening Him. So also, by St Mark, it is recorded of the temptation, that, when the devil departed from Him, angels ministered to Him. So that all these three marvellous incidents agree in this, that spirits from the unseen world came to strengthen and encourage Him, which proves the more what hath been advanced above of the terrible nature of the undertaking, and of the anxieties which lay heavy at His breast.

It is remarkable, and worthy of all observation, that those now glorified saints who came in the transfiguration to converse with Him of the death which He had to accomplish at Jerusalem, had each of them an experience similar to this temptation during their pilgrimage upon earth, and that they are the only two who had such an experience. Moses was in the mount with God forty days and forty nights, during which he declares unto the children of Israel that he did neither eat bread nor drink water. And Elias, when he fled from the face of Ahab into the wilderness, and out of the greatness of his sufferings laid himself under the juniper tree to die, received from the angel of the Lord a meal of meat, in the strength of which he went forty days and forty nights unto Horeb, the mount of God. These two instances resemble that before us too strongly, to be passed over in silence, especially when we have observed these were the very two of all the host of heaven that came to commune with Him when He was transfigured on the mount. The former of the two, Moses, had been called by God to go down to Egypt and rouse the slumbering and oppressed people, but remonstrated with the Most High upon the perils and unreasonableness of the undertaking. Whereupon the Lord gave him two proofs, making his rod a serpent, and turning his hand leprous, by which he might perceive the strength of Him whose servant he was. When he had delivered the children of Israel from the house of bondage, and had them in a place of safety and quiet, the Lord called him up to the same mount, and kept him forty days and forty nights with Himself alone. During these days He prepared him for the ministry to which He had called him, instructed him in the laws and statutes by which Israel was to be governed, and made such manifestations to his soul as might strengthen him to follow out his perilous embassage unto the people. God was sending him a warfare, and He sent him not on his own charges, but furnished him with a sufficiency of faith and confidence for the work. He annealed his soul, if I may so speak, with heavenly temper for the important work he had undertaken; and gave him such a foresight of the glorious issue of his work, and such a foretaste of his reward, as might go with him to his grave, and bear him up through all his trials, and in the very shadow of death. Elijah, again, had been very jealous for the Lord of hosts. He was the only prophet that durst raise a standard for God in the sight of Ahab and Jezebel, the king and queen of Israel; he had presented himself in the breach for God, and singly withstood all the prophets of Baal to their shame and ruin; and, notwithstanding his godly heroism, had to flee once more, and in the desert had stretched him out, and, like Job and Jeremiah, in the weariness of his soul prayed for death. The Lord had still high commissions for him to perform. By him by whom He had brought vengeance upon the friends of Baal, He was to bring sweeping vengeance upon apostatising Israel, and the bloody pair which filled the throne. But the heart of the prophet was broken, and his soul was weary of the struggle which it had to sustain. Therefore the Lord, to restore his soul, and shew him what He could do for him, delivered him for forty days and forty nights from the wants of the body, fed him with supernatural strength, until he came to Horeb; and there, after various sublime visions of His majesty, and various declarations of His providence and grace, He delivered to him His commission: "Go, return on thy way to the wilderness of Damascus: and when thou comest, anoint Hazael to be king over Syria; and Jehu the son of Nimshi shalt thou anoint to be king over Israel; and Elisha the son of Shaphat of Abelmeholah shalt thou anoint to be prophet in thy room." So Elijah departed thence, and never did his soul halt again or look back until he had fulfilled the commissions of the Lord, and was taken up, in proof of his fidelity, without tasting of death. In like manner, St Paul, about the beginning of his Gentile ministry, went down to Tarsus, and was no more heard of for three years; during which I doubt not the Lord was preparing him for his work, as he had prepared Moses and Elias in the former dispensation; and, to give him heart to endure its many sufferings, pangs, and death, He caught him up in a trance to the third heavens, where he heard unspeakable words, which it was not lawful for him to utter.

Now, if, for leading the children of Israel through the wilderness, and furnishing them with national laws and religious statutes, soon to come to an end, the Lord did prepare the man Moses by having him in the mount to Himself for forty days and forty nights, how much more for the greater work of laying the foundation of the everlasting kingdom of Christ, of giving it statutes and commandments, and exemplifying the same in practice—of rooting out, not a few Canaanitish nations, but of rooting out all error and sin which have possessed the world, and of establishing upon the earth a throne of judgment and a sceptre of righteousness;—how much more for those ends was it necessary to have Christ prepared by forty days' proof and trial of His strength and assurance of victory? If, again, to strengthen Elijah against the persecution of the murderous Ahab and his more murderous queen, it was necessary to have him for forty days and forty nights in the sustenance and strengthening of the Lord; and thereafter to fill his soul with sublime visions of the presence and providence of the Holy One of Israel, how much more was it necessary to build up and strengthen the humanity of Christ against the combined attacks of the devil, the world, and the flesh, which He had to stand against singly, without any of the people to sustain Him, but all to bear hard against Him? And if Paul, His Gentile apostle, in order to meet his buffetings, was plentifully furnished with visions and revelations of the Lord, how much more the Divine Master of Paul, whose footsteps he did but follow, and who Himself had to give the example unto all, to be the future hope of the human race in those regions of unsullied purity and unyielding virtue which no man had ventured on before?

Therefore the Almighty, in mercy and loving-kindness to the man Jesus of Nazareth, whom He had anointed for this perilous undertaking, led Him to the wilderness, far apart from the haunts of men, and kept Him there in perilous strife with the enemy of souls for forty days and forty nights, during which He ate no food, and conversed with no earthly creature. And these days of trial being ended, He permitted Satan to wax wanton against Him, and to put that humanity to proof, which, in the future incidents of our Lord's life, was to be sorely buffeted. This humanity was like the receptacle of His higher powers. It was the vessel which bore them about for the consolation of the sorrowful earth, and from which the earth might partake them, and be blessed. The fulness of the Godhead was embodied, the glory as of the Only-begotten of the Father was contained, in flesh. Now, the human vehicle, the manly body and manly soul by which that celestial freightage was borne about from place to place, needed to be proof against the sinful storms that assailed it. Had it in any place given way, then the whole enterprise had failed, and human salvation had been out at sea again, when in sight of shore, as far from our reach and knowledge as ever, and our souls had been once more in gross darkness, and this earth had been still in the region of the shadow of death.

Thus have we set forth, first plainly, then by analogy of others, and lastly by a figure, the use of this temptation so far as regarded Christ, whereof we had formerly set forth the use as it regarded mankind and the spirits of darkness. It was to put His humanity to the proof, that He might know His strength, and, knowing His strength, go to the work with courage. I pray you to follow me in a short analysis of the three trials by which Satan assailed Him; that you may discover how artfully they were laid by Satan against our Lord's humanity, and how wisely permitted by His Father, to assure the Son of man of the greatness of His strength. There are three sides upon which mankind are vulnerable by temptation. The first is through the lusts and appetites, and tastes and pleasures of the body, whether they be coarse or refined, vulgar or elegant. The second is through the world, its ambitions, its vanities, its occupations, its influences, its treasures and possessions, its titles, its thrones and dominions and powers. The third is through the deceivableness of the mind itself, whereby it becomes its own dupe, is taken in its own subtlety, becomes first self-deceived, and afterwards the deceiver of others. Besides these three instruments—the body, the outward world, and the soul itself—I know and can conceive no other means by which Satan can assail the nature of man. Upon each one of these ways he makes a descent upon the humanity of Christ; and though only by one experiment, yet that experiment being the severest possible in each kind, the most artfully and craftily devised, and the most difficult to be withstood, must be understood to include all the rest.

For these three temptations are not to be considered merely as a trial of hunger, of ambition, and of spiritual pride, but as the mode of those three classes of temptation with which Satan hath power to work against mankind. They are instances, but each is in its kind extreme, and by being extreme, including all the rest. First of all the demands which the body makes upon our attention, that of hunger is the most peremptory and powerful. The relishes of appetite, the delicacies of taste and smell, the beauties and proportions of visible things, all that is seen, tasted, handled, and heard, pass away from their sweet entertainment of the sense when the body craveth for the staff of life. These things will not appease that craving. It will not be bribed by them into silence. They must all give way for bread. Everything will be exchanged for bread. For bread the body will bow itself down to toil, sweat and labour long hours, deny itself sleep, clothing—everything for bread. Of which absolute dominion of this appetite, see a notable instance in the seven lean years of famine, from the effects of which God preserved Egypt by His servant Joseph. They parted first with their money, then with their cattle, then with their land, and finally with their own liberty, so masterful over all ornaments and possessions is this appetite of hunger. This extreme instance, therefore, includeth all the rest, and temptation by them includeth temptation by all the rest. So that this first assault of the devil is to be regarded as including one third part of his empire—his empire over the spirits of men through the medium of their bodily pleasures and sensations. The next thing after sensual pleasures, not so immediate as these, and therefore not so universal, but of a higher kind, and acting upon nobler faculties of the spirit, is the temptation of power. Having failed through the medium of the senses, the devil next makes his attempt upon the Saviour through worldly possessions; and here also he arrays the greatest possible of all temptations. Concentrating the whole world in his grasp, bringing it by some diabolical phantasm under the eye of the Saviour all at once, he offers it for the least of all returns—the return of one single prostration. "If Thou, therefore, wilt worship me, all shall be Thine." Here is all that Alexander sighed for, that Julius Cæsar accomplished, and that Napoleon attempted, and for which they fleshed their swords in blood, and stained their souls with dishonour, and made their hearts like flint towards their kind. All this—and under this, all inferior ambitions, sighed after by soldiers, politicians, lawgivers, and philosophers, are included—is offered to Jesus without loss of time, without expense of means. Bow Thyself, and all the world is Thine. In this instance, therefore, is contained the second part of the dominion over which Satan hath the mastery, and by which he assaileth the spirits of men. After sensual pleasures and worldly possessions, cometh a third and still higher region of his subtlety and art, by which he worketh the soul against the soul. This trial, which springeth from the deceitfulness of the heart, is of a far more subtle kind than either of the other two, and remains to be encountered after the temptations of sense and of the world have been overcome. It is the wandering of the mind in its own mazes, tending to superstition, delusion, and self-deception of every kind. Hence the infinite systems of philosophy which, age after age, have sprung up only to be demolished. Hence the infinite forms of false religion which have subjected men's minds, overthrowing reason when revelation is not present, and where it is, covering it with darkness, and disguising it with fable. Some of these have been invented for the purposes of worldly gain, coming under the second order of temptation; but far more are the production of self-deceived men, who have believed themselves right, who have fancied in themselves a higher reason, or a nearer fellowship with God than others possess, and have brought the power of intellect, the subtleties of logic, the mysteries of superstition, and the gathered stores of knowledge to defend and support their systems; and, so sustained, have sent them abroad to wield a more formidable sway over men than that of arms. And men, instead of adhering to their reason steadily, so far as it would guide them, and in things above reason, instead of examining nicely the evidence and observing the tendency of the doctrine, have been glad to find any food for those parts of the mind which long after the invisible and the eternal,—any religion rather than no religion; and so, contentedly have bowed their necks to some base superstition, altogether unworthy the credit, far less worthy the admiration and obedience, of man. Upon this, the deceivableness of the spirit of itself without any means, the tempter tries our Saviour in the last place—quoting the prophecy that went before concerning Him, that if He would cast Himself down from the pinnacle of the temple, the angels would bear Him up and save Him from any harm. The prophecy was intended for Messiah, and such guardian spirits were around Him; therefore it seemed safe to trust Himself thereto. The smallest particle of spiritual pride or of self-confidence, the smallest obliquity of understanding or presumption towards God, the smallest portion of that superstition to which religious people are very liable, of making the trial—of consulting God, as they term it, by opening His Word, or casting the lot, would have sufficed to give Satan the victory over the Saviour on this side. But that smallest obliquity of the mind was not present to His perfect rectitude; and, therefore, here also he failed. In which three regions of his subtle power being defeated,—in the sensual, by which he generally tempteth inexperienced youth; in power, by which he tempteth the prime of manhood; in superstition and self-deception, by which he tempteth hoary experience and wearied ambition or sated lust,—having failed, and having no fourth region on which to assail the great Champion of righteousness, he departed from Him for a season.

These three forms of trial it shall now be our endeavour to expound upon the principles laid down: first alluding to the individual case of trial as it is put by the tempter; and, secondly, to the way in which the tempted Saviour repelled it. Then from the individual case we shall reason to the class which it includeth; and out of the short sentence of Scripture with which it is repelled, we shall draw the doctrinal principle by the application of which that whole class of temptations is to be struggled with and overcome; so as to lay before you in full, not only the subtlety of the tempter, and the calm and consummate wisdom of the Saviour, as set forth in the narrative which Luke and Matthew have given of this mysterious transaction; but also to open up fully those three regions of the tempter's power, and the three corresponding regions of Divine wisdom to which it behoveth us to flee as unto a city of refuge.

LECTURE IV.

LUKE IV.

IN the life of trial and sore temptation for which Jesus of Nazareth had been anointed by the Spirit of the Most High, He was not to be exempted from the last and lowliest calamities of human life, which attend upon outcast and persecuted men. Without house or home or settled occupation, He was to wander from town to town, and from village to village, a dependent upon God's providence and upon the common charity of the people. His wants were few, and He had good gifts to give in return. For a piece of bread, He could restore a withered limb; for a meal of meat, He could recover a parent from the very article of death; for a night's accommodation, He could cast out a devil; and a good reception in any city He could conciliate, by recovering all its sick and disabled people. Yet these gifts of heaven, which, in His all-healing hand, had come down to bless the needy children of men, were not sufficient to procure for Him a regular supply of the necessaries of life; and, as we read in the Gospels, He was sometimes forced to take the hungered's privilege of rubbing a few ears of the standing corn. From which instance, recorded not on purpose, but for illustration of His doctrine regarding the Sabbath-day, and from the other instances of the precarious meals which He picked up from the hospitality of strangers, I doubt not that He must often have fared but scantily; and, not knowing where to lay His head, must often have known as little where to satisfy the cravings of nature. Many nights He passed under the canopy of heaven, taking no thought for the body; many days, I doubt not, He passed under the trial of hunger and of thirst. Of which, if any man make any doubt, let him think of the volumes which are spoken by these words: "Foxes have holes, and the birds of the air have nests, but the Son of man hath not where to lay His head."

And though, when thousands of hungry people were gathered around Him, and there were, in all, only five loaves and a few small fishes amongst them, He had the generosity to put forth for their sakes His creative power, and swell the morsel into the materials of an abundant repast, more than sufficient for all by many basketfuls; yet He took not for Himself any such privilege of helping Himself by a miracle out of the scanty or pitiful conditions with which He might chance to be encompassed. For He came not to escape by superhuman means the adversities of human life; but to endure, in the strength of flesh and blood, all the infirmities which flesh and blood are heir to, and all the evils which cruelty worse than human could add to these; and, except in two instances when He covered Himself with invisibility in order to escape premature death, and to reserve Himself for enduring more protracted mistreatment, and a more painful and ignominious death, we have the evidence of His whole life that He faced the whole cloud of trouble and trial which was brought against Him by the powers of the present and the infernal world, and came through them as the sun cometh out of a stormy cloud,—not abated, but increased in the brightness of His glory.

In the course of His pilgrimage among the evil conditions of humanity, having to travel through that region which is filled with objects of the greatest misery, where man is reduced to the most desperate shifts,—the region of actual want, of craving and raging hunger,—it was merciful in God to permit Him to be tried here, in the first instance, that He might know His strength, not only to suffer the pain and the exhaustion, but also to overcome the temptations which, in that moment of greatest weakness, the evil one suggested to human nature, and which human nature hath seldom the strength to resist. Accordingly, after the forty days have passed, during which the Lord was delivered from the natural wants of the body, for the supernatural contest which He then carried on, He is let down again into the conditions of humanity, and the body begins to make demands for its proper food. "When they were ended, He afterward hungered." And though we know not to what pitch of painfulness His hunger had arisen, it was a very auspicious moment for the tempter. He was in the wilderness, far from the abodes of men; not upon the skirts of the desert, but in the bowels of it, where the wild beasts prowled around. He was an hungered, after forty days' separation from food, and must endure the cravings of appetite until He reached a place where He could obtain bread. At this moment, when under the sorest call of nature—the call for the staff of life—the tempter, in what guise we know not, appears before Him, and suggests an expedient by which He might deliver Himself,—"If Thou be the Son of God, command this stone that it be made bread."

Whether this scene, and the others which follow, had an outward action, or not; whether the devil, in some human or angelic guise, did appear three successive times to the Lord, and utter these three successive speeches, and receive these three successive replies; or whether the whole be only an allegorical way of setting forth the thoughts which His human nature suggested unto Christ,—first, the thought of using the divine gift for His own personal pleasure; secondly, for the exaltation of His power; and, lastly, for practising upon the understandings of men,—has been disputed among the interpreters of Scripture. The German Neologists and Naturalists, who outdo even our Unitarians in their liberty with Scripture, have gone so far as to explain away all these things by allegory, and to disbelieve, as self-deception of the writers, all the miracles and prophecies of Scripture— calling themselves Christians withal; in which liberty the Naturalists of this country are fast following them, step by step. As to the main point of the question, it seems to us of small consequence whether they are taken as real outward acts between the tempter and the Saviour, or as inward promptings of spirit to spirit, such as those by which our minds are led into evil; for, whether in the one way or the other, the Saviour proved Himself superior to the guile and power of the Evil One, which is the chief thing for us to know. But while either supposition saves the constancy of our Saviour, and the good lesson thereby taught to us His followers, I beg to know of these rational men, what good end is served by turning plain narrative into allegory? Mystery, that terror of their minds, is removed; and at what expense, I would ask them, is it removed? At the expense of St Luke's credit as a historian. For, verily, if any man could conceive that St Luke, knowing this to have been an allegory, did set it forth so like a plain matter of fact, as he hath done; if any man will give me good and sufficient reason to believe that he could play such a trick with his readers, I would that moment cast his treatise upon the same shelf with clever equivoques, artful deceptions, and fairy tales, which please me by their ingenious and dexterous disguises. For the same end, of doing away with mystery, these Rationalists allegorise the whole person, character, and agencies of the devil, and bring all the books of Scripture into discredit; where he is as much spoken of as a real existence, as is God himself; and, after the same fashion, they explain away the Holy Spirit as a separate existence. But oh, rash and unadvised men! they know not whither they hasten. If it be mystery to conceive of the personality of one spirit, it is equally mysterious to conceive of the personality of another spirit; and then what becometh of the personality of God? The same rational tongue which laughs to scorn the existence of the devil, as a person, must laugh to scorn the existence of God, as a person; and this I do not despair of hearing one day from the pulpit, where He is even now preached of under the philosophic appellation of the Deity, the God of nature, and such titles as hide His personality, and are more proper to Pantheism than to Christian divinity. And for the separate existence of the human soul, as a spirit, these men of whom I speak have long been content to give up that matter as not worth the dividing upon. But the waters have now got so shallow upon these speculations, that soon their very footing must be discovered, and then a discerning people will see what they have to stand on.

But to return, taking St Luke to mean what he says—and to take him in any other sense is a liberty which a professed believer should be the last to take—the tempter came to Jesus when He was hungered, and said unto Him, "If Thou be the Son of God, command this stone that it be made bread." It is not credible that the tempter, when coming to address Christ through the strongest of His sensations, that of hunger, should by want of skill and management mar his own dexterous exploit: that by appearing abruptly, or undisguisedly, or in any unseasonable way, he should be the means of marring his own plot. When power was given him to tempt Job, by cutting off his all, liberty was left him to do it in the most masterful style. And in the most masterful style he did accomplish it, beginning with the least valuable of his estate, and mounting up to the highest, his sons and daughters, and arranging it so that messenger should arrive upon the heels of messenger, calamity be heaped upon calamity in the ear of the patient man, if possible to drive him to distraction, and to curse God unto His face. In like manner, when power was for good ends granted in heaven to try the Saviour of men by these successive trials, I doubt not that Satan was allowed the whole compass of his wiles, not only to take Him at the most seasonable times, but to circumvent Him with the most appropriate pretences, and to urge Him to the utmost extremity of his power. Therefore, the evangelists having said nothing as to the manner of his approach, you are at liberty to suppose it to have been in the most artful guise. Milton—who has rendered the whole scene into poetry, and whose muse was in better keeping than is the reason of the speculators whom we have alluded to above,—so that, though he embodies the scene by imagination, he doth never take liberties with the Word, much less defraud it of all its sense and meaning—hath thus imagined and described their meeting in the first book of his "Paradise Regained:"—

> "Till those days ended; hunger'd then, at last,
> Among wild beasts: they at His sight grew mild,
> Nor sleeping Him, nor waking, harm'd; His walk
> The fiery serpent fled, and noxious worm,
> The lion and fierce tiger glared aloof.
> But now an aged man, in rural weeds,
> Following, as seem'd, the quest of some stray ewe,
> Or wither'd sticks to gather, which might serve
> Against a winter's day, when winds blow keen,
> To warm him wet return'd from field at eve,
> He saw approach, who first with curious eye

> Perused Him, then with words thus utter'd spake:
> 'Sir, what ill chance hath brought Thee to this place,
> So far from path or road of men, who pass
> In troop or caravan? for single none
> Durst ever, who return'd, and dropp'd not here
> His carcass, pined with hunger and with drought.
> I ask the rather, and the more admire,
> For that to me Thou seem'st the Man, whom late
> Our new baptizing prophet, at the ford
> Of Jordan, honour'd so, and call'd Thee Son
> Of God: I saw and heard, for we sometimes
> Who dwell this wild, constrain'd by want, come forth
> To town or village nigh (nighest is far)
> Where aught we hear, and curious are to hear,
> What happens new; fame also finds us out.'"

And then, stealing by simple words upon the confidence of the tempted Saviour, the poet at length makes him to put the question thus—

> "But, if Thou be the Son of God, command
> That out of these hard stones be made Thee bread:
> So shalt Thou save Thyself, and us relieve
> With food, whereof we wretched seldom taste."

By these quotations you will not understand me to adopt for certain these imaginations of the poet, which may fall short of representing the cunning of the scene, but certainly can never surpass it. But, however it was, we may at least suppose that the method was as wary as the moment was opportune; which being granted, we go on to consider the proposal which he made—to turn the stones into bread. In this there was nothing difficult for one who had made five loaves into meat for as many thousands, and had converted water into wine. God is able, said the Baptist, out of these stones to raise up sons unto Abraham, and therefore able to make them bread to preserve the life of Abraham's promised seed. To have obeyed this suggestion was therefore both within His power, and within the pleasure of His heavenly Father, who was surely loath that His Son should starve of hunger. But, besides being possible in itself, it is suggested with such an inuendo of reasonableness, "If Thou be the Son of God,"—a suggestion by which very much is suggested. The fact is brought before His own mind that He was the Son of God, on purpose to inflame any spark of pride, if any was found in His breast, that, being such, He should be in such extremity. Therewith is suggested the doubt whether it were possible that He could be such, and He is solicited to the proof, and the proof such as all nature was craving for; and withal the tempter casts himself in the power of the Saviour, to put him to confusion by actually turning the stone to bread, and proving that He was the Son of God. He taketh Him when all nature is in arms for bread; he puts bread within the reach of a word; he suggests the word; he suggests that He had been deserted of God, and was no Son of the Highest; he offers to put it to the proof of that word, which would give Him bread. Suppose you were in want of bread, and craving for bread, that is what not one in a thousand could bear; suppose you were the king's son in want of bread, that were more humbling still, and more difficult to endure; suppose you were the king's son hungering for bread in the king's storehouse, with plenty of bread around you, and had only to put forth your hand to partake, and yet were withheld by some secret cause, so much the more painful; suppose, while nature and pride are thus tantalised in the midst of plenty, suppose some son of Shimei, some scoffing outcast fellow, who had been cast out long ago from your father's court, should come up at this perilous moment, and taunt you with such speeches as the following:—"You, the son of the king, and heir of the crown, come to this pass! You boast that all is yours, and you have not wherewith to fill your mouth! Vain boaster and pretender! If you be the king's son, why hesitate? Put forth your hand, take and eat. You now take one of the loaves, and I will reverence thee as the son of the king!" This is only to help you to imagine the truth; it is not intended as a description of the truth, but only to aid the conception. Now, I ask if it were not a sore trial to be thus taunted at such a moment when the irritability of nature was at its height? Nature would say, Dash the tempter to the earth; and I am very sure a hundred arms would be lifted up to do it, if any instance of such abuse were to appear under the eyes of our people. Suppose a lofty man upbraiding a beggar with his poverty, or a man able of limb upbraiding a cripple with his lameness, or one blessed with sight taunting a blind man with his blindness, what a burst of feeling it would raise in the bystanders, and what an emotion of contempt or wrath in the bosom of nature's needful child! Now, if Satan had betrayed the Saviour into a sin of temper, into an act of revenge, or a feeling of scorn, or a word of reproach, he had won the day, and our Captain, who placed Himself in the breach for our salvation, had been overcome. Or, if the Saviour, beguiled by the wily tempter, had listened to nature's call, and, under covert of confounding him by the proof to which He had been dared, created to Himself food, then He had been guilty of being outwitted, His human nature had been caught in the well-laid trap, and had used a subterfuge for His gratification. Or, if He had, without any hoodwinking of Satan's subtlety, but simply to satisfy nature's call, commanded the stone to be made bread, even though to defeat the bravado of the tempter, He had fallen into another trap of ruin, doubting the providence of God which watched over Him, and taking by a surreptitious method that food which He should have looked for in the ordinary course of the Divine procedure. So that the temptation was manifold; the snares set for the Saviour were many and deep. And if He had not been guarded by intellect, by temper, by humility, as well as by temperate contentment with the providence of God, He had been undone, and we undone along with Him.

Now, let us remark how the Lord delivered Himself from the complicated subtlety of this temptation. He did not revenge cruelty with wrath, nor resent indignity with scorn; He did not give way to offended pride, and overwhelm His enemy with the proof; nor did He yield to the gnawings of hunger, and create for Himself a morsel against His present necessity; nor did He suffer His intellect to be any way outwitted by the snares of this question, but coolly, piously, and with entire self-command, replied—" It is written, That man shall not live by bread alone, but by every word of God."

These words cast a strong light upon the employment of the Saviour's mind during the assault of the tempter upon the side of His bodily wants. Seeing for Himself no resource in that hoary waste wherewith He was surrounded, instead of sinking into the depths of despair, His piety rose with His emergency; He remembered the days of the right hand of the Most High, and the immutable word of His power, upon which He relied in this the hour and power of darkness. He remembered what was spoken by Moses, and the prophets, and the psalms, concerning Him. In that very psalm which the devil in the third temptation used against Him, He remembered how it was written, " Thou shalt tread upon the lion and adder: the young lion and the dragon shalt thou trample under feet. Because he hath set his love upon me, therefore will I deliver him." He turned in His distress to the former providences and preservations of the Lord to those that trust in Him, and remembered, perhaps, how through that very wilderness He had guided His people for forty years; how He had humbled them, and suffered them to hunger, and fed them with manna, which they knew not, neither did their fathers know, that He might make them to know that "man doth not live by bread alone, but by every word that proceedeth out of the mouth of God doth man live." The pious and well-instructed mind of Jesus had its refuge in this similar instance of God's ancient people, and was well assured that, if for forty years He so kept them suspended upon His providence day by day, in order that He might fulfil His promise to Abraham, much more now to the Chosen Seed, to whom He had just vouchsafed His testimony from on high, would He furnish a supply when He had sufficiently tried His faithfulness and trust. Therefore, unmoved by the tempter's art, He quoted that lesson which forty years' sustenance in the wilderness by quails and manna was intended to teach the people of God, that "man doth not live by bread alone, but by every word of God." Thus was the tempter foiled by our Lord's trust in the providence of God; and thus hath He taught all His followers how to foil him when they are in like manner tempted under the wants and cravings of nature.

LECTURE V.

Luke iv.

THE Saviour withstood the severest of all bodily trials, craving and raging hunger, upon the strength of a promise of Scripture, that "man shall not live by bread alone, but by every word that proceedeth out of the mouth of God;" and He withstood the offer of all the kingdoms of the earth, and the glory of them, in obedience to a command of Scripture, "Thou shalt worship the Lord thy God, and Him only shalt thou serve." From which two instances of His pious disposition, the devil, taking a lesson, and perceiving that this was no common man to be goaded into distrust of Providence by want, or bribed out of duty to God by glorious objects of the earth, at once changed his method of proceeding, and resolved to try whether he might not take Him by a skilful use of His own sanctified weapons, and an artful device of piety. But he did not cast away his wonted arts, but wrought his new attempts with his ancient artifice, and therefore chose a scene every way appropriate to the end he had in view. When he wrought by hunger, he had Him in the wilderness, far from any supply of hospitality or charity, or any power of purchase, and there, isolated with hungry want and desolation, he practised upon his victim. Afterwards, when he pushed Him upon the side of glory, he had Him to the top of a high mountain—some Alp or Appenine of the earth, from whose feet spread far and wide the objects of human ambition—and there, while in His eye was glassed all which men desire and hunt after, he offered to Him the glory thereof if He would but bow down before him in an act of worship. Next purposing, under the disguise of an angel of light, to practise upon Him with holy instruments for a holy end, he chooseth, in the first place, a holy scene, the pinnacle of the temple at Jerusalem, and there makes before Him his third and last great proposal. Upon the pinnacle of the temple, beneath which lay the sanctuary and the holy of holies, and Mount Zion, and the city of the living God,—upon the pinnacle of that house which, in His twelfth year, He had claimed as His Father's, when He said to His anxious mother, who found Him disputing with the doctors, "Wist ye not that I must be about my Father's business?"—here, where Simeon and Anna had welcomed Him in His earliest childhood, and where He was soon to put forth those powers with which He was commissioned, did the artful tempter plant Him, and said unto Him, "If Thou be the Son of God, cast Thyself down from hence; for it is written, He shall give His angels charge over Thee, to keep Thee: and in their hands they shall bear Thee up, lest at any time Thou dash Thy foot against a stone."

Not only was the scene chosen with the utmost skill, to raise in the mind of the Saviour such an enthusiasm of divine trust as might have brought Him into the most compliant mood with the artful request, but it likewise found Him in the mood in which He was the most likely to comply. The arch-magician of evil, by his superhuman arts, had brought before the eye of His mind, and perhaps, also, of His body, whatever is noble in the mastership and single sovereignty of the earth. He had wrought upon the natural desire which there is in man for glory and renown, shewed Him nations ready at His call, monarchs waiting upon His nod, wise men bringing the offerings of their wisdom, and great men the offerings of their services to His shrine. He shewed Him how busily the nations were working at his work: how the princes were partitioning the fair earth, pleased with the vastness of their dominion; how the warriors were reaping the fields of their bloody deeds, and politicians gathering in harvests of their political renown; how inventors were inventing arts, and poets inditing glorious imaginations for the honours of apotheosis and a seat among the gods,—all of them serving, as they thought, their own glory, while he, even the prince of this world, was the master for whom they wrought, who kept his secure seat upon the throne of their sinful hearts, working each several desire and inclination to his will, and from his high fortresses in the gay ornaments and strong delusions of the world, exercising an undivided supremacy over the decayed fancies and subject resolutions of men;—all which he proffered in full possession to Christ—not a monarch's lifetime of it, but that spiritual supremacy, that mastery within the veil, which he himself had held since the direful fall. Now, the Saviour was not a stock or stone, that these visions and this offer of things should pass before Him without power or impression. He was not an angel or unearthly being, that, being beheld, they should work in Him no human desires. It was of the very essence of His being to be touched by them, and moved with them, as another human being is. What, then, defended Him against yielding to that, the smallest portion of which daily overcomes the strongest of minds, and seduceth unawares the most pious and devout hearts, whereof they make constant confession to God, humbly seeking forgiveness? That which shielded and protected Jesus from this assault upon the noble parts of human nature, was the activity of other parts still more noble. His relation to God and to the world to come was present to His mind, and defended Him from falling. He remembered a higher Spirit than that powerful spirit before Him, and a nobler glory than the glory of the nations of the earth. He foresaw, also, a higher destiny, when, through much sorrow and tribulation, He should come to His kingdom. And though the prospect was distant and much overclouded, He descried through the vista of ages the coming of His kingdom, and the attainment, at length, of that very sovereignty which Satan now offered Him over the earth, when it should be held, not in allegiance to Satan, from whom by dishonourable prostration it had been purchased, but in right of redemption,—held, not for the interests of Satan, but for the interests of God. And I doubt not, that at this perilous moment the man Christ Jesus remembered all the grounds to hope and trust in Him which the Lord had given to Messiah since the world began—all which, by Moses, and the prophets, and the psalms, had been testified of Him—all which was figured of Him in the law and history of Abraham's seed—

all that had signified His coming and His work to the nations —and all that He had received of direct attestation from on high: as the sending of a messenger before His face to prepare His way, His own angel-announced approach, His arrival amidst heaven's glorious minstrelsy and the heraldry of angels, the homage of the country round, and the wise men from afar, to the new-born Son of God, His reception in the temple by the two old and hoary servants of God, the holy Simeon and Anna the prophetess, His preservation from the sword of Herod, the wonder which wrought within His youthful mind, and the tokens of the Lord's favour which He had received during His opening manhood, until at length He was proclaimed with God's own voice, and by God's own Spirit set apart, under the high denomination of God's own Son, for taking away the sin of the world. His mind being filled with these things, which appertained to Him as Messiah, much of which had been fulfilled, and the rest of which stood over for fulfilment upon His finishing His mighty work, there was no power in the worldly attractions. They were outdone by higher attractions. The love of God cast out the love of the world, and the veneration of God cast out the veneration of the god of this world; piety prevailed against power, as patient trial had formerly prevailed against appetite, and he said, I will worship the Lord my God, and Him only will I serve.

* * * * * * *

[It has been found impossible to give these Lectures at greater length. The MS. here terminates abruptly.]

HOMILIES ON BAPTISM.

"We utterly condemn the vanity of those who affirm the Sacraments to be nothing but naked and bare signs."—*Confession of Scotch Reformers.*

TO

ISABELLA IRVING,

MY WIFE,

AND THE MOTHER OF MY TWO DEPARTED CHILDREN.

My honoured and beloved Wife,

I BELIEVE *in my heart, that the doctrine of the holy Sacraments, which is contained in these Homilies, was made known to my mind, first of all, for the purpose of preparing us for the loss of our eldest boy; because, on that very week you went with him to Scotland, whence he never returned, my mind was directed to meditate and preach those discourses upon the standing of the baptized in the Church, which form the sixth and seventh of the Homilies on Baptism. I believe it also, because, long before our little Edward was stricken by the hand of God in Scotland, I was led to open these views to you in letters, which, by God's grace, were made efficacious to convince your mind. I believe it, furthermore, because the thought contained in those two Homilies remained in my mind, like an unsprung seed, until it was watered by the common tears which we shed over our dying Mary. From that time forth, I felt that the truth concerning Baptism, which had been revealed for our special consolation, was not for that end given, nor for that end to be retained; and therefore I resolved, at every risk, to open to all the fathers and mothers of the Christian Church, the thoughts which had ministered to us so much consolation.*

I desire most gratefully to acknowledge my obligations to the fathers of the Scottish Church, whose Confession of Faith concerning the Sacraments, and especially that sentence which I have placed as the motto of this book, were, under God, made instrumental in opening to me the whole truth of Holy Scripture concerning Baptism and the Lord's Supper; of which having been convinced by God's blessing upon these words of my fathers in the Church, upon consulting the venerable companion of my early studies, Richard Hooker, I found such a masterly treatise upon the whole subject of the Sacraments, that I scrupled not to rank as one of his disciples, and to prefer his exposition infinitely to my own; yet to both, to prefer that sentence of our own Confession which I have placed as the motto of my book. For this reason it is, that I have reprinted those parts of Hooker's treatise which concern the doctrine of the Sacraments.

And now, my dear Wife, as we have been sorely tried of the Lord, by the removal of two such sweet children, let us be full of prayers and fellow-feeling for those who are in like manner tried; and, above all, be diligent in waiting upon those children of Christian Baptism, whom Christ hath committed to my charge, as a bishop and shepherd of His flock. Unto all whom, even as many as by my hands have been admitted into His Church, I do now bestow my fatherly benediction in the Lord. May the Lord make you the mother of many children, to glorify His name for ever and ever. This is the prayer of your loving husband,

EDWARD IRVING.

[This Dedication was prefixed to the volume containing the Homilies on Baptism (published in 1828.) It was intended to publish another volume of Homilies on the Lord's Supper. That intention, however, was never carried out, and the Homilies are now printed for the first time from the author's MSS. The selections from Hooker's Treatise are of course omitted.]

HOMILY I.

THE SIGNIFICATION OF THIS ORDINANCE.

MATT. XXVIII. 19.

Go ye therefore, and teach all nations, baptizing them in the name of the Father, and of the Son, and of the Holy Ghost.

THE symbolical rites of religion differ from its ordinary observances in this, that there is couched under them a meaning, which expresseth itself in the symbols, and in the words which are appointed to be spoken over them. And the doctrines which are so embodied under a visible form are the most important doctrines; whose greater importance it is that giveth them the title to be recorded in a more expressive and enduring form. For that which liveth in a sensible sign not only speaketh more plainly, but hath also a greater security of life, than that which liveth but in oral or written tradition: as we see by the relics of heathen customs, which survive amongst the people even to this day, long after all trace of writing and memory of oral traditions have departed. Therefore the distinguishing characteristics of every dispensation are, for the sake of greater security, enshrined in a substantial form. The covenant with Noah, that no second flood should come up over the earth, but that we should get leave to sow and reap in security, was embodied to the sense in the sign of the rainbow. The covenant with Abraham, that in his seed the ends of the earth should be blessed, was embodied to the sense in the rite of circumcision. And even the leading facts of the Jewish history were secured in a similar manner: their deliverance from Egypt, and the standing order of the priesthood, by the preservation of Aaron's rod that budded; their receiving laws from God upon Sinai, by the preservation of the tables of stone; their divine sustenance in the wilderness, by the pot of manna; the presence of Jehovah, by the glorious forms above the mercy-seat; and the communications of Jehovah, by the Urim and Thummim, which the high priest wore upon his breast. All these are deep resources of wisdom for preserving what is most necessary to be preserved; sensible forms for containing spiritual meaning; new securities taken against the power of time, which changeth all things; the statuary of truth, which may endure, though the picturing and writing of it should be effaced.

Of these symbolical rites, two have been left by the Lord Jesus Christ, significant of what He did, and still continueth to do, for the children of men: these are, Baptism and the Lord's Supper: concerning which it is our purpose to discourse; having this day to administer the former, and soon to administer the latter, in the presence of this congregation. Which two symbolical ordinances, we shall shew, manifest, in the simplest and most expressive forms, the substance of what the Saviour hath done and taught unto mankind: so that, if the books of Scripture were lost, and these two sacraments, with the words pronounced over them, preserved, they would be sufficient to suggest to a reflective mind the great ideas of the Christian revelation. And to that great portion of mankind who are unable to read for themselves, they speak, whenever they are set forth in simplicity, the great truths upon which the world's redemption dependeth, and for want of which the world would shrink back into its former darkness and barbarism.

But for this very reason, that these two rites speak to the sense the most deep and mysterious truths of the Christian faith, they are liable to be abused to the degrading ends of superstition, by the natural sensuality and cunning artifice of man. For of superstition this is the essential character, that it seeketh the spiritual in the sensible; and transferreth to sensible things, first as emblems, afterwards as realities, the reverence which is due only to things unseen and eternal. Accordingly, the Roman Catholic Church, which out of the most spiritual of all systems of truth hath constructed one of the most perfect and debasing of all superstitions, hath fixed the whole meaning of the Christian sacraments in the worthless mixture which they consecrate instead of pure water, and in the bread and wine, which they worship as the very body and blood of Christ, the substance of the invisible God. And perceiving the power which they thereby acquired over that ignorance which the Sun of Righteousness came to scatter, (but they have used His coming to deepen it,) they have increased the number of the sacraments to seven; exalting ordinary services, which have no meaning further than what is plainly spoken, into mysterious and allegorical representations of subtle and sublime truth. And, pursuing the same course of bringing the spiritual into subjection to the sensual, they have introduced artificial emblems everywhere: lights and lanterns, to represent the illumination of the Spirit; holy water, to represent the purification of heart which God requireth of His worshippers; the sign of the cross, to denote our trust in the Redeemer of men. And even the facts of the gospel history they have set forth, by holy days, and processions, and mystical celebrations, to take the senses of the multitude. Which, verily, I cannot think of without abhorrence, I cannot speak of without detestation of those who, however well-intentioned, first brought these forms to eclipse the light of the gospel and enthral the souls of the people, and make, out of a spirit-quickening and spirit-sustaining religion, one of the most gross and sensualising superstitions upon the face of the whole earth.

On the other hand, and in direct opposition to them, the Famulists, and the Society of Friends, and other mystics, perceiving that the chief, and I may almost say single object of our faith, is to quicken the spirit, buried at present in sense and worldliness, and to give to the things unseen and eternal the victory over the things seen and temporal, have discarded the two emblematical ordinances of Baptism and the Lord's Supper, as not savouring of the spiritual character of Christ's discipline. Wherein they have certainly gone too far in a good direction. For though it be the chief, and perhaps single object of our faith to quicken the spirit, and give it the victory over the sense; to strengthen faith, and give it the mastery of sight; yet in bringing this to pass God hath always revealed

Himself through the medium of the sense. For what is the incarnation of Christ but a great demonstration of the Godhead to the sense? what His death and resurrection, but a declaration of life and immortality to the sense? So that God useth the sense in order to spoil the sense, as He used mortality in order to spoil mortality. Wherefore, if He saw it expedient, in making Himself known to the understanding and spirit of man, to give to His Son a body, and bring Him under bodily conditions, and so plant the gospel upon the earth, why should it be inconsistent to continue those two emblems, which were left to commemorate, through the sense to the spirit, those things which in that way were first revealed? And hence our Reformers shewed that spirit of wisdom with which they were endowed by nature and by the Spirit from on high, that, while they swept away those impositions which the Church calling itself infallible, at its pleasure, and for its aggrandisement, had added from time to time, as the ignorance of men would bear them, they were careful not to refine or spiritualise upon any of the institutions and establishments of the great Head of the Church, and have left us these two sacraments in the primitive simplicity in which they found them set forth in the Holy Scriptures.

These two holy rites of Baptism and the Lord's Supper, established by the Lord Jesus Christ, and by Him given in charge to His apostles, by His apostles established in the churches which they planted, and ever since continued in the Church, let us now, in devout dependence upon the grace of God, do our endeavour to examine and understand; that, so often as they are dispensed in the midst of us, we may be filled with their spiritual meaning, and praise the Lord our Saviour for having left us such signal manifestations of the great work which He hath wrought for the redemption of a fallen world.

The signs which embody any doctrine, and declare it to the sense of man, should be so well chosen as to speak their own meaning: for, if they needed any ingenuity or demonstration to help us to it, the end of their establishment would fail, which is, to render them independent of the frailty and

ITS SIGNIFICATION. 253

imperfection of oral or written tradition, by giving them the substantial or statuary form of expression. Therefore, in shewing forth the signification of baptism—which is the object of this discourse—we should speak not with the wisdom of words, but, as it were, with the dumb show of signs. Taking the symbols into our hands, we should ask ourselves what this and this meaneth, and must mean, to all who behold it: and that is the truest interpretation which is the most evident,—that the best demonstration which needeth the least to be demonstrated.

An infant, in the earliest age of its worldly existence, is brought by its father to a fountain of pure water, to be dipped therein by the priest, or washed therewith when the convenience of time and place admitteth not the former to be done. To immerse in pure water, or to wash with pure water, is, everywhere over the world, used for the purpose of cleansing away impurity, and to all men hath such a signification. But here is no visible, outward impurity in the child, for which it is brought to the fountain. Therefore, as the rite is emblematical of purification, and there is no outward impurity to be washed away, the impurity signified must be inward, or spiritual impurity. But this child hath not yet been conscious of good or ill, and cannot have contracted any guilt, being admissible to this ordinance as soon as born: it cannot, therefore, be intended against actual impurity contracted by itself: it must be for the sake of some impurity which it hath brought with it into the world, that Christ hath appointed it to be washed with the waters of baptism. Here, then, to any mind which reflecteth upon the rite of baptism, is revealed the fundamental doctrine of revealed religion—that we are shapen in sin, and brought forth in iniquity, and are transgressors from the womb of our mother. If the reflective mind goes on to inquire, And what availeth water to cleanse away the defilement of the immaterial soul? the question doth not admit of an answer, for it is of the very nature and essence of an emblem that it should not be a reality. If water could cleanse the soul, then the thing would not be an emblem, but a reality. It would be a real experimental truth, not a spiritual truth, exhibited, if the way how it came to pass could be seen through. And here we are upon the margin of deep waters, and touch the great distinction between truth of reason and truth of revelation, between philosophy and religion. The former is truth manifested to our senses and experience, occurrences and realities: the latter is truth never discoverable in the currency of life, or the labour of experimenting,—as it is written, "which eye hath not seen, nor ear heard, nor hath it entered into the heart of man to conceive;" but which God hath revealed to us by His Spirit, and manifested by revelation, through the help of emblems taken from actual life. And herein lieth the Hutchinsonian doctrine, which is the mother of all mystery, that, not content with what emblems God hath served Himself withal for the manifestation of what truth was necessary to man's redemption, it taketh a bolder wing, and holdeth that all visible things and philosophical truths are but emblems of spiritual truth, which it is the purpose of man's life to discover: thus extending the fact, that religion is truth discovered by natural emblems, into a universal system, that all nature is but, as it were, a visible impression of the spiritual truth which is behind: and as the day hideth the stars, so the vision of things hideth the spiritual meaning of things. But, to return to the emblem before us. Though we could not discover, from what is done or said in the administration of baptism, that the water serveth any purpose but as the emblem of purification; yet if we go into the Scriptures,—which is beside our present purpose, seeing we are reading their emblem only,—it is manifest, in every page, that it signifies no less than the blood of Christ, which taketh away the sin of the world; the fountain of the Holy Spirit opened in the house of David for sin and for uncleanness, whence Jesus is said to wash us with His own blood: "Unto Him that hath loved us, and washed us with His own blood." But upon this we do not insist.

The first doctrine, therefore, that is to be gathered from baptism is, that the natural pollution which we bring with us into the world is washed away. And if we go to search in the Scriptures, we further find, that it is washed away by the blood of Christ: but, adhering to the rigid principle of interpreting a symbol without foreign aid, this is not to be inferred from the rite itself.

While the infant is baptized with water, these words are pronounced over it: "I baptize thee in the name of the Father, of the Son, and of the Holy Ghost," in obedience to the last injunction laid by our Saviour upon His apostles: "Go ye therefore, and teach all nations, baptizing them in the name of the Father, of the Son, and of the Holy Ghost." Here is a declaration of the threefold nature of God, as the Father, the Son, and the Holy Ghost; and, being connected with the cleansing or washing of the child, doth imply that the Father, the Son, and the Holy Ghost are concerned in the great work of purging away the original sin of mankind: and its being said in "the name," and not in the *names*, doth imply that they are One. So that every time a child is baptized, there is a distinct avowal of the existence of a God; of the threefold personalities of the Godhead; and of the operation of each, and the co-operation of all, to the great work of purging away sin, which is shadowed forth. I purposely abstain from controversy; but if Christ be only a creature, and if the Holy Ghost be nothing at all but "an Eastern manner of speech," there never was such a method taken of disguising truth and of propagating error as this, appointed by Jesus, of baptizing in the name of the Father, the Son, and the Holy Ghost: for surely every one who heareth must conclude, that if the Father be a reality, the Holy Ghost is a reality; and if the Father be a Person in the Godhead, so is the Son, and so is the Holy Ghost. In baptism, then, we have further shewn forth to the world the doctrines of the Trinity, and of the co-operation of the three Persons in the Trinity in the taking away of the natural corruption of the human soul. And more than this is not said or done: more, therefore, than this, we think, is not signified: but this, simple as it is, sustaineth many conclusions, imparteth much consolation, and imposeth weighty obligation, into which we would now enter a little.

1. The symbolical ordinance which hath been explained

hath a threefold intention: first, to the beholders; secondly, to the child; and, thirdly, to the parents or sponsors of the child. To all men, who behold and witness this holy sacrament, it sheweth the way which is opened for the forgiveness of sins to be through the knowledge of God the Father, of Christ the Redeemer, and of the Holy Ghost the Sanctifier of men. And if they be worshipping God under the deistical notion of unity of person, it warneth them of the falsehood and unprofitableness thereof, and teacheth them, that, if they would be delivered from sin, they must contemplate Him under the Christian idea of Father, Son, and Holy Ghost. For the ends of salvation, and sanctification, and spiritual life, it teacheth us that this manifestation of the Godhead will alone avail;—that, however the words Deity, and God of nature, and Author of the universe, and such phrases, may amuse the mind; to sanctify and purify the mind, no conception, no faith of the Godhead availeth, but this Unity and Trinity, which is again and again and evermore pronounced in conjunction with the great symbolical rite of purification. If, moreover, there should be any one who believeth not in the original impurity and fallen condition of man, it rebuketh him of his error, and teacheth him that this is the very first and fundamental doctrine of our faith; that which every one who enters the Church must first bow to; that which is declared as often as a new member is added to the Church; the constant doctrine, the constant truth, without which redemption were folly and the gospel a fable. Moreover, if any one should doubt of the immortality of man, or the immortality of children, then let them behold it declared over them as soon as born, that not only do they live after death, but that God prepareth them from the beginning for heaven, by washing them with the waters of regeneration. If any one should have any doubts what becometh of the soul of a little child which is cut off before it is capable of actual transgression, let him take good hope from that which he beholdeth in baptism, that the God who admitted the infant to the rite of baptism, to be trained up in His Church, will admit it to the Church which is above, there to minister in His holy service. And if any one, groaning under the load of his sins, should say within himself, Who shall deliver me from this body of sin and death? here is "the figure of that which now saveth us (not the putting away of the filth of the flesh, but the answer of a good conscience toward God) by the resurrection of Jesus Christ." And, finally, if any one should be reposing his hope of pardon upon his own righteousness, here is the testimony against all such vain confidence; wherein an infant, before it hath conceived any good, is freely pardoned and cleansed, by the unbought and unmerited salvation of Christ.

2. As it respects the child, there is at this time a very strong controversy in these parts whether all that is signified in Scripture under the name of the new birth be or be not conferred in this ordinance upon the spirit of the child. Now, upon this subject, if those who are interested in the controversy will give me a candid ear, I doubt not to be able to say something towards adjusting the question at issue, while I open unto those who are in the better condition of not having made a controversy of it, the true benefit derived unto the child.

In the discourse of our Lord with Nicodemus, it is said, "Except a man be born of water and of the Spirit, he cannot enter into the kingdom of heaven." And St Paul, "Know ye not, that so many of us as were baptized into Jesus Christ were baptized into his death? therefore we are buried with him by baptism into death." From which it is inferred, that if the immersion in the waters of baptism be the emblem of our death, the rising out of them must be the emblem of our second birth. And, again, it is written, "Not by works of righteousness which we have done, but according to his mercy he saved us, by the washing of regeneration and renewing of the Holy Ghost." From these and similar passages, it is inferred, that what is said in Scripture of the new birth, and of regeneration, is to be applied to baptism. At which the more serious and spiritual take offence, as if it destroyed the necessity of a holy life, and threw the whole work and evidence of a man's salvation upon a rite, and so brought in the most fatal errors of the Popish superstition. There is no doubt that, by the apostles, baptism is referred to under the similitude of a burial and a new birth; because by that rite a believer was taken from the society of the world into the society of the faithful, adopted amongst the visible children of God, and made an heir of the inheritance of life. Therefore, to those to whom they wrote it was natural for them to appeal to this as the beginning of their spiritual life; and the act which marked their putting off of the old man, and their putting on the new; the death of the carnal, and the birth of the spiritual man. In the same spirit, the apostle, when writing to those converts who fell away, chargeth them with having "denied the Lord that bought them;" with having "trampled under foot the blood of the covenant, with which they were sanctified;" with having "crucified the Lord afresh, and put Him to an open shame." But though some had broken the covenant, it did not therefore lose its significancy to those who still lived under it: though some trampled the blood of it under foot, their unholiness did not desecrate it, but rather consecrate it the more, in the eyes of those who still trusted in Christ. And, in like manner, though many of those children who are washed with the waters of baptism in every Church, and especially in those Churches whereof the discipline is relaxed, grow up in ignorance and disobedience of Christ, and manifest themselves to be the children of the devil, and not of God, we are not, in order to get rid of them, to break up and destroy the meaning and purpose of the ordinance to those who continue steadfast in the faith, and by whom it should be regarded as the first testimony of Christ's love, and the public declaration of His willingness to save them. Therefore, while I would retain the doctrine of baptism as a new birth, and use that idea as freely as the apostles did, and urge it as I always do; I would not the less, but rather the more, inculcate the possibility of falling under the power of sin, and being lost in fearful apostasy; the necessity of conversion from our sins, by the Father's effectual calling of us unto Christ, and by the Holy Ghost proceeding, through Christ, to quicken those whom the Father hath given Him in all the life of holiness; with every particular duty and grace which appertaineth unto sanctification.

For as when we are born of our natural parents the seeds

of a corrupt nature are thereby conveyed to us, so when we are baptized into Christ the seeds of a spiritual nature are thereby conveyed to us: otherwise it were vain to hope that there could be any fruit of holiness yielded to our husbandry of prayer, faith, and instruction. Baptism declaring the child's natural deadness and inherent corruptness, placeth a bar against all dealing with the child; for who laboureth upon the dead? This bar it must remove, otherwise it were the inlet to no good hopes or painful labours of faith and love. If it declareth spiritual death, it must also declare spiritual life, or be utterly ruinous to all purposes and endeavours after holiness. But as the principle of natural life will soon cease, unless the means of natural health—food, raiment, and care—be afforded; so the principle of spiritual life is also made dependent upon the Spirit of God, who is given to the faith and prayers of the Church, to the spiritual affections, and the spiritual instructions, and the holy walk and conversation of parents. And as the evil born in every child is not developed but by the help of a fallen world acting thereon; so the seed of a spiritual life is not developed without a world of redemption acting thereon. The one world is the visible; the other world is the invisible, revealed in the Word of God, and brought into us by the Spirit. And as the eye and the other senses, when in the flesh, are our instruments of communication with the visible world; so faith, which is as strong and desirous in childhood as sense is, and as often called into exercise, needeth to be turned to the things invisible, that it may become acquainted with and repose its trust upon them. And so it is that the new birth of baptism no more answers to the perfect manhood of a saint, than the old birth of nature answers to the perfect manhood of the creature. But with more confidence than a parent trusts by proper care to rear his child to the maturity of natural life, may he trust, I think, to rear his child to the maturity of spiritual life: for the former is dependent upon the diseases, and accidents, and other forerunners of death; but the latter hath no necessary dependence upon anything but the Spirit of God, which no power can hinder from blowing, like the wind, whithersoever He listeth. Nay, more: as the child is secured in its life only by the force of nature in the breast of its parent, who, when it cries for bread, will not give it a stone to mock it; when it cries for a fish, will not give it a serpent to sting it; so have I the highest authority for saying, that the Father of men and children is more willing to bestow His Spirit, which is the only upholder of spiritual life, upon every one who asketh.

No man may take upon him to separate the effectual working of the Holy Spirit from baptism, without making void all the ordinances of the visible Church; which become idle ceremonies, or worse, save for the faith that the Holy Spirit may be and is in them of a truth, to all to whom the Father granteth the faith of His presence in them. On the other hand, no one may connect the Holy Spirit absolutely and necessarily with the administration of baptism; for thereby he would take the gift out of the electing will of the Father, and the redeeming love of Christ, and fix it in an outward visible act of an ordained priest: which act of a man will, in process of time and progress of ignorance, come to usurp the attributes of the Almighty Persons from whom the Spirit proceedeth. Therefore is it good and right to say, that every one who cometh to receive baptism, whether for himself or for his child, should come in the full faith and assurance of having his sins remitted, and of receiving the Holy Ghost: remembering always, that faith is not our work, but the gift of God by Jesus Christ; and believing that this faith being present, the Holy Spirit is assuredly present in this and every other ordinance of the Church?

Here, then, is the mystery of baptism revealed unto all believers—and a most glorious mystery it is—that no sooner is a child born into this world of sinfulness and sorrow by natural birth, than, by a spiritual birth, it is born into a spiritual world of grace and blessedness. The dispensation of redemption is placed coeval with the dispensation of recovery, the seed of immortality with the seed of mortality; and before the principle of ill hath gotten a hold, the principle of good is also implanted, to wrestle with and strangle it in its cradle: in order that the hearts of the parents may be encouraged to do for the sake of their unconscious babe the offices of spiritual parents no less carefully than they do the offices of natural parents; that they may be taught to place their confidence in Christ, for the sake of their little one, no less than they do for the sake of themselves; and that, as their little one grows conscious of good and evil, they may restrain the one, and encourage the other, in full assurance of the blessing of Him who allowed His thrice-holy Name to be named over it; and, when they begin to furnish it with natural knowledge for the business of life, that they may furnish it with spiritual knowledge for the life that is to come; inform it, from the very first dawn of intelligence, how God adopted it for His own, without any recommendation, calling Himself its Father; how Christ at the same time signified His interest in it as its Redeemer, and the Holy Ghost His work in it as its Sanctifier; that the Persons of the Godhead allowed their Name to be named over it, and its impurity to be washed away in the fountain opened for sin and for uncleanness;—that it may know that it is not its own, but bought with a price, even with the blood of Christ, as of a Lamb slain from the foundation of the world. To have the hearts of parents thus impressed, and thus assured, and thus bound over to spiritual duties; to have a child thus initiated into grace, thus commended to God from its mother's womb, thus possessed with spiritual strength as it grows into natural strength, and thus fortified with prayers beforehand,—this surely maketh infant baptism no unmeaning service, maketh this emblem of the new birth no unmeaning emblem.

And here, though I would not go out of the direct way of spiritual instruction for the sake of controversy, yet I do see it of so much importance to the justification of the orthodox faith established in the Churches, which is girded at by upstart innovations, as if it were an antiquated folly, and an unreasonable imposition of custom, that I cannot help saying one word to the opposers of infant baptism, upon what they lose by deferring this holy rite. They trust the instruction of the souls of the children to parents, as if it were an ordinary duty; whereas, to my thought, like the salvation of our own souls, it standeth out of the list of ordinary duties, in a place of solitary sacredness, above and aloof from all earthly vocations. Next, their children grow up without any assurance that the

Saviour hath taken any interest in them, or doth take any interest in them. There are no primitive bonds, no co-natal obligations upon their souls. Their religion cometh all from the future, in nothing from the past. They feel free to the question, whether they shall be Christians or not: and they feel out of all obligations, till they take them upon themselves by consent. Now, for the soul thus to fancy itself for so many years unobliged—which it must do when so much new obligation is left to it to take upon itself—is the most heinous of all things: for during this season Satan hath possession of all that ground of liberty, which waiteth for future occupation; and the probability is, he will so possess it as to bind them wholly over to himself. Certainly it were a very dangerous thing if our children were put away from us at their birth, and brought up remote until they reached years of maturity, when they might decide whether they would take upon them the obligations of children and enter under the obedience of their parents: so dangerous a thing it is to allow the children of God to grow up till a certain period without the idea of their being His children, and then leave it to themselves to decide whether they shall become so or not; as if an affection grew out of a reason, or everlasting relations were established by a process of logic. And as to the notion that they may be taught they are the children of God without any reference to the adoption of grace through Christ, I hold it to be a Deistical, and not a Christian notion; and to be proper discipline for the children of a Deist, but most unfit for the children of a Christian, who in everything sees Christ as the way unto God, and contemplates every relation which he beareth to God through the mediation of Christ.

But, to return. In the sense which hath been explained above, the sacrament of baptism may well enough be considered as a birth of grace, but a birth dependent upon the means of grace for its growth and perfection;—an assurance to all men that the seed of a spiritual life is bestowed by Christ upon them from the womb, and waits, in order to its growth, for the application of spiritual means, to which it will disclose itself more certainly than life will disclose itself by proper use of the means of health, (but without these means it will not be developed:) yet never departeth while life endureth, but there remaineth, a shame to the present lethargy of man, and a condemnation hereafter of his wickeduess. Baptism is the solemn sign which makes this great truth known to the world. It makes it known to those to whom it is not applied, no less than to those to whom it is applied; testifying, to all who have eyes to see and ears to hear, the everlasting truth, that Christ is the resurrection and the life, the immortality of every mortal creature, and the light which lighteth every man that cometh into the world. It is a manifestation, I say, to all; and it ought to be a conviction to all of you, whether baptized or unbaptized, who behold the sacred rite administered. But it is no assurance that the spiritual life will be developed in the little one: this dependeth upon the use of all the appointed means, and the blessing of God upon every one of them: for there are laws of the spiritual world no less than of the natural, in obedience to which it proceedeth; which laws are not discoverable by reason, but revealed to faith in the word of God. Though I call it, therefore, the new birth, or the manifestation of another nature than that which is visible, I do not preclude the doctrine of conversion. For if the child give way to the strivings of evil, rather than to the strivings of good within it, then it needeth to be converted or turned to the right way: and if it have borne the image of the old man, it needeth to bear the image of the new; if it have been obedient to the devil, the world, and the flesh, it needeth to be changed in the spirit of its mind, and regenerated after the image of God in righteousness and true holiness. So that while I preserve the symbolical meaning of baptism, and apply to it the language of Scripture, I introduce no Roman Catholic doctrine of salvation by works—or, rather, salvation by forms—but preserve the integrity and soundness of our Protestant faith.

3. Thirdly, This ordinance hath a special blessing and benefit in it to parents, which I now hold myself bound to open.

The parent, or the sponsor when the parent is not considered by the Church to be a responsible person, (and in every other case I consider the use of sponsors to be both unwarrantable and most destructive of parental obligation,) is by the sacrament of baptism placed to the child in a new relationship, which groweth out of the preceding doctrine, and is as follows: The parent, in the very act of presenting his child to be buried with Christ in baptism, doth declare unto the Church that his child deriveth from him nothing but sin and death; and in the act of baptism he doth, like Abraham, offer up his Isaac, who from thenceforth becometh dead and buried by the voluntary deed of the believing parent: so that I may say the relationship of nature existeth no longer, and a relationship of grace is constituted in its stead; which thus ariseth: God having permitted His Name to be named upon the child, it is, in the eye of faith, His by adoption through Christ; and being given to Christ to keep, He giveth it over to His Church, who hath all His charges on the earth given into her hand, being the sponsor and mother of the household: and from that time forth the infant is the child of Christ and His Church. Now, the Church, in order to discharge her sacred office, appointeth one who is willing, and whom she deemeth worthy, to be responsible for so high an office: and as Isaac, cut off in the flesh and raised in the spirit, was given to the faithful Abraham to be reared up for the Father of spirits; so deem we no one so fit, if worthy, to be honoured with this charge as the father; thereby sanctifying the ordinance of nature into an ordinance of grace. Nevertheless the Church standeth sponsor to Christ, and the parent to the Church; who, if she find the duty neglected, may, and doth, by means of catechists, and, if need be, I suppose, by actual separation from the neglectful parent, accomplish that which she is charged withal by the Head of the Church. And hence the origin and the duty of ministerial examination of adults, to ascertain their ability for this duty; and of children to ascertain that it be duly discharged. This, no doubt, is the standing of a parent or sponsor to any baptized child, that he is responsible to the Church, who is responsible to Christ, who is responsible to God.

And of the great blessedness of the relationship which is thus constituted, I have to observe, that though this sacrament doth not secure to you the salvation of your children,—

which, if they live, they must work out against many enemies, and enter into the kingdom through much tribulation,—yet I think it gives you the best grounds to hope that those of your children whom it may please the Lord to take away in childhood, He taketh unto Himself; for if He hath given a sign that their original impurity is washed away in the blood of Christ, and allowed His thrice-holy Name to be named over them, and they have not had any occasion of excluding themselves from the covenant, then I see not why we should doubt that the Saviour will take them unto Himself, and train their spirits up for glory—if training they need—in some more favoured region than this fallen world, in which we are working our weary way towards the city of our God. (The very question of a child's immortality would have been a difficult question, but for this holy sacrament, which proclaims its relation to the Father of spirits; and for several sayings of Christ concerning children, that of "such are the kingdom of heaven," and that their "angels continually behold the face of their Father which is in heaven.") But if the children be spared to arrive at maturity, the blessing bestowed upon a family in the sacrament of baptism is not the less that its infant spiritual life is cast upon all the uncertainties of ill-directed education, and all the temptations of an evil world: for baptism is the only assurance to you that its salvation is possible; that its natural corruption would not, like a millstone, have weighed it down in the grossness and darkness of wickedness for ever. This is your only hope of a holy and dutiful life here, and of life everlasting. All your parental affections are implicated with the assurances of this rite, and all your parental hopes do issue thence as from a fountain. Without this demonstration of heaven for your little ones, what had you to look for but the average chance of children, the haphazard of the world? But if you improve the assurance conveyed in this holy ordinance, you may almost be confident of an affectionate, dutiful, and pious offspring. Do you say, But this also depends on circumstances. I answer, And what does not? The life of your child depends upon circumstances; yet you are not hindered from rejoicing in its birth, and calling upon your friends to rejoice along with you. Your own salvation depends upon circumstances, by the means of grace; yet you rejoice not the less in the glorious gospel. The good of everything depends upon circumstances; and therefore there should be no joy nor gladness in the world, if we are not to rejoice in the baptism of our child, because, haply, its spiritual life may be shipwrecked amidst the evil disasters of time. But this is not a matter of hap or hazard, as I have already said. I think baptism is the assurance to a parent of a child's salvation, provided he, as its parent, take the even and holy course set forth to him in the gospel: at least, I am convinced every parent ought to act upon this assurance, and humbly leave the result in the hands of God. And certainly there could have been no expectation to us of meeting our children in the world to come, had it not been for this blessed rite, which takes off from them the guilt of their natural corruption, and cleanseth them of what they derive from us: thereby giving the best assurance of their being cleansed, by the same blood of Christ, from the guilt which they afterwards contract, provided they trust in His salvation, and walk in the obedience of all His commandments.

But certainly "without holiness no man shall see the Lord;" and our children, as well as their fathers, if they forsake the Shepherd and Bishop of their souls to follow after the devices of their own hearts, will descend to the chambers of the grave; but this condition, instead of being a painful one, is itself as sweet and gracious, and should be accounted as much our privilege, as was the first initiation into this divine way: for every deliverance from the power of sin is, as it were, the renewal of that first washing; and to the growing saint it is a continual washing of regeneration, and a continual rising unto newness of life. And this first act of purification is the assurance of all that are to follow; and all that follow should be ensued because of the earnest given to us before we could seek it or pray for it; and therefore parents should be thankful for this condition of progressive holiness being annexed to the primeval gift, as a continuation and realising of the gift.

To make this matter plain, by an illustration, of the benefit conferred by baptism upon the parents of a child, let me suppose this parallel case: That to the parents, while yet the joy over their new-born babe was fresh, and they had called their friends to rejoice along with them; into the joyful company the sovereign of the land, or one graciously commissioned by him, should enter, and, looking upon the child, declare towards it a dear and tender attachment, should take it in his arms and bless it: that of itself were an honour to make the parents happy, and talk of while they live. But suppose, further, that the gracious sovereign should declare that he would provide for their child in royal style,—that he would make for it a mansion in his royal palace, and a seat beside his royal person, and carefully watch over it, as if it were his own, during the years of its youth,—that when it arrived at maturity, he would take it to himself, make for it a coronet of honour, and bestow upon it a royal domain; and in every other royal way manifest the most exalted estimation of them and their dear little one;—in proof of the reality and truth of which his royal protestations, say that he should take from his bosom a testament, wherein it was all written, signed with his own hand, and sealed with the great seal of his kingdom, and, to make it doubly sacred, endorsed with writing of his blood, which he bestowed upon the parents in free bounty, to be afterwards fully implemented;—suppose such a thing to happen to the humblest family of the land, (and such things have happened in the providence of God,) how would the hearts of those parents be filled with indescribable gladness, how would they call upon their friends tenfold to rejoice, and how would they pray for long life to the honoured child, and diligently instruct him, and carefully rear him up for his distinguished inheritance! They would tell him of the high intention; they would stimulate him to be worthy of it: it would be the one idea, the master-thought of his mind, and the pole-star of all his course. And yet the fulfilment of the promise is crossed with many conditions. The child may die in his youth; but still the honour designed for him is the same, and the memory of it will remain. The child may disobey the laws, and render himself incapable of the honour; he may be banished to foreign parts; he may be put to a violent death for his crimes; he may, like Absalom, take arms and rebel against his more than father: but none of these conditions, I will venture to say, would ever cross the threshold of their fears, so as to trouble the fulness of joy with which they received so great, so unexpected, so undeserved a boon from their prince. They would not ask, that, besides going the extent of his royal prerogative, he should abrogate the laws for the sake of their child; that he should not only crown him, but, out of weak favouritism, suspend the regular process of law, and allow all things to run into disorder. Nay, such presumptuous thoughts would never enter into the most ungrateful mind on the reception of such a gift.

Such, parents, is the similitude; and the interpretation is plain. Your child—born in the meanest, most abject condition in the universe of God, in sin and misery; at the ban of the Divine law, which is holy, just, and good; rearing for the devil's service, to reap hereafter his reward—the Son of God and Saviour of men taketh, and with the waters of baptism washeth. These waters are His own precious blood, as "of a Lamb without blemish and without spot." He taketh your shipwrecked child as soon as his nativity, cleanseth him for heaven, prepareth for him a mansion and a crown that fadeth not away. He is minded to raise him to honour, and glory, and immortality; and giveth you the assurance thereof by the holy ordinance whereof we discourse. But He doth not abrogate the law of holiness, by which heaven is kept blessed, and without which heaven were like this earth, hardly worth the enjoying: He doth not open wide the gates to the admission of iniquity, or do away with the necessity of sanctification to every one who should be a partaker of its blessedness. The blessing consisteth in making salvation possible; in making it certain, through the obedience of faith and the regeneration of the Spirit. So that a duty is implicated with the gift, and the gift is the stimulus to the duty. The assurance of hope conveyed by this ordinance is the food of holiness and active well-doing, and the pledge of all necessary help from heaven.

How much more, therefore, ought parents to rejoice and be glad over this promise of eternal life, and rejoice over the second birth of their child among the sons of God, than over its natural birth into a world of sin and misery! So rejoice ye in the Rock of your salvation; so be ye glad in the Elder Brother of your family, who gave His life a ransom for the sins of all the rest, and hath prepared for them an inheritance of glory, if they continue faithful; whereof He hath given assurance unto all whom He alloweth to be baptized in the name of the Father, and of the Son, and of the Holy Ghost. Amen.

HOMILY II.

THE SEALING VIRTUE OF BAPTISM.

ACTS II. 38.

Repent, and be baptized every one of you in the name of Jesus Christ for the remission of sins, and ye shall receive the gift of the Holy Ghost.

SEEING, dearly beloved brethren, it hath pleased God, in His bountiful providence, to bring round unto us the near prospect of sitting down together to celebrate the Holy Supper of the Lord, I am moved by the remembrance of all His goodness in times past to make unto God the Father some offering of faithful and true doctrine, touching the person and work of His Son Jesus Christ, exhibited in the holy sacraments; and likewise some offering of painful and earnest exhortation unto all of you, His dear members, who have been baptized into His Church; that if it please the Father to accept the same, through the intercession of Christ, He may send forth the Holy Ghost, to sanctify therewith the ear of this congregation, to quicken your faith, and to work effectually on your hearts after what manner He wrought by this doctrine in the mouth of Peter, which when the multitude heard they were pricked in their hearts, and said unto Peter and the rest of the apostles, "Men and brethren, what shall we do?" And considering with myself, and finding from discourse with the brethren, how little alive the baptized are to the privileges which they have in Christ Jesus the Redeemer, and in the Holy Ghost their Sanctifier; and how Satan doth use this their ignorance to affright them, and keep them at a distance from the nourishment and strengthening of the Lord's table, whereby their weakness of faith is perpetuated, and their hardness of heart increased; I do now, in the name of God, and in the strength of His Spirit, draw near to every one who hath been sealed with the seal of baptism, in order to make known to them the very truth of their condition in the sight of God, from the day of their induction into the Church up to this hour. And this I do likewise for the sake of those whom I know to be established in the present truth, that your pure minds may be stirred up by way of remembrance; and that your hands may be strengthened to travail painfully and earnestly with the Lord in prayer for the sake of this people, and deal by wholesome counsel and well-timed exhortation with all His children whom you know to be lukewarm or asleep, or, like Felix, procrastinating and postponing the present and the pressing duty till some more convenient season. And now, may the Lord God of our fathers and forerunners in the Church be with us, while we endeavour to perform the good service which, for His glory and your health, we solemnly undertake!

When those men, whom it had pleased the Father, by the Holy Ghost, to quicken under that testimony which Peter gave on the day of Pentecost to the person and the glory of Christ, did cry out, under the strong and stinging conviction of the word brought home to their conscience, "Men and brethren, what shall we do?" Peter, without a moment's hesitation, as being prompted by the Holy Ghost, who had been just sent down from heaven, did make answer to them, "Repent, and be baptized every one of you in the name of Jesus Christ for the remission of sins, and ye shall receive the Holy Ghost: for the promise is unto you, and to your children, and to all that are afar off, even as many as the Lord our God shall call." The promise being made unto the parents and their children, every parent, who hath faith in Christ for his own salvation, may, and ought to have his child baptized, because his child is born in the covenant, and is holy: as it is written, "The unbelieving husband is sanctified by the wife, and the unbelieving wife is sanctified by the husband: else were your children unclean, but now are they holy;" that is, our children inherit a fellowship in the righteousness of Christ, which nothing but their own voluntary act of rejection and apostasy can deprive them of; and, as a seal of this righteousness, which they possess in virtue of their parents' faith, they are sealed with the outward sign of baptism, in order that it may be known and understood of all men that this is one of God's sealed ones. As the apostle argues in the fourth chapter of the Epistle to the Romans, that Abraham believed God, and it was accounted unto him for righteousness; which righteousness imputed to him possessing, in reward of his faith, he did then receive the sign of circumcision, as "the seal of the righteousness of the faith which he had yet being uncircumcised;" and therefore did transmit a holy seed unto his children, so that they also might, on the eighth day, receive the same seal of the same thing, even the righteousness which is by faith: so do I argue now, that our parents, having had faith, and made profession of the same upon every occasion in the presence of the Church, had likewise the righteousness which is by faith, and transmitted a holy seed unto their children; in the sign of which they also are, by the seal of baptism, set apart for a holy people unto the Lord. The sacrament of baptism signifieth, therefore, that we were born in covenant, and free to inherit all the privileges of the covenant, whereof the two principal are the remission of sins and the receiving of the Holy Ghost.

Whosoever, therefore, doth present himself or his child (for it is all one) to the Church for baptism, ought to be moved thereto by the strong desire to have the pledge of the forgiveness of his sins given to him from the hands of those whom God hath thereto appointed; but that of which it is the pledge he hath yet being unbaptized, as the necessary consequent upon faith: for where faith is, there also is remission of sins; and where faith is, there also ought baptism to be. "Believe, and be baptized." "Whosoever believeth, and is baptized, shall be saved." "Come and be baptized, and wash away thy sins," said Ananias unto Paul. And the eunuch said to Philip, "See, here is water: what doth hinder me to be baptized? And Philip said, If thou believest with all thine heart, thou mayest."

If any one hereupon ask me, And what need, then, of the sign or seal, when you say the righteousness is already present, as the sure consequence of faith? I answer, that faith is given by God for obedience, and righteousness is the power of obedience; and the first act of obedience, and the first fruit of faith, is our submission to the ordinance of baptism, which the Lord hath appointed. I answer, secondly, that faith is given to no man for himself alone, but for the whole Church of Christ; and therefore must he be baptized, in order to acknowledge his participation in and subjection unto the Church. I answer, thirdly, that though righteousness be already imputed unto him, it is not yet wrought in him: the imputation of the righteousness of Christ maketh him fit to enter into covenant with God, and into covenant he entereth by baptism; after which the Holy Spirit beginneth to work in his soul. There is an imputed righteousness of Christ, and there is an indwelling righteousness of the Holy Ghost: the former of which we have in consequence of faith while yet unbaptized; the latter of which we have in consequence of the covenant we have entered into by baptism. Whoso, therefore, refuseth the sign of baptism upon the plea of having already received the righteousness in virtue of faith, doth commit a double offence: one part, of the nature of ingratitude; the other, of the nature of indifference:—ingratitude for the great grace which he believeth himself to have received; and indifference to the great work which thereupon is begun to be wrought by the Holy Ghost.

The remission of sins, therefore, or the participation of Christ's justice, is that of which baptism is the seal in the present, and of which circumcision was the seal under the former, dispensation. This is what divines call the act of justification, in contradistinction from the work of sanctification, which till after the former proceedeth not. And towards that act of justification two things must concur: first, the sufficient ground of Christ's finished work, upon which a sinner may be justified; and this out of himself, seeing he hath as yet no righteousness wrought in him by the Holy Ghost: and, secondly, faith upon that outward ground of righteousness; and this must be in himself, in order to connect himself with the outward finished work of Christ. And to the concurrence of these two things two of the Persons of the blessed Trinity must conspire: first, the Father, to bestow faith, which is inseparably His own gift; and, secondly, the Son, to present the propitiation of His own sacrifice. The former of whom having pleased to bestow His gift of faith, as the latter hath been willing to offer Himself, there is no cause of hindrance why the person who hath been so graciously dealt with should not be admitted into the covenant; because he hath been freely justified by the blood of Christ, and, being so justified, he is a holy person in Their sight, and may not by the Church be counted unholy; and therefore may not be refused free admission into the holy covenant. And what I say of himself, I say also of his children, whom the apostle declareth that either parent rendereth holy. And having been admitted to the covenant, he is ever after to consider himself, and to be of the Church considered, as a justified person, in whom they are to look for, and assuredly to expect, the fruits of sanctification. And if such a one should at any time doubt of his justification by the blood of Christ; if he should be visited with fears of judgment; if the load of his sins should bear hard upon his conscience; it is to be treated as a temptation of Satan, leading him to doubt and disbelieve the great act of God, whereof he hath had the seal: and in all such cases the proper duty of the Church is to direct his attention to the instrument, and the seal of the instrument, by which God did solemnly ratify and confirm the act of his justification. For a man is not twice justified; he is justified once for all. Nor is his justification a work, but an act; of which act baptism is the seal. The work is sanctification, which therefore proceedeth ofttimes, yea always, by conviction of indwelling sin, by conversion of heart and mind, by rebukes for backslidings, and chastisements for slowness in the way of holiness. But if we ever lose sight of our justification, all is dark as midnight, and this work of sanctification doth necessarily stand still, and go backwards: for the Spirit proceedeth from the Father and the Son only into and upon those whom they have justified; not indiscriminately upon all, but only upon the just. Which justification, if, through the mists and blinds of Satan, we are brought at any time to doubt of—as indeed all may be, and perhaps at times are— the first thing to be done is to clear away that uncertainty by an explanation of, and a direct appeal unto, the sacrament of baptism, such as I am this day endeavouring to make. And for this end the seal is appointed, as well as for those others which have been mentioned above, in order that it may be the more signal and conspicuous in the eyes of a misled and misguided man. And until the uncertainty be wholly removed concerning our justification, it is a vain thing to think there can be any sanctification; and it is a vain thing to set the doubter upon this or that way and method of recovering himself. We must work *from* the faith of having obtained justification by the blood of Christ, not *unto* the obtaining of it; all work which otherwise proceedeth being a work of darkness, done in ignorance and in unbelief; yea, a work of sin and error, which thinketh to purchase the favour of God. And from all such blind working of penance it is the first effect of the blood of Christ to cleanse the conscience, in order to our being able to serve the living God: as it is written, (Heb. ix. 14,) "How much more shall the blood of Christ, who through the Eternal Spirit offered himself unto God, purge your conscience from dead works to serve the living God?"

And what brings the baptized into such doubtings, but the infirmity of their faith? They cannot believe that such an inheritance of undefiled righteousness is simply provided for them, without any doings of their own: and whoso will not believe this cannot receive the gift. There is but that one way, and no other, for every degree of guilt, and every dye of sinfulness. If you will not enter into the favour of God without money and without price, you shall never enter; for it is all of grace, from the first even unto the last. And, therefore, what I say to one I say to all the baptized who this day hear me: Ye are freely justified by the grace of God in Christ; ye have received the seal of the righteousness which is by faith; the possession of the Holy Ghost is your birth prerogative in Christ, if the possession of a sinful nature was your birth curse in Adam. And without faith in the justification which you have in Christ from the penalty and from the power of all your sins, simply, simply, you cannot be saved, nor proceed one step in or towards sanctification. And to encourage you unto faith, I do this day exhibit in your presence the great seal of God—even baptism. As one who would convince an unfaithful son of his inheritance doth shew him the seal of his father appended to the deed of bequeathment, so do I shew you this day the seal of your Father, in order, if the Lord will, to stir you up to know of what a holy stock you are, and to what holiness of life foreordained. But if you cannot believe, you cannot be established. And as it is the Father's prerogative to give faith at first, so I believe it to be His prerogative to revive and quicken faith; wherefore I commend all who doubt and misgive herein, to make their earnest suit unto the Father, and to plead all His promises, ever having their eye upon the seal of the covenant.—And so much for the first part of this subject, which is, "the remission of sins."

The other part of the dispensation of the grace of God under which the baptized are brought, is expressed in these words: "And ye shall receive the Holy Ghost." By which, they say, we ought to understand, not the outward gift of power, which hath ceased, but the inward gift of sanctification and fruitfulness, which we all believe to be co-essential in the salvation of a sinner with the work of Christ itself. But for my own part, I am inclined to understand both; for I cannot find by what writ of God any part of the spiritual gift was irrevocably removed from the Church. I see, indeed, that she hath lost the power which heretofore made her terrible as an army with banners; so also hath she lost the bright and glorious raiment which made her fair as the moon and clear as the sun; but why she may not hope, yea, assuredly believe, to have the former, when the Lord shall see it good, as well as the latter, is what I cannot see, the one being truly as supernatural a work of God as is the other. For that the works which the first disciples were enabled to work was a true fruit of the Holy Spirit, is not only manifest from their being constantly named by His name,—as in Acts x. 45, 46, "Because that on the Gentiles also was poured out the gift of the Holy Ghost: for they heard them speak with tongues, and magnify God," (this being the visible sign of the invisible grace,)—but is put beyond all doubt by the apostle's enumeration of the diversity of the Spirit's operations, as it is written in 1 Cor. xii. 7-11: "But the manifestation of the Spirit is given to every man to profit withal. For to one is given by the Spirit the word of wisdom; to another the word of knowledge by the same Spirit; to another faith by the same Spirit; to another the gifts of healing by the same Spirit; to another the working of miracles; to another prophecy; to another discerning of spirits; to another divers kinds of tongues; to another the interpretation of tongues: but all these worketh that one and the selfsame Spirit, dividing to every man severally as he will." Now, it is not for man, without some far more cogent reason than the mere fact of their being withdrawn, to preclude and prevent you from expecting the whole gift with which at any time it hath pleased God to endow His Church. It is not for any man, by an arbitrary distinction, for which I can find no warrant in Scripture, to name the one part ordinary and the other part extraordinary; and, upon the strength of this arbitrary division, to say the former was never intended to be continued, but the latter only. The better way of expressing the truth is to say, that in the first ages, the faith of the Church being great, her possession of the earnest of the Spirit was great: her expectation and her prayer being great, her answer and her receipt was great: but as she abused the day-spring which arose upon her from on high, and employed the glory of the morning in idle and unprofitable and wicked works; not valuing the gift of pure and holy light, of warm and vigorous life; the Lord from time to time withdrew His talents, and sentenced her to that poverty under which we now behold her;—and of which I will say, that while I bow with resignation to the will of God, I will never cease to use the withdrawal of these gifts as an argument of our being under the judgment and wrath of God; while I regard that account of the matter with which we content ourselves—that the extraordinary have been withdrawn from us, but the ordinary remain—as a poor shift to remove the blame off from our shoulders, and as making an unworthy use of the Divine purpose and intention. That it was a part of the Divine purpose to bring the Gentile Church under this deprivation of the Holy Ghost, as he formerly did bring the Jewish Church under blindness and deafness to the voice of their prophets, there can be no doubt: but, in like manner as they are continually rebuked, and were at length cast out from being the Lord's people, for this very cause, so do we underlie a present rebuke; and it ought to be the continual argument of the preachers of the truth, and to form the grounds of continual admonition and warning of judgment speedily about to come. And therefore I present it to you, my Christian brethren, as the ground of deepest humility in the sight of God, and most sorrowful repentance and painful intercession, like unto Daniel's, that we have been brought into this state of impotency, which argues a like state of unholiness. For these two, holiness in the inward parts and power in the outward, go together in the dispensations of the Spirit unto His Church. And being thus convinced in my mind, and moved in my spirit, I do not hesitate to affirm, that all we who have been baptized were baptized unto the fulness of the spiritual gifts, according as it might please God to divide unto every man, whether the word of wisdom, the word of knowledge, faith, the gift of healing, the working of miracles, prophecy, discerning of spirits, divers kind of tongues, or the interpretation of tongues; each one of these being the outward sign of a particular inward operation of the Spirit upon the soul, and qualifying the soul for profiting the Church with that inward gift which is given to it. These are the signs of the Spirit's presence: and observe what is the fruit of His presence: "The fruit of the Spirit is love, joy, peace, long-suffering, gentleness, goodness, faith, meekness, temperance," (Gal. v. 22, 23.) And again, "The fruit of the Spirit is in all goodness and righteousness and truth," (Eph. v. 9.) And again, "There is therefore now no condemnation to them which are in Christ Jesus, who walk not after the flesh, but after the Spirit. For the law of the Spirit of life in Christ Jesus hath made me free from the law of sin and death," (Rom. viii. 1, 2.) "But ye are not in the flesh, but in the Spirit, if so be that the Spirit of God dwell in you. Now if any man have not the Spirit of Christ, he is none of his. And if Christ be in you, the body is dead indeed because of sin; but the Spirit is life because of righteousness. But if the Spirit of him that raised up Jesus from the dead dwell in you, he that raised up

Christ from the dead shall also quicken your mortal bodies by his Spirit that dwelleth in you. Therefore, brethren, we are debtors, not to the flesh, to live after the flesh. For if ye live after the flesh, ye shall die: but if ye through the Spirit do mortify the deeds of the body, ye shall live. For as many as are led by the Spirit of God, they are the sons of God. For ye have not received the spirit of bondage again to fear; but ye have received the Spirit of adoption, whereby we cry, Abba, Father. The Spirit itself beareth witness with our spirit, that we are the children of God: and if children, then heirs; heirs of God, and joint-heirs with Christ; if so be that we suffer with him, that we may be also glorified together. For I reckon that the sufferings of this present time are not worthy to be compared with the glory which shall be revealed in us," (ver. 9-18.)

Now, brethren, never doubting that baptism is that solemn transaction of the Church, whereby she doth introduce believers, and the children of believers, into the inheritance of the Holy Ghost, because it is always so declared, as in our text, I solemnly charge you all, and with you the whole Christian Church, as being deficient, and destitute, and having been deprived of these things in consequence of your unbelief in that great and gracious promise of the Holy Ghost, whereinto Christ entered when He ascended up on high; which He received for the sake of men, yea, even of the rebellious; which He is always ready and most desirous to bestow wherever His Father hath bestowed faith to receive it; and to the end of for ever declaring and signifying the same unto His Church, He hath appointed this sign for the judgment of all, this seal of the righteousness of all who believe. If I understand anything of sound theology, this is the sum and substance of it, in a few words: That the Lord Jesus Christ, in virtue of His incarnation and humiliation to the death, hath received from the Father the gift of the Holy Spirit,—regeneration, resurrection, and eternal life, with all power in heaven and in earth; which now lie all treasured up in Him, not for selfish enjoyment, but for right welcome communication unto every one who hath received faith from the Father to apprehend and possess them. This only He waiteth for, that the Father shall have first bestowed faith: for without faith no gift can be apprehended or appropriated, and that faith is the gift of the Father. So that still, as is most natural, the Father hath the pre-eminency and the precedency, Christ the instant and necessary succession, and the Holy Ghost the continued operation: and these two, the Father and the Son, concur in the salvation of every sinner; and every sinner beareth testimony to the Father and the Son.

Now, our assurance of the Father's willingness to grant us faith, is derived from our knowledge that He hath sent His Son Jesus Christ to seek and save sinners, of whom we are the chief; and after bringing Christ through the experience of the most abject sinner, hath exalted Him above all height, and hath put into His hands this infinite store of righteousness and power, for the express purpose of distribution to the Church. And being thus taught that it is of God's good purpose to set His seal upon a Church, and perceiving that seal to be baptism, with which we have been sealed, what letteth or hindereth, what moveth not, what stirreth not up to draw near to the Father with all humble request and reverend acknowledgment of His only will, His sovereign right to save or to destroy; and to entreat Him with all earnestness to have mercy upon us, and grant us faith, that we may receive the Holy Spirit from the hands of Christ, and so testify to the glory of the Father and the Son? And I am well assured that such prayers presented to the Father, with such an enlightened knowledge, and in such a devout and reverent spirit, will be answered; because He is disposed, yea, and loveth, to bestow the Holy Spirit upon them that ask Him, with what affectionateness a mother doth love to give the sincere milk of her breast unto her child, or a father to divide his morsel with his hungry son.

And now, though this is not the proper place, being minded to treat largely of the Lord's Supper, I may observe in passing, and for the sake of the light which it reflects upon the subject of baptism, that as I have already presented to you the sacrament of baptism, as the seal of your justification, while yet out of Christ, I do present unto you the Lord's Supper, as the seal of your union unto Christ, of your fellowship with His body, of your membership in His Church.

This union you have consequent upon your baptism, not present in it. It is the work of the Holy Spirit to effect it by the progress of your sanctification; and the Supper of the Lord is the seal of your possessing it. And whosoever sitteth down at the table of the Lord doth, by his own act, declare that he is a member of Christ; and upon his declaration he hath a right to be so esteemed of by all the saints. The sealing is the last act of every covenant, and maketh it fast and sure. Now, there are these two seals connected with our salvation, "Baptism and the Lord's Supper;" and therefore there must be two distinct things which they seal up, conclude, and determine. These two things are our justification and our sanctification: the former of which we come to the inheritance of in right of our father's faith; the latter of which is a work accomplished in and upon ourselves, in virtue of which we may transmit the holy seed to our children also. Of the righteousness or justification which we have yet being unbaptized, baptism is the seal; and it is, at the same time, the promise of a work which is yet to be wrought upon us. That work is the sanctification of the Holy Ghost, wherewith we are sealed until the day of redemption. Of this work, begun and in progress, the Lord's Supper is the seal; and, therefore, every one who comes forward to the table of the Lord doth solemnly declare before the Church God's faithfulness to the promise which was made to him in his baptism; that already it is begun to be fulfilled; that already he is conscious of faith given, whereby he hath assurance of justification by the blood of Christ, and of the new life even now begun within his soul. To such an introduction and commencement of new life within himself, every one who cometh to the Lord's table giveth solemn testimony; otherwise how shall he be able to handle, to eat, and to live on spiritual food? But he testifies to nothing but the beginning and commencement of such a work, and least of all to its perfection. For while the Lord's Supper is doubtless a seal of the work of the Spirit begun, it is likewise of the nature of a nourishment or food for the continuance and growth of the same; there being therein presented that elemental life of Christ's holy humanity by which the Holy Spirit doth feed and foster up the children of Christ into perfect manhood. For as by Adam's fall, in him the well of life was corrupted, out of which, by natural generation, the evil streams have all proceeded; so, in Christ's resurrection, was the well of life purified, out of which all the holy streams of the Church proceed, by the Holy Spirit, to and into those upon whom the Father bestoweth faith. And as the universal death and corruption came to pass without any ubiquity or sublimation of Adam's body, so as to comprehend us all who were truly in it comprehended by the law of God which said "multiply;" so doth the regeneration and resurrection come to pass from the risen Christ, without any ubiquity of His body, or sublimation of it, or transubstantiation of bread and wine thereinto, or consubstantiation therewith; but by the will and purpose of the Father that it should so communicate its holy virtues unto all those whom He had seen it good to comprehend in Him in the purpose, and in the manifestation to give unto Him by faith. And the Holy Spirit, which proceedeth from both to execute their mutual covenant, doth proceed to carry into effect what the Father hath given the beginning to by working faith; what Christ hath given the materials for, in the work of His incarnation and resurrection from the dead. These materials, with which the Spirit worketh this work, are continually set forth to faith (for sense hath nothing to do with it, except as a help to faith when sanctified, and a hindrance when unsanctified) upon the sacramental table, which may be regarded as ever spread before the Church; and from these the Holy Spirit, quickening in us all spiritual appetite and desire, doth continually move us to partake the strength of a resurrection life: and so we are nourished up from strength to strength, and from holiness to holiness, and from glory to glory, by the Spirit of our God.

Such, brethren, according to my knowledge and ability, within the scope of one discourse, is the doctrine which I believe and teach from the Holy Scriptures concerning the personal seal of baptism, and such is the constant testimony of the orthodox Church unto this day. And I have now to press it upon the consideration of all who hear me, if haply it may please the Father to grant you faith to the acknowledging of the truth; if it may please Him to shew you your free justification by the blood of the everlasting covenant, your setting your seal thereto in the person of your father or sponsor, and His sealing thereto in consideration of their faith; if it may please Him to shine upon you with the light of that favour which you have in Him, unseal your eyes to look upon it, and, delighting your heart therewith, rouse you to desire strength to do Him honour. Upon the springing up of which desire, behold the table of spiritual strength is spread for you! Give me ear, while I lay this matter to every man's conscience.

Our fathers, men and brethren, receiving the word of the promise, which is written in all the Scriptures, and which hath been proceeded on in all the dispensations of the great God our Saviour, that the children of the believers are privileged to all and sundry the privileges of their faithful parents or sponsors; I say, having had grace given them to hold fast the true doctrine of the grace of God in Christ Jesus, and to be found unblemished and faultless before the Church, did present us, the fruit of their loins, unto God, and ask that we might be received into the number of the children, and named in the Name of the Father, and of the Son, and of the Holy Ghost. Whereby, in consideration of their faith, and in the eternal strength of the Divine promise, and in virtue of the unceasing honour with which God honoureth all His ordinances, and most chiefly the holy sacraments, we, who were so presented before God, and admitted by His Church, and hallowed with that most holy Name, do remain unto this day in the sight of God, and are not otherwise regarded than as, a "chosen generation, a royal priesthood, a holy nation, a peculiar people, that we should shew forth the praises of Him who hath called us out of darkness into His marvellous light." This I say in faith, nothing doubting—God grant that you may receive it in faith, nothing doubting!—that every one of you baptized in the Name of the Father, and of the Son, and of the Holy Ghost, are, to use the words of our text, living under a dispensation "for the remission of sins, and the receiving of the Holy Ghost;" or, to use the words of the Confession of our National Reformed Church, "are ingrafted in Christ Jesus, to be made partakers of His justice, by which our sins are covered and remitted;" or, to use the language of our Shorter Catechism, "are ingrafted into Christ, and made partakers of the benefits of the covenant of grace, and engaged to be the Lord's." Upon this ground I take my firm stand, and, feeling my footing sure, I proceed to wrestle with the enemy in the Church, who hath perverted many through unbelief, and would pervert all. And what I say unto one, I say unto all the baptized, that if you have not solemnly abjured the holy Name of the Father, and the Son, and the Holy Ghost, or by the Church been excommunicated for the pravity of your disposition and the wickedness of your lives,—which, I trust, is the case with none that heareth me,—you are, and have been, and shall continue to be, regarded by the Church as her children, to be instructed in all the liberties and immunities of the house of God; to be counselled with all the wisdom of the Spirit of God, and exhorted to enter into all the plentifulness of the grace of God. And he who would say you nay to any desire, request, or possession in the inheritance of Christ, is not a well-instructed steward over the house, but a hoarder of that grace bringing salvation which hath appeared unto all men; a grudger of that wine and milk which is to be given without money and without price; a fraudulent keeper of the keys of the kingdom of heaven, not permitting those who have a right to enter in, and this because they will not enter in themselves.

I solemnly do you to wit, therefore, brethren, every one of you who hath been baptized into Christ, that you have ever since been living under the dispensation of the grace of God; which consisteth of two parts,—the remission of your sins, and the receiving of the Holy Ghost. And at whatever time the Lord may be pleased to awaken you to a sense of your sinfulness—whether original, as derived from the corrupt stock of Adam, or actual, as wrought out by your own will—instead of being overwhelmed with the sight of them, and dispirited from undertaking the work of repentance and reformation, and plunged into recklessness and despair, or gradually lost again in lukewarmness and indifference—all which actings of natural doubt and fear, infant baptism is on very purpose contrived and established of God to prevent—you ought at such a time of awakening convictions to look to this dispensation of the forgiveness of sins under which you live, and behold the grace of God extended like a canopy of light over your head. As those who are not children of natural darkness, but of revealed light; who are not heirs of reprobation, but of salvation; and have God's faithful word pledged to your own selves, and His all-including covenant. sealed unto yourselves; you ought to look back unto the sacrament of baptism, and act faith thereon; and so, by the apprehension of faith, receive the forgiveness of sins assured unto your faith by that most solemn pledge: and being comforted with the assurance of God's grace in Jesus Christ, bless His name that He hath not left you to perish in your ignorance and impenitency, but at length by His Holy Spirit quickened you to the sense of your sinfulness; and by the same Spirit shewed you the promise which hath been made for your forgiveness in His faithful word, and sealed upon you by the blessed ordinances of His Church.

You ought not, therefore, dear brethren, to stifle the convictions of sinfulness which are brought to your minds whenever the prospect of the sacrament of the Lord's Supper is presented to you, but rather to bless God that He hath not seared your conscience with a red-hot iron, or given you up to judicial blindness: and you ought to say, "For I do know hereby that the Lord is dealing with me by His Holy Spirit; that He is stirring me up to perceive my true estate; that He is not leaving me alone: therefore now, O Lord, speak unto Thy servant all the mind of Thy Holy Spirit, for doctrine, for reproof, for correction, and for instruction in righteousness; and by Thy grace I will forego my evil thoughts, and forsake my evil ways, and turn unto Thee: for Thou hast mercy, and Thou dost abundantly pardon." But doth any one say, "How do I know that He will have mercy? and how do I know that He will abundantly pardon? for it is written, 'He will have mercy upon whom He will have mercy; and whom He will He hardeneth.' Now, how know I that I am not one of those whom He pleaseth to harden?" I answer: What kind of knowledge, or what kind of demonstration wouldst thou? Hast thou not the Holy Word in thy hand, continually inviting and entreating thee, which He taketh away from those whom He hath given over, that they may not trample it under foot? Art thou not sitting under a gospel ministry, which continually teacheth and admonisheth, and instructeth thee to be reconciled unto God; but which God maketh dumb or deceitful when He intendeth evil to any Church? Dost thou not behold His Spirit moving upon thy right hand and upon thy left, taking by the hand sinners as great as thee, and washing them white in the blood of Christ? Now, when God is visiting a people in His wrath, He doth withdraw His Spirit with His word, and no new branches are graffed into Christ, but those which seemed to be graffed drop off on every side. But still dost thou desire some more immediate and personal application of the matter home unto thyself? 'Tis well. Thou hast it in the sacrament of baptism, whereby thou wast admitted into the blessed bond of the covenant: to thee forgiveness of sin was promised; to thee the working of the Spirit was promised; to thee thyself, by thyself, and not in company with any other. And what more wouldst thou? Thou wouldst some sign of God's faithfulness done unto thyself? Indeed, thou art very hard of faith, my brother, and, like Thomas, dost tempt God exceedingly; but, as to Thomas, the love of the Lord doth grant this grace unto thee: for hast thou not the working of this conviction of sin in thy heart, whereupon we are reasoning together? Art thou not now stirred up to take a thought and concern about thy salvation? Art thou not ill at ease, and seeking for something to rest upon? Or whence cometh this earnest questioning of me for some ground of assurance that God hath not given thee up? I tell thee, that if God had given thee up thou wouldst have had none of those remorseful feelings, none of those alarming fears. If thou hadst been dead, thou wouldst have had no scent of the living waters. And so hast thou the sign thou soughtest, that God is desirous to accomplish upon thee that good work which He pledged to thee in thy baptism. And more than this thou never shalt have on this side the resurrection. If thou wishest for a visible sensible sign, beware how thou temptest God with thine unbelief: He may permit Satan to give it thee, in order to destroy thee. But wait for this in the Lord's good time, and in the fulness of that time it shall be given; when the glorious Lord, who is now hidden, shall come forth in His majesty and power; and we who have believed upon Him when not seen, shall be raised up in His likeness to look on the face of His manifest glory.

I say not but thou mayest be left a reprobate: it is not mine to deal out the Father's sovereign grace, with which my Lord and Saviour doth not intermeddle. But this I say, that if thou, having such significations made unto thee, such covenants sealed with thee, of His mercy and favour unto thyself, dost not accept the outward demonstration of the Father's good-will made unto thee; neither drawest nigh to inquire reverently at His oracle; and as thou hearest of the mystery of His free grace from the oracle of His only-begotten Son, dost not, with bended knee and suppliant spirit, entreat the sovereign Lord and Father of all, through the mediation of His Son and thy Brother Jesus Christ; then, seest thou, thou art worthy to be rejected, and rejected thou wilt be: for never since the world fell hath any son of man obtained any good and precious gift otherwise than by the hearty acknowledgment of the Father's sovereignty to grant or to withhold, and of our own willingness to be wholly at His disposal—for good, as not having deserved it; for evil, as having deserved it—according as it is most conducive to His own glory. Behold, then, how this doctrine of eternal election and eternal reprobation is only an acknowledgment of God's will to do what seemeth to Him good with the fallen creatures; to raise again, if it pleaseth Him; to visit with wrath to what extent it pleaseth Him: and if so with the fallen creatures, then so with me, who am a fallen creature; and so with thee; and so with all: and to shrink from believing and from declaring this, or to put in some salvo to soften it, is really nothing less than to deny the will and liberty of God to do with a fallen creature what pleaseth Him: if to save, then of His free grace to save; if to punish, then of His justice to punish. And the gospel begins to build upon this foundation of God's freeness to do His utmost wrath upon every fallen creature;

and whatever He saveth it giveth to the account of His free grace. Now unto all of you He hath made the overtures, and concluded the covenant of salvation: He hath shut you up in sinfulness, only that He might remember you in mercy; which mercy if you despise, then indeed you do prove the terrible power of sin in yourselves and against yourselves, and must be given up to eternal and unchanging perdition. One step forward unto which perdition is to reject the admonition of the Holy Spirit, pointing out your sinfulness; and, by my hand, pointing to you baptism as the dispensation of the forgiveness of sin.

HOMILY III.

THE DOCTRINE TAUGHT IN BAPTISM.

ROM. VI. 3, 4.

Know ye not, that so many of us as were baptized into Jesus Christ were baptized into his death? Therefore we are buried with him by baptism into death: that like as Christ was raised up from the dead by the glory of the Father, even so we also should walk in newness of life.

ALL the conclusions which we have derived in the two preceding Homilies concerning the standing of the baptized in the Church, and which we are hereafter to derive concerning the standing of the engaging parent or sponsor, flow necessarily from the doctrine of baptism, as we find it laid down in the Holy Scriptures; which, therefore, it may be necessary to examine at large, with a reference to the passages on which it is founded: and, first, we carry your attention to the text and context, where the apostle, having proposed the question, "Shall we continue in sin, that grace may abound?" immediately maketh answer, "God forbid. How shall we, then, that are dead to sin, live any longer therein?" In which words he represents the Christian Church to which he wrote, as having no longer any power to sin living in them: and what he says to that Christian Church he would, doubtless, have said to any. Now, from whence doth he derive this incapacity or deadness to sin? He deriveth it from baptism, in these words which immediately follow: "Know ye not, that as many of us as were baptized into Jesus Christ were baptized into his death?" And what is meant by baptism into Christ's death? This the apostle explains in the next verse: "Therefore we are buried with him by baptism into death: that, like as Christ was raised up from the dead by the glory of the Father, even so we also should walk in newness of life."

Baptism, it would appear, then, is a symbol of that death and resurrection in the members, which was accomplished in the fact upon Christ the Head, and remaineth to be accomplished in the fact upon every one of the members. If we inquire, then, what was accomplished upon Christ in the fact of His death and resurrection; we learn, that the body, in which He bore our sin and carried our sorrows, fell into the grave; and the body, free from the imputation of sin, according to the Spirit of holiness, arose in power and majesty from the grave. Of which, if baptism be the symbol, it must signify and seal that our natural body of sin and death is buried in the waters, and our spiritual body of holiness and power in the Holy Ghost ariseth thence. Upon which idea the apostle immediately adds, in the next verse, "For if we have been planted together in the likeness of his death, we shall be also in the likeness of his resurrection." Here he speaks of our "being planted" in the likeness of His death, as having been done at our baptism into Christ; which he had formerly called baptism into Christ's death, and a burial with Him by baptism into death. Which three expressions—"Baptism into Christ's death," "buried with Him by baptism into death," and "being planted together in the likeness of His death"—being all used as synonymous with the expression, "baptized into Jesus Christ," do put it beyond a doubt that the true meaning of baptism is a death and burial of the natural man under water. But lest any doubt should be left on this matter, hear what the apostle saith, in the 6th, 7th, and 8th verses: "Knowing this, that our old man is crucified with him, that the body of sin might be destroyed; that henceforth we should not serve sin. For he that is dead is freed from sin. Now if we be dead with Christ, we believe that we shall also live with him." Can there, then, remain a doubt upon your minds that baptism is intended by God to signify and seal our being put to death in the flesh, and crucified as to all fleshly desires and enjoyments; so that, with the members of our body and the affections of our mind, we should be under the law of sin and death no longer, but under the law of the spirit of life; that we should walk no more after the flesh, but after the spirit?

Doth baptism, then, leave us in the state of death and burial? This question is answered likewise by the apostle; first, in the 4th verse, "That like as Christ was raised up from the dead by the glory of the Father, even so we also should walk in newness of life." Which words define with precision another idea or doctrine signified in baptism, that the baptized are crucified and buried with Christ only that they may receive of that glory of the Father which raised Christ from the dead; that quickening power of the Holy Ghost, into the possession and disposal of which he then entered, and, being quickened therewith, might walk in newness of life. The same doctrine is taught in these words of the 5th verse, "We shall be also in the likeness of his resurrection;" and in these words of the 8th verse, "We shall also live with him." Which two expressions refer, not to the future life of the resurrection, but to the present life of the saint after baptism, or to the present life of faith, which is everlasting: according to the words of our Lord, "He that believeth on me hath everlasting life." That this is the true meaning of the expressions is manifest from the 11th, 12th, and 13th verses: "Likewise reckon ye also yourselves to be dead indeed unto sin, but alive unto God through Jesus Christ our Lord. Let not sin therefore reign in your mortal body, that ye should obey it in the lusts thereof. Neither yield ye your members as instruments of unrighteousness unto sin; but yield yourselves unto God, as those that *are* alive from the dead, and your members as instruments of righteousness unto God."

There can be no doubt, therefore, that baptism is intended by God to signify and seal, secondly, our vitality derived from the act and from the power of Christ's resurrection; whereof all the after-life of faith and holiness is but the various forms and actings. Both these effects of baptism in the believer—the death unto sin, and the life unto holiness—are the work of the Holy Ghost; even as, in the great antitype of baptism, it was by the Holy Ghost that Christ, though made sin for us, did offer Himself without spot unto God, and by the Holy Ghost was raised from the dead. And this work of putting us to death in the flesh, and quickening us in the spirit, the Holy Ghost worketh during all the days of the believer's life, yea, and in every act thereof: which is a twofold act; one part being mortification of nature, and the other part regeneration of grace: the former attended with sorrow and suffering and anguish; the latter with peace and joy and blessedness: the former being of the nature of an unwilling sacrifice all our life long; the latter turning it into a willing sacrifice: that which maketh it willing being not ourselves, but the Holy Ghost in us. But while we teach that this work of killing and making alive again extendeth over all our life, we regard it, with the apostle, to be all sealed, and given unto us like a deed or instrument at our baptism: and we maintain, that no one who hath neglected or rejected baptism, having it in his power, neither may expect, nor will receive, these effects and privileges of the Holy Spirit; seeing he hath not cared to possess himself of the instrument by which the tenure is held, nor to honour the great seal of the Head of the Church, which maketh that instrument valid. And I will say, moreover, that until believers will honour baptism as the great object of faith, and look back to it in all their struggles with the natural man, in all their longings and cravings for the Holy Spirit, they will not succeed so effectually either in the one or in the other. But into this it is not my present business to enter, but rather to confirm these positions of doctrine laid down above by some other passages of Scripture, of which I choose next that in 1 Pet. iii. 20–22, where, having occasion to refer unto the deluge, he thus expresseth himself: "When once the long-suffering of God waited in the days of Noah, while the ark was a preparing, wherein few, that is, eight souls were saved by water. The like figure whereunto" (or the antitype to which water) "even baptism doth also now save us (not the putting away of the filth of the flesh, but the answer of a good conscience toward God,) by the resurrection of Jesus Christ: who is gone into heaven, and is on the right hand of God; angels and authorities and powers being made subject unto him."

In this passage baptism is declared to be the antitype which answereth to the waters of the deluge: by which water Noah and his family were saved; the waters of the deluge being the means of Noah's preservation from the wickedness of the earth which they drowned. And as it is here declared that these waters were typical of the waters of baptism, which separate and preserve us from the wickedness and death of the natural man, we conclude, that baptism is to the world the token of their perdition, as it is to the Church the token of their salvation; drawing between them a sacred gulf, which cannot be crossed but by passing through the waters of baptism,—baptism being, as it were, the signification to the world that it is lying under the curse of the deluge: which was a fuller measure of the primeval curse than had been laid on man at the fall, bringing with it the shortening of the term of life; and, as I believe, the deterioration of all the elements on which life dependeth. For as baptism bringeth the nature of man into a state of suffering, crucifixion, and death with Christ, far more afflictive than what the unbaptized, who give nature its own curse, are liable unto; so seemeth it to me, that the deluge brought the whole elemental and animated earth into that state of disturbance and miserable travailing bondage into which they were not brought at the fall. And thus the deluge, while it hath in it of the nature of a punishment, hath in it of the nature of a redemption; and was truly, as I believe, the baptism of the earth and of human nature into a necessary miserable estate of longing pregnancy, until the time of its future baptism with fire should arrive. And now a Church was separated from the sinful mass of men, and holy things from the sinful mass of things, which might continue patiently to maintain the witness until the Lord should come to administer the second baptism of fire, and deliver all nature of her glorious birth. And in this way I conceive the deluge to have been typical of baptism, and baptism to be the antitype of the deluge. In confirmation of which, Paul, in the First Epistle to the Corinthians, declares, "That all the fathers were under the cloud, and all passed through the sea, and were all baptized into Moses in the cloud and in the sea." Where I observe again, that the water of the cloud, and afterwards the water of the sea, coming between them and the Egyptians, was the means of their preservation. And, moreover, in general, I may observe, that the emblem of the Holy Spirit under the present dispensation is water; and we are said to be born of water and of the Spirit, and our regeneration is called the washing of regeneration. And our Lord gave the promise of the Holy Spirit in these words: "If any man thirst, let him come to me and drink: he that believeth on me, as the Scriptures hath said, out of his belly shall flow rivers of living water."

That dispensation of this age was, as I judge, introduced by the deluge, and shall continue until the baptism with the Holy Ghost and with fire, which the earth in the day of its regeneration shall receive. And this is what I understand in the expression in the text before us, "Baptism, the antitype to which water." Now, with respect to the remainder of the text, for which indeed we quoted it, it is declared, that baptism now saveth us; which certainly any one will allow to be a very weighty declaration, especially when it is corroborated by such texts as these, "Repent, and be baptized, every one of you, for the remission of sins, and ye shall receive the Holy Ghost." "He that believeth and is baptized shall be saved." And again, "As many of you as have been baptized into Christ, have put on Christ." In the face of such expressions as these, no one surely ought to slight or undervalue the sacrament of baptism. Then the question is, What is this baptism that saveth us? And the apostle answereth it in a parenthesis, saying, "Not the putting away of the filth of the flesh," which water in itself can do, "but the answer of a good conscience towards God;" which cannot otherwise be done than by the application of the blood of Christ, in the hands of the Holy Spirit, according as it is written, "How much more shall the blood of Christ, who, through the Eternal Spirit, offered himself without spot unto God, purge your conscience from dead works!" So that the word "baptism," in the mouth of the apostle carried with it the whole substance of what baptism was appointed for; and was the name of the thing signified, importing the washing of the Holy Ghost; as indeed it doth in many other passages, of which I have quoted some already, and of which I may now quote some more. Eph. v. 26, "Christ gave himself for his church, that he might sanctify and cleanse it with the washing of water by the word;" where the washing of water is made to include the power of the word of Christ, which is spirit and life. 1 Cor. xii. 13, "For by one Spirit are we all baptized into one body, whether we be Jews or Gentiles, whether we be bond or free; and have been all made to drink into one spirit:" where the word "baptism" is made to include all that work of the Spirit by which we are taken out of the body of sin, and united into the body of Christ. It is therefore a most beggarly spoliation and wicked abuse of the mystery which that word and act were intended to convey, for the spiritualisers of these times to talk of water-baptism, and mock this holy sacrament as a ceremony, which the apostles ever laboured to deepen into a mystery, and exalt into a heavenly symbol. This baptism, the antitype of the waters of the deluge, doth save us, saith the apostle, by bearing up the ark of the Church, and floating it far above the wickedness which was consumed in the under-ground convulsions of the deep: and he addeth, that the thing which he speaketh of as being endowed with such wondrous virtue, is not the outward washing of the flesh, but the inward washing of the Holy Ghost, which is intended therein; and by being present in the act, doth sanctify it from an ordinary washing or ablution into a holy symbol and most sacred institution of the Lord Jesus Christ. And how it hath this virtue of saving us, he informeth us in these words, "By the resurrection of Jesus Christ, who is gone into heaven, and is on the right hand of God; angels, and authorities, and powers, being made subject unto him." To the power of Christ's resurrection he doth attribute the power of baptism to save the Church: from the exaltation of Christ in the heavens, and His session at the right hand of God, and the subjection unto Him of all angels, and authorities, and powers, the apostle doth derive the saving power of baptism. Baptism, therefore, must be no mean nor common thing, which is not to be accomplished save by such mighty ministry. Common thing! It must be the chief work of the Son of God to accomplish it: not the work of His flesh; no, nor yet the work of His death; but the work of His resurrection and ascension and omnipotent power. To baptize with the Holy Ghost and with fire, was the great work which John the Baptist set out for Him. "I indeed baptize you with water unto repentance; but he that cometh after me shall baptize you with the Holy Ghost and with fire." The end of John's baptism was repentance, "unto repentance;" but the end of Christ's baptism was "the Holy Ghost and fire." Now, on the day of Pentecost, when He had given the Holy Ghost unto His apostles, and Peter's preaching had converted many, who asked what they should do, "Peter answered, Repent and be baptized every one of you, in the name of Jesus Christ unto the remission of sins, and ye shall receive the gift of the Holy Ghost:" upon which I have two things to remark. First, that while John's baptism terminated in repentance, "unto repentance," that of the apostles, under which we now are, terminates in "remission of sins;" the one leading to the discernment of sin, the other to the taking it away out of our sight. Secondly, that the gift promised upon baptism was the gift of the Holy Ghost, and no more. Now, John had announced Christ as being about to baptize, not only with the Holy Ghost, but with fire also; and His apostles confine themselves to the Holy Ghost only, whose emblem, as hath been said, is water; even though they themselves had received the Holy Ghost in the form of cloven tongues of fire, they made no allusion thereto in the constituting of the Church, but restricted the gift unto the Holy Ghost. Because, as I said above, the baptism of fire yet awaiteth us who have believed in Christ, and shall be received in that great day when the Lord shall come in flaming fire, and the elements shall melt with fervent heat, and the earth and the works that are therein shall be burned up. Then when the earth receiveth her baptism of fire, and is restored to that blessed condition, of which Isaiah (lxv. 6) and Peter (2 Epist. iii.) make such glorious mention, we shall receive that second part of Christ's high office, for which the Baptist announced Him to the Jewish nation when he said, "He that cometh after me shall baptize you with the Holy Ghost and with fire." Christ himself, who is the great prototype of all His members, went through these two several stages Himself; the former at His baptism, when He received the baptism of water and of the Holy Ghost in the form of a dove; the latter, when in His grave, He put on

His resurrection glory, which is called (Phil. iii. 21) the body of His glory. But forasmuch as the baptism with the Holy Ghost, whose emblem is water, by which we are regenerated, and that other baptism with fire which we shall receive in the grave, and by which we shall be raised up in power and glory, do both follow upon and proceed out of the resurrection of Christ, we do not cease to maintain with the apostle, in both the texts which we have examined, that the baptism of Christ, or the baptism into Christ, which we administer in the Church, is a consequence of Christ's resurrection, and a perpetual token unto the Church, both that He is risen from the dead, and that He hath entered into power and glory; and every baptized person liveth by, and ought to live upon, the resurrection of Christ. And the life which the Church now liveth in the flesh, is a life of wrestling against, and suffering in the flesh and in the world, which she is able to carry on by no power inherent in the death of Christ, but by a power inherent only in His resurrection. The life of every member of Christ, the life of the whole Church, His body, a first-fruits of Christ's resurrection, is, in truth, a resurrection life, which we have given to us in a degree, to the end we may be sealed and pledged, (and, as we say in Scotland, *arled*,) by an earnest, and may not doubt, but believe and testify of the resurrection, first of Christ, then of His Church, then of all creation, which groaneth and is in bondage even until now; and without bearing it in mind continually, that the life of the believer after baptism is a resurrection life, you can neither understand the spirit of our Lord's life from His baptism in Bethabara till His agony in the garden; nor can you understand any of those Scriptures wherein the life of the believer is described; for example, such expressions as these: "We are quickened with Christ; we are raised up together with Christ, and made to sit with him in heavenly places, and blessed in him with all spiritual blessings in heavenly places." "If ye be risen with Christ, seek the things that are above, where Christ sitteth at the right hand of God." "He that hath suffered in the flesh hath ceased from sin." These, and many other expressions, are utterly unintelligible but upon the great principle which we have been this day laying down, that the mystery and meaning of baptism is a death and burial and resurrection done upon us in the body by the power of the risen Christ; and that our life in the Church is intended to be a resurrection-life, and the Church itself to be a great demonstration and continual witness, not by word of mouth merely, but by its presence upon the earth, its constitution, its holy doctrine and discipline, its whole conformation of that resurrection Church which is to be constituted over the kingdom of our Christ. And so well was this understood in the primitive times, that Satan himself caught hold of it, and perverted the Church by its means, gradually bringing it to pass, that the Church should set herself up to be the very resurrection Church, with her Melchizedek Head, and her worldly dominion, and other complements which were not permitted her to hold otherwise than by hope. And thus was the apostasy constituted, which is nothing but the converting of a part into the whole, of an earnest penny into the whole inheritance, and a cunning delusion to make men believe that it is so; which, though we Protestants have not accomplished in the same outward grandeur and visible puppet-show as the Papacy, yet have we committed, or rather we are committing, the very same substantial error in making the Pentecostal measure of the Spirit equal to the work of bringing in the kingdom: which error is the more to be condemned in these times, when really and truly, of the waters of the Spirit which then flowed forth, there seems to me hardly a spoonful present in the whole Church.

But, to return to the law and the testimony, I request, for the further confirmation of the doctrine which I have taught in this discourse, your attention to another passage of Scripture, which occurreth in the second chapter of Paul's Epistle to the Colossians, at the 11th verse. He is entreating them to be upon their guard against the invasion of philosophy, and the entering in of traditions into the Church of Christ; and, to the end of declaring his completeness for all knowledge and for all faith, he saith, "In him dwelleth all the fulness of the Godhead bodily:" to whom, therefore, nothing could be, nor might be, added. Then, to the end of declaring their full participation of this all-comprehending fulness of

Christ, he addeth, "Ye are complete" (filled) "in him who is the Head of all principality and power." And, to the end of guarding them against the temptation of returning to the bondage of the ordinances and beggarly elements of the law, he addeth, (verse 11,) "In whom also ye are circumcised with the circumcision made without hands, in putting off the body of the sins of the flesh by the circumcision of Christ." To understand which expression, you must bear in mind, that circumcision cut the Jew off completely from all participation in the superstitions of the rest of the world; and so the apostle means to say, that the circumcision of Christ cut the Christians off from all participation in the ordinances of the Jews: and therefore, after being circumcised therewith, that it was as wicked a thing for any one to go back to Moses and his beggarly elements, as it would have been for Moses and the Jews to go back to the superstitions of Egypt. Now, what meaneth he by the circumcision of Christ? It is said to be done without hands; and, therefore, a supernatural and spiritual act. It is said to be attended with the putting off the body of the sins of the flesh; and, therefore, to deliver from all those burdensome ablutions and purifications, and other carnal ordinances, which, having for their object the keeping of the flesh clean, are necessarily abrogated when the flesh itself, or the body of the sins of the flesh, is altogether put off: this supernatural and spiritual act, called the circumcision of Christ, doth therefore put away that body of sin and death whose presence the ceremonial law declared, and whose uncleannesses it had a fashion of purifying. And what is this act whose virtue is so wonderful? Read the next verse, (ver. 12,) and you will find that it is nothing else but baptism: "Buried with him in baptism, wherein also ye are risen with him through the faith of the operation" (or energy) "of God, who hath raised him from the dead." This is not a new subject, nor yet a new sentence, being grammatically as well as substantially a part of the whole idea included under the term "the circumcision of Christ," and pointing out to us, that baptism in the mind of the Spirit is the name of the spiritual work, and washing with, or dipping in, the water of baptism, is the act outward, which is intended to signify the act inward, done without hands, of putting off the body of the sins of the flesh: for what is a burial, if there be not first a death? And what is the death of a saint but the putting off the body of the sins of the flesh? If in baptism, then, we be buried with Him, as it is said, then in baptism we die with Him: if in baptism we die and are buried with Him, then from thenceforth are we regarded by the Spirit as having suffered with Christ in the flesh, as being dead with Him unto the power of sin, yea, and unto the power of death. "Knowing that Christ being raised from the dead, dieth no more, death hath no more dominion over him." Wherefore it is added in this passage, as in all the rest, "In which baptism also ye are risen with him." So that thenceforth our life is, as hath been said, a resurrection life nourished and fed upon the risen body of Christ: which food, accordingly, is handed down to us in the sacrament of the supper, and thereby is made a constant declaration of the nature of our life in the Church. And by what act in us, the subject of baptism, is this great work of dying unto sin, and living unto God, accomplished? It is immediately added, "Through the faith of the energy of God, who hath raised Christ from the dead." It is, then, through faith that this baptismal regeneration proceedeth. But faith of what? Faith that Christ came in the flesh? No! that is not the act of faith which worketh the baptismal regeneration. Faith that Christ died for our sins? No! What then? Faith of the energy of God, who hath raised Him from the dead. And he, who will not pass beyond the cross and tomb of Christ, to look with an eye of faith to the act of the resurrection, and to apprehend the energy of God, put forth therein, need never to expect the baptismal regeneration of which the apostle in all these passages speaketh, and of which, after their example, I take liberty to speak; meaning always by baptism what they mean, not a sign, but the thing signified also,—not a shell, but a shell with its kernel in it.

In order to justify myself, and, what is much more important, my doctrine, against the ignorant suspicion of novelty, I shall conclude this discourse upon the doctrine which the Church holdeth concerning baptism, by quoting, and shortly paraphrasing, the answer to the question : "How is our baptism to be improved by us?" as it is given in the Larger Catechism of our Church: from which you will see how exactly these our views of baptism accord with those entertained by the Westminster divines, and the last council of the Protestant Church, as we have already shewn its accordance with the symbols of our Reformers. "The needful, but much neglected, duty of improving our baptism, is to be performed by us all our life long, especially in the time of temptation, and when we are present at the administration of it to others." Here baptism is wisely considered as a great safeguard against the snares of the world and the temptations of Satan, and as a sacrament, whereof the administration should be fraught with great advantage to the whole Church; seeing temptation, and the ministration of it, are the only times which they have specified, though they consider that it ought to be present in our mind, and improved by us at all times. And how is it to be improved? The answer thus continues,—"By serious and thankful consideration of the nature of it, and of the ends for which Christ instituted it." Our divines, therefore, dear brethren, considered it as no empty and idle ceremony, but as an institution whose nature, that is, whose form and substance, and whose ends were at all times worthy of serious and thankful consideration: therefore do ye justify me in endeavouring, with all diligence, to present this subject before you, and condemn yourselves for slighting it, as you have been accustomed to do. Further, "By serious and thankful consideration of the privileges and benefits conferred and sealed thereby." So, brethren, the compilers of our Catechisms did not hesitate to think that there were great privileges and benefits conferred upon the baptized; and that it was not left to chance or circumstances, yielded to some as a special favour, but withdrawn from the multitude, but both conferred and sealed upon all in the act of striking that covenant; for sealing is of no import, except as it signifies the confirmation of a solemn deed and testament by a solemn act: and that the engagement here referred to by sealing is not on our part, but on God's, is shewn by the connexion, "conferred and sealed;" he that conferreth being the same that sealeth. If now you ask, what these benefits are, I shall enumerate them from the previous question, "What is baptism?" where they are enumerated thus: "Ingrafting into Christ, remission of sins by His blood, and regeneration by His Spirit, adoption and resurrection unto eternal life, and whereby the parties are solemnly admitted into the visible Church." Now, I am sure, if you think that I have gone far, you will allow that the Church, of which I am a minister, goeth still further than I do, in extending the blessedness of this ordinance, and without any of the guards or cautions which I have continually interposed, in dutiful consideration of your weakness. To all which covenanted blessings, the collateral engagement on our part is thus added, "We are to improve our baptism at all times, by serious and thankful consideration of our solemn vow made therein;" of which, if you inquire into the burden, then I give it you in the words of the previous question, "We thereby enter into an open and professed engagement to be wholly and only the Lord's." It is the vow of self-denial, renunciation of the world, and contending against the devil, to stand fast in the faith, and to keep all the commandments and ordinances of the Lord blameless, to be wholly and only the Lord's, into which we have entered. But the pregnant answer of the framers of our Catechism goes on to unfold the matter in a most excellent way—thus: "By being humbled for our sinful defilement, our falling short of, and walking contrary to, the grace of baptism, and our engagements." Why humbled for our sinful defilement? Because it was washed away in baptism, and ought no more to be present; and in being present doth shew that we are not improving the grace of baptism, which would cleanse us thoroughly, nor fulfilling the covenant for which God would strengthen us by His sufficient Spirit: and therefore there is conjoined with this article of our humility, in order to explain the grounds of it, "our falling short of, and walking contrary to, the grace of baptism, and our engagements;" of which the former is sufficient to wash away all our sins, and the latter to strengthen us for standing to all our engagements. But our baptism is further to be improved, "by our growing up in assurance of pardon of sin, and of all other blessings sealed to us in that sacrament." Now, what meaneth it, if our sins be not pardoned in baptism; if it be only a shew of doing it, but not the very doing of it; that the rulers of the faith of our Church have expressed themselves in such language as, that pardon of sin is sealed to us in baptism, and have called upon us to grow up into the assurance thereof? And is it not my part to speak to the baptized as to men pardoned, who hence ought to have the blessedness of those whose sins are forgiven, and whose iniquities are covered; and this, not only of the pardon of sin, but of all the other blessings therein sealed to us? Moreover, in accordance with the spirit of this homily, it is said, "Exemplified by drawing strength from the death and resurrection of Christ, into whom we are baptized, from the mortifying of sin, and quickening of grace: looking to His death as that after which we are to be conformed in all deadness unto sin, and looking to His resurrection as that after which we are to be conformed in all the life of holiness:" that is, seeing in His death and resurrection the reality of our spiritual death and resurrection in our baptism, and from our baptism all our life long, as much as of our natural death and resurrection: further, "by endeavouring to live by faith, to have our conversation in holiness and righteousness, as those who have therein given their names to Christ; and to walk in brotherly love, as being baptized by the same Spirit into one body."

From these expositions of the Scriptures which treat of baptism, dearly beloved brethren, it must be manifest to you, that it is a far greater mystery than in these times it is wont to be regarded, and that it is well worthy the most profound meditation of every believer in Christ. Now, the sum of what hath been gathered from the Word of God at this time concerning it is this, that in it is done over beforehand, in an emblem, the death and burial and resurrection of that which is born of our parents. When I say it is done in a symbol, I do not mean that it is merely done in a show, or representation as it were, to help the conception and instruct the mind; for this would be much better done by a plain discourse upon death and resurrection than by dipping in water or sprinkling with it; which act doth not naturally carry with it any resemblance or signification of death, burial, and resurrection. But I mean, that to faith, the death, burial, and resurrection of the child is actually accomplished, and that the symbol of baptism is to faith the very self-same thing which death, burial, and resurrection are to sense, and that the eye of faith should behold, the prayer of faith believe, and the actings of faith entreat a baptized child, as one that is dead and buried with Christ, and risen and seated with Him in the heavenly places. And while the mystery of baptism requireth us thus to entreat the baptized, it requireth us thus to entreat ourselves: we ought to feel that we are as dead men in respect to sin, and that, as dead men cannot act, so we cannot sin; and we ought to feel ourselves alive only unto God, and not only having power to please God, but having power to do nothing else but please Him. I know how strangely these expressions will sound in your ears, and what odium they may chance to bring on him that utters them; but that they are apostolical, that they are the constant language of the apostles when speaking of baptism and the baptized, I have this day sufficiently proved: nor shall any fear of the face of man hinder me, by God's grace, from speaking the language of the Spirit in the midst of the Church.

Wherefore, brethren, I exhort you to look upon one another as being indeed dead unto sin and alive unto righteousness; look upon the death-warrant of your natural man as issued from the court of heaven: yea, look upon him as slain and buried too in the purpose of God, and go to him with a divine purpose and assurance, to take him and bind him, and sacrifice him with all his powers and faculties unto the Lord your God. Put me in no *ifs*, nor conditionals of any sort; there are no such words in the decrees of God. I tell you, it was not only worded in baptism, but it was done, if only ye have faith to believe it; and without faith ye can never be established. It was to the very end of destroying doubt, and putting demur out of the question, that God had you every one baptized in your childhood, in order that ye might never doubt; but, from the first dawn of reason, believe in God, who slayeth and who maketh alive. Go about your crucifixion and your mortification, like men who have Almighty power at their back, and the Almighty Word for their standard, before their face; and go about the work of life and holiness, of resurrection life and holiness, as mighty men of God who are disencumbered of the clayey tabernacle, with all burdensome weights. Thus believe, dear brethren; for these are the truths of faith, these are the lessons of the Spirit, these are the doctrines of Christ, under which to act, under which to overcome. Sense will meet you, and clog you; and sight will cast stumblingblocks and rocks of offence before you: you will find that you are still amongst the impediments of things seen and temporal; and that there remaineth to be done for sense and sight a work kindred to that which hath been done for faith. But how, I ask,—and I ask it in the name of human frailty,—how shall you do battle against these visible and invisible enemies, unless you have the victory already achieved in your faith, and that not dependent upon a word, which is common to all, but upon an act which was done upon yourself? Therefore, oft look upon, and oft strengthen yourselves by the wonderful mystery of the work of God, which was declared unto you, and sealed upon you, in the holy sacrament of baptism, when you were first admitted into the Christian Church, and enrolled as the soldiers of Christ to fight all the days of your life against the devil, the world, and the flesh.

HOMILY IV.

THE NEW STANDING INTO WHICH BAPTISM BRINGETH THE CHURCH, AND THE ENGAGING PARENT OR SPONSOR, TOWARDS THE CHILD.

PSALM CXXVII. 3.

Lo, children are an heritage of the Lord; and the fruit of the womb is his reward.

IF then, as we shewed in the former Homily, the mystery of baptism be the death of our natural manhood inherited by generation from our fathers, and the resurrection of our spiritual manhood derived by grace from the risen Christ; and if the high privilege of this mystery be unto our children, the question is, To whom belongeth the right of presenting a child to have such an act done upon it? This right manifestly can belong to none but the parent, or, failing him, that person nearest of kin whom the laws of God and man consider as holding property in the child. For it is no slight and trivial ceremony which is to be done upon the child, but a high and holy transaction of God and His Church, which is to make it all its life long responsible for the sinlessness of a naturally dead person, and the holiness of one who is spiritually alive from the dead. It is to root out all natural affections, and to plant all spiritual affections in their stead; it is to cut asunder all natural ties, and to bind fast all religious obligations; and, in one word, it is to sacrifice upon the altar of faith the infant's natural life and natural inheritances, looking unto the promise of a spiritual life, and an unseen inheritance. Which, although it be a great advantage unto the child, is yet such an advantage as groweth out of a great sacrifice; and who hath a right to make that sacrifice in the prospect and the promise of that advantage I know not, if it be not the parent or the kinsman who hath natural right in, and is held obliged to act for, the child. And thus it was under the former covenant, that the father of children, and the master of slaves, were bound unto God for their circumcision; as it is also a law in the new dispensation under which Cornelius presented his house, as also did the jailer of Philippi, and Lydia, of whom every one upon believing was baptized, with their whole house.

This question being settled, another immediately ariseth; which is, And what is the nature of the act which a father doth when he presenteth his child to baptism? And the answer is, He doth offer it to be slain and buried, which, as we have shewn in our former discourse, is the first thing done in every true and rightly-administered act of baptism. Now, I would pause here a moment, and endeavour to impress upon the minds of all present, what a deep and pregnant significance this gives to the act of presenting a child to baptism; by which act the father declareth before the Church, though not by words, yet by that sacramental act, which is more solemn than words,—he declareth, "I believe this child of mine to be wholly conceived in sin, shapen in iniquity, born into a life of sorrow, and the heir of an everlasting death: all that it hath derived from me is misery and mortality, and I take pity upon the sinful and wretched thing which hath sprung from my loins: all this I know through my faith in the revelation of God in Jesus Christ, where I am also informed that from among the creatures so produced in sin and doomed to misery, there is a portion chosen of God unto eternal life, which are begotten 'not of blood, nor of the will of the flesh, nor of the will of man, but of God,' to this election. I do find, since it began in Abraham, that there hath been an outward sign or mark given heretofore by circumcision, and now by baptism; and though I know that this hath ever included more than the true election, yet know I likewise, that the true election hath ever been found included therein; and perceiving that the promise hath ever been unto the children, as well as unto the parents, I do now come to seek, for this my child, admission within the pale of the Church, wherein are these holy ones; and though I know that I do thereby sacrifice, and put to death, and bury in the tomb, my child's natural life, and by this act renounce all right of nature in him from henceforth, yet am I willing to make the sacrifice ; and though I do know that Satan doth only rage the more violently within the Church, and that it is God's purpose he should prevail against many for the trial of the rest, yet perceiving that there is hope there, and no hope elsewhere, and having a good faith in the promise of God, as it is set forth in this very sacrament, that He will raise this child from the dead, I do present him to be offered by the hands of the Church, to whom pertaineth the keeping of Christ's priestly office." All this, I say, is virtually declared by the parent in the act of presenting his child, and that in a far more solemn manner than words can do.

Now, another question ariseth, By what right is a parent entitled to ask, and upon what terms is the Church permitted to grant this boon ? First, with respect to the parent's right : it standeth solely and wholly in his faith, of which the Church being satisfied may not refuse the boon. For if the Church be satisfied of his faith, then must she also be satisfied of his possessing that justifying righteousness of Christ, which is imputed to and received by faith alone. It were to subvert the foundations, and to confound the word of God, to separate the Father's gift of faith from Christ's gift of righteousness, so as that, being satisfied of the presence of the one in any individual, we should not be satisfied of the presence of the other also. I do not say that our being satisfied of the presence either of the one or the other causeth it to be present, or insureth that it is present : nay, I know the very contrary, that the Church is both deceivable and deceived in her judgments ; and that there is no infallibility in any man, or in any judgment of man, but in Christ the Judge of all, at the judgment of the great day : but this I say, that with her means of judgment, if the Church be satisfied as to the faith of a man, she may not for an instant doubt as to the righteousness of Christ, which He hath imputed to him in the sight of God. Now, if God regardeth children as being in their parents during their incapacity of believing for themselves, then, whatever is imputed to the parent for his faith, is imputed also to the infant as a part of him, and thus the infant, who by generation shared the pollution of his father's nature, doth by grace share the justification of his father's faith, according as it is written, "The unbelieving husband is sanctified by the believing wife, and the unbelieving wife is sanctified by the believing husband: else were your children unclean; but now are they holy." And in virtue of this derived holiness, this inherited holiness of faith, it is that a creature born in sin, whom God could not look upon in itself, but must for ever abhor, becometh capable of being taken within the holy bond of the blessed covenant; and of having performed upon it the utmost efficacy of the work of the Holy Spirit which is signified therein. And the child thus admitted is as truly a member of the Church of Christ as the oldest saint upon the earth, because the Holy Spirit is as free and as powerful to work His work upon the babe, or the child unborn, from the first moment of conception, as He is to work His work on the hoary sinner, who, instead of having any advantage, hath verily the disadvantage, if so it may be called, of years of sinfulness and prodigality; but I call it not a disadvantage, because grace is free to the fallen creature, and not proportioned either to the term of his life or to the degree of his guilt.

Having thus settled the question of the parent's act, and the parent's right, we now come to the act of the Church, what it is; and to the right of the Church to impose obligations, whence it is. With respect to the Church, there can be no doubt that as it appertained heretofore to the sons of Levi to offer up the sacrifices which the children of Israel brought to the door of the tabernacle, so it doth appertain to the holy ministry, ordained by the laying on of hands, to offer up the sacrifice of the fruit of his own loins, which the parent of his free-will and faith presenteth. I say sacrifice, not in a meritorious, but a eucharistical sense; for I consider it no less, as I have often said, than the great Abrahamic act of faith, wherein a father, on the strength of a promise of God, is willing to forego his own right and interest in his child, and doth make overtures to the Church that it should be by her hand put to death and buried. Yea, I rise not high enough, when I say it is the Abrahamic act of faith, which was but typical of this act, done by every Christian father in presenting his child to baptism: for Isaac's natural flesh was not offered upon the pile of wood, whereas truly and really the flesh, the body of the sins of the flesh, is slain, and buried by baptism, in every elect child of God. The true act which Abraham's offering of Isaac, and every act of Christian baptism, doth shadow forth, is not less than that first and greatest act of God the Father, whereby from all eternity He did offer up unto the death, in a body of fallen yet sinless manhood, His own co-eternal consubstantial Son. And as this stupendous act on the part of the Godhead, is that out of which groweth the eternal covenant between the Father and the Son, including all the manifestations of creation, of redemption, of regeneration, and eternal glory, so doth this act of the Christian father, offering his own son in baptism unto death and burial, open the covenant of grace unto the new-born fallen creature, and begin the work of his exaltation from the death and grave of nature up to the co-inheritance of the throne of Christ; and therefore I call it a sacrifice, as being the continued memorial, and the very continuance, in a lower kind, by the Church, of that sacrifice from which the Church hath her beginning. I call it a sacrifice, moreover, because, little as it is thought of, it ought to be as painful to flesh and blood as was that which Abraham was prepared to do. For, though it may startle you when I say it, yet doubt have I none, that, in the sight of God, the true time of the separation of a parent and his child is in the act of baptism, in which the name of another Father is named over him, and the service of another Father is imposed upon him. It is true, that, to the eye of sense, the child is present still; but that is of the nature of a temptation, and not of an enjoyment,—for to eye him after baptism with the love of sense, is to covet that which is the Lord's. He is as much separated from us as was John the Baptist, when he was in the wilderness until the time of his shewing unto Israel; and that child which we then renounce, if indeed we did renounce him, shall be shewn to us again in glory as a child of God, in the day of the manifestation of the sons of God. But, alas! alas! let me remember that I speak to human frailty. O God, how little we are able to fulfil any of Thine ordinances; how little we walk by faith, how much by sight! Remember that we are dust, and that our foundation is in the dust. Nevertheless, dear brethren, as I am a minister of faith, for the establishment of your faith, I must render a faithful account of the mysteries of God, praying always for myself and for you, that we may be more and more perfected in the faith and observance of them.

The Church, then, by her ordained minister, doth receive from the father the offering of his child unto God, and she gladly approveth it as another fruit of faith and of righteousness. But, before doing the act, she wisely weigheth with herself what will be the consequences of the act which she is about to do. She believes, according to the doctrine of Holy Scripture taught above, that from the lowly bed of this death a new life, spiritual and eternal, ought to arise. I say ought to arise, because that, in many and most instances, it doth not arise, is due not unto God but unto ourselves, though by God foreseen and provided for. The Church, therefore, as the handmaiden of God, and the spouse of Christ, believing Him to be faithful, and feeling herself set for a witness of His faithfulness against all doubters and disbelievers, doth never permit herself to doubt that a new life will come from the lowly bed of this death and burial. She believeth that unto God's elect this sacrament is made effectual to kill the natural and to quicken the spiritual man. And though she humbly acknowledgeth herself quite unable to discern the election of God, yet, acting in her vocation of a witness, though not of a judge, and expecting her office of judge when Christ as Judge shall come, she doth, yea, must believe, that a life will arise out of the grave of baptism, and upon this faith she must necessarily act.

Proceeding, then, upon faith of a spiritual life, about to be begotten in the tomb of the natural creature, she, like a good mother and guardian, questioneth with herself, "But who is to care for this new-born life? The parent is parent only of the natural life, which he hath laid upon the altar of faith, he hath no right as natural parent in the spiritual life; for that were to make the spiritual life born of blood: moreover, in this act which I am to do, the God and Father of our Lord Jesus

Christ, by His name, the Father, doth appropriate this child unto Himself; and from henceforth this child I must regard and deal with as a most holy thing, even as the child of God. And surely there lieth here a great burden and charge at the door of some one. And with whom doth it lie?" The Church can answer in no way but this: "The charge must lie with him who is the instrument of doing the deed. As the act of generation constituted this parent the guardian of the natural life, so must the act of regeneration constitute the party into whose hands it is intrusted the guardian of the spiritual life. I, therefore, in the eye of God, am the guardian and parent of these children, because I, and I alone, am intrusted of God with the power, and do perform the act, of bringing them into this covenant-standing, in which, and in which alone, the fallen creatures can be made partakers of eternal life." And this reasoning of the Church I hold to be irrefragable. Heaven and earth shall pass away, but the responsibility of the Church for all her baptized children shall not pass away. The obligation of the natural parent is not stronger than this; yea, and, I may say, is not so strong; inasmuch as the pledge in question is infinitely more precious. This being fixed and declared, we shall advance another step towards the complete discovery of this mystery.

The parent having resigned his right of nature, the Church, with the full apprehension of her responsibility for the surrendered child, doth proceed to offer the sacrifice unto God, in the assured expectation that, as under the law, when the sacrifice was laid upon the altar, the fire from heaven descended upon it, so shall this sacrifice in due time also be baptized with fire. In due time, I say,—that is, in the resurrection after the death, which to faith is seen in baptism, hath been accomplished to sense in the very grave; for baptism, like every other ordinance of the Church, is a reality only to faith,—the reality to sense occurreth afterward in the progress of the curse, and so in like manner the reality of the resurrection, which to faith is present in baptism, becometh present to sense in the day of the coming of the Lord; and thus the whole Church is but, as it were, a foreshewing, for the help of faith, of that which, in the fulness of the times, shall be realised in the purpose of God. God is not content with foretelling it, but doth shadow it forth by visible symbols, of which baptism is one. In due time, therefore, when the figure of baptism shall be realised in the fiery deluge of the resurrection, shall be fulfilled the true meaning of the ancient sacrifices which God accepted, by sending fire to change the visible corporeal substance of the animal into an invisible aerial substance, a change similar to that which in the resurrection our bodies shall undergo.

This sacrifice the Church being disposed to offer up in faith, and taking counsel with herself concerning the spiritual life which she believeth will follow to faith, she seeketh about to discover into whose hands she may best intrust the rearing of the child of God. And here she acteth, as I conceive, according to her own wisdom, and not after any commandment of God: and so it is our Church hath adopted, I think, a much better order than the Church in these parts, preferring in every case the parent to any other sponsor or sponsors; and if not competent to the charge, seeking the nearest of kin whom she judgeth to be so. This order of proceeding I prefer, because it maketh the ordinance of the Church to run parallel, as far as may be, with the ordinance of law and nature, committing the spiritual guardianship into the same hands in which the providential guardianship must ever rest. And as the Holy Spirit, in His regenerating office, doth never despise His work of creation, however fallen and marred of sin, but entering thereinto, doth cleanse the sinfulness and stay the dissolution thereof, proving Himself thereby kindly to His former handiwork, and glorifying Himself over its infirmity, and shewing forth the oneness of idea in the creation state of the fallen state, and of the regenerate state of the creation; even so it is to be believed that it will be congenial to the Holy Ghost to enter into the natural relationship of father and child, which hath been laid as a sacrifice upon the altar of faith, and regenerated into a spiritual relation, rather than rejecting this, which hath been so generously sacrificed unto God, to constitute a new relationship between the child and sponsors, who have in it, and to it, no natural affiance, and have made the sacrifice of none; and, therefore, I think it is both more agreeable to the whole principle of the regeneration, as well as more dutiful to the faithful parent, to cleave as close as can be to the natural relationship, and to avoid, as much as may be, foreign sponsorship. But, as hath been said, this is an ordinance of the Church, grounded upon views of expediency alone; because, virtually, she continueth responsible for the life which she is made instrumental, under the Spirit, of begetting, and no act of those constituting either parent or other sponsors can absolve her from the obligation.

Nevertheless, the covenant which the parent entereth into with the Church is a most solemn covenant, which she hath a good right to require, and which he should have a willing heart to ratify. She hath a good right to require it, inasmuch as she, and she only, hath the boon to bestow. True, she hath it but in trust for the benefit of Christ's members; but still it is in trust for all His members that she hath it, and especially for the infants who are not capable of caring for themselves; and, therefore, as the mother may well claim of the father industry to support the child, whom she hath conceived in pain, and in travail brought forth, and is nourishing with the milk of her substance; so may the Church, who presenteth the father with a spiritual child, through her sufferings, and the sufferings of her Head, well require of him the functions of a spiritual parent. And what on her part it is both rightful and prudent to require, on his part it is both reasonable and dutiful to grant: for what is it that induces him to come forward and offer up his child unto the death? Is it not the hope of receiving it from the dead in a figure? Is it not the desire of having it brought into the inheritance of a better life, even an eternal? And having this desire, how can he but rejoice to become the guardian of that better life? Not to enter into the obligations, therefore, which the Church imposeth on him, would be to deny and make void the holiness of the purpose with which he offered his child, and would convert it into a deliberate act of casting off and slaying the child of his bowels, converting the faithfullest act of Abraham, the father of the faithful, into the most horrid act of the worshippers of Moloch, who offered their infants on his altar. And here, again, I see a higher ground than any of those alluded to above, for which the father should be preferred to every other sponsor, in order to justify and validate and sanctify the act of presenting the child to baptism, seeing to refuse him now, as incompetent to the charge of his child, were to deny the act of faith in the offering of his child. For surely if a man hath offered his child in faith to baptism, he hath done the highest act of Christian faith, and may be trusted with any other. And observe, further, that it is that very act of faith which constitutes the child admissible, for otherwise there were no righteousness to cover it withal. On all accounts, therefore, the father is pointed out as the proper person with whom the covenant of sponsorship may be stricken by the Church; and if the Church consenteth not to take him as such, neither should she consent to his presenting the child, because of whom she receiveth the act of presentation, to him she may with safety, and ought in duty, to commit the charge of sponsorship.

But to whomsoever committed, whether to the parent or to another, the obligation is one and the same; an obligation contracted with the Church, to watch over one of the children of the Church; an obligation, through the medium of the Church contracted with God, to train up in His nurture and admonition one of His children, upon whom His name hath been named; an obligation to believe, and pray, and hope, and wait until Christ be formed in the child, the hope of glory; an obligation, moreover, to check, to prune, to eradicate, and utterly destroy every shoot of sin and wickedness which proceedeth from the old stock of nature, the eye of faith did in baptism behold cut down and extirpated. Now, if in baptism the eye of faith beheld our natural man dead and buried, what, I would ask, is there left alive unto the eye of faith, if it be not the spiritual man? so that he who denies a spiritual life to be present after baptism, hath only one or other of the alternatives left him: either he must deny that baptism means the death and burial of the body of the sins of the flesh, which no one can who receiveth the word of God as it is plainly written; or, if he admit this, and deny the spiritual life, then what doth he believe to be present? nothing at all; and this nonentity is the other alternative.

Now, no one in his senses will say, that after baptism a child is to be believed to be a nonentity; and no one that believeth the Scriptures will say, that its natural life is not dead and buried. What, then, is there left to work upon, but the faith of a spiritual life which it hath received? I do not say that it hath received a spiritual life; but that it is ours to assume that it hath, to believe that it hath, and to act upon that assumption and belief, leaving secret things, and things not revealed, unto God. God forbid that I should prejudice the decree of election. God forbid that I should be guilty of the Papal error of separating the acts of the Church from, or preferring them before, her glorified Head. God forbid that I should bind the Spirit to an outward ordinance, or make Him to proceed from the hands of a priest whose goings forth are from the eternal Father, through the risen God-man. All I undertake is to explain a revealed thing, an instituted ordinance of the Church of Christ, for the use of the Church of Christ. And I say again, that it is the duty of the Church, and of the parent, to believe that there is a spiritual life in every baptized child; and in so believing, and acting on the belief, they are sure to carry themselves rightly towards the election of God. And if they carry themselves in like manner towards those who prove themselves not to be the election of God, they do so by reason of the present infirmity and deception which are in all things visible: they commit no offence against God by so conforming themselves to His own holy institution, wisely adapted to the infirmity of sight: they do no injury to themselves, but, contrariwise, act upon a principle of faith and charity, instead of acting upon a principle of sight and judgment: and, finally, while they nourish the election in the Church, by such an open avowal of spiritual life in the baptized, they do no injury to the reprobacy in the Church; but, on the other hand, are continual monitors of what they ought to be, exposers of what they actually witness for God, and fully justifying Him in the reprobation of those who, having light continually shining, prefer darkness to light, their deeds being evil.

If, then, it be both so dutiful and advantageous for all the baptized thus to carry themselves towards one another, how much more is it so in the case of a parent towards his child, for whom he hath entered into covenant with the Church? His own professed faith in the promise bindeth him; his own act of bringing the child into this new standing towards God bindeth him; the inestimable benefit which he hath received at the hand of the Church bindeth him; the solemn covenant into which he entered bindeth him; and I may say, all the yearnings of a spiritual parent over a spiritual child, all the bowels of regenerate nature towards its regenerate offspring, draw him to discharge the offices of a spiritual guardian and sponsor, for which he now standeth pledged unto the great Head of the Church. And in the fulfilment of this holy parentage, he ought never to doubt that there is a holy seed given in charge to him, that he may rear it up to be a flourishing tree in the courts of the house of our God. To doubt or to disbelieve in any one instance, is to doubt or to disbelieve in all, and utterly to make void the sacrament of baptism; and making this void, to make void the whole institution of the Church, of which I have no other idea than this, that it is a representation unto faith of those very things which are hereafter to be represented unto sight, and therefore symbolical, because they are looked upon by faith for a symbol, standing to faith exactly in that relation in which an object standeth to sense.

The parent, therefore, is never to doubt that a spiritual substance is in his child after baptism; and he is never to cease to pray, to hope, to speak, to act, towards his child as one who so believeth: and whatsoever perversity, and obstinacy, and malice, and wickedness, he may discern in it, he must still hope, and pray, and speak, and act, in the same holy spirit, because God hath nowhere said at what time of life He shall effectually call His own elect, and the experience of the Church commonly findeth that they are not effectually called until they have first suffered the bondage of Egypt, and oft also the captivity of Babylon: though we do surely believe that the election of God are, like Jeremiah, known of Him before they are conceived in the womb; yea, every one chosen in Christ before the foundation of the world; yet doubt there can be none, that the Spirit doth seldom shew

Himself in the saint from his mother's womb, but rather suffereth the sinfulness of the creature to shew itself by a period of prodigality, or of world-service and flesh-obedience, in order that he may afterwards wage a more strenuous and successful warfare, by having been brought acquainted with the enemy's camp and stratagems of war: and, therefore, conversion ever hath been, and ever ought to be, regarded as an important epoch in the life of saints, though by no means the same, nor of the same importance with regeneration: for conversion is proper to one who is already adopted into the family of God; whereas, regeneration is that which gives him a right thereto. The prodigal was converted when he returned from alienation back again to his father's house. Simon Peter was converted when he repented of the denial of his Lord, and returned with bitterness of spirit to his fidelity. But Simon Peter and the prodigal son were both of them children of God before they went astray. Oh, brethren! these subjects which I thus touch discursively as I pursue the train of my thoughts, are worthy to be treated of in many separate sermons; and none more so than this the true relationship to God, in which we stand from our baptism to our conversion; of which I will just say this in passing, that it is a standing in the covenant and household of faith, wherein we perform the part of disobedient and perverse children, and experience the long-suffering patience and yearning love of our heavenly Father. And I will add, that to disentangle the nature of this Gordian knot of Divine love, which our spiritualisers cut, is one chief end of all God's dealings with the Jewish Church up to this day, whose perpetual backslidings from God, and God's perpetual restorations of them, do shadow forth the perversity of the children of God, and His unwillingness to let them go; whose ejection at length, and present outcast condition, doth shadow forth the prodigal state of the children of God; whose restoration, as it is contained in the promise, and will yet be performed in the reality, doth shadow forth the certain conversion and eternal perseverance of every elect child of God. And I could say much more of the estate of a saint between his regeneration and conversion, particularly respecting the light which is thereby cast on God's fatherhood, the tenderness, the unwearied tenderness, of His parental love, the yearnings of His bowels over all such strayed children, the rejoicings, the hundredfold rejoicings of His heart, over their return; all which hath its emblem in the natural constitution of a parent's heart, which loves its offspring for a long time before it returns any love; yea, which loves it for a long time only the more, and follows after it the more, because it hath failed to return a parent's love. This mystery of nature, which all observe, and which no one can on any reasonable grounds account for, is fixed there in a parent's heart, for the end, I believe, of shewing forth the fatherhood of God towards His children, in the season of their prodigality and alienation; and therefore it is, that I cannot away with those murderers of holy doctrine who will neither allow nor hear of any fatherly relationship between God and man till after conversion, thus abolishing the sacrament of baptism, and the doctrine of the Holy Scriptures concerning it; the relationship of God to His prodigal children; the relationship of the Church to her sponsors; the relationship of the sponsors to the baptized children; leaving the baptized children free from all these obligations, to be tossed like a ball into a large country, and lost in the wilderness of the nations.—But further into this subject our time permitteth me not, at present, to enter: God willing, I shall resume it in some of our future discourses.

In the meantime, holy brethren, I pray you to lay these things to heart, and to believe assuredly, that it is no High-Church error or superstition that I am advocating, but that I am standing for the very existence of a Church,—whether we shall have symbolical institutions for the help of our faith, or whether we shall have them not. Dearly beloved brethren, I am endeavouring to restore a spiritual meaning unto the relationships of the Church, to treat you as redeemed persons, and to shew you how to entreat one another in the same kind. It is, that we may have a substance—a spiritual substance— under all our forms; that we may not be the hypocritical performers of those ordinances of which we see not, and believe not, the mystery. I say again, it is whether we shall have a Church founded upon the doctrines, and ruled by the institutions, of Christ; or a Church founded upon the understanding, and ruled by the prudence, of men;—in short, whether the ritual and worship and sacraments of the Church shall offer to the lips of the people an empty vessel, or a vessel full of waters, and these the waters of the Holy Ghost. And I, as a minister of the Holy Ghost, who believe that the ordinance of the laying on of the hands of the Presbytery is no vain or idle ceremony, but doth constitute a man a minister of the Holy Ghost, have this day been standing up for one of the great ordinances of the Spirit; which, methinks, but for the creeds and standards of the Churches, would be swallowed up in the vain, extravagant, and all-absorbing trust which they repose in the written word. And, therefore, I do entreat you, as believers in the Holy Ghost, to weigh well the truths whereof I have this night discoursed; and, as you are convinced of them by the Spirit, to lay them to heart, and to seek the power of the Spirit to carry them into effect: for the days are exceeding evil, and the venerable ordinances of the Church are pecked at by the vain and idle multitude; but, by the grace of God, they shall prove life and strength to every one who believeth and revereth them.

HOMILY V.

THE DUTIES OF THE CHURCH AND THE ENGAGING PARENT OR SPONSOR.

Prov. XXII. 6.

Train up a child in the way he should go: and when he is old, he will not depart from it.

THE views of the doctrine of baptism which we set forth on the last Lord's day amount to this,—That in the mystery of that sacrament is represented as finished and completed the whole work of human redemption, consisting of these three parts, "death, burial, and resurrection:" the first being the extinction of the first life of the creature; the second, the dissolution of its substance; the third, the restitution of its life and substance in a new and abiding form. Which symbol of the complete redemption of the fallen creature being done upon any subject by the hands of the Church, duly ordained thereto, and in the name of the Father, the Son, and the Holy Ghost, whose power and offices are all directed to accomplish the same, this act doth introduce him on whom it is done into relations altogether new, both towards God and towards the Church. Towards God, it placeth him in the condition of one who is honoured and privileged with all the promises which have been made since the world began, and who, by his own act, hath declared himself to be responsible for all the great and mighty ends for which these promises were given; and therefore liable to all the penalties which are written against those who, having been so kindly entreated of God, and solemnly engaged unto God, do yet despise His grace, and trample His covenant under foot: and this is the exact definition of a reprobate. To the Church, again, this act of baptism doth change the relationship of him upon whom it is done, inasmuch as she must from henceforth regard him as one upon whom, in the solemnest manner, the work of Christ, from the beginning to the ending of it, hath been sealed, as God hath appointed it to be sealed to any child of Adam. In which light, if she refuse to regard any baptized person, then she doth invalidate the ordinance altogether to every person, and becometh guilty upon those awful accounts "of changing the ordinance, and breaking the everlasting covenant," upon which, as you will see in Isaiah xxiv., the whole world is subverted and destroyed. Which indignation and vengeance of God, if the Church would avoid, then must she stand fast by the ordinances, uphold their eternal obligation, and, though all things should reel to and fro like a drunken man, keep the stability of her footing upon these foundations of Christ.

To the end of bringing back this church over which I watch, from the tottering instability of private opinions, and from the expedient measures of the multitude, who drift with wind and current; after setting forth these views of the doctrine, I proceeded to shew the nature and obligation of those new relations into which all parties are brought by this solemn sacrament; and had advanced so far as to shew, that the Church is responsible unto Christ for every baptized child, and the sponsor is responsible to the Church: and we now proceed to shew in what way these two responsible parties should fulfil their obligations.

The Church, as distinguished from the unbaptized world, is a body of men living and walking by the faith of things invisible; whereas the world liveth and walketh by the sight of things visible. That visible state of things, which is to the world the substance of its possessions and the materials of its enjoyment, is to the Church the cloud of its darkness, and the materials of its temptation. Wherefore God, perceiving how unequal a combat the Church would have to maintain, hath, in His great mercy, accorded unto her present weakness certain symbols of the invisible things for which she is to contend. Which symbols addressing the sense, or rather the faith through the sense, might help her in contending against sight. If the battle could have been waged without these symbols, they would never have been instituted by the appointment of Christ; but, being instituted, I believe they cannot be dispensed with. Now, this symbol of baptism having presented unto the faith of the Church any child as dead and buried and risen with Christ, the Church, as one who liveth by faith, should ever look upon that child as really dead and buried and risen, pray for him as such, speak of him as such, and act towards him as such; and this she must do notwithstanding the fearful evidences to the contrary which he displays: yea, and when remonstrating against his natural propensities and actual sins, as they are ever shewing themselves, she should, like St Paul, ever proceed upon the principle, that he became dead to sin when he was baptized into Christ. This is exactly the trial of her faith, to believe that a new creature is in him, according to the promise, notwithstanding the wickedness which appeareth: just as she believeth that, in the elemental world, there is a new and sinless and immortal creature groaning for redemption, notwithstanding the meanness and wickedness and corruption which now pervade it. Could Abraham, when his body was dead, and Sarah, after the deadness of her womb, have any reasonable hope of a child? But they believed against hope, and so became heirs of the promises. And where is the faith of the Church, if she cannot believe in the covenant of baptism made with a person, because that person seems hitherto to have been barren, and at present to be dead? or doth she think that she shall have the end of the promise upon the instant of its being given, as if she could trust God for a day or a year, but not for ten, or twenty, or thirty years? or must she have sight to help out faith? then let her look unto the emblem, which is the only help of sight which God hath seen it meet to grant unto faith. Oh, but she would have certain grounds upon which to believe and hope and act, besides those given in the emblem! Then she lacketh faith in God, and in so far forth must suffer loss.

I do not say, dear brethren, but that the Holy Spirit, when He beginneth to work in any of the election according to grace, will produce the fruits of righteousness, by which you shall know, and ought to discriminate them: but I am speaking of the period which intervenes from baptism until effectual calling, and not of the period after effectual calling; of the period from the time that Sarah received the promise until she conceived the child, not of the time afterwards; for it requireth little faith to believe then, when experience properly beginneth; so likewise, there is little faith, except, indeed, the faith of perseverance, of which at present I discourse not, required for the sake of any one after the Holy Spirit hath begun to bear fruit in his soul, when it becomes no longer the faith of a promise, but the experience of the faithfulness of a promise; not the work, but the reward, of faith, which reward, that she may in due time reap, if so it seemeth good unto God, in all her baptized children, I am shewing the Church how to labour in the work of faith, while as yet there is nothing to build upon but the promise of God, being well assured that her remissness during this the sowing-time of faith, is the reason why she reapeth such a scanty harvest, and is found in such an impoverished condition. It is the duty of the Church, therefore, to believe most surely of every baptized child, that in the fulness of time fixed in His own counsels, God will fulfil His covenant engagements towards it. I say it is her part to believe that He will, and to act out that belief: this is her office, and the rest she must leave to God; if the covenant should not be fulfilled to any one, there is a day when that secret thing will be openly justified, in which day she will be reproved if it shall appear that she hath not believed and acted to that one as to the rest of God's saints.

I know, from the parable of the tares and the wheat, the mystery that there are reprobates as well as elect within the bond of the holy covenant, that it is God's will and purpose that it should be so; but I likewise, by the same token, do know, that it is not given to the servants of the Sower to separate the tares from the wheat, and that they must grow together until the harvest. Now, I hold that it is to take this forbidden office upon ourselves, for which we are not qualified, if we shall go to make distinctions among the baptized, and have faith for one, but not have faith for another: it is even to judge and discriminate before the plants have shewn themselves above the ground; or, without a figure, it is not to believe at all, but to usurp the office of judgment, and to make this day of faith and hope the day of judgment and doom.

But if any one hesitate to grant me what I conceive to be the first principle and chief end of the Church, that she should have a most inviolable reliance upon the word of the covenant for every one thereinto admitted, then I ask such a one, upon what principle he would have us to proceed in taking care of the soul of a child, and training it up? I take for granted that the objector believeth the doctrine of our fallen and helpless estate by nature, and our incapacity of originating any spiritual life within ourselves: now, I ask such a one what he meaneth by labouring upon such a dead stock as this? Who would nurse a still-born child? Who thinketh of ministering the offices of life to one that is dead? And yet you hope for this creature that is born spiritually dead that it will live unto God; you labour for it that it may live unto God, and you train it up in the nurture and admonition of the Lord. I ask wherefore you do this, seeing you believe the child upon whom you bestow your pains to be dead? It is needless to tell me that it is your duty to do so, for it never can be your duty to expect life from the dead, unless you have a promise of God to that effect; and what promise have you for this child, if it be not in baptism, which you reject? Do you direct me to some general promise of the written Word? I ask, to whom is that promise made? There are only two possible answers: Either to those in the covenant, or to the election according to grace. If you say the former, then is not baptism that which introduces to the covenant, and gives the privilege of the promise? If you answer, the election according to grace; then I answer, how can you use it until you know that this child is one of that election, which in this life you can never know, and therefore use of it have you none?

But, lest I should become unnecessarily subtle and minute, I return from this digression to the more profitable work of instructing the Church of God concerning their duties to the baptized. And of these, I place first, after faith, the duty of instruction, which must ever be preceded by the belief that there is in them the capacity of being instructed in spiritual things. I say not that this capacity is given in baptism. The Spirit is free to impart it to the elect of God from the very womb; but I say, that after baptism it may not be doubted to be in any one. Nor do I say that it is in any but in God's elect; but as these are not known, and cannot be known to us, to any but God, it would have been impossible for the Church to have served unto them any of the purposes of God, but for this sacrament, which defines the class amongst whom they are found. And because of the election that are found amongst the baptized, God requireth His Church to carry herself towards them all, as if they were His election, and permits not to any power on earth the right of discriminating amongst them for any end but that of discipline. Now, all discipline of the Church, even to excommunication itself, proceedeth upon the assumption that the subjects of it are children of God, whom Satan is seeking to delude; and even in excommunication, as saith the apostle, the flesh is cut off, that the spirit may be saved in the day of the Lord. And for the Church to ask, why she should be required to act upon an assumption which is not the very fact, is merely to ask, why she hath not the attribute of God to search the heart and try the reins. For her to desire a more clear line of acting and faculty of judging unerringly, is merely to complain against the present dispensation of charity, and to forestall the future dispensation of judgment. Seeing, then, that the baptized are to be entreated of the Church exactly as if they were all elect, we say that the first duty the Church oweth to them is instruction, or enlightening in the privileges and conditions of that covenant wherein they stand. The time from baptism till the partaking of the Lord's supper is the period which should be occupied in instruction, and up to that period the children of the Church are in the condition of catechumens; and for these the Church hath drawn up the Shorter Catechism; and no one, according to the discipline of the Church, ought to sit down at the Lord's table who is not perfectly instructed therein. And to this day I make trial of their thorough knowledge and perfect understanding in that section of the catechism which concerneth the holy sacraments. Now, as parents are sponsors under the Church, each for his baptized children, and the Church has seen it good to put into the hands of every parent this most sound and precious form of words, I hold it to be a distinct dereliction of duty for any parent to neglect instructing his children, the children of the Church, in this manual, or to take upon him to change it for another. And I most solemnly protest here in my place against the use of catechisms which the Church hath not authorised, be they written by whom they please; and if in such matters you will prefer your own private judgment to the judgment of the Church in the matter of your children, then you break the vow of sponsorship. You are guilty concerning your child, and you so far forth cast your family out from the inheritance which the Church hath in the favour of God. But, dear brethren, if you have done it ignorantly and unwittingly in these years of indifference to all ecclesiastical order, then I pray you, now when the matter is rightly stated to you, to give it serious thought, and reform the abuses which have crept over us in the tract of time, and by the heedlessness of the Church.

But, to return to the subject of instruction, if you ask me to what objects it should be chiefly directed, I answer,—Instruct the child to do that which the sponsor, according to our sister Church, undertakes for the child; to "renounce the devil and all his works, the vain pomp and glory of the world, with all covetous desires of the same, and the carnal desires of the flesh, so that thou wilt not follow, nor be led by them." Respecting these the forms of wickedness as they arise in its own heart, and are presented to it by the world, the engaging parent is bound to instruct the child,—for how shall it be able to renounce the evil, unless it first know the evil?—to do which requireth a full acquaintance with the law of God, by which all evil is discovered; and no instruction is so fit for children as that which proceedeth by commanding and forbidding.—Secondly, The child should be taught all the heads of the Christian faith, and be required to believe them; I say, required to believe them, as the great principles of the Christian Church, for the faith of which it hath been already pledged. And if Satan should so far prevail with it as to pervert its conscience to the disbelief of them, then is it the duty of the sponsor to submit such a case to the rulers of the Church, to whom he is responsible, that it may be dealt with according to their greater wisdom; and if that should fail, and the youth, after being waited for and dealt with by all means, should remain unbelieving, let him be cut off, first by the act of lesser, and then of greater, excommunication: for nothing is so unseemly as that there should be an unbeliever in communion with Christ's Church.—Thirdly, The baptized person should be instructed in all God's holy will and commandments, and his obligations to walk in the same all the days of his life. And, in one word, to finish this subject of the instruction which a sponsor owes to his charge, let me quote again from the most excellent baptismal service of the Church of England:—" Forasmuch as this child hath promised by you his sureties to renounce the devil and all his works, to believe in God, and to serve Him; ye must remember, that it is your parts and duties to see that this infant be taught, so soon as he shall be able to learn, what a solemn vow, promise, and profession he hath here made by you. And that he may know these things the better, ye shall call upon him to hear sermons; and chiefly ye shall provide that he may learn the Creed, the Lord's Prayer, and the Ten Commandments, in the vulgar tongue, and all other things which a Christian ought to know and believe to his soul's health; and that this child may be virtuously brought up to lead a godly and a Christian life; remembering always, that baptism doth represent unto us our profession; which is, to follow the example of our Saviour Christ, and to be made like unto Him; that, as He died, and rose again for us, so should we, who are baptized, die from sin, and rise again unto righteousness; continually mortifying all our evil and corrupt affections, and daily proceeding in all virtue and godliness of living."

Such of you as are natives of Scotland can bear witness how much this duty was felt by our fathers: and it may be instructive to our English brethren, to inform them, that till within these thirty or forty years, a Sabbath school was not known through all the bounds of the Kirk of Scotland;—every father fulfilling this office in his house as constantly as the minister fulfilled his office in the Church; and this in the house of the cottager, in the house of the farmer, in the house of the laird or esquire, all alike; and I may add, also, in the house of the nobles. Of which diligence I will give you this curious proof, that no head of a house liked to take a servant into his family who was not already a communicant; thereby signifying, that till that time it was not proper she should be removed from under the sponsorship of her parents. And, in cases where this religious rule was deviated from, it was understood to be the duty of the head of the house to examine such a one along with his own children. Yea, and so tender were our fathers wont to be upon the subject of these baptismal obligations, that in such cases where a master was discharging the office for which a father was responsible, it was the custom to permit the servant to go home to his father's house on the Sabbath evening, that his father might thereby have an opportunity to take knowledge of his soul's health, and deal with him as one who had come under solemn engagement to the Church for the same. Now, while all this husbandry of baptized children was proceeding in every family, and under every roof of our native land, the Church was not inactive in performing her part; but as the mother of the whole family of families, responsible unto God for the instruction of the children, and for the faithfulness of the sponsors, she required the minister of every parish, with the elder of each particular division of it, to visit every family from house to house, and, amongst other things, to take proof of the knowledge of the children in presence of their parents. This being finished, and one whole year was allotted to it, the next year was devoted to the examination of the communicants themselves, including parents of both sexes, old men and old women, for which office the Larger Catechism was appointed by the Church to be used. On which occasion the minister himself was expected to resolve any doubts or difficulties, or questions of doctrine, that might arise. And the year following, he began again with the visiting of the families, and the examining of the children; and so on, in an unceasing round, proceeded the wholesome discipline of the Church, and the edification of the whole land;—all, all growing out of the root of this sacrament of baptism, which you would fain have extinguished as an everlasting covenant, and brought into the insignificance of an outward ceremony. But, as the Lord liveth to reward His faithful ministers, and as the Head of the Church liveth to require the obedience of all His members, I will not cease from my duty of sharply rebuking every one who undervalueth this holy ordinance, whose augustness our fathers held in such esteem, that they would not administer it privately, except in extreme necessities; and when these occurred, they gave public notice from the pulpit on the Lord's day preceding, mentioning both time and place, and requiring all the brethren in the neighbourhood to assemble there for the exercises of public worship: on which occasion the minister delivered no short address, but a regular sermon; and the people assembled in no chamber of a house, but generally in the largest barn which was to be found: and such was the good understanding between the Church and Secession, and the reverence paid by all classes unto this sacrament, that I am old enough to remember my father's granting his barn, as being one of the largest in the town, for this end, to a most holy father of the Burgher communion, to whom I owe a debt of gratitude of which I delight ever to acknowledge.

Truly, dear brethren, when these things we think upon, we may well mourn and weep, and rend our garments, and cast dust upon our heads, and be unclean until the evening. Ah, when I compare the silent steady working of an invisible principle of an ever-felt obligation like that of baptism, setting in motion the hearts and minds of a whole people, linking into communion, and yet preserving in due subordination, the various ranks and degrees of men, regenerating the affections of nature, and hallowing the relationships of kindred, sweetening the bitterness of adverse conditions, sanctifying all the offices of the Church, and displaying her as the true and liberal mother of all her children;—when this harmonious and effectual working of the Holy Spirit, through the institutions of Christ, I do compare with the present condition of the Church, concerning which there is such triumphant boasting: if I observe, first, the relaxation on the part of the rulers of the Church, and their indifference to the spiritual charge of their children, their ignorance of the state of families for which they are responsible, and the abuse, I had almost said profanation, of the sacrament itself, the profaneness, the privacy, the indecent haste of its administration; the ignorance of its bonds and obligations, and the practical, if not open denial, that it involveth any: if I observe, next, the discipline of families, how little system and order, how little instruction and discipline, how little worship, how the father hath ceased from the priesthood of his house, and the children from the devout honour of their father; how the mother hath ceased from the gentle office of kindly carrying into effect the details of a father's plans; and how the servants are kept without the family circle which our mild and gracious discipline bringeth into one: if I observe, again, the state of the schools, in which these defects are intended to be supplemented, and witness the secularity and ostentation which run through them, insomuch that I regard the Sunday school, as it is ordinarily conducted, to be no Sabbath work, and likely to be of no advantage to the Church of Christ, having in truth little or no relation to the Church, and no reference whatever to the ordinance of baptism, as the origin out of which it grows, or to the communion, as the end to which it aims, or to the spiritual seed, as the material upon which it works, but being in truth little holier than our week-day parish schools: if next I observe the outward and visible machinery of the present religious world, as it well nameth itself; their endless, and often prayerless committees, their multitudinous, and often unhallowed meetings, their hustings and hustings-like harangues, their numerous travellers upon commission, their flaming, and often fallacious reports, with all the hurry, haste, and bustle of the evangelical and methodistical machinery; can I be but grieved at the fall and declension of the Church's glory, and the common weal? Can I be but indignant when they call themselves better than their fathers, and dare to say that a millennial age is beginning to dawn in those churches which are hastening to their downfall and destruction? Can I be but desirous to restore the spiritual meaning, and the spiritual power of the ordinances of the Church, and especially of this the sacrament of baptism, which I may call the *pri-*

mum mobile, the moving power of the whole? Brethren, you must bear with my zeal: it is not the zeal of a fanatic or enthusiast, but of one who has lived much with the fathers, and is stricken in spirit with the degeneracy of the children; of one who would fain turn the hearts of the children unto the fathers, lest God come and smite the earth with a curse.

The end of that instruction which the sponsor, under the watchful eye of the Church, should impart, is the fitting of the baptized for sitting down at the Lord's table, which may never be permitted save to those who are of sufficient knowledge of the faith that is within them. When they have attained unto this degree in the Church, they are no longer under sponsorship, but free to become sponsors or catechists in their turn; and therefore, every parent or sponsor should long for the time when he can thus deliver up his burden into the hands of the Church: and the rulers of the Church should be most ready on their part to receive the burden from the shoulders of the sponsors, and to advance another child to the freedom of Christ's house: yea, the elders in their several wards should be diligent to travail with all the youth until they persuade them to seek admission to the table of the Lord; and when it so happeneth, as in our city congregations it doth, that the youth are found separated from those who have the charge over them, there seems to me only two ways of answering the end and intention of baptism;—the first, by the elders and deacons dealing with their several charges in the congregation; the other, to restore the discipline of the primitive Church, by appointing catechists from amongst the brethren: but these are only resources to be substituted in those cases where the youth are, in the providence of God, separated from their sponsors: wherever they are not, let the discipline of the Scottish Church, which hath been described above, proceed under the sponsor each Sabbath during the hours of intermission from public worship.

And so much have I to say upon the matter of instruction: and next in order I place discipline, or the exercise of authority over the child; to train it up according to the laws and commandments of God; for, from the time that a child is admitted into the Christian Church by baptism, it is not only entitled to all the privileges, but subject to all the commandments, and amenable to all the penalties of the Christian Church; and being given into the sponsor's hand in full and complete charge, he is bound not only to instruct it in all these, but likewise to enforce obedience thereto: and this latter is what I understand by discipline. Now, brethren, you will observe that a child or youth is placed by God under obligations proper and peculiar to the estate of childhood and youth, for the fulfilment of which we may never doubt that the grace of the Holy Spirit will be granted by God: and, proceeding upon this faith, we make no allowances for childish folly, but by instruction endeavour to correct it; neither do we make any abatement for childish waywardness, but by temperate authority endeavour to restrain it. Now, a sponsor, who is at the same time a father, ought never to forget his parental relationship; for the spiritual doth not annihilate the natural, but doth quicken and regenerate it: therefore ought the sponsor to require the obedience of the child to himself, and to enforce his obedience to his mother, and never to spare the rod in order to teach this first lesson of obedience. And as the wife is represented in her husband, and bound with him in every obligation to which he is bound, it is her part also, being crowned with his authority, to carry into effect this and every other duty incumbent upon him as a sponsor. The Church ever regardeth them as one flesh, and indivisible save by ecclesiastical divorce; and, therefore, what she imposes upon the husband, she imposes also upon the wife, in her place of subjection. And be assured, that in the co-operation of the two, the work of training the souls of the household will prosper. Now, so little were our mothers, and their mothers before them, acquainted with the modern tact of bringing up their children without chastisement, that I remember to have often seen the instrument of correction hanging up in the sight of the children, to be taken down indeed as seldom as possible, but not to be spared when necessary, lest the child should be lost. And I believe that every one here present who can look back with satisfaction upon a well ordered household, can say, with the apostle Paul, "We have had fathers of our flesh who corrected us, and we gave them reverence." And if you would have your children to give you reverence, you must put forth your authority in some way or other; for of reverence, superiority is an essential element, and without reverence a child or youth is worse than a fool. The Church, therefore, expecteth at the hand of every parent or sponsor the discipline of the *will*, as well as the instruction of the *mind*, of the young Christian: at the same time, she expecteth it to be done in the spirit of love; for all discipline doth proceed from love, and in love is perfected: therefore we say with the apostle, " Fathers, provoke not your children to wrath:" " Fathers, provoke not your children to anger, lest they be discouraged." But from this the Church hath little to fear in these times: from forwardness and irreverence she hath everything to fear. Now, the ground of all reverence, whether to mothers or to sponsors, to magistrates, or to the king as supreme over all; whether to the members of the Church or to its office-bearers, or to the ministers of the Word, or to the Church in general, or to Christ her Head, and God in Him, is ever laid, and in a great degree built up, in the reverence of a child to its parents; for if we reverence not our father on earth, whom we have seen, how shall we reverence our Father in heaven, whom we have not seen? It being so necessary, therefore, on every account, that the parent or sponsor should take upon him this duty of obliging by all authority of love and fear, his child to be obedient to the commandments of God, and at the same time, being so profitable for the growth of that reverence which ought to be an element of every action and every thought of a child, the sponsor placed by the Church in the plenary office of guarding over that spiritual charge, must never cease from the discipline of love, however painful it may be, must never suffer natural fondness to come before positive obligation, but patiently persevere in exacting what is holy, as well as in teaching what is right; trusting for the performance, as well as for the understanding, of duty, that the grace of the Holy Spirit will be granted. And remember, that, as it is in the endeavour to understand that the divine faculty of understanding is conferred, so in the endeavour to obey, the power of obedience is granted. Do not say, We will postpone it till riper years, and a more favourable occasion; but say, This child hath the promise of the Holy Spirit from its baptism, at all times and seasons: therefore let me trust in the Lord's covenant, and go steadily about the fulfilment of my office, however painful.

And here I can perceive a very good use which might be made of the separation of the sponsorship from the parent, and which I would now mention, as a compensation for the many disadvantages of it which I pointed out in my former discourse: it is this,—That as the chief part of a child's obligations for a long time lieth towards its parents, who are oft, by natural affection, betrayed into the neglect of their office as sponsors, and indulge in their own children what they would censure in the children of others; these sponsors being separate from such an influence, might take knowledge of the shortcomings and transgressions of the children towards all, and especially towards their parents, and report the same to the Church, if they are not able to prevail by their own private admonitions: and, no doubt, this is the office to which the sponsor doth solemnly engage himself, and for which he is responsible to Christ and to the Church. And I make no doubt that this natural infirmity of parents to indulge and overlook the sins of their children, was one reason, amongst others, why the Church ever had recourse to sponsors. Yet, though I have presented this apology for the custom, I do not the less on that account disapprove of it: for the Church, though she be tender to all, ought never to indulge the infirmities of any; and still less ought she to make provision for a neglect of duty in any of her members, because she believes that the grace of God is sufficient for the weakest of them, and that His strength is perfected in their weakness. While, therefore, like a good guardian, she keeps a watchful eye over all her family, occupied in their several charges, she rather rejoiceth to see any one performing his appointed task, than desireth to interfere with foreign help; and this the more, because the parent, in presenting his child, doth of his own accord surrender and sacrifice parental affection in its natural estate, that he may receive it from the Almighty Father in a spiritual state, such as it is in His own bosom towards His own Son. For I hold that parental affection in the Church is the issue and ought to bear the likeness of parental affection in the Godhead: and seeing that the Church hath accepted this the faithful sacrifice of the father's natural affection in the life of it, she ought not to consider it as living any more, nor make provision for the acts of its life; and seeing that she hath endowed the parent with a spiritual fatherhood like unto God's, she ought in all her future dealings with this person to regard this heavenly form of the union between father and child, as the only one which now subsisteth: and therefore, instead of providing extraneous administrators to supplement what should never be supposed to exist, she should stir up the gift that is in his parents, by setting out to them, in all its sublime and affecting manifestations, the way in which the Father shewed forth His affection to His own Son when He had come into the estate of fallen manhood; how, in order to exalt Him to be Head and Lord of all, He did first wound Him and bruise Him and put Him to grief, hiding the tenderness of a Father's love, and for a while repressing the outgoings of a Father's joy: even so ought the Church to teach all fathers to carry themselves to their baptized children, who, though buried and raised again in the symbol to the eye of faith, have yet a body of sin and death present to the sense, until it be deposited in the grave; which body of sin and death answering to our Lord's flesh, it is the part of every spiritual father, so constituted by the Church, to wound and bruise and put to grief, yea, to mortify and crucify, and put to death so oft as it shall shew any signs of life. I do not mean to put to death in the letter, but in the spirit; that is, whenever the fruits of the flesh shall shew themselves in our children, it is our part, as spiritual parents, to extinguish their appearance, and, if possible, to annihilate the root from which they sprung.

For I consider every parent, after he hath been constituted by the Church sponsor for his child, to be a servant of the Holy Spirit, and His minister, for the end of bringing that little one unto Christ. The Church, which is the temple of the Holy Ghost, and the fulness of the body of Christ, hath gifts of grace and power and holiness to bestow. And as Christ, through her hands, doth bestow the grace of wisdom and teaching and rule and government upon the presbyters and deacons of the Church in ordination; and as Christ, by her hand, doth bestow the nourishment and the communion of the body of Christ, and the blessed covenant of His blood, upon all the members of His body in the holy supper; even so doth the great Head of the Church, our Christ, at once the Anointed and the Anointing One, bestow, by the hands of the Church, upon the responsible parent, grace to fulfil the spiritual office with which she hath invested him, even as she bestoweth upon the child the faculty of receiving the ministration of the same; and if thereafter either parent or child should be found failing of the grace given unto them, it is to be charged upon them from their want of faith to believe, and of faithfulness to ask and obtain that which is freely given unto them of God.

Now, if any one start back at the hearing, or stagger under the force of these things which I speak concerning the Church, I can only say, that I have them from God's holy Word, and may not hide it in a corner; for there it is written, that the gifts which Christ received for men, when He ascended up on high, He gave unto the Church, in various measures and proportions, according to her various offices; "to some apostles, to some prophets, to some evangelists, to some pastors and teachers; for the perfecting of the saints, for the work of the ministry, for the edifying of the body of Christ." And, again, it is written of the Church, that by her "is made known unto principalities and powers, in heavenly places, the manifold wisdom of God." I have too much value for the Church of the living God, which is the pillar and ground of the truth, and too clear a perception of her denuded and despised condition in these Protestant lands and infidel times; and withal, I have too keen a sense of our guilt,— above all, the guilt of the children of the Scottish Church, in slighting and dishonouring the mother of saints, to be deterred from standing on my watch-tower, and proclaiming aloud what invaluable gifts of God the Church of Christ, since the day of Pentecost, hath been fraught with, and is still fraught with, unto all who believe in Christ, her living and glorious Head: for without faith in Christ her Head, would I ask you to have faith in the Church? I might as well ask you to go and worship at the footstool of the Pope, and kiss his toe. It is the Church in Christ, and under Christ, her Head, from whom you should expect living waters, in the cisterns of His ordinances: it is from the Church, the body, the temple, the servant of the Spirit, with which she is anointed by the Anointed One, that I tell ministers, bishops, presbyters, deacons, communicants, and sponsors of children, to expect their several endowments of grace, for the service of their several offices. And I will tell a word of my mind further, to those who can hear it, that when the Church ceaseth thus to be trusted in, the Holy Ghost will cease to be trusted in; as certainly as when Christ's manhood and incarnation cease to be trusted in, His Godhead and His Christhead cease to be trusted in; for the Church is truly the manifestation, the visibility, the variety, and manifold formations of the Spirit: but enough of this to an unbelieving generation.

And I now return to speak further concerning the sponsorship of the Church and of the engaging parent; for I cannot separate these two; seeing, between them, they constitute the link of communication between Christ the Head, and this yet incompetent member of His Church. I have shewn their obligations to believe for the child, to instruct the child, and to discipline the child in the way which a child of God should go; and what further remaineth to be said, in order to the complete exposition of this subject, than that I should advert to the fruit which is reaped from such faithful labours?

And, first, I observe that, though all should be disappointed; though the father should grieve over a prodigal, and the Church mourn over a fruitless family, God and Christ will never be disappointed of their glory, nor defeated of their ends; which is, by means of the Church, to shew forth unto all beings now existing, or hereafter to exist, the awful and cumulative enormity of sin, and the almighty triumphings of grace over it. Now, if to the latter God honoureth not the faithful labours of the Church and her sponsors to be subservient, then, certainly, to the former; for without such laborious ministry of the servants of the Holy Ghost, the exceeding sinfulness of sin would never have appeared so clear and manifest. If the apostle saith, that by the law sin was shewn to be exceeding sinful, by that which in itself was holy, just, and good, then how much more is that sinfulness shewn to superabound, by its working death through the better and more merciful ministry of Christ and His spiritual Church; and according as the might, and deadliness, and antichristian spitefulness of sin is exhibited the more perfectly, so much the more gloriously is the power of God, and of Christ, and of the Holy Ghost glorified in triumphing over it. Now, this is a view of her high calling which the Church should never lose sight of, lest at any time she faint and weary in her mind; and she should also remember, that it is the first part of every office, before she can arrive at the second; her sowing in tears, before she can reap in joy; whereof her great Head and prototype gave her the example, by suffering under sin, and for the exposure of sin, before He entered into the reward of the travail of His soul. So hath the Church, as Satan changeth his form of wickedness, first to expose the hideousness thereof, and to suffer in that cause, before God will give her the triumphs over it: so she proved, first against paganism, over which she triumphed, after three centuries of suffering; then against Popery, over which she triumphed in the Reformation, after she had endured nine centuries of suffering; and now she will prove it again against infidelity, over which she will receive the victory, after she hath suffered for a season—though I think this latter victory is not to be achieved by means of the Gentile, but by means of the Jewish Church. What the Church hath thus proved upon the large scale, with respect to her works, she must also prove in the smaller scale, in every one of her works. First, exposing the form of sinfulness in the natural man of every child, and thereafter, if God will, reaping the reward in the life and triumph of the spiritual man, and therefore, though we should see no fruit of holiness in the children, over whom we have the charge, we should not the less labour in the work, watering it the while with our tears, and remembering always, that if, after all our painful labours, we should bear no sheaves home to the garner, we still have not laboured in vain, nor spent our strength for naught, having proved the barrenness of the soil, and justifying God, in committing the thorns and the briers, and the soil itself, to the burning flames.—Thus, dear brethren, would I fortify your hearts against disappointment, and shew you that there is no such thing as disappointment in labouring for the Lord, but that, in due time, we shall reap, if we faint not.

And, secondly, though I thus speak the language which becometh the present mixture and disorder of the Church, and, indeed, which is proper for her best estate; seeing, as hath been said, she consisteth of tares as well as wheat; language also, which becometh our present condition of faith and not sight, and harmoniseth with our great fundamental article of election in Christ Jesus before the world began: yet is it most just to observe, in the second place, that to such faith, instruction, and discipline, as I have set forth above, it is that God granteth the harvest of many souls; for in spiritual things as well as in temporal, there is a proportion established, in the Divine purpose, between labour and fruit, between obedience and reward: wherefore it is written, in a certain place, "God is not unrighteous to forget your work of faith and labour of love, which ye have shewed towards His name, in that ye have ministered to the saints, and do minister." I can therefore assure this church, and every engaging parent in this church, that, according to their faith in the sacrament of baptism, and their labour proceeding in that faith, shall be the reward in the salvation and edification of many souls; which labour if ye would frustrate, labour without faith in the sacrament,—as, indeed, is the case with most parents, with most catechists of Sabbath schools, and with most ministers of churches. They labour *without* the ordinance, not *in* the ordinace; they labour without the assurance of the covenant, not *in* and *from* the assurance of the covenant, and therefore they labour so much in vain. To remedy this, and to enable you to labour in hope and in full assurance, I have set forth, in your hearing, the true doctrine of baptism, and the true standing in which it placeth us to one another: but I have been careful all along to preserve the great doctrine of God's sovereignty, and of our election in Christ, as the only ground of the covenant; and seeing that the covenant resteth upon this ground, we ought to consider all the contents and fruits of the covenant, as likewise rested thereon; and, therefore, though we consider our children in covenant, and travail with them as the subjects of a divine engagement, we should ever bear in mind, that the covenanted Church is for the testimony of God's sovereignty, as much as of any other of His attributes; and, therefore, in all our pleadings of the promises, in all our assurance of His faithfulness to His covenant, we should bear in mind, above all other things, that grace is free to be refused, as well as to be granted: this being forgotten, all is marred. For if we suppose God to be under compulsion; then what is it that compelleth Him? for that which compelleth Him will be the true God. Hence proceeded the root of the apostasy, who said the Church—the ordinances administered by the Church—compelleth or obligeth Him; and so the Church became the infallible God: and we now say, in our Bible-mania, the written Word obligeth Him; and so the written Word becometh God. But no; neither written Word nor sacramental ordinances oblige God; no, nor the Son that came forth from His bosom; nor the Holy Ghost which proceedeth from the Father and the Son. The Son was manifested, and the Holy Ghost proclaimed: by the former the Word was revealed, and by the latter the Church endowed; all for the end of teaching us what the will of the Father is; of setting the will of the Father supreme over the universe, fallen and unfallen, redeemed and unredeemed; and he who hath learned aright, in the school of Christ, is taught to exalt the will of the Father as supreme; and to expect everything which he doth expect, and to receive everything which he doth receive, as proceeding from the same. Not, therefore, to remove you from dependence upon that will, which alone is independence and liberty; not to bring you into bondage to any Church, or to the ordinances of any Church, but by the exposition of the Church and of its ordinances, to shew you the will of the Father, His free and sovereign grace, that ye may trust therein; this hath been the object and end of our discourse.

The object of faith is God, and not a word written or spoken. The end of faith is the invisible God, and not any visible person or visible thing; for, brethren, even Christ is not the end of faith, but the Father which sent Him. Therefore, I pray you, dearly beloved, by the help of Christ, the living ladder, whose foot—whose bruised heel—is His Church on earth; whose head is the Son of man in glory, to ascend into the knowledge of the true God, whom to know is life eternal. But not without that living ladder think ye to ascend into the sublime and secret mysteries of the Father, whom no eye hath seen nor can see; and remember that, of that ladder, baptism is, I may say, the first step which manifesteth the purpose of the Godhead to regenerate the fallen creature, and to raise it at length into the fellowship of the exaltation of Christ.

HOMILY VI.

THE STANDING OF THE BAPTIZED IN THE CHURCH.

PSALM CIII. 17, 18.

But the mercy of the Lord is from everlasting to everlasting upon them that fear him, and his righteousness unto children's children; to such as keep his covenant, and to those that remember his commandments to do them.

HAVING ministered, last Lord's day, both by word and sacrament, to the consolation and strength of one portion of the Church of Christ committed to my ministerial and pastoral carefulness, I have been much pressed in spirit during the week for the rest, who, though baptized into the same family, and entitled to all the privileges of the house and family of God, do yet, for some cause or other, deny themselves the sweetest, strongest token of their Father's love, and abide far off from the table which He hath spread for their spiritual refreshment in the wilderness of the present world: to whose doubts and difficulties, scruples and fears, I would now, in the spirit of a shepherd's love and care, address my words; earnestly praying unto the Lord that He would enable me rightly to express, and graciously to convey unto their souls, the most affectionate message and tender invitation with which His ministers are charged towards them. In fulfilling which purpose of grace, let me first place before all who have been baptized into the Church of Christ, in what relation that covenant placeth them generally towards God, and more particularly towards the sacrament of the supper. And, secondly, let me endeavour to deal, by explanation and argument, with the most influential of those obstacles which Satan interposeth in the way of the baptized to lead them from the sacrament of the supper. And, lastly, by expostulation and entreaty, do my part to stir you up, in a righteous and holy spirit, to give obedience to the commandment of the Lord.

I am therefore, according to the gift which is apportioned unto me of the great Householder, first, to lay before you who have been baptized into Christ, at whatever age and in whatever communion, so it hath been one of His ordained ministers, the true scriptural doctrine of your privileges and obligations, and the condition generally in which you stand towards God and His Church; that, being possessed of the true doctrine, you may be able to judge of the resolution of doubts, and expostulations of duty, which I am afterwards to offer. "Know ye not," saith the apostle, "that so many of us as were baptized into Jesus Christ, were baptized into his death? Therefore we are buried with him by baptism into death; that like as Christ was raised from the dead by the glory of the Father, even so we also should walk in newness of life." And, again, in another epistle, he saith: "For ye are all the children of God by faith in Jesus Christ. For as many of you as have been baptized into Christ have put on Christ." And, again, in another epistle, he saith: "In whom also ye are circumcised with the circumcision made without hands, in putting off the body of the sins of the flesh by the circumcision of Christ; buried with him in baptism, wherein also ye are risen with him through the faith of the operation of God, who hath raised him from the dead." From these explanations of, or inferences made from, baptism, there can be no doubt that, however much abused, the doctrine contained in the standards of our Church, and the sister Church of England, concerning baptism, is the true doctrine; that is, That it is a sign and seal of engrafting into Himself, of remission of sins by His blood, and regeneration by His Spirit; of adoption and resurrection into everlasting life, whereby the parties baptized are solemnly admitted into the visible Church, and enter into an open and professed engagement to be wholly and only the Lord's. Now observe, my baptized brethren, that it is not the sign of these blessed doctrines, but also the seal of them, stamping the privilege and possession of them upon every one; and holding him, if he be found wanting of these precious gifts, to be so wanting as one who hath squandered away his portion like the prodigal son, or, for present profit, sold it, as profane Esau did his birthright; and that he is to be blamed, not as one who hath not known, but as one who hath known and shut his eyes upon the light; not as one who hath not possessed the inheritance of the New Testament, but hath possessed it and put it away. For the doctrine that the sacraments are but signs, which hath got the sway out of the Church, and within the Church even, hath obtained a hearing, through the miserable ignorance of the believers, and the idolatry of the formalists, is a doctrine upon which the Reformers of our Church thus express themselves in the first symbol of faith which they drew up:—"And thus we utterly condemn the vanity of those that affirm sacraments to be nothing else but naked and bare signs. No; we assuredly believe that, by baptism, we are engrafted in Christ Jesus, to be made partakers of His justice, whereby our sins are covered and remitted. And also, that in the supper, rightly used, Christ Jesus is so joined with us, that He becometh very nourishment and food to our souls; and yet, notwithstanding the far distance of place which is between His body, now glorified in heaven, and us, now mortal on this earth, we most assuredly believe, that the bread which we break is the communion of Christ's body, and the cup which we drink is the communion of His blood." There never hath been a doubt in the Christian Church, from the times of the apostles to the present time—always excepting those who deny the Divinity of Christ, who have wandered into all errors of doctrine—that baptism is the most solemn act whereby a soul is introduced into the full inheritance of Christ's purchased redemption, and made a member of the visible Church, to live in His faith, and to walk by His faith, and to inherit the kingdom of His faith. The Papal apostasy, though it dared to add to the number of the sacraments, and to cover them with veils of sense, durst never take the sealing virtue out of the sacrament of baptism; nor yet the Greek Church, nor any of the communions of the Reformed Church: it was left to the silent sapping and mining of the intellectual apostasy of this age to have so wasted all the strongholds of faith and everlasting institutions of the gospel, as to leave this sacrament in the minds of professors no more than a shell without the kernel; a husk without the food; a sign without anything signified; a rite, a ceremony, a form, anything or nothing—certainly not the thing written of in Scripture under the name of baptism.

You will not err, brethren, as the formalists of this day do err, in supposing that the outward act of washing with water brings with it, as of necessity, any saving virtue, or worketh, as by magic, a cleansing of the corrupt soul; for, on the other hand, as we have oft taught you, for a man without faith to have to do with these sacraments is an abomination to the Lord, and bringeth down upon his spirit some visitation of God, as sure, though invisible, as that which fell upon the profane, though otherwise exalted, king of Judah; yea, and to his child no blessing descendeth from the dry fountain of his father's faithless act, but rather an inheritance of barrenness, and a visitation of wrath, according to the threatening of the second commandment against idolatry; for is there grosser idolatry within the Romish Church than that which is taught in this land of the sacrament of baptism,— that on that rite, discharged in due form, there is present a virtue to regenerate the soul of the little one, and to look for any other regeneration is but a vagary of idle and enthusiastic brains? But, nevertheless, though the parent who presented us at the laver of regeneration, and the priest who washed us therein, and the people who were witnesses thereof, had been all faithless and idolaters, and the little one made but a cold, unfathered, unbefriended entrance into the Church; yet within the covenant it is now found, and being there found, it is an heir of all the promises which are the everlasting inheritance of the faithful disciples of Christ. So that I have no hesitation in saying, it is as fully privileged to enter in by faith into the riches of the inheritance as any other, however more favourably conditioned, and more dutifully introduced to the Church. There are rough inclemencies which such a little one shall have to pass through—disabilities, disadvantages, and hindrances; such as prayerless parents, ungodly acquaintance, an untutored childhood, an unspiritual ministry, infinite temptations of worldliness—

accumulated upon its head in consequence, it may be, of a long line of ungodly ancestors, or by the withdrawing of God's candlestick from the Church, or from its being the day of His wrath upon the country; and from a thousand other dispensations of His righteous government, over which we have no control. For it is a poor and shallow notion of God, that He is the God only of individuals, and not also the God of families, and the God of nations, and the God of generations and of ages. There is a scheme of justice and government; there is a recompence of reward, and a recompence of vengeance, which reacheth far and wide, both over the Church and over the world. The Church hath her discipline of heaven, however much she may hold discipline cheap; and she is suspended from her ministry of grace to the world, and her light is eclipsed, and she is stricken, smitten, and afflicted: she is excommunicated also, and given over to Satan to be accursed, if she forsake the testimonies of the Lord. The milk of her breasts being dried up, her children are left to pine and perish, and the land where she tabernacleth is defeated of its blessings, and scourged with every evil. All this happeneth, and hath happened, to every Church which hath existed in Christendom; ay, and will happen to us, if we continue in our Laodicean condition, neither hot nor cold, full of boasting and self-sufficiency, and golden bravery, when there is no faith, or almost none, in the midst of us. And what were the Church without such government?—a house of all iniquity, and not the house of God; Satan's temple, not the temple of the Holy Spirit; another prison-house of slavery, instead of being the citadel of the free; dark and plagued as Egypt, and not peaceful and untroubled as Goshen.

Of this Church, with its promises, its privileges, and its government, and of all its visitations of blessing, of affliction, of mercy, and of wrath, we become the children by baptism, to be blessed with its blessings, and afflicted with its afflictions, and to take our fare in the same vessel with it; or, if we do not become its denizens and citizens by baptism, I am here who know not how or when we become its denizens and citizens, or what reality there is in a visible Church. It is altogether an invisible Church and a spiritual dispensation, if baptism be taken away from these high uses which it serveth. But baptism doth not only bring us into the visible Church; it doth also, being accompanied with faith—without which it is not baptism solemnised, but baptism profaned—bring us into the invisible Church. If there is faith in the receiving of it, it doth bring with it rich grace, both to the parents and to the child; in which faith if the child continue as its faculties unfold themselves, then it will grow up before the Lord, increasing more and more in favour with God and men; and surely the first act of interruption is never in God's unreadiness to bestow, but in our unwillingness to receive. And, therefore, I do exhort every parent to come to the sacrament with no scanty faith, and to expect no scanty blessing to himself and his little one. And I do, moreover, exhort every one who hath been neglectful herein, even now to exercise faith in the Redeemer and in the regenerating Spirit, both for his own sake and for the sake of those whom he, in an unworthy manner, brings to the laver of regeneration.

But to all those who, having been baptized, of whatever spirit may have been the functionaries of the holy act, I have this day undertaken to explain their common privileges, which are all the privileges of the visible Church; amongst which I reckon, first, the written Word of God—a treasure in itself more to be prized than all the labours of the learned, and all the knowledge of the skilful, and all kingdom, and all wisdom, and all wealth, and all glory. This is the first gift which is made to you at baptism—the Old and the New Testament, comprised in the blood of Christ. Yours it is in full possession; your right to it is the right of all saints. Those who inherit heaven had no better birthright or title than you received at your baptism. For you, Moses writ the law; for you, David poured forth the rich strains of his harp; for you, the prophets were anointed with the fire of God's altar; and for you, the apostles were baptized with the Holy Spirit and with fire. For you, also, came the Prophet of prophets, and the Apostle of apostles, the Shiloh, the Messiah, the Sent of God; and for you have been preserved the gracious words which flowed from His lips. And thus, in your hands, under your eyes, in your knowledge, and, perhaps, in your memory, is the testimony of God since the world began;—the record of His acts, which are wonderful; the records of His Word, which are sure and steadfast; the praises of His saints, which are fearful; the discovery of His purposes, which are holy—light, spiritual light, to the soul sitting in darkness and the shadow of death. What say you? Is not that a glorious endowment for memory, and for expectation, for knowledge, for wisdom, for redemption, and salvation; containing such insight into your inward state, such admonitions of the outward hazard, such pledges of help, such assurances of blessing, such soul-supporting consolations in adversity: is that naught? Say ye that it is little? or say you, that it is an unspeakable gift? What, though it condemn you, and violently accuse you, you would rather part with houses and lands, with liberty and with life, than part from this seed and nourishment of an immortal life, this revelation of an inheritance that fadeth not away. All this ye have in virtue of your baptism; it is the dowry of the visible Church, and the expectation of the ends of the earth.

There is next the infinite privilege of the Christian ministry, which, when it is what our Lord intended it to be, passeth the former, inasmuch as it is a combination both of the word and the Spirit; the word in the mouth, the Spirit in the soul: and however formal and imperfect it is, so that it speak not heresies, nor declare errors, (when it becomes the ministry of the deceiver, not of Him whose name is Faithful and True,) it is, perhaps, the greatest blessing which a land can be endowed withal: a ministry of religion, from Sabbath to Sabbath, is the greatest blessing of a nation, and ought to be the greatest care of the rulers of a nation; and the late-fledged notion that this is, and ought to be, no care of the State, doth strike at the root of God's government of States. For if you have not the people cared for, in respect to religious instruction,—care for them as you please in respect to the freedom of trade, the administration of justice, the preservation of the peace, and the spreading of knowledge,—you do but clothe the members, fill the head, without caring for the heart; and we all know that the members of a fool may be swathed in purple and gold, and the head of a miscreant may be filled with knowledge, but the soul which is cultivated by the Christian religion must be furnished with knowledge, and endowed with industry, for the profitable discharge of all its occupations. Such an unwearied ministry of word and prayer have ye continually, my beloved brethren, in the Churches of Christ; and there is no minister of Christ who would not welcome you to a more private and particular ministry of the same, if you would seek it at his lips.

To us also have been the blessings of a religious education, for few in our Church are without this unspeakable advantage. The most of you have had the inheritance of the prayers of godly forefathers, and, perhaps, are even now endowed with the prayers of pious and watchful parents, wearying the Lord, till you shall be joined in spirit to the body of His Son. You have all the inheritance of the prayers of the Church invisible. For the true and spiritual Church of Christ is not now of the temper of the elder son, who grudged his prodigal brother's liberal welcome; but we do continually pray our Father that He would be pleased to forgive you, and touch your hearts with the sense of His mercies, and with the shame of your contempt of His long-suffering. And here I must speak, likewise, of the inheritance which we have in the faith, and patience, and prayers of those martyrs in whose blood our Church was planted, and of those most faithful ministers who laboured and wrestled with the Lord for this Church, which hath been planted in the midst of us. Yea, and the odour of our orthodox and enlarged doctrine is well pleasing to the Lord, in this age of limited and heterodox doctrine; and our simple primitive forms of ordinance and sacrament cannot but be well pleasing to Him, in the midst of pomps and ceremonies. And the sister Churches which remember us in their prayers, as we remember them, cannot remain without an answer in the ear of the Lord. In short, brethren, you stand, in virtue of your connexion with the visible Church, ensphered with a multitude of blessings, which time would fail me to enumerate. These, all these stand inviting you, soliciting you, to enter into the possession of the very things; for the written Word speaking to your natural man, to have the living Word formed within you the hope of glory; for the ministry of the preacher, to have the ministry of the Holy Spirit; for the teaching of parents, to have the teaching of the Holy One; for the mediate blessings, to have the immediate blessings of the house; and for the tidings of your Father's love, to have the very experience of His love; the communion of the Father, and the Son, and the Holy Ghost, to which you were introduced and welcomed at baptism—to which you are ever privileged to enter by faith, and to which, without faith, no one did ever enter.

Such is the inheritance, brethren, whereinto we are introduced by the sacrament of baptism;—a spiritual heritage, compared with which, the rights of kingdoms, or the titles of nobility, or even royal honour and power, sink into nothing. But these same privileges are guarded by awful sanctions, which are all included in the word judgment to come. One who is in covenant with God shall be judged otherwise than one who is out of covenant with Him: we shall be judged as prodigal children, who have lavished away our inheritance; not as strangers, who have never possessed any: we shall be judged as a wife, who hath been contracted and espoused unto the Lord; not as a strange woman: we shall be judged as those who have trampled under foot the blood of the covenant, with which we should have been sanctified. There is no error more fatal, than to have forgotten this the exact standing of the baptized in the Church, and to have commenced the term of our responsibility as Christians from conversion. Conversion is a most important point in our Christian course, when we return from our prodigal state to our Father's house: but conversion is not a sacrament; it hath no visible nor sensible form, although they oft labour to constitute it into such. It is no sign nor seal of the covenant, that the covenant should be looked upon as beginning then; and before it we are not as heathens. Oh that I could persuade myself the multitude of unconverted persons were as heathens! my soul would be more at ease concerning them; for to the heathen it shall be greatly more tolerable than to them. But they are Christians, whom God hath endowed with all Christian privileges, and overlaid with all Christian sanctions. And let me tell you, brethren, that the history of God's dealings with your soul, His long-suffering, His frequent calls, His visitations of trial, His instructions and His warnings, His forbearance and forgiveness, before conversion, is as wonderful a part of the divine book of our spiritual history, as His dealings with us after our conversion;—how He forbare with us, and entreated us while yet enemies, more instructive of His love, than how He hath entreated us while friends, reconciled unto Him, and obedient children of the house. And let me tell you, my beloved brethren, that the waters of repentance are made many times more bitter and medicinal; and the godly sorrow, which worketh salvation, many times more grievous; and the whole work of humiliation and contrition, many times more heavy, when we look back upon the period of our baptism as a period of broken and rejected vows, neglected privileges, judgments heaped up; than when we look back upon it merely as a blank or waste in our life, during which we stood in no relationship whatever unto God.

It may seem to you strange, that in virtue of that which is commonly held in no better esteem than a ceremony or rite, the Lord should bear to you so exquisite a love, and follow you with such inquisitive desire;—so strange was it that He should, in like manner, entreat Abraham's seed for the faith of their father; so strange, that He should, by His Son, open the covenant to the idolatrous and wicked Gentiles, and give His life for the sinful and rebellious world. Strange, passing strange, and wonderful is it all, an unsearchable mystery of love! But as St Paul saith of Israel, so I say of those who have been baptized into Christ, that they are beloved for the election's sake: for the sake of the Church are they beloved of God, who honoureth and will honour His own ordinances, however they may be abused; and will continue to make them, unto the hand of faith, the storehouse and supply of all spiritual grace. Within the temple of His Church,—sanctified and separated by these holy sacraments, ministered by an ordained priesthood,—He is to be found present, and out of it He is not to be found as a God in covenant; for the

Church is that for which Christ did enter into covenant, by the sacrifice of Himself; and whosoever believeth in Christ must be baptized; and whosoever hath been baptized into Christ, hath been baptized into His faith. But my wicked life, say ye, my life of unbelief! Concerning that we shall come to speak in its place; for there is a government of God over the Church, as over the world; but as in the world, a man's wickedness doth not curtail the earth and heavens of their sweet influences, nor make the fruits of the earth less kindly, or the breezes of the air less refreshing, or the light of the sun less plentiful, though by his wickedness he be greatly mistuned and molested for the enjoyment of the same; so, in the Church, the formality and faithlessness of the wicked do not prejudice the fruitfulness of God's grace, and the light of His countenance, and the joy of His Spirit, and the certainty of all His promises. These peculiar blessings of the spiritual world continue to inhere in the Church, to abide upon her, though, through want of faith, she may receive none of them; and the moment she exerciseth true faith, another spring and summer and harvest shall burst forth as at the first; even as in Palestine, and the fairest countries of the world, which were once a garden, there doth still abide all the powers of fruitfulness, ready to burst forth so soon as industry shall arise to guide and direct them. And as these people are visited with poverty, and wretchedness, and barrenness of all good, for their base and brutal apathy, and shall be held responsible for the abuse of God's good gifts of creation; so, also, shall the professing but unproductive Church be held responsible for all the promises which are written in the book of God, for a real endowment to her, if she use them not, and be not crowned with their fruits.

Therefore, my beloved brethren, who have been baptized into Christ, this is the sum of the doctrine concerning your condition: That there is not a promise, blessing, or privilege of the true and spiritual Church of Christ on earth, and of the everlasting kingdom of heaven, which hath not been constantly in your power, and continually offered to you since you became members of the visible Church. No offices of the Father to lead you unto Christ, no offices of the Son to redeem you from all unrighteousness, no offices of the Spirit to restore you to the image of God, no revelation of their love, no assurance of their help, which were not made patent and free to you that day ye were baptized in the name of the Father, the Son, and the Holy Ghost. It doth not bring with it as by necessity the baptism of the Holy Ghost, which cometh not save by faith, and in the proportion of our faith; but it is the symbol of that baptism, and the free declaration of it: yea, it hath to the baptism of the Holy Ghost, the same relation which the written Word hath to the living Word, which the Church on earth hath to the Church in heaven. There is to every spiritual reality a visible and intelligible representation, which being impregnated with faith, becomes the spiritual reality; and, until so impregnated, is only a representation, but such a representation as is devised of Infinite Wisdom to remove all our fears, and surmount all our objections, and open the way into the real presence; sufficient, moreover, to save the soul, which will give reverend heed thereto; and sufficient to condemn the soul which will not: so that, as the word is either the savour of life, or else the savour of death, to the soul of every one who heareth it; so is baptism, to those who receive it, either the seal of regeneration, or the seal of condemnation, (and that Christian condemnation,—condemnation without excuse,) according as they exercise faith and are regenerated, or do not exercise faith and are not regenerated.

Taking the Scriptures, therefore, for our only guide of faith, with the writings of all orthodox divines, and the symbols of all orthodox Churches, to help our interpretation thereof, there can be no doubt, dearly beloved brethren, that every baptized person who now heareth me, whatever may have been the unworthiness of his parents, or of us the administering priests, is as much, in the eye of Christ, a member of His Church, and free of His covenant of grace, as were the Jews of His day, who, though they had lapsed into the uttermost formality, and were ripe for the sickle of vengeance, and the wine-press of wrath, were treated by Him, and entreated of Him, with all patience and affection; their law reverenced and fulfilled; their priests honoured in their places; their immunities preserved; yea, the preaching of the gospel religiously restricted to them; and the promise which Messiah had been appointed to fulfil, all by Messiah fulfilled; just as if the rebellious and hard-hearted nation had been of one gracious heart and believing soul; as if they had been recapitulated into one man, and that man the friend of God, and father of saints, the faithful Abraham; insomuch, that Christ wept over that city, the wickedest perhaps in the world, hardly excepting imperial Rome, and certainly, considering its knowledge and privileges, the far wickedest in the world; so that Josephus, its citizen, hath said, that if God had not destroyed it by the Roman sword, he thinks it would have perished, like Sodom, by fire from heaven, or convulsive throws of the earth, to be eased of such a vile and pestilential load; yet over the children of that city, remembering its dearness to His Father, and its sacred inheritance in the promises of His Father, the Saviour wept! He sat Him down upon the brow of the overhanging hill, and looked upon the beloved city, and wept! saying, "O Jerusalem, Jerusalem! thou that stonest the prophets, and killest them that are sent unto thee; how would I have gathered thee as a hen doth her chickens under her wings, but you would not!" And, in like manner, ye children of the Christian Church, by baptism—however unworthy and wicked in yourselves, and however unworthy your fathers may have been—are beloved of Christ for His Church's sake; and for the honour of His covenant, into which you have been brought by the observance of His holy ordinances, He doth weep over you with a still tenderer lamentation, saying, "Come unto me, my children; why stand ye afar off? Come unto me, all ye that are weary and heavy laden, and I will give you rest: take my yoke upon you, and learn of me, for I am meek and lowly; and ye shall find rest unto your souls." He hath bidden you to the wedding, and ye are unwilling to come. But He sendeth other servants, saying, "Tell them which are bidden, Behold, I have prepared my dinner; my oxen and my fatlings are killed, and all things are ready: come unto the marriage." Oh! ye know not the love and longing with which He longeth over you, nor the welcome with which He will receive you to the house of which ye are the children, the beloved children; and though your course of unnatural disobedience, and wicked apostasy, had been like the prodigal's, when you return in the spirit of the prodigal, you shall receive from Him the prodigal's welcome and blessing; the fond, the exuberant, and unbounded entertainment of the prodigal. And I tell you, there shall be more joy in heaven that day you come home into the kingdom, than over ninety and nine of those who are resting and remaining constant to the engagement of our Father's house. Search the books of the prophets, who had words put into their mouths from the Lord to His ancient people; take the most pathetic of the Lord's complaints, the most tender of His entreaties, the most warm and earnest of His expostulations, and the most home-felt of His appeals; take them and apply them unto yourselves, for surely they are to the full, and even more fully, your right than they were of the children of the former dispensation. Hear what the Lord saith unto you by the prophet Isaiah: "Thou hast not called upon me, O Jacob! but thou hast been weary of me, O Israel! yet I, even I, am he that blotteth out thy transgressions for my own sake, and will not remember thy sins." And again, by the prophet Ezekiel: "Cast away from you all your transgressions whereby ye have transgressed; and make you a new heart and a new spirit: for why will ye die, O house of Israel? For I have no pleasure in the death of him that dieth, saith the Lord God; wherefore turn and live ye." And again: "Seek ye the Lord while he may be found, call ye upon him while he is near. Let the wicked forsake his way, and the unrighteous man his thoughts: and let him return unto the Lord, and he will have mercy upon him; and to our God, for he will abundantly pardon. For my thoughts are not your thoughts, neither are your ways my ways, saith the Lord. For as the heavens are higher than the earth, so are my ways higher than your ways, and my thoughts than your thoughts. For as the rain cometh down, and the snow from heaven, and returneth not thither, but watereth the earth, and maketh it bring forth and bud, that it may give seed to the sower, and bread to the eater: so shall my word be that goeth forth out of my mouth: it shall not return unto me void; but it shall accomplish that which I please, and it shall prosper in the thing whereto I sent it," (Isa. lv. 6–11.) And again: "O Israel, thou hast destroyed thyself; but in me is thine help," (Hos. xiii. 9.) And again: "Go and proclaim these words toward the north, and say, Return, thou backsliding Israel, saith the Lord; and I will not cause mine anger to fall upon you: for I am merciful, saith the Lord, and I will not keep anger for ever. Only acknowledge thine iniquity, that thou hast transgressed against the Lord thy God, and hast scattered thy ways to the strangers under every green tree, and ye have not obeyed my voice, saith the Lord. Turn, O backsliding children, saith the Lord; for I am married unto you: and I will take you one of a city, and two of a family, and I will bring you to Zion: and I will give you pastors according to mine heart, which shall feed you with knowledge and understanding; and it shall come to pass, when ye be multiplied and increased in the land, in those days, saith the Lord, they shall say no more, The ark of the covenant of the Lord: neither shall it come to mind: neither shall they remember it; neither shall they visit it; neither shall that be done any more," (Jer. iii. 12–16.) But though these exclamations of the prophets be very tender, they come not up to the spirit which our Lord hath embodied in the parable of the prodigal son, to which we have so often referred; of the labourers in the vineyard, where the last that came was paid as the first; of the marriage-feast, where the highways and most promiscuous resorts were visited with inviting messengers: and perhaps His words upon the cross pass all example, when He said, "Father, forgive them, for they know not what they do."

But time would fail me to enumerate the words and acts of God's longing over His Church: and enough surely has been said to lead you to serious thoughtfulness and consideration; and I trust, by the blessing of God, enough hath been said to stir you up from the lethargy in which you are held, by reason of the veil which Satan hath cast over all these your high privileges and blessed conditions; and that without delay you will be moved to meditate the Word of God whether these things be so; and pray unto Him to deliver you from your sins, and lead you by His Spirit into that temple of glory and blessedness which Christ hath set open to your souls.

HOMILY VII.

THE STANDING OF THE BAPTIZED WITH RESPECT TO THE LORD'S SUPPER.

MATT. XXVI. 27.

—— *Drink ye all of it.*

HAVING laid before you, in the former homily, what are the privileges of those who have been baptized into Christ, and what the grace to which they have had continual access, and which even now is open to every one of them, I now proceed, as was proposed, in the second place, to deal with some of those difficulties and objections which present themselves in the way of their approach to the table of the Lord. In the primitive Church baptism was called the enlightening, in order to signify the natural darkness out of which we are brought into the marvellous light of the gospel; and therefore it is rightly administered to infants, because infancy and youth is the season at which the light of knowledge, either natural or spiritual, is to be introduced into the mind for the direction of the future life: the Lord herein, as in everything else, conforming the institutions of the gospel to the natural condition of the mind, which is not required to act for itself until after it hath been long placed under parents, teachers, and guardians. Which period of instruction and discipline being past, the pupil is released from his tutelage, and takes upon him the offices of the man, and is regarded as a person in the eye of law and of society. Whereupon the light of instruction becometh the life of action, and the discipline of the will changeth into the freedom of the will; at which entrance into self-directed life we have the sacrament of life given in the elements of life, as at our birth and nonage we had the sacrament of the spiritual birth: the one releasing us from the guardians under which the other had placed us, and presenting to us the manly food of spiritual strength; whereas the former did but purify the soul from the uncleanness, and deliver it from the darkness, of its natural birth. Yet, as the birth doth give the promise of manhood, and the child doth contain the rudiments of the man, and is never properly instructed or disciplined but with a view to future self-government; so the sacrament for spiritual infancy doth contain the rudiments of the whole spiritual life, and is often used, both in the Scriptures and in the Standards of the Church, as indeed we formerly quoted, to signify and contain all the privileges of the covenant of grace. But though completely contained therein, the principle of personal and independent life by union to Christ Jesus, is only fully and properly revealed to us in the symbol of the Lord's supper.

Therefore it was the custom in the primitive times, before admitting the converts to the faith and privileges of the Church by the sacrament of baptism, to consider them as wards of the Church, and to appoint over them catechists, who might instruct them in various classes until they were enlightened and thought fit to stand for themselves, and perform their various offices as members of the Christian body. And from this also, I doubt not, arose the custom of godfathers and godmothers, in order that the Church might have the pledges and securities of holy persons, that its infant members would not be left in ignorance, but early introduced to the knowledge of the blessings freely given to them in Christ Jesus the Lord. Which custom our Church, in her more rigorous and severe discipline, would not permit, but doth require this duty solemnly at the hands of the parents, and oblige the ministers, in their rounds of visitation, to examine and take order that in every family it be dutifully discharged. And every Church, without any exception, doth signify, by its provisions of discipline, that there is a period in the Christian life between baptism and the Lord's supper, during which the disciple is under the guardianship of the Church, and preparing by instruction for becoming his own master, and joined to Christ, but in subordination and subjection; and afterwards, when he is deemed worthy by the rulers of the Church, to be admitted to his liberty and freedom in Christ. Wherefore, at the supper we are well said to renew the baptismal covenant, and to take the vows upon ourselves.

Now, it will easily appear from these premises, that the baptized who are not communicants, are to the communicants of the Church not as heathen men and as publicans; but, if they have not fallen away from the faith, are to be regarded by us as our children in Christ Jesus, over whom we have with tenderness and care to watch until they shall be sufficiently enlightened and prepared for assuming to themselves a personal standing in the Church; and that as I now, in my office of minister, deal with them by instruction, so were it comely and right for you, in your office of members of Christ, to deal with your friends and brethren who are in this condition, to come and partake of the waters of life freely. And to the end of fulfilling my duty, and shewing you how to fulfil yours, I shall now, as the Lord giveth me the ability, endeavour to consider their case, and to administer to it the counsel of the Word of God.

If those who have been baptized into Christ Jesus continue to maintain their faith in His person, as the Son of God; in His offices, as their own Redeemer and Mediator with God; in His Church, as the pillar and ground of the truth, and the minister of His grace unto the world; then are they, as we taught in the former homily, to consider themselves as having the title to some portion in His house; from which if they be withheld, they withhold themselves; forasmuch as there is nothing which another possesses, that they may not, by the same application and diligence, possess, to the comfort, and enriching, and salvation of their souls. But if they have renounced the faith of Christ altogether, and denied Him who bought them, holding Him for a deceiver of the earth, then I speak not unto such; their case is indeed very hopeless; and truly I know not whether any hope at all remaineth for such: but for the rest, who continue as pupils and children in His house, there is nothing which ought to prevent their becoming free and privileged men, but these two things, ignorance and wickedness. If they have been neglected by their parents, and their guardians, and the Church, and when they come to listen to the gospel ministry, find no answer of the conscience to its spiritual exhortations; or when they read the Scriptures, find no spiritual discernment of their meaning, nor inward experience of their truths; and have no higher notion of religion, than to obey the natural conscience of right and wrong, and act an honourable and upright part between man and man,—then I say not that in this state they should come unto the table of the Lord, for they are not yet acquainted with the first principles of the doctrine of Christ, and are still in the condition of babes, who must be fed with milk, the food of babes, not with bread and wine, the food of full-grown men. But they ought not to remain a day, no, not an hour, in this condition of darkness and doubt; but address themselves to God, into whose name they were baptized, as to a Father, praying that He would lead them into truth, and guide them in righteous judgment; and they ought to apply to the ministers of Christ, whose lips should ever keep knowledge, in order to be instructed with more simplicity than is convenient in public sermons, and with more plainness than is proper to a mixed multitude, concerning those things in which they feel themselves to be in doubt and perplexity. And to the end of receiving such inquirers, ministers do fix for the people certain times at which they may instruct them. And on such occasions you should open your heart and mind to the minister of Christ, that he may inform you wherein the views you entertain are right, and wherein they are wrong; not coming to him to be excited, by eloquent or tender discourse, into a soft and pathetic mood, but coming to be resolved of doubts, and instructed more perfectly in the ways of righteousness. Ye are inexcusable, therefore, on this score, who have a ministry of the gospel, and opportunities of private communion with your minister, if you continue in ignorance or uncertainty concerning the mysteries of your salvation. Why should a man be afraid to confess his ignorance? If he know that he is ignorant, and seek not to have it removed, he is worse than a fool, and there is no hope of him; for knowledge cometh before action, and light cometh before life; and the Word of God is revealed before the Spirit of God.

At the same time, be careful to understand and believe, that there is a light which is not attained but in the way of a holy life; and that there is a discernment of the Word of God, which is not to be had but by the teaching of the Holy Spirit; and a knowledge of the truth, which cometh only from the doing of the truth, according to that which is written by the apostle John, "He that doeth the truth, shall know of the truth, that it is of God." Whence I draw these two inferences: That your ignorance of the true faith may proceed from no want of early instruction, but from the blinds which are cast over all spiritual knowledge by the power and presence of the carnal man within you; and in this case, the true cause of your incapacity for the communion springing from wickedness, which we are to treat of forthwith. But if this be not the case, then I observe, secondly, That you are not to withhold from the communion because your knowledge is imperfect; or wait till the mysteries of all doctrines have declared themselves to your souls, for this cannot be but by progress in the actual life of godliness, for which the Lord's table is the nourishment. At the same time I think, that no one ought to give himself to the communion of the Church who holdeth opinions adverse to the great fundamental doctrines of the Trinity and the redemption; although, even in respect to these, we are far from requiring those clear and determinate convictions which come only by progress in the spiritual life: there ought to be an entire reverence for the doctrines of the orthodox Church, and an open, teachable disposition to be nourished up in them, according to the teaching of the Word and the Spirit of God. And, above all, you ought to remember continually, that for this very end ye were baptized, that ye might be enlightened in the knowledge of Christ; and that the Lord holdeth out no false promises, neither maketh any fruitless covenants; and, therefore, you may assure yourselves, that day you were baptized, the temple of spiritual knowledge was thrown open to you, is now open to you, into which you may enter, and pass onward and inward, until you have possessed as much of the precious doctrine as your vessel is able to contain. Therefore, as I said, ye do not well to remain another day, another hour, without the gate, as if ye were Gentiles, and not circumcised with the circumcision of Christ.

Now, for the second disqualification,—namely, The indulgence of sins which are inconsistent with the discipline of the Church of Christ on earth; and are denounced in the Word of God, as excluding from the kingdom of heaven,—I have this much to say: That no one ought to bring with him into the Church of Christ any habit of body or of mind which would justly entitle him to be challenged and rebuked while abiding therein; and, if not amended, would justify the Church suspending him or excommunicating him from her communion. I do not now stop to make the enumeration of those immoralities and unchristian tempers, having solemnly read, in your hearing, when fencing the communion-table, several lists of that kind, which you will find written everywhere in the Holy Scriptures. To become members of the Church, while either publicly or wittingly indulging in these habitual sins, would be a great profanation of the holy communion of Christ's body, which hath no fellowship with sin; and a grievous offence to His little ones, of whom the very least is defended and protected from offence by the most severe denunciations; and therefore I, as a minister of the Church catholic and universal, must for ever protest against the shameless remissness of the Churches in this respect, and the indiscriminate giving of the bread and wine to whosoever approacheth the altar, or the giving of tokens to whosoever may ask them. The ministers and overseers of the Church who permit such prostitution are much to be blamed; and still more to be blamed are the men, who, educated in a Christian land, dare, without repentance and the renunciation of sins, trample under foot the holy fence which the Lord hath placed around His fold. And again: if any one, maintaining a fair outward character, while he is conscious of secret and hidden offences, presumeth upon the secrecy thereof, to present his claim to be admitted amongst those whom God seeth always; what doth he but condemn himself of hypocrisy, and present himself to be challenged and cast out by the Father of our Lord, when He shall come in to behold the guests? for all things are naked and open to Him with whom we have to do

At the same time, I am too well acquainted with human frailty, and the warfare of flesh and spirit, within the breast of every child of God, to set this mark too high. The best men are worsted of their enemies : Job himself sinned with his lips ; and St Paul had a messenger of Satan to buffet him, lest he should be exalted above measure; and Peter, James, and Barnabas, both dissembled with their consciences and subjected themselves to the carnal elements of the Jewish dispensation ; and they write to all the churches, as to fallible men, and men who had fallen, and were in daily danger of falling, through the soreness of the conflict which they had to maintain with the devil, the world, and the flesh. Therefore, I am far from excluding from the Church any one who is labouring in the contest, because he hath not yet prevailed at all points ; but so that his soul is set within him to resist, by the strength which is in Christ Jesus, I do the rather encourage him to come to the table of the Lord, that he may be filled with the food of strength. So that his spirit is awakened and aroused, is stirred up and in arms against its enemies, is wounded and grieved with its sins, and looking around for the strength which it findeth not within itself. I do heartily encourage such an one to maintain the conflict from the Christian citadel, and with the armour of Christ, and within the lines of the Christian army. Wherefore there is no better sign of a young communicant, than that he should be humbled under the sense of his own sinfulness and infirmity, and crying out, "What shall I do to be saved ? Who shall deliver me from the body of this death ?" And there is none worse, than to deem himself worthy, or that he hath already attained, and is already perfect.

From which remarks you will perceive, dearly beloved brethren, that if ye have erred from the way of your Father's house, into which you were introduced by baptism, and lavished the goods which were given to you, or, with unnatural hardness of heart, have despised your Father's continual overtures of kindness, and disbelieved His protestations of love, and set His messengers of good tidings at naught, ye should not continue to do so any longer, adding iniquity to iniquity, and ingratitude to ingratitude, but return with convinced and sorrowful hearts to the house of your Father; and whenever you do lift up a penitent voice, and set your face to return, I, or any minister of Christ, am here ready to assure you of welcome, and conduct you on your way in peace; and having clothed you, and comforted you, and strengthened you, to lead you into your Father's banqueting house, whose banner over you shall be love. The penitent, the soul-stricken, the heart-broken, the heavy-laden and oppressed, are indeed very welcome, the most welcome, to the house of God: over whom there will be more joy, than over ninety and nine of those who are already standing fast in their integrity. I would not therefore, my well-beloved brethren, have you to stifle the motions of conviction within your soul, or to quench the Holy Spirit; but to cry unto God for help, knowing that ye have an Advocate with the Most High, even Christ Jesus the righteous; who also is "an High Priest, that can be touched with the feeling of our infirmities; being tempted in all points like as we are, yet without sin." Come like good children of the Church, and open your hearts to some brother of the Church, in whom ye have confidence, or to the elders of the Church, or to the minister of the Church, or to some one of the body of Christ, who can give you discreet counsel, and lead you in the way in which you should go. But I am led away by my sympathies, from the expository discourse which I am striving to maintain.

It is, indeed, a very dangerous condition, in which many permit themselves long to remain undecided, whether, having been baptized, they shall join themselves to the body of Christ by the sacrament of His flesh and His blood; and it must be very provoking to that good providence of God, which gave them this best of all inheritances, to be endowed with all the privileges of His house; and the longer they abide in this doubt and uncertainty, the more they do provoke His Holy Spirit, and render powerless the blessed doctrines of the gospel, which they daily hear, and daily hear in vain. It must be that they wax harder and harder of heart, deafer and deafer of hearing, more and more dead and spiritless. If ye believed not, if ye had rejected Christ, and all the blessings of the baptismal covenant, then I know not, as hath been said, but your case were hopeless; and I fear it will come to this pass with you, if you continue to be deluded by the world, the devil, and the flesh. It cannot be but they will work more and more out of you that light of knowledge and life of faith which there is in you, and leave you but a name to live; for they are blank and ignorant of God themselves, and they shall soon reduce to the same utter blankness that human soul which embraceth them as its chief good, or communeth with them as its closest companions. You must grow worse and worse, or better and better; there is no standing still. The soul will not stop its various motions, and either God or an idol must be its glory; and whether that idol be itself or another creature, it mattereth not; when death hath disposed of self, we know not where, and sealed up the creature in utter darkness. I would not treat this matter with eloquent or pathetic discourse, but use words of truth and soberness. And I ask any father here present what would be the effect upon his parental heart, if the son, whom he had cherished from youth in his bosom, and fed from day to day at his table, did, each day that he arose, arise to neglect his duty, and forget his father's love, and disobey his commandments, and dishonour his name, and trample under foot all the reverend ordinances of his house? But, say you, will it mend the matter that I trample another, and the holiest of all, under my foot? Now, I will condemn thee out of thine own mouth: If thou fear to trample upon the sacrament of the supper, why shouldst thou not fear to trample upon the sacrament of baptism, whose inheritance we shewed in the former homily did take in the whole scope of the Christian kingdom? And why shouldest thou not fear to trample upon the ministry of the word, and the solemnities of public worship, and whatever other holy ordinance or observance appertaineth to the Church of Christ? But if thou sayest, All these I do my endeavour to keep, and have from my youth upwards; then say I, Yet thou lackest one thing: turn thy back upon the world's tent, and pitch thy tent with the host of the Lord.

I have long been convinced in my own mind, and the conversations which I have held with young communicants have confirmed me in it, that a great deal of honest purpose, and endeavour after a holy life cometh to no point, from being designed and undertaken in complete ignorance of the only means whereby good can be effected upon earth. There is a certain measure of righteousness (if so it may be called; but I use the word only in accommodation to custom, for righteousness there is none, save that which is wrought by Christ in His people) which may be reached in the strength of natural resolution, without any help of God, which serves to mark the standard of heathen morality; but in a Christian country, where sound doctrine hath long prevailed, as in ours, that standard hath been so raised, conscience hath got such a flood of light from the neighbourhood of Divine truth, that I defy any one to work up to the pitch of its satisfaction. Now there are many, both young and old, who are straining after this impossibility—to stand straight with their own conscience—who, if they would draw nigh to that Word which gave their conscience such discernment, would find that it was never in the mind of God that any man should, in himself, fulfil His holy law!—which is, therefore, always called the minister of death, not of life; the accuser, not the advocate; the condemnation, not the justification of men. For which very end, I have oft taught you, it was given to drive men to distraction, and force them to flee for another fountain of justice, another principle of obedience, another strength, another system of means, than those of nature. And, therefore, I do most solemnly entreat all who are moved to holy living, or are wearied of the world's dissimulation, and cannot endure that conscience should be so trampled under the foot of sense and worldliness, to draw near to Divine instruction, and apprehend for their consolation another and a better way of entering into righteousness and holiness, through the redemption of Christ and the regeneration of the Holy Spirit. It is to fight without your host, to try the battle in your own strength. We might as well say to the flesh, Be pained no more, as say to it, Rule me no more; and to the carnal mind, Be careful and anxious no more, as to say to it, Envy no more, or be no more stirred up with pride: and to the physical world, your will might as well say, Become Eden again, thou wilderness; and thou cruel, blood-thirsty tenant of the wilderness, man-slaughtering man, become thou as Adam was in Eden; or say unto it, Overcome me no more, O world, with thy wiles and deceptions! and, ye men of the world, lead me not astray into your wicked courses! If man, in his own strength, could have done this, then that man might have been made our mediator, and Christ had died in vain. To give force to the human will against the law of the flesh and the world, to condemn sin in the flesh, and to overcome the world, required the union of the Word of the Godhead; and to this day, the reunion of that Divine Word is as necessary as ever in each one of us to the achievement of the same superhuman work of stemming the stream of nature which setteth against us. Therefore, if you think to wait until, in your own strength, ye have pruned yourself to a certain form of godliness, ye do utterly mistake the matter. Ye may deceive your conscience, ye may deceive the Church, ye may corrupt the gospel into a legal ritual; but ye shall never bring yourself, but by the operation of the Spirit, through faith and prayer, into any meetness for the Church on earth, or for the kingdom of heaven.

O my brother, what waitest thou for? Not for knowledge; for now I tell you, that the door of knowledge is opened to thee; and, if thou have no better, I will myself become thy teacher. Not for entreaty: I do now entreat thee, in the name and behalf of the Father, Son, and Holy Ghost, whose child thou wast acknowledged in the Church. What waitest thou for? Not for liberty: I give thee liberty, as one of the messengers sent into the streets and the highways, saying, "Come ye unto the feast." Wait you till you have something of your own to offer? I tell you it is without money and without price; and that no one was ever admitted on the plea of aught which he had to give in exchange; for the whole material world is no equivalent for one transgression of a spirit. What, then, waitest thou for? I earnestly entreat thee to meditate. "For the sight of my sins, and faith in the Redeemer, and a humble, penitent frame of soul." Dost thou wait for this, my brother? It is well. And whence dost thou expect it? From the world?—it is ungodly. From the carnal mind?—it is vain-glorious. From nature?—it is dark, dark as midnight. Where, then, is it to be found? It is to be found in God—in the revelation which He hath made of Himself by His Son. And what saith that revelation? "Ask, and ye shall receive; seek, and ye shall find; knock, and it shall be opened unto you." Of whom? Of Him who hath it to give, even of the Father, who hath sent forth His Son, that whoever believeth in Him might not perish, but have everlasting life.

This, therefore, is the conclusion of the whole matter;—that you must betake yourselves to your Father, who gave you the full and free privilege of His gospel, by the sacrament of baptism; to the Son, who, by the same, declared His death to have been for your redemption; to the Holy Ghost, who, by the same, declared His sanctification, and teaching, and consolation, to be directed to you for good; in whose life-giving and life-cherishing beams you have since been ensphered, but have loved darkness rather than light. Wherefore, I fear that this abundant declaration of mercy and grace will also be ineffectual; which may the Lord, in His great mercy, forbid, making it profitable to stir up some soul now sitting in darkness and the shadow of death.

But I am only one of the many who, last Lord's day, declared themselves to be of the Church of Christ. And will ye not also put forth some strength for the kingdom of Christ, my fellow-communicants? Will you not wrestle with God in prayer, for the sake of their souls? Will you allow Satan's ceremonious courtesies to divide you from your brother's salvation? Will you see your sons and daughters, your brothers, sisters, and near kindred, about to perish from the grace of God, living out of communion with His Church, and put forth no desire, no entreaty, no instruction? The Lord forbid! Gather yourselves, my beloved brethren, together, and take counsel for the Church, for the prodigal children of the Church. Encourage one another in the grace of the gospel. Talk with one another, pray with one another, comfort and edify one another. Ye are my helpers; ye are my eyes; ye are my voice. And, oh, how sweet then were it to my soul to labour in the word and in prayer, meditating my thoughts, and going myself to Christ my strength, and to the communion of the Holy Spirit!

This duty which the Church—I mean the whole visible Church—oweth to baptized children is little thought of. Yet she is responsible, if the proper sponsor fail in his office; for by her hands the covenant was sealed, and upon her responsibility she took such and such persons sponsors. She, therefore, is responsible to Christ for the sponsors: and hence one ground of domestic visitation, to see that the children are instructed, that the duty covenanted for is fulfilled to them. And when this is neglected by the rulers of the Church, then cometh to supplement it the institution of religious schools, for teaching the children of the Church what their parents do not teach them; for otherwise the Church will suffer loss. Therefore I regard every Sabbath-school teacher as a catechist over the baptized children of the Church; and as such I cannot conclude this discourse without a word to those of my flock who have given themselves to this work.

In every work of Christian charity, dearly beloved brethren, it is not enough that there should be present mere natural good-will and benevolence to all, or natural pity and compassion of the poor and the destitute—which alone may well enough constitute a work of worldly benevolence; but inasmuch as it springs of nature, it is a work of the natural, not of the spiritual man; a work of the world, not of the Church; —but to constitute a work Christian, there must be at the foundation of it a Christian principle, and it must be built up in a Christian spirit, and intended to answer a Christian end. And if benevolence and pity and generosity and disinterestedness be the best and most amiable parts of human nature, they are the most worthy offerings upon the altar of Christ, who hath redeemed human nature; and not being offered unto Him, you may rest assured Satan, the lord of the natural man, will convert them into his strongest hold against the Lord of the spirit. And forasmuch as, for want of a clear knowledge and apprehension of this distinction between natural philanthropy and spiritual well-doing, it hath come to pass in the Church that, through the avenues of our religious operations, the pernicious doctrine of works is creeping in, and out of the Church morality and benevolence make a direct head against the gospel,—I lay before you the care of Christ's ignorant members as being the true Christian principle and Christian end for which we ought to labour, even more diligently than we ever have done, in the work to which so many of this Church have addressed themselves, of instructing the young, of all classes and denominations, in the principles of the doctrine of Jesus Christ, the Son of the living God, and the Redeemer of the world. To all of you who engage in instructing baptized children, these points of doctrine which I have expounded are of the utmost necessity, though they be fallen into great neglect; shewing you the fearful obligations under which the children of this land are brought, and the spiritual relation in which they stand, to the Church of Christ, and the Church of Christ standeth unto them: out of which relation, as I judge, doth spring the great duty of instructing the young in Christian doctrine and duty.

And, brethren, if these be the privileges of every one baptized into the Church of Christ, it is surely monstrous cruelty that they should not be instructed therein. How shall they ever possess their inheritance, if they never know that they are heirs to it? How shall they ever become attached to the Church of Christ, if they know not the blessedness of that Goshen,—the security of that ark? And how shall they forsake the world, if they know not the Egyptian darkness, the unhallowed practices, the hopeless condition, of all who dwell therein? The rite of baptism, done upon the unconscious babe, cannot bring that knowledge as it were by instinct or legerdemain: nature doth not grow up into it, the world doth not teach it, and their sponsors do neglect it most awfully; and it is neglected, and it is clean omitted, among thousands and tens of thousands and hundreds of thousands of the baptized, so that I say not, go to the children, but go to the full-grown men of the streets around, and ask them to explain what profit or peculiar advantage they have from being members of the Church of Christ; or what is the mystery of the Church, for which it should be called the pillar and ground of the truth, the holy nation, the royal priesthood, the chosen nation and peculiar people, the temple of the Holy Ghost, and the body of Christ; and you shall find them profoundly ignorant, dark as midnight upon the whole matter, as if there neither were Bible nor Christian ministry, nor holy sacraments, nor any religious offices, within a day's journey of them, within the reach of intelligence, or within the land, and, I might almost say, in being. But, men and brethren, if the doctrine I have taught be the doctrine of Holy Scripture, and of all Christian Churches, reformed and not reformed, Conformists and Nonconformists—and I tell you it is so—is it not a shame that we, who know what a loss these men are suffering by their ignorance, do not speak of the responsibility they are incurring? I say, is it not a sin, seeing the Christian Church is one body, that any member should thus be fruitless, gangrenous, when a little instruction, a little exhortation, a little prayer, and other Christian diligence, on our part, might be blessed of God to make him lively and active and profitable to Christ the Head, and to all the members of the Christian body?

On these grounds, I hold it to be the duty, not of one man, the pastor, but of every man, the members of Christ, to watch for the interests of His house; first of all for those for whom they are severally responsible—that is, these our children—whom they have brought into the great inheritance, and the equally great responsibility, of the Church of Christ; and in those Churches which admit of sponsors besides the parents, it is the duty of the sponsors, and indeed the very meaning of the office, to see that those for whom they have offered themselves in that responsive situation be made acquainted with the infinite privileges and awful sanctions of the Church of Christ, that they may lay hold of the one, and flee from the other; and of every Christian church—that is, body of Christians worshipping in one place, for truly there is but one Church,—of every Christian community, it is the bounden duty to see that all the baptized of their body, that all the younger children, be reared up, and all the prodigals of the house be brought back to their Father's love, and to their Father's yearning bowels of compassion. And this, let me say unto you, the catechists of my church, is your first office, to be, under your pastor, labourers for the sake of the younger members of our church,—you to be instructed by him, and the younger to be instructed by you. But we are not alone; we are the brethren of all that are joined to Christ in the sacrament of baptism; and if we be the brethren of all Christ's members, then ought we to feel a brotherly tenderness towards those who are around us, of every condition and of every name, who are entitled to the same privileges, and amenable to the same judgment as we are; one with us in the blessing of believing, or in the woe of rejecting the gospel. The little children of the poor who surround us cannot escape the painful sanctions of the covenant into which they have been brought. When the time for judging the professing formal Church shall come, they shall share the judgment. It did not hinder the people of Israel from being destroyed that they lacked knowledge, or that their priests had failed in their holy functions: no more will it hinder them from being destroyed that they lack knowledge. Their ignorance is the beginning of their curse, and the beginning of their judgment. Ignorance is mental darkness; ignorance is mental barrenness; ignorance is God's judgment already revealed in the mind. Now, if these your neighbours were suffering in the fields by blasting mildew, and in their houses by famine, would you not feel it your duty to go forward and relieve them? If the Lord had palsied the father of a family, if He had inflicted a universal plague upon the children, would not nature take pity upon them? And shall nature's bowels be more melting than Christ's bowels? Shall the desolateness that sight beholdeth be more grievous than the desolateness which faith beholdeth? Shall the sufferings of a few years be more pitiable than the sufferings of eternity? Shall the world be better and more friendly to its denizens than the Church of Christ to her members? If I thought, brethren of this flock, that we would be less pitiful of the children of the Established Church, or of the Dissenters from the Established Church, than of our own, I, who am a minister of an Established Church, would rebuke your evil, rather than commend your good example, before the Jerusalem above, which is the mother of us all. For, oh! the sacrament of baptism entaileth upon all the same penalties of ignorance and disobedience. Were not our fathers of one Protestant Church? Hold we not the same doctrines? have we not the same sacraments? Therefore, I say unto you, go unto the hedges, and the lanes, and the by-ways, and invite all to your feast; instruct all, edify all, that it may not be said that, in a Christian land, with Christian neighbours, multitudes perish without ever knowing the glad tidings of salvation: for assuredly the judgment of God will come upon us, if we knowingly allow of such abominations.

Wherefore, brethren, I say ye are yet under the spirit of the world in this work which ye have undertaken, if you execute it merely in the spirit of natural philanthropy or pity, as to children in a state of nature, and do not carry with you all these great truths of the Church of Christ, and act under them in the spirit of Christian love and brotherhood towards the strayed and prodigal, after whom the heart of the Father longeth so affectionately, that He maketh mirth and gladness beyond all measure when any of them returns, saying, "For my son was dead and is alive again, was lost and is found." And when any of the sheep wandereth, He goeth forth into the wilderness, and patiently ploddeth over the weary waste, and returneth very glad that He hath found him. And when one of them repenteth, there is more joy in heaven than over ninety and nine persons who need no repentance. And as our Father in heaven is, in His longings after them, so ought we to be; and as He is patient in His requests, so ought we to be; and as He is joyful in His success, so ought we to be. We ought to go forth boldly and courageously; we ought to seek patiently; we ought to invite largely; we ought to threaten fearfully; and, when we succeed in bringing any back to the fold, we ought to return very cheerfully, and rejoice right gladly. And so, being filled with the doctrine and with the Spirit of Christ, we will not weary in our work, knowing that to us also there remaineth a rest and a great and glorious reward; as it is written in the prophet Daniel, "And they who turn many from darkness into light, shall shine as the stars in the firmament for ever and ever.

HOMILY VIII.

CONCLUSIONS OF DOCTRINE FLOWING FROM BAPTISM.

HEB. VI. 1, 2.

Therefore leaving the principles of the doctrine of Christ, let us go on unto perfection; not laying again the foundation of repentance from dead works, and of faith toward God, of the doctrine of baptisms.

HAVING now exposed to you at length, dearly beloved brethren, in many discourses, the true scriptural and orthodox doctrine concerning the sacrament of baptism, I shall, before closing the subject, open to you the conclusions of doctrine and practical effects which such views ought to have upon us. And for this end I interrupt our ordinary subject of discourse this morning and evening, as I purpose from this day to begin my catechetical instructions to the younger part of my flock, in the view of the next communion. And may the Lord enable me to set forth this subject with so much power and persuasion of the Holy Ghost, that there shall not be any one in all the congregation, of mature years and ripe understanding, unmoved with a sense of the obligation which he oweth to God, in virtue of his baptism, to come forward and partake of the Lord's supper, for his spiritual nourishment and growth in grace.

The first and most obvious conclusion of doctrine which we derive from the sacrament of baptism is, that the Holy Ghost, who proceedeth from the Father and the Son, is to be expected at any age of life, and by no means to be limited to the years of reason and thought. This follows clearly from baptism being, like circumcision, the privilege of the infants of believing parents; of which two signs and seals of the covenant of grace, circumcision was appointed to be done on the eighth day, no doubt for some great typical end; to point out, perhaps, that not until the eighth day of time—that is, not till after the Sabbatism of the millennium—will the uncleanness of flesh be wholly taken away, the pollution of sin wholly cut off, and cast into the lake that burneth, and the perfectly holy estate of the creature established for ever in unchangeable blessedness. But, however this may be, it is enough for our present purpose, that on the eighth day— before intelligence and reason, and the capacity of knowledge and reflection, almost before distinct sensation, and any human function of speech, sight, or hearing had begun to dawn into existence, the unconscious babe was admitted to that covenant of righteousness by faith, whereof circumcision was the seal, and did receive "circumcision, the seal of the righteousness which he had yet being uncircumcised." And baptism being confined to no stage of our being, but permissible at the very moment of our birth, doth carry, if it were possible, this point to a higher degree of evidence and conclusiveness. Now, if Christ, by so appointing it that the seal of the covenant should be dependent upon no condition but the life of a human creature, and the faith of its parent or (in his incapacity) of a sponsor, it is most clear, that all the gifts, privileges, and immunities which the sacrament bringeth to any one being, no less than "the remission of sins and the receiving of the Holy Ghost," are proper to be given and warranted by God to the unconscious babe; yea, to any seed of man in which there is life. Otherwise, if the Holy Spirit were not free to be communicated to all ages of the living human creature, but only after life had put forth the functions of thought, of intelligence, of reason, the sacramental sign and seal of His communication would not have been permitted to be given till that function was become manifest. And those who refuse baptism to infants, do in fact bring themselves to this awful conclusion, that the Holy Spirit is not given, and may not be expected, till a human being is capable of faith, which implieth knowledge and thought and reflection, and the other functions of reason. Now this is a great limitation of the Holy One, and a confinement of the Redemption within narrower limits than the Fall; which certainly sheweth itself in the pains and diseases and deaths of infants; yea, of childbirth, and of premature births and abortions. It goes far, as I think also, to deprive infants of the hope of salvation, seeing to salvation I consider the anointing with the Holy Ghost to be as indispensable as the redemption by Christ, who, in truth, is Christ only as He anointeth with the Holy Ghost. And to whomsoever He is Jesus or Saviour, to that person is He also Christ; and if you deny that He is Christ to any one, by refusing to Him the Holy Ghost, then to that one you deny Him to be Jesus or Saviour also. I know how obstinately the Anabaptists deny this conclusion in words; but I maintain, that a tenet of doctrine, conveyed by an ordinance or sacrament of the Church, is not to be met by a denial of words. It is on all hands allowed, that baptism is for receiving the Holy Ghost; and if that sign and seal be not permitted till a certain age, what other reason can be alleged for the refusal but this, that this thing, signified and sealed, is not till then to be expected; or if before this to be expected, why before this may the sign of it not be administered?

It is not, however, to dispute, but to teach, that I have undertaken this subject; and, as a teacher of righteousness, I do instruct you all, dear brethren, that the openness of this ordinance to the unconscious babe, who hath no righteousness, nor faculty of any kind for receiving any; who can work no work, set forth no prayer, and act no faith, but is wholly born in sin, is the clearest demonstration in the world of the freeness of Divine grace, and the willingness of the Father to bestow the Holy Spirit upon any age and upon all ages of human life. The only thing which is preferred before this gift is faith. If a parent have faith for himself, he may not, without a denial of God's promise, fail to have faith for his baptized child. And any one who hath been baptized may not, without casting dishonour upon his father, and upon the Church which judged his father worthy to receive the sacrament for his children's sake, doubt of his full right and title to this inheritance of the forgiveness of sins and of the Holy Ghost. And because many children are wont to puzzle and perplex themselves about the question, whether their parents had faith or not; I say positively, that they take too much upon them to go about to judge a question which hath already been judged by the Church. Not that I infringe the right of private judgment, which I consider a most essential point of the protestation which we have lifted up against the Papacy, but that I will not permit a decision to be reviewed by private judgment which God hath not left to private judgment, but fixed in the rulers of the Church. Your parent did not himself take it upon his own private judgment to decide whether he was worthy to have his child baptized: he left it to the rulers of the Church, into whose hands the sacraments are committed, to decide to whom they should be administered. The Church decided favourably in your case, and then the thing resteth upon the Church's responsibility. For your part, ye may not doubt thereafter that you are freely admitted to all which the Church hath thus to share in common among her members, be it much or be it little. The same say I, in answer to all doubts with respect to the minister of the Church by whom it was done, who is only a minister or servant of the Church, not the Church herself; whose gift ye received, whether it came through the hand of a dishonest or a true servant; seeing, as is well set forth in our Catechism, " the sacraments are made effectual, not from any virtue in them, or in him that doth administer them, but only by the blessing of Christ, and the working of the Holy Spirit in them who by faith receive them." Remember that I do not say the Holy Spirit is actually given to every baptized person; for that dependeth upon the previous gift of faith, which is from a higher source than the Holy Ghost, even from the Father, and which the Father giveth to whom it pleaseth Him;—but that the Church having judged one to have faith, she may not refuse to judge that he hath righteousness imputed to that faith which she judgeth him to have, nor that his children have the fellowship of the same, nor that his baptized children are declared to have righteousness also, and the Holy Spirit. The first judgment involveth all the following ones; and in all her acts of discipline towards that baptized child, she ought to proceed towards him as towards one who is in covenant with God, and a privileged member of the Church.

This leadeth us to observe, secondly, that the work of

Christ hath an equal respect to all ages of human life, from the first to the last moment of it. This follows directly from the former; because, if the Holy Spirit is free to proceed from the Father and the Son upon every age of life, the Father and the Son must be willing to send Him; for He cometh not without their permission and commandment. "Whatsoever He shall *hear*, that shall He speak." "I will send you, ... my Father will send you, another Comforter, even the Holy Ghost." It follows, not only from the orthodox doctrine of the Trinity, but also is contained in the nature of the sacrament itself; for baptism is *for the remission of sins*, as well as for the receiving of the Holy Ghost. And without the shedding of the blood of Christ, there is no remission of sins, nor purging of the conscience "from dead works to serve the living God." Therefore, an interest in the death of Christ is part of the thing which is signified and sealed to us in our baptism. Yea, not only is this interest in Christ's death of the substance of the grace of baptism, as well as the work of the Holy Ghost, but it is previous thereto—as, indeed, it ought to be—in the order of the Divine idea. Because, previous to baptism, there must be a believing parent; in order to a holy child, there must be an imputation of righteousness; and in order to an imputation of righteousness, there must be a righteous One to be believed on, from whom the righteousness may, through the channel of faith, be derived. To take an unholy nature into covenant with the holy God, before there had passed upon it an act of absolution proceeding from Christ, is totally subversive of the Divine idea and revealed purpose. Such a thing would mingle heaven and hell, reconcile God and Belial, Christ and Satan. Therefore, previous to the striking of the covenant, there must be a fountain opened for sin and for uncleanness; and from this opened fountain the capacity of coming into covenant must be derived. By the cleanness thereof applied to the uncleanness of the creature the great eternal impossibility must have been got over—I mean, the impossibility of God entering into covenant with an unclean thing. Therefore, we draw our second conclusion of doctrine, That the righteousness of Christ is freely imputed, and the work of Christ freely imparted to children as to men, to infants born or unborn, in whom is the spirit of life, and the seed of faithful parents.

Now, as the former head of doctrine was most demonstrative of the irresistible and insuperable power of the Holy Ghost to perform a work of sanctification upon the unconscious babe, which passeth far above and beyond the power of human teaching, but surpasseth not His power who gave it a living soul,—He who gave to the material germ a living soul being able to give the Holy Spirit to sanctify the creature thus constituted; which mysteriously connecteth at the same dark and inaccessible fountain-head the two great streams of life,—life natural and life spiritual, life mortal and life immortal, making the Redemption run up as high as the Fall,—to prevent its evil effects wherever faith is; to the end that faith should be as large as, and a more powerful organ than, sight;—I say, while this mystery of Divine power is set forth in its fair and mighty proportions to our faith by the former conclusion of doctrine, by this second conclusion is set forth the infinite dimensions of the love and grace which is in Christ Jesus, its unconditional freeness, its all-sufficient fulness, its all-embracing tenderness, its unwearied delight with the children of men. As He despised not the virgin's womb for His own bed, and as the Holy Spirit sanctified Him there from His conception, so are we to understand the same Spirit, through Him proceeding, despiseth not the womb of any sinful woman, nor refuseth to sanctify the fruit of her womb from its conception; and as He despised no period of childhood, but went the full round of opening sense and dawning reason up to manhood, in order that He might have the knowledge and the fellow-feeling of all its trials and every infirmity thereof, so is He tenderly attached and most closely knit to every child, to every youth, to every man, to every son of the human race, who have faith to receive and entertain His unlimited affections. I say faith, because without faith we cannot have any of that love of the Son of God, or influence of the Holy Ghost; which comes not in wild and unpremeditated liberty, nor is scattered abroad in wasteful diffusion, but directed according to the purpose of Him from whom originateth both the Son and the Spirit, even the Father, who, in Christ Jesus, electeth unto eternal life whom it pleaseth Him to elect, from amongst the fallen creatures; and upon them whom it is His good pleasure to save, sendeth the love of the Son and the power of the Holy Ghost.

And now, concerning this—the highest head of orthodox theology, without which all the rest are most unprofitable and deceptive—I have to observe, that the sacrament of baptism yieldeth to us this third conclusion of doctrine, That the election of the Father is not limited to any age of human life, but doth include all ages, from the first imparting of the living soul, to the last moment of its presence in the body, immediately before it departeth to Him who gave it; that is to say, that He electeth at any age, and at all ages of human life, the sinners of mankind to everlasting life. For if this were not true, and there were a time before which, or a time after which, the election of the Father did no longer apply, baptism would be prohibited until or after that time; for baptism is of no meaning or effect if it include not the election of the Father; seeing that is the first act of redemption, whereby the Father giveth one of His chosen ones unto His Son, who thereupon anointeth Him with the Holy Ghost. And seeing that baptism is effectual through faith unto the remission of sins and the receiving of the Holy Ghost, it presupposeth the will of the Father, in which every act of the Son and the Holy Ghost originateth, unto whose obedience they have respect, and in whose glory, and honour, and worship they terminate; which combined and co-equal, though subordinate presence of Father, Son, and Holy Ghost, that it is the act of grace signified, and to the faithful sealed in baptism, is sufficiently demonstrated by the name, "the Father, the Son, and the Holy Ghost," into which we are baptized; and without this acknowledgment of the Father's election as a part, and the first part, of baptism, we would fall into the most fearful conclusions, either of superstition, if we keep to the letter of the ordinance, or of infidelity, if we depart from the letter of the Scriptures, and interpret it according to *common sense*, (that substitute for the Holy Ghost in these enlightened times.) For without this electing love of the Father, preceding the work of Christ and the operation of the Holy Ghost, we would have no room for faith as the indispensable prerequisite to baptism. Here is a baptismal font, signifying the waters of the Holy Ghost, flowing from the rent and smitten side of Christ, which, like the rock of Meribah, had till then hid them all within its own bosom, and here is an unclean child of Adam to be washed in it; but where is the connecting power to bring the one unto the other? The priest can take the child, and wash or dip it in the waters; but who hath a right, or who hath the power, to absolve the guilty substance, and fill it with the spirit of righteousness? Who, but He who hath judged the soul guilty, hath the power to absolve the soul from guilt? Who, but the Father of the spirits of all flesh, having the power to kill, and who, in virtue thereof, hath killed all Adam's race, hath power to make alive again? And how doth He manifest the same? He manifesteth it by bestowing faith; to which faith Christ bestoweth righteousness; upon which righteousness, imputed from Christ, the Holy Ghost proceedeth to work salvation. Now, faith requireth knowledge; for how can they believe in Him whom they have not heard? And knowledge requireth understanding and the exercise of all our creation gifts; so that here the creature cometh into direct communication with the Creator; and the Creator hath in His hand the account of the creature's creation gifts, and no doubt bestows the redemption gifts of grace, with a respect to the use which the creature hath made of the former. And at this point, Christ comes in as the Prophet or Preacher of His Father's will unto the creatures, opening to them the purpose of the Father; and leaving off there in His character of Prophet, he waiteth for the Father to bestow faith according to His will—according to that unrevealed will of His, which He giveth no account of, in order that every creature may be hung up in continual suspense thereon; because this is the true standing of the creature, to have no will of its own, but to hang evermore suspended upon the Father's will. Then, when the Father hath given faith according to that purpose which He hath purposed in Himself, Christ cometh to exert His office of Priest; because the Father's gift of faith doth point out to Him another of the chosen ones, and consigns that one over to His care, whom, certainly, He will not leave, but bring out to glory. And now cometh in the sacrament of baptism, which pertaineth not to Christ as Prophet, but to Christ as Priest; and, therefore, it is not merely a preaching ordinance, but a purifying ordinance; not a sign, but a seal also. And though I have written the first homily upon what it doth signify, as it were to break the ground, yet the result I came to was, that it signified certain things concerning His priestly office, which things also it did—not only *signified*, but *did*. Be it understood, therefore, that faith, the gift of the Father, is previous to baptism; as the prophetic office of Christ, of which the end is *faith*, is previous to the priestly office, of which the end is *holiness;* and, moreover, that faith is not bestowed on any one, but in the exercise of creation gifts, though freely and of will bestowed; and not, as it were, in reward for this or that occupation of them.

And thus ye have the subject completed, which standeth thus:—That to whom the Father is pleased to bestow faith, He doth indicate His electing love; and such an one is free to the participation of all the benefits of Christ: not free himself, but also his children free, on this very account, that the election extendeth to children as well as men, because the promise and the seal of the promise extendeth to children as well as men. The father of a family, therefore, hath such dignity given to him in the purpose of God, that he should cover with his faith all the members of his household who are yet incapable of faith; and the children, when they begin to pass out of this included state, are not to think that they enter upon a new probation for faith, (there is no probation whatever now, and hath been none since Adam fell out of that estate,) but that they have been growing up into faith, and should make progress in it as they do in reason or in any faculty of natural life; that it is a gift of grace, with which they are as truly invested of God as the gift of nature; and upon the expectancy of which they should proceed about the works of faith as they do about the works of nature. This, no doubt, was the end of God, to make His Church perpetual and progressive, this is the doctrine which cometh out of baptism; in the understanding and faith of which the work of God will be most effectually promoted.

These conclusions, with respect to the purpose of God and the offices of the Persons of the Godhead, are of an incalculable value in theology; and, though not altogether dependent for their demonstration upon the sacrament of infant baptism, do obtain thence a prominence and importance far beyond that which is to be derived from any number of texts of Holy Scripture. For those principles, and those only, which are of the last importance, are deemed worthy of being represented and fixed in a symbolical and sacramental ordinance. The only other principles which have been so embodied are those contained in the Lord's supper, which are, the nourishment of the Church upon Christ's fleshly body, and their sealing unto the kingdom of Christ in the day of His appearing. We are at liberty, therefore, to conclude, that there is no more important principle in Divine revelation than that which is embodied in the three foregoing conclusions of doctrine,— that it is the Divine purpose to gather His Church out of all classes, and conditions, and ages of human life. And if we consider this conclusion we shall see how important it is:— First, In that it gives a great and unspeakable value to a living creature, however existent, born or unborn, setting the gift of life infinitely above all the circumstances of life. Secondly, In that it opens the mouth of preaching to every living creature, baptized or unbaptized, without any limitation. Forasmuch as the sacrament of initiation, and the decree which it representeth, containeth no exception nor exclusion of any kind, to the baptized we preach their privileges in Christ, that they may possess and occupy them; to the unbaptized we preach the wrath of God, which abideth on them, and shall overtake them, if they repent not and believe not the gospel of Christ. And thus, though there be a decree of election which containeth only a portion of the creatures, yet is the mouth of the minister of God opened to every creature under heaven, in virtue of those conclusions which we have stated above as directly resulting from the sacrament of infant baptism.

The fourth conclusion of doctrine is with respect to the Church, into whose hands this holy symbol is entrusted; that by the right use of it she may make it fully to speak forth, and not in any way to contradict, these great fundamental truths of the purpose of God,—that the election of the Father, the righteousness of Christ, and the sanctification of the Holy Ghost, are equally and alike applicable to mankind in all the stages of their life, from the first beginning to the last ending of it. It is from this sacrament that the Church hath her existence as a visible and ostensible communion upon the earth; and by the right use of this sacrament it is that her existence will be perpetuated, and from the abuse of it that she will be subverted by the fearful judgments of God. The Church grows out of this sacrament, in virtue of its being the seal of a covenant entered into between God and certain of the fallen creatures; and if it be no seal of a covenant concluded and done, there is and there can be no Church, under obligations distinct and different from the rest of the creatures. For how can there be obligations beyond those which are natural to man, without an act imposing them by the authority of God? And what act is that, if it be not baptism, which imposeth upon us the new obligations of Christians? Now, is it of the nature of Christianity, I ask, to impose an obligation without conferring a grace? Cometh the gospel or the law first in the order of Christian truth? The gospel surely. If, then, baptism impose Christian obligations, then, I say, baptism must bring grace sufficient to fulfil these obligations; otherwise it is no gospel ordinance, but a legal ordinance merely. Whosoever, therefore, refuseth not to allow the obligation imposed upon us by our baptism, cannot deny a grace bestowed therein to meet the demands; for surely, at the least, the gospel answereth its own demands. And should any one deny that baptism is either for the imposing of obligations or the receiving of grace, I know not what to say to him, less than that he denieth the very existence of the Church of Christ as an objective outward thing, and cannot be the recognised member of any Church; and is, by his own act, an excommunicated person, with whom we have nothing more to do, and to whom we have nothing more to say. But to all who have had any conviction of the things set forth above, it necessarily resulteth, that the baptized are the Christian Church, the body of men which is spoken to and written of, beloved, and threatened, and prophesied of, in the Scriptures of the New Testament: and if so, then are we all brought to act together as the body of Christ, and responsible to the Head in the several stations which He hath appointed to us. We are responsible to Him for the use of that measure of the Spirit which hath been dealt out to each of us; and we are called upon to honour one another, according to the offices which He hath appointed us severally in His house; because the offices are of His appointment, and those who fill them are of the selection of His providence. And because He hath appointed subjection unto some, and rule unto others, and subordination unto all, there necessarily ariseth the sacred and Divine right of government in the Church, for which gifts of the Spirit are to be expected ;—in those who govern, the gift of holy ruling; in those who are subject, the gift of holy subjection: of which two conditions, that which is the highest is also the lowest, because it ministereth to all; and that which is the lowest is also the highest, because it is ministered unto. Now, it is to be observed, that, though there hath been different opinions of what kinds those office-bearers in the Church are—though, in truth, there be much less than is generally imagined among the Protestant Churches, who agree very nearly as to the three orders of bishops or pastors, or ministers of the word, and elders or presbyters or priests, and deacons—these questions do not at all affect the Divine right of government in the Church, as an institution of Christ, which all admit; and this is all for which I am arguing at present, as proceeding out of the covenant of baptism: that, by virtue of its being a sealing act, there ariseth the separate body of the Church of Christ under its own Divine government, with which nothing may interfere, and against which no one may rise without rebelling against the Spirit. And thus discipline ariseth out of the same sacrament of baptism; the baptized being regarded as of the election of the Father of the body of Christ, and under the guidance of the Spirit, and held responsible to the laws of God which are written in His Word.

The fifth conclusion of doctrine which we draw from the above premises, is with respect to parents, the mystery of whose relation to their children is in no way taught or exhibited as by this holy sacrament. The doctrine may be thus expressed,—that the parent is the medium through whom God will convey all needful grace unto the children, during the time of their own incapacity of faith, and in what respects they continue incapable of faith, until by the Church they be judged worthy to sit down at the table of the Lord. It is of the substance, not to say of baptism, but of circumcision, and all the covenants and promises of God, that they should be unto the father and his children. It began to be so in the Fall, and it continueth to be so in the Redemption: yea, and it is of the very constitution and law of our being that it should be so ; for, if otherwise, then is there a period in the existence of every soul for which God hath made no provision, and of which man can render no account. I mean, from the first beginning of life in the womb until the time that we are capable of understanding and believing the revelation of God, or hearing the preaching of the gospel—which age, let me observe in passing, was not thought by the primitive Church to be so early as it is in these days. What are we during that important period of existence? Souls we have, and bodies we have; therefore we are persons. And how stand we to God? What connexion have we with our Maker? What purpose serve we amongst His creatures? How are we responsible? And how are we dealt with? When, moreover, it is remembered, that within this period more than the half of human souls are called away from their earthly sojourn, these questions are of a very large application, as well as of the most deep concernment. To these questions a Baptist can make no answer: he can neither say the child is a believer nor an unbeliever; he can neither make it the subject of hope nor of fear. So far as the world to come is concerned, that child is a nonentity, or at best an isolated, solitary thing, without relation to God of any sort.

And what state is this for a soul to be in; an immortal, responsible soul? This barrier, which ariseth in the mind of every person, is at once opened and set to a side, by the fourth head of doctrine which we have derived from the sacraments of baptism and circumcision; whereby it is concluded, that the parents, through whom God hath seen it good to bring that soul into the world, is by God regarded as verily and truly responsible for the souls which God hath given him, until they be capable of responsibility for themselves; unto which reason itself gives its assent, in the laws of all well-regulated States. And it is consistent with the very ordinance of nature that it should be so; for if God honours two human beings so highly, as by means of them to bring into the world those immortal souls which He alone can create, and which He alone doth give, is it to be wondered that He should honour them to convey to that soul the sustenance of His grace, through which alone it is capable of existing in a healthy and happy state? No one, I suppose, will say that the law of generation concerneth more than our material part; the soul, surely, is not linked to the body by a necessary law: otherwise we have one of two conclusions,—either that it hath no separate existence after death, or that it sleeps away the time during which the body is dissolved; either of which conclusions all orthodox divines and sound-minded men utterly abhor. If, then, the soul is the gift of God, coeval and coexistent with the first pulse of life, which God, by the ordinance of death doth again separate, and call unto Himself, and retain apart till the resurrection of the dead, then is it after the nature of a trust unto the parents, of a bequest, of a great grace and honour, and may well stand connected with future acts of grace necessary to its well-being, with future supplies to those parents for the rearing up of the infant for immortal life, and with vows and pledges taken of them in token of their acknowledgment, designed for enlightening their minds concerning their charge, and for the assurance of their responsibility. Therefore marvel not that God should accept the parents as sponsors for this His gift; rather marvel if there should not be an ordinance to that effect. This ordinance is infant baptism, wherein is declared and taught unto the parent the whole mystery of this little creature's immortality, and of its relationship to the Father, the Son, and the Holy Ghost. But, forasmuch as this name, the Father, the Son, and the Holy Ghost, is God's name in Christ, which is not otherwise known but through revelation, it is necessary that he who receives the charge of a soul in this name should believe in the record which God hath given by His Son concerning Himself. Were it permitted to any one without faith in revelation, it were to give up the greatest point of theology, that this name of God is not otherwise to be named but by faith in Jesus Christ. But so soon as any one declareth himself able to name that name, he is free to have his children baptized—that is, to receive and to accept the immortal souls of his children, and their bodies likewise, in solemn bequest from Him of whom every creature in heaven and earth is named. But doth God give him the life without the means of its support? Verily not: He who giveth milk to the mother's breast, and conception to the mother's womb, will not fail to give for the immortal soul the only nourishment upon which it can live,—the grace of God in Jesus Christ. But how shall it be conveyed to him, seeing without faith it cannot be received? Surely through the parents, who were counted worthy to receive this pledge of God's favour, and have been glad to take it in the revealed name of God. For them the investment lieth in the purpose of God, if they will seek to obtain it through the channel of faith, and prayer, and knowledge, and obedience, and the other fruits of faith, by which they receive for themselves. But if this they refuse, then they are found faithless to God, treacherous to the child, and unworthy to be called members of the Church of Christ. Oh, what a sublime dignity this giveth to the ordinance of father and child! —the child, though outward, and another person, being still one with the father in the counsel of God; and the father including in himself the faith and the responsibility of his child, until the child disengageth himself by efforts of faith and conscience, and is judged by the Church ripe for the functions of separate manhood: from which time forth he is called upon to answer for himself before her tribunals, and to bear with an equal shoulder the burdens of the faith and testimony of Jesus.—I have not time to open these ideas, but they are most pregnant with practical conclusions.

The sixth conclusion of doctrine concerneth children who die in infancy; concerning whose standing in God's sight there is much very unwholesome discourse; some alleging that they must needs all be saved, without considering whither such a conclusion leadeth them. I hold this to be a preclusion of God's electing grace from that region of human life, which cannot anywhere be precluded without denying His sovereign right to do with and for the creature whatsoever it pleaseth Him. It is the spirit of universalism applied to children: and if permitted here, here it will not stop. Besides, they see not that if this assurance were established among men, that children do all of a certainty go to heaven, it would act upon many minds, yea, more or less upon all, to the prejudice and destruction of that care of their infancy which needeth to be so watchful. Who would apprehend death for their child, or guard against it so diligently, if assured that the moment it leaves this world it is removed to a state of blessedness? God hath more wisely covered this subject with an impenetrable veil, which I thank no man, although I have two infants sleeping in the dust, to remove from it. I perceive such fatal consequences would flow from it, in separating the religious affections from the natural affections, and distracting the relationship of parent and child, which it is of God's purpose, as it is of the very constitution of human nature, to sanctify and confederate more and more. On the other hand, and at the other extreme, there be those who discourse on this subject as if a child were not capable of receiving the Holy Spirit, because it is deficient in reason and conscience: as if the Holy Spirit were commensurate, not with natural life, but with only a certain season of it. To this I make answer, that the soul of a child, yet unpractised in wickedness, in its first faith and first love, is a fairer and more congenial abode, so to speak, for God's Holy Spirit, than the soul of a man, hardened as most men are in sin; and that it is an express limitation of the Holy One so to discourse;—that our Lord's doctrine is literally as well as symbolically true, that we must become as little children: we must untwist the web of wickedness, and become simple and sincere as in the beginning. To say that the Holy Spirit doth not take hold of childhood, is simply to say that no child can be saved; for if there be a principle in orthodox theology more certain than another, it is this, that the first creation is all fallen and corrupt, and doomed to death, and can only be saved by being anointed with the Holy Ghost from the hands of our great High Priest. For if one fallen creature can be saved without the communication of the Holy Ghost, then can every fallen creature be so saved, and Christ is dead in vain. Now, between these extremes—of saving all, and so destroying God's sovereignty; or of saving none, by denying the power of the Holy Ghost to act upon the unconscious babe—we are enabled to declare the true doctrine from the principles which have been laid down. It hath been shewn, first, that the offices of the Father, and the Son, and the Holy Ghost, in salvation, are exhibited equally for the unconscious babe as for the man of ripest reason: and, therefore, no one may doubt that God doth save infants, and may save all infants, if it so pleaseth Him, but this He hath not revealed. He hath simply made it sure and steadfast, that the unconscious babe is as proper a subject of salvation as any other. We have shewn, secondly, that He regardeth the infant, during the years of irresponsibility, as included in the parent, not by a fiction, but by a reality, of a verity. And being so, if the child be taken during that season of irresponsibility, who is answerable to God for its life? The father surely. And how shall the father be assured of its salvation? By becoming assured of his own. If he hath found favour for himself, it is with all the perilous load of his sins upon him that he hath found such favour, and with the responsibility of his unconscious children likewise, which is but a part of his own responsibility. And though the child was taken from him when he thought little of baptism, and little understood the ministry of a Christian parent's dignity and prerogative before God, and have the burden lying upon his conscience of broken vows, neglected privileges, and violated duties, this is only a part of that burden which Christ hath borne for him, if so be he hath believed in Christ. This I say, not as determining the question of the child's salvation, which I leave wholly in the secrecy with which God hath covered it, but as shewing how a father is to be comforted over his solicitude. Let him believe for himself, and find acceptance for himself, and he findeth acceptance for those included in himself. The child's soul is from God; and its connexion with an earthly father doth not, as it were, obliterate its connexion with the Father of spirits, who will see to His own creation, and justify Himself in His dealings with it: but for its connexion with the earthly parent, this which I have given is, I think, the true account of the matter, That seeing God doth regard the child, during its incapacity of faith, as included in the father, he, the father, believing that himself is accepted, doth therein believe also that his child, included in him, is also accepted. And I, for my part, would wish the doctrine to stand on no other ground. I count it a great privilege which God hath given us parents, to believe for our little children as for ourselves; in their life, as in our own life; in their death, as in our own death; in their eternal condition, as in our own eternal condition.

But the question is altered when the child begins to emerge from the shades of ignorance and the waste of unconsciousness, into the knowledge of God and the conscience of good and evil. This is a season intervening between the former condition of irresponsibility, and the condition of full responsibility, which must be otherwise discoursed of. For the mind is capable of knowledge and righteousness long before it is ripe for admission to the Lord's table. This is the season of spiritual growth, during which the responsibility becomes divided between parent and child—the one being a help to the other's weakness; and they must walk together before God hand in hand. The child is now to receive those stores of faith, knowledge, and experience which God hath stored his believing, responsible parent withal; and the parent is to open them with what delight every creature doth nourish its young. And those whom God taketh away in this mean season are responsible for so much knowledge and belief as they were capable of. The parent also is responsible for the same measure. If he hath failed to feed the appetite and fill the fountains of his offspring's strength, God will not hold him guiltless; and if his son or daughter hath refused to receive that which he willingly tendered and earnestly impressed, God will not hold that child guiltless. And so the two proceed together in an intercommunion of offices and of responsibility, until the time come when the Church accepteth the charge from the parent's hand, and admitteth the youth amongst the number of the communicants of the Church; and, from that time forth, I consider such a one to be fully responsible for all the knowledge, faith, and duties of a Christian, to press on to the highest perfection, and not to rest until he is pure as our Father in heaven is pure, and perfect as He is perfect. How important a point of duty is it, then, for every parent to press his children, when they have attained to a competency of knowledge, to come forward to the Lord's table, and perform their vows unto the Lord! And for those who have no parents to watch over them, or are removed far from their care, how needful is it to present themselves unto the ministers and elders of the Church, that they may be well instructed in these matters, and, being rightly informed, may come to some wise resolution upon the question! Those who are so situated in the providence of God are truly and properly under the Church. The parental sponsorship being invalidated by death or otherwise, the trust reverteth to the first authority, or the Church, who originally made it over to the parent or sponsor; and, therefore, all such should present themselves to the Church, as their proper mother, in order to be instructed in everything which concerneth the holy ordinance of the Lord's supper. To the instruction of all such as, being moved by the parents, or by their own minds, shall come forward, I propose devoting myself for a portion of each Sabbath, during the three months which are to occur before the administration of the holy sacrament. And to the end of stirring up the minds of all of you, by opening to you your privilege and freedom in Christ, I have set forth these great conclusions of doctrine, and in the evening I shall continue the subject. Meanwhile, I do commend these considerations most earnestly to every one who, having been baptized, is still as it were an infant in the Church, not having taken his vows upon himself at the Lord's table. And now, may the Father, and the Son, and the Holy Ghost, bless all these endeavours which we make to restore the true import and obligation of His holy ordinances, and move many, yea, all, with such a lively sense of their privilege, that no one will fail to desire it with their whole heart. Amen and amen.

HOMILY IX.

PRACTICAL CONCLUSIONS FLOWING FROM BAPTISM.

ROM. VI. 11–13.

Likewise reckon ye also yourselves to be dead indeed unto sin, but alive unto God through Jesus Christ our Lord. Let not sin therefore reign in your mortal body, that ye should obey it in the lusts thereof. Neither yield ye your members as instruments of unrighteousness unto sin: but yield yourselves unto God, as those that are alive from the dead, and your members as instruments of righteousness unto God.

THOSE who maintain that the sacrament of baptism is nothing more than a sign demonstrative of some truth, but not communicative of any grace, do not only contradict the whole tenor of Scripture, and deprive themselves of all the advantages which have been set forth in the foregoing homilies, but likewise involve themselves in certain errors and inconsistencies, which I would open a little before proceeding to state the practical conclusions to the Church and the individual, which derive themselves from the doctrine of baptism.

The first inconsistency which resulteth from the false principle that the sacrament of baptism is but a bare sign, is with respect to the visible Church; by which I mean, a company of men who are professedly under the law of God and the Headship of Christ. None will deny that there is a visible Church. I ask of whom it consisteth? They answer, Of all who believe in Christ. I ask, How am I to know those who believe in Christ? What ostensible sign is there by which I may know them? There can be no answer, but either baptism or the Lord's supper. If they take the latter, and say those only who sit down at the Lord's table are the Church of Christ; then I ask, And why, in that case, is it that, when a heathen is converted and professeth his faith in Christ, you do not at once set the bread and wine of the supper before him, instead of requiring him to be baptized? And, being baptized, why do you take him into your arms, and call him brother, and give him all the benefit of the discipline of the Church? Beyond a doubt, it is manifest that no Church nor sect in Christendom—except the Quakers, who are out of the question in all controversies of this kind—but holdeth that baptism is the act whereby a man declareth his faith in Christ, and becometh a member of the visible Church, to be dealt with after the laws and ordinances thereof. If, then, baptism be that act which bringeth a man under the new obligations of the Christian life, as every Church and sect confesseth, both by word and deed, I have next to ask, Does the Christian religion impose any duties upon a man without conferring also grace upon him, to enable him to perform them? Or, I might say, if I were reasoning with a divine of any depth, Doth the Christian religion talk at all of duties until the question of sin and guilt hath first been set at rest? Is there not a justification freely, by the death of Christ, from our sins through faith, before there is one word of Christian duty, except the duty to believe? And, besides that justification by free grace through faith, is there not also a gift of the Holy Ghost to be supposed previously to the power of fulfilling any Christian duties? To these questions, no divine, who hath any respect to orthodox doctrine, can answer otherwise than in the affirmative: That in the order of the Divine purpose, and in the preaching of the gospel, the work of justification by the blood of Christ, and the free gift of the Holy Ghost proceeding thereupon, must be always supposed before speaking of Christian duty, and, in speaking of Christian duty, are actually taken for granted as present in those whom we address. Well, then, as we have seen that upon a baptized person all Christian Churches, and even sects, do impose straightway the obligations of a Christian walk and conversation, and proceed to discipline if they be contravened and transgressed, they must suppose that in the baptized person there is that justification through faith and presence of the Holy Ghost which, it is confessed, must precede the former, and prepare for the performance of Christian duty. Otherwise, the Church is most foolish and unreasonable in expecting that which she believeth there is not power to perform. And if baptism impose these obligations, then the gift of faith, upon which justification ensueth, and the gift of the Holy Ghost, which ensueth on justification, must be before baptism, or at baptism; otherwise, in all good doctrine and conscience, you expect your men to make bricks without straw.

Furthermore, all Churches do require a profession of faith, and do take some scrutiny of its honesty before they will admit a catechumen to the sacrament of baptism: and not without a true conviction, so far as man can discern, that the faith is sincere, will they grant the privilege. Now, I ask again, Is anything necessary to justification besides faith? Surely not, saith every Church under heaven. And they who hold works to be likewise necessary, do egregiously err from the truth. If, then, faith only be needful to justification, and you believe that a man hath faith, must you not believe also that he hath justification? You would not grant him baptism without a belief in his faith already possessed; and having granted him baptism upon your assurance of his faith, can you turn about upon him, and say, I doubt whether thou hast faith or not? Or can you believe him to have faith, and at the same time believe him not to be a justified person? Then faith may be believed to be, where justification is not believed to be! And why? doth justification depend upon something else than faith? Is the Father's gift of faith not necessarily connected with Christ's gift of righteousness? Then the Father and the Son are divided in their substance, and may be opposed to one another in their mind, and Christ is no longer the faithful Witness; which are conclusions that no divine will dare to entertain within his mind. Well, then, if justification upon the imputation of Christ's righteousness may no more be doubted, to any one who is believed to possess faith, and baptism is not given but upon our assurance of faith possessed, we must admit we cannot, without the subversion of the foundation, believe but the person baptized is already a justified person, in virtue of the faith which we believe him already to possess.

Let me proceed one step further as a questionist. You have been forced to admit that the baptized person must be believed to be a justified person, otherwise the baptism is a hollow falsehood, and no holy sacrament. I ask next, If one may believe a man to be justified for the righteousness of Christ imputed to faith, which is the Father's gift, and at the same time believe that the Holy Spirit may be withheld from him? To open this question, which, from the ignorance that prevaileth upon the subject of the Trinity, may be found somewhat difficult, I observe that the true doctrine concerning the Holy Ghost is, that He proceedeth from the Father and from the Son in all His actings, and without them never proceedeth anywhere. The Father shews His will in granting to the object of His election faith to believe on Christ; and Christ sheweth the harmony of His will in granting the righteousness of justification to His faith; upon which consent of the Father and the Son, to say that the Holy Spirit might refuse or hesitate to proceed upon and dwell in that chosen person, were again to divide the substance of the Godhead, and to contradict the essential unity of God. It is not, therefore, for a moment to be doubted, that faith being present from the gift of the Father, and justification from the righteousness of Christ, the Holy Spirit is also present for the illumination, the information, and, in one word, the sanctification of this subject of grace. It may not be said, that there is any interval when the act of the two former Persons is present, and the act of the latter is not also present. Be it so then: and let us now proceed to the question again. Here is a person that you are baptizing in the name of the Father, the Son, and the Holy Ghost. Why do you so? Because I have a good faith he believeth with all his heart, and therefore I may not refuse him the ordinance of baptism. Thou dost well; and, believing that he hath this faith, whence thinkest thou that he had it? From the Father, whose office it is to draw souls from this darkness, deadness, ignorance, and disbelief, to believe on the true Light which He hath sent into the world. Thou hast well answered again. And, having such a faith, doubtest thou whether he may have justification through the righteousness of Christ? I may no longer doubt of that, because whom the Father pleaseth to give, Christ delighteth to receive, and it were hideous to suppose any division between the Father and the Son, who are united on this very matter in the bond of the eternal covenant. Well, and now that thou no longer mayest doubt of his being accepted in the Beloved, and hath the act both of the Father's election, and of Christ's justification, canst thou doubt that the Spirit will proceed upon him, and that he is a holy person in the sight of thee, and of all who entertain the same belief concerning him? Truly, I may no longer doubt it, without dividing the Holy Spirit from the Father and the Son, and denying the most orthodox and needful doctrine of His procession, and raising insurrection in the very bosom of the harmonious Godhead.

Thus, brethren, have we shewn how it is impossible to separate that view of baptism which is upheld in the standards of all orthodox Churches, from the very ground-work of all doctrine: that however men may reject it, it is only an effect of their ignorance; for if they would reflect, and were capable of any insight into truth, they must believe it as all their fathers did. One thing more suffer me to observe, before proceeding in my discourse, that the act which declareth the Church's belief in a man's faith, and involveth all the consequences in the act, not of the minister who performeth, or of the kirk-session who approveth it, but the act of the whole Church, it may be of Scotland, or of England, in which the act is .done, without being challenged or reversed by the superior powers, who review the actings of the inferior. And, therefore, from the time the Church hath so declared concerning any one that he is a believer, and gives him the seal thereof, he must be so accounted of, and cannot otherwise be accounted of than as a believer, without setting up our own private judgment against the Church, and actually becoming dissenters or seceders from her communion. And such an act is so desperate and daring an act of uncharitableness, that I would advise no man to be readily guilty of it. So very jealous are the Churches themselves upon this subject, that they will not rebaptize any man who may desire the privileges of them, though baptized in another communion. This is the great act of uncharitableness whereof it is the peculiar distinction of the Baptists to be guilty. But, excepting amongst them, it is not known in the Christian Church.—After this reasoning, I shall now proceed to draw out some of the practical conclusions.

First, The Church, or community of the baptized, is to be regarded as a family of God the Father, a holy priesthood, redeemed unto God by the blood of Christ, and cleansed by the washing of regeneration, and the purifying of the Holy Ghost;—seeing the one act of baptism doth necessarily imply no less, and therefore it ought to bring forth the fruits of the Spirit, and keep all the commandments and ordinances of the gospel blameless. We may now expect, we have now a right to require, such a walk and conversation as becometh the gospel of Christ, seeing we believe grace to have been vouchsafed sufficient for our weakness. And, therefore, next to the continual reverence of one another, as the chosen of God, ought to be the observation of one another as the obedient disciples of Christ. And if we discover any brother erring from the truth, denying the faith, or walking disorderly, we are called upon in all love and faithfulness, to warn him against the danger of such a course. And so we will be apt to do if we consider him to be a brother, and one with us in the Lord Jesus; for there is no bond so close and tender and enduring as that of the household of faith: but if we regard him as nowise concerning us, not of our kindred, not of our acquaintance, not of our city or nation, and far out of our circle, we say, What have I to do with such a one? he is nothing to me, and I am nothing to him. But if we feel that to the baptized we are knit by the most intimate of all relationships, the oneness of baptism, the oneness of the Father, the oneness of the Spirit, then is there a fulness of the heart, out of which to speak unto every one, though he were the lowest menial of our house, or the poorest drudge upon the highway. There is a fund of charity and love, there is a divine interest of Christ, whose name is either to be honoured or blasphemed in this member of His body; there is a near interest of the catholic Church and the communion of saints, which is either to be strengthened by this her child's faith and love, or to be vexed and grieved with his perverseness, and by his worthlessness dishonoured in the presence of Christ her spouse. Under the influence of such strong and abiding sentiments, every Christian is attracted to every other Christian; and the communion of the saints becomes more than a name, and passeth into the life of continual love, and overcometh the uncharitableness of the world, and the diversity of rank, and nation, and kindred, and tongue, and every other divisive and malicious affection of the human heart. There ariseth, thereupon, a bond of union and a various articulation of the body, which knitteth the members of Christ into one, and thence proceedeth a circulation of love which, coming out of the gracious fountain of God's mercy in Christ, to all in covenant with Him, doth circulate far and wide in acts of grace unto the furthest limits of the Church.

To this an objection is wont to be taken of this kind; But how can I regard such a one, whom I clearly perceive to be under the power of the devil, the world, and the flesh, as a member of Christ, or treat him as a brother, though he have gone through the form of baptism? I answer, Call not baptism a form any more: we have settled that question. Call it a holy sacrament for the remission of sins and the receiving of the Holy Ghost. But thou sayest, thy friend is utterly without the sense of sin, or the apprehension of the Holy Ghost. And wast not thou so also at one time? Is it so rare a thing for a soul to be first a prodigal, under the bondage of Egypt or in the stronghold of Babylon? Thou knowest little, if thou thinkest so. Go the round of thy most pious and faithful acquaintance, and ask them if it was ever so with them; and hear them answer with one voice, Alas! brother, dost thou put such a question to me, who was the chief of sinners? Ask thou, then, how they were delivered from such a state of degradation and bondage? They will tell thee, that it was by some kind brother or faithful minister cleaving to them with wholesome instruction and patient perseverance. And if thou thyself, O uncharitable questioner! and thy friend being heretofore in the gall of bitterness and the bond of iniquity, were brought to the knowledge of the truth by some true and faithful words uttered in love to your souls, dost thou go about to ask what thy duty is to one or to many who are found in the same estate, and are privileged with the same privileges as thou wast, and need the same forgiveness which thou hast obtained? I grant thee, that he is under Satan's power: so wast thou heretofore; and thou wast delivered: so also may he be. Therefore, go not to set him at naught or to treat him unbrotherly, lest God set thee at naught, and harden thy heart. So true, dear brethren, is this to which I now exhort you, that all discipline of the Church towards the baptized proceedeth upon this principle up to the last act of the greater excommunication. Every censure and rebuke, public or private, proceedeth from love to the soul of a brother, and the endeavour to reclaim him from some temptation of Satan; every deprivation of privileges, or temporary suspension from them, proceedeth from the same tender regard to a brother's conscience, lest, partaking unworthily, he might only partake the greater judgment. And when it comes to the worst, that we are forced, by the contumacy of any one, to cut him off with excommunication, greater or lesser, it is still the same holy spirit of love; as Paul teacheth concerning the man who lived in open incest: "In the name of our Lord Jesus Christ, when ye are gathered together, and my spirit, with the power of our Lord Jesus Christ, to deliver such an one unto Satan for the destruction of the flesh, that the spirit may be saved in the day of the Lord Jesus," (1 Cor. v. 4, 5;) so also our Lord, before any member of His Church shall be reckoned a heathen man and a publican, doth first require that the person whom he hath offended shall go and speak to him as a brother by himself alone, then with a mutual friend, then lay it before the church: after which discipline of brotherly love he may be cut off and cast out of the church. And upon this principle, I say, all discipline proceedeth; and discipline which doth not thus proceed is the worst of all tyranny. It is, therefore, no new commandment that I give unto you, when I require you to look upon each other as brethren; but the commandment which we have had from the beginning, and which hath been observed in all the Churches of Christ until these times; when the total breaking up of all discipline hath brought us into the most unholy condition of treating Christ's baptized members as heathen men and as publicans, before even we have mentioned their offence to themselves privately, or treated it by the arbitration of a friend, or sought the judgment of the church. Every man doth now take judgment into his own hand; and when it pleaseth him to consider any one in an offence against sound doctrine or holy living, he doth, without warrant of any kind, proceed at once to excommunicate him, and to speak of such a one as of the world, who have no inherent relation in Christ. This is evangelical discipline: and I will tell you what the result of it must needs be; to erect in that body who so carry themselves, not the Christian spirit, but the spirit of the Pharisee; for the Christian spirit is not to judge but to exercise the discipline of love, and to be in subjection to the rules which Christ hath given for His Church; but the Pharisaical spirit is to preserve the outward profession of Christ, and give certain lesser tithes of spiritualities, but to have another rule, by which we regulate the greater acts of our obedience. The Pharisees, under the law, did not outwardly despise Moses; but to the very letter, and beyond the letter, to the last demands of tradition, exacted a scrupulous conformity. In like manner it will be found, that the Pharisees under the gospel will not reject Christ, but will supplant the liberty of His Church by the addition of many spiritual impositions, under which they will form themselves into a sect, in the bosom of His Church, zealous of their own peculiar traditions, instead of giving themselves to walk by the ordinances of the Church of Christ which He himself established. Against which, brethren, I do solemnly warn you all, and put you upon your guard against it, as the spirit most like to the Christian spirit, and most difficult to be resisted; and I charge you, upon your responsibility to the laws and institutions of Christ, to love every baptized person as a brother, and to teach him as a brother, with all faithfulness; and not to take upon you the office of the Church, in dealing with one that is contumacious, but to obey the Lord: and if you find, as no doubt you will, much hindered and hampered by the ruins of the dilapidated Church, why then mourn and weep, and let the affliction of your souls, for the despoiled glory of His Church, enter into His ears.

In thus loving and in thus treating one another as brethren in the Lord Jesus Christ, you should ever bear in mind that all are not Israel who are of Israel, that there is a reprobation as well as an election in the Church, which is known to God, though not unto us. But it is asked me, Are reprobates among those who are sealed with the seal of baptism? I answer, Yes; and for that very reason, that they were so sealed. The very meaning of a reprobate is one that is rejected, from that to which another is elected; in order to shew that everything dependeth from the will of another, even of God: and in order to shew that it dependeth upon the will of God only, it is necessary that they should stand in exactly the same condition; for if they stood in different conditions, then it were imputable to this diversity, and not to the will of God. That the will of God, the only uncaused cause of itself, may clearly appear to be the only cause of the difference between the elect and the reprobate, it is absolutely necessary that they should stand in exactly the same condition. In order to constitute, therefore, an act of rejection on the part of God, we must have the rejected one brought into the Church with the same fulness of privilege, and promise, and grace, and goodness as the elected one; to the end that it may be shewn out and seen, how far the fallen nature of man can go in withstanding, despising, and trampling under foot the fairest, fullest endowment and inheritance of God.—But doth not this invalidate the ordinance of baptism, and subvert all the doctrine above stated? Not a jot. The work of Father, Son, and Holy Ghost, as I have stated it fully out, is freely presented in baptism to the reprobate as to the elect: it is not a false presentation to the one, and a good presentation to the other, but a *bona fide* presentation unto both: and both, if left to themselves, would reject it; would entirely and for ever reject it; such is the obduracy of human hearts,—such the degradation of fallen, sinful creatures. The elect do not accept it because they have power to accept it, but because God giveth them power to accept it: and the reprobate reject it, because they have not that supernatural power given to them; and because the power of a fallen nature is totally unequal in itself to this or any other act of obedience or dutifulness to God, let God solicit it never so warmly, never so graciously.—And why should there be a difference made? Because God pleaseth it should be so; because He will shew His will in heaven, and earth, and under the earth; because His will should never have been contravened, and, having been contravened, must not always be contravened, but acknowledged, at length, everywhere; finally, because it is the only way to redemption, recovery, and blessedness, that we should acknowledge God's will to be over all, and in all, and above all; which, if you have not consented unto, then are you still in your sins, and still unconverted unto Christ.

Be it so, then, that, in order to manifest the will of the Father in the Church as out of the Church, there must be a reprobation and an election mingled together therein, in such a manner as man cannot discern the difference; for if we could discern the difference, then to that difference would it be imputed, instead of being imputed to the will of God, to reveal which is the good end of the intervention. And seeing, moreover, that it is of His purpose, and written in all the prophecies, that the Church is to end in a total apostasy, and at length to consist almost entirely of reprobates, we ought not to wonder that we find our brotherly affections scorned and set at naught; yet ought we not on that account to discontinue them: we may be silent—our Lord was oft reduced to such a case—but we must love still, with the love of a wounded and afflicted spirit, of a groaning and grieving spirit; yet ought we to be faithful, and to expound to such the awful condition of a reprobate, and shew them, out of various parts of Scripture, of what nature apostasy is, and the sin against the Holy Ghost, and how it is utterly impossible to renew such unto repentance, seeing they crucify the Son of God afresh, and put Him to an open shame. This is what our Lord doth, and what St Paul oft doth in his Epistles, and what I believe God to be daily doing in His providence, and at the present time more than in any former period of the

Church. It ought not, therefore, to be hidden by us from one another, that there is such an open gulf upon the left hand : and while we are faithful to state out the perilous risk in which every prodigal standeth of passing into a reprobate, we should address them by all the tender mercies of God ; shewing them with what fatherly love they have been followed by God since the hour of their baptism ; with what tender compassion of Christ, and urgency of the Holy Spirit, and everything besides, with which the bounty and grace of the most gracious Giver of all good hath stored up in Jesus, for the chief of sinners : then we should pass on to shew them what a hard heart and rebellious spirit, what a dead and barren soul, it revealeth towards God, that, in defiance of the whole gospel-grace held out to them, they have gone on in their perverseness and obstinacy, trampling honour, glory, grace, love, and every noble thing; daring power, threatening, indignation, wrath, and every awful attribute of God! and thence prove to their satisfaction that it is not in man to accept of any good thing from God, that he is possessed with a most irradicable, incurable alienation from God, and cannot cease from sin ; that neither Bible, nor preaching, nor Christ, nor heaven, nor hell, nor anything whatever can convert the human will and bring it back again, so as to become concentric with and moved by the will Divine. And what, do you ask me, is the use of being brought to such a conclusion ? I answer, It is the perfection of all which man can do for his brother-man, to shew him his own total impotency in himself ; and this is exactly the point at which Divine grace findeth the sinner. Then, when the rebellious will is humbled, and the poor creature is conscious and convinced of utter helplessness, he may be glad to hear of another will which is able to overcome and subdue this will of his own. He will no longer kick against the will of God, nor refuse to have His salvation of free grace ; now that he hath an idea of what human depravity is, and of what Divine grace is, and of what reprobation is, and of what election is. But while he stumbleth at this stone there is no hope of him whatever.

And how can you ever bring a man to this pass of good hope, if you withhold from him the knowledge of God's gracious dealing with him ever since his baptism? and what ground have you to argue with him at all? The man is a step-son from his birth, a bastard, and no legitimate child: he hath had a dry breast to suck, and an empty spoon hath been held to his lips: how could he thrive? What grace hath he had? None whatever. And will you talk to him about the perversity of his nature? What hath it perverted? You gave him naught, and how could he pervert it? Is it your preaching that he hath set at naught? He will tell you, because you are not worth the hearing. Is it your love? With what love have you loved him, treating him always as, and calling him, a heathen man and a publican. But transfer the question from yourself, from the preacher, from everything visible, and shew him that, ever since his baptism, God hath been yearning over him with love, treating him with a full cup, and doing for him whatever He doeth for the most favoured of men; that he hath had share and share alike with the Church, and hath been no step-child, nor foster-child, but a true son of the house and sharer of the inheritance which he hath rejected. Do act thus with him, and you put the question upon its proper bearing, and nonplus all his retorts; unless, indeed, he be of such a terrible mood as to retort against God: in which case, say to him as Paul did, "Who art thou, O man, that contendest against God?"

II. The practical conclusion with respect to individuals is, that we should bear in mind for ourselves, that from the day of our baptism we have been entreated with God's unceasing grace; which, if we have till now rejected, then have we accumulated upon our heads a weight and load of guilt wherewith the heathen are not at all chargeable. I say heathen, and not world; because, properly speaking, in a nation of baptized persons there is no world, but a reprobate Church. If by the term "the world" be understood a people who have broken covenant, I object not to its use, seeing our Lord useth it in the same sense when speaking of the Jewish nation; but if by the term be meant that which is expressed under the symbol of the sea—that is, the ignorant and unchristian nations—I reject it as utterly inapplicable to any man within the pale of the Church. For though he may be in his moral life as bad, and even worse, and in his opinions hardly better than a heathen man, yet is he not therefore to be acquitted and absolved from the more heinous guilt of having trampled under foot the Son of God, and sinned against the light of His gospel. It is totally to deny the profitableness of a visible Church, for any one to seek out of the Church the infinite advantages which a man holdeth thereof; and where it is commonly done, as amongst the Dissenters and the Evangelicals, it hath the invariable effect of extinguishing all sense of the vast benefit, and corresponding responsibility, of being born and baptized and educated in a Christian Church; and, to the extent of the prevalence of such sects, it hath the effect of subverting, not only the natural thankfulness for an established Church, but for a visible Church altogether. And when the use and profit of the visible Church—that is, of all ordinances, and, I may add, the written Word itself, which is only the prophetical ordinance—hath been lost to the sense and the sight of man, it is a proof that the invisible Church is about to expire, and, without any prophetic foresight, you may pronounce, that in a generation or two it will expire. The only thing which preserveth the visible Church in being is the faith, that in its ordinances all the blessings of the invisible Church are held, as the water in a cistern, and through them conveyed to the lips of the elect of God. And because I believe that this is a great and fundamental truth, and that God will at no time dispense with the ordinances in the communication of His grace, save where they are not in existence, I know full well that when the ordinances are set light by, or when they are all overlooked for the single glorification of one of them, the written book, as is the case at present, we are near to be dissolved and broken up by death. I do the more earnestly, therefore, call upon every baptized person who now heareth me, to rest assured that, in possessing the ordinances of God from his youth, he hath possessed the continually overflowing cistern, where is contained the waters of the gospel;—that you have been setting at naught the love of God in Jesus Christ, the affection of a Father to His children, which, indeed, swalloweth up all fatherly affection in its infinite comprehensiveness, as the heavens include the earth and all the planets, and all the stars which softly move therein;—that you have been setting at naught the infinite honour of being accounted a son of God, which is so great that the apostle upon that name alone inferreth Christ's superiority above the angels; and David was amazed that one of his loins should be honoured with that high degree;—that you have been rejecting the infinite condescension and self-humiliation of the Son, who descended from the incomprehensible dignity of the Only-begotten of God from all eternity, and forewent the boundless blessedness of inhabiting the Father's bosom, in order to find for you favour and forgiveness in the sight of God, which you, for your part, have for long years been declaring your total indifference and unwillingness to receive or partake;— that you have been withstanding and effectually resisting the infinite diligence of the Holy Spirit in the Holy Scriptures, and in all the ordinances of the Church, especially in the preaching of the word and the administration of sacraments; whose condescension to reason with you, to remonstrate against your wickedness, to wait upon you soon and late, and in every way to insinuate Himself into your nature, by all its avenues of affection, you have withstood, and do withstand unto this hour. O brethren! doth this make no difference in your guiltiness? or, rather, doth it not make all the difference which is conceivable, and constitute the condemnation, that light is come into the world, and men have loved darkness rather than light, their deeds being evil? Is it no aggravation of a son's crime, that he hath broken the hearts of the tenderest parents that ever lived? Is it no aggravation of a servant's crime, that he hath betrayed the trust and pilfered the treasures of the worthiest master who ever breathed? of a friend, that he hath cast off the truest friend? of a lover, that he hath been treacherous to the faithfullest, truest lover? of every relative offence, that it is committed against the best and noblest, most generous and forgiving disposition in those who are offended against? Why, dear brethren, these are the very head and front of offences. It is not the quantity of dust that hath changed hands, it is not the piece of matter which hath got a new master, that makes the complaint; but it is a rent heart, a violated trust, which crieth for vengeance. And if this be so, as you all know well how truly it is so, I affirm, that to have belonged to the visible Church, to have been baptized, and to have known God in the various relations of Father, Friend, Lover, Master, Redeemer, Saviour, and Lord, and whatever else is tender, reverend, and awful amongst men, and yet to have rejected Him, to have turned a deaf ear to Him, to have defrauded Him of the kindred affection and service, doth heap upon our head the accumulated amount of the penalties which, in the statute-book, are found written against the various violated relationships of righteousness, and doth add to the amount thereof, all which poets have truly imagined, and sentimentalists have represented in the most romantic and incidental relationships, whereof the statute-book taketh no cognisance. Such is the nature of the guiltiness of a man in covenant with God: and do they call this nothing? Is this to be lost sight of, and not spoken of? Are men who have thus offended to be dealt with as the ignorant and unconscious, the superstitious and idolatrous heathen, called the world, and understood to be as if they had never known and never despised the knowledge of God? As the Lord liveth, while I have the privilege and the vocation of dealing truth from the pulpit of a Church established in these lands, I will never suffer such a thing to be said or thought without the most instant and urgent appeal to the law and the testimony of our God. To which if you give heed, and perceive the way in which God speaketh to Israel, is it in the way He doth to the heathen? It is as a husband, the tenderest of husbands, doth to the wife of his bosom; as the most loving father doth to the son of his love: "O Ephraim! how shall I give thee up! all my bowels yearn over thee: how shall I make thee as Admah or as Zeboim!" "O Jerusalem! Jerusalem! how oft would I have gathered thee as a hen doth her chickens under her wings!" &c.—And thus, by their blindness to the sacrament of baptism, and the consequences which it involveth, have they lost the whole effect of the revealed mind of God to the sinner, and the manifested sinfulness of the sinner, and destroyed the very possibility of a covenant; and they have lost all the prophecy which beareth against the apostate Church, and indeed the whole mystery and meaning of a Church. But I must not insist: for there comes from this fountain of infant baptism a thousand streams, of which I have been able to follow only one or two; but let these suffice for the present.

Such, dear brethren, is the way in which this great subject comes home to our own souls and to the Church: and in this way doth it prove itself to be most profitable unto holiness; and in this way, I pray you, to use it for the edification of one another in love. And give heed now to our application of it; for which, indeed, I have preached these two concluding discourses of this series upon the sacrament of baptism. You heard, in the morning, in our enumeration of conclusions from the doctrine of baptism, how parents stand towards their children, and how children stand towards their parents; and now ye have heard how all the Church stand towards one another. Well, let us bring these instructions to bear upon this one point, of urging all the baptized, who are of sufficient knowledge, sound in the faith, and inoffensive in their lives, to come unto the table of the Lord, or to present themselves for instruction in the view thereof. Let us first state to you what is the nature of the offence which a baptized person commits in not partaking of the Lord's supper. Taking baptism to be the true thing, and not the sign of the thing merely, he who hath been baptized in the name of the Father, and the Son, and the Holy Ghost, doth, in so doing, first, Refuse the only food on which his new life can be sustained; and as life cannot be sustained without food, he may soon expect to die. Secondly, He doth despise the communion of the saints, in refusing to partake with them of the common bread and common cup, and so may not expect any share of the prayers, intercessions, blessings, and gifts of the Church, from which he voluntarily exileth himself. Thirdly, He dishonoureth the Church which admitted him to the privileges of Christ, and acteth most ungratefully by the father who took upon him the vows of responsibility for his sake; but he will not even have his privilege, or take it up for himself, but counteth nothing by it. Fourthly, He dishonoureth God the Father, who hath spread this table for him; Christ, who hath given Himself as the Paschal Lamb to be eaten; the Holy Ghost, who doth prepare guests for the banquet, washing them in the blood and robing them with the righteousness of Christ; and how can he look to be blessed when thus standing stoutly against the blessed Trinity? Finally, He doth what he can to abolish the Church from the earth; because, it is manifest, that if all were to follow his example in abandoning the most holy of all the ordinances, not only would this, but every inferior ordinance, be soon brought into desuetude and contempt.— Such is a small reckoning of the sins which every one committeth who abstaineth from the Lord's supper. It is not for me to enter into any justification of such conduct; there is, there can be none—any apology will only make the case worse. What, though it be your wicked life?—then add that to the rest. What, though it be your ignorance?—add that also. What, though it be your having no time to think about it?—and add that also. Thou reprobate, wilt thou justify thyself by shewing how wicked and how obstinate thou art? If thou art ignorant, come and be instructed; if thou art wicked, forsake thy wickedness; if thou art such a drudge to the world, be so no longer. These additional acts of wickedness will certainly not justify the other.

Therefore, dear brethren, we ought to look with a tender and pitiful eye upon those who stand aloof from this holy ordinance, as men who labour under some strong delusion, or who are given over to some very evil spirit; and we should address ourselves to seek them with all diligent instruction and earnest correction, knowing that they must stand stock still until they be delivered from their present snare. And, therefore, I do most solemnly entreat you, as you love one another, to do your part faithfully by one another, and not to suffer brethren, for whom Christ died, to continue in such ignorance and error. Tell them plainly how they offend against all; shew them what precious things they make shipwreck of; shew them what promised blessings they lose; rehearse to them the profit ye have had in every way since you became joined members of Christ's Church. This office apperteineth chiefly to the minister, and the elders, and the deacons of the flock ; but it appertaineth in a measure unto all—it is a brother's love unto a brother. Be watchful, therefore, for each other's soul, and let us endeavour to present before the Church the aspect of a congregation of worshippers, in which every baptized person, of sufficient knowledge, is found continually to pay his vows to the Lord in the sacrament of the body and blood of Christ.

HOMILY X.

JUSTIFICATION AND RECAPITULATION OF THE WHOLE DOCTRINE CONTAINED IN THE ABOVE HOMILIES.

ROM. IX. 31, 32.

But Israel, which followed after the law of righteousness, hath not attained to the law of righteousness. Wherefore? Because they sought it not by faith, but as it were by the works of the law.

THE ignorance which existeth upon the subject of baptism is so great, and the tendency to an intellectual apostasy so violent, that, although I have at every hand sought to guard the orthodox, and I may say catholic, doctrine which I have delivered, against being misapprehended and misconstrued, many will roundly assert that I have preached what is commonly known by baptismal regeneration: whereupon I have resolved, in the strength of God, to give this additional discourse for the sake of my flock, who have an ear to hear the truth, and a mind exercised to discern differences; but as to those who come amongst us to spy out our liberty in Christ, and to make an evil report of our doctrine, we have no hope of ever becoming to them anything but a stumbling-block and a rock of offence, unless the Lord should be pleased to change the spirit in which they come, and the temper in which they listen to the preaching of His Holy Word.

By *baptismal regeneration*, when that term is used for reproach, is meant the doctrine that the work of Christ is done and finished in baptism, and that it is idle to speak of anything else under that name. This doctrine is supposed to be held by the Church of England, from these words in the baptismal office which are pronounced by the priest over the child after it hath been baptized :—" We yield Thee hearty thanks, most merciful Father, that it hath pleased Thee to regenerate this infant with Thy Holy Spirit, to receive him for Thine own child by adoption, and to incorporate him into Thy holy Church." I have shewn at length, in former discourses, that this is the very language in which the apostles and the Church, in all her creeds and confessions, have spoken of and to the baptized: but this is not enough in these intellectual days, which require of us to square the thing by human understanding, and shew the usefulness of such a doctrine, which they conceive must be very dangerous. I shall first, therefore, defend it from the charge of baptismal regeneration; and, secondly, shew what is the consequence of taking the low ground which men, in these times, are wont to take; and conclude with a repetition and reinforcement of the whole doctrine.

The error of baptismal regeneration consisteth, not in holding that the true children of God are regenerated at their baptism, and from thence should date their admission into the household of faith, which, with all my orthodox fathers in the Church, I hold to be the only true doctrine, but in holding, that every person who is baptized doth virtually thereby become regenerate and possessed with the Holy Spirit; or, to speak the language of theologians, that the inward grace is so connected with, or bound to, the outward ordinance, that whosoever receiveth the one doth necessarily become partaker of the other. This is an error of the most hideous kind; bringing in justification by works, or rather by ceremonies, destroying the election of the Father, the salvation of the Son, and the sanctification of the Holy Ghost, and exalting the priest and the ceremony into the place of the Trinity. This is exactly what the Papists have done, and against nothing have the Protestants more sedulously guarded; and I am sure, that I have taken, more than a dozen times, a solemn protest against such a vile notion. I have struck at the very root of it, by shewing, that among the baptized there is a reprobation as well as an election; and I have endeavoured even to prevent the imputation of it, by shewing, that faith, true faith, the gift of the Father and the manifestation of His electing love, is necessary to the receiving of any baptismal gifts, is necessary to the receiving of the ordinance itself. I have shewn, in many discourses, how the Holy Spirit once given will never be recalled; and that the perseverance of the saints is as sure a doctrine as the unchangeableness of the Father's will or the sufficiency of the Son's salvation, being nothing else than the irresistibleness of the Holy Ghost expressed with reference to the subject of His possession. And if the Holy Ghost is irresistible, and there is a reprobation in the Church, how could I say that the Holy Ghost is necessarily tied to the ordinance of baptism, or to any ordinance whatever?

Yet, while thus we most steadfastly hold that God among the baptized hath His own people, endowed with all grace, and Satan hath his, entirely destitute of grace,—for we allow of no secondary influences of the Holy Ghost,—we are not the less steadfast in maintaining, that it appertaineth not to us to make the distinction or division between them, which God only maketh, nor to speak of baptism otherwise than God speaketh of it. But because the Church is limited in her power of discerning the efficacy of the ordinance, shall she, therefore, strip the ordinance of all efficacy whatever, and speak of it in a lower style than the Scriptures require her to do? If so, she changeth the everlasting ordinance. We must still treat the baptized as the children of God, who have been brought into covenant with Him. If they have forgot their 'privileges and their engagements altogether, the more need have we to remind them diligently of that which God hath not forgotten, though they may. My brethren, what say you, if a man is forgetting the dignity of his name, and the honour of his station, is it friendly, or even honest in you, by silence, to acquiesce with him therein; or, by diligently avoiding the subject, to indulge him in his wicked forgetfulness? But if his Father be waiting for him with all tenderness of affection, and earnestly desiring his return to the path of duty, ready to forgive, is it right of us to keep this matter hidden from such a one? Now, dare any one, who heareth me, declare that this is not the case with respect to any baptized person? If so, with respect to what class of them, or what individual of that class? If you cannot answer me, tell me how you dare take upon you to speak otherwise of all and to all than as children of the covenant, to whom God is openly reconciled, and for whom He earnestly waiteth till he shall be converted? Therefore, we dare not do otherwise than use the language quoted above. It is a necessary consequence of our present ignorance, and the invisibility of the Church. It is written, that baptism is for the receiving of the Holy Ghost; and, therefore, we will ever hold up baptism as the ordinance in which the Holy Ghost is received by the faithful: and having baptized any one upon the ground of our belief in his faith, we will speak of him as one that hath received the Holy Ghost. If he should not, then we do continually convince him of his want, and of the exceeding danger of his estate of reprobacy. He may take it to heart, and repent of his great wickedness: he may harden himself the more, and be given up to believe a lie,—that he is regenerate, when indeed he is not: what then? we cannot prevent the judgment of God, and have, for our parts, fulfilled our vocation. But even reason and common proverbs say, that putting a man in good company is one of the best ways to make him good; and that to give him a bad name, or to suppose him bad, is the sure way to make him so. No one would say, that a society of worthy men should change the purity and gravity of their discourse, because one or two foolish or ignorant fellows pestered them with their presence: but because we have got amongst us those who are ignorant and foolish, they would have us to speak other language than that which Christ hath taught His disciples. The Lord forbid: I, for one, by the grace of God, will never consent to such an unwise, unprincipled, and rebellious course.—I have only to say further upon this their charge against us of maintaining baptismal regeneration, that I believe he who doth not look to his baptism as the covenanted promise of God to regenerate him, will be very imperfectly regenerated, if regenerated at all.

But one may say, If the regenerate be at baptism regenerated, why from baptism do they not exhibit the signs of a regenerated person? I answer, first, That the way of the Holy Spirit is commonly to teach unto the souls their wickedness, by leading them into temptations of various kinds which may expose it, and to train them for future service in Christ's army, by making them acquainted with the enemy's camp, and weapons, and stratagems of war : but He never suffereth such a soul to commit the sin against the Holy Ghost which cannot be pardoned ; and in due time He converts him to the way into which God from the beginning had appointed him.—I answer, secondly, That when such a one doth awake from the torpor and insensibility of sin, he hath no ground to expect favour, but by acting faith upon his baptism. God hath not judged a general promise to be sufficient, otherwise He would not have instituted a special covenant. I know full well, that, of late years, the greater part of the conversions which have been made, have been made upon the missionary principle of dealing with the people as heathen. But of what kind have they been ? with little or no assurance, with very narrow views and exceedingly indistinct apprehensions of the truth ; arising from their taking hold of loose promises, catching at everything which floateth in the stream of God's Word, instead of resting upon the rock of the everlasting covenant.

If any one say, But I am sure I had no faith till such and such a period of my life; and without faith there can be no gift of the Spirit ; I answer, But art thou sure, thou boaster in thy shame, that thy father had none, or thy mother, or the Church which received thee as her child ? And what brought thee that faith which now thou thinkest thyself to have ? Came it to thee because thou wast a profligate and a trampler upon the Son of God ? or cometh it not to thee because He hath a regard to His covenant and His Church which doth faithfully administer it ? Thou wouldest fain isolate thyself, and transact thine own business with God for thyself; wouldest thou ? God will not let thee, try how thou mayest. We do not deny that there are generally two divisions in the life of the saints ; the season of their prodigality and alienation, and the season of their love and obedience to their Father : but we hold, that the mystery of the one is as deep a mystery of godliness as is the mystery of the other ; that the season before conversion revealeth the mystery of our sinfulness and of God's love to the sinner, even more than the season after conversion, which exhibits rather the mystery of His power in subduing us to Himself. But, oh, who that knoweth it would forego the delight of contemplating the love of God towards him while he was yet in his sins! It is not for any one, therefore, of God's elect children to say, that he had not the love of God, nor the righteousness of Christ, nor the presence of the Holy Spirit, till it became manifest to himself or to others. This is to contradict the whole tenor of Scripture, which representeth the elect as chosen in God even before the foundation of the world.

So much have we to say in answer to the charge of our connecting baptism and regeneration together as cause and effect, or inseparable attendants. We connect faith and regeneration together in this way; and where we believe that there is faith, we must, to be consistent, believe that there is regeneration: but our believing so, doth neither make the one nor the other to be present. But as we must use some sort of language to the baptized, and apply some sort of distinction to the members of the Church, this is the distinction which we find sanctioned in the Word of God, and in the use of all orthodox Churches, and of our own Church; and therefore we will abide by it, God helping us.

I have not pressed the adversaries of our doctrine very closely, as neither designing to attack nor to defend, but peaceably to open the matter to my people; but being now, at length, provoked by their malicious representations, I will be at the pains to spend a few minutes upon their vain and frivolous view of this great head of Christian doctrine, which is much as follows:—That the Church conferreth the outward sign, water-baptism, which is all that she can do, and thereby admitteth to the outward visible Church; that the Spirit, when it may seem good to Him, conferreth the thing signified, generally at conversion; and then beginneth his Christian experience; after which he may be admitted to the Lord's table, having set forth at length the way of his conversion and the details of his experience. This, you will allow, is the current notion among the Christians which pay any respect to discipline. Give ear while I sift it a little.

I observe, first, That there is no ground from any part of Scripture to speak thus slightingly of baptism, thus peremptorily to separate from it the Holy Ghost, thus to magnify conversion into the importance of a sacrament, and thus to date Christian experience from the time of conversion, and thus to exclude a portion of the baptized from the table of the Lord, instead of freely inviting them all. These are gratuitous suppositions and mere accommodations of Christian doctrine: I say it again, they have no ground whatever in the Word of God, or in the creed of any Church.

Secondly, If baptism be thus a mere water-washing, and may not be connected with any inward grace, what is the use or meaning of it as an ordinance of God's Church? It must be only for outward form; and I have yet to find any institution of God which was appointed only for form's sake. What advantage is it for a child to be baptized, if it only impose obligations, without conveying any power to discharge them? It is a burden, it is a heavy yoke, which we bind upon the necks of our children; and I do not wonder that parents, who are accustomed to such doctrine, should make baptism a matter of conveniency, or feel indifferent to it altogether. Truly, for my part, if I held such notions, I would consider it an act of injustice to bring my child under any such bondage, and I would openly practise adult baptism; not out of any persuasion of that way, but out of the feeling of the perfect unmeaningness of the other.

Observe, thirdly, What would become of any other ordinance if treated in the same way? For example, of the reading of the Word. If any one should say, that to read God's Word was an exercise which the Spirit might bless or not bless as it pleased Him, but upon which we had no right to expect any blessing till after conversion, what would be the consequence of such idle and wicked discourse? To make the Word of God not to be read at all; or, if read, read only as a formal custom, and with less attention than any other book. Again, if any one should say of the preaching of the word, that it was like any other address made by any individual to an assembly of men, which must be judged of by the same rules, listened to in the same spirit, and altogether used in the same manner as any other argument or oration held in other places; and that it is a most vain and superstitious notion to think that, because a man is ordained by a presbytery, or standeth up in a pulpit, or readeth a text out of the Bible, his words should have any new meaning, or his arguments any more cogency. What were the end of such discourse? Wholly to destroy the efficacy of preaching, which is the foolishness of God that is wiser than the wisdom of men; to make the Christian Church a company of sophists, critics, and censors, or a company of spectators and observers, and perhaps even admirers, of the intellectual performer, and to turn the poor Christian minister into a gazing-stock, or a laughing-stock, a courter of public favour; or, at best, a disputer against public vices, and skilful user of his natural faculties for natural ends. And what were the consequence of such a relation between minister and people? Lukewarmness, infidelity, and death. Once more, not to multiply particulars, treat prayer as baptism is by the religious world treated;—tell men that prayer is a very good thing for exciting in their minds such or such devout and charitable emotions; but as to expecting that God should yield any supernatural and extraordinary answer thereto, that He should bestow His Spirit in the very act of prayer, that He should never fail to answer a faithful prayer, and that prayer is that which the Church in heaven offer in their censors before God, which God delighteth to receive; that all these are superstitious notions, which may by no rational man be entertained. Let this discourse, I say, be maintained, and this opinion received among any Christian people, and what will the result be? Either to convert prayer into a system of self-excitation, and so to nourish all manner of self-love and self-idolatry, or else to nourish a spirit of formality, and totally to destroy the very idea of a faithful prayer, and consequently to change the everlasting ordinance of God. But the limitation of the subject of this discourse forbiddeth us to enter into particulars; and, therefore, we conclude this second part of our subject by observing, in general, that it is nothing less than wholly to pervert the advantages, and in a short time to destroy the very being, of a visible Church, thus to separate the forms which are presented unto the sight and fulfilled by the natural understanding, from the influence and power of the Holy Ghost, and the various graces of the spiritual man, and the various enjoyments and gifts of the invisible Church. What, under heaven, would or should move men to keep the ordinances of God, and to worship Him, but the hope and assurance that, in so doing, they shall enjoy the presence of His Holy Spirit? But if you go about to persuade them that they may not, or they will not, you do so far forth prevent them from honouring these services, and defeat the end of God in their appointment. And this is not all the evil. You not only defeat the ends of the visible Church, and in time destroy it altogether, but you prevent the invisible or spiritual Church from flourishing, and in the end destroy it also; for without faith there can be no gifts of the Holy Spirit. Now, the visible Church, or the ordinances of God, are all helps unto our faith, shewing us at what time and in what manner we may expect the grace of God; but if these helps to faith be removed away, how shall she prosper without them? Much worse, certainly, than with them. But if faith faileth, then this stream faileth at its fountain, and the fruitfulness of its banks is parched. This, alas! is the case with the Church in these times, through her neglect and misuse of the ordinances of God; and the end will be entire infidelity, unless the spiritual import of these ordinances be revived. Nevertheless, I abhor the opposite extreme of connecting the spiritual grace necessarily, and tying it indissolubly to the visible ordinance; so as that those who have performed the one may believe that therefore they are possessed of the other; which introduced the spirit of the Pharisee into the former dispensation, and hath perfected the apostasy in the latter dispensation. God forbid that I should teach you either the one or the other of these errors, while I endeavour to preserve the ordinances of the Lord's appointment in their sanctity and importance.

I do now proceed to conclude this subject, by stating over again the sum of the doctrine which we have taught.

The Church, in her prophetic office, interpreteth the symbolical institutions of Christ, and doth not take upon her the office which the objectors would take upon themselves, of sitting in judgment. Having taken proof of the baptized person's faith—whether from himself personally, or from his responsible parent—and being satisfied therewith, the Church doth feel that she is not at liberty to doubt that the baptism which she hath administered is a true baptism, done according to the mind of its Divine Author, and may be spoken of, as we have shewed that the apostles ever speak of that holy ordinance, as being effectual for the washing away of sins, and the receiving of the Holy Ghost. For her to speak otherwise would be either lamely and imperfectly to interpret baptism, or to insinuate that she had been guilty of a rash and unwarrantable act in administering it in this particular case. If the former, she is faithless to her prophetic calling, which is fully and truly to interpret the ordinances and mysteries of religion; if the latter, she is guilty of violating the ordinance. Now, it is not to be expected that any Church would permit or enjoin her ministers to set forth an imperfect or a false account of the ordinances; which were at once to constitute an apostasy: nor would she justify her ministers in loosely and licentiously squandering the holy ordinances upon any one who may desire them. What, then, is left for a Church to do, but to state out broadly and plainly to all her members what is contained in the ordinance of Christ, and what is therein communicated to the faithful, and to require of her ministers, upon every celebration of it, to make the same fully known? This is what the Church of England, with every orthodox Church under heaven, hath done: and to have done less would have been the greatest of dishonour to Christ, the great Appointer; to the Holy Ghost, the great Executor; and to the Church, the receiver of the benefit. And I may add, that from neglecting fully to state what is contained in the ordinances and sacraments, and ever presented there to the faithful, for the great encouragement of their faith, and for preferring to state only so much as the intellect of the natural man can perceive, and the natural heart relish and desire, it cometh to pass that orthodox doctrines and the influences of the Holy Spirit are found at so low an ebb amongst all those sects who exhibit no standards of faith to which the eyes both of ministers and people might be directed.

But while the Church, according to the practice of the apostles, doth never speak of baptism as less than it really ought to be, and always is, to a believer; nor of the baptized as less than they ought to be, if they have faith; she doth not thereby enter into the secret counsels of God, and determine whether the person who hath received the seal of righteousness by faith, be one of God's hidden ones who are chosen in Christ, or whether he be one whom Satan hath introduced into the fold, and to whom God permitted His most faithful ministers unwittingly to open the door: as, for example, in the instance of that arch-heretic Simon Magus, baptized by Philip. I have shewn, in a former discourse, that, let discipline do its best, (and it ought never to attempt less,) the Church will ever find it impossible to discriminate and distinguish between the election and the reprobation, which are brought into exactly the same visible, intelligible, and cognoscible condition, in order that the eternal difference which is to be placed between them may be known and believed to result simply from the will of God. For man is so indisposed to trace things up to God, and so willing to rest in second causes, that if anything were discoverable to the sight or intellect of man, which could account for the difference between the elect and the reprobate, to that the difference would be referred as to its cause; and so God's will, as the ultimate cause of all things, would be lost sight of by the Church, of which it is the chief end to maintain the remembrance, and continually make mention thereof, in the midst of the fallen creatures. A Church, therefore, which holdeth that a reprobation as well as an election is at all times present amongst the baptized, and every orthodox Church holdeth so; a Church which referreth the difference between these two classes of the fallen creatures, as due only to the sovereign will of God; and every Church which prefaceth and concludeth her ordinances with prayer to God, that He would grant the Spirit therein, doth acknowledge His sovereign will to be over all. Such a Church must not be condemned because she speaketh out to the baptized what manner of sacrament they have been sealed with, and what manner of covenant they have joined themselves to, and what manner of persons they are ever after to be regarded, in what language spoken of and spoken to at all times, until they shall be removed from the number of the faithful by some deliberate and decisive act of discipline.

When the Church, therefore, speaketh to a baptized person as one whose sins have been remitted, and who hath received the Holy Ghost; who hath been buried with Christ, and raised up together with Him to a resurrection life; who also is seated in the heavenly places, and made a partaker of the heavenly blessings;—which language of St Paul's is still stronger than the office of any Church;—she doth by no means declare that all those blessed effects of Divine grace hath been done upon him, but that the ordinance which she hath bestowed upon him is for the communication of all these spiritual gifts to every faithful person, and that they cannot deny them to him, or by her language imply that he hath them not, without expressing her conviction that he is an unbeliever and a hypocrite; which is a conclusion she will not come to without holding a deliberate assembly of judgment, and coming to a solemn conclusion of discipline. For the Church holdeth charity to be so much the breath of her life, and judgment so much her strange work, that while she expecteth the former from all her ministers unto all her members, she committeth the latter to her rulers, and suffereth them not to proceed thereto without the solemn convocation of themselves, in the name of the blessed Trinity, and the earnest invocation of the Holy Spirit; only when they are gathered together in the name of the Lord Jesus Christ, and in the Holy Spirit's, and with the power of the Lord Jesus Christ, (1 Cor. v. 4.) If, then, she will not, without a solemn adjudication of any one, believe that he is other than he professeth himself to be, and that she hath at the time of his baptism declared him to be, what can she, without offence both to charity and to justice, and to consistency, do but continue in that faith, until in the regular way of rule and government and process of discipline, she hath seen it right to change it? To do otherwise would be to destroy the very being of rule and government and discipline, and of everything else which doth keep the Church together as a community, and fit it for holding within its rough casket, and somewhat representing to the sight the form of that most precious jewel of the faith, the communion of the saints, and the Holy Catholic Church: while, upon the other hand, it would introduce amongst the brethren a system of judging and suspecting and censuring one another, and otherwise engender the Pharisee spirit, which is the most widely opposed to the true principle of love by which Christ intended His Church to be bound together. I know to what a hideous state of corruption every community of baptized persons have come, and how extraordinary it soundeth to address them as a communion of saints: but whether is it better to make known to them the covenants which they are breaking, and have broken, or not to mention them at all; to speak to them of the privileges and rights which they are trampling under foot, or by our silence to signify that they have lost and forfeited nothing at all. How, I would ask, hath this hideous enormity grown in the Church, but by the neglect of discipline? And how, I ask again, is discipline to be revived, without making known to the people whereon it proceedeth? And wherein doth the right of taking cognisance of any Christian proceed, but upon the baptismal act? and according to what rule proceedeth it, but according to the rule of the new life, which every baptized person ought to live? But if you forbear to teach or to preach to the baptized that it is the rule of a new life which they are under, and you shrink to tell them that they have power to walk in the Holy Ghost, then how preposterous, how tyrannical and unjust, to exercise judgment and discipline upon them according to that rule whereof ye have studiously kept them in ignorance! For if there be an axiom in Church affairs, it is this: That all discipline in the rulers, which is not preceded by doctrine in the preachers, will turn to tyranny. And, for my part, I confess myself totally in the dark concerning the principle upon which discipline proceedeth in those Churches which regard baptism as merely an outward rite, and never intended to seal the righteousness of Christ, and communicate the regeneration of the Holy Ghost. I say it is so intended, and so it always doth to those who have faith; and, therefore, when I judge any one to have faith, I must likewise judge him to be both accepted and regenerated: and when, upon my conviction of his faith, I baptize him, that solemn act of mine, or rather of the Church—for baptism is no one man's act, but the act of the whole Church—doth preclude me from using any other language to him than that of an accepted, adopted, and regenerate person, until another act of the Church permitteth me: yea, and if I do speak of him otherwise, he may impugn me before the proper tribunals for daring to do so; and the Church would be justified in rebuking me for uncharitableness and presumption. Such is a short explanation and justification of the use of such language as that which I quoted from the baptismal service of the Church of England, not because it is there—for I use the same every time I baptize—but because it is the ground upon which the objection is commonly raised.

If it be alleged against this, How many of your baptized and regenerate people are found to live in a state of ignorance and wickedness, and to die in impenitence, or even in unbelief! What, then, is regeneration, if it is to be spoken of as having proceeded upon such as those, of whom there are thousands in every city, and tens of thousands in every province of Christendom? To this I answer, with St Paul, that "their unbelief doth not make the faith of God without effect." Reasoning upon such a principle, would Caleb and Joshua ever have rested in the covenant which God made with the children of Israel at Sinai for the land of Canaan, when they alone of all the hundreds of thousands who had the same promise, believed that God was able to accomplish it? Yet the covenant of God abode steadfast to the two faithful witnesses, notwithstanding the hundreds of thousands towards whom it failed. And why did it fail upon them? "They could not enter in because of unbelief." So say we, that the baptized have no privilege without faith; but, having faith, they have every privilege, not of an outward visible Church merely, but of an invisible Church: which faith, we do never pretend to bestow upon them, but do constantly declare, that it is the gift of God. But if any one come to us, professing to have faith, and we see no ground to doubt his profession, we dare not refuse him the seal of the righteousness of faith, which is baptism; nor may we refuse it to his children, during the years of their incapacity for conceiving faith. If we see ground of uncertainty, we may postpone and put him under probation; but we may not peremptorily refuse any one who seeketh, nor, without a good and sufficient cause for doubting his sincerity, may we refuse at all. And having consented to do the solemn act, are we to do it in part, or to do it in whole? And having done it, are we to speak of it as done in part, or as wholly done? I can find no authority in the Scriptures, and surely there is none in reason, why we should make any division in God's holy ordinance, of which it is the character to be one and indivisible. But while this proceedeth in full faith at the hands of the Church, and, in consistency, she continueth to hold such language, it all proceedeth upon her faith in the man's profession and appearance; which may be assumed for a deception to others, or taken on through a deception which Satan hath wrought in himself. But as we do not take upon us to judge the heart, or to try the reins, which is the prerogative of God only,—and for which, as He hath not given us the faculty, so He exacteth not from us the responsibility,—we are content, though sorry, to be deceived, in all instances where we are deceived—content, because it is God's appointment, and sorry that men should be found so deceitful and so deceivable. For all such we never expected the sacrament of baptism, or indeed any other ordinance of Christ's appointment, to work any fruit of good, but rather much fruit of evil; because they had not faith, and without saving faith did dare to ask for the seal of the righteousness which is by faith. It is a point of faith with us, that there are always such in the Church, and, therefore, we are not disappointed, though vexed, when they make themselves manifest; but do warn the brethren, that Satan's chief subtlety and strength are in the Church, and we exhort them to make their calling and election sure against all his arts. And, moreover, we see the wisdom of God in revealing to us this great truth, that we might always be upon our watch-tower, and not sink down into the assurance of repose, while we are filled with the assurance of victory. For these two things are necessary to every great exploit: first, a great heart to undertake it; and, secondly, a great perseverance to accomplish it; of which we have the former in looking to our baptism, where all might and triumph are assured to us the better by looking to every hand of us, and seeing the enemy everywhere active around us. It is nothing to us, therefore, to be told that there is a great number of the baptized who are without God and without hope in the world, dead in trespasses and sins: we know it already, and we know the wisdom of it, yea, the necessity of it, in the present warfare of the Church. But when you would infer from this, that baptism is without any effect upon them who believe, we challenge you of that error of logic which consisteth in changing the subject: you ought to have concluded, that it hath no effect upon those who do not believe. The gift of faith we never set forth as a consequence of baptism, but as the act of the Divine will: we did not baptize that they might receive faith, but because they professed, and we believed, that they had already received faith. And how many soever you point out to us as not having any fruits of baptism, we do answer, Well, if it be so, (but we warn thee to beware of uncharitableness,) it is so because they never had faith: but for the efficacy of baptism to the faithful, the question is not altered by these thousands in every city, and tens of thousands in every province of Christendom, who are faithless.

Here two observations suggest themselves: the first, Of what importance it is to set forth the sacraments in all their awful solemnity and pregnant meaning, in all their privilege and responsibility, that men may not rush forward in ignorance to partake of them, and not as mere signs commemorative, or external rites and ceremonies, which any one who believeth human nature to be corrupt, and Christ to have died on the cross, may well enough discharge. The preachers who make so little discourse concerning them, and set so little store by them, are the very men who open the door to those thousands in every city and tens of thousands in every province of Christendom to break through and vex the Lord:

and we who are blamed, because we hold them with apostolical force and earnestness, are the men who endeavour to defend the sacred passage with all the thunders of the wrath and indignation of God.—Secondly, Those who open not the inexhaustible privileges bestowed in the sacraments upon believers, do not present the proper reward of faith to move men to entreat the Father for the gift of it: neither do they keep faith, in its distinctness, as the gift of the Father, and of no other person in the blessed Trinity, (the Son being the object, the Holy Spirit the operator, but the Father, and Him only, the giver of it:) neither do they keep it separate from all works, and prior to all forgiveness and grace, itself the Father's grace, which includeth every other ; which distinctness and separation is admirably preserved by the sacrament of baptism, which joins us to Christ, and bestows upon us the Holy Spirit; and, therefore, proveth that all which went before was from the Father: but by their blundering here they blunder everywhere, confuse the personalities of the Godhead generally, divide their substance, set forth every one of them as God complete, and most commonly forget that there is a Father, from whom the Son and the Spirit proceed. They remove the great steps and progressions of the work: first, a work done by the Father while we are yet out of Christ, which is before baptism, the grace of accepting Christ's sacrifice instead of us, and bestowing upon us faith to believe upon Him whom He hath sent; then the work done by Christ upon us, after we are joined to Him, in baptizing us with the Holy Ghost, and rearing us up in the principles of the new and everlasting life, and enabling us to feed upon His body. They blunder also sadly in respect to the means of obtaining that faith from the Father, very often setting forth these very sacraments as means to that end; whereas the truth is, that if faith in Christ be not received from the Father before our baptism, our baptism, so far from being a mean to that end, will work unbelief and the hardening of our hearts; and so the Lord's supper, instead of being a mean to receive the Spirit, will, to one who hath not the Spirit, be the most effectual hindrance thereto: and why? because to both we come with a lie in our right hand, and without any raiment proper for the solemnity. The proper mean to faith is to receive Christ in His prophetic office, coming forth to declare the Father's will, or in His ordinance of preaching, which He hath established during His absence. This openeth the Father's purpose to include an election in Him, and to bring them through all perils and perplexities; which encourageth prayer to the Father, that He would include in them. And so faith cometh by hearing and praying; and being come, we are ripe for baptism, when we receive Christ as our Priest, and are endowed with the Holy Ghost to be kings and priests unto God.

And here, brethren, I conclude this testimony, which I have lifted up amongst you, for the orthodox doctrine of the Church concerning baptism; in the full assurance that ignorant and wicked tongues cannot prevent it from producing, unto all of you who believe, the fruits of righteousness and holiness: for, surely, a full vessel is more profitable to a weak and sickly people than is an empty one; and it is better to drink from the cisterns which God hath consecrated, than to hew out others for ourselves. Oh, therefore, seek ye, dear brethren, faith from the Father; and having it, possess yourselves of all the treasures of Christ, which the Spirit presenteth unto you in the sacraments of baptism and the Lord's supper. And we shall grow together into a communion and fellowship of holy men, nourished up in faith unto good works. Which may the Lord grant unto us all; and to His name be the praise.

This now is the conclusion of the whole matter concerning baptism, that every one, whether for himself alone, or for those also for whom he is responsible, should believe that God hath entered into covenant with him, in the most awful name of the ever-blessed Trinity, and that he is a person entered into the most solemn covenant with God; which covenant God will not abrogate, and man cannot. This covenant apprehendeth us as altogether sunk in sin, and destitute through every infirmity; and, apprehending us thus, doth, of free grace, endue us with forgiveness of sins, and the powers of the Holy Ghost: "Repent and be baptized every one of you, for the remission of sins, and ye shall receive the Holy Ghost." From the celebration and solemnisation of that holy covenant, we ought to abide under the continual state of men forgiven—not once forgiven, but forgiven for a continuance; seeing we sin for a continuance. To doubt of our forgiveness at any time, or for any sin, (except the sin against the Holy Ghost, of which I speak not,) is to doubt, not the word merely, nor the promise merely, but the covenant of God: which, as it is the most solemn of all God's transactions, may not be doubted, or disbelieved, or despised without the most aggravated sin against God, who is very truth, without variableness or shadow of turning. This is the very end of the covenant, to transfer the general promise to an individual soul, and seal it upon him as his own. The faith, therefore, of a baptized person is, that he himself is forgiven, and anything short of this is to make void the covenant. Secondly, From the moment of his baptism, and ever onward till the separation of soul and body, we ought to look upon our body as a pure and cleansed substance, inhabited by the Holy Ghost, and by Him empowered to live the life of Christ, and keep the commandments of God blameless. Nothing should appear too difficult for us, because the Holy Spirit, that dwelleth in us, is irresistible. In the habitual exercise of these two continued states of the renewed soul, peace with God, through the imputed righteousness of Christ, and sanctification unto all obedience, through the indwelling of the Holy Ghost, a baptized person ought to live: in thus living, he believeth the word and honoureth the act of the covenant of his God. And if, at any time, the clouds of doubt, and the fears of infirmity and falling away, are permitted by God to come over the soul of a baptized person, they are to be looked upon as temptations of Satan through the infirmity of our faith; and the only way which I know for effectually removing them is, to turn the eye of such a one unto God—as a covenant-keeping God, and to that covenant which He hath made with him in the sacrament of baptism.

HOMILIES ON THE LORD'S SUPPER.

HOMILY I.

ON SELF-EXAMINATION.

1 COR. XI. 27-29.

Wherefore whosoever shall eat this bread, and drink this cup of the Lord, unworthily, shall be guilty of the body and blood of the Lord. But let a man examine himself, and so let him eat of that bread, and drink of that cup. For he that eateth and drinketh unworthily, eateth and drinketh damnation to himself, not discerning the Lord's body.

THE duty of self-examination hath always been regarded by the Church as standing next in order to the invitation which we give unto all the baptized. We invite all, and we add, "But let a man examine himself." Now, in discoursing of self-examination, the first inquiry must be, whether a man that is in Christ can discover himself to be in Christ? for if it be an uncertain and problematical thing whether he can discover this or no, it seems an idle thing to set him upon the search. The second part of the subject will be to give directions as to the best method of conducting this duty; and the third will be to propose the proper arguments and inducements for proceeding in it.

Now, for the opening of the first head, which is the ground of the whole, being the answer or assurance of the conscience, which a man may attain unto, I desire that you would read and consider with me the last chapter of the Second Epistle to the Corinthians, where this subject is specially treated of, and which I would make the basis of this head of discourse. The apostle Paul is stirred up with mighty zeal, in the three chapters preceding, to defend his own authority as an apostle of the Lord, which had been shaken in no small degree amongst the Corinthian brethren; and in the third verse of the thirteenth chapter, he bringeth the question of his apostleship to a direct issue, saying, "Ye seek a proof of Christ speaking in me." He then proceedeth to give them one; and what think you that proof of Christ speaking in him is? The proof is their own selves; and therefore he desires them (ver. 5) to examine themselves, to prove their own selves, and see that Christ is in them: from which we would infer, that Christ had spoken by him; for unless Christ had spoken by him, how would Christ be found in them? Observe now, word by word, how he constructs this argument, (ver. 3:) Since you seek proof that Christ speaketh in me, Christ, who to you-ward is not weak, but is mighty [giveth might] in you; for although He was crucified out of weakness, yet He liveth out of the power of God. For we also are weak in Him, but we shall live with Him from the power of God towards you; try yourselves, whether ye be in the faith; prove yourselves. As hath been said, his object is to give them a proof that Christ spake in him, which proof is their own selves. That this might be a proof, it was necessary that Christ should have been manifestly powerful in them; for if Christ had not been powerful in them, there would have been no evidence derived from that quarter that He had spoken by the apostles. But that they had received into themselves the mighty power of Christ's Spirit, enabling them to speak with tongues, and to heal, and to interpret, and to do miracles, and whatever else is proper to the Christian spirit, is manifest from every part of these two epistles. For the reason, then, of recalling this to their mind, and using their consciousness of it in his argument, he introduces the parenthesis half of the third and of the fourth verse, asserting that Christ was not feeble towards them, but mighty within them; referring to the powers of the Spirit, with which they had been endowed, just as to the Galatians he doth the same, (chap. iii. 2:) "Received ye the Spirit by the works of the law, or by the hearing of faith?" and (ver. 5,) He therefore, ministering to you the Spirit, and implanting [energising] powers in you; did he it from the works of the law, or from the hearing of faith? In this place he is defending the doctrine of justification by faith only; in the place before us he is defending his apostolical vocation under Christ; but in both places he doth it by the same appeal unto the Spirit, the powers of the Spirit, which had followed his preaching. Christ unto you, saith he, is not weak, but is mighty within you. And forasmuch as they had spoken contemptuously of his bodily presence, saying, (chap. x. 10) "His bodily presence is weak, and his speech contemptible," he taketh occasion, in this same parenthesis, to connect his own weakness and his own power with Christ's weakness and Christ's power; saying, (ver. 4) for although he was crucified from weakness, yet liveth He from the might of God; and, for we also are weak in Him, but we shall live with Him from the might of God to you-ward. Having stated that Christ was not weakness, but might in them, he explains that the cross of Christ was His weakness, and that His resurrection and life is God's might. So, also, the apostle saith of himself, that he had become weak in Christ; that is, entered into the fellowship of His sufferings, and been made conformable to His death, emptied himself out, impoverished himself, weakened himself, as Christ had done on the cross; yet, as Christ lived mightily in the Spirit given unto His Church for the pulling down of strongholds, so the apostle lived along with Christ from the same might of God exercised towards them, making out that the might of God towards them was an effect flowing out of his personal self-inflicted weakness, just as Christ's might in the Church was an effect flowing out of His self-inflicted weakness in the flesh and on the cross. And having thus explained to them how power in them was not incompatible with weakness in himself, but in truth the very consequence thereof, he then directeth their attention to the power of God in themselves, as the proof which they desired of Christ having spoken in him: You ask a proof that Christ hath spoken in me; try yourselves whether you be in the faith; prove yourselves. Know ye not your own selves, that Jesus Christ is in me? Here ends this part of his argument. The words, "except ye be reprobates," should be, as in most versions they are, and as they are in the most approved editions of the original, connected with the following part of the argument. His argument therefore is: I refer for my credentials to yourselves. Would you try me? try yourselves if ye be in the faith; and if ye be in the faith, then am I in the faith, for ye are the fruits of my ministry. Ye would prove me, prove your own selves; for in yourselves—in your true discipleship—standeth my true apostleship. Ye ask whether Christ speaketh in me; are you ignorant whether He be in yourselves? The same method of reasoning with these troublesome and vexatious people—who proved how far ingratitude could go in Christian disciples without subverting the grace of God in the heart, how far forbearance could go in a Christian apostle without weakening his love—he adopteth in the third chapter of this Epistle: Do we begin again to commend ourselves? or have we need, like some, of commendatory epistles to you, or from you? Our epistle ye are, written in our hearts, known and perused of all men; being manifested to be Christ's epistle, ministered by us, written not with ink, but with the Spirit of the living God; not in tables of stone, but in fleshly tables of the heart. There can be no doubt, therefore, that in both these passages, as well as in that of the Galatians and many others, the apostle resteth his apostolical calling upon the knowledge of his disciples, that they were in the faith. If, now, it were a difficult or a doubtful matter for a disciple to know whether Christ was in him or not, then surely the apostle would never have appealed to a doubtful test of the truth. If the Corinthian church had been of a like mind with the present Church, which looketh upon a state of doubt and uncertainty with respect to the indwelling of Christ within a man as a more frequent, ay, and a more wholesome state of a Christian than is that of full certainty and assurance, then, how utterly inconceivable would it be that a wise man like Paul should over and over again refer to this doubtful and uncommon thing, as the best and strongest proof he could give that Christ had spoken by him? It seems to me to put it beyond a doubt that in the Corinthian church it was a common thing, and a constant thing, and by the apostle taken for granted to be such, that every disciple that was in Christ should know that Christ was in him. But this will more clearly appear by following the train of his argument.

The apostle having referred them to self-examination for the proof of his apostleship, adds these words, as containing the only possibility of its proving an uncertain and fallible test, "except ye be reprobates." The word "reprobate" is, in the original, a word applied to counterfeit and base coin—literally unproved, unexamined, untried; being applied sometimes to metals unpurified from dross, and sometimes to money that is not sterling. Now, the argument of the apostle is, that they would find proof of his genuineness in themselves, unless, somehow or other, they themselves should not be genuine, whereby it is distinctly declared that the only cause wherefore a Christian might not be able to find the faith in himself, might not be able to discern Christ in himself, is his own want of genuineness; and therefore every ingenuous and true Christian may surely expect to discover the work of grace within himself. This is the right conclusion from the apostle's words, as they read in the original. In our version, the question, instead of ending at "in you," includes the words "except ye be reprobates;" and thereby is given a good enough sense, that Jesus Christ was in them except they be reprobates, but not the sense which cohereth with the apostle's argument. His argument is, not to cast doubt upon their being in the faith, or upon the indwelling of Christ in their souls; for he had already said that God was might in them, and not weakness; then there would have been no meaning nor sincerity in the test of his apostleship to which he referred, which was, that from their own standing in Christ they should discover his commission from Christ. Therefore, though the collocation of the sentence in our English Bible gives a simple meaning, yet certainly not the meaning which the apostle's argument and the collocation of the original require. But that which we have given is very pertinent and very powerful, and altogether coherent with the context both which precedes and which follows. Prove, saith he, your own genuineness; take trial of your own purity; discover if Jesus Christ be in you. This is the proof I give of my apostleship, and this must stand me good, unless, indeed, ye are spurious and will not bear trial; then, indeed, Jesus Christ is not in you, ye are not in the faith, and I must seek some other test of my apostleship. Then he proceeds to express his hopes and his prayers: Unless somehow ye are unproved. I hope, however, that ye know that we are not unproved. I pray, indeed, unto God, that you do not any evil, not that we may appear proved, but that ye may do what is honourable, though we be as unproved. For we can do nothing against the truth, but for the truth. For we rejoice when we are weak, and ye are strong; and this also we pray for, even your perfection. This noble, disinterested, and holy conclusion of the apostle is to the intent of declaring that his anxiety for their growth in goodness was far greater than his anxiety to make out the genuineness of his apostleship. He would rather be unattested by them than that they should depart from what was honest in order to give him testimony. He wanted not glory nor power unto himself, but he wanted honour and righteousness unto them.

Such, dear brethren, is the context in which the subject of our discourse lies involved. I have drawn it out in order, giving to every expression its true import and its proper weight, to the end you might see that self-examination, trying our faith, and proving our standing in Christ, and Christ's dwelling in us, is a work in which a Christian not only ought to engage, but in which, if he do engage, he shall surely discover the certainty of his calling and election; and if he do not be able to discover it, he ought to look upon himself as an ungenuine, insincere, hypocritical professor, and, concluding so, turn from his hypocrisies and dissimulations, and seek a true heart and a right spirit, that he may serve the living God. It is no death-blow to a man to discover that he is a hypocrite, but it is a death-blow to be a hypocrite. It is no harm or injury to a man, but contrariwise a great good, to be put in the way of ascertaining whether he be a dissembler or a genuine believer; and therefore when we deduce the inference from the whole context, that every man who is not an ungenuine, counterfeit Christian shall be able to discover himself to be a true and faithful and sincere believer; and that he who cannot make that discovery, who cannot examine and prove himself, and know that Jesus Christ is in him, ought to regard himself as a spurious, insincere man, deceiving and being deceived;—when this, I say, we give forth, as the fair conclusion from the context, do not, I pray you, take offence, because self-deception and Satanic delusion, yea, and wilful hypocrisy, are sins which can be forgiven, and for detecting which in us we ought to be exceeding thankful. It is not true, then, that a man may be a Christian, and yet not know that Christ is in him. It is not true that a man may be in the faith, and yet not feel that he is in the faith. It is not true that a Christian may go to the work of examining himself, and yet after all not find the thing which he is seeking after. When, therefore, our Church requireth of a person before the communion to examine himself whether he be in the faith, it meaneth not that the examination should end in uncertainty, but that it should end in conviction, according to the question in the Catechism, or form of examination before the communion: To whom should this sacrament be given? To the faithful only, who can "examine themselves," or prove themselves. It is the same word which is used in 1 Cor. xi. 28: But let a man prove himself, and so let him eat of that bread, and drink of the cup. This self-proof is required by the apostle, in order to protect men from the guilt of the Lord's body, and of the Lord's blood. Now, brethren, if this self-proving is to end in no knowledge or conviction the one way or the other, how can it be any protection? If a man after self-examination is to be left in the same dubiety and uncertainty as before, then what serveth it for opening and clearing his way to the Lord's table and delivering him from blood-guiltiness? The meaning of the apostle is, that a man should not only be able to discern, but should actually know his right to come unto the Lord's table, in order to be fed and nourished in the life which he feeleth to be in him, and out of which cometh that knowledge to discern the Lord's body, faith to feed upon Him, repentance, love, and new obedience, which are the five particulars required by the Church to be ascertained. I am far from saying that such an examination will not issue often in self-condemnation, and when it does, there is good hope that such a one is in the way of attaining unto self-approbation. The fear, therefore, of self-condemnation ought not to paralyse the diligence of our inquest. But note you well, that if a man go to examine himself without the belief of finding a certainty the one way or the other, then the inquest of such a one is effectually paralysed. For he will say, Though I look my best, and try my best, yet I may not find the thing I seek. But if you tell him, Thou canst certainly, if thou be in Christ, know that thou art in Him, then if he discover not the same, he concludes that certainly he is not yet in Him. And is the man the worse for knowing that hitherto he hath been trusting in a falsehood? or is it such a wonderful and such a dishonourable thing for poor frail man to be deceived by the devil? or when he doth discover that his profession of faith is not the possession of faith, is he hopeless, is his case desperate? or, rather, is he not in a more hopeful and favourable condition than before? I do not say that this self-examination or self-trial may not be attended with many difficulties and issue in many doubts. The difficulties I shall attend to in a future part of this discourse. For the doubts with which it may be attended, and in which it may issue, I have this to say, that whenever the verdict is doubtful, our wisdom and our righteousness would be to give it against ourselves. And this I say not only because no man is inclined to think too hardly of himself,—for I believe there are doubting spirits which actually do so, though there be not so many as those who give self an undue preponderance,—but I thus advise you to give the verdict against yourselves when the examination issues against yourselves, because the text declares it should issue in knowledge and conviction of our being in Christ, and not in doubt whether we be in Him or not. And this self-persuadedness that we are in Christ is by all Churches, and in the standards of all Churches set forth, as the thing to be possessed by the saints; and therefore it is the thing which should be set before all the communicants. I know that the Church dealeth tenderly, and none more tenderly dealeth than our own, with those who doubt of their being in Christ, or of their due preparation for the Lord's Supper, upon which the Larger Catechism thus expresseth itself: "One who doubteth of his being in Christ, or of his due preparation to the sacrament of the Lord's supper, may have true interest in Christ, though he be not yet assured thereof; and in God's account hath it, if he be duly affected with the apprehension of the want of it, and unfeignedly desires to be found in Christ, and to depart from iniquity: in which case (because promises are made, and this sacrament is appointed for the relief even of weak and doubting Christians) he is to bewail his unbelief, and labour to have his doubts resolved; and so doing, he may and ought to come to the Lord's supper, that he may be further strengthened." I think that these words are cautiously and considerately written, and ought not to be abused, as they are too frequently, into the palliation of doubt, and even the encouragement of it. It describeth only a possibility, that one not assured of his true interest in Christ may yet have it. It does not describe a common or a probable, but a possible case; and therefore we are at liberty to conclude, that the common and probable state of matters contemplated by the Church is, that a man who is standing in Christ will, upon self-examination, discover it; which if he cannot do, then is it a probable and very likely, though not a certain thing, that he is not in Christ. Now, observe, secondly, that this answer and resolve of the Church not only stateth it as a bare possibility, but likewise proceedeth to guard this limited permission from being turned into evil, by requiring that he be duly affected with the apprehension of the want of assurance—that is, feels it as a shortcoming, grieves over it as an offence, and earnestly desires to be delivered from such a state of uncertainty; which, let me say it, brethren, is far from being the case in these days, when this state of unassured salvation and of continual doubt is held up as the best sign of a believer. Having thus limited the possible case, and guarded against resting and abiding therein, the fathers of the Church add this further, that such a one should not resist the doctrine of assurance, or make light of those who declare themselves to have found it, or count it an exceeding difficult thing to find; but that he should "unfeignedly desire to be found in Christ, and to depart from iniquity:" in which well-limited and well-defined case, saith the Catechism, he is to bewail his unbelief, and labour to have his doubts resolved; and, so doing, he may and ought to come to the Lord's supper, that he may be further strengthened. The Lord's table is presented to such as the means under God for removing these very doubts and uncertainties. His state is called unbelief,—he is to bewail his unbelief; he is called a weak and doubting Christian, and the sacrament is for his relief. I am sure, dearly beloved brethren, that while this question of the Larger Catechism opens the door of the Lord's table unto persons not yet assured, it doth in the most striking terms discountenance such a state of the Christian. If any one now should ask me, And why doth the Church, at one and the same time, stigmatise such doubtfulness of spirit, and yet open the table of the Lord to their approach? I answer, that I know no other reason but this, lest a man's judgment of himself should come to be exalted into a ground of confidence, by being made of the Church an invariable prerequisite to his sitting down at the Lord's table; lest man should be encouraged to consider himself as able by the Holy Ghost to pronounce infallibly concerning himself, which would be to make void the judgment of Christ. Infallible judgment is as truly the prerogative of Christ alone as is infallible salvation. We may expect the gift from Christ of infallible judgment as to our own state; but we may not arrogate it to ourselves. And to the end that He may let all His people know how specially and essentially it is His own gift, He may be pleased to withhold it from some, and at times to weaken it in all. This I take to be the reason why the Church, while she so severely censureth the want of assurance, doth yet not utterly condemn it, lest she should clog faith in Jesus Christ, with a condition which proceedeth from a man's own self. Just as we would say that the agonies and tortures of an awakened conscience are not a necessary prerequisite unto faith, are not of the essence of faith; so we say that assurance, or a judgment passed by ourselves upon ourselves, is not of the essence of faith. But while this we diligently maintain, for the honour of that only foundation which is laid in Christ, we do never doubt that when the love and holiness of God in Christ met together are laid out to the soul of a poor sinner, and he is entreated to believe this, which God hath done for him, and doth believe it, then doth he well and clearly know that he hath believed it. If he might believe it, and yet not know that he had believed it, why would God ask him to come and be baptized? Baptism is not a thing which a man may do at a venture, or upon an uncertainty; but wittingly, deliberately, and out of firm and resolved purpose. And how could a man do so if, upon believing, he were left in darkness, doubt, and conjecture whether he had believed or no? Now this certainty of his having believed is not a thing which the unbaptized man is to gather, or which the Church is to gather, from his life, as these Anabaptists foolishly and ignorantly talk; for behold how the apostles in every instance baptized their converts the same day, and often the same hour, that they believed. From the depths of legality came forth the three thousand who were baptized on the day of Pentecost. From the depths of heathen darkness came forth the jailer, who was baptized that same hour he believed. There must, therefore, doubtless, accompany our faith a clear knowledge and conviction of the same. Now he that believeth hath everlasting life; such a one, therefore, as hath believed hath entered into everlasting life. It doth not require a training to entitle him, nor yet to prepare him, unto eternal life. The work of the Spirit, which is the life of Christ in the believer, is not a work antecedent to or separate from, but coincident with, and a part of, everlasting life, being Christ's everlasting life put forth in the believer: a part, not a precursor, of everlasting life. The same act of faith which receiveth Christ as our sacrifice for sin receiveth Him as our life and resurrection and blessedness. The gospel is not the gospel of reconciliation merely, nor of sanctification merely, but it is the gospel of a kingdom, the good news of a kingdom, prepared for us, prepared for all who will receive it,—in Christ prepared for the believer, as surely, and more securely, than the world was prepared for Adam. Therefore, a man who hath believed hath entered into life, and shall never come into death. This is a sure thing, never to be resisted or gainsaid. The gates of hell shall never shake this truth; but observe, that it is a thing of no small importance for a man to be able to prove himself to be in the faith. Nay, it is absolutely required of him to examine himself whether he be in the faith, and the continual presentation of the Lord's supper to believers doth continually require of them all diligence in the duty of self-examination. The question now is, not whether thou believest, but whether thou hast been quickened by the Spirit. Baptism sealeth up our remission of sins, and openeth up the work of the Spirit. The Lord's supper cometh with an inquiry, Hast thou profited in the Spirit? art thou quickened with divine life? The food which it presents is food for the everlasting life, not for the mortal life; food spiritual, not food carnal. The communion which it speaketh of is the communion of the living body of Christ, the Church of the first-born, whose names are written in heaven; therefore it is necessary that a man examine himself whether he have that spiritual life for which that food is prepared; whether he be of that body of living ones; whether he be come unto the Church of the first-born, whose names are written in heaven. Baptism sealed unto us our faith and the remission of our sins, but the Lord's supper sealeth unto us our life in the Holy Spirit; and therefore it is most necessary that we should have received that life already, and be conscious of having received it. I say not always be conscious of it, for there is a life before consciousness of life; and our mother is conscious of our life before we are conscious of it ourselves; and therefore the Church permitteth the exception above referred to. Yet not the less, as the general rule, which the exception but confirmeth, a man should both be able to examine himself, and should have examined himself, and have found himself to be in Christ, before coming to the table of the Lord. It now remaineth that we endeavour what we can to direct this self-examination, and then that we urge upon you by the terms of the text, to undertake and perform this duty. Taking it therefore as a thing certain, that the end of self-examination in view of the Supper is to discover whether we be in Christ or not, and that this may in almost, if not altogether, all the members of Christ be discovered, we go about now to inquire into the right and the wrong method of following this most important Christian employment. It is written, (2 Cor. v. 17,) "If any man be in Christ, he is a new creature: old things are passed away; behold, all things are become new." And again, "We walk by faith, and not by sight." And again, "We look not unto things which are seen and temporal, but unto things which are unseen and eternal." And again, "The flesh is dead because of sin, and the spirit is alive because of righteousness." And again, "We have put off the old man, with his corruptions and lusts, and have put on the new man, which is created in righteousness and true holiness." In these and such expressions are set forth the life of the new man, and the death of the old man; or rather, the quickening of the new man in the bosom of a corrupt nature, which is daily contended against, and triumphed over, and put to death, and at the resurrection is quickened with divine life. But forasmuch as the law of the flesh continueth during our present pilgrimage opposed to the law of the spirit, no one can acquit himself of the guilt of a wicked nature, nor yet be unconscious of the movements of corruption within himself, and therefore I place the chief part of self-examination in the discovery of a renewal in the spirit of our mind, rather than in any alteration or surceasing of the desires of the flesh. The sinful nature with which we are on every side surrounded is restrained by the power of a renewed spirit, but is not changed until the regeneration, when we receive the adoption, to wit, the redemption of the body. That, therefore, whereof a Christian should be chiefly importunate to examine himself is, whether he hath been awakened from the oblivion of God and of Christ into the belief and the love of God and of Christ; whether power hath been given to him, through faith, to will and to do of God's good pleasure; whether he hath that within him which delighteth in God, and desireth to have no fellowship with the wicked one; whether he hath been delivered from the spirit of fear and bondage into the spirit of love and freedom; whether, in one word, there is within him a controversy against himself for God; whether he feeleth the flesh lusting against the spirit, and the spirit lusting against the flesh. He who hath been thus exercised cannot be ignorant of it; it is not done in a corner of his heart, but is a dispute for the throne and sceptre of his heart, and thereto agree the words of the first Confession of our Church:—

"For so soon as the Spirit of the Lord Jesus (which God's elect children receive by true faith) taketh possession of the heart of any man, so soon doth He regenerate and renew the same man, so that he beginneth to hate that which before he loved, and to love that which before he hated; and from thence cometh that continual battle which is between the flesh and the spirit in God's children. Still the flesh and natural man, according to their own corruption, lusteth for things pleasant and delectable unto itself, and grudgeth in adversity, is lifted up in prosperity, and at every moment is prone and ready to offend the majesty of God. And the Spirit of God, which giveth witnessing to our spirit that we are the sons of God, maketh us to resist fleshly pleasures, and to groan in God's presence for deliverance from this bondage of corruption, and finally to triumph over sin, that it reign not in our mortal bodies. This battle hath not the carnal man, being destitute of God's Spirit, but doth follow and obey sin with greediness, and without repentance; even as the devil and then our lusts do guide them on: but the sons of God, as before is said, do fight against sin, do sob and mourn when they perceive themselves tempted to iniquity, and if they fall, they rise again with earnest and unfeigned repentance; and these things they do not by their own power, but by the power of the Lord Jesus, without whom they were able to do nothing."—*Scots Confession*, Art. xiii.

Now, it is possible that this controversy within a man, which the Spirit of Christ stirreth up, may be mistaken for the natural workings of conscience in the breast of every man; and therefore I would endeavour to draw a distinction between the two. The natural conscience knoweth not the grace of God, as seemeth to me, but only His holiness and righteousness, and therefore it worketh fear and apprehension of His righteous judgment, rather than faith and hope of His forgiveness and favour. It is God's witness to our being sinners. It is that whereunto God's law is addressed. Law is the light of conscience, and by the law the conscience is enlightened. But the law knoweth no mercy, and therefore the conscience, however enlightened, bringeth no consolation, and in this, a work of natural conscience may be distinguished from a work of grace, that the former is fearful and apprehensive of evil, the latter is joyful, and apprehensive of good; the former looks at duty mainly, the latter looks at grace mainly; the former looks to a righteousness which is to be wrought in us, and puts this in the foremost place, the latter looks to a righteousness which hath been wrought in Christ, and puts this in the first place, and makes it of the chief importance. And because I find the Church in these times much more concerned about what they call practical holiness, which is certain feelings and states of the mind, accompanied by certain actions, than they are about that complete and finished righteousness which is wrought in Christ for all who believe, and not only righteousness, but wisdom, and sanctification, and redemption, I am very much inclined to believe that the Church hath ceased, or is fast ceasing, to be evangelical, and hasting to become legal. The natural conscience doth accumulate upon itself a load of guilt from which the blood of Christ alone can cleanse it: and it must be cleansed from these dead works before it can serve the living God; being cleansed from these dead works, it hath peace, and standeth under grace, and hath boldness in hope of the glory of God. The work of the Spirit, therefore, applying to the conscience the blood of Christ, is a work of peace-making and peace-giving; whereas the work of natural conscience is a work of self-condemnation and peace-breaking. The one ends in love, the other ends in fear; the one operates by law, the other operates by grace; the one engenders a fearful bondage to outward observances, the other a joyful liberty in the obedience of God's holy commandments: and with these lights it will not be difficult to distinguish the working of natural conscience from the working of the Holy Spirit. Now, I make this distinction, not as it were to undervalue the light of nature, or the testimony of the conscience against the wickedness of our lives, but simply that this may not be mistaken for the work of faith concerning which we are teaching you to examine yourselves. I believe indeed that with many, the Holy Spirit proceedeth by the method of awakening the conscience, and presenting to it the terrors of the law, and delivering it by the knowledge of Christ, whose righteousness is the fulfilment of the law, not for Himself only, but for all who believe. But while I allow this to be at times the method of God, I will no more permit it to be called a work of God, than I would the very sin itself of which the soul feeleth the remorse. God leadeth His own children through bondage and captivity of sin, from which He sometimes delivereth them in the way of remorse; but there is no work of Christ in that remorse, which oft endeth in plunging deeper into the guilt. The work of faith beginneth not by looking into ourselves, but by looking outward to Christ; and when the soul becometh conscious of God's love to her in Christ, and of a righteousness provided for her in Him, out of the mercy and love of God, then it is that she proceedeth towards sanctification, and then it is that the warfare between the spirit and the flesh commenceth,—the Spirit ever presenting God's love in Christ to justify the soul against those accusations which conscience deriveth from the flesh. Conscience is the great accuser; the flesh furnisheth the grounds of that accusation. The Spirit is the great justifier, and the grounds of His justification are all derived from the work of Christ; and it is a continual warfare between man's way of inherent righteousness, and God's way of imputed righteousness. The conscience is, as it were, ever yearning for a righteousness unto which in this life it can never attain,—a noble instinct, yet capable of being sorely perverted. The instinct is noble, first of all, because it furnisheth a key whereby to unlock the mysteries of God's holiness in the law, and a channel whereby to convey the righteousness of Christ into the soul; wherefore it is well called God's vicegerent over the turbulence and rebelliousness of man's soul, and it might be called a witness there for Christ, the only Righteous One. A noble instinct, secondly, because it prophesieth, predicteth of a time when the soul of man shall be endued with a nature which is capable of inherent righteousness, when the righteousness of the law shall be fulfilled in us, who walked not after the flesh, but after the Spirit. We shall yet apprehend that perfect righteousness for which we are now apprehended in Christ. We shall yet stand in our own strength, but a strength derived, not from Adam, nor from creation, but from the second Adam, the Redeemer of creation. Therefore, this conscience in man is a noble faculty, but not in itself capable of any sanctification or consolation: the great peace-breaker, that will not let the fallen rebel be at ease, but stirreth him, and stingeth him with troubles infinite, and openeth his ear to terms of peace through mediation of another, and to terms of hope through redemption of another. But when these Socinians, and Arminians, and Free-willers of every name, go about to persuade the conscience that she hath a power to deliver herself, and set on foot a righteousness of her own,—when they represent remorse, or repentance, as they misname it, (for repentance, in the Scripture use of that word, is not a work of the conscience in the unbeliever, but a gift of the Prince of life to the believer,) to be a partial or a complete satisfaction unto God for sin, then do they at once make void the righteousness of Christ purchased by His death, and the inherent righteousness which He will bestow upon us in the resurrection of the just; when, indeed, we shall not be law-fulfillers only, but law-defenders, and law-judges, and law-executors, governing the world by the righteous judgment of the law. Now, the Spirit of God doth take the righteousness of Christ, and so comfort the conscience therewith, and so possess it with peace, and love, and joy, that it magnifieth the Lord its Redeemer, and trusteth in His might. The poor soul, flesh-oppressed, being told of Him who had redeemed his soul, likewise flesh-oppressed, and who hath obtained power unto Himself to do likewise for many, in doing it for Himself, hath in fact done it for many,—the soul, thus comforted, and thus reposing confidence, doth receive the mighty power of God, whereby she mastereth, bendeth, and restraineth the members which are upon the earth, and waiteth with patience, yet groaneth within herself for the day when the body also shall be redeemed. And thus possessed with the Spirit of Christ, the soul contendeth with power against the devil, the world, and the flesh. When I say the soul, it is all the same as if I said the conscience; and thus it is that the conscience is entreated with help and with deliverance: no new spiritual substance is created, the identity of the person is preserved, the work is wrought in us by means of us; we are the instruments of our own redemption; we are acted upon as intelligent creatures; God's work of creation He doth avail Himself of in redemption; redemption is proved not to be an after-thought, but the stage of a great progress towards the perfection and stability of the creature; and, in brief, conscience, to which the law addressed itself, and by which it was understood, feeling it utterly ineffectual to produce righteousness, doth give up, and suspend for a season, the fruitless undertaking of working out an inherent righteousness,—doth suspend it, I say, until the weakness of the flesh shall have been removed; and then, the power of the law being restored, the righteousness of the law shall be fulfilled in us, who presently suspend ourselves by faith upon the righteousness of another, and by hope look forward to a righteousness which we shall inherit in the world to come. All of which most orthodox and comfortable doctrine concerning conscience is expressed in these words of the holy apostle: "There is therefore now no condemnation to them which are in Christ Jesus, who walk not after the flesh, but after the Spirit. . . . For what the law could not do, in that it was weak through the flesh, God sending his own Son in the likeness of sinful flesh, and for sin, condemned sin in the flesh; that the righteousness of the law might be fulfilled in us, who walk not after the flesh, but after the Spirit." O thou Apostle of the Gentiles! to thee indeed was wisdom given; thou mightest well boast of thy many revelations; and surely thou hadst been more than man, if thou hadst not needed a thorn in the flesh to keep thee humble! I, who am a sinner of the Gentiles, to whom thou wast sent, do bless God, who hath enabled me to understand these blessed mysteries. Thou hast taught me that the law is a very holy thing, and that the flesh of man is a thing most unholy, utterly incapacitating the soul from keeping the law; wherefore the law would drive the conscience mad, if in the law there had not been a sacrifice: unto which sacrifice we, who are called under the gospel, as well as they called under the law, do flee from the terrors of the law, and abide before the altar with prayers, and supplications, and confessions of sin, until our great High Priest shall come forth from His intercession, and bring with Him the remission of sins unto all the holy nation; whereupon we shall stand up, in cleansed, purified flesh, clothed in white robes, and now with joy shall we keep the law, magnify it, and make it honourable; and having fulfilled the perfect righteousness of His creature, and satisfied God's holy law, we shall then come into His presence, and stand before Him, and minister for Him, according to that rank, and station, and dignity which He may please to appoint us; and thus the end of man's creation is attained unto. He, through a fall, and through a redemption, hath arrived at the condition of keeping God's law without spot, and without blemish, and perfecting righteousness, and receiving from the Father an appointment of priestly government, whenever it pleaseth Him to give it.

Now, after these explanations, no one can be at a loss to distinguish between the workings of natural conscience without any help of faith, and the working of faith unto the redemption of the natural conscience. The one hath its origin in ourselves, and its end also there; the other hath its origin in Christ, and its end also in Him. The one looketh unto the purification and obedience of the natural man in this present life; the other looketh for his subjugation, and the enforcement unto obedience in this present life, and for his willing obedience in the age to come, and the resurrection from among the dead. The one is an effort of the creature to redeem himself, of the fallen creature to erect himself; the other is the acting of faith, and love, and hope, through Jesus Christ, towards God. Now, forasmuch as in every man who is brought unto Christ, there must be a struggle and strife, we consider it enough to have distinguished this from the natural struggle between good and evil which is felt in the bosom of every man; and having made this distinction, we ask you all to examine yourselves, whether there hath been wrought in you such a power to contend with the flesh, whether with the will you do serve the law of the Spirit, though with the flesh you do serve the law of sin, even as Paul saith of himself, "So then with the mind [or, the spirit] I myself serve the law of God; but with the flesh the law of sin." Then out of the obedience of the law of God by the mind, there will come forth certain fruits, which are called fruits of the Spirit, and of which every one doth proceed out of the roots of love, and grow in the liberty of the sons of God. They are these—love, joy, peace, long-suffering, gentleness, goodness, faith, meekness, temperance; and, on the other hand, the works of the flesh, which warreth against the Spirit, are—adultery, fornication, uncleanness, lasciviousness, idolatry, witchcraft, hatred, variance, emulation, wrath, strife, seditions, heresies, envyings, murders, drunkenness, revellings. The law of sin, which the apostle saith he obeyed, inclineth to these things. The flesh of a fallen man cannot help being under their dominion. It is intended of God that it should be so, and God's glory cometh of its being so; for there would be no might in redemption, there would be no demonstration of the Spirit of Christ in us, had we not this perverse and wicked ever-present law and love of the flesh to overcome. Therefore it is a vain and fruitless thing to ask Christians to examine whether they have been delivered from the consciousness of this law, which must exist until the resurrection of the body,—ay, and lust and war against the Spirit,—ay, and ofttimes prevail against the Spirit; not, indeed, through the weakness of the Spirit, but through the weakness of our faith in the Spirit; but still the soul, renewed by the Spirit, doth perceive the viciousness of these sinful motions of the flesh, and, having confidence in God, doth repent of the same, and receive remission, through the blood of Christ, whereby the overladen conscience is purged anew from dead works. This continual acting of repentance and of remission, I believe to be one of the invariable signs and attendants of the Christian life; and he who is not acquainted herewith is either ignorant of the work of grace altogether, or in some great error concerning the method of our sanctification, which in our Catechism is thus defined:—" Sanctification is the work of God's free grace, whereby we are renewed in the whole man after the image of God, and are enabled more and more to die unto sin and to live unto righteousness." So that it is a work of daily dying unto sin; and how this is otherwise than by a daily repentance on account of sin, I cannot discern. But to put this matter beyond a doubt, as the orthodox doctrine of the Church, I recite unto you another answer to the question in the Larger Catechism, "Whence ariseth the imperfection of sanctification in believers?" "The imperfection of sanctification in believers ariseth from the remnants of sin abiding in every part of them, and the perpetual lustings of the flesh against the Spirit; whereby they are often foiled with temptations, and fall into many sins, are hindered in all their spiritual services, and their best works are imperfect and defiled in the sight of God." This occasional failure, therefore, this perpetual shortcoming, ought not to be taken as an evidence against a man's being in a state of grace; but if attended with hasty repentance, and with the continuance of faith in Jesus Christ, ought to be looked upon rather as a sign of his being in a state of grace. For what is repentance, but an act in which the Spirit obtaineth a triumph over the flesh? If two laws or forces be contrary to one another, that proves itself to be the stronger which possesseth and impelleth the body under their influence. Now, here is the soul of man under two contrary laws or forces,— the law of the flesh, and the law of the Spirit,—and repentance being a work of the Spirit, being a state of the soul under the dominion of the Spirit, doth surely prove that the Spirit hath obtained the mastery in this instance and at this time, and therefore is a sign and token of a state of grace, and not of a state of nature. But it may be said, And what availeth repentance unless it be perfected into obedience? I answer, just what the conviction of mind availeth to the actings of the man. Repentance is the cause of new obedience,—yea, is the beginning of it,—yea, is the chief part of it, and that without which, of new obedience there shall be none; and he that hath heartily repented of his sins, through the knowledge of God's mercy in Jesus Christ, even though he were instantly to be cut off, shall be regarded as a righteous man in the sight of God, and shall obtain salvation through our Lord Jesus Christ. These Pharisees lay great stress upon the outward work which man discerneth, because they have a chief eye to the approbation of man: but the believer, to whom God's eye is all in all, looketh rather into his heart to see whether or no the work of renewing the will, of enlightening the understanding, of captivating the affections, of sanctifying the heart, be proceeding under the power of the Spirit of God; whether another law of love hath begun to reveal its mighty power within him; whether light hath sprung up in the midst of darkness, peace in the midst of trouble, and joy in the midst of sorrow. I say not that the outward manifestations will be wanting; I say not that the tongue will not be bridled, and the various members brought into captivity to the spirit of godliness—surely they will; that which sight looketh upon will be subjected to that which faith apprehendeth;—but it will be an unwilling subjection, for that which sight beholdeth, which a brother can look upon, is the same as that in which Satan sits enthroned. The more need have we, it may be said, to come forth against it, unto these his quarters. Be it so, but we never shall come forth against his power until we come forth in the power and might of a liberated redeemed soul. The soul, as hath been said, is God's warrior against the devil, the world, and the flesh. With and by man God subdues the enemies of God and man. Therefore see to it, that the soul which fighteth is endued with the might of the Spirit of Christ, is redeemed, is free, is bold, is brave, is armed at every point for the fiery conflict,—and to this, the inward accomplishment of the soul, it is that I would have one examining himself mainly to look. If I were calling upon the Church to examine him, then it would be to the outward rather than to the inward I would direct her observation; but when a man is examining himself, I desire him to look to that larger field, of which he himself is conscious, according to that word, "What man knoweth the things of a man, save the spirit of man which is in him?"

The sum and substance of what we have said is this: That the natural conscience, bearing a testimony for complete righteousness of body and of spirit, cannot attain unto it, because both body and spirit are in bondage to the law of sin and death. And Satan, when he would gall a man and drive him to distraction, doth enthrone himself in this conscience, and useth its whips and scourges to mangle his peace. Then comes the priest, whether pagan or papal, with his quietus of penances, sacrifices, purchases, and other works of expiation, and drives a most unsanctified traffic with the fears and alarms of the conscience—living by tears, and groans, and misery. But not so the High Priest of our profession, who cometh to the awakened conscience with salutations of peace, saying, "Peace be still; God is gracious; I have redeemed thee. Thou art safe, thou art saved. Expiation, sacrifice, purchase, redemption, everything which stood between thee and God, behold in me ended and made away with." This is the gospel which giveth peace; and being at peace, quiet and composed, He gently taketh the man whom He hath delivered from a legion of terrors, setteth him at His own feet, and teacheth him wisdom, teacheth him how the Holy Spirit will perfect in due time that work of completeness which conscience crieth out for. But this is not the work of a day, nor of the present life, but is perfected in the resurrection. Meanwhile, saith the Lord, "Behold in me your present completeness made sure to you, and lay hold upon it by faith and hope. The Spirit will take of the completeness that is in me, and shew it unto you with such power that you will feel it to be your own, in as complete possession as if it were your own inwrought, and not mine inwrought, because you are in me, and I in you; we are one, and may not be separated." Faith, therefore, in Christ hath a perfection; while out of Christ, and as we are in ourselves, we are in everything imperfect. This is the imputation of Christ's perfection. It is imputation, and not inherency. Sin still dwells in me, sin still reigns in me; but yet it is not imputed to me because I have faith in Christ, and cleave unto Him with a complete and undivided faith. To put any perfection in myself as a creature, to say that my soul is holy or my body is holy, is to take away the single honour which pertaineth unto Christ, and to Christ alone. And thus faith worketh by love, for such a faith of our own unworthiness and of Christ's worthiness doth so exalt in our hearts the tender mercy and grace of our God, that we are lifted up and locked in the embraces of His love. Out of ourselves are we carried, in Him we dwell, to Him we devote ourselves, for Him we live and move and have our being. And thus it is, that being suspended upon the Father, we fulfil His will against the strain of nature, against the fallen inclinations of the creature, against the corruptions of the flesh, against the power of the devil in us and about us, —we do, I say, sustain the battle of the Lord, and bring forth the fruits of righteousness. Our fears are laid, our conscience is quieted, our selfish desire of self-sufficiency is put an end to. The diabolical ambition (diabolical, though angel-like) of being perfect in our present condition is put an end to: and if we glory, we glory only in the cross of Christ; and if we glory, we glory only in the resurrection of Christ; and if we glory, we glory only in the perfection of Christ. Such I conceive to be the true standing of an approved and approvable man, and such I hope is the standing of all who purpose approaching the Lord's table. Vile in their own selves, beautiful in Christ; all-imperfect in themselves, all-perfect in Him.

Now, forasmuch as many, yea, most, understand a thing best in its details and examples, I count it good not to conclude this discourse without a short exhibition of the graces of the Holy Ghost, which flow out of such a self-humbling and Christ-exalting condition. And for my guidance I will take the word which is written in Gal. v. 22: "But the fruit of the Spirit is love, joy, peace, long-suffering, gentleness, goodness, faith, meekness, temperance." The fruit of the Spirit, which the Spirit produceth in us, through that love to God which is begotten by faith, not in ourselves, but faith in Christ Jesus. Now, examine yourselves, beloved, whether the Spirit of Christ bringeth out of you these affections of the renewed man. First, *love;* that is, the affection which seeketh not its own, which desireth union to another, which desireth union to all. Love, such as in God subsisteth; who loveth not that any should perish, but rather that they should turn and live; who maketh His sun to rise upon the evil and the good, and sendeth rain upon the just and the unjust. Love, which straineth forth from the soul, as light and heat do from the sun : and as the light and heat of the sun beateth upon the unfruitful water as well as upon the fruitful earth, and lieth upon the flinty rock as well as upon the fruit-bearing tree, and guideth and warmeth the wicked as well as the righteous; so doth love, benignantly beaming, all-insphering, all-comforting, send itself without schism to embrace and to bless all : yet promoteth it not unholiness; it is very holy, yea, love is very holy, and because it is holy the wicked cannot receive it. Love embraceth the wicked, but the wicked are not cherished by it, as light shineth in darkness, but the darkness comprehendeth it not. He that loveth not, knoweth not God. He that is wicked cannot love Him, and this is the curse, this is the blight of wickedness, that it can neither love nor receive love. God's love beameth into hell, it lieth upon the foul pit, but doth only quicken, doth only aggravate the corruption of the second death; even as the light of the sun, shining so lovely upon the green meadows and fertile fields, and little hills covered with sheep, doth, when it falleth upon the stagnant pool, exhale from it corruption and poison, and cherish in it the elements of more corruption and poison. Ah, what a thing is love! how good, how blessed a thing! Would we were all made perfect in love! then were we all perfect in holiness. Next cometh *joy;* which well may walk in the train of love, for where love is, there is joy: joy to be the companion of God, to be the member of Christ, to have fellowship and communion with the Father and the Son; joy to see the salvation of God in Christ, to see that glorified which Simeon was glad to see incarnate, which Abraham rejoiced to see afar off. The Holy Spirit is a Spirit of joy and of enjoyment, as the evil spirit is a spirit of care, carking care, malice, remorse, grief, trouble, and despair and misery. But the renewed man is joyful in the Lord; the kingdom of God within us is peace and joy in believing; and in tribulation the Holy Spirit worketh joy, and in conflict there is the joy of victory, and in duty there is the joy of strength, and in affliction there is the joy of contentment, and in adversity there is the joy of resignation, and in everything there is the joy of knowing the Father's will and discerning the Father's hand; and evermore the holy man rejoiceth. The Spirit worketh joy, but the flesh worketh death. Oh that I could carry this to your experience, and rebuke your want of joy! Oh that I could dispel moroseness and gloom, moody melancholy, abiding sadness! These things are not of the Spirit, they are of the flesh. In the world ye shall have tribulation, but in Christ ye shall have joy. The mother is in anguish in her pains, but she rejoiceth that a man-child is born into the world; and so we have sharp conflicts, but out of them ever cometh joy. Take it not on my illustration, dearly beloved; take it out of the text that the Holy Spirit is joy,—joy to be redeemed from death by Christ, joy to be included in the chosen of the Father, joy to be in the communion and fellowship of the saints, joy in God, through Jesus Christ our Lord. Next to joy comes *peace:* peace from an accusing conscience; peace from a broken law; peace from an offended God; peace with men, even our enemies; peace from fears of evil to come, through the knowledge that all things work together for good to them that love God, and are the called according to His purpose; peace from the fear of judgment to come, knowing that no condemnation awaiteth us. Well sung the angels over the Babe of Bethlehem, "Peace on earth!" Well is His blood called peace-speaking, His message peace-preaching, His work peace-making to them which are near, and to them which are afar off! Have ye peace? have ye quiet and rest within? are the voices of stormy passions hid? are the voices of angry quarrels hushed? are the tumults of men's contending opinions stilled? are ye at peace within your own bosom? bear you peace upon your tongue? and in your hand is there the olive wand of peace? It ought to be so, for peace is the fruit of the Spirit. And next to peace, *long-suffering;* patient endurance, like unto God's, who hath borne with the world's wickedness until now. Wrath is a fruit of the flesh, but long-suffering is a fruit of the Spirit. Charity suffereth long, and is kind. He that is risen with Christ forbeareth and forgiveth much. And when they speak evil of us, as evil-doers, by our good works we put to silence their evil speeches. Easy to be entreated is the wisdom that is from God; but the wisdom that is from the earth is full of strife and contention, and every evil work. Why do ye not rather endure, suffering wrongfully? for this is thankworthy with God, who when He was reviled, reviled not again, when He was threatened, threatened not, but committed Himself to Him that judgeth righteously. Oh, I wish that we were long-suffering with one another, of a patient mind, not hasty, not heady, not high-minded, but adorning the gospel of our Lord Jesus Christ, by having in us the same mind which was also in Him. Then cometh *gentleness;* which is sweetness and amiableness of spirit,—that is, not self-willed, but giveth itself up easily to the guidance of God, and of His holy Word, and of His providence, whatever it be; neither fretteth at the bit with which our mouth needeth to be held in, nor is galled by the spur with which our indolence

ON SELF-EXAMINATION. 461

needeth to be prompted forward. Gentle, like a little child in the hand of its parents; pliable, like the flax in the hand of him that dresseth it; easy to be entreated, gentle towards all, is the man of God; inclined by sweet disposition of the Spirit to whatever is good. How gentle was the Lord Jesus Christ! I would that such poverty of spirit reigned amongst us: every one thinking of himself less highly than of another; to ambition dead, to violence dead. Oh, I desire this grace; I pray for this fruit of the Spirit to be upon us, for it is most lovely. It judgeth not another, but it judgeth itself; it commendeth not itself, but another it commendeth in Christ, in Whom it boasteth and greatly rejoiceth. Examine yourselves of this, beloved; pursue this, seek earnestly to obtain it; we want it much, and to our faith God will assuredly grant it. Then cometh *goodness;* which is as it were a constellation and combination of excellences, but, above all, opposed to evil and wickedness. Goodness, which is in God, and being in God, is in the Spirit of God; goodness, which is in every perfect work of God, which was in man, but now in man is blemished and overlaid with the rust and earth of wickedness; and the law also is good, and the Spirit worketh goodness in the members of Christ. Goodness is the obedience to every good commandment of God; goodness is the performance of the good-will of God; goodness is the right use of every gift of God; goodness is the fruit of the Spirit working in us to will and to do of God's good pleasure. The Spirit of Christ moveth us to goodness, against the grain and temper and spirit of our nature. The fruit of the Spirit is in all goodness and righteousness and truth. Then cometh *faith;* which believeth, feedeth upon, and liveth by every word of God. Faith, whose object is Christ; faith, which heareth Christ's word, which longeth to see His face, and which doth indeed see His face in the word; faith, which eateth His flesh and drinketh His blood, and maketh us one with Him, as He is one with the Father. Faith doth not want sense; it fighteth against sense. It wanteth promise, and that sufficeth it. Faith, which ever heareth and ever greedily devoureth the word, which acteth by meditating and remembering the past, by acting the present, by realising and hoping in the future. Faith, the great witness against things seen and temporal, which resteth upon, and rejoiceth in, things not seen and eternal. Faith hath nothing to do with sensation, with frames and feelings, which belong to the fleshly man; faith riseth out of self, as hath been said, and rejoiceth in Christ. Above all, faith rejoiceth against doubt, as love rejoiceth against fear; and as perfect love casteth out fear, so perfect faith casteth out doubt. A doubting Christian is not a believing one. I do not say he hath not faith, but his faith is weak. Faith fighteth against works, and yet it is the parent of all good works. It seeth no works out of Christ, and good works in us it seeth only by seeing us to be in Christ. Faith hath ever reference to another; it believeth another, and having believed another, it is perfected. The fruit cometh under another name, the general name of goodness, but it is all consequent upon faith. And, finally, faith is the gift of God, and a great grace of the Spirit it is to believe all things. And besides these, there be only two others enumerated as the fruit of the Spirit; which are meekness and temperance. Now of *meekness;* the meek are of those whom our Lord blesseth: "Blessed are the meek; for they shall inherit the earth." And such are those who fret not because of evil-doers, neither are envious against the workers of iniquity; who, though they mourn over wickedness, do not sorrow without hope, neither in darkness make their moan, but know God to be present in all things; and so they are comforted. A meek man is full of trust in the Lord, and he committeth his way unto the Lord, in Him also he trusteth. A wilful man would have everything his own way, but a meek man is contented that all things are ordered of the Lord. He submitteth his will and surrendereth his interest to the will of God, and the interest of Christ. These three—long-suffering, gentleness, and meekness—are chief fruits of faith in God. They have an eye ever to the overruling providence of God. Moses was very meek, and Job was very patient, and Daniel was very wise, and Noah was very righteous. I would the Lord would bestow on us the like gifts, for we lack them greatly. They came all out of Christ's fulness, and faith is the channel through which they flow to us. I desire greatly, brethren, that we might make progress in the wisdom which cometh from above, which is first pure, peaceable, easy to be entreated, full of mercy and of good fruits, without partiality, and without hypocrisy. While I am inditing these things, I am examining myself; and while I preach them, I hope you are likewise examining yourselves. If you fall short in meekness,—and I know not but that it is the shortcoming to which men agitated with worldly cares are most liable,—then, I tell you, go to the fountain, and fill your pitchers, and drink, yea, drink abundantly. Christ is that fountain, faith is the pitcher, and the hand which holdeth it, and the lip which drinketh it. Go to Christ by faith, and see your meekness in Him. There it is, bless God for it; and in honouring Christ and blessing God, ye come to partake of it. Oh, it is not the workings of a child that breatheth in it the faculty of reason; but it is God that implanteth it and bringeth it to full-grown stature. And so it is not working, chafing our own cold bosom with our colder hand, agitating our too-much troubled conscience; it is not self-discipline,—no, but it is worship of the good in Christ, and the faith that it is in Him for us: this it is which moveth God to enkindle the life in us; and, as it is enkindled, maketh us more to know and more to acknowledge that the fuel of the fire is from Christ. And now, lastly, cometh *temperance ;*—not in matters of eating, and of drinking, and sleeping, and other fleshly appetites, but restrictive moderation in all things; a careful measurement of ourselves by the standard of God in Christ, by the Word of God applied in the Spirit. God himself limiteth Himself, and every son of God must limit himself. Not losing himself in diffuse speculation, nor wasting himself in idle undertakings, nor wandering in boundless imaginings, nor declining from the laws and ordinances of life, into a wild luxury of wilfulness; but measuring, bounding, and contenting himself with his condition: if a servant, to be in obedience; if a child, to be under authority; if a parent, to be mindful of a parent's duty; if wealthy, to be ready to communicate; if poor, to be willing and thankful to receive help; if unlearned, not to despise learning; if weak, not to despise them that are strong; and so on through all degrees. This is temperance, or, as it is restraint and government, to keep within the bounds which God hath prescribed to us by our creation, by our calling, by our condition, by our station in the Church. It is a grace, a very great grace; and I desire nothing more for myself and for my flock, than that they might be enriched with it. Your time, dearly beloved, doth not permit me to enlarge on these things, nor is there need to do so; with those who seek the Spirit, and who have the Spirit, enough hath been said to stir up and somewhat to guide self-examination. Now, I call upon you to prove your own selves; try whether you be in the faith or not. If these things be in you and abound, ye shall not be barren nor unfruitful in the knowledge of our Lord and Saviour Jesus Christ. Add these things to your faith, and you shall make progress in the knowledge of Christ. Attempt to do without these things, set them to a side, undervalue them, and you shall become purblind, unable to discern things afar off, and forgetting that you have been purged from your former sins.

We come now to the third head, which will shew the awful sanction with which this duty of self-examination is bound upon us. If men had a right estimate of the holiness of the sacrament of the Lord's supper, I may say there would be no occasion for handling this part of our subject at all. Their reverence for the ordinance would be sufficient to protect it against all rash intrusion; and their fear of the consequences would supply their want of reverence, where that was really wanted. There needeth no formal instruction to inform a loyal people of the honour bestowed upon them in being permitted to appear before their king. The sentiment of loyalty within their breast teaches them of itself, that by every means they should prepare themselves not to dishonour the royal presence into which they are permitted to come. But custom hath made the table of the Lord to be common, and we have forgotten the solemn sanctions with which it is fenced around. Let me, therefore, endeavour to open to you what is implied in these words: "Whosoever shall eat this bread, and drink this cup of the Lord, unworthily, shall be guilty of the body and blood of the Lord;" and in these other words, "He that eateth and drinketh unworthily, eateth and drinketh damnation [judgment] to himself, not discerning the Lord's body;" and in these other words, "For this cause many are weak and sickly among you, and many sleep." First, then, what is meant by these words—"Whoso eateth and drinketh unworthily shall be guilty of the body and blood of the Lord?" By many this is interpreted as if it were merely, guilty of some offence against the body and blood of the Lord. But this gives no satisfaction to the mind; which immediately inquires, And what kind of offence is he guilty of? Now, I think that the words of the apostle are intended to declare the nature of the offence, just in the same manner as the expression, "guilty of theft," "guilty of manslaughter," or as it is in Mark iii. 29, "He that shall blaspheme against the Holy Ghost hath never forgiveness, but is guilty of eternal judgment;" and as in James ii. 10, "Whosoever shall keep the whole law, and yet offend in one point, is guilty of all;" that is, of all the laws or commandments. What, then, is the precise amount of that guilt which is expressed in the words, "guilty of the body and blood of the Lord?" It seems to me that it is parallel with what is expressed in the other words, "eateth and drinketh judgment to himself." And of that which is signified by these words, we have an exposition in the next verse: "Therefore many are weak and sickly among you, and many sleep;" and then it is added, "For if we discerned ourselves, we would not be judged; and being judged, we are chastised by the Lord, that we may not be condemned with the world." This whole passage I consider to be one of no small difficulty, and to be understood it must be interpreted as a whole. Here is a guilt—the guilt of the body and blood of the Lord; here is a judgment upon that guilt, shewing itself in weakness, sickliness, and death; but these are not the amount of the judgment, but only, as it were, a chastening of the Lord, to the end we may not be condemned with the world; all which signifies to me, that in the Church there is a discipline of God, dependent upon the worthy or the unworthy receiving of the Lord's supper; and this a discipline specially applicable to the body, consisting in the infliction of weakness, and sickliness, and even death. Few think of this, yet nothing is more distinctly asserted than that it is so. And what proportion, it may be asked, is there between bodily afflictions and unworthy partaking of the Lord's supper? I cannot answer this question otherwise than by saying, that I believe the elements, especially the bread of the Lord's supper, when partaken in faith, doth reach its efficacy unto the bodies of the saints,—not by any physical or sensual alteration thereof, for the flesh of the greatest saint is as wicked as the flesh of the greatest sinner; and, even if it were allowed that a substantial change could be produced, there is no substance to produce it withal, unless we were to hold the papal abomination, that the bread and wine are by consecration transubstantiated into the muscular flesh and circulating blood of the Lord. But though we abhor all such sensual explanations, we believe the revealed truth, nevertheless, that the worthy receiver is endowed with health and strength of body, and preservation from sudden death, and, haply, length of days itself; while the unworthy receiver is, according to the text, visited with weakness, and sickness, and premature disease. Believe this who can, I believe it upon the authority of the apostle; and shall even encourage myself, and the Church of Christ, to expect, not only spiritual strength, but likewise the restraining of bodily disease, and the postponing of death itself. And why should it be a hard matter to believe this? Did not the body of our blessed Lord, while it abode on earth, extend its energies to the bodies, as well as to the souls, of men? Did He not bear our sicknesses and our diseases, as well as our sins? (Matt. viii. 17;) and, bearing our sins, did He not bear the cause of all sickness and of all disease. And if such was the virtue of that body which He offered whole and entire upon the cross, should its virtue be anything diminished by His having entered into His glory, and received power to communicate of the same gifts unto as many as believe? For my part, I have no difficulty whatever in believing this; and though I had, I would believe it not the less, when I find it vouched for by an apostle of the Lord. It is needful to guard this great and salutary truth, that Christ is Chief Physician of body as well as soul; that the Lord's supper is health to the body as well as soul; and that good health and long life are objects of faith to one who comes to the table of the Lord, as well as sanctification and resurrection, and changing into the substance of Christ's glorious body, and an eternal inheritance as kings and priests in the redeemed world;—this salutary doctrine of the application of the Lord's supper to the body as well as to the soul, it is necessary, I say, to guard against that fanatical abuse which would thence infer, that when diseases do come, they are not to be treated with the proper remedies of the physician, but healed by an act of faith, without any means whatever. That faith in Christ, the Chief Physician, ought to be uppermost, both in the mind of the sick person and of the physician who attendeth him, there can be no doubt; that when any one is sick, he should send for the elders of the Church, and avail himself of the promise made to them in visiting the sick; yea, and though our Church, to prevent superstition, doth not favour it, yet can I see good reason why, a little congregation being assembled in the sick man's room, the sacrament of the Lord's supper may be administered as a means of bodily health, as well as a means of spiritual edification; yet all these things are not to prevent, but rather to encourage the more, the use of all means. For what are these but means and ordinances of grace? In using these spiritual remedies, you are using means; and therefore all those pious methods of entreating the sick which God hath appointed in His Word, are, in truth and verity, God's way of sustaining the doctrine of the use of means; and he who will not use means for the remedy of nature's ailments, will soon fall away from the use of the means of grace. The truth is, that the world, with every plant, and every animal, and every inanimate substance, is as truly the work of Christ, the Word, as is the written Word itself; and the frame of man's natural body is, as a creature of God, made not to depend upon, but to rule over, and to possess, and to enjoy, and to be benefited by all these things. The varieties of meat and drink, the varieties of cordials and medicines, which the world containeth, are the wealth and possession of the body; and whoso casts them away rejects God's gifts, is presumptuous, is puffed up in his own mind, is weak, is in danger of falling. In using these remedies, however, we should always use them as gifts of God through Christ; and with faith, with adoration, and worship of Him who hath created all things, ought we to receive them, and ought the Christian physician to give them; which faith in the Feeder and in the Healer we express in those ordinances of the Church, the visitation of the sick, and the use of the Lord's supper. This error of neglecting the use of means in the remedy of diseases is attended sometimes with another, of a more ruinous and fearful kind; which is, to derive from this passage some sort of an assurance that, if the Corinthians had rightly partaken this ordinance, they would not have died, and that, therefore, if we do the same, we shall not die. Now, I believe that those in the Corinthian church, referred to in these words, "For this cause some of you sleep," would not have been so visited with premature death had they not profaned the ordinance. But is this to say that they would have lived for ever? The apostle says that the great Bishop had visited the Corinthian church, as He threatened the church in Thyatira, saying, "I will kill her children with death." But because He had visited them with death for their sins, is it to be concluded that, if they had not sinned, they should never have died? The like silliness of interpretation would draw out of such words of the Lord as these, (John vi. 49, 50,) "Your fathers did eat manna in the wilderness, and are dead. This is the bread which cometh down from heaven, that a man may eat thereof, and not die," the doctrine that one who truly eateth in the supper shall never taste of natural death. But what saith the Lord in the same discourse, not once, but four times over? "Whoso eateth my flesh, and drinketh my blood, hath eternal life, and I will raise him up at the last day." So that not dying is perfectly consistent with being raised up at the last day. But how can we be raised up, unless the body first descend into the grave? The not dying, therefore, the eternal life which we have in Christ, is not the perpetuity of this body of sin and death, but the perpetuity of that living union which we have unto Himself; because He lives, we live also. Now, as in the fifth commandment there was a promise of long life to those who honoured their father and their mother, so in the Lord's supper is there an assurance of health and life unto those who worthily partake thereof. And if you will reflect a little upon the peculiar nature of this ordinance, you will see the reasonableness of such an outward sanction as I am now explaining. It is an ordinance for life, for the nourishment of that life which we receive in baptism; we come as regenerate persons who have been intrusted with a new life, to nourish it up in godliness. We may nourish it, or we may neglect it. It may come to perfection in our hands, or it may die in our hands, according as we rightly use the table laid out for its nourishment. If we use the table of the Lord wisely, temperately, faithfully, our spiritual life will grow apace; if, on the other hand, we neglect the table of the Lord, or use it intemperately or unfaithfully, then we may starve our life, and die through weakness, or by surfeit bring on disease, and die through plethoric fulness. If, now, the perfection or the destruction of the spiritual life be dependent upon the right or the wrong use of this holy table, then ought we to expect some outward visible indication of those realities which are in it. Such outward manifestation was given in the Corinthian church, by weakness, sickness, and death; and such, I believe, will continue to be given in every church. Now, this is one reason for which every communicant should examine himself of his worthiness to sit down at the table of the Lord; for these ailments and mortal sickness of the Corinthian church are expressly said to have come from their not discerning the Lord's body; that is, not perceiving the Lord's body as present under the elemental signs. They ate of it as of a common meal; and instead of feeding them, like a common meal, it turned into starvation and poison. Their ignorance not only made the ordinance of none effect, but absolutely made it of evil effects: and I believe the same with respect to the ordinance of baptism, when it is not discerned as containing the regeneration; and of the ordinance of preaching, when it is not discerned as containing faith; and of the ordinance of laying on of hands, when it is not discerned as containing power; and I may say of every other ordinance, that the stupid ignorance of the partaker doth change its property, and make it of the very opposite effect to that which it hath unto them who rightly partake thereof. But while this we undoubtingly declare, as a consequence of stupid ignorance in the matter of the supper, and in the manner of Christ's presence therein, (for there be many who, like Queen Elizabeth, consider it a matter of nice and subtle speculation, and many are not ashamed to profess their total ignorance thereof,) that if a person will come ignorantly, they must come unworthily, and eat judgments to themselves, you are not to suppose that these bodily inflictions are the whole of the guilt contracted by unworthy communicating; for they are called (ver. 32) a chastisement of the Lord, to the end we may not be condemned with the world; which chastisement, if we be exercised withal, then will we guard against the like offence in time to come, wisely instructing ourselves, and reverently conducting ourselves, whenever we approach to the table of the Lord. But if, upon the other hand, we should not be rightly exercised with the chastisements of the Lord, but continue to profane the holy ordinance, ignorantly approaching and heedlessly partaking of it, then the question ariseth, And what guilt is incurred? The answer is, The guilt of the body and blood of the Lord. And if I be called upon to explain words so awful, I will do it by referring to the only passage of Scripture which is parallel to this, and an awful passage it is, (Heb. x. 29;) but for the sake of the connexion, you may read from ver. 26: "For if we sin wilfully after that we have received the knowledge of the truth, there remaineth no more sacrifice for sins, but a certain fearful looking for of judgment and fiery indignation, which shall consume the transgressors." This I take to be the judgment of which one that unworthily partakes maketh himself guilty, and in the verses following are contained the nature of the offence: "He that despised Moses' law died without mercy under two or three witnesses: of how much sorer punishment, suppose ye, shall he be thought worthy who hath trodden under foot the Son of God, and hath counted the blood of the covenant, wherewith he was sanctified, an unholy thing, and hath done despite unto the Spirit of grace?" Now, it seems to me that being guilty of the body and blood of Christ, is the same with treading under foot the Son of God, and counting the blood of the covenant a common thing. For is not the cup called "the blood of the testament" or covenant, and is not the bread called "the body of the Lord?" If, now, as I believe, the guilt and the judgment be the same in these two places, then we are at no loss to explain of what an awful kind they are. For in this passage of the Hebrews, it is without doubt the sin against the Holy Ghost which is committed,—that sin, to wit, for which there remaineth no more sacrifice; that sin of apostasy which can be committed only by those who have come to the knowledge of the truth; that sin which is especially designated wilful, because it is an act of the will, the will made conscious of God's Spirit, yet deliberately resisting that influence, or, as it is in the text, doing despite to the Spirit of grace. Now, concerning the nature of this sin, which is called being "guilty of the body and blood of Christ," I have one or two things to express. First, That it is a sin proper to an enlightened man, and which every enlightened man is capable of committing. To understand this, it must be remembered that election, and regeneration, and the efficacy of the Spirit, are all done upon a being possessed of a will, and done consistently with the constitution of a will, as hath been already said in this discourse. The human soul is the instrument with which itself, the body, and the world are redeemed. The will in the renewed man doth not cease to be a will because now it is free, whereas formerly it was in bondage. It is not driven by the necessity of an almighty influence, but it is released from its bondage, and put into the condition of choosing the good which is promised in Christ, and rejecting the evil which is seen in the world, and, by preferring God, the soul doth glorify God. Such is the condition and standing of a renewed will. But most manifest it is that the same will which, being redeemed, doth prefer God, might likewise prefer evil. If it be said No, then every redeemed will must be under the necessity of preferring God; which were to yield God no honour. If, then, a redeemed will possessed by the Spirit may prefer the devil in the world to the Spirit of Christ, shewing God in the ordinances of the Church when it doth so, it committeth the wilful sin. It sins, not under bondage, but willingly; being redeemed from the bondage, and having proved the liberty, it nevertheless preferreth the bondage, saying to the evil, "Be thou my good." This I take to be the sin of apostasy; this I take to be the sin against the Holy Ghost; and for such sin there can remain no sacrifice, either in this life or that which is to come. It is the fearful alternative upon the one side into which the enlightened are brought; and the joyful and blessed alternative upon the other side is, that of the first resurrection, and the kingdom and the glory of the Lord. Paul seems to have felt himself to be standing between these two most awful alternatives when he said, (1 Cor. ix. 27,) "Lest that by any means, when I have preached to others, I myself should be a castaway,"—that is, a counterfeit or spurious person, or, as it is translated in 2 Cor. xiii. 5, a reprobate. In the Epistle to the Philippians, again, the substance of the following remarkable passage seems to me to prove that he still rested in some fear or apprehension of the possibility of the awful alternative: "That I may know him, and the power of his resurrection, and the fellowship of his sufferings, being made conformable unto his death; if by any means I might attain unto the resurrection of the dead. Not as though I had already attained, either were already perfect: but I follow after, if that I may apprehend that for which also I am apprehended of Christ Jesus. Brethren, I count not myself to have apprehended: but this one thing I do, forgetting those things which are behind, and reaching forth unto those things which are before, I press toward the mark for the prize of the high calling of God in Christ Jesus." This was written some six or seven years after the former, and indicates some considerable dubiety in the apostle's mind whether he had attained unto the high calling of Christ; which I conceive to be the calling up from the grave of certain ones to meet Him in the air, and to reign with Him on the earth. But some three years after this again, when he wrote his last epistle, he was delivered from all doubt, (2 Tim. iv. 6,) "For I am now ready to be offered, and the time of my departure is at hand. I have fought a good fight, I have finished my course, I have kept the faith: henceforth there is laid up for me a crown of righteousness, which the Lord, the righteous judge, shall give me at that day: and not to me only, but unto all them also that love his appearing." I believe that the apostle felt himself placed in that very alternative, between reigning with Christ and apostasy from Him, in which he placed the Hebrews so frequently, and in which, I believe, every one enlightened by the Spirit is placed. This is a deep mystery, and it is not given to every one to discourse aright thereof; nor do I mean to say that what I have set down is the very truth, yet do I believe it is substantially true, and, if I mistake not, it is the very condition in which I feel myself to be placed. For when God enlighteneth a man concerning the first resurrection, and the glory which follows, that man, if he press not forward to the mark of this high calling, must fall back into the sin of apostasy, and commit the unpardonable sin against the Holy Ghost. Now, forasmuch as the table of the Lord doth contain the mystery of His advent and kingdom, and is the pledge and seal of the resurrection body, and the inheritance of the new testament, I do certainly conclude that those who, being enlightened therein, do yet profane the ordinance, are guilty of the body and blood of Christ, in the same sense as those spoken of in the Hebrews, who trample under foot the Son of God, and count the blood of the testimony with which they were sanctified a common thing, and do despite unto the Spirit of God. While I thus interpret the expressions "eating and drinking judgment," being "guilty of the body and blood of the Lord," you will not mistake me, as if I meant that every one who profaned this ordinance had committed the sin against the Holy Ghost. They may have done it ignorantly, or in unbelief of the great mysteries which it containeth; and in such a case, like these Corinthians, they will be visited with chastisements, that they may not be condemned with the world. But if upon coming to know that the bread broken in the supper is the body of Christ broken for us, and that the wine partaken in the supper is the blood of the new testament shed for the remission of sins, any should have the hardihood, without examining themselves, to come and partake of it, as if it were a common thing; then verily they do shew themselves to be hardened in the last degree, and to be in that state of apostasy out of which it is the apostle's desire to preserve them. For, certainly, of all the ordinances and sacraments of our religion, the Lord's supper is the most pregnant with the Holy Ghost—where, we may say, He delighteth to dwell. And the man who consciously doth despite unto this holy ordinance, doth, in the most glaring way, do despite unto the Holy Ghost; and it may be said of that man, that it is impossible to renew him again unto repentance, for he hath vilified the Son of God afresh, and put Him to an open shame.

This great truth, which I have argued out concerning the Lord's supper, holdeth likewise with respect to every other ordinance of the Church of Christ, and the ordinance of the Church itself; for all of these are vessels for containing the Holy Ghost, vehicles and channels of communication between Christ, who possesseth the Holy Ghost, and every one of Christ's members upon the earth. The Holy Ghost, unto those who have these ordinances, cometh not otherwise than through these ordinances. To deny, then, that there is any virtue given unto these ordinances, is, in effect, not only to reject the Son of man, who instituted them, but likewise the Holy Ghost, who worketh through them; to call these ordinances mere signs, teaching signs, is therefore the high road to apostasy; and flatly to deny that there is any grace communicated in them is, it seems to me, apostasy consummate. To think, for example, that preaching is no more than a man's account of his own opinions and method of maintaining them, and that the Spirit is not in the ordinance of a preached gospel to work faith therein, but that this faith is some after work, which the individual, by prayer and other means, obtaineth for himself; to say and believe that baptism is but a water ordinance, in which no spiritual grace of regeneration is present, and that this is to be wrought out afterwards without an ordinance, by some work of prayer in the individual; and, after the like manner, to unspiritualise the various ordinances of the Church, which Christ hath instituted, and to treat them as common things,—this is, as I conceive, the sin against the Holy Ghost, which shall never be forgiven in this world or in that which is to come. I do not mean that every ignorant person who taketh this abominable and horrible doctrine from his favourite spiritual guide is guilty of this sin. He may be doing it in ignorance and unbelief; he may not have been enlightened, and his spiritual guide may be in darkness—there is yet hope of them both. They have committed a great sin, but it may be forgiven. But after they have been once enlightened in the spiritual fulness which every ordinance containeth, and, being enlightened, have come and partaken thereof, and tasted the good gift of God and the powers of the world to come, and then thereafter fallen away, to look upon them, or act towards them as common things, and come unto them without any self-examination,—they do, I make bold to say, commit a sin which cannot be forgiven, and they shall never be renewed to repentance. These, now, are awful words, but they represent the certain conviction of my soul, and they mark out the condition in which I feel myself to stand, and which I believe to be the standing of many in my flock: to wit, that, enlightened as we now are in the mysteries of the sacraments, there is no middle course between the full assurance of hope unto the end, and irremediable, irrecoverable apostasy; and of this most awful truth I warn all the beloved brethren who have entered along with me into these the mysteries of the Church, that if we fall back, we fall back for ever. There remaineth no second repentance, no second renewal for us. We know the good, and if now we should elect the evil, then we shall be exhibited before this generation as direful examples of apostates; and it shall be again seen to what fearful lengths of heresy and wickedness apostates can go. But, as the apostle writeth to the Hebrews, "I hope better things of you, brethren, and things becoming salvation, though I thus speak." But the time is coming that will try us all, and therefore I am urgent. I feel also that, in setting forth these truths unto the Church, concerning the mystery of the sacraments, I am putting those who read and hear into the fearful predicament of either receiving or rejecting the great and mighty power of God. If they receive and are enlightened, then I feel again that they are brought into a high standing, and one of great trial, and from which the fall is irremediable destruction. But are we therefore discouraged in our work of faith and labour of love? No, verily; God is faithful, who hath promised, and His promise He hath confirmed with an oath, "that by two immutable things, in which it was impossible for God to lie, we might have a strong consolation, who have fled for refuge to lay hold upon the hope set before us." " Stand therefore, having your loins girt about with truth, and having on the breastplate of righteousness; and your feet shod with the preparation of the gospel of peace; and above all, taking the shield of faith, wherewith ye shall be able to quench all the fiery darts of the wicked [one.] And take the helmet of salvation, and the sword of the Spirit, which is the word of God."

Now, then, having thus explained the responsibility which is incurred, the guilt which is contracted by the unworthy, the judgments which they eat and drink unto themselves, the chastisements which they receive in the body, and the fearful consummation of apostasy to which they draw onward, I have little to add with respect to the uses and ends of self-examination, for this will now speak for itself. To preserve against these catastrophes, to protest against these unspeakable wickednesses, this is the first aim and use of self-examination; which therefore directeth itself to the discernment of our faith in the presence of the body of Christ in the ordinance. We examine ourselves of our knowledge to discern the Lord's body, for he who cannot discern the real though spiritual presence of Christ's body in this ordinance, must be liable to abuse it. Indeed, not to discern the Lord's body is, according to the apostle, the ground of all the mischief and miscarriage. They eat and drink judgment to themselves, not discerning the Lord's body. Without such a discernment there can never be any reverence for, faith in, or profit from, the ordinance. You cannot make men reverence a shadow, or a symbol, or a sign, till they know the substance, the sacredness, and the sufficiency of the thing signified; and if you say the substance, and the sacredness, and the sufficiency of the thing signified is not there contained, how can you ask of men to put any reverence or faith upon it? They ofttimes make a jest of, and even minister rebuke unto the Reformers, for their violent controversies upon the kind and nature of the presence of the body of Christ in the supper. But this is the root of the matter, and he who hath not much inquired into this, will, almost to a certainty, be found ignorant of, and unprofited by the ordinance. The holy apostle, and, after his example, the Church of which we are members, requireth of us, first of all, to examine ourselves of our knowledge to discern the Lord's body; for, coming unworthily, we eat and drink judgment to ourselves. The next end of self-examination is to discern our right to partake of Christ, which standeth not in this or that degree of attainment, but singly and simply in our faith in God, through Jesus Christ. If we believe in God, that He hath loved us, and given His Son to save us, to feed and nourish our souls, we may come and be fed and nourished. But if of this we doubt, it is the greatest of profanations. Therefore, it is said that we should examine ourselves, secondly, of our faith to feed upon Him; that is, our belief that God has given Him to be fed upon, and that we may feed upon Him. Another end of self-examination is, that we may discover that our faith hath not been a vain and fruitless one; that it hath not been without works, which is dead; that it hath not turned to apostasy, which is twice dead; that it hath been attended with godly sorrow and genuine repentance for sin; that it hath turned our hearts towards God, from ourselves, from the vain and wicked world: and, therefore, we are required to examine ourselves of our repentance. And because the Lord's supper is the communion of His body, wherein we have fellowship one with another, and all with Christ, we are required to examine ourselves also of our love, because faith without charity profiteth nothing: our love to God, who hath first loved us; our love to Christ, who hath so loved us as to give His life for our sake; our love to the brethren; our love to all men. And because repentance and faith, without the obedience of good works, do prove themselves to be but a deception, we are to examine ourselves next of our new obedience,—that is, obedience springing from the new principle of love, and not from the old principle of fear. There can be no doubt that, according as our self-examination in these great heads of Christian life is proceeded in, so will be our holy exercise of soul, and our most comfortable edification at the table of the Lord. But these five heads of the Christian experience—knowledge, faith, repentance, love, and new obedience—are so large and fruitful, that I know not in what way I can better stir up the graces and the desires of the faithful, or instruct the simplicity of the ignorant, or better prepare the way of this holy mystery, than by discoursing on them, and shewing how much they are excited by the near prospect, and how fitly they prepare for the profitable partaking, thereof.

Suffice it, in this homily, to have shewn, first, the duty of self-examination to be proceeded in at all times, but never to be neglected before coming to the table of the Lord; to have encouraged all who are in Christ to undertake this duty, by the good hope, yea, and almost certainty of discovering that they are in Christ, and Christ in them the hope of glory; to have exhibited at large the fearful consequences of neglecting this most solemn duty: and, after what I have said, I do trust that every one who hath heard will solemnly undertake this duty, being encouraged therein, yea, and forced thereto, and terrified out of the neglect of it, by all these solemn truths.

This, therefore, dear brethren, I would give you, as the sum and substance of what I have said on self-examination: Every baptized person amongst you is answerable for a spiritual and eternal life. He that doth not believe this doth neither know what baptism means, nor hath he realised the benefits of his baptism. He hath not even comprehended them; and such a one, who knoweth not of a new life pledged to his faith, and believeth not in a regeneration, cannot use the Lord's supper as it ought to be used. But those who see that baptism is God's covenant for a new life, and who believe that they have such a life in Christ, are in a state of belief which enableth them to eat the supper; and if they come not to the supper, they do voluntarily suffer that new life to die for want of nourishment. And I believe that there are many, very many, who, through abstinence from the Lord's supper, abide in continual weakness and continual peril of death. In which course they justify themselves by these two considerations: the first, that they feel within them such unworthy thoughts, dispositions, and passions, and are led astray by the natural man into such evil acts, as make them afraid to draw near so holy a table. But while I am the last to encourage wilful sinners, and perverse, malicious persons, to approach unto the table of the Lord, I ask of those who are endeavouring to contend with the flesh, How ever they can expect to prevail, otherwise than through the holiness and power which Christ put forth upon His own body, and by which He presented it for ever blameless? and if so be that it is only by Christ's holiness of body, communicated unto, and partaken of by, us, that we are to attain unto such purity and power as we yearn for, then I ask next, Where is this participation of Christ's body to be received save at the table of the Lord? To suppose that otherwise than by this table, to suppose that anterior to the use of this table, we can obtain power over the body, power over the natural man, with all his corruptions and lusts, is to make the table void, to make it unnecessary to the Christian warfare, to make the Christian victory independent of its help. Be therefore advised, dear brethren, who believe in Christ the regeneration and the life, and who are seeking perfection through the ministry of the Spirit of Christ, who are conscious of indwelling sin, and grieved by reason of it; be persuaded, I say, not to avoid this table, as if it were spread for unfallen angels or perfect men, but to apply yourselves to it, as a weak and hungry man doth to food for the sake of strength, as a sick man doth to medicine for the sake of health. It is for the Church militant, that giveth and that taketh blows, that is oppressed by the enemy and sometimes overcome,—for the Church militant, growing daily in grace, in strength, in wisdom,—that this table is spread; whereof I wish you, with a good understanding of its uses, to come and partake with a true desire of profiting thereby, in the enjoyment of peace, and in the ways of holiness. Now, the second consideration with which some are pressed and prevented from coming to the table, is their worldliness, their much occupation in, and battle with, this world's affairs; and oft have I heard the neglect of the Lord's table excused by the consideration of being distracted with worldly cares, and prevented by worldly occupations. But what meaneth this? Do they mean, as I was once told by foolish and impertinent young men, that in order to fill offices in the Church it was necessary to have nothing to do with business, and to be retired from the world? Do they mean, I say, that in order to sit down at the Lord's table, a man must first have made his fortune, and taken his degrees, as a monk or a hermit? Idle, foolish puritanism! The Lord's supper is for the very end of enabling men to combat with the world, and to overcome it. Whence hath the world its mighty power? Is it not from its possessions,—its houses, and lands, and honours, and friendships, and other ties? But how expect ye ever to overcome these, but through the knowledge and the faith of an inheritance in the heavens, wherein, as kings and priests, ye shall dwell and reign for evermore? And where have you the assurance of this but in the cup of the Lord's supper, which is the pledge of the new testament of our Lord Jesus Christ, by which He bequeaths to you a share of His inheritance, of His kingdom, of His throne, and of His glory? It is the entering in of this better hope which casteth out the power of things seen over the soul. It is the assurance of this glorious possession, noble prerogative, and highest preferment, which enables the soul to cope with and overcome the allurements of avarice, ambition, honour, and the like; which enableth her to reject this world and its kingdoms, for the hope of the world to come and its kingdom. But where is this firm assurance and glorious hope to be attained, save in the cup of the Lord's supper? And he who thinks to conquer the world without the use of that cup, doth in truth make void the cup, as much as he who thinketh to overcome the body without the use of that bread. Therefore, setting aside these two excuses, I call upon all men who believe in the regeneration and life which they have in Jesus Christ, and desire through that life to make an effectual debate with the flesh and the world,—all such I entreat to come to this table, in a serious purpose of serving and glorifying God, with that strength which we seek, and believe that we shall receive. It is not our weakness, nor yet is it our imperfection, that disqualifies us for the table of the Lord; nay, but it is our coming thither with a careless indifference or with a presumptuous boldness. To come in a state of unawakened and insensible nature, is to err exceedingly; for it is not a life-quickening but a life-feeding ordinance,—not for conversion but for edification. Men must know of the life they have in Christ, and be persuaded of it, before they come hither. They must be desirous to do His will in all things, yet conscious of the need of strength to do the same, and not doubting but they will receive it,—looking to God as to a father, and looking to His table as to a father's table. So coming, I say, with love and with unity, with faith and with confidence, with conscious infirmity yet desire of perfection; who is he that will let you, who is he that will disappoint you? Come, then, I pray you, with a good heart and with a right mind, that your souls may be filled with the abundance of the goodness and the grace of God.

HOMILY II.

THE THING WHICH IS SIGNIFIED IN THE LORD'S SUPPER.

1 COR. XI. 23-25.

For I have received of the Lord that which also I delivered unto you, That the Lord Jesus the same night in which he was betrayed took bread: and when he had given thanks, he brake it, and said, Take, eat: this is my body which is broken for you: this do in remembrance of me. After the same manner also he took the cup, when he had supped, saying, This cup is the new testament in my blood: this do ye, as oft as ye drink it, in remembrance of me.

LUKE XXII. 19, 20.

And he took bread, and gave thanks, and brake it, and gave unto them, saying, This is my body which is given for you: this do in remembrance of me. Likewise also the cup after supper, saying, This cup is the new testament in my blood, which is shed for you.

THE passage which we have read from the Corinthians consisteth of two parts: first, the narrative of the institution; and, secondly, the apostle's conclusions therefrom for the instruction of those to whom he wrote. In this discourse we shall confine ourselves to the former of these, and endeavour to explain the several parts of this service, following no plan but the order of the parts, and bending our discourse to no object but the edification of those whose purpose it may be to present themselves at the Lord's table.

The institution of the ordinance of the supper, of which we have accounts given us by the first three evangelists, was in this wise. On the night of the passover, when all the Jews from Judah and Israel, and the regions round about, assembled in Jerusalem, and sat down together in small companies to eat the paschal lamb, in commemoration of their deliverance from the house of bondage, Jesus, who had come up to the city of Zion with the intent of offering up the great passover for the sins of men, was not the less careful of the observance which He was about to supersede by the sacrifice of Himself. He called two of His disciples, and said unto them, "Go ye into the city, and there shall meet you a man bearing a pitcher of water: follow him. And wheresoever he shall go in, say ye to the goodman of the house, The Master saith, Where is the guest-chamber, where I shall eat the passover with my disciples? And he will shew you a large upper room furnished and prepared; there make ready for us. And his disciples went forth, and found as he had said unto them; and they made ready the passover. And in the evening he cometh with the twelve. And when the hour was come, he sat down, and the twelve apostles with him." While they ate of the lamb dressed with bitter herbs, and drank of the wine which was partaken therewith, He gave them to know that it was the last time He should partake of it upon earth; and said, "With desire I have desired to eat this passover with you before I suffer." Likewise, during the paschal supper He held with them that sorrowful discourse, recorded by all the evangelists, concerning the traitor Judas, who dipped with Him in the dish; and stirred up their minds with zeal and love, and every strong attachment. And, the more to touch their souls with evidences of His great love and condescension, He arose, and having poured water into a basin, and girded Himself with a towel, the Son of God, who took upon Himself the form of a servant, went round the table, and, one after another, washed and wiped His disciples' feet. By which forebodings of His approaching end, and lamentation over him that should be the cause of it, and condescending kindness to them all, having filled their minds with sorrowful solemnity, and wound them up with expectation of His oft-predicted death, He straightway proceeded to institute this holy ordinance, whose emblems and words were in harmony with the deep emotions which must have occupied their breasts. For in the Saviour's ministry of salvation there is nothing more remarkable than the suitableness of the word to the action, the propriety of time and place to both, and the harmony of all with the feelings of those who were addressed; and which arose from His soul's being attuned by the deep relations of truth, unbroken in its perception, undisturbed in its emotions, rich in feeling and harmony, responsive to every secret association of nature, whereof He was the Creator, and acquainted with every deep and secret movement of the human soul, to whose mysterious sympathies He was always ready, in His great grace, to accord whatever He had to say or do. In this sweet and harmonious spirit, having touched the souls of His apostles by these various notes of warning, He proceeded to the institution of this holy service. He took bread, and gave thanks, and blessed it, which was the sign of a new and distinct service from that in which they had been engaged, and brake it, and gave unto them; and while their minds, already moved with the mysterous meaning of all that had been said and done during the supper, burned for an explanation of this solemn commencement, He said, "This is my body which is given [or broken] for you: this do in remembrance of me. And he took the cup, and gave thanks, and gave it to them, saying, Drink ye all of it; for this is my blood of the new testament, [or, this is the new testament in my blood,] which is shed for many for the remission of sins."

Such was the institution of the holy ordinance whereof we have taken in hand to explain the meaning, according to the principle formerly laid down, that every ordinance which is set forth by signs should explain itself by help of the ordinary signification of the signs and of the words pronounced over them. Following this rule of interpreting, with the elements in our hands, and the words in our mouths, we remark, with respect to the signs, that, as the element used in the sacrament of baptism is the emblem of purity, and the action of washing or dipping therein is the sign of purification; so bread and wine, the elements used in the sacrament of the supper, are the emblems of strength and cheerfulness, and the action of eating and drinking is the sign of sustenance and nourishment. Bread is the staff of life; and wine cheereth the heart of man. Also, to sit around the table of any one, and be permitted to eat of his bread and drink of the wine which he hath mingled, is, on his part, a sign of hospitality and friendship, and on ours a pledge of faithfulness and truth. Which sentiment that our Saviour felt keenly is manifest from what He said of Judas: "He was troubled in spirit, and testified, and said, Verily,

verily, I say unto you, that one of you shall betray me." "Behold, the hand of him that betrayeth me is with me on the table." "One of you which eateth with me shall betray me." In which expressions it is manifest that He felt the criminality to be aggravated by the breach of that good faith which is signified in eating and drinking with a man at his table. Thus are these two things, therefore, the very face and outward show of this ordinance: first, a pledge of friendship and faithfulness to Him around whose table we are seated; and, secondly, that we are come thither for the sake of sustenance and refreshment.

So much is discernible by the eye from the visible emblems and actions of the ordinance, which being taken along with what is gathered by the ear from the words that are appointed to be spoken, giveth its whole meaning and significance. Now the words spoken over the communion have a twofold intention: the first, spoken over the emblems to tell what they signify and shadow forth, "This is my body, which is broken for you; this is the new testament in my blood;" the second, spoken to the people who partake them, "This do in remembrance of me. This do ye as oft as ye drink it in remembrance of me." These two parts of the declaration require to be considered apart.

When the Lord Jesus presented the bread to His disciples, He said, "Take, eat; this is my body which is broken for you;" or, as it is in Luke, "This is my body which is given for you." Upon this the Romanists have founded their doctrine of transubstantiation, that the bread is no sooner blessed than it changeth its nature, and from being bread becometh the real body of Christ, in which, not in a spiritual manner unto faith, but in a visible manner unto sense, He is present, and entereth into union with all who partake thereof. And hence, upon the exaltation of what they call the host or victim, they require reverence to be done by all present upon their bended knees, and understand the mass as a renewed sacrifice of Christ;—doctrines, for the denial of which the best blood of England was shed, and upon the denial of which the Church of England may be said to have been built. Now, this doctrine of the Papal Church is not of ancient date,—going back no further than to a few centuries before the Reformation, begotten in the brain of a subtle friar, and by the orders of friars propagated over the Church; which, in its adoption, condemned not only the primitive times before a papacy was heard of, but also the first and best age of that usurpation, during which such a notion concerning the communion was never broached. They infer, in like manner, from the language used over the other element, that the wine, upon being consecrated, becometh transubstantiated into the blood of Christ, and, as the blood of the Redeemer, enters into and incorporates with the substance of every one who partaketh thereof.

The chief end for which this doctrine was so sternly and bloodily maintained by the Church of Rome was to raise the clergy to a super-eminent place above the power and authority of princes, seeing that into their hands had been conveyed the power, as they blasphemously express it, of creating God the Creator of all, and offering up the same God before the face of God the Father, for the redemption and salvation of the whole world. Its effects upon the people are as debasing as the purpose of it was blasphemously ambitious in the priesthood: for they are taught to look upon a wafer, and believe it to be God the Creator of all; they are taught to partake of a wafer, and believe that they have entered into union with Christ, and are cleansed from their sins. By which all inquiry into the spirit and meaning of things is put an end to; all searching into the manner of the spirit they are of is disannulled; repentance and a holy life are made void; and that trust in outward forms, so fatal to religion and morality, is not only sanctioned, but is sustained and kept up by the delusion, that there lieth in the form whatever virtue lay in the crucifixion of Christ for the sins of men. Whatever is awful and overwhelming to the spirit in the death of Christ, whatever is consoling to poor sinners in the cross of Christ, they transfer to a rite and ceremony which the priest daily performeth; and the people, thinking they eat and drink of the body and blood of Christ, with which so much holiness and virtue is associated, are stimulated with earnestness to procure it, and then with false confidence, when they have obtained it.

The whole fabric of this delusion resteth upon a literal, or rather sensual, interpretation of the words, "This is my body," "This is my blood;" and is to be overthrown by discovering in the habitual discourse of our Saviour the same expression, used not in a literal, but in a figurative sense. Such an example we have in the 6th chapter of John, to which I request attention, as not only resolving this question, but as proving the best commentary which is to be found in Scripture upon the words of the communion. The people required a sign from heaven, such as their fathers had received in the manna of the desert, as it is written, "He gave them bread from heaven to eat." To which Jesus replied, "The bread of God is he which cometh down from heaven, and giveth life unto the world. I am the bread of life: he that cometh to me shall never hunger; and he that believeth on me shall never thirst." "The Jews then murmured at him, because he said, I am the bread that came down from heaven." To which, among other gracious things that He said, He replied thus, "I am the living bread which came down from heaven: if any man eat of this bread, he shall live for ever; and the bread which I give is my flesh, which I will give for the life of the world. The Jews therefore strove among themselves, saying, How can this man give us his flesh to eat? Then Jesus said unto them, Verily, verily, I say unto you, Except ye eat the flesh of the Son of man, and drink his blood, ye have no life in you. Whoso eateth my flesh, and drinketh my blood, hath eternal life; and I will raise him up at the last day. For my flesh is meat indeed, and my blood is drink indeed. He that eateth my flesh, and drinketh my blood, dwelleth in me, and I in him." Such was the discourse our Lord held with the Jews in the synagogue at Capernaum, in allusion, doubtless, to this sacrament; very similar in its mysteriousness to that which he held with Nicodemus in allusion to the sacrament of baptism, "Except a man be born of water and of the Spirit, he cannot enter into the kingdom of God." And as Nicodemus took offence at this declaration of the first sacrament, and said, "Can a man enter into his mother's womb, and be born the second time?" so the Jews, and even many of His own disciples, took like offence at this declaration of the second, and said,

"This is a hard saying: who can hear it?" And in precisely the same style in which He retorted upon Nicodemus, "If I have told you earthly things, and ye believe not, how shall ye believe if I tell you of heavenly things?" He retorted upon His disciples, who could not hear this saying concerning eating His flesh and drinking His blood, saying, "Doth this offend you? What and if ye shall see the Son of man ascend up where he was before?" Then, having rebuked them for the slowness of their apprehension, He addeth the explanation of the mystery in these words, "It is the spirit that quickeneth; the flesh profiteth nothing: the words that I speak, they are spirit, and they are life." The flesh concerning which I speak, and ye take offence, profiteth nothing: it is the Spirit within me which quickeneth your spirits. "The words that I speak they are spirit, and they are life." In this way doth He resolve His own figurative language, by telling them that, in its literal sense, being understood of His flesh and blood, it profiteth nothing; but in its spiritual sense, being understood of His words or doctrines, it quickened, it was Spirit and it was life. So, also, he resolved it to Nicodemus, by saying, "That which is born of the flesh is flesh; and that which is born of the Spirit is spirit." The reason why He put the truth in this symbolical form to the Jews was, doubtless, because they required a sign similar to the manna in the wilderness, which He told them they had in His own person, which was the bread that came down from heaven. But to us it serves the more important purpose of ascertaining what it is which He hath embodied to all ages under the symbols of bread and wine, or of His body and blood. For if He hath spoken so unequivocally and so repeatedly of His flesh and blood as meaning the spirit of His doctrine, then in that sense He must be understood when, under these emblems of body and blood, He handeth down some mysterious significance to His disciples in all future ages.

This manner of speaking under material emblems concerning the spiritual life and nourishment which existed in His doctrine is not confined to the discourse held with Nicodemus and with the Jews in the synagogue of Capernaum.

But whenever occasion served, He used the same figurative manner of speech. To the woman of Samaria, He said, "Whosoever drinketh of this water shall thirst again: but whosoever drinketh of the water that I shall give him shall never thirst; but the water that I shall give him shall be a well of water springing up into everlasting life." Again: "In the last day, that great day of the feast, Jesus stood and cried, saying, If any man thirst, let him come unto me, and drink. He that believeth on me, as the scripture hath said, out of his belly shall flow rivers of living water." Of this allegorical language the evangelist hath given us this interpretation in the next verse, saying, "But this spake he of the Spirit, which they that believe on him should receive: for the Holy Ghost was not yet given; because that Jesus was not yet glorified." It is also used in the Old Testament in several places. Thus Wisdom saith unto the simple and those who want understanding, "Come, eat of my bread, and drink of the wine which I have mingled." And again, Isaiah: "Ho, every one that thirsteth, come ye to the waters, and he that hath no money; come ye, buy wine and milk without money and without price. Wherefore do ye spend your money for that which is not bread? and your labour for that which satisfieth not? hearken diligently unto me, and eat ye that which is good, and let your soul delight itself in fatness." In which passage wine and bread are made to produce fatness in the soul. And the apostles, following the phraseology of their Master, have used this language in all their epistles: "Know ye not that your bodies are the members of Christ?" "For we are members of his body, of his flesh, and of his bones." "So we, being many, are one body in Christ." From all which examples it is manifestly the use and wont of Scripture, as well as the practice of our Lord, interpreted by Himself, to use these words, "This is my body," and "This is my blood," never in a literal but a figurative sense; and, as such, it is to be understood in the words of explanation pronounced on the elements of bread and wine.

But the earnestness and heat of this controversy hath

somewhat, I think, withdrawn the minds of the Protestant Churches from the true spirit of the expository sentences which are pronounced over the bread and wine used in the communion. Christ did not say merely, "This is my body," but "This is my body broken [or given] for you." Now in the latter clause the feeling and endearment of the sentence lieth: "This is my body broken for you;" "This is my body given up for you." He referreth to His death, and giveth them to know for whom He died: "For you who sit around the table, and for those who shall follow in your footsteps, and become my disciples, I have been born, and afflicted with sorrow, bruised, buffeted, spit on, and crowned with thorns, nailed to the accursed tree, pierced with the spear of the uncircumcised, poured out unto death, and brought to the dust of the grave." But, higher still: "This is my body broken for you;" or, according to a frequent idiom of the Greek tongue, "This is the breaking of my body for you." "As I now break this bread, and divide it among you all, which ye partake in common, and, partaking, become nourished by a common good, which heretofore was whole, but now is diffused over you; so this my body is to be broken up and to be divided piecemeal, as it were, amongst my disciples, who are thus to constitute my body upon the earth, and to be united in one, as the many members of one body are united in one." Hence the apostle Paul never faileth to call the Church the body of Christ; and from this, as if it were no figure, but a reality, he enforceth all his lessons of charity, which is the bond of perfectness. And speaking of the same ordinance, he saith, "The bread which we break, is it not the communion of the body of Christ? For we being many are one bread, and one body; for we are all partakers of that one bread." This, therefore, I conceive to be the high theology of the sign, and the words pronounced on it: that the bread denoteth the body of Christ; the breaking of it denoteth the change which took place in His body at death, which, from being one individual upon the earth, was broken into the form of many individuals, that is, of His true and faithful disciples; and that we who are truly of Him are to regard ourselves as in Him, and representing Him. His body, therefore, is still with us in the Holy Catholic Church; and every time this bread is broke, it doth recall to us the change which passed by death upon the body of Christ. That from being a visible shape it should become the unity or community of all the saints which are upon the earth, this seemeth mysterious. It is so; but religion without mystery is as absurd as knowledge without mystery. And there is as much mystery in the principles of our knowledge as in the principles of our faith; which, by the grace of God, we shall demonstrate at large when once the holy season of the communion is past.

And now that we have arisen out of the region of the visible and intelligible, which sight and understanding possess, into the region of the unseen, which faith alone can enter into and discourse of, we ask your ear a little longer, the circumcised ear of your heart, while we open a little further insight into the mystery of the bread.

By nature all mankind hold of one fallen man, even Adam: of whose substance, with all its attributes of sin, depravity, and misery, we are by natural generation partakers, both of body and spirit; for whatever notion may be held concerning the invisible spirit which God communicates to each man, there can be no doubt, from the time that it is ours, it is full of alienation, rebellion, and disobedience, under the law of the flesh, the partner, yea, and the mover of all its wickedness. This state of sin and infirmity which is derived to us all was not the original constitution or nature of the human substance, but one which it was free, under the temptation of Satan, to assume, for the manifestation of God's greater glory in the work of recovering it and reconstructing it in infallible and perfect blessedness. And this derivation of a sinful substance unto all his posterity is what the divines mean by original sin; which if any one deny, then must he hold the notion that we are born as Adam was created, in the possession of all his creation powers, and, like him, are tempted to sin by the power of evil from without, and the infirmity which is within us. This is the Pelagian, which is now palmed upon the people for Arminian doctrine, and necessarily leads to three consequences:—1st, A power in man to do good as well as to do evil, to resist temptation or to yield to it. 2dly, The power to do without supernatural help; for if we may stand of ourselves, then we may not need another's hand to hold us up. 3dly, The conclusion that we are in a state of probation, as Adam was. And then what is the gospel? It can only be a thing to call in or not according as we need it: something which those who give way need, but those who give not way need not. But if it be confessed that all give way, as Adam did, then how is it with them? Why, just as it was with Adam; they have done an evil work, and must pay the forfeit of it. And what is that forfeit? Some inward disagreeable feeling, some painful sense of the loss of virtue. And how is our peace to be restored? By regret, and repentance, and reparation. But will God accept of this? Yes, certainly, because He is merciful. And how know ye that? Christ hath come to declare it. And so Christ becomes the great indulger of man's licentiousness. Such is the sum and substance of Pelagian and Arminian doctrine; such is the consequence of denying the doctrine of original sin, which we all believe, and proceed upon as the basis of all doctrine and the ground of the gospel—a part of it, and yet the foundation upon which it rests.

Well, then, believing the total depravity and entire helplessness of this visible estate of manhood, by virtue of its connexion with and laying hold upon Adam, our great head, we desire to know the hope which remaineth for creatures whose power of good, whose very power of life, hath thus departed from them. What shall we lay hold upon in order to lift us out of this fearful pit and miry clay, into which we have sunk, and in which our feet are holden fast? There is nothing which we can lay hold of for that great end of redemption and resurrection but the risen body of Christ: as it is written, "If Christ be not risen, then are we still in our sins." It is nothing that Christ was crucified and laid in the grave, unless He be also risen: for to die is the very consummation of our lives and demonstration of our helplessness, in which every one that shareth doth so far forth demonstrate his taking part with the rest of the fallen creatures. But if such a one as hath been born and lived and died like other fallen creatures, have likewise arisen from the dead and liveth for ever; then, indeed, there is a door of hope opened to every poor, mortal, corruptible creature who holdeth the same nature. On the other hand, again, there would have been no ground of hope if He had not died, but been translated like Enoch and Elijah; because in that case it would not have been made manifest that He was bone of our bone, and flesh of our flesh, partaker in all respects of the substance of fallen manhood. He might have been an angel who had but taken human form and appearance in order to accomplish some errand and message of God, as the damnable Arian heresy feigneth. But being proved to be very man and partaker with man in his doleful condition, by His having borne it first and last, and all its sorrows and infirmities, and having risen incorruptible from the tomb, and entered into an eternal life and infinite power, all eyes and all hearts of mortal kind ought to be turned unto the risen body of Christ, as the great demonstration of the possibility and of the fact of redemption and resurrection from this our low and lost estate.

For what hope is there else? The rest of mankind, all the children of Adam, lie mouldering in the dust: the worm hath fed upon them, and corruption hath devoured them. There is no memory of them, and their name is perished. They had no power against death while they lived, and when they came to die they were fain to yield themselves, and the grave closed her mouth upon them, and they are not. To look for help from them is utterly vain; they need a helper more than we, for we are still in the narrow strait and isthmus of life, but they are swallowed up in the gulf. But here is one Man who, his life long, prevailed against sickness and death; who said that He had power to lay down His life, and that He had power to take it up again; who entered into the house of death, and spoiled the strong man of the house, contending with him for His own body, and overcoming him, for it saw not corruption. There it lay, the seed of the regenerated world, and death and Satan sought to destroy it for ever; but it endured all their malignant power, and arose in glory and in strength into the possession of an eternal life at the right hand of the throne of God; whence the risen Man shall come again to judge the world in the last day.

If, therefore, the children of Adam are ever to be helped out of their present evil plight of sin and death, it must be through the power and prevalency of that Son of Adam who is now in the heavens, far above death and sin, and all principalities, and powers, and dominions, and every name that is named both in this world and in that which is to come. Here the resurrection of Christ is the tomb-stone of His divinity, whereby He was declared to be the Son of God with power: it is also the strong point of the gospel, to the preaching of which the preaching of the cross is but preparatory, to shew forth His true manhood, His being truly in the estate as well as in the stead of fallen manhood, in preparation for the shewing forth His resurrection, which is the proof that now fallen manhood hath been exalted from its lowly bed into the condition of risen and immortal manhood, and in that condition will take its superior place of primogeniture above all other beings, upon the right hand of the throne of God.

These things being so, what have we in the supper but this risen body of Christ, this headship of risen manhood, unto which the eyes of all fallen creatures should be directed, and the hands of all creatures sinking, drowning in death should be stretched out, and to which the supplications of all that fell with Adam should be lifted up? This our risen and glorified substance we have presented to us in the symbol of the supper; which, presenting us with bread, doth say, "This is my body broken for you," and presenting us with wine doth say, "This is the blood of the new covenant, which was shed for you; drink ye all of it." Christ doth as it were let down His body in this sacred symbol from its regal dignity to the capacity of the present weakness of man, and present it under a figure to all who have believed upon Him, and have their hopes directed upwards to that pole-star of the night, in order that their faith therein may be strengthened, and that they may receive a pledge that they shall be partakers thereof. He doth not present His very body, which is in the heavens, far removed from mortal sight; He doth not convert wine and bread into His glorious body, for that is to go quite beyond the mystery of which the end is in the day of the resurrection, —to transubstantiate then the fallen substance of the believer into the true substance of Christ; but not to transubstantiate bread and wine into that most glorious substance. He doth not consubstantiate His body and blood with the elements of bread and wine; which dogma of obdurate Luther, left to teach us not to trust in man, hath indeed no touch of the mystery at all, which transubstantiation hath, though out of all time and out of all subject. For there is a time when there shall be a transubstantiation, and there is a subject upon which it shall be. The subject which shall be transubstantiated into Christ's real body is the substance of fallen manhood in the believer; and the time at which it shall be done is at the resurrection of the just, before the setting up of the millennial kingdom, in which they are to reign as kings and priests upon the earth. But that baked bread and fermented wine were to be transubstantiated into the real body of Christ, now or at any time, is a beastly sensual folly, which was never heard of amongst Christians till that mother of abominations made every holy thing abominable. But that anything is at any time to be consubstantiated with the body of Christ, as poor obstinate Luther, to punish his obstinacy, was permitted to hold with fierce contention against the Reformed Churches, is an idea for which there is no foundation anywhere. We, indeed, who believe and receive this pledge of the supper in true faith, shall be consubstantiated with Christ; but that taketh not place through the conjunction of any other substance with His glorious substance, but through the changing of the substance of fallen manhood into the new state of the risen manhood, by the same change in the day of our resurrection which passed upon Christ in the day of His resurrection. But as to making this transubstantiation upon bread and wine, and making it now by the power of priestly consecration,—which is never to be made but by the power of the voice of Christ extended upon His sleeping saints in the renewal of the Church,—it is a monstrous figment, which should be hunted out of the earth with the fire of the Holy Spirit, and the sword of the preached word of Christ.

To the eye of faith, and to the handling of faith, and to the receiving of faith, there is indeed that present transubstantiation of which they ignorantly and foolishly say that it is made unto the sense. Faith doth, indeed, behold, and handle, and eat, and feed upon the risen body of Christ, although invisible to the sense, and incomprehensible to the understanding of the sense; and we believe that Christ is truly and really present in the holy sacrament unto every believer, and is there and then partaken of in a high and spiritual sense, with which sight and reason have nothing to do, but which is accomplished wholly by the Spirit through faith. And that faith may ascend as by a ladder unto the exaltation of Christ's body, He doth let down, from His high and holy place, this symbol from time to time unto His Church, to the very end that they may know and most assuredly believe that His absence, the absence of His body, divideth Him not from their care, neither divideth Him from their presence, but that, according to His promise, He is with us always;—with us, not by bodily or visible presence in bread and wine, for in that case there were no need for Him so graciously to comfort His saints under His absence by this sacrament, if so be that He was present in a wafer, which could be kept in the corner of a chest, and produced upon all occasions;—oh, you miserable, wretched deceivers of ignorant souls! if yon paltry wafer which you lay up and parade about with you, be the body of Christ, what need hath the Church to be comforted with this sacrament over His absence? for ye say He is present, and this sacrament is constituted till He come again to be present;—I say, in order to comfort those who believe on Him, with His very and true presence in them, and their union unto Him through faith, He doth continually present this sacrament of the supper, wherein, by sensible signs, His death is shewed forth, and thereby His having truly partaken of man's substance in its fallen estate; for that is the great use and end of His death, to demonstrate that He was truly in the state of the fallen, sinful creature: and not only is this shewed forth, but the worthy partakers thereof are, not after a corporeal and carnal manner, but by faith, made partakers of His body and blood, to their spiritual nourishment and growth in grace; or, to use the words of our Reformers, as expressed in the 21st Article, which is entitled, "Of the Sacraments:"—

"We utterly condemn the vanity of those that affirm sacraments to be nothing else but naked and bare signs; no, we assuredly believe that in the supper, rightly used, Christ Jesus is so joined with us, that He becometh very nourishment and food to our souls: not that we imagine any transubstantiation of bread into Christ's natural body, and of wine into His natural blood, as the Papists have perniciously taught, and damnably believed; but this union and conjunction, which we have with the body and blood of Christ Jesus, in the right use of the sacraments, wrought by operation of the Holy Ghost, who by true faith carrieth us above all things that are visible, carnal, and earthly, and maketh us to feed upon the body and blood of Christ Jesus, which was once broken and shed for us, which now is in heaven, and appeareth in the presence of His Father for us: and yet, notwithstanding the far distance of place which is between His body now glorified in heaven, and us now mortal on this earth; yet we most assuredly believe, that the bread which we break is the communion of Christ's body, and the cup which we bless is the communion of His blood. So that we confess, and undoubtedly believe, that the faithful, in the right use of the Lord's table, do so eat the body and drink the blood of the Lord Jesus, that He remaineth in them, and they in Him; yea, they are so made flesh of His flesh, and bone of His bones, that as the eternal Godhead hath given to the flesh of Christ Jesus (which of its own nature was mortal and corruptible) life and immortality; so doth Christ Jesus His flesh and blood, eaten and drunken by us, give unto us the same prerogatives. Which albeit we confess are neither given unto us at this time only; neither yet by the proper power and virtue of the sacraments only; yet we affirm that the faithful, in the right use of the Lord's table, have such conjunction with Christ Jesus as the natural man cannot apprehend; yea, and further we affirm, that albeit the faithful, oppressed by negligence and manly infirmity, do not profit so much as they would in the very instant action of the supper, yet shall it bring fruit forth as lively seed sown in good ground; for the Holy Spirit, which can never be divided from the right institution of the Lord Jesus, will not frustrate the faithful of the fruit of that mystical action; but all these, we say, come of true faith, which apprehendeth Christ Jesus, who only maketh His sacraments effectual unto us. And, therefore, whosoever slandereth us, that we affirm and believe sacraments to be naked and bare signs, do injury unto us, and speak against the manifest truth. But this liberally and frankly we confess, that we make a distinction between Christ Jesus in His eternal substance, and between the elements in the sacramental signs; so that we will neither worship the signs, in place of that which is signified by them; neither yet do we despise and interpret them as unprofitable and vain, but do use them with all reverence, examining ourselves diligently before that we so do; because we are assured by the mouth of the apostle, that such as 'eat of that bread, and drink of that cup, unworthily, are guilty of the body and blood of Christ Jesus.'"

The one idea, therefore, which is contained in the bread of the supper is this, "that our faith layeth hold of the risen body of Christ, and feedeth on it." As by nature we all lay hold of the fallen body of Adam, and grow into its sin, death, and corruption; so by faith we all lay hold upon the risen body of Christ, and hope, yea, are assured, that we shall arise unto the honour, and glory, and immortality thereof. This we do not in the sacrament merely, but always; for it is the only object for a fallen creature to look unto—the subject of all preaching, the object of all believing. In the sacrament we receive the seal and the pledge of that holy union which we already have through faith before sitting down at the sacramental table, or partaking of the sacramental elements. And every one who proposeth himself to the Church, in order to receive this seal and pledge at her hands, doth in that proposal of himself make honest declaration of his belief that he is united to Christ already, and desireth to make profession thereof, and to receive the confirmation thereof in the holy supper. So that as baptism is the seal of the righteousness which we have by faith while yet unbaptized, so is the supper of the Lord the seal of the union which we have with the risen body of Christ while yet unsealed with the seal of the sacrament. Baptism is, therefore, the seal of righteousness imputed to us; the supper is the seal of a union unto Christ, wrought in us since our baptism. Imputation is from an outward source, which is separate from the sinner; union is the oneness of these two heretofore separate. And this is the difference between the two sacraments, and the higher, nobler, diviner character of the latter, that it represents, and seals, and declareth a union to be wrought, which in baptism was declared not to be yet wrought. But besides this idea or doctrine of union with our risen Head which the supper sheweth forth, there is another idea, of nourishment derived from our Head in virtue of that union, whereby we are enabled to live His life in the flesh, to die His death, and to partake in His resurrection. For as bread and wine are the nourishment of strength in the body, and without some such nourishment of an outward substance the body would decline and die, so is it signified that the risen body of Christ is that outward object of which the life of every regenerated creature is nourished, and without which it would utterly decline and die. Inasmuch that as if there had been no Adam, there would have been no creatures in Adam's sinful likeness; so had there been no risen son of Adam, no Christ, there would have been no creatures of the fallen stock graffed into the risen stock, partakers of its righteousness, its wisdom, its sufferings, and holy obedience, its hopeful death, and most glorious resurrection. Natural generation bindeth the link with the first and fallen Adam; faith bindeth the link with the second and risen Adam; and as we all are children of the former by nature, so likewise are all believers children of the latter by faith. Of which two mysteries I know not whether is the more wonderful: that I, and all of you, living here some six thousand years from the creation, should be possessed of the substance, and fulfilling the evil condition of a being who hath for that very long tract of time ceased to be a visible being; or, that I and all of you believers should be partakers of the substance, and fulfilling the blessed condition of another Being who hath ceased to be a visible being for a much shorter space. Indeed, I think the body of Christ to be the less mystery of the two, because we know He is exalted God over all, and hath all power in heaven and earth. Whereas Adam died in weakness and became a prey to worms, Christ's body rose in power, and ever liveth to declare and to execute the mighty power of God. Nor is it to me more mysterious that my spiritual life should be fed and sustained upon the body of Christ, now in glory, as its outward nourishment, than that my natural life should be fed and sustained upon bread and wine, and the other fruits of the ground. There is a further mystery here which riseth upon my view, but which I do not now undertake to discover until I have better apprehended it; which is, in what sense Christ's risen body shall be the nourishment of the life of His saints in their risen estate, as the bread and wine is the nourishment of our bodies in their fallen estate. I perceive this much, and have oft declared it, that as all believers hold their resurrection hope of Christ's risen body, so do all the inferior creatures of the earth hold their resurrection hope from the resurrection of the saints: for as they fell with man, their master, so with man, their master, shall they arise again. So that Christ's body is in truth the hope of the resurrection of all visible things which fell with man: out of whom He is forming unto Himself first a spouse in the elect, and then a numerous progeny in the days of His kingdom; and out of all, a church of risen creatures, and a redeemed habitation of risen creatures upon the earth, with whom, in the ages to come, to carry on, as I take it, the government of the universe. Now, in what relation this Church of the first-born and general assembly of all the children shall stand to the purchased and possessed inheritance of the earth, and its various races of creatures, and its various productions, is to me a mystery upon which I dare not say anything, but which I do see some shadow of in the choice of bread and wine, and the use of eating, in the sacrament of the supper.

Let it suffice that we have opened to you the great doctrine of the mystery, which is the headship of Christ, and the membership of all believers; and the nourishment of the whole body proceeding from and through the head;—the great end of the mystery, which is the transubstantiation of the fallen manhood of all believers into the new manhood of Christ in the day of their resurrection, and their holding

ITS SIGNIFICATION.

thereof for ever, as verily and really as all mankind do now hold of the fallen substance of Adam—so that we shall say, "I am of Christ the God-man," as naturally as we can say, "I am of Adam, our first parent;" and we shall shew forth and be patterns of the nature of Christ, the visible Godhead, unto all angels and spirits which set their eyes upon us, and hold converse with us, as we are now exemplars of fallen man. To keep up the memory of which high and holy distinction of mankind, and that the Church might not lapse and decline away into low conceptions of herself through a voluntary humility, is the very object and end of this sacrament,—the most precious jewel and the most fragrant mystery which the Church hath in all her storehouses.

HOMILY III.

THE INVITATION, ADMONITION, AND ARGUMENT FOR ALL BAPTIZED PERSONS TO COME UNTO THE TABLE OF THE LORD.

MATTHEW XXVI. 27.
Drink ye all of it.

HAVING now before us, dearly beloved brethren, the near prospect of the administration of the sacrament of the Lord's supper in this place, I desire, by the grace of God, to discharge two duties unto all who statedly attend here the ministration of divine ordinances: the first, to point out the obligation which resteth upon every baptized person to partake of the supper of the Lord, and the sin which is contracted by every one who neglects the same; the second is to point out the privilege of partaking worthily, and the peril of unworthily partaking this holy sacrament: and these two offices of the ministry I now solemnly desire to discharge, with the view, not only of testifying to the truth as it is in Jesus, but also of leading you into all truth.

In virtue of your baptism, as we have already taught, you are brought from the standing of nature into the standing of grace, and are no longer, before God and His Church, abiding in the flesh, but abiding in the Spirit; no longer carnal, but spiritual. It doth not alter this your spiritual standing before God and the Church, that you have been led astray by the temptations of Satan, the desires of the flesh, and the attractions of the world, and that you are still suffering under their grievous oppression, which hath been the case with almost every member of God's Church now advanced into glory. It is the common, and I may say universal method of God, in bringing His elect ones unto glory, to shew them their own sinfulness and weakness, by suffering almost every sin to have the dominion over them. For it is the sad and sorrowful reality, that we are not otherwise able to be convinced of our own vileness, and our own weakness, than by the experience of the same. Pride and self-sufficiency are so bound up in our fallen nature, that we do ever incline to please and flatter ourselves with the conceit of our own freedom from, and superiority to those transgressions of the divine law which we have not been proved to be guilty of. Therefore, God's discipline with His chosen ones most commonly proceedeth by suffering them for a while to abide in the same evil conditions in which the world around them abideth. But they are not less His elect ones while thus oppressed by the devil, than after they have been delivered from his oppression; for God knoweth His own from the beginning, and in every stage of their earthly being His purpose according to election is working in them. Go not, therefore, ye who are sitting with the scorner, and walking astray in the counsel of the ungodly, to say, "I am far from Christ, and have no part in Him, and need not to trouble myself with His ordinances, for it is vain, seeing they belong not to wicked persons like me." Go not to say, ye Sabbath-breakers, if any such hear me, ye worldly, covetous, luxurious, and vain, "I have no part in this matter;" for such were some of us, who are now washed and purified by the Spirit. Go not, ye prayerless, thoughtless, heedless, to say, "As for us, we make no profession, and would not add hypocrisy to our other sins; therefore let us refrain from the table of the Lord, and not stain its holiness with our pollutions:"—for be it known unto you, all ye unawakened, unconverted men, that, to the end of teaching you not to despair, not to doubt, but to believe and be saved, I stand here from Sabbath to Sabbath, ministering the words of the gospel of Christ. And now hear what I declare to you, that it is Satan's arch-deception thus to have persuaded you that you are aliens from the commonwealth of Israel, and strangers to the covenants of promise. All your sins are nothing, when compared with this sin of not believing the grace of God manifested unto all men in Jesus Christ, and the work of the

Spirit manifested unto you by your admission into the Church. The sins which you have committed, and under the dominion of which you still abide, are indeed rendered the more heinous by being committed in your persons, who are members of Christ's Church, and by your standing therein should be holy as He is holy. The sins which ye have done since your baptism are sins done against light, the light that is in the Church; and done against covenant,—the covenant of God to wash away your pollution, yea, to kill and bury the flesh, —the covenant of God to give you the Spirit, and raise you unto newness of life. The sins which you have done since your baptism, all the sin which is committed in the Church, is a vexing and grieving of the Holy Ghost, with whom you have been sealed. It is a sinning against the risen, glorified Son, who baptizeth with the Holy Ghost; and for this sin of the Church it is that the risen, glorified Christ shall come against her with overwhelming judgments. I do not wish to extenuate your sinfulness. God forbid! when I do not the less declare it unto you, that this sinfulness doth not by any means hide you from the love of the Father unto His own chosen ones, seeing that all His chosen ones have been guilty of the same, and, notwithstanding, been forgiven of God, and gathered unto the Church in glory. There is nothing in your sinfulness which is not common to the sinfulness of all. We are bone of each other's bone, flesh of each other's flesh; God hath fashioned our hearts alike. Every one hearing me this day, every member of the Church on earth, and every inhabitant of the new Jerusalem above, may say, and ought to say, "In me, that is, in my flesh, in my natural man, dwelleth no good thing." My sin, brethren, before God, is not counted by the number of my ostensible transgressions and innumerable frailties, but by my inheriting and possessing a fallen nature, along with the rest of the brethren. Every sin is in me, and I am chargeable with every sin, thought or not thought, acted or not acted. The infant who thinketh, who willeth not, is chargeable as I am chargeable. Our complete, thorough, and radical sinfulness, is a matter of faith, and not of experience. Experience, alas! it likewise is, but by experience is not to be measured, though thereby we become conscious of it. But far more blessed is he that believeth than he that waiteth for the experience. He that believeth his total sinfulness will not need to be convinced that he must seek righteousness elsewhere; but will flee at once to the Son for imputed righteousness, and to the Holy Ghost for the empowering him to possess and perform the same. But he that believeth no further than he hath proved by experience, or by conscience hath felt, is in a case to be led astray again and again into new paths of wickedness, and to be deluded by Satan; ay, and until he can receive original sin as a great doctrine of faith, which doctrine, if ye unconverted men will now believe, as it is shewn to you in your baptism, then, from this time forth, ye may be at once delivered from the experimental demonstration of your sinfulness. But until you do so believe, God hath, I may say, no other way permitted to Him to convince you of the same, save by suffering you to fall more and more egregiously; and I believe that this your present sinful condition, over which you make your moan, and which hideth grace and hope from your eyes, is in very truth caused by nothing else than your uncertainty and doubt concerning the total depravity and incurable infirmity of human nature in its best estate. Take my counsel, therefore, I pray you, and be intreated, for your soul's sake, to believe this great article of faith, and to act accordingly, by seeking a righteousness which is not in you, nor in the Church, but in the great Head of the Church, by whom it is dispensed through the ordinances of the Church to all the faithful. And know assuredly, that it is no proof whatever of your being out of Christ, and out of the Father's election, that you have been found in sin, and are still under sin's dominion. Therefore go not to stand afar off from the subject of this discourse, or from the desire of God's holy ordinance, but give me good heed while I shew you, in the second place, the sinfulness and the peril of abiding in your present state of listlessness, indifference, neglect, and perhaps contempt of this holy ordinance. And this I sum up in one head: that you do in a manner excommunicate yourselves from the Christian Church, by refusing in your own act to confirm the action of your parents by which you became a member of Christ's Church in the sacrament of baptism; and while you continue so, you stand in great peril of that apostasy which cannot be renewed unto repentance. I do not say that you are able by any act of your own will, or by the neglect of any ordinance, to undo and, as it were, make void the act of your parents in your baptism. It is possible for a man in his sober senses to take away the life which he hath received from his parents by an act of violence done upon himself, but this he cannot do without rising up against God, and against nature, and against the laws of human society, and committing the most heinous, the most enormous of crimes: wherefore, in all well-regulated countries, his lifeless body, all that remaineth of him, is disgraced from Christian burial to the common highway and the most public resort thereof, ignominiously cast into the earth, and thrust through with a stake. Even so, a man may, it is true, deprive himself of that new life which the faith and piety of his parents sought and obtained from the Church in the sacrament of baptism, but this he cannot do without committing a crime which shall neither be pardoned in this world nor in that which is to come; for thereby he doth rise up against the life, not of nature, but of the Holy Spirit, and he doth offend, not against the venerable laws of human well-being, but against the most holy ordinances of the Church of Christ, doing his part to make void that which God hath purposed and set forth in His Son, for the stability and support of all the creation. Seeing, therefore, this act of spiritual suicide to be of such hideous guilt, I would indeed be very guarded in saying that any of you have committed it, while I am bold to say that every one of us may commit it; and in so far forth as you refuse by any act of your own to confirm this act of your parents, you do, so far as man can witness, dishonour and disallow that gravest and solemnest act of baptism, and you stand in peril every day of falling into that fearful apostasy or act of self-destruction whereof I have represented the terrors above. Far be it from me to say that any one who heareth me hath been guilty of this violent act of spiritual self-destruction; for then there were no hope of such a one, it being impossible to renew such apostates unto repentance. Still further from me be it to say that by not coming to the Lord's table you do commit this act. Nay, I believe that all ordinances may be neglected, and are neglected, that the recommendations and injunction of the Church may be set at naught, and the act of excommunication be inflicted in its heaviest form upon the stout-hearted rebel, and yet this act of immediate self-destruction not be committed. In which judgment I am borne out both by the instance mentioned in the Corinthians, which excommunicates to the end of saving the soul, and restores again to the end that the excommunicated person may not be swallowed up with too much sorrow; and I have also the support of the excommunication service in all orthodox Churches, which is not unto the death and reprobation, but unto the recovery and restoration, of the diseased member of Christ. Nevertheless, though the neglect of the ordinance of the Lord's supper, and of all ordinances whatever, be no evidence that a baptized man is cut out of Christ, and thenceforth good for nothing but to be cast into the fire and burned; yet it is possible, I would have you to be assured, for every baptized man to commit this great sin against the Holy Ghost, after which there remaineth nothing but a fearful looking for of fiery judgment to consume the transgressor. Nor am I willing too nicely to define this most fearful act of the human will, lest any timorous and doubting soul might haply seize upon my imperfect definition, to its own distress, and even haply to despair. I do simply leave it there, in its undefined form given by the Lord and His apostles, assuring every baptized man that he can commit it, and pointing out to him the way which leadeth to that fearful precipice and direful abyss of spiritual life. And assuredly, brethren, the way is first to stand still in our progress, and then to go backwards, and finally to fall away. The holy apostle, in his Epistle to the Hebrews, rebuketh them for having so long stood still; and because he knew that this was the beginning of apostasy, he, for his part, resolved that he would not stand still in his instruction of them, but would go on steadily unto perfection. Then he addeth as his reason, that it was impossible to renew again to repentance those who were once enlightened, and had tasted the heavenly gift, and been made partakers of the Holy Ghost, and tasted the good word of God, and been make partakers of the world to come, if they should fall away. Now, dearly beloved brethren, ye who stand aloof from this holy ordinance because of your confessed unfruitfulness in the Spirit, do thereby declare that you are from year to year standing still, and not going forward, and therefore you are in the case of those whom the apostle warneth of the peril of apostasy. It is true you do not forsake the assembling of yourselves together, you reverently attend the ordinances of public worship, and haply you express your faith in Christ by bringing your children to the font of baptism; but, behold! by your own confession the word preached doth not savingly profit your souls. The prayers offered up to the Majesty on high are not accepted nor answered unto your necessity, and the vows of sponsorship you discharge not, you cannot discharge, while, according to your confession, you are living in a state which may not permit you to approach the table of the Lord. Is not your case, then, exactly the same with that of the Hebrews, which the apostle illustrates by the following emblem?— "For the earth which drinketh in the rain that cometh oft upon it, and bringeth forth herbs meet for them by whom it is dressed, receiveth blessing from God: but that which beareth thorns and briars is rejected, and is nigh unto cursing; whose end is to be burned." Even like such an unfruitful field are those who, sitting under my ministry, or the ministry of any orthodox preacher of the saving truth, do yet, time after time, as the table of the Lord is spread for nourishing the children, withdraw themselves from the same, because they are not bringing forth fruits meet for repentance, but are still abiding in their sins. The word, the precious seed of the word, is ever being sown upon them; the dews, the softening dews of the Spirit, are ever descending around them and upon them; the labour of the great Husbandman is ever pruning, and dressing, and digging around them, and He looketh that they should bring forth unto Him good grapes: but, lo! they are fruitless, or yield only the sour grapes of a degenerate vine. For whom what can be said, what can be done, but, after having faithfully warned them of the peril of the unpardonable sin, to gently intreat them with good hope and tender love, saying unto them, with the blessed apostle, "But, beloved, we are persuaded better things of you, and things which accompany salvation, though we thus speak?"

I have likened the apostasy from Christ, which precludeth all hope of repentance, unto the act of suicide, which a man committeth against his own natural life, because I believe that every baptized person is brought into responsibility for a new life. Now, I cannot help making an observation which is suggested to my mind by this comparison. It is well known to you that in inquests holden upon suicides, the great point to be ascertained is whether the act had been committed in a sound or an insane state of his mind—the latter being justly accounted no crime, the former a great one. This confirms by a solemn practice what most of you may have observed or read of, that when men fall into a state of insanity, they are very liable to do the act of suicide; as, indeed, I have personally known in the case of two of the most holy and benevolent men; and this action, being done in the absence of reason, is not looked upon as a crime for which they are responsible to the laws of men or of God. Now, it hath been affirmed to me by the most competent witnesses, that there is nothing which so much prepares the way for insanity as indulgence of parents to the wilfulness of their children. I remember to have been told by a physician who had the charge of the asylum of the most populous county in the empire, that nine out of ten of all the cases were cases of persons who had been indulged and spoiled in their childhood. Whether the disorder seated in the constitution led to this wilfulness, or whether the wilfulness of the child produced the madness of the man, he took not upon him to say; but he did solemnly assure me that the fact was as I have stated it above. Taking it, therefore, to be so, I have to observe that it casts much light upon the mysterious act of apostasy or spiritual suicide; shewing us, first, that the madness which leadeth thereto doth begin in the resistance of the authority and rejection of the love of our parents. And whom baptism doth constitute our parent the ordinance itself declareth: "I baptize thee in the name of the Father, of the Son, and of the Holy Ghost." Being thus brought into the family of the Father, we testify the first beginnings of that spiritual malady which endeth in apostasy by rejecting the love and refusing the commands of our Father which is in heaven. And what is His love, and what is His commandment? Is not His love the giving of His Son to be crucified for us? "God so loved the world, that he gave his only-begotten Son, that whosoever believeth in him should not perish, but have everlasting life." And what is His commandment? Is it not to honour the Son, even as we honour the Father? And how do we honour the Son but by keeping His commandments? And is it not His dying commandment, "Do this in remembrance of me?" In His death upon the cross, the love of the Godhead shone most gloriously. In the holy supper, commemorative of His death, the commandment of Christ is as it were centred and fixed. And methinks it is the last act of wilfulness in the children to set at nought this meat, which hath been prepared at so much cost, and is fraught with so much benefit and blessedness. It is as if a child should refuse the wholesome bread for which his father's brow hath sweat, and which his mother's hand hath carefully prepared. And truly as wise parents in such a case of frowardness are wont to act, by setting aside the despised meat, and suffering the little recreant to prove the pains of hunger, and come to his senses again, and then to present before him that which he had rejected; so doth the Church, your mother, patiently and lovingly put forward, from time to time, the manna from heaven, angels' food, the flesh and blood of Christ, which with so much cost the Father prepared, and serveth the Church withal, for the nourishment of His house. This meat, I say, which is meat indeed, and this drink which is drink indeed, we do set forth to you again and again; which if you again and again reject, it will come to pass that the nourishment of life, the only nourishment of spiritual life, being by you refused, starvation, death by starvation, will ensue; which will not be the less wilful self-murder, because there hath been no other act of the will, no absolute voluntary renunciation of, and blasphemy against, the Holy Ghost. And thus truly it is that multitudes pass into eternity guilty of the unpardonable sin of apostasy, who have never, by any actual renunciation, but by the neglect of the means and ordinances of life, brought themselves to that hideous perdition. But wherever an act of wilful apostasy doth supervene upon the neglect of ordinances, it can, like the suicidal act, most frequently be traced back to the rejection of our heavenly Father's affection, and the refusal of His commandment to bear testimony to the death and resurrection of His Son for our reconciliation and justification. Therefore, dearly beloved, I give you timeous warning to beware of standing aloof from the holy family of Christ's Church; for these are times in which that wilful act of renouncing Christ is not rare, but very frequent, amongst us. Leaves never drop faster from the tree in autumn than men do now fall away from the Church; denying the spiritual substance of baptism, refusing the authority of the Church, proudly setting at nought all the ordinances of God, and finally denying Christ and the Holy Ghost to be persons of the Godhead. Is it rare for men brought up in the bosom of the Church to fall away to infidelity? The question ought rather to be put the other way: Is it rare for young men brought up in the bosom of the Church to abide by their mother, and to remember the holy name by which they are called? Yes, this is rare, this is very rare, for it is confirmed unto me by the testimony, not of tens, but of hundreds, now hearing me, most sponsible members of this church, that in their workshops and places of business, the scoffers at the name of Christ far outnumber the believers therein, and oft, yea, most frequently, they stand alone, like Lot testifying in Sodom. Now, therefore, is not a time for men to straggle away from the banner which God hath uplifted amongst us; when, on every side, not single soldiers but whole companies are cut off. Now is a time for every man to stand to his arms, and encompass the banner of the Lord. And as when our brave countrymen were set upon at unawares in their march through the deep fields of standing corn, which covered the enemy from their view, they did on the instant betake themselves to their military discipline, and close their squares on every side, and so preserve their lives and their arms ; we ought, in these times, when apostasy, under covert of toleration, liberality, charity, and every fair disguise, cometh on from every region of our fellowship, to betake ourselves to our ecclesiastical discipline, and be assured that thus we shall live in honour, or die with the benediction of our Captain. I do pray you, dearly beloved, by the bonds of our mutual love, that ye withstand not these our most urgent intreaties, but give good heed to the peril of apostasy and perdition, which doth stare, as it were, in the face all who make light of it, or neglect the holy sacrament of the Lord's supper because of their alleged unworthiness to partake thereof. Oh, even now, put away your sins! See your sins buried in baptism; and not your sins only, but the very substance of sin—the flesh, the body of sin. Act faith upon your baptism, I say. Do it even now. See yourselves therein not only dead to sin, but raised to righteousness; born again of water and of the Spirit. Oh, go not to disbelieve God's holy covenant; for remember that they could not enter into the rest who disbelieved. Wait not for a season and a time until you shall have experienced such convictions of sin and such fruits of righteousness as you fancy may justify you, or entitle you to approach the holy table. Nay, calculate not on time, for our times are in His hand; and time is not an element necessary to the acts of God, nor yet to the actings of our own spirit. Faith doth not require time to germinate and bring forth justification. Justification is not a work, but it is an act of God. Believe, I say, in the covenant of baptism, which expresseth original sin buried, together with all actual sins which proceed from it, which expresseth new life, regeneration, together with all the fruits of the Spirit. Act faith herein, I say, and come to the Lord's table, freely and fully privileged. Oh, my brethren, it is not to put a bar that we ministers make so much previous instruction, and that the Church appoints so much previous preparation. Still less is it to beget the most fatal pharisaical error, that a certain measure of attainment and advancement in the divine life is necessary. It is not to search you with the dim candle of our discernment. It is not to try you in any scales of our own construction. It is not to sist you until you can read off from your changed mind this and that experience. Oh no; far be these things from an orthodox catholic Church: they savour of schism and of sect. Ours is quite another; we meet our intending communicants and the youth of our flock, in order to instruct them in the excellence of this holy sacrament, and to stir them up with zeal unto the desire for the same; and this we shall endeavour to do for the whole congregation this very day, postponing to this higher object our ordinary instructions, and endeavouring what in us lies to bring it to pass that no one of the flock should be without the nourishment of these green pastures, and the refreshment of these quiet waters. Meanwhile, we do most earnestly entreat you to lay to heart the matter of this discourse, wherein we have endeavoured to remove obstacles out of the way, to expose the peril of standing afar off, and to encourage you to draw near to the table of the Lord.

We come now to consider, in the second place, the obstacles which arise before the minds of baptized persons, to be removed from the way of the Lord's table, and shall endeavour, by the help of God, to present unto all the baptized that grace of the Spirit of God, and those benefits to the soul of the believer, which should induce us, with one consent, to draw near and partake of this holy ordinance; a duty of the holy ministry which is at all times incumbent upon the preachers of the word, but then most especially incumbent, when the Lord's supper is about to be administered, and, above all, in times like these, when the privilege and the duty of communicating are alike forgotten or neglected by the great multitude of those who belong to the Christian Church: for, if we were to compare the numbers of those who partake this holy ordinance with the numbers who partake it not, we should find a most lamentable defection, calling loudly for the strenuous endeavours of those who are stewards of the mysteries to recall the attention of the Church to this most precious and much-neglected ordinance. In setting forth the value of any ordinance, we conceive the duty of a Christian minister to be, first of all, simply and sincerely to state the place which it holdeth in the institutions of the great Head of the Church, without any respect whatever to the misrepresentations and misapprehensions of men, that the truth may speak for itself, and the ordinance be commended upon the ground of its own worth. Baptism, then, is for the manifestation of a new life, which is born, not of blood, nor of the will of the flesh, nor of the will of man, but of God. The written and preached Word is for the information, and enlightening, and edification of this new life of the Holy Ghost. As the new-born child is cherished with the love, and nourished by the milk of its mother, so ought the infants and children of the Church to be nourished with divine instruction, and to receive the sincere milk of the word from the Church, the mother Church, that they may grow thereby. And as the infant is not fed with bread and wine, and the other nourishments of full-grown manhood, but extracteth the milky juices thereof from the breast of its mother, so may not the infants and children of the Church be nourished upon the same strong food which the Church herself partaketh in the supper of the Lord, but with the milky extract of the same, dropping from the lips of a Christian father and a Christian mother—of the hundred fathers and the hundred mothers which Christ hath promised to His people in this world, when He promised to them life eternal in the world to come. And every full-grown man in the Church of Christ should feel that he is a father, to instil wisdom, and every full-grown woman that she is a mother, to drop affection and loving-kindness, upon all the children of the Church of Christ. We who are ministers of the gospel unto the Church, and the highest, most learned, and most profound instructors of the Church, ought chiefly to attend unto the nourishment and the growth of those who are fathers and mothers in Israel, while we press it upon them, and refuse not ourselves to shew them the example, of breaking down the bread unto the children, and giving them their food in due season. Such is the nurture and admonition of the Lord, in which the baptized infants should grow up to the stature of full men in Jesus Christ. But as children do but for a short time depend upon their mother's breast, and as youth is not always to be dieted by the rules of the nursery, but doth in good time arrive at that stage when the sense becometh exercised to discern both good and evil; so in the Church the time is anxiously expected when every one of her members shall desire the food of full-grown men, which is communicated in the elements of bread and wine at the table of the Lord.

The table of the Lord doth, therefore, fix an epoch in the life of every Christian, at which he may step out from the guardianship of others, and become responsible for himself. Now the Church, which, as hath been said, is not, like the world, under the conditions of time and place, doth not fix any number of years at which this spiritual majority may or ought to be taken up; but simply requireth that the baptized should be of such maturity of knowledge as to be able to examine themselves, lest, coming unworthily, they should eat and drink judgment to themselves. And the office which the rulers of the Church fulfil, as the stewards of the mysteries of Christ, is merely to have a care that no one ignorant or deficient as respecteth knowledge, that no one blamable and offensive as respecteth life, should with a veil over his eyes, and with his unrepented sins upon his head, sit down to debase by superstition, or to profane by wickedness, this the sanctuary of the Church of God. But it is, as hath been said, our constant desire and entreaty unto all to come and partake of the waters of life freely. And I do now, as the consecrated and ordained minister of this Church, present unto all who are wont to worship and hear with us, the most cordial invitation, and the most pressing entreaty, to come unto the table of the Lord, and to eat and drink abundantly of that which the Lord hath prepared. And to the end of encouraging and enticing them, I do present the following most grave considerations.

First, In this holy sacrament you have set forth to you the elements of spiritual life, the body and blood of Christ. Hitherto you have held of Christ through the intermedium of another. You might not hitherto approach unto Him but through those who hold over you the sponsorship under the Church; nay, and if you did, you might not expect the blessing, save through whom the Church hath appointed over your childhood. Whether we may, or whether we may not, reverence the persons whom the Church hath taken as our sponsors, Christ will reverence them; and acteth in such wise as not to deal with us but by their intervention, or, if they should neglect their office, by the intervention of some others whom he may please to use. But for the substance of the inferiority it remaineth the same, in order to be a continual inducement for us to seek the standing of full-grown men, of free men in His Church. If the great Head of the Church were to put no difference in His communication with the baptized and the communicants, then would there be no difference to induce the baptized to sit down at His table, and the spiritual administration within the veil would not answer to the visible administration without the veil. I say it, therefore, because I believe it, that one who standeth apart from the supper of the Lord never shall have the personal and close communion with the great Head which is enjoyed by him that seeketh the same in the observance of the holy ordinance. If I understand anything of the Lord's supper, it presenteth unto the faithful a full measure of the manhood of Christ. When it is said over the bread, "This is my body," and when we in faith do receive the bread, I understand that the Spirit communicateth unto us the perfect and complete communion of the body of Christ; that is to say, the Spirit proceeding from Christ doth, without intervention of another person, communicate unto the believer, directly and immediately, the full participation of humanity redeemed by Christ. I say not of Christ's personal body, but of humanity cast in that very mould, instinct with that very Spirit, and heir of that very holiness, beauty, and glory. We receive from Christ, by His Spirit, the complete and perfect likeness of His manhood, just as truly and verily as we receive from Adam the complete and perfect likeness of his sinful manhood. As a child differeth from a man in his understanding, his independence, his power, so doth the gift in baptism from that communicated in the supper of the Lord. All the arts of the world cannot convert a child into a man, so that he should become an intelligent administrator of his affairs, a husband, or a father; so I believe no arts of instruction can convert a baptized person into a full-grown man; which degree I believe to be attainable only by the faithful use of the ordinance of the supper. For ordinances are not barren things without fruit, neither are they idle things without usefulness; He that appointed them will take good care that His appointment be not nugatory and vain. If, therefore, you desire to have the Holy Spirit operating in you all the functions of a perfect man,—understanding to fathom the Scriptures, wisdom to guide your affairs with discretion, courage to encounter the enemies of the Church, skill to command her forces, discretion to conduct her councils, love to be a father or mother in Israel, honour to fulfil her offices, together with all other qualifications for being an active member of the Christian Church,—then must you seek for those gifts at the table of the Lord. In every other ordinance there interveneth between you and the Head of the Church another person,—in baptism, both your father and the minister; in preaching, the preacher; but in the Lord's supper there interveneth no one. It is the nearest approach unto the great Head of the Church. Every Christian transacteth for himself with his living and risen Head. It is a personal act, which every man in his own free-will and agency acteth for himself; and therein consisteth its special power of characterising Christian manhood. Now, before leaving this our first inducement to the Lord's supper, let me observe, that so much was this idea of childhood and manhood connected with baptism and the Lord's supper in the primitive Church, that the whole discipline of the Church towards the baptized was but an expression of this one idea. The baptized were placed under the catechising and supervision of others—aye, and until they were judged to be of sufficient maturity to sit down at the Lord's table; whereupon they ceased from that restraint and supervision, and were ripe for taking upon them the offices of catechists, of deacons, of elders, of pastors, in their turn. And I may observe that this likewise is the discipline of the Reformed Churches. Of our Church, as is well known to you, it is as constant a provision to have a parish school as a parish church; the one for the instruction of the children, the other for the instruction of the men in the oracles of God and the offices of the Church. Schooling is now looked upon as a thing apart from religion. At the Reformation it was not so, nor is it so in any of the institutions which grew out of the Reformation. In the Church of England, also, all schools and seminaries of learning were but nurseries of the Church; and, in both Churches, the parochial ministers are required to take as diligent an oversight of the children as of the full-grown men. These things are neglected in practice, they are even forgotten in principle; but to one acquainted with their origin and principles, they do all but shadow forth the great idea expressed above, of the difference between the grace communicated by baptism and the grace communicated by the holy supper. I do call upon you, therefore, beloved brethren, by all the dearest and noblest desires of liberty, by all the holy and heavenly ambitions of the new man, by all the propensities which make a youth aspire to the station and function of a man,—I call upon you also by the wants and necessities of the Church, her need of brave soldiers, her need of wise counsellors, her need of eloquent advocates,—I call upon you by the distresses of the Church of Christ, her schisms needing to be healed, her losses needing to be repaired, her unproductive wastes needing to be cultivated, her active occupations needing to be extended,—by whatever it is praiseworthy for a youth to aspire to, by whatever is dutiful in a redeemed child of God, and by whatever is tenderly affectionate to the members of Christ,—I do call upon and entreat you, young men, not to abide any longer in your tutelage, in your ignorance, in your weakness, but to come to the table of the Lord, and, in receiving the nourishment, to receive the strength, might, wisdom, and activity of full-grown men.

The second consideration by which the Lord's supper presseth itself upon all the baptized is, for the remission of sins, according to that word pronounced over the cup, "This is the new testament in my blood shed for the remission of sins." Baptism is for the remission of sins, and, as hath been said, for the death and burial of the sinful flesh. But, notwithstanding this seal which we receive of death unto sin and life unto righteousness, we do, through want of faith in that holy covenant, fall into divers sins, which are vexations of the Holy Spirit; for after baptism we stand no longer in the flesh, but in the Spirit. Of these sins, also, we have the forgiveness in Jesus Christ through faith, and the consciousness of indwelling sin is our continual argument unto repentance and unto faith in the atonement of Jesus. But as the unbaptized, through believing in Christ, and through that faith having remission, do nevertheless long for the seal thereof in the baptismal covenant; even so the baptized person, though he believeth to be forgiven for the sins done in the spirit, as for the sins done in the flesh, doth nevertheless desire to have the seal thereof; which is given him in the sacrament, whereof the cup doth convey the seal of the new testament for the remission of sins. Those, therefore, who are burdened with their sins, instead of being deterred from coming to this holy table, ought the rather upon that account to be moved thereto, that this burden may be removed from their shoulders, for Christ is exalted a Prince and a Saviour to grant repentance and remission of sins unto Israel. He, the great Head of the Church, doth within the vail evermore present unto the Father His own sacrifice with His own flesh and blood, and doth ever give the seal thereof unto His Church without the vail, in the sacrament of the Lord's supper. And every one who is conscious of sin ought, with grief and sorrow of heart, to repent of the same, and so, coming to the table of the Lord, receive remission. Be assured that the great High Priest, the Prince and the Saviour on high, will grant first repentance and then remission of sin to every believer, by this holy ordinance. Now, out of this second idea, or doctrine, of the supper, arise some of the most constant and holy customs of the Church. For example, the Sabbath, as it is called, of preparation, immediately before the administration of the supper; on which day the minister is required to exhort the people to self-examination and forsaking of all known sins, to the forgiving of all offences, and the healing of all divisions; after which a day is set apart for solemn fasting and humiliation on account of the sins which exist in the midst of the flock. And in the apostasy, through whose disguises the forms of the primitive Church are easily to be discerned by the skilful, this point of doctrine is expressed in discipline, by their being required, oftener, I believe, than once, to go unto confession and to receive absolution before partaking of the sacrament,—all proving that remission of sins is considered by the Church to be of the essence of this ordinance. I have further to observe, that the apostle, when contemplating Christ at the passover, doth represent the Church as purged from the old leaven of malice and of wickedness: "For even Christ our passover is sacrificed for us: therefore let us keep the feast, not with old leaven, neither with the leaven of malice and wickedness, but with the unleavened bread of sincerity and truth." There is, therefore, in every administration of the supper, a solemn pledge given unto the faithful that their sins are forgiven; and, therefore, that day ought to be to them a day of joy and gladness, a feast, and a good day; and, like the Jews upon the fall of Haman, and the issuing of the king's decree for their release from death, the Church should have light, and gladness, and joy, and honour. Out of this most valuable doctrine of the holy supper hath arisen the abomination of the mass, wherein the priest pretendeth to offer up the true body of Christ, and to make atonement for the sins of all who receive the same. Most pernicious blasphemy, yet revealing to me a great mystery of godliness beneath the mystery of iniquity. The mystery of godliness is, that every time we administer the supper, Christ is visibly set forth crucified in the midst of us; and that every one who in true faith partaketh doth indeed receive the remission of his sins; and therefore right wisely hath our Church appointed a solemn service of thanksgiving on the day following the holy action. Wherefore, well beloved, I do entreat as many of you as groan and are burdened under the sense of your sins, to examine and prove yourselves in the sight of Almighty God; to confess and mourn over all your sins, as being done against light and against the Spirit; and to pray unto Christ, the Prince and the Saviour, for repentance and remission: then to come unto the holy table, and receive the most comfortable sacrament of His body and blood, in seal and in testimony that the burden is removed from off your shoulders; after which you may go on your way rejoicing, giving honour and glory unto the Father through the Lord Jesus Christ.

The third and last consideration by which the Lord's supper commendeth itself unto all the baptized in Christ

Jesus, is for the continual nourishment of that new life which baptism bringeth unto light. I consider baptism in the economy of the Church to be the generation of a new life, which seeks its nourishment from the great head and fountain of life,—that is, Jesus Christ, our risen Head. This life is quickened by the seed of the word which liveth and abideth for ever. And being quickened through the Holy Ghost accompanying the word, it receiveth strength and nourishment upon the body of Christ, just as the child in the womb is nourished upon the body of its mother; and if separated from that body by any evil accident, it becometh an abortion, and never arriveth unto the birth, which is the resurrection of the saints. Like as, therefore, the unborn child hath its being, hath the continuance of its being, only through union to, and nourishment derived from, the body of its mother; like as the branch cannot bear fruit except it abide in the vine, and continue to derive its nourishment through the root and stem of the vine, and falleth into decay, fruitlessness, and corruption from the time that it is separated by any accident; like as any member of the body cannot subsist alone, but doth straightway, when separated from the living body, perish, and corrupt, and return unto its dust ;—even so a baptized person who is brought into the communion of Christ's body, and, as it is written in our Catechism, graffed into Christ, cannot subsist alone, but hath his being only from the life which was manifested in Christ ; and he may not expect otherwise to live, for the Holy Spirit is not given to generate and support a life independent on or out of Christ, but to bring the creature which hath not life, but death in itself, into communion with Him who alone hath life in Himself. The operation of the Holy Ghost is not an independent acting of an independent person unto independence of being, but is the acting of a person who hath subordinated himself unto Christ, to the very end of bringing so many of the creatures as the Father hath given unto Christ out of that state of natural independence, in which, by reason of sin, we fancy ourselves to be, or rather really are; and to reconstitute them, to reconstitute all the election in Jesus Christ, even as branches are taken out of the wild olive, and graffed into the good olive, which is the Root out of Jesse, the Branch of renown, the true Vine, in whom and upon whom all the fruitful branches do grow, flourish, and bear fruit. Now, dearly beloved brethren, to express this union to Christ, this our oneness with Him, this our growth upon Him, this our life by Him, the holy supper is on very purpose instituted and preserved in the Christian Church. And the Holy Spirit, which the faithful have given to them in their baptism, doth, no doubt, without any exception, testify unto every man who hath been quickened by Him, that his life is not a life inhering in himself, or proper to himself, but a life wholly contained and invested in the risen God-man, and from Him propagated unto as many as the Father pleaseth to bestow upon Him; and therefore the Holy Ghost doth testify unto the Father and the Son. And when an ordinance is thus constituted in the Church, to the very end of signifying this union and dependence of life, the Holy Spirit will never fail to induce the child of Jesus to come unto this ordinance, in order to receive from the Father his nourishment, through the Son, by that channel of conveyance which the Son, ever obedient unto the Father, hath Himself instituted in the Church until He come again. And you may rest assured, my brethren, that if you have no urging and impulses of the heart towards this blessed ordinance, it is so either because you are not yet enlivened by the Spirit, or because you understand not the ordinance aright. If you are not enlivened by the Spirit, it ariseth from your not exercising faith upon the covenant sealed by God with you in baptism to give you the Holy Spirit. And all that I can do is to assure you of God's faithfulness to His covenant, and entreat you to believe therein, and pray continually of God to quicken you with His living Spirit, the living Spirit of Christ. But if it be ignorance of the ordinance, then have I this day done for you a minister's part, and do again explain to you that it is an ordinance for receiving spiritual food, in order to support a spiritual life. What bread and wine, entering by the mouth, and eaten, and passing into the body, do for the sustenance of the natural life, that same office doth the Lord's supper, spiritually received, for the nourishment of the spiritual life.

The great Head of the Church, who in baptism communicateth the Spirit to generate the life, doth in the Lord's supper communicate the Spirit to feed and nourish the life; and without this ordinance I believe He will not communicate nourishment unto the Church. I, the minister, neglecting it, or not faithfully receiving it, shall cease from my knowledge and utterance of the truth. We, elders, not receiving it in faith, shall cease from our love, care, and comfort of the flock. We, deacons, not receiving it, shall cease from our faith in God's providence over His house, from our care of the poor and the orphans, from our watchfulness over the Church's outward wealth. We, parents, not receiving the supper in faith, shall cease from our sacred sponsorship over the children of the Church. We, members of every name, who sit down at the table of the Lord, not partaking thereof in faith, shall surely fail to be nursing fathers, nursing mothers, tender brothers, tender sisters, kind and gentle friends, charitable nurses of the flock of Christ. And the whole body of the Church shall grow famished, sickly, pallid, diseased, vile, and corrupt, communicating from itself nothing but loathsomeness, poison, and death; even as hath come to pass in the places where this holy ordinance is converted into the most concentred superstition,—a very focus of hellish error and abomination. Now, I ask you to tell me, what such a mother, all diseased and defiled, can from her bosom yield unto her baptized children but disease, leanness, death? So completely doth baptism, the preaching of the word, prayer, praise, watchfulness, faith, hope, and charity, depend for their fulness and efficiency upon the holy sacrament of the Lord's supper, which is to the family of the Lord exactly what it names itself to be, the table of the Lord, the bountiful board from which the household are all fed, and without which the household pines and dies. Oh, let the thing speak for itself. What can a table, decently spread, encompassed with the baptized only, served by the ministers, elders, and deacons of the Church only, who being the greatest are yet those that do serve, on which table bread called Christ's body, and wine called Christ's blood,—what, I say, can this mean but this, that this spiritual family, this united brotherhood, this body corporate, is nourished and sustained by the power and virtue which God the Father hath given unto His own crucified and now risen Son? Truly he that runneth may read what is meant by the table of the Lord. A wayfaring man, though a fool, will not err therein. Like every other work of God and institution of Christ, it speaketh for itself, and needeth no interpreter. Would that men would look at it with simplicity, and interpret it with simple honesty! Then should they not err nor be easily led astray by the subtleties of the deceiver. Add to this the constant doctrine of ordinances, that no one despising the ordinance may expect to receive the work of the Holy Ghost therein exhibited. And how important, how unspeakably important, doth this holy ordinance become,—so important as bread is unto life, so important as a well-supplied table is to the life and activity of the household. Where were the father's sinewy strength, and where the mother's nourishing bosom, where the children's healthful happy hours, where the servants' patient toil, if the bread and the oil and the water of the house were drained? It is because the Church is stored,—the poor widowed Church's barrel is not, nor her cruse of oil, run out,—that the Church ceaseth not to bear children, to rear children, to present children perfect unto her living Lord.

Now then, beloved brethren, ye have heard in this day's ministrations a large discourse upon this precious ordinance, intended to remove all obstacles out of the way, to shew the peril of apostasy, of self-destruction, and utter perdition in which they stand who keep aloof from the same, and to open and explain the manifold great and precious advantages which come of the right administration and reception thereof. Take this as my offering of love and faithfulness unto all the baptized who have not yet partaken of the Lord's supper, and especially to such of them as the Lord hath brought to sit under my ministry. Suffer, I pray you, the word of exhortation, remembering that all Scripture is with me, and preaching, "for doctrine, for reproof, for correction, and for instruction in righteousness: that the man of God may be perfected, thoroughly furnished unto every good work." What I have done in my ministerial capacity, let us, the elders of the Church, do in our pastoral capacity,—let all the deacons and members of the Church do in their personal capacity, entreating, remonstrating, patiently instructing all the baptized who are arrived at sufficient maturity of understanding, to give heed to these most concerning truths, and to be zealous for the ordinances of the Lord. Then shall the Lord, the great Head of the Church, when He beholdeth in us such endeavour to do Him honour, come near to us with the sweet influences of His Spirit, send forth among us the sweet fruits of righteousness, make us the mother of many children, and the nurse of more: we shall live in His sight, we shall prosper in His favour, we shall advance in strength, we shall increase in number, and the gates of hell shall not prevail against us. Our sons shall be as plants grown up in their youth; our daughters as corner-stones, polished after the similitude of a palace; our garners shall be full, affording all manner of store: our sheep shall bring forth thousands and ten thousands in our streets: our oxen shall be strong to labour; there shall be no breaking in, nor going out; there shall be no complaining in our streets. Happy is that people that is in such a case; yea, happy is that people whose God is the Lord!

HOMILY IV.

THE INVISIBLE GRACE SIGNIFIED AND CONVEYED TO THE FAITHFUL IN THE RECEIVING OF THE BREAD.

LUKE XXII. 19.
This is my body which is given [broken] for you.

TO the understanding of this text, it is necessary that we should seek in the Holy Scriptures what is understood by the body of Christ, and what is the special virtue of its being offered for us. And to the end of ascertaining these points, no passage of Scripture occurs to me as more profitable than the tenth chapter of St Paul's Epistle to the Hebrews, where the subject of Christ's body and the offering of it is thus treated of:—Ver. 5, " Wherefore when he cometh into the world, he saith, Sacrifice and offering thou wouldest not, but a body hast thou prepared me: in burnt-offerings and sacrifices for sin thou hast had no pleasure. Then said I, Lo, I come (in the volume of the book it is written of me) to do thy will, O God." From these words, which the Holy Spirit putteth into Christ's mouth upon the eve of His coming into the world, we learn that His body is that human nature which was prepared for Him by the Holy Ghost; not merely the body, but the body in a living state—that is, the soul and the body united in one. To prepare this body is represented as the work of God, and to take it, as the work of Christ, to the end of His coming into the world, or becoming manifest unto the creatures in a creature-form. This body, therefore, or His human nature, is a new thing, prepared on purpose by God the Father, through the efficiency of the Holy Ghost—is, in short, the substance of manhood possessed and up-borne by the Holy Ghost. Now, observe how both the Spirit of God in the holy psalmist and in the holy apostle doth set this body—the taking of it, and the offering of it—in opposition to all manner of sacrifices and offerings for sin made under the law. You have heard the quotation from the psalm, hear the apostle's reasoning thereupon:—Ver. 8, "Above when he said, Sacrifice and offering and burnt-offerings and offering for sin thou wouldest not, neither hadst pleasure therein; which are offered by the law; then said he, Lo, I come to do thy will, O God. He taketh away the first, that he may establish the second. By the which will we are sanctified through the offering of the body of Jesus Christ once for all." Not, therefore, unto atonement for sin, yea, not even unto the pleasure or acceptance of God, were the sacrifices offered under the law; but only unto the keeping up the memory of sin, and the faith of a body most precious, which was about to be prepared for an offering, did they avail; by which body, prepared by the Holy Ghost of sinful materials, when the Son had apprehended and taken loving hold of the former types and shadows of it, which God had no pleasure in, and which were taken away, in order that His good pleasure and satisfaction might shine forth in this offering of the body of Jesus Christ, which He had prepared for Himself;—by which body His Son was enabled to become a servant, and the Father was able to lay upon Him and perform in Him whatever His pleasure was, and so to get His mind expressed in the sight and hearing of all creatures, and this is meant by these words, "Lo, I come to do thy will, O God." By the divided personalities of the Godhead, now manifested in separation, the Godhead is able, through its own device and energy, to make plain its own being and its own attributes; and this is the prodigious virtue of the Son's taking a body, that the Godhead, being thereby manifested as three distinct personalities, might bring its own secret purposes into light. None but the Son could do the Father's will, which He had from all eternity done, but in the incomprehensible mystery of the Godhead only; but which He is now to do by means of a body in the visible regions of knowledge, and comprehension, and feeling, within the limited sphere of word and reason. "Lo, I come to do thy will, O God:" these words contain the end for which the body was prepared and taken. He who was the Word to reveal the will now becometh a body to do the will: "The Word was made flesh." But in order that the Word might become likewise the doer of the work, He must have in Himself the virtue of the Holy Ghost also, through whom alone any part of the divine will is acted and done; and accordingly Christ's body is the Holy Ghost's containing vessel or reared temple; —a temple far more august than the work of creation, which fell under the bondage of sin, over which Christ's body triumphed gloriously. Unto this work of the Holy Ghost, created not out of nothing as heretofore, but created out of the fallen thing by the Holy Ghost, did Christ join Himself, that having in Himself both the word and the effect of God's will, He might for ever perform the same to all eternity, in the sight, knowledge, feeling, and experience of all things created and made. It is not a mere active or passive obedience in the days of His flesh to which the words, "Lo, I come to do thy will, O God," have their proper reference and application, but unto the entire counsel and purpose of the secret Godhead, which Christ in His body, and by the Spirit resident there, shall perform, and cause to be performed, by all created beings and existent things in the universe of God and the eternity of ages to come. But, amidst the infinite variety and the stupendous magnitude of actings upon actings which arise before the comprehensive and contemplative spirit, through the amphitheatre of creation and the endless vista of ages, there is one act in that body performed which the apostle singleth out as the means of our sanctification, in these words, "By the which will we are sanctified, through the offering of the body of Jesus Christ once for all;" which act is, no doubt, that very same to which the words of the text have reference when it is said, "This is my body given [or, offered] for you." This act, whatever it is and whatever is its virtue, concerning which we hasten to inquire, is, like all the rest, a performance of the will of God; because it is said, "By the which will we are sanctified, through" this act, "the offering of the body of Jesus Christ once." And I have no doubt in my own mind, that one, and perhaps the principal end of the agony in the garden, where Christ is manifested in torture and in weakness, through the access of His torture, to this very end of proving that in this act of offering His body there was such an abhorrency to His personal inclination, that He did, as it were, cleave unto it with such an excessive love, that He did part from it with such pangs and struggles of reluctancy, as nothing could have overcome but His knowledge that it was the will of His Father. And to put it beyond all doubt that the offering of His body was a part of the Father's purpose, hardly less important than the taking of it at first, He is made three times to declare so with an agony of acquiescence in that stern decree and sore commandment. Now, if we inquire what mighty efficacy there was in this act of offering the body, whereto the word of consecration in the communion steadfastly looketh, it is answered by the text before us, "we are sanctified thereby;" and more fully is it declared in ver. 14 of the preceding chapter: "How much more shall the blood of Christ, who through the eternal Spirit offered himself without spot to God, purge your conscience from dead works to serve the living God?" Now, with respect to the question how this act of Christ's offering His body upon the cross should take away our sins, though I have discoursed much and thought more, I am chiefly comforted by simply believing, upon God's declaration that it is so, and that it was His will it should be so; and I hope that the more firmly I am enabled to rest upon the cross of Christ for the forgiveness of sins, the more will God open to me this great mystery, and help me to teach you how it should be so, that the offering of Christ should purge our conscience from dead works to serve the living God. No doubt it was the perfect holiness of the offering, His offering Himself without spot, which gave to the offering its value. This is taught in all the sacrifices under the law, and especially in the paschal lamb. And wherein consisted the value of His spotless holiness? In this, as it seemeth to me, that He did the Father's will in all things on this side the grave: the Father at length obtained in manhood the end for which manhood was created,—the end, to wit, of fulfilling His will in the region of reason and of body joined together. This, doubtless, is in itself a great accomplishment, not to be undervalued because it occupied so brief a period, and was performed in so narrow a space. For brief as was the period, it was enough for all combinations of sin against the Holy One; and narrow as was the space, it was compass large enough for the encounter of all the powers of darkness visible, and darkness invisible. Oh, flesh itself was space enough,—existence in flesh, however momentary, was duration long enough, for this great controversy. How short time suffices for bringing sin, and death, and all our woe! It is not the time employed in the work, nor is it the amount of the work suffered or done, but it is the act itself of taking the body, and in it doing God's most holy will, which doth constitute its unspeakable worth. But I have not told all when I have said that He brought a holy, spotless offering to the accursed tree. There is more than this in these deep and solemn words, John x. 17 : "Therefore doth my Father love me, because I lay down my life, that I might take it again. No man taketh it from me, but I lay it down of myself. I have power to lay it down, and I have power to take it again. This commandment have I received of my Father." These words do raise into a prominent place of merit this one act of giving His life for the sheep, for which He declared the Father loved Him, as it passed all other acts of obedience, and took for itself an unrivalled place in the Father's estimation. No one will persuade me that the secret of this deep thing lieth merely in the sufferings and pangs of death ; and, I confess, I can rather tell where it doth not lie, than where it doth lie ; but my ignorance is no prejudice to the unerring Word of God, which I undoubtingly do believe. However, I do perceive, from this my text, that the secret lieth somewhere in this fact, that no power could take His life from Him, and that He himself had the power both to give it up and to resume it again. Yet, nevertheless, He was willing, at the Father's commandment, to do this great thing. Now, in reflecting much upon this subject, it looks to me to be best explained thus: that the Son and the Holy Spirit together did put forth their fullest energy of manifested and proceeding Godhead upon this living body, which the one informed with all His powers of vitality, and unto which the other joined Himself with all the strength of His cleaving love; the life was manifested in it,—it held, I may say, the strength of all life in itself. Thus the Son, with all the manifested power of Godhead, embraced it round; the Holy Ghost, with all the powers of indwelling Godhead, informed it throughout; and in giving this thing up to death at the Father's commandment, did demonstrate this grand truth, that the fondest love of the Godhead, manifested in the person of the Son, and the strongest energy of the Godhead, communicated in the person of the Holy Ghost, both concentrated to keep this body in life, were yet at all times, and in all things, and to all extremities, only serving the commandment of the Father. In other words, by giving that precious object of their mutual labour of love and life unto death, they shewed that all creation, even in its regenerated state, should be willing, ever willing, to go back unto death, if the Father commanded so. But by the issue of that death unto glorious resurrection and everlasting fulness of glory, it was proved that such perfect obsequiousness of the Word-informed and Spirit-possessed creature would always issue in the creature's own infallible exaltation. Oh, I do see at length the mystery of Christ's death and love—it is the abolition of sin, and the assurance of sanctified obedience for ever! Well might the Father make Him ever after the great trustee of the creature's obedience, when He had surrendered up His own body. Into whose hands could He commit the accomplishment of His electing purpose, but into the hands of this One, who had not shrunk from yielding unto Him His own elected and sanctified body? By that offering, He did in deed and in truth perfect for ever all them that are sanctified. "Though he were a Son, yet learned he obedience by the things that he suffered; and being made perfect, he became the author of eternal salvation unto all them that obey him." Such was the virtue of the offering of that body which is given unto us in the supper. Take now further into consideration what that commandment of the Father was, for which this subjection and submission of Father, Son, and Holy Ghost was made. As the giving up of life, their own proper work, this commandment was no other than the commandment of His holiness, that the soul that sinneth should die. Death is the wages of nothing but sin,—death is the grand sign of God's hatred of sin. This commandment, therefore, which gives law, and form, and punishment to the fallen world, Christ consented unto, not in the article of dying merely, but in the article of living in a body composed of fallen elements; but death was the seal and sufficient testimony of that great act of His obedience, that He did not shrink from the lowest abyss of creation, in order to prove His Father's holiness in creation. In this act of the manifest Godhead and the indwelling Godhead, surrendering that which they had won from the power and curse of sin, and giving it up to death because of its sinful origin,—in this act, God's holiness and hatred of sin was more illustrated than it could be by the ruin and destruction of all creation; for it is not the creatures, but the Creator, not the life-holding creature, but the life-giving Spirit, who make the offering unto the Father's holiness of this living body, in which they had set their strength, and by which they had achieved their victory over all sin. In Christ's death, therefore, in the offering of His body, the end of permitting sin in the world was finally attained. This end is to shew the nature of God unto the creature, by shewing the nature of the creature unto itself; to shew the holiness of God, by shewing the unholiness of the creature; to shew the grace of God, by shewing the undeserving of the creature. These, and every other end intended by the fall, were all accomplished to the uttermost in the act of Christ and of the Holy Ghost, yielding unto the death that body unto which they had joined the strongest love and mightiest effort of the manifested and indwelling Godhead. And thus Christ's offering cometh to be an offering for the sin of the world, or, in the abstract, an offering for sin. And from henceforth the Father, having effected the purpose intended by a fall, doth proceed to effect the purpose of resurrection from the dead,—the purpose of election from amongst the creatures, and regeneration of as many as He pleaseth to ordain unto everlasting life. And here beginneth the second part of our discourse—to wit, the communication or impartation unto others of that holy humanity, of that body which was prepared for Christ. And this is indeed the substance of the thing acted in the supper, which is Christ's giving His offered body for the nourishment of His Church. To this part of the Father's purpose, Christ maketh frequent reference during the days of His flesh; as, for example, "When the Son of man is lifted up, he shall draw all men unto him." But still more remarkable are these words, "Verily, verily, I say unto you, Except a corn of wheat fall into the ground and die, it abideth alone: but if it die, it bringeth forth much fruit." Let us then proceed to inquire into this great subject of the communication or impartation unto the elect of Christ's body. The expression, "Christ's body," hath in Scripture a twofold application: the one unto His personal human substance, which was born of the virgin, crucified upon the cross, and raised from the dead, and is passed into the heavens; the other unto His Church, which is in Him, and of Him, and not out of Him, but made one with Him, of the same substance of redeemed humanity; so much and entirely one with Him, as He is by His divine substance one with the Father: "The Church, which is his body." "That they all may be one; as thou, Father, art in me, and I in thee, that they all may be one in us." "For we are members of his body, of his flesh, and of his bones." "For the edifying [or, building up] of the body of Christ." "Even as Christ is the head of the church; and he is the Saviour of the body." These passages, which are according to the tenor of all Scripture, do shew us that God's elect are brought into such union with the Head, as to be of the same substance with Him, or rather of the same substance with that which was offered on the cross; for Christ is not any longer in that body which He offered, but in that body changed by the resurrection. Christ now subsisteth in a glorified body, having offered upon the cross the body of His humility. Now, in the supper, it is the body offered, not the body raised, which we receive: or, in other words, we receive that power of the Holy Ghost which enabled Him to subsist without sin in flesh and blood; and thereby we are mystically united to Him. He, however, is not mystically united to His glorious body, but hypostatically united to it,—that is, subsisting with it in one person. In like manner, He was personally united to His body of flesh and blood, united to it in a manner in which He is not, and cannot be, united to any person or thing. This, though it may seem to you somewhat a subtle matter, is nevertheless one of the greatest importance in the whole scheme of divine truth. To enter into which, you must understand that by all sound divines there are distinguished these three unions: first, the union of the three Persons in the one substance of the Godhead, which is called the divine unity; secondly, the union of the second Person to manhood, which is called the hypostatical union; and, thirdly, the union of believers unto Christ, wrought by the Holy Spirit, which is called the mystical union. Now, if you confound the two former, you bring the manhood of Christ into the Godhead; and if you confound the two latter, you bring believers to be equal unto Christ Himself, and so confound the distinction between the Head and the members; and, finally, if you confound all three, you make no distinction between God and the creature, and so destroy all worship, rule, and government, all providence, and all grace. If, then, as the Papists say, it is the flesh which Christ is invested withal that is here present and that we partake, then, indeed, I who have partaken it am one with the Godhead, by the same mode of union with which Christ's human nature is one with the divine nature, and there is no longer a difference between Christ's person and my person, and I may apply to myself or to the Church all the attributes, names, and works which the Holy Ghost, in the Scriptures, giveth unto Christ,—a hideous conclusion, which hath verily realised itself in the apostasy, by their claiming infallibility, lordship, merit, forgiveness of sins, intercession, and all other mediatorial offices which pertain to Christ, and to Him alone. I do not argue against transubstantiation upon the common ground of its contradicting the sense, because this is to give the sense too great a say in the matter; nor yet upon the ground of Christ's body being essentially local and limited to one place, because I know not well the properties of matter in the resurrection form; but I argue against it upon a higher and surer ground than either, when I say that I cannot be included in His personal body, without losing my personality in His personality, and being covered with the very honour and glory with which the God-man is invested. Observe, also, I am not speaking of the manner of the presence, whether corporal or spiritual, which we will come to speak of in due time, but of the thing which is present under the name of Christ's body: for present something must be besides bread, seeing we are to examine ourselves of our knowledge to discern the Lord's body. Having, then, set at nought the papal idea that it is Christ's personal substance which is present, there only remaineth the other idea, namely, that it is His mystical substance which is present,—that is, the substance of which His body the Church is composed. Now, let us examine this idea a little, and make it clear, which will be best done by looking upon it in the type, which type is Adam. Out of Adam hath proceeded the substance of all mankind; yet Adam is a distinct person from all his descendants, as they are distinct persons from one another. And what is it that constitutes this distinct personality? What but the act of God breathing into each one of us the breath of life, whereby we become living souls? This God doth in the person of the Holy Ghost; for all life is an effect of the Holy Ghost. It is not the word spoken unto our first parents, "Be fruitful, and multiply, and replenish the earth;" but the Spirit of God working in that word, and blessing the obedience of that commandment. For it is that same breathing of God into our nostrils which constituted Adam a living soul, that constitutes us likewise living souls. Our personality is not given to us by Adam, but by God; and, therefore, we are responsible to God for all the actings of our personal will. But our substance is derived from Adam: we are of one substance with him, though different persons. Now, from this turn to the Antitype which it was all intended to shadow forth. Here is Christ the second Adam—a person such as none was ever, nor ever shall, nor ever can be; being no other than the second Person of the Godhead—the Word made flesh. He, according to the Father's purpose, was appointed to be the father of a spiritual seed—the father of the eternal; ay, He received power to beget sons unto God. "As the Father hath life in himself, so hath he given to the Son to have life in himself," who quickeneth with eternal life whom He willeth; for He willeth as the Father willeth, and as the Father and the Son will, the Spirit effecteth. Now, according to this purpose of the eternal Godhead, the Spirit from Christ proceeding doth quicken a new life in God's elect ones. And as life is opposite to death, He doth quicken the life by mortifying the death,— that is to say, the substance of life, which we receive from Christ, doth act against and overcome the substance of death, which we receive from a fallen creation; which is a creation in death subsisting, yet not the second death, but the first death, over which Christ hath obtained power, and which, by the resurrection, He will wholly receive,—not in part receive, but wholly receive;—one part to the resurrection of life, another part to the resurrection of judgment, which judgment is unto life, or unto the second and eternal death. Those living ones, therefore, whom Christ begetteth out of the creatures dead in Adam, He begetteth by an impartation of that substance which He now enjoyeth in the state of redemption and immortality. But the substance which He communicates is not His own personality, His own self, but the Holy Ghost proceeding from Himself. The Holy Ghost is now His to give—the Holy Ghost doth now dwell in Him; and that which proceedeth from Him is the Holy Ghost. Therefore, beyond, and apart from His own person, Christ is only known and felt through the operation of the Holy Ghost. Christ, therefore, is in the elect only in the substance of the person of the Holy Ghost. The Son is not personally united to the elect; but the Holy Ghost personally doth dwell in them, as He also dwelleth in the body of Christ. It is the energy of the Son which claspeth unto and for ever embosometh in Himself the human nature; but it is the energy of the Holy Ghost which joineth, and, I may say, claspeth the elect unto the human nature of Christ. The Son doth not proceed from Christ, but formeth Christ by enfolding the humanity. The Son's is an act of love, dwelling, and resting, and rejoicing over human nature. He doth not Himself go forth; but He sendeth forth His human nature, the Holy Ghost, of whose substance His human nature is, as it were, the containing vessel, from which the Spirit proceedeth at the will of the Son, which is also the will of the Father, into and upon the elected people of God, who thereupon become members of Christ's body, and being taken together become the body of Christ. And when thus explained, you will, I think, have little difficulty in discerning the body of Christ in the bread and wine of the supper. We are of Christ's bodily substance as we are of Adam's bodily substance; and yet we are different persons from Christ, though consubstantial with His body. We are consubstantial with His body, not merely by our common holding of Adam, which is true of all men, but by a common operation of the Holy Ghost, which is distinct from His operation to create or to generate, and is His operation to create and generate anew. The energy of the Godhead put forth in creating Adam, is a different thing from the energy of the Godhead put forth in creating Christ; and the energy of the Godhead put forth in generating from Adam, is different from the energy of the Godhead in regenerating from Christ. The former is the energy of giving existence to the creature, the next is the energy of giving salvation to the creature; the one an energy unto a fall, the other an energy unto infallibility. There is no greater mystery, however, though there be a higher effect, in the one energy than in the other. And, as every one sees his unity of substance with Adam, and feels his distinctity of person from another man, so ought we to believe that every regenerated man is of the substance of Christ, though distinct from Him, and far beneath Him in respect of personal attributes and powers. So much for the distinctness of Christ from His body the Church, which, I think, the papal idea, that Christ's personal substance is given to us in the supper, doth subvert. Seeing, then, from what hath been said above, Christ's personal substance cannot be extended beyond Himself, and that He doth not include us, as it were, within the limits of Himself, and cast the mantle of His body over us; seeing, also, that it is by the Holy Ghost proceeding from Him that all redemption and regeneration is accomplished, the question, what is meant by eating His flesh and drinking His blood, is not of difficult solution, but doth signify our being made partakers of that special work of the Holy Ghost, which was exercised in sanctifying, and redeeming, and raising from the dead Christ's very flesh. That Christ's flesh should not have fallen into the same sinfulness, and remained under the same corruption under which all flesh of Adam, save Christ's own, fell and remaineth, is due to a power of the Holy Ghost, which then, for the first time, was put forth. How to designate this action of the Holy Ghost, or rather this finished work of the Holy Ghost, we know not, save by saying that it produced Christ's flesh and blood. As we would designate the work of the Holy Ghost in creation, by saying that from it flesh and blood of man arose out of dust, out of nothing, with all the thought, purpose, and work which flesh and blood is capable of; so say we that the second forthputting of Holy-Ghost energy brought out of fallen flesh and blood the flesh and blood of Christ, which prevailed over death and the grave, and sin and hell, and is capable of the seat at the right hand of God, and the superintendency of all created things, visible and invisible. That is, flesh and blood of Christ, which, coming out of fallen humanity, is capable of wrestling with sin and condemning it, of going to death and overcoming it, of rising unto immortality, shewing forth the glory of God, and bearing and upholding the sceptre of all creation. As flesh and blood is the word to describe briefly the region of the will and power of man, so flesh and blood of Christ is the word to describe briefly the region of the holy will and mighty power of Christ. And when Christ is said to impart to us His flesh and blood, and we are said to receive the same, it is verily and truly declared that we receive that energy of the Holy Ghost which put itself forth in His holy life and in His resurrection from the dead ; and we are assured through faith of a holy action in us, to the effect of bringing us out of our corruption and infirmity to the inheritance of His holiness and power. When I say that I partake of Adam's flesh, I do not mean that I am a morsel, as it were, of his very body; and yet I am truly of his flesh and of his bone; but I have upon me that same created word, and in me that same law of being, which Adam was the first to exhibit. So, when the Church is said to be Christ's body, it is signified that every one member of the Church hath that same holy law of creature being, and is destined to the same offices in creation, unto which Christ's flesh and blood first attained; of the same species, as they say, nothing differing save in this, that one portion of the redeemed creature hath been brought into personal union with the Son of God. Such, we conceive to be the right explanation of our partaking His flesh and blood.

Now, observe further, before leaving this subject, that the energy of the Holy Ghost put forth upon Christ, though one, had three manifestations: the first, from His conception until His baptism, during which He was placed under the law, and kept the law, and answered the faith of those worthies under the law who had looked forward to Him as about to keep it; the second, from His baptism until His resurrection, during which He was not under the law, but under the Spirit, and fulfilled such a holiness of grace, and not of debt, as we, under the gospel, are called on to fulfil; the third manifestation of the Holy Ghost's energy in the Christ, was in raising Him from the dead, and setting Him in the heavenly places, far above all principality, and power, and dominion, and every name that is named both in this world and in that which is to come. These, I say, were three manifestations of the same energy of the Holy Ghost, to sanctify the substance of the creature, rising higher and higher above each other, but all agreeing in this, that it is an energy of regeneration and not of creation. Now, this same energy Christ is exalted to impart to the election of God; but it is no longer imparted in the legal manifestation, because we are not debtors to the law, that which is debtor to the law being buried in baptism, but it is imparted first to work in us the life of Christ, conformity to His life and death, and, in His good time, conformity also to His resurrection. So that the end of the Spirit in this present life is to produce in His Church the redeemed flesh and blood of Christ, and in due time the resurrection glory of Christ. With respect to the question, therefore, whether we are made partakers of His passive or impassive, of His mortal or immortal body, we answer, of neither, so far as His personal substance is concerned; but so far as consubstantiation is concerned, we are partakers at present of His holy flesh and blood in the state before its death, to pass at the resurrection into the state in which His body now is. In as much as the origin of the gift is concerned, it proceedeth from Christ in His immortal state. He had not the power to beget sons unto God by the impartation of the Spirit until He ascended up on high. It is, therefore, in the power of the risen God-man, and as the great Head of the Church, that He doth feed us with His flesh and blood. He sits at the head of His table, in His present glory, and He distributes His gifts with the bounty, and precision, and assurance of the great God our Saviour. But that which He doth bestow at present is power to live the life which He lived from His baptism to His death, with assurance of being raised from the dead in the glory of His resurrection.

We do now, therefore, receive His redeemed yet mortal flesh and blood, to the end of receiving hereafter His immortal body. Or, to speak more correctly, being of the natural substance of fallen manhood, doomed unto death, as He was doomed, the Spirit, given unto us to redeem our flesh and blood, as His flesh and blood was redeemed, doth not remove from off our head the curse of death, but in comfort thereof assureth us of victory over death in the resurrection. These ideas expressed above do certainly contain the truth of the connexion between Christ's body and the believer. They are not given as an exposition of the words, "This is my body," so much as an exposition of the thing which these words point at. And now, when we understand what thing it is which the Church partaketh from Christ, we shall not find much difficulty in understanding the symbol by which that thing is signified to all, and sealed to the believer. And what is that symbol? A loaf of bread, homogeneous, or of one substance throughout, is placed upon the table, around which the members of Christ's Church are seated. This loaf of bread, the blessed Lord, by the hand of His minister, breaketh into parts, and bestoweth a part upon each of His members seated around the table, saying, during the action, "This is my body broken for you," or given for you. Take this action and these words, together with the action of all the Church eating all the parts of that loaf, and what have you represented to your meditative mind? The loaf was once one undivided lump; by the Lord himself it is divided into as many portions as there are disciples; and these portions are eaten by these disciples, and consubstantiated with their bodies, so that what was once one lump is now become living substance of many living men. This one lump, Christ calleth "my body, broken and given for you." Take this the name which He imposeth upon the bread, and what then doth the action amount to? It amounteth to this: that Christ's body given for us, once an undivided substance, hath been broken into as many parts as there be members of His Church; and being by them eaten, is now in living union with their living persons; or, in other words, that which hath before lived in one person now liveth in many persons,—that which once was the body of Christ hath now passed to be the nourishment and sustenance of His Church, and in them is a living and life-giving substance. Now then, let us reflect a little upon this action, and draw it into comparison with what hath been said above concerning the mode of communication of substance from Christ to His members. Christ calleth the loaf or lump of bread His body, given for us. Now, what was it that was given for us? Not, certainly, the immortal and glorious body in which He now subsisteth, for that He never will part with, but abide in for ever and for ever. If not the immortal body, then the mortal body of flesh and blood, in which He did tabernacle upon earth. This indeed was given for us. That form of subsisting He hath given up, —He hath changed it for one more glorious. But it was not after the manner of a bargain, gainful to Himself, that He gave up His life in flesh and blood subsisting, for a life in glorious immortality subsisting. Nay, He cheerfully, lovingly, and most meritoriously gave His life for the sins of the world, as it is written in that most memorable discourse, John vi. 51: "And the bread that I will give is my flesh, which I will give for the life of the world." He gave His life into His Father's hands, because His Father wished it for the manifestation of His grace in the remission of the sins of sinful flesh. He gave it, indeed, believing that His Father would not leave His soul in hell, nor suffer His Holy One to see corruption. And His Father, satisfied with the sufficiency of His Son's act in giving His life, loved the Son of man, and raised Him from the dead, according as it is written, John x. 17, "Therefore doth my Father love me, because I lay down my life, that I might take it again." The thing, therefore, which was given for us was His subsistence in flesh and blood. He took it sinful, He offered it sinless; and He bequeathed the redeemed thing unto His Church. The Godhead, when the fulness of the time was come, came forth together to operate in the fallen sinful substance of flesh and blood. And having perfected and completed the work of redeeming it through incarnation of the Son, it was offered upon the cross, and laid in the grave, but passed not into the heavens until the Father had invested and irradiated it with the mantle, with the being of His own good pleasure and glory. For though my Lord now subsisteth in a body, and though that body be numerically the same body in which He lived on earth and died, —be, atom for atom, the virgin's substance transfigured and transmuted by resurrection-energy of the Holy Ghost,—yet I would be slow to say that He subsisteth now in flesh. In flesh, changed indeed, He doth subsist; but what changed flesh may be, or may be capable of, passeth all my understanding; and, therefore, I would be slow to name it by the word flesh, of which such things as these be said in Scripture: "All flesh is as grass, and all the glory of man as the flower of grass." And again: "The flesh lusteth against the Spirit, and the Spirit against the flesh." And again: "In me, that is, in my flesh, dwelleth no good thing." If these be the attributes of flesh, I am loath to call Christ's glorified body by the name of flesh, though, as hath been said, it be numerically, and atom for atom, the very substance of the virgin. And this I am still the more reluctant to do, when the apostle, treating of this very subject, taketh the following broad distinction: "It is sown a natural body; it is raised a spiritual body. There is a natural body, and there is a spiritual body." True it is that Christ, after His resurrection, during the forty days that He abode with His disciples, said unto them, "Behold my hands and my feet, that it is I myself: handle me, and see; for a spirit hath not flesh and bones, as ye see me have." But this was spoken before He ascended up into glory and was clothed with His glorious body concerning which I am now taking the distinction. Besides, He was only addressing the outward senses of His apostles, to convince them that He was a body, a substantial body, and not a merely assumed shape. Nor have I any hesitation to call Christ's risen body flesh, provided it be understood to be flesh transfigured and transmuted by the resurrection-energy of the Holy Ghost that is signified; just in like manner as I have no hesitation to call my own flesh, or the flesh of other men, by the name of dust, from which, by the putting forth of the creative energy of the Holy Ghost, it did arise. But when I witness the difference between inanimate, inorganic particles of idle dust, and the soul-animated body of man, instinct with every sense, informed with reason, various thoughts, and directed by reason's high and sovereign power; when I further reflect how much more excellent and sufficient is the resurrection-work of God than His creation-work, I am filled with amazement and astonishment at the change which must have passed upon the body of Christ,—at the wide difference between His subsistence in flesh and blood and His subsistence in glorified humanity. But to return again to the very words with which He defineth the body, given under the element of bread. He calleth it, "my body given for you," "my body broken for you;" which two things can in no wise be predicated of His risen, but only of His fleshly body. Be it then on these accounts believed that the thing which is under the species or element of bread contained is the subsistence of Christ in flesh and blood, which is no longer a thing in being, a thing that was, but no longer is in union with the person of the eternal Son, and the question is, What hath become of it? where is it gone? and the answer is, It is given for His people; it is broken in pieces among His people. It still abideth on the earth, in the divided members of Jesus Christ. It hath passed from being one lump to be many fragments, which form the nourishment and the subsistence of all believers. Now, some may think that this bringeth us back to transubstantiation, or to consubstantiation; but those who deem so have only to reflect upon what was set forth in the former head of discourse. So far as Christ's fleshly substance personally united to His divine is concerned, we have nothing to do or to say, except that it cleaveth to Him still; and being changed, atom for atom, and transmuted into incorruptible and immortal substance, it passed into the heavens. Of this, I say, we neither are, nor can be partakers. It neither is, nor can be joined to any person but the person of the Son of God. It neither is, nor can be anywhere beyond the limits of the body of the God-man. It is transubstantiated into nothing. It is consubstantiated with nothing whatever in heaven or on earth, but abideth in its own hypostatical union with the person of the Son of God. But that putting forth of divine power which did redeem the flesh and blood of Christ from the power of sin, and present it on the cross, holy, harmless, undefiled, and separate from sinners, did not end there; because it thereupon wrought the mightier work of raising Him from the dead: for if it ended there, then there doth sanctification and redemption of fallen manhood likewise end, which, however, we know well is continued in the Church until now, and will continue until He come again. That working of the Holy Ghost in the flesh of Christ, whereby it was sanctified and became His body,—for without the Holy Ghost, Christ had had no body,—that mighty working which created Christ's body of the virgin's substance, and wrought in Him to uphold it against sin and corruption, and make it victorious over them, ceased indeed for Christ's behoof when He passed into glory, beyond the reach of infirmity and temptation; and it became His to bequeath in His risen estate, as it had been His to receive in His incarnate estate. He had that energy of the Spirit unto the redemption of flesh and blood while He abode on earth, in virtue of His faith upon, and exact obedience of, the Father; but when He ascended up on high He inherited it, in rightful reward of the work which He had wrought; and possessing it in Himself, He doth put it forth to work in His Church, in the Father's elected ones, to produce that same redeemed flesh and blood, sin-conquering, Father-obeying, which He first exhibited and first possessed. As His immortal body is His mortal body, atom for atom, transmuted and transfigured by a greater measure of the Spirit's re-creating power;

so hath He now the privilege, and faculty, and right in Himself to bid the Spirit go and put forth upon elect persons in flesh and blood of sin, and deliver them from the power of sin, and enable them to be flesh and blood of Adam no longer, but flesh and blood of Christ, of the second Adam; and so enable them, in flesh and blood, to overcome sin, and to please the Father. This is eating of His flesh and drinking of His blood, that we should receive another action of the Holy Ghost than creation, which is regeneration and renewal in the image of God; which action of the Spirit, being put forth first in Christ's flesh and blood, did give it that power, holiness, and righteousness which is recorded in His life. And, therefore, we are said to partake of His flesh and blood—to partake of His body, given and broken for us.

Now, though this exposition of the matter will appear to the Church in these times, which liveth mostly by sight of the natural understanding, to be very mystical, they will be, perhaps, not a little surprised when I inform them, that it is not only not sufficient for the Papists, nor for the Lutherans, nor yet for the Calvinists themselves; for what saith Calvin?—" Those, therefore, give me as little satisfaction who indeed allow that we have some fellowship with Jesus Christ; but when they shew us wherein this fellowship consists, they declare that it is in the participation of His Spirit only, without making any mention of His flesh and blood; as if these words of our Lord, 'My flesh is meat indeed, and my blood is drink indeed,' 'Except ye eat the flesh of the Son of man, and drink his blood, ye have no life in you,' with many more relating to this subject, were spoken to no purpose." Now, I say that it is the participation of the Spirit only; but unto what end? Unto the end of creating in me flesh and blood of Christ, of changing me from unholy flesh and blood of Adam into holy flesh and blood of Christ. What constituted the body of Christ different from mine, but that the Spirit was present in it under another law and ordinance of the Godhead than He is present in the fallen nature? Flesh and blood of man is made out of nothing, and is nothing but the Godhead putting forth its power according to its will. There is no substance of matter in itself as old as God, eternally co-existent with God, or in God; for God is a Spirit. Flesh and blood, therefore, which is matter's royal form, is no more than a word of the Godhead, effected by the Spirit, and continued from generation to generation; because the word of God liveth and endureth for ever, because what God doeth once, He doeth for ever. And what is flesh and blood of Christ, but the same nothing, subsisting under another and a higher word of God, under another and a higher efficiency of the Spirit? It is not that God, by the incarnation of His Son, giveth unto matter of creation an existence which it had not before; but that He advanceth it unto a degree and dignity which it had not before, but which from the beginning He purposed that it should have. And what signifieth He by the propagation of flesh and blood, under this new law subsisting, unto other persons besides His Son, but that the same new working of the Spirit was to reveal itself in the substance of their persons also; that is, of as many as the Father had chosen unto His celestial degree? So that Calvin's difficulty, as expressed above, ariseth from inexact ideas of the Spirit's work, which he vaguely apprehendeth as some influence short of the work of changing our flesh and blood into those of Christ; whereas this is the only work of the Spirit in the Church which I know of. He never worketh short of this,— He never worketh anything but this, to change us from unholy flesh and blood of Adam into holy flesh and blood of Christ. But this is a mystery so little understood, and so necessary to the understanding of everything besides, that I count it worthy to be opened a little more largely.

It seemeth to me, after weighing this controversy much upon all sides, that the real cause of the confusion and disputation would be removed, if men could be delivered from certain vague and incorrect ideas of the Spirit's work in our salvation, which many view as a sort of help and assistance derived from above, in order to enable us to believe upon Christ and obey His commandments. But the truth is, that the work of the Holy Spirit, in the regeneration of a fallen man, is not merely to help his faculties already existing, but to possess them all, and to expel from them the power of sin and Satan, and to renew the whole man after the image of

God, in righteousness and true holiness. It is not a partial, but a complete work: the delivering of humanity from the fall into the redeemed state. This you may observe in baptism, where the old man, the flesh of Adam, is buried, and, consequently, in the divine economy, can have no more existence. These would, therefore, remain a nonentity, unless the Spirit created a completely new man. Baptism doth not partially destroy the flesh, but completely; the Spirit, therefore, does not partially renew the flesh, but completely. We may not speak of the old man as living after baptism; or, if we do so, we ought thereon to ground an accusation of a broken covenant through deficiency of our faith. In the eye of God, and in the word of God, we are buried with Christ in baptism, our old man crucified with Him, the body of sin destroyed, that we should henceforth not serve sin; and if so, the work of the Spirit must be unto the generation, the quickening, the forming of a new man, complete in all human functions and faculties: otherwise, we were only parts of men, which is a solecism not to be found in the renewed creatures of God. The work of the Spirit, therefore, is not to help the natural man, and lift him up a little towards the elevation of God, but to take possession of, to inhabit, or, as the word in the original, "to take up house in," the creature, and to put to death all his fallen propensities, to crucify the flesh with its corruptions and lusts, and to keep them in a state of suppression, binding the rebel to the horns of the altar, and offering him up there, all our life long, a willing sacrifice;— to accomplish, in fact, that death and burial of the flesh which is signified and sealed unto us in our baptism; and, while this work is doing, and as it proceedeth, to quicken the new man, and to fill the soul and the body with holy desires after God's glory and Christ's service; and enabling us, as we had yielded our members servants to uncleanness, and to iniquity unto iniquity, even so now we may yield our members servants to righteousness unto holiness. This doctrine of the Holy Spirit's work is taught continually by our Lord and the holy apostles; is fixed in the very words, "new generation," "new man," "new birth," "child of the Spirit," "sons of God," "newness of life," "new creation;" and it is made the groundwork of all righteousness, as in this passage, (Rom. vi. 11-13:) "Reckon ye also yourselves to be dead indeed unto sin, but alive unto God through Jesus Christ our Lord. Let not sin therefore reign in your mortal body, that ye should obey it in the lusts thereof: neither yield ye your members as instruments of unrighteousness unto sin: but yield yourselves unto God, as those that are alive from the dead, and your members as instruments of righteousness unto God." It is a vain thing, therefore, and greatly to be discouraged, and to be treated as highly dishonourable to the Spirit, and derogatory from the completeness of Christian life, to speak of His common and His peculiar gifts—His common gifts unto all men, and His peculiar gifts unto God's saved ones. There is, indeed, a work of the Spirit common unto all, which is the work of our creation. That we are not inanimate dust, that we are men, capable of all the functions of living souls, is due unto the sustenance of God's Spirit. Thou takest away their breath, they die and return to their dust; Thou sendest forth Thy Spirit, they are created. For this work of the Spirit in our creation, we are all responsible unto God. And herein lieth our sin, that though created by Christ, and upheld by the Spirit, for the service of God the Father, we yield ourselves to be the servants of sin. And from this complete and radical corruption we cannot be delivered otherwise than as Christ's human nature was delivered—by the virtue of the incarnation of the Word, and the baptism of the Spirit. By virtue of which two Divine Persons, co-operating in their proper modes, the created man, which hath become the fallen man, doth become the redeemed man, in all the three cases, a complete man, and a perfect man. It is true, the redeemed man is not yet manifested in his glory and his might; but he is spoken of as such in Scripture, as sinless, and perfect, and without blame, before God, in love; and we are called upon to look unto this, and to believe the Spirit to be irresistible and infallible in His production of this perfect and holy man: "Till we all come in the unity of the faith, and of the knowledge of the Son of God, unto a perfect man, unto the measure of the stature of the fulness of Christ," (Eph. iv. 13.) "To the end he may stablish your hearts unblamable in holiness before

God, even our Father, at the coming of our Lord Jesus Christ with all his saints," (1 Thess. iii. 13.) "That he might present it to himself a glorious church, not having spot, or wrinkle, or any such thing; but that it should be holy and without blemish," (Eph. v. 27.) Therefore the true Scripture idea, with respect to the work of the Spirit, is, that He destroys one man, to create in us another man; that He destroys the flesh-and-blood propensities of Adam, to create the flesh-and-blood propensities of Christ. He undoes all that the fall hath wrought in us, by doing all that the Godhead did in the body of Christ. The Father by giving His Son to be united unto fallen manhood, and the Son by giving Himself and uniting Himself therewith, and these two, the Father and the Son, by sending the Holy Spirit into the virgin's substance, with which the Son united Himself, it was brought to pass that a body, sinful in its substance, was made perfectly holy in all its acts, passions, and operations. By the same divine co-operation of Father, Son, and Holy Ghost, continueth to come to pass that unholy manhood, sinful, fallen manhood, should, in God's elect ones, be changed and converted into holy, harmless, undefiled manhood, confirmed not now to the similitude of Adam's body, but to the similitude of Christ's body. For the Father, with what free choice He chose the virgin's substance to be first changed and converted into redeemed manhood, doth still choose whom it pleaseth Him, sinners like the virgin, sinners in and with Adam, for the purpose of shewing forth His regenerating power upon them. Then the Son, receiving the Father's mind, and hastening to obey it, doth accept of such a one, and fix His love upon him—love like unto that with which He loved the human nature, unto which he wedded Himself for ever. And forth He sendeth the Holy Ghost, bearing with Him the good-will and harmonious consent of the Father and the Son, who doth forthwith take up His abode in the chosen one, and make him partaker of the redeemed flesh and blood of Christ,—doth work in him "according to the working of his mighty power, which he wrought in Christ when he raised him from the dead," (Eph. i. 20.) Now, besides this, I know of no work of the Spirit, except His work in creation, which is not now under consideration. Short of this impartation of the body of Christ, I know of no influences of the Holy Ghost. I belief in no half measures, no co-operation between nature and grace, no mere helping of us to do this and to do that duty. I know only of the Holy Ghost the generator, the quickener, the informer of a new man in the likeness of Christ, flesh of His flesh, and bone of His bone. And therefore when I say that in the Lord's supper we do receive nothing corporal nor carnal, but the Spirit only, I fall not short of the mark, as Calvin allegeth, but am fully up to the measure of the stature of the fulness of Christ. And I do truly and really say, that in so partaking the Spirit, we do partake the flesh and blood of Christ. As by generation we receive that work of the Spirit which supporteth flesh and blood of Adam; so by regeneration we receive the higher work of the Spirit, which supporteth flesh and blood of Christ. And thus, brethren, have you the complete exposition, according to my ability, of the gift communicated unto the faithful, through the element of bread, in the ordinance of the supper, even the nourishment of a perfect and complete manhood, formed according to the likeness of Christ's body, and capable of the imitation and performance of Christ's life; and not only so, but having itself the capacity and the destination of an eternal and ever-glorious life through the resurrection. I pray you, therefore, as many of you as would understand doctrine, as would attain unto holiness, as would possess the same mind as is in Jesus Christ, that you would come unto His table, which is so soon to be spread amongst us, and would receive the pledge, the seal, the sum of that perfect and complete manhood, that ye may be holy, as He is holy, and perfect, as He is perfect, in all manner of conversation.

Before concluding this subject, allow me to impress upon your minds, dearly beloved brethren, what an unspeakable value there is in the holy sacrament, which, to the believer, doth impart such a gift as we have described above. Christ's holy humanity, in flesh and blood subsisting; not a partial holiness, but a complete holiness; not a partial strength, but a complete strength; the gift not of this and of that grace, but the gift of all grace, to complete the new man created in righteousness and true holiness; the gift of the Holy Spirit, not unto this or unto that attainment in knowledge, or in virtue, but unto the attainment of a complete man, of the stature of the fulness of Christ. You receive the regeneration, you receive the edification, you receive the salvation, of the body of Christ,—of that body in its holiness, and in its power against sin and the devil,—of that body after it had been offered, and attained unto the very good-will of the Father; and so do you attain unto that same good-will when, by faith, you partake of the fellowship of Christ's broken body. I pray you, therefore, to be stirred up with desire and with earnestness to long for the participation of this His body, and at all times to exercise such lively faith thereon, as shall bring you into the possession of the gift; but, above all times, then, when at the table of the Lord, you shall have the symbols of it presented before you, and the assurance of it dressed out by an ordinance of the Lord's own appointment.

HOMILY V.

THE RECEIVING OF THE CUP.

LUKE XXII. 20.

This cup is the new testament in my blood, which is shed for you.

WE now come to unfold the second part of the sacrament of the supper, which is contained under the symbol of the cup. The words of the text, which were spoken by the Lord over the cup, are reported by Matthew and Mark with some little variation. By the former, "This is my blood of the new testament, which is shed for many for the remission of sins;" and by the latter, "This is my blood of the new testament, which is shed for many." But by St Paul, in the 11th chapter of First Corinthians, it is reported in the words of Luke, "This cup is the new testament in my blood." These four accounts of our Lord's words, spoken on that memorable occasion, do agree together in these three particulars: first, that the thing conveyed in the cup is the new testament; and, secondly, that this new testament was purchased by the blood of Christ; and, thirdly, that it is conveyed to us by drinking of the cup. And to these three particulars, Matthew and Luke add two more, likewise of much importance, which are—first, that the wine is His blood unto the eye and lip of faith, in what sense the bread is His body; that the new-testament right and title are not only conveyed in the cup of wine, but that faith is to look upon that wine as the blood of Christ. Secondly, it is added by these evangelists, that this blood was shed for many, for the remission of sins. These five particulars do contain the great and most precious privilege of partaking of this cup, and they all depend upon the right interpretation of that which is contained under the name of the new testament. For the right understanding and interpretation of that which is implied in the expression, the "new testament," we must study together what is written thereof in the 7th, 8th, and 9th chapters of the Epistle to the Hebrews, beginning with the 15th verse of the 9th chapter, where the two testaments are set in opposition, the one to the other, and may be studied in the way of contrast: "And for this cause he is the mediator of the new testament, that by means of death, for the redemption of the transgressions that were under the first testament, they which are called might receive the promise of eternal inheritance." What the first testament here spoken of is, we are sufficiently assured in the 18th verse: "Whereupon neither the first testament was dedicated without blood. For when Moses had spoken every precept to all the people according to the law, he took the blood of calves and of goats, with water, and scarlet wool, and hyssop, and sprinkled both the book and all the people, saying, This is the blood of the testament which God hath enjoined unto you. Moreover, he sprinkled with blood both the tabernacle, and all the vessels of the ministry. And almost all things are by the law purged with blood; and without shedding of blood is no remission." This passage doth sufficiently determine the first or old testament to be that book of the law and ordinance of the ministry which Moses received from God upon the top of Sinai, and which he read in the hearing of the people, and confirmed with them by a solemn sacrifice, as you have it all recorded in the 24th chapter of the Book of Exodus. This first testament bequeathed unto the Jewish people, and unto them alone, a gift of the Holy Land, from the Red Sea even unto the sea of the Philistines, and from the Dead Sea unto the river; and assured it unto them against all their enemies, in quiet and safe possession, provided, and upon condition, that they kept the laws, and the ordinances, and the judgments, which are written in the 20th, 21st, 22d, 23d chapters of the same Book of Exodus. Of this testament, Moses was the mediator, according as we have it declared in the Epistle to the Galatians, chap. iii. 19: "Wherefore then serveth the law? It was added because of transgressions, till the seed should come to whom the promise was made ; and it was ordained by angels in the hand of a mediator." Here, then, have you that old testament, and that mediator; into contrast with which, the new testament, and Christ, its mediator, are drawn in the 7th, 8th, and 9th chapters of the Epistle to the Hebrews. Now, observe, by recurring to the 15th verse of the 9th chapter, wherein this contrast is placed, and what was the need of a new testament. It is there said that, under the first testament, there were transgressions unredeemed ; to wit, the transgressions of the ten commandments, and those other laws, on condition of keeping which the first testament was bequeathed. These laws were broken by all who were under that testament, even by those who had been called by the special grace of God. For that law, God, when He gave it, did well know that no man could keep, but doth daily break it, in thought, word, and deed. And wherefore, then, did He place them under such a law? Because He must ever express His own holiness for His own part, and for theirs He would shew them their transgressions, that they might take refuge in the promise given freely without law unto Abraham, and look forward to the great atonement which was to be made by Christ for all sin. But being placed under that testament with a law, by breaking that law they became excluded from the bequest of the promised land, and so are found at this day deprived of it because of their transgression. This I speak of the whole nation; but in the passage before us the apostle is speaking only of them which are called, or, as it is in the original, which have been called,—that is, the chosen ones of God ; as it is written, (Rom. viii. 30:) "Whom he did predestinate, them he also called; and whom he called, them he also justified; and whom he justified, them he also glorified." These called ones under the first testimony had transgressed against the law of that testimony, even as all the rest; but through the effectual calling of God, they had grace to look forward to the great Redeemer who was to come, and so they were justified by their hope from all things from which they could not be justified by the law of Moses. And so, when Christ came, and in His death had offered the sacrifice for their transgressions, they were loosed from the bondage of God's broken law, and so were at liberty to receive, not the inheritance of Canaan in their lifetime, which their transgressions had forfeited, but the eternal inheritance which had been promised unto Abraham, and unto all the heirs of Abraham's faith; and therefore it is said, "might receive the promise of eternal inheritance," in which expression, both the word "promise," and the word "eternal," distinguish the inheritance procured by means of Christ's death, from the inheritance contained in the first testament, which was not given under promise, but given under stipulation of law, to the very end that the condition being broken, the possession of it might be taken away—might be temporal, and not eternal. And I may add, in passing, that when the children of Israel shall hold their land by an eternal tenure, it shall be held under the tenure of the promise made to Abraham, and not the testament given to Moses. Now, before they can arrive at the tenure of Abraham's promise, they must be delivered from the transgressions done under the first testament; for God's law is perfect and holy, and when He hath put a people under it, they must keep it or they must die, or, not keeping it, they must be redeemed by Christ; and therefore I conclude, that whatever storms of wars the unconverted tribes shall yet raise with the Gentiles around that troublous stone of Jerusalem, they shall never come to sit down in peace, and dwell in it in safety for ever,—shall never receive it for an eternal inheritance according to all the prophets, until they shall have believed upon the death of Jesus Christ, whereby the sins done under the first testament may be remitted to them, and so they may arrive at the better standing of the promise of faith given unto Abraham. That land can never be held otherwise than in right of that seed in whose behalf Abraham received the promise of it. This is explicitly taught in these words of the Epistle to the Galatians, chap. iii. 18, 19: "If the inheritance be of the law, it is no more of promise: but God gave it to Abraham by promise. Wherefore then serveth the law? It was added because of transgressions, till the seed should come to whom the promise was made."

Now, then, observe, how from the above true and faithful

account of the first testament, and especially from these last words quoted from Galatians, Christ becometh the mediator of a new testament. If the first testament, or the law given to Moses, was given for the end of shewing forth transgressions,—that is, of shewing forth God's holiness in visiting His Church with the judgments which, from the beginning, He had purposed in Himself,—then, when Christ came, and by His death had shewn the sinfulness of the flesh and the holiness of God, by that demonstration which God had purposed to set up for ever, and of which all former demonstrations, such as the fall of man and the law, were only the preparations and the shadows; then there remained no room for them any more, for who desireth the shadow who possesseth the reality? which reality, God and man having attained unto in Christ's death, the first testament was removed out of the way, or, in truth, Christ having fulfilled the conditions of it in all respects, claimed it as His own of the Father, and, having obtained it in full right to Himself, He nailed it to His cross and crucified it there. Likewise all those called ones who, under this sore bondage and penalty of law, had lost all personal right to the land, and held only in the right of that Seed upon whom they believed, being now honoured and acknowledged by Him, whom they, by their faith and hope, had already honoured, He becometh their surety for the possession of the promised inheritance; and not theirs only, but the surety of all who had rested upon the promise thereof as given to Abraham. And because it was the purpose of God to take out a people from the Gentiles for His name, and not at once to possess the saints of the inheritance, it became necessary that the intervening time should be occupied by some instrument of God in Christ, and that the Gentiles in gathering should have some assurance made unto them of their full participation in the inheritance promised unto the Father,—that is to say, the covenant made with Abraham, for an inheritance unto him and to his seed, must undergo a change in its form, though it remain the same as to its substance. The form which it had, as given unto Abraham, was that of a sovereign grant and unconditional promise, without any requirement whatever from him, save faith upon the Seed which was to come. But now that the Seed is come, and hath purchased the inheritance, and possessed it in full right, it would be want of acknowledgment to His work and title were it still to stand as an unconditional gift of God. There was a condition in it from the beginning, but not of man's performance, but to be performed by the eternal Son of God; under the knowledge of which, God the Father promised the inheritance to all who should believe upon His Son. But now that His Son is come, and by incarnation and death hath performed the condition of the everlasting covenant between the Father and the Son, He entereth into full right and title unto the whole inheritance, and from henceforth, as His own possession, He must be represented as disposing of it. That which formerly proceeded from God the Father, must now proceed from Christ; that which formerly was given in the view of conditions to be performed, must now be given as the reward of the performance of the same,—that is, from being a covenant of promise, it turneth to be a testament of bequests. But it is the same thing, and the very same thing, which is given in the one case and in the other. The inheritance promised unto Abraham, the blessing promised unto Abraham, are the very same which are promised unto us, according as it is written, (Gal. iii. 13, 14:) "Christ hath redeemed us from the curse of the law, that the blessing of Abraham might come on the Gentiles through Jesus Christ; that we might receive the promise of the Spirit through faith."

Now, God foreseeing that after His Son was come, the covenant would change its form into that of a testament, and that all the Gentiles would be called under this testamentary form of His grace, did, when giving the Mosaical economy to be a type and shadow of the good things to come, cast it into the testamentary form,—the death of Christ, the testator, being prefigured in the death of animals, and the inheritance of the saints being prefigured in the promised land, and the believing seed of Abraham being prefigured in the natural seed of Abraham: and so it is called the first testament by reflection from the second testament; but, properly speaking, there is only one testament and the prefiguration of it.

Now, forasmuch as the figure or shadow is only for a time until the reality come, and was intended by God at that time to be removed, the promises were all made under conditions to be performed by those to whom they were given, that upon the failure of the performance, the former testimony might be removed without prejudice to, but rather with honour of, the truth and the faithfulness of God. Now, this is the key to all that is said about the first testament in these three chapters of the Hebrews; as, for example, (chap. vii. 22:) "By so much was Jesus made a surety of a better testimony." And, again, (chap. viii. 6:) "By how much also he is the mediator of a better testimony, which was established upon better promises; for if that first testament had been faultless, then should no place have been sought for the second." Better promises means promises without conditions, promises of free grace without a law; a better testament, because it is everlasting, and not temporary like the former; the only testament which is unto salvation, the former testament being unto condemnation: not but that even under it there was salvation, but a salvation which flowed not from it but from the covenant made with Abraham, which was fettered with no law. The former testament, so far from bringing salvation, did bring an obligation which no one but Christ could perform, and, in the absence of its performance, did bring a condemnation and a prevention from the inheritance which none but Christ could remove. And as I have said above, had Christ not died for the sins of the saints under the former testament, not one of them, no, not Moses himself, nor David, nor Daniel, could have come into the possession with Abraham, Isaac, and Jacob. And this is the meaning of the 15th verse of the 9th chapter: "And for this cause he is the mediator of the new testament, that by means of death, for the redemption of the transgressions that were under the first testament, they which are called might receive the promise of eternal inheritance."

Such we conceive to be sound doctrine concerning the new testament. And now let us inquire further concerning the substance of the gift therein bequeathed. This I think to be expressed in the passage last quoted by the words "eternal inheritance," and the word with which it is connected. The promise of eternal inheritance doth shew that it hath been promised unto those who were under the first testament, but could not be attained by them until Christ had atoned for their sins done against the law. Now, while this passage proves that the eternal inheritance was present by promise under the law, the passage quoted above from the Epistle to the Galatians, (chap. iii. 18,) "For if the inheritance be under the law, it is no more of promise: but God gave it to Abraham by promise," doth prove that it was present also by promise unto Abraham. Therefore we see from these two passages that the inheritance which we have from Christ, by testament bequeathed, is the same which was given to Abraham by promise. Now, what was it that was given unto Abraham for an inheritance? Read with me in the 17th chapter of Genesis, at the 7th verse: "And I will establish my covenant between me and thee and thy seed after thee in their generation for an everlasting covenant, to be a God unto thee, and to thy seed after thee. And I will give unto thee, and to thy seed after thee, the land wherein thou art a stranger, all the land of Canaan, for an everlasting possession; and I will be their God." Such is the form in which the covenant of an everlasting inheritance was given unto Abraham and unto his seed; which seed, be it observed, is distinctly declared at this same time to be not one nation, but many nations, for, in the act of making this covenant, God changed his name from Abram to Abraham: Ver. 4, "As for me, behold, my covenant is with thee, and thou shalt be a father of many nations. Neither shall thy name any more be called Abram, but thy name shall be Abraham, [that is, father of a great multitude;] for a father of many nations have I made thee. And I will make thee exceeding fruitful, and I will make nations of thee, and kings shall come out of thee." In this passage it is that the apostle perceiveth the Gentiles to be included: Gal. iii. 8, "The scripture, foreseeing that God would justify the heathen through faith, preached before the gospel unto Abraham, saying, In thee shall all nations be blessed. So then they which be of faith are blessed with faithful Abraham." This passage shews us also that our blessing passeth not the blessing of Abraham, but that we are introduced into the fellowship thereof; as, indeed, we are more fully instructed in the 11th of the Romans, in these words addressed to the Gentile Church: Ver. 17, "And if some of the branches be broken off, and thou, being a wild olive tree, wert graffed in among them, and with them partakest of the root and fatness of the olive tree; boast not against the branches. But if thou boast, thou bearest not the root, but the root thee." That is, we Gentiles support not Abraham and the Jews, but they us; or rather Christ supporteth us both with an equal hand, they having the preference in respect of time, we in respect of the clearness of the revelation. Be it so, then, that the inheritance promised unto Abraham is the same which is bequeathed unto us, we go on to examine what more is said concerning it in the Holy Scriptures; and we find in the 37th Psalm that the inheritance is extended unto the whole earth, which, indeed, is covertly contained in the original covenant made to Abraham: Ver. 9, 18, 29, "Those that wait upon the Lord, they shall inherit the earth. . . . The Lord knoweth the days of the upright, and their inheritance shall be for ever. . . . The righteous shall inherit the land, [the earth,] and dwell therein for ever." And again: Ver. 34, "Wait on the Lord, and keep his way, and he shall exalt thee to inherit the land, [or, the earth.]" This remarkable song is addressed to those who do not fret themselves because of evil-doers, who cease from anger and forsake wrath, or, in one word, unto the meek. And our Lord, amongst the beatitudes, doth, in one word, express the substance of the psalm: Matt. v. 5, "Blessed are the meek; for they shall inherit the earth." The apostle Paul gives to our inheritance a still wider range, even the whole creation, in the 8th chapter of the Romans: Ver. 17, " And if children, then heirs; heirs of God, and joint-heirs with Christ; if so be that we suffer with him, that we may be also glorified together. For I reckon that the sufferings of this present time are not worthy to be compared with the glory which shall be revealed [not *in*, but] *unto* us." Then follows what this glorious inheritance is: Ver. 19, " For the earnest expectation of the creation waiteth for the manifestation of the sons of God. For the creation was made subject to vanity, not willingly," &c. . . . . . "But if we hope for that we see not, then do we with patience wait for it,"—that is, "the adoption, to wit, the redemption of our body." This passage includeth the redemption of the body in our inheritance, and bequeaths to us in the redeemed body the lordship of creation in its redeemed state. Now, that no doubt may remain upon this our inheritance, co-inheritance with Christ, I ask your further attention to the 11th chapter of the Hebrews, where both the universality of the inheritance and our participation of it along with Christ are fully stated. The apostle, in the 4th verse of the 1st chapter, having declared that Christ is in His generation so much better than the angels, as He hath by inheritance obtained a more excellent name than they,—that is, the name of Son,—doth, in the 5th verse of the 2d chapter, declare what that inheritance is, in these words: "Unto the angels hath he not put in subjection the world [in the original, "the habitable or inhabited world"] to come, whereof we speak." Then quoting in the following verses the 8th Psalm, which putteth all whatever, visible or invisible, under Christ, he argueth that the brethren also, the many sons whom He was bringing into glory, should be altogether one with Him in that future habitable world which He is to inherit; nay, he goes so far as to make His suffering of death and humiliation for a while beneath the angels to be for this very end of delivering us from the bondage of corruption, and bringing us into the fellowship of His glory. Besides this I will direct your attention to one other passage only, where this our inheritance is declared to be now in the heavens, but ready to be manifested in the last times: 1 Pet. i. 4, "God hath begotten us to an inheritance incorruptible, and undefiled, and that fadeth not away, reserved in heaven for you, who are kept by the power of God through faith unto salvation ready to be revealed in the last time. Wherein ye greatly rejoice, though now for a season, if need be, ye are in heaviness through manifold temptations: that the trial of your faith, being much more precious than of gold that perisheth, though it be tried with fire, might be found unto praise and honour and glory at the appearing of Jesus Christ." In this passage two things are added concerning our inheritance:

the first, that it is at present in the heavens, which meaneth not among the stars or in the empty space, but in the invisible condition in which Christ is, and the spirits of just men made perfect, and the angelic hosts, being truly those new heavens and that new earth, and especially that new Jerusalem, the metropolis of both, which cometh out of the heavens from our God. The second thing added by this passage of Scripture is, that it is to be revealed, or made manifest, in the last time, which is also declared to be the time of the revelation of Jesus Christ. So that this passage being taken along with that quoted above from the Romans, we have these three contemporaneous revelations or manifestations: 1st, The manifestation of Christ; 2d, The manifestation of the sons of God; 3d, The manifestation of the eternal inheritance, which is the habitable world to come—Christ the heir, we the joint-heirs, and the redeemed creature the inheritance. Now, be it observed that a testament, a last will or testament, is, in all languages, and in all nations, and hath been in all ages, a deed or instrument whereby one person conveys unto others the right to his inheritance or possession. When it is an inheritance properly so called,—such, for example, as in the land of Israel, whose laws and ordinances form the basis and ground of the New Testament language and New Testament ideas,—then the inheritance, or heirship, descended in the direct line, from father to son, in the first-born. This forms the key to a good deal of scriptural language: for example, the first verses of the Hebrews; where the Son, in right of His generation as Son, is said to be appointed heir of all things, and to have inherited a better name than the angels; that is, the name of Son, in right of which He is heir. Moreover, into this name and degree of sons all the elect ones of the Father are taken by adoption. The Father adopteth us in virtue of Christ's righteousness, for He cannot adopt an unholy person; and whom the Father hath adopted through imputation of Christ's righteousness, Christ doth baptize with the Holy Ghost, which is not the inheritance, but the earnest of the inheritance, until the redemption of the purchased possession, (Eph. i. 14;) which is not the adoption completed, but the seal of the adoption, according as it is written, Rom. viii. 23, "Ourselves also, which have the first-fruits of the Spirit, even we ourselves groan within ourselves, waiting for the adoption, to wit, the redemption of our body." And having thus received from the Son "the Spirit of adoption, we are able to cry, Abba, Father. The Spirit itself beareth witness with our spirit, that we are the children of God: and if children, then heirs; heirs of God, and joint-heirs with Christ." Thus we come at a fellowship in the inheritance which Christ hath purchased unto Himself, through the free grace of the Father adopting us, through the baptism of Christ sealing us with the Holy Ghost; but, as hath been said, we have not yet received the inheritance, because Christ himself hath not yet received it, as the apostle declareth, Heb. ii. 8: "But now we see not yet all things put under him." How then do we hold it? We hold it by a testamentary grant; Christ hath bequeathed it unto us. But unto whom hath He bequeathed it, and how doth He signify this His bequest? He hath bequeathed it unto all the Father's election, whom He hath baptized with the Holy Ghost; and He doth signify and seal it openly by the cup in the supper of the Lord. This cup is the new testament, this cup is the blood of the new testament,—that is to say, this cup is that blood with which the new testament was purchased; that new testament including under it our redemption, the redemption of our body, and the redemption of the inheritance;—being redeemed not with corruptible things, such as silver and gold, but with the blood of Christ, as of a lamb without blemish and without spot. The apostle's discernment findeth in this language another force; which is, that it points out to us the death of the Testator, which maketh His testament irreversible: "For where a testament is, there must also of necessity be [added] the death of the testator. For a testament is of force after men are dead: otherwise it is of no force at all while the testator liveth." So that in drinking the blood of the Testator, we do, in fact, receive the assurace that this second testament shall never be reversed as that former one was; that there shall be no third testament; that there shall be no codicil appended to this second testament; that we receive in the cup the full fellowship of that inheritance of all things, which Christ hath purchased for Himself, in full possession, and which He bequeaths to those that overcome, according as it is written, Rev. xxi. 7: "He that overcometh shall inherit all things; and I will be his God, and he shall be my son." Observe, then, what we have made out under this first head: that the new testament referreth directly to the inheritance of Canaan, promised unto Abraham,—of all the earth, covertly promised unto him, and openly to the prophets,—to all things created and made, purchased by Christ. The inheritance is the object of the testament; but that inheritance includes a redeemed body to possess, as well as a redeemed world to be possessed. The seal of this testament is given in the cup. And to whom is it given? Unto all those who have been sealed with the Holy Ghost, born again of water and the Spirit. Therefore, with lively faith lay hold upon the cup which containeth such a regal dowry, such a princely inheritance. With eager faith, lay hold upon the cup; and, in tasting that wine which rejoiceth the heart of God and man, think of the eternal joy and blessedness unto which you are adopted as the kings and priests of God. Think of the time when your Lord shall drink the wine of joy new with you in His Father's kingdom; and be no more,—after ye have been thus sealed to an eternal and universal inheritance of creation, and of creation's various productions,—set upon the things of this present evil world. O brethren, having these treasures in the heavens, and having the assurance that they shall in due time be manifested, set not your affections upon earthly things, but upon the things that are above, where Christ sitteth at the right hand of God. And having in this cup, moreover, the assurance of a redeemed body, capable of possessing and of enjoying all these things, be not taken or captivated with the present enjoyments or recreations of the sense. Regard the flesh as buried, and bethink yourselves evermore of its redemption about to come. When pleasure presents itself at every inlet of the soul, remember that ye have drunk of this cup, which, for fading pleasure, hath insured you of eternal blessedness—blessedness, brethren, unto the body;

yea, unto the body, for which let our very flesh cry out, as in a parched land wherein there is no water. From the cross of this holy life, upon which the quivering limbs of the lustful flesh are extended, lift up your cry unto God, and wait patiently for Him; for you shall be redeemed from the grave, your flesh shall arise immortal and incorruptible, and the world shall be redeemed for a fit possession and inheritance unto your holy flesh, unto your redeemed body. And then, in happy society, free from the reality, free from the suspicion, free from the possibility of evil accident, of evil intermixture, shall we enjoy that jubilee which hath no apprehension of change, of satiety, or of termination. Thus blessed shall we be in the city of our God, in the new Jerusalem which cometh down from heaven; and we shall walk by the rivers of His pleasures with great contentment; and that world which was to us for a wilderness, shall be made to us for a garden more blessed than Eden. Oh, by such thoughts and meditations as these, dearly beloved, let this cup, which sealeth to you this inheritance, be exceedingly precious! Drink ye all of it; drink, oh, drink abundantly, O beloved! "The Spirit and the bride say, Come. And let him that heareth say, Come. And let him that is athirst come. And whosoever will, let him take the water of life freely."

Having thus explained what the new testament is, we come now to explain the important addition contained in these words, "in my blood," or, in other words, to shew forth and estimate the purchase and price of this new testament, which being well and rightly opened to us by the great Prophet and Counsellor of His Church, will add much to our esteem and love of this most precious token, the cup of the communion. The inheritance contained in, and bequeathed by, the new testament unto the adopted sons of God doth, as we have seen, include all things created and made. These things, according to the fore-ordained purpose of God, were every one brought under the bondage of sin and corruption, as we see them and feel them at this day to be; and through the corruption of the flesh and the fall of the world, the spirit of man, which by God is given to constitute a living soul, doth come into a fearful bondage of the flesh and of the world, in which it struggleth ineffectually, but cannot redeem itself, nor by any means obtain redemption. The earth said, It is not in me; and the sea, or the abyss, answered, It is not in me. But destruction and death said, We have heard the rumour thereof with our ears, because the rumour of that redemption was older than destruction and death, or rather death and destruction had the precedency in time, but not in effect. They were in being, they came into being, as soon as Adam fell; but they took not effect until they had heard the rumour of the redemption: before they drew their sword against God's fair creature, or touched him with their ruthless fingers, their ear was poisoned with the rumour of that wisdom and way of understanding which should destroy them both, and the might of their right hand was paralysed with the knowledge of their own death and destruction in the fulness of the time. Between the fall and the first stroke of death, came that rumour of death swallowed up in victory, of death cast into the lake of fire, in these words: "The seed of the woman shall bruise the head of the serpent." Therefore, the soul that came from God to be thus under the bondage of a fallen creation, was never left without a witness, was always treated by its Creator as a prisoner whom He loved, as a wife whom He fondly loved, and whom He would yet redeem from her thraldom. The love of the Son of God unto the soul of man was before the foundations of the world were laid, His delights were with her even from everlasting. A woful thing, a very sorrowful thing it was, that the soul which He loved from the depths of eternity should come forth to be thus oppressed; but it was the same sorrowful thing unto which He had devoted Himself in the fulness of the time: and, therefore, if the all-sufficient One, the eternally-begotten Son, was to undertake such a perilous voyage into the unredeemed creation, be clothed upon with its poverty, and weakness, and wickedness, and upbear its weight and load of rushing ruin, and pillar it up again in stable infallibility and glorious majesty,—then why should the created soul mourn that she should undergo the same passage, through infirmity and imprisonment, unto glory, and liberty, and strength? And thus are we sent, creatures of His hand, souls immortal and indestructible, into tabernacles of clay, whose foundations are in the dust, and which are crushed before the moth, to bear, through imparted strength of Christ, the rushing ruin of the world, that we may afterwards inherit with Christ its fixed stability for ever and ever. This bondage of the will or spirit of man is beautifully expressed by the ancient fable of Prometheus, as it is set forth in the Greek tragedian; who representeth this man, that had stolen or obtained, as it were, not in a full, but in a sort of insecure and fraudulent possession, the ethereal fire. This man, who, no doubt, is Adam, having in him a soul that once was free, but afterwards became bound, the ancients did represent as bound upon a rock, and his vitals continually torn by the harpies, which are the evil birds that would have taken the pieces of Abraham's offering, the spirits of evil which torment us with wicked thoughts, and vex the soul continually; and the ancients pictured the mystery thus: that aye as the heaven-born man lay stretched upon his rock impotent and tormented, the gods—children of terror and Satan, that is, of the earth and time, even the fallen powers of the natural world—came to him and entreated him to their captivity and to their inheritance; which is Satan tempting Christ with all the powers of this world. But aye the impotent and suffering man refused their bribes contemptuously, preferring to possess a will, though thus oppressed, preferring the consciousness of a will oppressed, unto all the glory and all the power which are to be found in the fallen heaven and in the fallen earth. Such is the true mystery set forth by the most famous of the Greek tragic poets, picturing out to the very life the condition of the human soul, of a reasonable soul, of a will enduring the bondage of all the creation, and groaning within itself, waiting for the redemption of the body, and meanwhile saved by hope, and in the strength of that hope preferring its bondage to all the power and liberty which is contained within the bounds of creation under its present laws.

Now, that new testament which was purchased by the blood of Christ, combineth, as we have seen, the redemption of the soul out of this bondage of the body and the fallen creation into the liberty, the glorious liberty, of the raised body and the redeemed creation. The question, therefore, which ariseth is, how the blood of Christ should accomplish this great emancipation, and secure to us this great inheritance. By the blood of Christ, is to be understood the life of Christ; and by His blood shed, is to be understood His life offered up. For, from the beginning, even from the time when the hope of redemption was given unto the first man, it was signified by the institution of sacrifices, that a life was required to accomplish the great redemption, and that a life in due time would be given. This condition of the redemption was continually indicated by the reconstitution of sacrifices at different times: even until the Redeemer came, God was never approached but under the sanction and protection of blood. Everything under the law was purified with blood, and without shedding of blood there was no remission. Now, observe how the apostle reasons in the 9th chapter of the Hebrews upon these ordinances: Ver. 23, "It was therefore necessary that the patterns of things in the heavens should be purified with these; but the heavenly things themselves with better sacrifices than these." And what these better sacrifices are, whereby the heavenly things are sanctified, is declared in such passages as these: "Neither by the blood of goats and calves, but by his own blood he entered in once into the holy place, having obtained eternal redemption for us," (ver. 12;) and, "But now once, in the end of the world, hath he appeared to put away sin by the sacrifice of himself. . . . . And unto them that look for him shall he appear the second time without sin unto salvation," (ver. 26, 28.) It was, therefore, the sacrifice of Himself, the blood of Christ, who through the eternal Spirit offered Himself without spot unto God, the blood presented to us in the cup, as being shed for the remission of sins,—this it was which sanctifieth the heavenly things themselves; whereof the tabernacle and service of Moses were but the patterns. Now, what are these heavenly things which needed sanctification of the better sacrifice of Christ? They are the good things to come, the greater and more perfect tabernacle, not made with hands, whereof He is the High Priest, and into which He entered to purify them by the blood of His own sacrifice, as the high priest entered once a year into the most holy place to purify it. Now, of what were the things in the most holy place the patterns? The Shechinah, or glory between the cherubim, was the pattern of Christ's own body, from which the glory and the word of the Godhead shall for ever shine and speak forth. The cherubim, between and upon whom the glory sat enthroned, are the Church in its golden purity, inheriting all dominion over the earth, both clean, as the bullock, and unclean, as the lion, and over the heavens, in which the eagle possesseth the supremacy. This Church, kings and priests, is standing on the mercy-seat, the monument of God's grace; and this same mercy-seat covereth the ark of the covenant, wherein the law lay enclosed, symbol of righteous government; and the rod that budded, symbol of royal priesthood; and the pot of manna, symbol of immortal, incorruptible nourishment, derived from an incorruptible state of the all-producing earth. These were the things in the most holy place which the high priest purified once a year, and these are the things in the heavens whereof they are the patterns—even Christ's own body, the Church of the first-born, the elements of earth and air, and all which abideth in and passeth through the same. These are the things which the sacrifice of Christ availeth to sanctify; and they are now sanctified in the word and act of God, and do only wait His good pleasure to come forth and be manifested, when the High Priest himself shall come forth and be manifested. Then shall the body of Christ, which heretofore was in the form and likeness of sinful flesh, be manifested in the form and likeness of sinless flesh; and the Church over which He is High Priest, the holy temple, built up of living stones, shall be manifested in its beauty unto all men; and the habitable world to come, sun, moon, and stars, and habitable earth, shall come forth in their new and perennial glory. These are the heavenly things which could not be purified by a less costly sacrifice than the blood of Christ, being the inheritance of the saints, bequeathed unto them by the new testament of our Lord and Saviour Jesus Christ.

Now the deep question ariseth upon us again, How should

the blood of Christ avail unto the sanctification and eternal redemption of the flesh, and of the world which was made for flesh? We have seen how the bondage lieth most heavy upon the human soul. We have seen, also, how, from the beginning until the coming of Christ, redemption through blood was foretold. And now the third and greatest question ariseth, How should that blood purchase redemption from that bondage? Let us consider the terms of this question. By blood is understood life: "The life thereof is the blood thereof." By blood shed, is understood life taken away. And when it is said over the cup, "This is the new testament in my blood, shed," it is signified that the new testament, the redemption of the body, and the redemption of the inheritance, are obtained by the purchase of the death of Christ. As it is written, "Redeemed, not with corruptible things, such as silver and gold, but with the blood of Christ, as of a lamb slain without blemish and without spot." Now Christ, inasmuch as He is God, can never die, can never change, but is the same yesterday, to-day, and for ever. Inasmuch as He is man, however, having taken to Himself a body, He can die; and it is, therefore, through the offering of the life of His body that He hath put away sin, as it is written, "By the which will we are sanctified through the offering of the body of Christ once." Now, then, the question becomes, Doth the offering of that body on the tree make an end of sin in the creation of God? I answer, not because it changed God's mind towards the creation, but because it allowed His mind to open and to unfold its everlasting and unchangeable purpose. The purpose of God from the beginning was to bring the creation into that state of perfect holiness and infallible blessedness, unto which it is about to arrive through the purification of the blood of Christ. The purposed method of accomplishing this was, from the beginning likewise, that very method which hath come to pass: to wit, by His Son's taking a body, and offering it upon the cross. Wherefore He is called "the Lamb slain before the foundation of the world." And if so that the end of God was a faultless and infallible creation, and the method of God the offering of the body of His Son, then all things must work together under the Divine government unto the attainment of this end by this very means. The creation of all things in the heavens and in the earth, and of Adam, lord of this earth, the palace of the universe, was not inharmonious, but harmonious with the method of Christ being put to death. Adam was created not sinful, not mortal, in the view and purpose of his becoming both sinful and mortal, to the end that Christ, when He came, might die; and, in dying, quicken all already dead, or yet to die. The fall of Adam was the bringing of all creation under death, to the end that Christ, when He became a creature, might also be under death. Death, therefore, had its perfect and consummate work in Christ; and if so, then also sin, for death is only the wages of sin. In Christ, therefore, behold and see the sin of creation concentrated, and the power of death likewise concentrated. Put, therefore, Adam, and the fall, and Moses, and the sacrifices, and the law, and the sin of all men, and all men, out of the question, and look simply at Christ made sin for us, made a curse, made flesh and blood in order to die. Look at Him, for the whole mystery of the question is wrapped up in Him. Suppose nothing in creation but Himself; suppose yourself an angel looking down upon this creature, and the question will be greatly simplified. Here are, then, in Christ, the Son of God, the soul and the sinful creation. In His flesh, the sinfulness, the devilishness of all creation, its mortality, its corruption, its alienation, its misery, its poverty, its wretchedness, all inhere and inhabit. And into this concentrated power of a fallen world cometh the soul. Such a soul as our souls, a reasonable soul, cometh with power of the Holy Ghost to quicken this germ of sin. And thus far the formation of Christ's body differeth nothing from the formation of Adam, save in this, that Adam's substance was not sinful, but Christ's was sinful; for in quickening Adam, a soul possessed with power of the Holy Spirit to quicken came to his body. Or look at it in Eve: a soul came with Holy-Spirit power, and took of Adam's flesh, substance, which it enlivened, and Eve was a living soul. So a soul with Holy-Spirit power came and took of Mary substance of Christ's body, and quickened it, and Christ was a living soul. Each being the same creation-act, with this only difference that the one was an act upon a creation unfallen and sinless, the other upon a creation fallen and full of sin. To this human nature, thus creation-wise composed, the eternal Son unites Himself, and imposeth upon it the honour of His own personality; that is, through it He acteth, in it He is seen, through it He looketh, by it He speaketh. And thus the strength of God, in the person of His Son, and the strength of sin, and the strength of death, and the strength of corruption, and, in one word, the strength of creation fallen and sinful, sun, moon, and stars, and fallen angels,—in one word, the strength of Satan,—come into diametrical opposition, direct controversy, closest strife, who shall win that soul—whether the Son of God shall prevail to redeem it, or Satan and his powers, visible and invisible, shall prevail to bind it. One sin, and all is over; one rebellious wish of that soul, and all is lost: Satan hath made good his usurpation, and the soul, reason, the human will, is bound for ever. But, otherwise, let every wish, and every thought, and every act of that soul be harmonious with God, and averse from evil, and the soul is redeemed for ever. This is the nature of the work which Christ wrought in the flesh, and in which He prevailed. The ignorant and foolish men who will not hear of the sinfulness of His flesh, but will put some difference of some kind or other —whether understood by themselves or not understood, God knows—between His flesh and ours, do merely make redemption void, and Christ's work void, for fear they should defile Him by the wicked thing which He laid hold on to prove His strength and holiness to be greater than its weakness and wickedness. When God had thus proved, in the person of His Son, that He was the almighty and the all-holy One, and that the devil was but a tool of His, and the creation but a lump of clay in the potter's hand, and the soul of man His own chosen vessel, reason His own temple, for the Godhead to inherit, to inhabit, to illuminate, to inform,—what further did He with His Christ but proceed, through Him, to execute the original device and purpose of an infallible and glorious creation, by the method which He had purposed within Himself of taking the life of His Son? Not the life of the soul; nay, for the soul, always immortal, is now, above all measure, glorified to be the Life-giver, the Life of life; but to give unto that soul, now redeemed, a worthy tent wherein to abide, to change the state of the body, and to glorify it, and with it to change and glorify the body's dependent materialism, which is, the earth its footstool, the air its breath, the light its element of vision, the world its domain. These, the Father had purposed should become infallible, sinless. And now that His Son is cut off by death, without a spot, perfectly holy, the Father can have His will accomplished without offence unto His holiness; and Christ's body may pass into the infallible state. If Adam could have come by death without sinning, Adam might have passed into the infallible state; but this could not be, therefore Adam and all creatures lay in the corrupt state until One should come who could die though He had not sinned. And why die? what the importance of death in the purpose of God? Vast importance—all important. And why so? That creation might be proved to itself to be nothing but dust; that the future rulers of creation, the destined lords of the universe, might, by dying, know that the soul in itself hath no power to give life, or preserve life when given, and, knowing this, might be able to govern all, and to teach all, in whom is life, from whom is breath, and all things. This is the importance of death, and, therefore, death must supervene upon the creation before resurrection supervenes; fallibility must be proved before infallibility be given, This was the purpose, this the commandment of the Father; and, therefore, Christ died. But Christ, being sinless, died not for His own sin, but for His Father's glory, in the putting away of all sin. His death is the great act of grace unto the creation, as the fall was the great act of holiness unto the creation. And what grace, say you, in putting the guiltless One to death? The guiltless One was willing to go to death, for His Father's great ends. Learn thou to be likewise willing. Demonstration of the Father's grace, I say, by putting away sin and fallibility from the creation altogether, and communicating to it sinlessness and infallibility. Askest thou, How, and where? In the resurrection of that body which, as I told thee, was the concentrated infirmity, mortality, and sinfulness of creation. In changing this, the Father changed all, for nothing in its essence or substance is worse than this. And if the Father sheweth His power in changing this, it is law to all the rest. All the rest may look for this change unto infallibility and blessedness through the grace and the power of God; and if all receive it not, the not receiving of it ariseth out of some other thing posterior in the purpose of God. I say posterior, not in time, but in purpose. Hell, and those who shall inhabit it for ever, form another mystery, having its origin in the pre-supposition of this universal grace and power of God. It is the manifestation, not of a power resident in the devil, or in the flesh, or in creation, or in death, or in corruption, which have all been vanquished and are effete, and, I may say, annihilated, by the grace and power of God; but it is the manifestation of a power resident in the soul itself, and demonstrative of the terrible grandeur of its being, by the terrible potency which it hath within itself of setting at naught not only creation-power, as the angels did, but redemption and resurrection powers. The very great capacities of that form of being which God was to take for His own created substance must be proved; and it is proved by its power to set itself up against God and its own salvation, when all the angelic wickednesses and all the material wickednesses have been put, as we may say, out of the controversy, and God's own Son and Spirit superadded on the side of its salvation. But this our rejection of Christ is a subject of such great depth, and the everlasting consequences are of such an awful kind, that I cannot do more in this place than merely to look at them as I have done, and pass on to the further consideration of the redemption by the blood of Christ. The thing which is redeemed is the soul of man, and the bondage from which it is redeemed is the bondage of a fallen and sinful body, with which the world, depending from it, hath likewise become fallen and sinful. The way in which it is redeemed from this bondage of a sinful nature is by Christ taking upon Him that very nature, in that very state of sinfulness, and triumphing over and against all its evil conditions; and having brought it into a holy state, so offering it unto His Father, to do with it according to His mind, who doth require of His Son to pour out its life, and leave it in the Father's hand, to do with it according to His will. And the Father, taking the redeemed thing, which not only hath not sinned, but hath prevailed against all sin, doth make it the seed of a redeemed world, doth prevent it from seeing corruption, doth raise it from the dead, incorruptible and immortal, doth place it at His own right hand, united unto the Divinity for ever; and doth constitute the redeemed soul, quickening the redeemed body of Christ, the great second nature of His eternal Son, in which His person may gloriously appear, and through which His will may be effectively acted in all, and upon all. Jesus, the redeemed One, becometh the Redeemer in virtue of His most precious death, the great price which purchased the inheritance. And in virtue of His resurrection, installation, and investiture with immortality and incorruption at God's right hand, He doth become the Administrator of that universal estate which He hath purchased by His death,—the Dispenser of resurrection gifts,—the Mediator between the Father and His elect ones, receiving gifts for men, and bestowing them upon men,— the great Baptist and Sealer with the Holy Ghost,—the great Head of God's elect in heaven and on earth, giving unto some apostles, unto some prophets, unto some evangelists, unto some pastors and teachers, for the perfecting of the saints, for the work of the ministry, for the edifying of the body of Christ,—the great Intercessor and Advocate with the Father, interceding for the sins which are continually committed, repented of, and confessed by His Church on earth, and advocating in the court of the eternal Father the various petitions, prayers, and intercessions which His Church in flesh is continually making unto the God and Father of her Lord and Saviour Jesus Christ. In one word, being now the great Head of the Church, and being yet about to be the great effecter, as He hath been the great purchaser, of the universal redemption, He it is through whom the Father shall put down all rule, and authority, and power; He it is, and no other, who shall in person come to effect that great redemption of the Church whereto we look with outstretched necks, and for which we pray with uplifted hands,—to break the bonds of wicked kings and raging peoples,—to become terrible unto the kings of the earth, to rule them with a rod of iron, and dash them in pieces like a potter's vessel. And to this it is that the apostle Paul looketh as the time at which all Israel shall be saved, as it is written in the prophet Isaiah: "And the Redeemer shall come to Zion, and unto them that turn from transgression in Jacob, saith the Lord." This is the great breaking of bonds, opening of prison doors, and setting of captives free, unto which the prophets constantly looked; when the yoke of the Assyrians shall be broken, and the two-leaved gates of Babylon shall be thrown wide open; when also the groaning creature shall be redeemed from its bondage of corruption, and the dust, the sacred dust of His saints, shall arise incorruptible, and the government shall be upon His shoulders, and He shall be called Wonderful, Counsellor, The mighty God, The everlasting Father, The Prince of Peace. But still there shall be bondsmen and bondage likewise, even those who heretofore possessed the wicked and usurped dominion,—Satan and his angels in the bottomless pit, and the bodies of the wicked in the loathsome grave, whom haply, whose vile and polluted dust haply, the purified earth shall have ejected from her bosom into that place of the carcases of wicked men, whereto such frequent allusion is made in the holy prophets. Slaves and bondsmen indeed there shall be during the season of the millennial kingdom, wherein the enemies of Christ shall be made His footstool, and under His feet the head of the serpent shall lie bruised in the dust. This great effecting of the redemption, which we believe in, is a different mystery from the purchasing of the redemption, in which we also believe: the former is the acting of faith prospectively, the latter is the acting of faith retrospectively. The one, even the purchase, we have received; the other, even the effecting of the redemption, we believe to receive at the coming of the Lord to judge the quick, to raise the saints, and to deliver the earth and the air from Satan's bondage. Therefore it is that the coming of the Redeemer is fixed by the apostle at the time when the fulness of the Gentiles have come in, and all Israel are about to be saved; therefore it is that he saith in another place, that "we groan within ourselves, even we which have the first-fruits of the Spirit, waiting for the redemption of the body." And in another place: "After that ye believed, ye were sealed with that Holy Spirit of promise, which is the earnest of our inheritance until the redemption of the purchased possession." And in another place: "Grieve not the Holy Spirit of God, whereby ye are sealed unto the day of redemption."

HOMILY VI.

THE INVISIBLE GRACE SIGNIFIED AND CONVEYED TO THE
FAITHFUL IN THE RECEIVING OF THE CUP.

MATT. XXVI. 27, 28.

*And he took the cup, and gave thanks, and gave it to them, saying, Drink ye all
of it: for this is my blood of the new testament, which is shed for many for
the remission of sins.*

IN a former homily upon the signification of the Lord's supper, we explained the meaning of the words, "This is the new testament in my blood;" shewing at large how that which to Abraham was given as a free promise, became in the time of Moses burdened with conditions of a law, and that a law which no mere man in this life is able to keep: to the end that when the man Christ Jesus should come and fulfil all righteousness, He might in His own right claim the inheritance from which all the rest under the Old Testament were prevented by their sins; and, receiving it, might shew forth His love unto the elect ones of the Father by freely bestowing upon them, without any condition, the fellowship of the inheritance which He had purchased. Without repeating anything which we have already said upon this subject, we now proceed to unfold the spiritual grace which is conveyed unto the faithful under the symbol of the cup of wine; for every sacrament, besides the outward sign, containeth an inward and invisible grace. Over the cup these words are pronounced, "This is the blood of the new testament." Two questions arise hereupon: first, What is meant by the blood of the new testament? and, secondly, What is meant by its being in the cup? Now, with respect to the first of these questions, upon which the second turns, we have much to say, derived chiefly from the Epistle to the Hebrews. When

Moses had received from God the substance of the old testament, he came down from the mount, intrusted by God, on His behalf, to confirm it with the people. The people had entreated to be spoken with through a mediator, and for that office had made choice of Moses. God accepted Moses, and intrusted him with all the words of the testament. But before the people could be made possessors of it, so as to call it their own, and claim under it, it was necessary that victims should be slain, in the blood of which the solemn pact was stricken between God and them, as it is written, (Heb. ix. 19:) "For when Moses had spoken every precept to all the people according to the law, he took the blood of calves and of goats, with water, and scarlet wool, and hyssop, and sprinkled both the book, and all the people, saying, This is the blood of the testament which God hath enjoined unto you." From this is derived the word, "This is the blood of the new testament," or, "This is the new testament in my blood," spoken over the cup; which signifies, that the testament which Christ hath obtained for us is valid only in His blood; that though, by His perfect obedience to the law, He became rightful heir of all bequeathed in the old testament, upon the condition of perfect obedience, we, who were disobedient, could not attain unto the fellowship thereof otherwise than by His death; that as the old testament which Moses had received on the mount became extended to the people through the sprinkling of blood, both upon the book which contained it, and upon the people who received it, so the new testament, which for Himself, without a death, Christ by perfect righteousness had obtained, is obtained for others only by the purification of His blood passing upon that which containeth the testament, and upon those who receive it. Now, what is it that containeth the testament, as the book which Moses sprinkled contained the old testament? that is to say, what is the thing sprinkled with blood? and who are the people sprinkled with blood of the sacrifice of Christ? The thing sprinkled with blood of the sacrifice of Christ is contained in these words, (Heb. ix. 23:) "It was therefore necessary that the patterns of things in the heavens should be purified with these; but the heavenly things themselves with better sacrifices than these." These heavenly things, then, whatever they be, are the things purified by the blood of Christ. And what are these heavenly things? Not certainly the angels, or the archangels, nor the sun, moon, and stars, but that kingdom and inheritance which is now reserved in the heavens, and which is to be manifested in the last times for us,—that new Jerusalem which cometh down out of heaven,—those things which God hath prepared for them that love Him, which eye hath not seen, nor ear heard, neither hath the heart of man conceived;—the inheritance of this world, in its regenerated or heavenly form, which was promised unto Abraham, and the inhabitation of the New Jerusalem, until the earth itself be delivered from the bondage of corruption and death. And how did the blood of Christ purify these? The blood of Christ did not make any alteration on God's original purpose, that creation should at length come to a glorious and immortal state, but it was the great mean to that end. And how was the death of Christ the mean towards the regeneration of the world? Because, in His death, God's hatred to a sinful creation was amply, sufficiently, and is for ever sufficiently, demonstrated. God shewed, by putting His own Son to death, that holiness is beyond everything in the Divine mind. Christ had called that body His own, He had embraced it in His person, He had taken it into union with His divine nature for ever. No union, then, no love, no fellowship, is there like that between the two natures of Christ, which one personality for ever embraceth; and surely no love nor unity is there like that between the Father and the Son, which, being embraced in the infinity and eternity of the Divine Being, no creature is able to discourse of. Yet both these fastest concentrations of love were suspended in the death of Christ. His person parted with a portion of itself; and the Father struck off this separated part, all because it was a portion of the sinful creation; wherein, I say, the holiness of God had a supreme exaltation beyond all conception and utterance. His hatred, His inalienable hatred, towards the sin-possessed creature, is likewise most wonderfully exemplified. If anything could have preserved sinful flesh from suffering and dying, surely its having been taken into the person of the eternal Son would have prevailed to do so; which, not being permitted, it is proved beyond all contradiction that God loves nothing so well as His own holiness. After this, all minor inflictions are, as it were, of no import; and therefore God, having told out the sum total of His hatred to a sinful creation, and placed His holiness beyond all imputation or infringement, He doth straightway proceed to His ulterior purpose of bringing from the womb of the fallen creation the heavenly thing; beginning the work upon that very body of Christ which had exhibited and borne the weight of His wrath and indignation against the fallen, earthly things. The first of the heavenly things, then, which are purged with better sacrifices is the body of Christ itself; which, had it not died for sin,—had it not exhausted the indignation upon sin,—had it not borne the penalty of all sin,—would never, no, never, have risen again: but because He brought in eternal redemption to the creature, He therefore obtained eternal life to Himself—that is, His body—and to the creatures. Hell is another mystery, which holdeth of a deeper root than the fall. The evil of the fall accumulated and accumulated, until it spent itself and exhausted itself in slaying Christ, in whom all are made alive. And thus it is that the blood of Christ, or the death of Christ, cleanseth the material creation which hath no consciousness,—that is, our bodies, and the fallen earth, and fallen heavens,—by opening the way for God to carry His purpose into effect, without any, the least, sacrifice of His holiness. It was as much an original purpose of God that man should rise from the dead and the world be regenerate, as it was that man should fall and the world be degenerate. But when sin had brought in the one, the other could not be brought in until the foundation-stone of it should be laid in perfect holiness. The sinful world in passing away must leave behind it a stone of memorial; and upon this stone of memorial, as a basis, must the regenerate world be built. That stone of memorial is the body of Christ, which was dead, and is alive again. Christ will ever be remembered as Him that was born out of death. He is the child of the resurrection, the first-born from the dead. "I have been dead," is written upon His forehead;

and that writing is the emblazonry of God's holiness. "I was dead, and God is most holy;" and, forasmuch as He is the basis of the new creation, and its supporting Head, it doth, as it were, lie between these two extremes, whereon are written, "God is holy, God is holy." And this is the meaning of the heavenly things being purged with better sacrifices than these.

And now we come to examine how the blood of Christ, that is, His death, should be made available, not only to the restitution of all things, but likewise to the purging of the soul or conscience of man from the defilement of sin. "This is the new testament in my blood, shed for the remission of the sins of many." It is true of the soul as of every other creature, that God, from the beginning, did purpose that it should be regenerate and holy, as surely as that it should fall;—the very end of election being that it might be holy and blameless before Him in love; and forasmuch as the soul had sinned, and was indeed the origin of the sin, it was as necessary to its regeneration and blessedness that the death of Christ should intervene, as in the case of every other creature: God's holiness must be justified, before His grace can appear unto the sinful. The death of Christ, therefore, hath as much to do with the redemption of the soul, as with the redemption of the inheritance of the soul. For though Christ's soul never sinned, it was by the same laws and affinities united unto His flesh as in the case of any other man, and therefore was conscious to all approaches and assaults of evil, and therefore it was made liable to death, which had been pronounced upon every living soul. The soul of Christ, therefore, suffered the pains of death, together with all other pains, though it could not be holden thereby; and thus upon the righteous soul of Christ was the wrath of God against sin visited, as well as against His body; and therefore the death of Christ is the act of Godhead, with which the indignation against sin is accomplished, and after which the grace unto the sinner may be extended. There is a divine order in these things which cannot be broken. In the divine purpose, there is a harmony which is of the very essence of God; and whosoever would expect good before knowing and believing in the cross of Christ, must be for ever defeated. Being then that the death of Christ is the resurrection of creation, and maketh the preaching of a resurrection possible, it remaineth to examine how the conscience is purged from dead works by the blood of Christ, in order to serve the living God. The conscience, or soul of man, is accessible only by knowledge. Material blood hath no congruity with the conscience whatsoever, neither can any action or event, or purpose of God whatever be available for any effect whatever upon the conscience otherwise than by the knowledge of the same. When it is said, therefore, that the Holy Ghost applieth unto the conscience the blood of Christ, it is meant that the Holy Ghost maketh the conscience acquainted with that knowledge of God which is made known to men by the shedding of the blood of Christ. The question therefore is, and what point so important and influential concerning the knowledge of God is therein communicated? These two—the holiness and the grace of God. His holiness, in the way which hath been explained above; His grace, in that He should have freely given His Son to such an ignominious and dishonourable condition. Why did He so afflict and humble His Son, and why did His Son so please to be humbled and afflicted? Because God loved the world, and wished that we should not perish, but have everlasting life. The knowledge of such love and such holiness met together is that by which the Holy Ghost worketh in the conscience. The applying of the blood of Christ to the conscience, in order to satisfy it, is nothing more than the Holy Ghost carrying home to the soul first the sense of God's love manifest in the death of Christ, to put her fears to flight, and then the sense of God's holiness, likewise manifest therein, to put to death her sin; and he who seeth not the love of God to sinners, and the hatred of God against a sinful condition, in the death of Christ, may talk what he pleaseth concerning the cross, and the blood of the cross, and the atonement made upon the cross, but he talketh empty words which signify nothing, either to the profit of him that speaketh, or to the profit of him that heareth. But whoso discerneth the love of God unto the soul of man, and the hatred of God against its sinful condition, met together in the death of Christ, the same doth possess the benefit of that death, which is peace with God and introduction into the standing of grace; and the continual presence in the soul of that sense of peace towards God and sense of hatred towards sin, is the evident proof that the blood of Christ is effectually purging it from dead works to serve the living God.

And this much have I to say with respect both to the application of the blood to the things bequeathed by the new testament, and to the persons to whom it is bequeathed. But, to explain this matter clearly and fully, I must refer particularly to, and regularly explain, a passage in Hebrews, chap. ix. 14, 15, which is the best commentary upon these words, "This is the new testament in my blood, shed for the remission of sins." The apostle had stated in the 9th verse, that the gifts and sacrifices under the law could not make him that did the service thereof perfect, as pertaining to the conscience, but only as pertaining to the flesh; and here saith ver. 13: "The blood of bulls and of goats, and the ashes of an heifer sprinkling the unclean, sanctifieth to the purifying of the flesh." Now, what this may mean I cannot well say, nor is it very material to our argument that it should be fully understood; but according to the best of my judgment it is, that the law, and the revelation made under the law, were really addressed only to the fleshly, that is, to the natural man; and that the spiritual man was not in being until Christ became the quickening Spirit, and gave the Spirit to bring men into the condition of new creatures, or a new creation. Those under the law were merely natural men, who understood not the things which God hath revealed unto us by the Spirit; yet they lived by faith,—that is to say, those of them that were effectually called lived by faith, but it was the faith of bare precepts, under which they were in a state of bondage. These precepts, accompanied with promises, were, when violated, visited with certain judgments which they were required to observe. These judgments were either sacrificial or baptismal, in blood or in washings. The Jew who rightly observed these judgments, upon his breach of God's statutes, having always a view unto the great Sacrifice that was to come, was justified by his faith in God and in the coming One, which faith was counted to him for righteousness; for in the blood of a bullock or of a goat there was no more fitness to cleanse the sin of a natural man which is born of the flesh than of the spiritual man which is born of the Spirit. They had their effect only in virtue of the faith whereof they were signs and tokens: all blood being a token of Christ's blood, and all water of purification a token of the Spirit's purification. Now, the apostle having expressly declared that the blood of bulls and of goats, and the ashes of an heifer, did sanctify to the purifying of the flesh, doth from that, as a given thing, go on to argue the greater and higher purification of which the blood of Christ was capable. But first he must shew how the blood of Christ, fountain of all purification, doth acquire its own purity, and this he doth in these words: "Who by the eternal Spirit offered himself without spot unto God;" in which it is asserted, first, that Christ came to His cross without a fault, without an imperfection, without blemish, and without spot; secondly, that this spotlessness He perfected in Himself by means of, through virtue, power, and operation of, the Holy Ghost. Not, therefore, by any difference of His flesh and blood; not, therefore, by any supralapsarian immortality and incorruption in His flesh and blood; not, therefore, by any Adamic purity: but by that cleansing, by that sanctification of the Holy Ghost, by that new and better generation, which, beginning in the beginning of His human being, continued actively to preserve Him pure and holy against all the affections and attributes of flesh, against all the liability of the soul to be influenced thereby, against all the load of a fallen creation which lies upon a human will, did the Holy Spirit effectually sustain Christ, and, though brought to every brink, and every extremity, did effectually sanctify Him; and thus using the Holy Spirit in preference to the fallen world, preferring God through faith to the world through sense apprehended, He did offer Himself faultless upon the cross. The Lamb taken out from the flock to be a sacrifice was bone of their bone and flesh of their flesh; only He needed to be faultless. So Christ was very man—bone of the bone and flesh of the flesh of the brethren whom He would redeem; only He, of them all, was faultless. Here, then, is the holy fountain opened in the house of David for sin and for uncleanness. Here, then, is blood of a perfect man; and as the blood of a sinful man corrupted many, so this blood of a perfect Man shall sanctify many. Now, the language of blood-purging is still figurative language, and we must strip it of the legal figure before we can bring it into contact with the spiritual mind.

There is yet one word which remaineth to be explained before we can say that we have completely expressed the benefit of the cup; which is the word "many,"—"shed for the remission of the sins of many,"—of which we have the most perfect exposition in the 2d chapter of the Romans. Of this there can be no dispute amongst orthodox Christians, that those who shall inherit the benefit, are not all, no, nor yet many, but few, according to the word of the Lord, "many are called, but few chosen." The only question is, whether the expression "many," used in the text,—"shed for the remission of the sins of many," —be used to the exclusion of the rest, or be simply used to denote that the sacrifice He offered should shed its influence beyond His own Person, unto many persons; whether, in truth, by this expression, the propitiation which He made be confined unto a part or extended unto all mankind. For the ascertaining of this point, let us examine together the 5th chapter of the Romans, at the 15th verse: "If by the offence [or, forfeiture] of one many be dead, much more the grace of God, and the gift by grace, which is by one man, Jesus Christ, hath abounded unto many." In this passage the word "many" is not used to the exclusion of some, but merely for the inclusion of several, because he had asserted in the 12th verse that death had passed upon all, and, therefore, we should naturally infer, that the "many" in the latter clause is likewise merely used for the inclusion of several, and not for exclusion of any. But this natural inference is put beyond a doubt by the conclusion of the argument in ver. 18: "Therefore as by the offence of one judgment came upon all men to condemnation; even so by the righteousness of one the free gift came upon all men unto justification of life." The "many," therefore, of

THE SIGNIFICANCE OF THE CUP. 587

the 15th verse is now written "all" in the 18th verse; but to put this beyond all doubt, the 19th verse again reverteth to the use of "many:" "For as by one man's disobedience many were made sinners, so by the obedience of one shall many be made righteous." There can be no doubt, therefore, that in this passage of the Romans the word "many" is used, not for exclusion of part of mankind, but for the inclusion of a number, without any specification as to the extent; yea, with the understanding that it extendeth unto all, for the "all" and the "many" are interchanged at pleasure. Now, with the same liberty would I use the word "many" in the text, understanding it to mean simply "many," without either asserting or denying anything with respect to the "all." I do not think that our Lord goes further in these words, "shed for the remission of the sins of many," than merely to assert that His sacrifice was applicable to others besides Himself. When I say besides Himself, I mean, not that Christ had any sin of His own, original or actual, but that, having taken flesh and blood with the brethren, He behoved, like the brethren, to die, and, by dying, did attain unto the resurrection. I say, His resurrection and His glory were the consequence and the reward of His death. Now, He meaneth to say that this reward was not for Himself alone, but for many; that "he was exalted a Prince and a Saviour to give repentance and remission of sins unto many;" that however many it might please the Father to give unto Him, there was in His death an offering presented for them all; that, therefore, there needed no other offering for sin—that this one offering had for ever "perfected all them that are sanctified." The Lord's supper was intended to be a social ordinance, at which many were to sit down together; and therefore it was a very appropriate and, one may say, necessary addition to say, that His blood was shed "for the remission of the sins of many." However much, therefore, I value the doctrine of particular election,—and I consider it by far the most valuable point of Christian doctrine,—I do not think it is stated here in the word "many," but otherwise do think that here it would have been altogether out of place; for these words were intended to be spoken to believers and not to unbelievers, to elect persons and not to reprobate, to the

Church and not to the world. And though our Lord doubtless contemplated the mixture of reprobate and elect in His Church, and therefore requireth a man to examine himself before coming to His table; yet is it not to be believed that, in the words of institution, intended for the nourishment and confirmation of His people, there should be introduced one word which should occasion doubt or dismay within their minds. But whatever may be thought of this, I stand to my conviction, that the word "many" in this place, as in the 5th of the Romans, is used inclusively of several, and not exclusively of any,—to signify merely that this was the one sacrifice for all His Church, that this was the only sacrifice that ever should be made for the remission of sin. And so much have we to say of the benefit contained in the cup; and we now come to speak of the manner in which it is therein contained.

HOMILY VII.

THE LORD'S SUPPER AS A COMMEMORATIVE ACT.

1 COR. XI., 25, 26.

This do ye, as oft as ye drink it, in remembrance of me. For as often as ye eat this bread, and drink this cup, ye do shew the Lord's death till he come.

IN the preceding homilies we have opened, at length, the desires, exercises, and resolutions of the soul which are proper to be entertained in the view of the holy sacrament; and we have likewise set forth the substance of the sacrament itself, and the meaning of the action in all its parts, together with the doctrines couched under the elements and the words of consecration; and now it doth remain to us to recompose the parts, and, regarding it as one great whole and complete action, to consider what be the chief aspects which it beareth unto the Church, and under which the Church should speak and reflect upon it. These, judging from the use and wont of the Church in times past and at present, are the four following:—First, As a great open commemoration and confession of Christ's death. Second, A solemn sacrament, or oath of fealty and service, into which we enter with the Lord. Third, An act of close communion, wherein the members of the Church do most charitably embrace and unite as one. Fourth, An act of thanksgiving, so singular in its kind, and exalted in its degree, as to have obtained for it in the primitive Church the common name of the Eucharist, or thanksgiving. These four views of Commemoration, Sacrament, Communion, and Eucharist, have been so universally sanctioned by the Church, and, as we shall see, so fully warranted by Scripture, that we greatly prefer to open what remains of the subject under this method, rather than to adopt any other of our own. Let us, then, in this discourse, contemplate the Lord's Supper under the aspect of a commemorative act, according as it is declared to be, in the words of our text, "For as often as ye eat this bread, and drink this cup, ye do shew the Lord's death till he come."

The view of the Lord's Supper as a commemorative rite grows out of its character as a sign, and hath nothing to do with its higher character as a seal and a pledge: and in these times, in which the base and heretical doctrine, that the sacraments are but naked and bare signs, hath obtained such alarming influence, this idea of mere commemoration hath obtained a corresponding popularity; and many be the eloquent and pathetic appeals with which the Church is solicited to remember the dying love of her Lord; and many be the comparisons drawn from persons famous in the annals of men, whose names are borne down to distant ages in the hearts of their admirers, and the monuments of their country. Many, also, be the well-meant endeavours of good men, but insufficient divines, to point out the circumstances of His death, and the benefits thereby derived unto men, in all the charms of poetical imagery, and with all the power of eloquent discourse; to which well-meant labours of the ministry it is far from my purpose to object, if they were not put forth as the whole service of the Lord's table, whereas, they ought to be but lively pictures to the memory, to the feelings, and to the understanding of men, in order to awaken them to the higher discourse which grows out of the higher aspect of the sacrament as a seal, and as a pledge. But wherever the doctrine of the sacrament as a sign is presented as a whole, these appeals do only serve, in a somewhat higher kind, the purposes which are attained in other churches by altar-pieces and ceremonial pomps. Yet, seeing that commemoration is, indeed, no mean part of the holy action, it is at all times both convenient and dutiful to set forth in order the substance and the circumstance also of that event which is commemorated. Let us, therefore, with due reverence, and with exact tradition, deliver unto you the amount of our Lord's sufferings and death.

The ever-memorable passion of our Lord began, as seemeth to me, from the time at which the Greeks were brought to Him by Philip. Then, and by that sign, He appears to have known that His hour was come; for instantly He said, upon hearing thereof from the mouths of Andrew and Philip, "The hour is come that the Son of man should be glorified," (John xii. 23;) and again: Ver. 27, "Now is my soul troubled; and what shall I say? Father, save me from this hour; but for this cause came I unto this hour;" and again: Ver. 31, "Now is the judgment of this world; now shall the prince of this world be cast out." These expressions, together with the whole strain of the discourse then pronounced unto the people, shew me that a new crisis in the history of His life did then begin; which I take to be the crisis of His passion. Perhaps He knew by some admonition of His Father, that when the Greeks, or Gentiles, should be brought to Him, His ministry, His peculiar ministry to the Jews, was come to its close. And to this conclusion not only do the words quoted and the general tenor of the discourse well agree, but likewise the action with which He closed it: "These things spake Jesus, and departed, and did hide himself from them." The same day on which this happened, He had entered with triumphal state into the city of Jerusalem; and the day before, Mary the sister of Lazarus, had anointed Him with ointment of spikenard, very costly, upon which Jesus made this remark: "Let her alone; against the day of my burying hath she kept this." Now this happened six days before the passover; and, therefore, the day following, on which He entered Jerusalem triumphantly and received the Greeks with such mournful presentiments, was five days before the passover, being the very day on which the lamb was required to be set apart; and as the Jews reckoned their day from evening until evening, it was on the same day that Mary anointed Him unto His burial; whereby is signified and clearly shewn out, that as the sacrifice, the Lamb of God, our passover, she did anoint Him. Now, from the time the lamb was separated from the flock, its life was forfeited, and, had it been a conscious thing, the sufferings of its death did commence; which falleth in with our conclusion stated above, that His passion began from the day the Greeks were brought to Him. Now, be it carefully observed and wondered at, that as the lamb had to be taken unto the priests, and certified of them to be without fault, so

Christ, from the evening that Mary anointed Him, had one ordeal after another to pass through; and every one of His examiners were fain to attest Him as without fault and blameless. First, in the morning, the people, as He entered the city—the people of the country, and the villages, and the city also, even all who had known Him best, an innumerable multitude—shouted hosanna to Him as the Son of David, and blessed Him as coming in the name of the Lord. The like testimony were His greatest enemies, the chief priests, forced to give, when, after suborning many false witnesses, they could establish nothing against Him; and were fain to condemn Him upon His own declaration, that He was the Christ, the Son of God. The same testimony, that He was a Lamb without blemish and without spot, gave Pilate forth when, having washed his hands before the multitude, he said, "I am innocent of the blood of this just man." And, verily, because accusation was laid against Him that he had stirred up the people in Galilee as well as in Jewry, He was sent to Herod, the chief governor of Galilee; of whose examination Pilate thus speaketh: "Behold, I, having examined him before you, have found no fault in this man touching those things whereof ye accuse him: no, nor yet Herod; for I sent you to him; and, lo, nothing worthy of death is done unto him." The same testimony to His innocency was enforced from Judas the traitor, who, in the agony of his remorse, hanged himself. The same testimony also was enforced from the Roman centurion, who, having seen all the accidents of His crucifixion, His bearing of Himself in the agony of death, under the torments of His persecutors, did say, "Certainly this was a righteous man." Thus was He carried about and about to receive the attestation of priests and people, of Jew and Gentile, and thus was He declared, with one voice, to be a Lamb without blemish and without spot, fit to be sacrificed for the sin of the world. Now then, believing Him to be innocent and without guile by the common confession of all men, I ask you next to look at the indignities and cruelties which He received under their eyes, from their hands, and by their permission; and, in the light of His innocency, behold the darkness, the blackness of their depravity. Judas, His most trusted apostle, over whose avarice and dishonesty, though He knew them well, He had cast a veil in the presence of the rest, hoping that His tender affection and gentle rebuke would have won him out of the devil's hands,—this one of the twelve men whom He had chosen, to honour them with His private confidence and with apostolical dignity, did betray Him, and he did it with a kiss of love. "Betrayest thou the Son of man with a kiss?" These words shew how His tender and delicate soul felt even the manner of the treacherous act; and how He felt the act itself is still better evinced by that trouble of soul with which He is said, at the supper, to have broken the matter to the twelve. The base following of the traitor, the armed midnight rabble, who went to take Him, seems also to have grieved the perfect dignity and harmless innocency of His spirit. "Be ye come out, as against a thief, with swords and staves?" were His words unto the chief priests and captains of the temple. "When I was daily with you in the temple, ye stretched forth no hands against me: but this is your hour, and the power of darkness." Behold Him now led in the cold and damp night unto the high priest's hall, and there submitting to the inquisition of His deadly enemies and the false accusations of their suborned hirelings; and when this midnight conclave of Satan's synagogue could find no charge that would fasten upon Him, see them condemning Him to death, because of the adjuration of the high priest He had told them who and what manner of person He was. "Then did they spit in his face, and buffeted him; and others smote him with the palms of their hands, saying, Prophesy unto us, thou Christ, who is he that smote thee." And, while suffering the injustice of the chief men of His nation, the indignities of the meanest and most cruel, behold Him also deserted and denied three times within hearing of His ear, at last within sight of His eye, by Peter, on whom He had put such frequent honour. From this scene of perverted judgment, base cruelty, and universal desertion, see Him led unto the governor bound, and accused of perverting the nation and raising sedition against the king. After one hearing, the governor, finding no fault in Him, but yet fearing the phalanx of iniquity that was combined against Him, is glad, in order to escape from his conscience on the one hand, and his policy on the other, to send Him unto Herod, who had slain the Baptist in cold blood, and had longed to see Jesus, that, like Samson, He might, with His miraculous power, minister amusement to his court, before whom, when the Son of God stood in dignified silence, answering him never a word, Herod, with his men of war, set Him at nought, and mocked Him, and arrayed Him in a gorgeous robe, and sent Him again to Pilate, who, having attested His innocence again, as hath been said, and having put Him in the balance with Barabbas, a murderer and a raiser of sedition, they preferred the life of Barabbas, the murderer and raiser of sedition, to the life of Christ, crying like demons, "Crucify Him, crucify Him;" and Pilate, the representative of Rome, the empress of the world, gave sentence that it should be as they required: "And he released unto them him that for sedition and murder was cast into prison, whom they had desired; but he delivered Jesus to their will." And how they exercised their barbarous will upon the innocent man, you well do know. How they took Him into the common hall, and gathered unto them the whole band of soldiers, and made Him the subject of the rude mockeries of a military guard-room. How they stripped Him, and put on Him a scarlet robe, and when they had platted a crown of thorns they put it on His head, and a reed in His right hand, and they bowed the knee before Him, and mocked Him, saying, "Hail, King of the Jews," and they spat upon Him, and took the rod, and smote Him on the head. And after that they had mocked Him, they took the robe off from Him, and put His own raiment on Him, and led Him away to crucify Him; and so He went forth from that city gate, cast out, despised, and rejected of men, a man of sorrows, and acquainted with grief; out of that city over which He had sat and wept, and spoken words of tenderness, which proved His love to be of the deepest: "O Jerusalem, Jerusalem, thou that killest the prophets, and stonest them which are sent unto thee, how often would I have gathered thy children together, even as a hen gathereth her chickens under her wings, and ye would not!" And that this superabundant and overflowing love suffereth no abatement from the complicated and wearisome cruelty to which He had been subjected, from the awful scene of a cursed death unto which He was proceeding, is sweetly betokened in those words which He spake unto the tender-hearted women who followed Him without the city to the place of skulls: "Weep not for me, O daughters of Jerusalem, but weep for yourselves and for your children; for behold the days are coming in the which they shall say, Blessed are the barren, and the wombs that never bare, and the paps that never gave suck." And when they were come to the place which is called Calvary, there they crucified Him, and the malefactors, one on the right hand, and the other on the left. And still He bare with the meekness of a lamb led to the slaughter; and as a sheep before her shearers is dumb, so He opened not His mouth,—He opened not His mouth to speak that word unto His Father which would have called down upon the instant twelve legions of angels to consume the transgressors; He opened not His mouth unto His Father, save to pray that they might be forgiven, saying, "Father, forgive them, for they know not what they do." And they parted His raiment, and cast lots upon His vesture; and the people stood beholding, and the rulers also with them derided Him, saying, "He saved others, let him save himself if he be Christ, the chosen of God." And the soldiers also mocked Him, coming to Him and offering vinegar, and saying, "If thou be the King of the Jews, save thyself;" and one of the malefactors which were hanged railed on Him, saying, "If thou be Christ, save thyself and us." But the other, answering, rebuked him, saying, "Dost not thou fear God, seeing thou art in the same condemnation?" And he said unto Jesus, "Lord, remember me when thou comest into thy kingdom." And Jesus said unto him, "Verily I say unto thee, To-day shalt thou be with me in paradise." What truth so striking, what evidence so strong, that when lifted up upon the cross, and made a curse, it was for us, for sinners, for the forgiveness of sinners, that He was thus accursed, from one of whom, and that one of the greatest sinners, He could not receive a prayer without answering it in peace! Such, dear friends, was the outward combination of cruelty and wickedness which He endured unto the death; but who shall tell, or what language can express, the inward anguish and agony of soul which He underwent during this season of His passion, from the time the Greeks came unto Him until the time that He bowed the head, and gave up the ghost! It was not the fear of princes, or of the sons of men, in whose presence you see He stood unmoved, in the dignity and in the strength of innocence; it was not the cruelty, the mockings, the scourgings, the torments which men could perpetrate upon His body; it was not the desertion and denial of His friends, which wrung from Him in the garden those shuddering petitions, pressing from His veins those drops of blood which fell from Him like drops of sweat upon the ground, which covered His soul with the darkness of midnight, and hid from His spirit the light of the countenance of His Father. The scene of the garden, and the more awful scene of the cross, when He exclaimed, "My God, my God, why hast thou forsaken me?" are not to be explained by the wisdom, nor to be understood by the experience, of man. There never was sorrow like unto His sorrow. It passed all bounds of utterance, it passed all bounds of comprehension; and I seek not to lay it open, because I cannot. In the midst of such a sorrowful season, unexampled in the annals of creation, what was it that engaged the Sufferer's heart, and upon whom was it that He thought? To whom spake He words of comfort? "Let not your hearts be troubled; ye believe in God, believe also in me." For whom interceded He with His Father? To whom promised He the Comforter? For whom did His Spirit vent itself in long-drawn discourse of peace, and joy, and blessedness? in long and fervent prayer for unity, sanctification, preservation, and glory? For you, believers, for all who should believe in Him through the preaching of His apostles. "Neither pray I for these alone, but for them also who shall believe on me through their word; that they all may be one; as thou, Father, art in me, and I in thee, that they also may be one in us: that the world may believe that thou hast sent me. And the glory that thou gavest me I have given them; that they may be one, even as we are one: I in them, and thou in me, that they may be made perfect in one; and that the world may know that thou hast sent me, and hast loved them, as thou hast loved me. Father, I will that they also, whom thou hast given me, be with me where I am; that they may behold my glory, which thou hast given me: for thou lovedst me before the foundation of the world. O righteous Father, the world hath not known thee: but I have known thee, and these have known that thou hast sent me. And I have declared unto them thy name, and will declare it: that the love wherewith thou hast loved me may be in them, and I in them." What words so sweet, what thoughts so excellent, what blessings so precious, what love so divine! For the memory of this love, shewn forth at such a moment, for the commemoration of such a scene for ever in the Church, was the sacrament of the supper instituted by our blessed Lord; and for the shewing forth of this love in death, stronger than death, stronger than agony and anguish, let the Lord's supper be observed and sanctified for ever. Now, then, that ye have heard the narrative of the event commemorated, let us proceed, in the next place, to consider and reflect upon the reasons for which this ordinance is specially set apart for the commemoration of this event.

Our blessed Lord and Saviour, upon giving the bread into the hands of His disciples, added these words of exhortation, "This do in remembrance of me." And so likewise spake He when He presented them with the cup; and the holy apostle, not content, as it were, with this double injunction of the Lord, doth, in the words of our text, repeat it the third time in the form of a declaration, making, however, an important addition by these words, "until He come." No doubt, therefore, can remain but that the commemoration of Christ's death, and the lively remembrance of Him in our hearts, are in some way or other most dutiful and becoming in every one who eateth of this bread and drinketh of this cup. Let us now endeavour to discover the reason why it should be so. The chief reasons wherefore our Lord did prefer to connect His memory with this, rather than any other ordinance of His Church, are, as it seems to me, because, first, it containeth the great fact that He took unto Himself a body; and, secondly, His great act of love in giving it for

His Church. Every one wisheth to be remembered by that which is peculiar and proper to himself; and if there be many such peculiarities, by that which is most excellent amongst them all. Now, herein doth Christ stand distinguished from all men—that He was the fulness of the Godhead in a body; not merely a living soul, but the living God, united to a soul and body. This was the divine act of love, that the Son of God should be willing to take a body,—an act also necessary to retrieve the ruin, and found the stability of creation for ever; whereupon God could effect His purpose of communicating infallible blessedness unto the creatures whom He had made, and is about to make. For straightway upon this condescension of the Son, He, by the Holy Ghost, prepared a body for His condescending Son, and through the perils of this mortal estate, and the passage of death itself, He, even the Father, acting by the Holy Ghost, did bring that body into the estate of infallible creation which He had purposed in Himself to do through the one and only means whereby it was possible to test the willingness of His Son to unite Himself to it. From the overshadowing of the virgin by the Highest, until the resurrection, God was preparing the body which, under covenant, He had promised for His Son; and His Son, acting in it, and personally embracing it, did, in the state of its humiliation, make atonement for the sin of the world, and dispossess the devil of all which he had gained by the fall. This act, therefore, of Christ, whereby He took a body which was to be offered, being entirely an act of grace for us undertaken and done, He doth desire to be remembered by during the season of His absence. And because the supper doth specially set out the giving of His body and the shedding of His blood for us, He doth most appropriately select that ordinance as the monument of His great act in time past, by which He would be remembered in the season of His absence, and until He shall come again. The thing, therefore, of which we make continual commemoration in the Christian Church is, that the eternal Son of God did take upon Him our human nature, our body, "and being found in the likeness of sinful flesh, did condemn sin in the flesh, and by death destroy him that had the power of death." In the

Jewish Church there was a continual remembrance of sin made from year to year; but in the Christian Church there is a continual remembrance of sin for ever remitted by Christ's sacrifice of Himself. In the Jewish Church there was a remembrance continually made of one to come who should die for the sins of the people; in the Christian Church there is a continual remembrance made that Messiah hath come, and by His death brought in a universal righteousness: so that with us that is perfected which with them was hoped for. Whenever, therefore, a Christian church doth seat itself around the table of the Lord, and keep this high solemnity, it doth shew forth in the sight of the world that great act of God and of Christ, of which this world was the theatre, but the whole universe the deeply-interested beholders. We lift up unto the world the ensign of its salvation, plucked from the hand of the devil by the mighty power of Immanuel, God with us,—that ensign which, while it is all stained with His blood, yea, rolled in His blood, is surrounded with the glorious trophies of a redeemed world. We lift up unto perishing sinners that emblem of health and life eternal, unto which their eye being turned, their souls shall live. "For as Moses lifted up the serpent in the wilderness, even so must the Son of man be lifted up, that whosoever believeth in him might not perish, but have everlasting life." Whenever this sacrament of the body of Christ is celebrated, we do give note of remembrance unto all men that He is the bread of life which came down from heaven, which giveth life unto the world; and we do sound the trumpet unto all the tribes of Israel sojourning in the wilderness, calling them forth from their tents, even every living man, and entreating them to gather nourishment for their souls. And so might I go over all the forms and similitudes for expressing the inestimable benefit of Christ's death, and shew you how they are worthily commemorated in this holy act, wherein His body is exhibited and His death represented: the one to commemorate His incarnation, the other to commemorate the remission of sins which is thence derived unto us. But after the large exposition which hath been given above of this most pregnant mystery, I need not go into such detail, but in one word recapitulate the whole by saying, that whatever of good procured by the offered body and shed blood of Christ,—whatever of precious inheritance bequeathed by Him in the new testament,—whatever of present earnest and firstfruits is conferred upon us by the Holy Ghost in this present life, or the amount and value thereof, is solemnly given by the Church unto the merit, the only merit of Christ's taking to Himself a body, and offering it upon the accursed tree. But no memorial of what Christ hath done would be sufficient to represent what He, the living One, is doing still, and is yet to do,—no memorial of His death were faultless, unless it contained likewise a memorial of His abiding and eternal life; for by His death He brought life and immortality to light. No grateful acknowledgments of His presence heretofore in a body upon this earth were sufficient, unless it contained the assurance that He was to be present in that body upon the earth again. Therefore, when the Lord instituted this supper, He added to it these words: "For I shall not henceforth drink of this fruit of the vine, until I drink it new with you in my Father's kingdom." And the apostle, following His example, doth add words of the same import, when he saith, "Ye do shew forth the Lord's death until he come." Here, then, is the important addition which preventeth all error and incompleteness from attaching themselves unto the ordinance of the supper, seeing that by these words is made known unto the Church the great truth, that Christ, though dead, is still alive—though absent, is still purposed after a season to be present with us again upon this earth in His body, which shall be such a body as can drink the fruit of the vine; and further, it is signified that with us—with the apostles who first observed, and with us who have since continued to observe, this ordinance—He will eat and drink in His Father's kingdom, for which we continually pray in these words, "Thy kingdom come, Thy will be done on earth as it is in heaven." This bringeth us to consider—

In the second place, the limitation of time, and the presentiment of a glorious change, which is put and given by this ordinance in these words, "until I come." Remembrance is proper only of a thing past, or of a person absent; and when that person returneth again, we no longer think of remembering, but of enjoying Him. So when Christ shall come again, as He always promised He would do, there will be no need of keeping up the remembrance of Him as one that was present, but now is absent, for, behold, He is present with His Church again. But it may be asked, And will the Church likewise cease thenceforth to make memory of that death by which He accomplished eternal redemption for her and for the world? The language of the apostle doth, I think, rather incline one to believe so: "As often as ye eat this bread and drink this cup, ye do shew forth the Lord's death until he come." This seemeth to me to bear that when He comes we will have to shew forth His death no longer; that the ordinance shall then have done its office, and with all other things shall be changed at the coming of the Lord. Not that the act of Christ's death shall ever be obliterated or obscured from the annals of creation, but shall grow more and more bright and glorious unto eternal ages, being, in truth, the groundwork and support of the redeemed world. Doth not the work of creation grow in glory by every revolving year, which, as it revolveth, doth obey the commandment of the Creator then given forth, and the law then laid down for every creature? Even so shall redemption, which was begun by Christ's taking a body and offering it upon the cross, only acquire new glory at the coming of the Lord to redeem the body, and to redeem the purchased possession, and to establish the kingdom. Let it not be thought, therefore, that the death of Christ shall ever cease to be the burden of eternal thanksgiving, as we know it to be the cause for which the Father shall heap upon Him fresh tokens of His love, as it is written, "Therefore doth my Father love me, because I give my life for the sheep." Nevertheless, I do firmly believe that against the day of the Lord's coming this ordinance shall cease from its present form. For behold how each one of its parts shall then be accomplished! The Church, which is the broken body of Christ, shall then have been completed, and be no longer broken, but gathered into one. As it is written, (Ps. l. 5,) "Gather my saints together unto me; those that have made a covenant with me by sacrifice." Then shall the angels have gathered together the elect from the four winds of heaven, when the Lord cometh with all His saints, to be glorified in them that have believed. Then also shall they have received the thing which was pledged to them in the bread, being raised in the likeness of His glorious body. Then also shall the Church have received the complete remission of sins, when corruption shall have been cast out of their body and their souls alike, and death, which is the wages of sin, shall have been spoiled. Then also shall the inheritance bequeathed in the new testament to Abraham and his seed, heirs of the world, have come to its proper possessors, the adopted sons of God,—even at the blowing of the seventh trumpet, when "the kingdoms of this world are become the kingdoms of our Lord, and of His Christ, and the time of the dead, that they should be judged, [that is, justified,] and that thou shouldest give reward unto thy servants the prophets, and to the saints, and them that feared thy name, small and great." Now, if that for which God impledgeth Himself unto the Church in the supper shall have then been all accomplished; and if He, whose death is there commemorated, shall then be manifested as the great and only Lord of life; and He, whose absence from His Church on earth is there commemorated, shall then with all His Church be present upon the earth to reign in it for ever and ever,—how could this ordinance in its present form subsist any longer? What new form of commemoration the work of Christ in flesh shall take, or whether it shall by any ordinance be commemorated, I have no authority from Holy Scripture, and therefore attempt not any resolution of the question; and yet methinks that the resolution of the question is contained in those last chapters of Ezekiel, which set forth the worship of the Jews after the rebuilding of their city and temple. But in the new Jerusalem that came down from heaven, which is the dwelling-place of the saints, there can be no ordinance but the ordinance of a continual obedience and service unto God and the Lamb, for the apostolic seer saw no temple there. The city is the temple, whereof the saints are the lively stones. The saints are the commemoration, in their holy bodies, in their union with Christ, in their righteous government of all things;

they are the very thing which in the supper is commemorated: as Christ was the end of the law and all its ordinances, so is the new Jerusalem the end of the Church and all its ordinances. As circumcision passed away when Christ was cut off in the flesh, or rather, I should say, when Christ had fulfilled the law, and been baptized of John into a new condition of subsisting; and as the eating of the paschal lamb passed away when Christ our passover was sacrificed for us; so reckon I that baptism shall pass away when the Church shall arise in its spiritual body, which baptism signifieth and pledgeth; and the Lord's supper shall pass away when the Church shall be one in bodily substance with Christ, and have received the co-heirship of His inheritance. But whether or not amongst those who still subsist in flesh upon the earth, under the supremacy of the Jewish nation and metropolitan authority of the re-edified Jerusalem, there may not be instituted ordinances of a more advanced kind, which may be proper to their dispensations, and what these ordinances are to be, I take not upon me to decide.

By these explanations, therefore, dear brethren, you will perceive how, while the Lord's supper is an ordinance for calling to remembrance, it is likewise an ordinance for exciting unto hope and desire; because if it look backward to the former coming of Christ, it doth likewise look forward to 'His coming again; because if it make mention of what He did and what He suffered, it maketh mention of what He is to do, to enjoy, and to communicate unto all His people. Therefore, it is not to be partaken of without that faith which the apostle defineth to be the substance of things not seen and the evidence of things hoped for. Because, as he doth in the glorious celebration of faith speak of it both as that by which we understand the worlds to have been made by the word of God, and things that are not seen to have been made of things which do appear; and likewise as that which looketh forward to the inheritance and better resurrection to come; so in the supper do we need this realiser of things past and of things future, inasmuch as we have in the supper a symbol which bringeth together into one both the things which Christ hath done for us who believe and which He is to do, inasmuch as the Lord's supper holdeth of the former advent by remembrance, of the latter advent by hope. I would, indeed, that communicants had been in all ages of the Church as mindful of the latter as they have been of the former. I would that the mouth of the Church, which is her minister, had been as diligent to deliver the Spirit's witness in the Scriptures and in the primitive traditions of the Church, as it hath been diligent to declare His testimony of the latter. I would that the faith of the Church had been carried prospectively forward to the glory which is to be revealed, as it hath been retrospectively to the sufferings which have been endured. Then, indeed, the high, holy, and most wise purpose of the Lord to connect His two advents into one great ordinance of strength and nourishment would not have been lost and defeated as it hath been, and the Church would not have been found as now it is—one part of it worshipping an impostor and his imposture as Christ and His kingdom, the other worshipping a kingdom and a king of their own imagining and of their own bringing to pass. But seeing it hath pleased God to deliver us, beloved brethren, from this fearful mutilation of His holy ordinance, I do trust we shall be found ever walking together in the beauty and freedom of strength, trusting in the death of Christ, testifying unto His resurrection, and waiting for His coming in the clouds of heaven to take possession of His kingdom. And now, to the end that you may be awakened to a right, worthy, and sufficient act of remembrance, I shall do my endeavour, as was proposed, in the third place, to stir up your pure mind by way of remembrance, shewing to you some of the most excellent acts and worthy causes for which He should be remembered of all His people.

HOMILY VIII.

THE SUBSTANCE OF THE DOCTRINE CONTAINED IN THE LORD'S SUPPER.

JOHN VI. 40-54.

And this is the will of him that sent me, that every one which seeth the Son, and believeth on him, may have everlasting life: and I will raise him up at the last day. The Jews then murmured at him, because he said, I am the bread which came down from heaven, &c., &c.

IT hath often been argued, in opposition to the Papists, who lay so much stress upon this discourse of the Lord, concerning the eating of His flesh and drinking of His blood, that it hath no reference to the sacrament of the Lord's supper whatever: which is true, inasmuch as the magnet may not be said to have reference to the needle; for as the needle pointeth to the magnet, so doth the Lord's supper point unto the substance of this discourse. As baptism referreth to the discourse delivered unto Nicodemus concerning regeneration, so the Lord's supper referreth to this discourse concerning faith. Every visible ordinance hath its reality in some great spiritual truth, whereof it is the continual monument, and, as it were, the express effigy; and every visible ordinance hath its sacredness and value, in being unto the believer ever filled to overflowing with the nourishment of that grace whereof it is also the outward expression. Now, as baptism hath for its spiritual object the great work of regeneration, or the new birth, unto which it doth continually direct the faith and hope of man, generated under the curse of sin and death, even so doth the supper of the Lord, both with visible index and with audible voice, direct the attention of mortal men to that source and nourishment of immortal life, which is to be found only in the body of Christ, and to be received only by faith.

Concerning which object in the invisible,—now, indeed, in the invisible, but then in the visible world,—and concerning which principle of faith, our Lord holdeth this discourse with the men of Capernaum; and, therefore, the Protestants argue rightly when they say it concerneth not the supper, because it concerneth that which the supper concerneth;—but they argue very foolishly, if they would therefore say that it is not to be applied in exposition of the supper: it is, in fact, the only true exposition of the mystery of the supper, which it explaineth in the true spiritual sense, by explaining that act of the spirit-living faith whereof eating and drinking are the proper expressions; and that spiritual subject, the flesh and blood of Christ, whereof bread and wine are the proper sensible expressions. If you were to ask a man to discourse to you of magnetism, and he should bring a compass into your presence, and make a few experiments upon it with a magnet, and say, "There you have the nature of magnetism explained," he would do exactly what the Papists do when they would satisfy an inquirer by explaining this discourse by their abominable tenet of transubstantiation. The language indeed of transubstantiation we find in this discourse, because, as we shall see, no other language is able to express the facts of that which is to be explained; but when these facts are expressed by the language, "eating my flesh, and drinking my blood," the cause, or principle, or divine operation of faith, is no more explained than would the science of magnetism, by saying that a steel bar pointed continually to the north pole of the magnet. As the falling of an apple unto the earth drew the attention of our great philosopher to the law of gravitation, and enabled him to resolve a thousand and ten thousand disjointed problems in the system of the world; and as the continual turning of the needle to the north drew men's attention to the subject of magnetism, which promises to embrace electricity also, and, perhaps, other branches of science; so exactly did our Lord, by fixing the ordinance of the Lord's supper in the Church as a standing ordinance, seek to direct the attention of men to this discourse, that they might find therein the great principle of the origin and continuance of spiritual life explained. Being well assured, therefore, that in this discourse of our Lord is contained the true mystery of faith, and that the eating Christ's body and drinking His blood in the communion, is but the description of the great evidence of this faith, as we say the falling of a stone is the great fact and evidence of the law of gravitation, we shall shew that this sermon of our Lord hath no other object than to explain the nature of faith; and we shall, from the Lord's own words, examine what is the proper object of this faith.

That faith is the subject of this sermon will appear sufficiently from a short examination of its parts. He had fed the multitude of five thousand upon five barley loaves and two small fishes, whereupon they said, "This is of a truth that prophet that should come into the world;" and being minded to take Him by force, to make Him a king, He departed again into a mountain Himself alone, and passed over to the other side of the sea, whither they having crowded after Him, He said unto them, "Ye seek me, not because ye saw the miracles, but because ye did eat of the loaves, and were filled. Work not for the meat which perisheth, but for that meat which endureth unto everlasting life, which the Son of man shall give unto you: for him hath God the Father sealed." In these words is contained the whole substance of the discourse, for here is the meat enduring unto everlasting life, which He afterwards declareth (ver. 51) to be Himself. Next, it is to be given to them, not now, but hereafter: "which the Son of man shall give unto you." That is, as is explained in ver. 51, His flesh, which should be offered, or given, for the life of the world; and He addeth, "for him hath God the Father sealed;" that is, as He himself explaineth it, "whom the Father hath sanctified and sent into the world;" which I understand to be spoken of Him as the Lamb set apart to this very end of taking away the sin of the world, and being the nourishment of His Church,—the body prepared for Him by the Father, whose sacrifice was to bring all sacrifice to an end, as it is written, "My substance was not hid from thee, when I was made in secret, and curiously wrought in the lowest parts of the earth. Thine eyes did see my substance, yet being unperfect; and in thy book all my members were written, which in continuance were fashioned, when as yet there was none of them," (Ps. cxxxix.) This, the opening of His discourse, doth therefore set the meat of His holy and sanctified body in opposition to the loaves and fishes for which the people would fain have followed Him, and He calleth upon them to work for that better meat, just as He said unto the Samaritan woman, "If thou knewest the gift of God, and who it is that saith to thee, Give me to drink; thou wouldest have asked of him, and he would have given thee living water, . . . which shall be in thee a well of water springing up into everlasting life." And again, as He saith of Himself, "My meat is to do the will of him that sent me, and to finish his work." Having proposed to them this food of everlasting life, His body about to be offered, which would in like manner nourish in them the disposition to do His Father's will, and make them messengers of God sent unto the world, as He into the world had been sent; He calls upon them to labour or to work for this meat, and not for the meat which perisheth: unto which His exhortation and request they did promptly answer, thinking that He would propose to them some enterprise of royal state worthy of the triumphant and powerful Messiah, whom they believed to be before them, saying, "What shall we do that we might work the works of God?" He had called upon them to work for the meat of everlasting life, and they ask Him how they should go about it. Here, then, is the very knot to be untied. The discourse, on all hands, is allowed to be a discourse concerning nothing else but the eating of His flesh and blood; for when He opened it by calling upon them to labour, they asked Him how. And what answer maketh He? Ver. 29: "Jesus answered and said unto them, This is the work of God, that ye believe on him whom he hath sent." Here, then, is a categorical declaration that faith is the work of God, whereby they should obtain the meat which endureth unto everlasting life. Faith, therefore, is that which layeth hold upon, and obtaineth, and possesseth, and eateth, and drinketh the meat which the Son of man hath given. It is called a work, to liken and parallel it to that labour of the body and the mind, by which man procureth the meat that perisheth, to signify that it must be ever doing, and is never done withal. For as it hath come to pass, by reason of the ground which God hath cursed, that not without labour will the earth yield food, there being no where any sabbatical and jubilee year wherein it produceth of itself; so must the bread of immortal life be attained unto by a diligence and toil of faith, called here the work of God, and by St Paul the work of faith; which proceedeth by the labour of love, as he saith in another place: "Faith worketh by love;" and which ever fighteth a battle and achieveth the victory, as is said in another place, "This is the victory that overcometh the world, even our faith;" and which, finally, is the very use of that meat, even to strengthen us for the work, and make us mighty for the battle, according to the word of our Lord already quoted, "My meat is to do the will of him that sent me, and to finish his work." Therefore is faith called a work, because it obtaineth meat by diligent and fervent meditation of the truth, apprehension of the promise, performance of the commandment, and upstirring of all the soul's faculties, and moving of all the body's forces, under the main strength of God's Spirit inhabiting and empowering us to this very thing, that we may lay hold on Christ, and feed upon Him, and do the will of His Father which is in heaven. But we have not yet come to that part of our subject which treats of faith, what it is in him that hath it, but only shewing that it is the subject of our Lord's discourse in the passage before us, and that it is the hand which layeth hold, the mouth which eateth, and the life which rejoiceth, in that divine meat. In further proof of which position, observe with me what is written at the 35th verse: "And Jesus said unto them, I am the bread of life; he that cometh to me shall never hunger; and he that believeth on me shall never thirst. But I said unto you, That ye also have seen me, and believed not." These words occur in our Lord's discourse, after He had corrected them in their misapplication of that passage of Scripture, "He gave them bread from heaven to eat," which they would have to be spoken of the manna, but our Lord to be spoken of Himself; because the manna was no bread from heaven having virtue of immortal life, but only common nourishment of this mortal estate. Wherefore, also, that corruptible manna, before it was laid up in the ark of the covenant before the Lord, in the most holy place, which is the figure of heaven, had first to be inclosed in a golden pot before it could receive its virtue of incorruption, to signify that no flesh should be able to nourish immortal life until it should first be inclosed and encompassed with the divine nature, by which it should attain incorruption, and the presentation in God's presence, and the faculty of coming down from heaven again in the substance of the Holy Ghost, and giving life unto the world. By the magnificence of these our Lord's words, being mightily attracted, overpowered, and borne along, they said, "Lord, evermore give us this bread;" even as the woman of Samaria said, "Sir, give me this water that I thirst not, neither come hither to draw." In reply to which their unconscious assent and impatient request, heedless of the mystery of His words and fascinated by the beauty of them, He replied, "I am the bread of life: he that cometh to me shall never hunger; and he that believeth on me shall never thirst." In which words I see the second proof that faith is the subject of our Lord's discourse in the passage before us. For having avowed Himself, the man speaking unto them, to be the very bread of life, the very bread of God come down from heaven to give life unto the world, He asserteth that every one who came to Him should never hunger, consequently, should have eaten that meat; and every one who believed on Him should never thirst, consequently, should have drunk that drink. The act of coming to Him, therefore, is the same with the act of eating Him, because it issueth in a man hungering no more; and the act of believing on Him is the same with the act of drinking His blood, because it issueth in thirsting no more.

Now, with respect to these two expressions, "coming to Him," and "believing on Him," the former hath special reference to Him as an object present upon the earth, and the latter hath a larger and wider reference to Him, not only as present, but also as absent for a while to be present for ever; but that the expressions are one in substance, and that "coming to Him" is for those then present as strong an expression as that of "believing on Him" is to us, we have put beyond a doubt in the 37th verse: "All that the Father giveth me shall come to me; and him that cometh to me I will in no wise cast out." We have it, therefore, beyond a doubt that there is no more mystery in the expressions used afterwards, such as "eating my flesh," and "drinking my blood," than there is in the expressions, "coming unto me," and "believing on me," because the two mysteries issue in the same result, which is a life that needeth no sustenance nor repair, that is, an immortal life. We shall see in the sequel why it is that the expression is changed from "coming and believing" into "eating and drinking;" but for the present we rest in the conclusion, that the expressions are used to signify the same mystery. But that this point might be more strongly confirmed, He referreth them in the verse following to a former declaration which He had made, concerning their unbelief, (verse 36): "But I said unto you, That ye also have seen me and do not believe," referring no doubt to the words with which He began His discourse: "Ye seek me, not because ye saw the miracles;" that is to say, not out of any belief produced by His works which they had seen; for they had challenged Him: "What sign shewest thou then, that we may see, and believe thee;" in reply to which He says, "And ye also have seen me and do not believe;" Me, the sealed One of God; Me, God's own gift; Me, the bread of life; Me, the thing signified by every sign of God; even Me have ye seen and believed not. For, brethren, we greatly err in signaling out particular works of Christ, and particular words of Christ, as specially demonstrative of His divinity; which resteth upon the completeness of His wisdom, and power, and holiness, upon Himself the sanctified Man, separate from all men, though yet the Brother of all. To see Him, to hear Him, was evidence enough to Nathanael, and ought to have been evidence enough to every guileless Israelite; and that which hindered them from coming unto Him was their having been given up by the Father, in consequence of their misuse and neglect of Moses and the prophets, as He Himself declareth (ver. 65):

"Therefore said I unto you, that no man can come unto me, except it were given unto him of my Father." To see Him, therefore, ought to have been a sufficient satisfaction of faith, as He said unto Thomas: "Thomas, because thou hast seen me, thou hast believed me;" and to believe without seeing Him, as we do, is a great blessedness, as in the same place He declareth: "Blessed are they that have not seen and yet have believed." To which agree the words of 1 Peter i. 8: "Whom having not seen, ye love; in whom, though now we see him not, yet believing, ye rejoice with joy unspeakable and full of glory." This sight of Him they had had, and yet believed not; which shews us, as I said, that belief is the great subject concerning which the Lord holdeth this discourse. But that this may still more clearly appear, we draw your attention to the 40th verse, where the declaration is made more explicitly still. To this He draweth on by the following connexion of thought:—Having declared to them that they were not believers, He proceedeth to explain how it came to pass that they believed not; referring them to a higher and remoter origin of unbelief than they dreamed of in those times, than is commonly dreamed of in the times in which we live,—even to that origin of causes and fountain-head of all effects—the will of the invisible Father, the absolute will of the Godhead, as distinct from, and standing above, the manifestation of the same which is made in Jesus Christ. These are His words:—All whatsoever the Father giveth me [unto me] shall come: and him that cometh unto me I will not cast out. Because I have come down out of heaven, not that I may do this will of mine, but the will of him that sent me. This now is the will of him that sent me, that all whatsoever he hath given to me I shall not lose of it, but shall raise it again in the last day. For this is the will of him that sent me, that every man whatever beholding the Son, and believing into him, should have eternal life, and him will I raise in the last day. Here Christ referreth back as always, unto His Father, as the mainspring, and moving power, and succeeder of the work of salvation; and Himself, He doth present as receiving His Father's chosen and elected ones after the nature of a gift, and preserving them from being cast out into the outward darkness, unto which the fallen creature must of itself, and by the decree of God, come at length. And He further representeth that He had come down from heaven, and put Himself into the conditions of a creature, with a creature will, not for the end of doing that will of the creature, but for the end of still doing the will of the invisible Godhead; in which you may recognise the obedient Son, the Man of Faith, the Prophet of Truth. Now, saith He, seeing I may not, and purpose not, to set up any will of mine own, but faithfully and truly to preach my Father's will in the great congregation—by the which will, saith the apostle, we are sanctified—hear ye, saith the Son, what is the Father's will which hath sent me;—it is this, That of all whatsoever He hath given me I shall lose nothing at all by its being cast into the second death, but shall raise it up again in the last day. But lest they should hereupon draw off from Him, as an incapable and insufficient Saviour, and think to find the way unto the Father's mighty grace by some other means—to link the invisible Godhead with the visible Godhead, as well as to advance it above it—and to shew, that while the invisible essence was to be looked at through the visible manifestation, it could not otherwise be known, He further giveth them to wit concerning that absolute and abysmal will in these words: "For this is the will of him that sent me, that every one whosoever beholdeth the Son, and into him believeth, should have life eternal, and him will I raise up in the last day." Whereby He doth not mean to gainsay what He hath said concerning the absoluteness of God's will in the matter, but to declare and reveal another fact with respect to that absolute decree; which is, that eternal life was appointed unto those who saw the Son, and believed into Him;—which is to say, that besides and beyond this category of sight, or of faith, there was no other which contained one particle of the substance that was to be raised up in the last day,—but that of this category of faith not a jot should perish. And what, then, we may ask, in passing, is this last day's resurrection, wherein all the given quantity, and all the believing substance, and not a jot more, shall be raised up? It cannot be that resurrection of good, bad, and indifferent, of all that have ever lived and died, whereof the sleepy Church now dreameth. Far, far otherwise. It must be that first resurrection spoken of in the Apocalypse, wherein every one that hath a part is blessed and holy, on whom the second death hath no power, but they shall be priests of God and of Christ, and they shall reign with Him a thousand years. It must be that resurrection unto life which it is the object of our Lord's discourse, recorded in the preceding chapter, to distinguish and define from the resurrection unto condemnation; wherein, after having set forth eternal life as the reward of hearing and believing, and that the dead should hear the voice of the Son of God, and they that hear should live,—and to this having added the other mystery counterpart to this, that God had given Him authority to execute judgment also, He breaks out into these words, (chap. v. 28:) "Marvel not at this: for the hour is coming, in the which all that are in the graves shall hear his voice, and shall come forth; they that have done good, unto the resurrection of life; and they that have done evil, unto the resurrection of judgment." And who will go to tell me that the righteous rise to a resurrection of judgment, of whom it is said, (Rom. v. 1:) "There is therefore now no judgment to those that are in Christ Jesus;" and to whom it is said, (Heb. ix. 28,) that not unto judgment, but in direct contradistinction thereto, without charge of sin, He appeareth? And who shall tell me that the wicked rise to a resurrection of life, when they are adjudged unto the second death? How opposite, therefore, to all correct interpretation, how opposite to all correct ideas, is it to place these two resurrections as one mystery of God's work, and to include them under the same category, and to bring them into the same time, seeing they are thus separated by contradistinction of words and things, and do in truth form the two opposite poles of almighty power: whereof the first is His great concentrative power to redeem, and eternally quicken the fallen and dead creatures; the other, His concentrative power to destroy but not annihilate, to endow with immortal capacity of enduring the second death!

Forasmuch, then, as it is solemnly by the Lord declared to be the will of the invisible Father, in whom is hidden the incommunicable Godhead, that every one who seeth and believeth upon Christ, who is the manifested Godhead, should inherit the resurrection of life and immortality,—which is the last, the greatest, and the best gift which God hath to bestow upon the creature,—we may not add, unto the faith that came by sight, and now cometh by hearing, anything more, signified under the expression, "eating and drinking;" because there is not anything more to be bestowed, for which some higher qualification or attainment of God should be required. Faith, therefore, beyond a doubt, is the ultimate thing concerning which our Lord discourseth; and that word ought, being properly interpreted, to contain under it all which is afterwards expressed by eating His flesh and drinking His blood. Let us now advance another step in the examination of this discourse. The Jews, it is said, murmured at Him, because He said, "I am the bread which came down from heaven." And they said, "Is not this Jesus, the son of Joseph, of whom we know the father and the mother? How then saith this person, I have come down from heaven?" If, indeed, Jesus had been a mere man, as they supposed, the son of Joseph, as was reputed, their objection would have been a sufficient one; for how could He claim to be descended from the heavens, more than another man? Unto whom Jesus replied, by repeating what He had already said: "Murmur not among yourselves. No man can come to me, except the Father which hath sent me draw him: and I will raise him up at the last day;" as if He had said: Do not take it amiss that I have thus spoken, for otherwise I cannot speak, because it is as I have declared unto you. Neither grieve yourselves with yourselves, as if the power lay with you to come; nor be vexed with me, as if the power lay with me to draw you, but of a verity believe that there is an unseen power which must co-operate with its visible expression, a will besides and beyond the Word, which I am, another Person, from whom I have mine origin, yet approachable only through me, with whom I am one, and yet am not He. To this Person, who worketh in me, and who is seen in me, make your petition, and in Him place your dependence, instead of murmuring as now you do. For if you doubt the word which I have declared unto you, and will not believe me, whom to believe is life eternal, then believe ye Moses and the prophets, in whom is it not written, "And they shall be all taught of God?" Every man, therefore, that hath heard and hath learned of the Father cometh unto me. And now we see the appropriateness of the language which He continually useth of Himself as the person seen, because He was the person spoken of in all the prophets. Hitherto they had heard of Him, but now they saw Him; and as John's privilege of laying his hand upon His head gave him preeminence above the prophets who had all told of Him, so the prerogative of that generation above the generations past was to see Him, of whom their fathers had but heard. And yet, because it is not the method of God to cast away His words like pearls unto swine, but to make them more precious than the gold of Ophir, Jesus declareth that those who had not heard the testimony of Moses and the prophets, neither listened to the teaching of God, who had spoken at sundry times and in divers manners by the prophets unto their fathers, either would or could come unto Him to recognise in Him the Messiah foretold and shadowed forth in the former messages of God, which is an awful warning unto you who will not give heed to what is taught in all the Scripture concerning His second coming in power and glory. Ye dream on, ye laugh scornfully, ye shoot out the lip and mock at our folly, and the folly of those who hunt what in your ignorance and superciliousness you are pleased to call a fable; look here for your correction, and take warning by what you see and hear of a people whom God had taught by prophets commissioned from Himself, who had the keeping of the Scriptures, and were even more faithful than the faithfulest of us can boast of, and yet, behold! when He cometh, they can neither recognise nor receive Him, because Satan, the subverter Satan, whose eye prophetic scanneth the forms of coming things, had taken them as he is now taking you with a false conception of, and endeavour after, that millennial age, where He, and He alone, is able to bring in the beauty and the blessedness by casting Satan out. But they were too wise to be contented with the Scriptures, and did cleave to the traditions of the elders; and so they failed and were broken upon Him, who was appointed to be a stone of stumbling, before He became the Shepherd and the Stone of Israel. Unto whom the Lord, having made this quotation from their prophets, doth straightway, lest they should suppose these prophets had any priority over Him in dignity as they had in time, add these words assertive of His own singular prerogative: "Not that any one hath seen the Father, save he which is with God, or beside God, he hath seen the Father." Being parallel with that other declaration, "No man hath seen God at any time; the only begotton Son, which is in the bosom of the Father, he hath declared him;" and with that other declaration of our evangelist, "Of his fulness have all we received, and grace for grace; for the law was given by Moses, but grace and truth came by Jesus Christ." This His unrivalled dignity of inhabiting the bosom of the Father and dwelling with Him in the bosom of invisible and inaccessible glory before the world was, having asserted to Himself, to the rebuking of the prophets and Moses into their own level as the forerunners of His Majesty, He doth, in His most solemn mood, asseverate the truth so oft repeated to them from the beginning of His discourse, which is the truth we mention as the great burden of the whole sermon, "Verily, verily, I say unto you, He that believeth on me hath everlasting life. I am that bread of life. Your fathers did eat manna in the wilderness, and are dead. This is the bread which cometh down from heaven, that a man may eat thereof, and not die. I am the living bread which came down from heaven: if any man eat of this bread, he shall live for ever: and the bread that I will give is my flesh, which I will give for the life of the world." In these words again, belief is with the Lord's most earnest manner declared to be the means unto everlasting life; bread, indeed, He is, of that life from heaven descended, but faith is that in us which layeth hold upon the bread, and eateth it and turneth it unto life. But there is added here, besides, another idea, which is, that the bread is His flesh, to be given for the life of the world. This referreth to His body, His fleshly body, bone of my bone, and flesh of my flesh—that body which He took when God willed not sacrifices nor offering; and this flesh, declareth He, He will give for the life of the world. Both, as seemeth unto me, for an atonement, to take away its sin, according to that word, "This is the Lamb of God, which taketh away the sin of the world;" and likewise for a nourishment, and sustenance, and source of strength of life to that world which was dead in trespasses and sins. I think certainly that the transition which is now made in this divine discourse from bread unto flesh, ariseth from the idea of a sacrifice, which He now presenteth to their consideration. It refers to the custom of eating the flesh of sacrifices after the feasts proper to God had been offered by the priests upon the altar; and likewise, in particular, and perhaps entirely, to those sacrifices, by which life was redeemed, as, for example, the paschal lamb, whose blood stricken upon the door-posts redeemed the life of the first-born in the house, whose flesh also nourished them all. I think, therefore, that at this point of the discourse the idea of sacrifice begins to be introduced. Still, however, this eating His flesh by us is no more than that act of faith which makes Him one with us and us one with Him, because at the beginning of this passage it is said, "He that believeth on me hath everlasting life." True saving faith doth eat the flesh of Christ, which is the bread of life, the manna that came down from heaven, and giveth life unto the world. There is still another idea, as I think, contained in these words, "The bread that I will give is my flesh, which I will give for the life of the world." Christ's flesh is no longer in existence, because He arose into heaven, not as flesh and blood, which cannot inherit the kingdom of heaven, but in that body proper to a spirit with which the dead shall rise, and which, in the fifteenth chapter of first Corinthians, Paul doth, by so many contrasts, set in opposition to this natural body, which falleth into the earth. If, then, Christ's fleshly body be now transformed into that glory which it put on in the mount of transfiguration, where is His flesh and where is His blood?

It is given, resigned, delivered up, for the life of the world. When the Son of God, the eternal person in the blessed Trinity, had taken a body of flesh and blood, according to the conditions of the fallen creature; when He had made this a part of Himself, and preserved it free from sin, holy and blameless, He could likewise have preserved it from death by that eternal life which was first manifested in Him; as it is written, "For the life was manifested, and we have seen it, and bear witness, and shew unto you that eternal life, which was with the Father, and which was manifested unto us." He whose voice shall quicken the dead, could have preserved His body from the power of death. It was a great act of humiliation to come into creature form at all, and a greater act of humility was it to take upon Him the form of the fallen creature; but a third, and still greater act of voluntary humility it was, to give up His life, which no one taketh from Him. This was the act contemplated in the eternal counsel, and revealed to us under that word, "The Lamb slain from the foundation of the world." Surely His death was a part of the eternal purpose and covenant between the Father and the Son, from which lowest point of humiliation His exaltation was to begin. And wherefore was this act of slaying the Lamb of God a part of the eternal purpose? It was a part of the eternal purpose, for the end of shewing the creature that it had no life in itself; that existence which it hath anterior to the manifestation of its life in Christ, must be proved not to be very life by the act of dying, and in that state of disproved life it must receive life from the Son of God by the regeneration and resurrection of the Holy Ghost. Now, Christ's coming into death and giving up His fleshly body, was the completion of that purpose of God, which death had from the beginning foreshadowed, and it accomplished the great humiliation of the creature, by which it becometh separate from the Creator. This death, as it came not into the world without a purpose of God, so neither did it come without a cause in the creature, which is the disobedience of the commandment of God, which is sin; for sin is well defined to be any want of conformity unto, or transgression of, the law of God. Death, therefore, is in time the monument of sin; and the second death shall be the monument of it through eternity. If, then, through sin in the creature death came, how can resurrection from death come otherwise than by taking away the guilt of sin? Christ, therefore, in whom the resurrection was manifested, as well as the life, must take away that guilt of sin from as many as are raised from the dead. For as it is written, "The sting of death is sin, and the strength of sin is the law." Under the law, therefore, came He, that He might keep the law, and be proved sinless, the holy and the righteous One; and under death came He, that He might be proved to be not only life in the living, but also life from the dead—that He might be proved not only a quickener of life in mortal flesh, but a quickener of life in the hollow tomb. Wherefore He is called the resurrection and the life. But seeing that Christ shall quicken with immortal life those only who have done good, and shall raise unto the second death all the rest, all who have done evil, why is it said, in the passage before us, that he giveth his flesh for the life of the world? and in other passages, as, for example, "Behold the Lamb of God, which taketh away the sin of the world;" whereas, in other passages, again, He saith, on the contrary, "I pray not for the world, but for them which thou hast given me out of the world." To understand this seeming contradiction, you must recollect that man being the head of the world, in his death the world died. The creatures together with one fall came under the power of death, so that the world is subsisting in a state of death. Now when Christ, the true man, arose from the dead, He drew up with Him, though not at that instant, yet in the fulness of time to be accomplished, every one in his own order, yet with Him truly and virtually arose first they that are Christ's at His coming to the earth, when the earth shall be delivered from Satan, but not from death; and during the millennium He shall reign, and His living saints in their immortal glory, having visible bodies, over the kingdom of flesh and blood, upon the earth, until the time cometh, in the fulness of the Divine purpose, for the destruction of death itself, at which time the resurrection unto judgment shall proceed, and the wicked be cast out into the outer darkness of the second death; and the kingdom, now delivered from death, and delivered from wickedness, as it had been delivered from Satan and his angels, shall be delivered up, blooming in the beauty and standing in the strength of immortal life, unto the Father; and then shall this word be accomplished, that He hath given His flesh for the life of the world; seeing that the world, now living in immortal life, and for ever to abide therein, hath received the same from the act by which Christ gave His flesh upon the cross a sacrifice for us. When in other places He saith, "I pray not for the world," He means the unregenerate part of the world, which the Father hath not contemplated in His purpose of resurrection unto life, but doomed to be cast out into the waste of the second death. Now, though I have said thus much concerning Christ's sacrifice of Himself for us, the most fruitful idea in this passage is not yet exhausted, which concerneth the eating of His flesh. But as the Jews proposed this to Him as a distinct question, we had better follow onwards the verses, as they lie in order. Ver. 52: "The Jews therefore strove among themselves, saying, How can this man give us his flesh to eat? Then Jesus said unto them, Verily, verily, I say unto you, Except ye eat the flesh of the Son of man, and drink his blood, ye have no life in you. Whoso eateth my flesh, and drinketh my blood, hath eternal life; and I will raise him up at the last day. For my flesh is meat indeed, and my blood is drink indeed." Now, dearly beloved brethren, ye have heard how I said above, that the flesh of Christ and His blood were in existence no more; but that His human nature is passed into that immortal form which flesh and blood cannot possess, though out of flesh and blood it ariseth by the power of the resurrection, even as flesh and blood is dust in itself, and unto dust returneth; but yet, being builded up into its present form by the creative power of God, doth become the fit abode for the immortal soul, and a proper instrument whereby the living soul may inherit, know, and possess all things;—so from the body of Christ, as it lay in the tomb under death and liable to corruption, though not to corrupt, as in life it was liable to sin, though it sinned not, did arise that eternal and immortal form of risen glory, wherein the Godhead, as in a spacious temple, shall shew forth its beauty, its majesty, its power, and, in one word, its will unto all creatures whatsoever. If, then, the flesh and blood of Christ have been so transfigured and transformed in their elemental principles, though not numerically changed, what meaneth He in this passage by such solemn asseveration: "Verily, verily, I say unto you, Unless ye eat the flesh of the Son of man, and drink his blood, ye have no life within yourselves;" for how can we eat that which hath no more a being? There are two questions here necessary to be separated from one another, whereof the first is, what is this flesh, that we might eat it? and what is meant by the eating of it? His flesh and His blood are His true body, not in its present but in its former state—during the days of His flesh. Of that body, now no longer existent, He saith, Verily, verily, we must eat in order to have life in ourselves. Well might the Jews say, "This is a hard word, who can hear it?" It is a hard word. I feel it to be a hard word, whether in the hearing or in the expounding of it, and I do not wonder at the Papists falling into their error of transubstantiation, by which they affirm that the priest doth first make the bread and wine into flesh and blood, before the people can have flesh and blood of Christ to eat and to drink. For, certes, there is no flesh and blood of Christ in being; and if it is to be eaten, it must first be. That the consecration by the priest, therefore, of the elements should turn them into flesh and blood, is a necessary preliminary unto the eating of them by the people. If eating, therefore, be literal, eating then the bread and wine must be literal flesh and blood; and how it is to become so, I see no better way than by the consecration of the priest. But if that which we have proved by the examination of this discourse from the beginning be true, to wit, that eating and drinking is all along synonymous with believing, and a form of speech used to express some very high mystery of faith, then are we delivered from the dilemma of the Papists, which reduceth them to the making the flesh and blood of Christ before they can eat it. But yet, as there is something very startling indeed in this express and oft-repeated language of Christ, I crave your patience to pause with me a little longer, while I fortify the position that I have been building up, concerning the identity of the act of faith with the act of eating, by an examination given by our Lord Himself of this hard word in the 63d and 64th verses : " It is the spirit that quickeneth [that maketh alive]; the flesh profiteth nothing: the words that I speak unto you are spirit, and are life. But there are some of you that believe not. . . . Therefore said I unto you, that no man can come unto me, except it were given unto him of my Father." This word was spoken unto His disciples, to reassure their minds, which had been skaken, and were quivering in doubt ;—and unto what amounteth the explanation ? It amounteth unto this: that the flesh had in it no profit nor value of life, but the Spirit which inhabiteth the flesh,—that is, the Holy Ghost, which came unto His body, and was the cause of its quickening in the womb, and continued to be the informing principle of its life. My flesh therefore, saith He, that which ye see and handle, is of no avail to give ye life; therefore think not, O ye most faithless men, that by eating this flesh I mean you to attain unto life; but know that by reason of the Holy Ghost who lodgeth in this flesh of mine, and will not separate Himself from thence for ever, is the life quickened, and to Him who now is mine, and from me, and by me, proceedeth forth, do you direct your faith, and hear the words that I speak by the Holy Spirit with which I am anointed, to preach glad tidings unto you, for these words of mine are spirit and they are life. Therefore it is that Christ is called a life-giving spirit, in contradistinction to Adam, who was but a living soul. And doth, then, all this earnestness and repeated asseveration about eating His flesh and drinking His blood amount to no more than this—that we are to hear His words and believe them ? Is this all ? Ay, this is all; and how great an all it is will appear when we come to consider what faith is, of which I will say at present that the only definition which I can find capable of expressing it is, that it eats the flesh and drinks the blood of the Lord. This is regenerating faith to take us out of the body of Adam, in which we are by nature, and join us unto the body of Christ.

This is living faith,—that we draw near unto Christ; that we close with Him; that we lay hold upon Him, as the child upon its mother's breast, and draw nourishment from His living body. And what is that nourishment? It is the Holy Ghost; He is the life in the state of procession now flowing out from the Head into the members, who during the days of Christ's flesh was in Him in a state of fixation, like the waters in the rock before it was smitten by the rod of Moses. And what is the consequence unto us of thus drawing forth by faith, or of Christ deriving unto us, by grace, the flowing stream of the Holy Ghost? The consequence unto us is this, that the flesh and blood of our human nature becometh changed into the flesh and blood of Christ's human nature; for whereas we heretofore were all corrupt, unclean, and defiled, and unto every good work reprobate, we do become, through the power of the Holy Ghost dwelling in our flesh, holy, blameless, heavenly-minded, members of Christ, and sons of God. And our flesh, which heretofore lusted after worldly and wicked desires, doth now long for God, as the hart panteth in the wilderness for the water-brooks. "Our very flesh and heart cry out for the living God." "Our flesh longeth as in a dry parched land where there be no waters." I say, that there is another law propagated by the Spirit throughout the flesh of man, upon which, no doubt, there still lieth the bondage of corruption, and the curse of death; but yet, not the less truly is it in a sanctified state, because it is obnoxious to all temptation. Nay, let me tell you, that this is our fellowship with Christ, that this is Christ's fellowship with us. Were we delivered from the pressure of sin in the flesh, we would have no fellowship with Him who overcame sin in the flesh. Were we delivered from the controversy which the Spirit causeth in the flesh, against the powers of darkness and of death, we would have no fellowship with Him, who therefore was brought under the power of death that He might overcome him that had the power of death. It is of His flesh and blood subsistence that we partake, not of His resurrection subsistence; and to that flesh and blood subsistence an outward openness unto, and contact with, the powers of wickedness, is as necessary as an inward presence of, and indwelling and empowering of, the Holy Ghost, to overcome and preserve us holy, against all the corrupt, and corrupting, and oppressing powers of the fallen world. Therefore, when a man in flesh and blood hath received the Holy Ghost, proceeding from Christ, he is brought—his flesh and blood are brought, his body is brought—into the self-same condition of existence in which Christ's human subsistence was, in which His flesh and blood was, from the time that it was quickened in the virgin's womb by the Holy Ghost, until the time that it was transformed in the tomb by the Holy Ghost, out of the state of flesh and blood into the state of immortal glory in the which it now subsisteth. So that verily, verily, in deed and in truth, there is no other way of expressing the effect and consequence of the baptism of the Holy Ghost but by saying, that it giveth us to partake of a new substance or subsistence, which is not the substance or subsistence of the fallen Adam, as by generation transmitted; which is not the substance or subsistence of the second Adam, by resurrection communicated; but is the subsistence intermediate between these two, which the Holy Ghost gave unto the body of Christ, found in the virgin, as to her it had been transmitted from Adam, enabling and empowering it to live that holy life, and to fulfil those offices of power and holiness, and utter those words of grace and truth which Christ in the days of His flesh, and He alone, ever did and ever uttered. Now, that same Holy Spirit findeth in each one of us a living substance of the fallen Adam, which cannot cease from sin; and He doth quicken it, by regeneration, with life divine, and doth enable it to subsist as Christ subsisteth; to war against Satan, to overcome sin, and to do good, and to love God, and to keep His commandments, and not to sin. This, I say, is partaking of Christ's flesh and blood; this is being one with Him, as He is one with the Father; this is to have the Spirit; this is to be regenerated; this is to have the spirit of adoption; this is to be an heir of God and a joint-heir with Christ. And there is no language which is able, with so much beauty, and with so little ambiguity, to express it all, as that which is so often used, as " eating his flesh and drinking his blood;" where you have only to guard against the error of literally eating that which never could be literally eaten, unless it had been eaten alive or during the hours it was in the tomb, being never afterwards in existence as a thing, but commemorated as a former state of a thing now existing in a different state. This error, I say, being guarded against, and nothing but Satan's incredible ability could, by the doctrine of transubstantiation, have perpetuated this literal interpretation of the men of Capernaum, and you have it at once, the whole work of the Spirit expressed in the words, "eating my flesh and drinking my blood." That is translating you from flesh and blood of Adam to flesh and blood of Christ.

In order to open this a little more distinctly and fully, you must keep a good reckoning and account of the difference between Christ's state of humiliation and His state of exaltation, as they are set forth in the Shorter Catechism, whereof the humiliation is the state of continual oppression; the other, the state of triumph and of continual victory,—of which oppressions now triumphed over by Christ, of which captivities now led captive by Him, flesh and blood was one of the three chief. To be in flesh was a part of the humiliation of Christ, and in flesh to be holy was a chief part of His mighty work. Christ shewed a constitution of flesh and blood, perfectly holy, perfectly harmless, perfectly obedient unto God,— a thing which never had been exhibited in existence before; and this He did exhibit through the fulness of the Holy Ghost, which abode in His manhood;—and this fulness of the Holy Ghost He received of the Father, in virtue of that great act of devotedness to His Father's glory by which He joined His eternal divinity to the fallen substance of manhood. Now, this holy subsistence of flesh and blood which Christ brought into being, and which is no longer in being in the united state of one individual person, He hath broken up into pieces and bequeathed to all His true disciples, that they, partaking of the same, may grow into the same likeness of His humility, enter into the fellowship of His sufferings, and fulfil all the good will and pleasure of God. This I hold to be the true idea of Christ's broken body; and it is an idea both simple in itself and analogous with the constitution of human nature: for you see the counterpart of it in the first Adam, who became a sinful substance, and, in a sinful substance, disobedient to God, and full of sin, before he became the parent of children. These brought the sinful substance of flesh and blood into existence by the fall, and there they stood, having it all included in themselves; but soon, by birth of children, was it broken, violently broken, into parts; and in parts it now continueth. We are, though individual persons, but parts of that sinful substance which was all included in Adam. And this is the only true account of human nature: that it is a system of sinful flesh, once united in one person, but now broken into many parts, that it might be the inheritance of many persons. Now, with this fact before our eyes, and this the only visible account of the fact of our fallen nature,—which also, by generation of children, is continually kept before our eyes, whereby the sinful substance of the parents is taken into parts, to become the inheritance of many persons in their children,—I say, with this before our eyes, let us consider the idea which hath been given above of Christ's broken flesh, and see if it be not the very counterpart thereof. Christ, the second Adam, having accomplished the redemption of that sinful substance of human nature which Adam had introduced,—and by union of the Godhead therewith, and consequent full possession of the Holy Ghost, having prevailed to drag it out of the miry clay and the fearful pit into which God's word had doomed it,—having constituted it a righteous substance, the habitation of light, life, and holiness, which before had been the habitation of darkness, sin, and death,—He held the righteous, holy thing wrapped up in Himself, yet unbroken, yet undivided into parts. Inhabited only by one person, and that the person of the Son of God, who, having created the creature in its first estate, had thus redeemed the creature into its second estate, and stood in it, and to it, eternally united,—having made it of Himself to be, and no longer out of Himself to be,—which is the great distinction between the creature's creation estate and the creature's regeneration estate: that, in the former, it is out of the Creator and the Creator out of it; but, in the latter, it is taken into the Creator, and the Creator eternally united with it;—this mystery, I say, of redeeming the fallen system of flesh and blood, and presenting it pure and spotless unto the Father, Christ having prevailed to accomplish, He stood the very counterpart of Adam and Eve after they had fallen, and before the conception of children—Christ, the antitype; Adam, the type—Adam, the producer of the sinful thing; Christ, the bringer up again of that sinful thing into a holy estate. And now, shall the correspondency of the type and the antitype end here, and go on no further? If Adam, being the container of the sinful substance, did, as it were, fall into pieces innumerable, each of whom became, as it were, a part of his broken body, inheriting and conveying unto all posterity the very fellowship thereof, shall not Christ likewise, when about to lay off flesh and blood, and ascend into another estate with which flesh and blood hath no fellowship, divide that holy substance of flesh and blood, which He was, amongst His children by regeneration of faith? that they partaking thereof, may be the manifest election of God, as the rest were the manifest reprobation of God; so that they, by partaking of that Holy Spirit in manhood which enabled Him from the mother's womb to sanctify the sinful vessel of His humanity, and present it without sin, may be able in like manner to sanctify the sinful vessel of their own humanity, and be in due time presented blameless in the presence of the Father. When, therefore, the loaf is set forth in the holy supper, one lump, and it is said over it, "This is my body," what doth it, what can it signify, but that faith should therein discern that holy substance of flesh and blood which Christ was before His ascension, but which He is no more, and which hath no more an objective reality to sight, but is in truth a remembered and commemorated thing,—is, in truth, a thing that was, and is no longer, existent in an individual, undivided form,—therefore an object to the memory of sight, even as Adam is in his individual capacity;—but as truly an object of presence in the faithful in its divided state, as is the substance of Adam in its divided state—yea, I may say is the only object of presence in the inward man of faith, even as the substance of Adam is the only thing present in the outward man of nature and of sense? Though the bread, therefore, in the communion be properly and rightly presented first as one unbroken loaf, to signify to the memory of faith that this broken substance of holiness, now present in all the election, was once present only in the chosen and holy One, and thus maketh the ordinance commemorative, (which, indeed, I may observe, in passing, is lost in the sister Church, by presenting the bread already broken into pieces, and in the apostasy by presenting it in wafer,) it doth, while it remains in that unbroken state, serve only for commemoration; but straightway, when it is broken, it serveth as an object, as I may say, to the present sense of faith; for Christ's holy subsistency in flesh and blood is as much present in His members as Adam's wicked subsistency of flesh and blood is present in all mankind; and when we do eat a part of the broken bread, we do by faith eat a part of the broken body of Christ, and so become of His flesh and of His bone. Faith, therefore, discerneth in the broken bread the subsistency of His flesh and blood in a broken state, until He shall come again, as really and truly as faith discerned in the son of Mary the same holy subsistency in an individual and undivided state. I say faith in both cases, for sense truly had nothing to do in either. Peter did not say, "Thou art the Son of God," by any act of flesh and blood, nor by reflecting upon the miracles and words which he saw and heard, although, no doubt, these had a certain influence upon him; but our Lord expressly declared that flesh and blood had not revealed it unto him, but His Father, which is in heaven. To the eye of sense He was truly man, a lowly man, a broken-hearted man, a man of sorrows and acquainted with grief; but to the eye of faith He was the Son of God, "which is, and which was, and which is to come," the Almighty. Even so He hath presented the substance of His broken body to faith under the larger symbol of bread and wine, in which sense discerneth but bread and wine, but in which faith discerneth the broken body and shed blood of Christ. It is not His personal subsistency, otherwise the Papists were justified in worshipping the sacrament. His personal subsistency is now in the risen man, heretofore it was in the man of sorrows; but Christ is no longer personally subsistent in the Church, but subsistent in it by the Holy Spirit, which dwells in His manhood. He is personally subsistent in the son of Mary, now in the estate of glory, God and man in two natures and one person for ever; but He is not personally subsistent in any one of the members of His Church, nor in all the members put together, otherwise the saints and the Church were proper objects of worship. The union with Christ, which we eat and drink into in the holy supper, is not a union of personality such as existeth between the seed of Mary and the Son of God, but a union of the sameness of substance with His manhood, though not the sameness of substance with His Godhead. As He and the Father are one substance in the Godhead, yet different persons, so are believers and Christ one substance in the holy manhood, though different persons. And as the unity of the substance of the Father and the Son in the Godhead is maintained and carried on by the intercommunion, or, as the old divines called it, the vinculum of the Holy Ghost, so is the union of substance between the manhood of Christ and that of all His members preserved through the operation and circulation of the Holy Spirit descending from the head to the utmost extremity of the body, and preserving through the whole the communion of saints. Now, if Christ is not in such a way present in any of His members or in His Church corporate as that He should be made an object of worship, how much less is He present in the broken bread, which doth but represent to sense the sign of that membership of His Church—is He present in such a manner as to be worshipped? And if faith, discerning His true presence in the membership of His Church, doth not worship His Church, or use its intercession, or set value upon its merits, how much less ought faith, though discerning the presence of Christ's broken body in the bread, to bow down and worship the same? And wherefore? Because He is personally present neither in the one nor in the other, but in the son of Mary alone, with whom He is consubstantiated two natures in one person for ever and for ever. Faith discerning His presence in the son of Mary, did rightly bow down and worship Him, because the Godhead was wholly present therein; but faith, discerning

His presence in the bread and wine, or in His Church, may not worship Him, because the person of His Godhead is not present therein, but the nature of His manhood, as informed by the Holy Ghost. If any one ask here, And why may we not worship that which the Holy Ghost inhabiteth? I answer, that this honour is reserved only for the Son of man, because He is also the Son of God, whom we should honour even as we honour the Father; and this honour hath the Holy Spirit dwelling in Christ, which He hath not dwelling in a member of Christ, because in the member of Christ He is, as it were, subservient to Christ, even as Christ in human nature was subservient to the Father, though in the undivided substance of the Trinity neither Christ nor the Holy Spirit be under any obligation of service. But into this subject it is not proper that we should enter further, seeing our present object is not at large to open the Lord's supper, but to shew wherefore the language of eating His flesh and blood should be used to denote the true nature of faith. Yet neither is this a digression which we have made into the subject of the supper, which, as we said at the beginning of our discourse, is like the needle which pointeth to the magnet, because it is of itself a part of the great magnetic substance, or brought under the power of magnetic influence;—so wisely doth the Lord's supper continually point to this the true act of saving faith, which appropriates the very subsistence of Christ unto ourselves, or eats His flesh and blood. Nor is the Lord's supper a mere index pointing thereto, and suggesting continually this the true acting of faith, but it is like the needle, a part of the same—that is to say, in the Lord's supper that faith is acted, and then specially acted; acted with all the special advantages of a visible ordinance; acted also with special promises made unto the faithful, to meet them there, as it were, upon the holy mount; to feed them there, as it were, with the fallen manna from heaven; to refresh them there as when the water flowed from the rock; to entertain them there as when Moses and the elders eat and drank in the holy mount, and saw God, and were preserved. Oh! there is little danger now-a-days of making the sacrament superstitiously sacred; that door, I think, is closed for ever upon the Protestant

Church. But, ah! what danger presseth on every side, lest, from converting the sacrament into a commemorative rite, we should altogether make shipwreck of the true character and meaning of faith as an act of the Holy Ghost in us, in our flesh and blood, kindred with that act of the Holy Ghost in Christ's flesh and blood, whereby the will or soul of man is redeemed from the main oppression of sin and death, and left free to obey God, to love Him, to delight in Him, and to fulfil all His pleasure;—which openeth the avenue into a most beautiful field of discourse concerning the condition of the soul from the time it is joined unto the body until the time that it is redeemed from the power of the body of sin and death by the Holy Ghost. But into this subject I shall not be tempted, however much disposed and inclined, to enter thereon; but that you may see in a few words, and, as it were, with a glance round the whole subject of faith, which we have undertaken to teach, I will crave your good heed to this which I am about to say, still further, before leaving this first head of matter, which is, in a word, to shew you why the expression "eating and drinking" and not the expression "hearing and reading" is so much insisted upon in this discourse concerning faith, which, however, will better appear after reading the words which still remain of this divine discourse.

Ver. 56–58, "He that eateth my flesh, and drinketh my blood, dwelleth in me, and I in him. As the living Father hath sent me, and I live by the Father: so he that eateth me, even he shall live by me. This is that bread which came down from heaven: not as your fathers did eat manna, and are dead: he that eateth of this bread shall live for ever." Now, brethren, if our Lord had, by a mere figure of speech, excited this tumult in His audience, He would certainly soon have allayed it by explaining their misapprehension of His meaning. If He meant merely that they should receive His word like the words of any other prophet or messenger from God, eat His words as the prophet Ezekiel eat the roll from God—if the whole mystery of His language amounted only to this, (which I ask your pardon for even supposing, and I do it only because it is in fact the supposition which they take up who believe the sacraments to be but naked and bare signs, and who would say, "This is the sign or symbol of my body," instead of saying, "This is my body);"—I say, if the Lord had perceived that the Jews were misunderstanding Him in taking up His words to signify a literal eating of faith, and not a mere hearing, He would instantly have set them right; so far from which, He doth repeat and confirm, with a twofold asseveration, the very words which He had spoke. Jesus, therefore, said to them, "Verily, verily, I say to you, if ye eat not the flesh of the Son of man, and drink not his blood, ye have not life in yourselves. Whoso eateth my flesh, and drinketh my blood, hath eternal life, and I will raise him up in the last day; for my flesh truly is meat, and my blood truly is drink. He that eateth my flesh and drinketh my blood, remaineth in me, and I in him. According as the living Father sent me, and I live by the Father; also, whoso eateth me, that same person shall also live by me. This is that bread which descendeth out of heaven, not according as your fathers eat manna and died, he eating this bread shall live for ever." In the whole compass of the Holy Scriptures, perhaps in the whole compass of recorded speech, there is not such a strong reiteration and earnest enforcement of one truth, and that the same of which the first mention had set the audience into a tumult of contention; the one truth, to wit, that nothing less than eating and drinking His flesh and blood would ensure eternal life, and the resurrection thereto in the day of the Lord. There is added upon the foundation of this truth two forms or variations of the same: the first, that this act of eating His flesh and drinking His blood did constitute a permanent and abiding union unto Himself, and not only so, but a permanent union and an abiding of Him in us; we in Him, and He in us. The second variation of the same truth is, that this life, thus constituted between us and Christ by the act of eating His flesh and drinking His blood, is life in the highest form—yea, is the very life of life; being no other than that which subsisteth between the Father of life and His own eternal Son. Which expressions, I doubt not, bring to your mind those parallel expressions in the last prayer of the Lord; which, observe, are made not to flow from eating and drinking, but from faith, which, as we have all along maintained in our discourse, is the act—the spiritual act—whose approximating, appropriating, uniting, and possessing power, the Lord laboureth so hard to express by the act of eating His flesh and drinking His blood. The passage I refer to is in John xvii. 20–23: "Neither pray I for these alone, but for them also which shall believe on me through their word; that they all may be one; as thou, Father, art in me, and I in thee, that they also may be one in us: that the world may believe that thou hast sent me. And the glory which thou gavest me I have given them; that they may be one, even as we are one: I in them, and thou in me, that they may be made perfect in one; and that the world may know that thou hast sent me, and has loved them, as thou hast loved me." This passage in the intercessory prayer, being compared with that passage in the discourse of eating His flesh and blood, doth sufficiently shew that they contain and express the same most intimate, most abiding of all unions, the union of Christ and believers, which hath no similitude nor equivalent in creation, but is of the same kind, and degree, and subsistence, which existeth between the Father and Christ Himself. The Lord, being desirous to put forth unto the men of Capernaum the whole power of this great doctrine of union between the person of Christ and the person of the believer, doth find no other language by which to express it but that which he useth, to wit, the eating of His flesh and the drinking of His blood; being as much as to say, that the believer through faith doth enter into the substance and subsistence of Christ, and dwell therein, endued with all its strength, and pervaded with all its life, and furnished with all its powers, and graces, and beauties, and perfections, and, in a word, as entirely one and the same with it, as our bodies would be one and the same with His body, if we were actually (monstrous supposition which the Papists have sanctified!) to eat His flesh and drink His blood. The great object of the discourse, and it is an object of surpassing moment, is to teach His disciples of what nature, power, and faculty is that which he calleth faith, and which the Father alone can give. That it is of such a potency to discern, appropriate, and assimilate Christ unto us, and us unto Christ, as is the eating of nature to discern, appropriate, and assimilate the food unto itself; so that of two things, the food and the living body, one thing after eating should be composed. The like power, saith Christ, hath faith to take hold of the body of Christ, which now is another thing from the believer, and to make it one thing with the believer, and the believer one with it.

In these remarks, which we were led into by the quotations from John, I have a little interrupted the regular progress, and anticipated the conclusion of our discourse. Let us return then again to the 6th of John, at the 59th verse, where we left off:—These things spake he in the synagogue, when teaching in Capernaum. Many therefore of his disciples who heard, said, Hard is this word, who can hear it? Jesus, however, knowing in himself that his disciples murmured concerning the same, said to them, Doth this scandalise you? Were you then to see the Son of man ascending to where he was before; the Spirit is that which maketh the life; the flesh profiteth nothing: the words which I speak to you are spirit and are life. But of you there are some who do not believe. The words which He had spoken were of so corporeal, and, I may say, material a sense, that the wonder is not that some should have taken them literally, and do yet take them literally to mean an eating and drinking by the sense of a material flesh and blood, but the wonder is, upon the other hand, that all should not have taken up this interpretation of them. We wonder not that the error of transubstantiation, all absurd as it is, should have come into the Church, when we read this discourse, and consider the language of the Lord's supper: "This is my body, and this is my blood." But we do wonder that any man of common honesty, having such words in the communion, and such an interpretation of these words in this discourse, should dare to say that there is not any real presence of the body and blood of Christ in the supper, or any real eating and drinking of the same by the faith of every believer; that it is a mere memorial of His death. Oh, I cannot express my abhorrence and detestation of such an ignominious, shameful deprivation of this holy mystery, which the Lord hath so defended; and I say it again, I would rather, many times, be guilty with those who ignorantly believe transubstantiation, interpreting our Lord's words to the sense to which He never spake, instead of interpreting them to faith, to which He always spake, than with those who contradict both the letter and the spirit, and speak neither to sense nor to faith, but to a mere acknowledgment of a fact which no well-informed man ever dreamt of doubting, that the Lord Jesus Christ was crucified upon Mount Calvary. If the Lord had meant merely that He was to die, and that His death was to be kept in remembrance, what were there so astounding in this to the ears of man, as that they should call it a hard word which no one could hear? and what were the meaning of wrapping it up in language which seemed constructed on very purpose to be offensive to the ear and common sense of man? If that, indeed, were His meaning merely, His words were ill-chosen words; and His disciples did well to be offended. But if, as hath been said, He would express an assimilating and uniting power of faith, such as there is no other language for expressing but the language of eating and drinking; and if the only object of that faith be His human substance, what other way was there to express the nature, the virtue, and the effects of that act of faith upon His human subsistence, but by eating His flesh and drinking His blood? No discourse of the eye with the objects of vision will express this consubstantiating act of faith; for when the object of sight hath been perused, yea, and devoured by the sight, it continueth an outward and separate object still; and when the ear hath listened to the sound of the human voice, or of any instrument of music, the object which caused the same continueth outward still. Nor is there any other act or function of human life which bringeth its object into consubstantiation with it, but this one of eating and of drinking; wherefore, I say, there is not any language capable of expressing that uniting act of faith but this which the Lord employeth. Not that the use of seeing and of hearing is thereby excluded from the mystery of faith, but that they are only lower and preparatory parts of the mystery. For Christ took a body which was beheld by the sight of His disciples; and He uttered words which were heard by the hearing of the ear; but the sight of His body and of all the works which it did, the hearing of His voice and of all the words which it spake, did only prepare the way for that saving act of faith which taketh the substance of His humanity and appropriateth it to ourselves: so that He shall dwell in us, and we in Him; and as He was seen, we shall be seen; and as He spake, we shall also speak. While He is merely beheld, He is but outward; while He is merely heard, He is but outward; and how can He then be represented as becoming inward, but by being eaten, and by being drunk? In like manner, I reckon that all which is recorded of His life, from the cradle unto Calvary, yea, and of all the miracles which He did, is but answerable to that beholding of His person which is proper to the eye. This is what they call historical evidence; which, I say, though it may be preparatory to the faith of consubstantiation, hath in itself no part thereof, being only a well-meant endeavour to recall the certainty of the Lord's incarnation and abode upon the earth. Answerable also to the faith of the ear, is the hearing of the voice of the preacher of the gospel, which, again, is also preparatory to, but is not itself, the consubstantiating act of faith. Most necessary is it, therefore, and of the last importance, that in addition to the written word, which is, as it were, the portraiture of Christ's visible living substance, set forth in promise, in type, in law, in history, and every other form by which the wisdom of God could prepare the expectation, and retain the remembrance, of that life which occupied but three short years and a half; and in addition to a living ministry, and a system of visible ordinances, which do, as it were, continue the voice of the Saviour to all ages, and make it heard over all countries; and which, taken at the best and highest estimate of it, can only approach to, and never surpass, the very living voice of Christ,—I say, it is most necessary that, in addition to these two subjects for the eye and ear of faith to peruse, there should be a third and far more important subject for the eating and drinking of faith, which may continually keep before the Church that function of faith, so much higher than the function of sight and hearing, to wit, the function of taking hold of Christ Himself, and consubstantiating Him with ourselves. Now, this third and highest office is served to the believer by the sacrament of the Lord's supper; whose distinctive peculiarity is this, that passing beyond the written word, which addresseth Christ's person to the eye of faith, and passing beyond the preached word, which addresseth Christ's voice to the ear of faith, it doth present the body and blood of Christ, that is, the very human subsistence of Christ, unto the mouth of faith, to be, by eating and drinking, consubstantiated with the life of faith, and to impart unto the inward man of faith those very self-same properties, and qualities, and thoughts, and acts, and words, and sufferings, and rejoicings, which belong unto Christ as He is the Son of man. Take away this mystery from the sacrament of the supper, and you take away the doctrine of union from the Church. Take away the real presence unto faith of Christ's body and blood from the communion, and you take away from faith the hope, the power, yea, the very idea of realising any such union with Christ, as Christ hath with the Father; and the saving faith of Christ is reduced to what indeed it hath become, the mere vision of the intellect, the mere approval of the evidence of written or spoken testimony; and from henceforth, amen to the communion of the saints; amen to the unity of the Church, which I endeavour, however rudely, to represent that holy communion; amen, also, to the indwelling of the Holy Ghost, to the headship of the Son, and to the faith-bestowing prerogative of the Father.

Our fathers, at the Reformation, found this doctrine of the real presence of Christ in the sacrament depraved by the priesthood of Rome by the most damnable adjunct of transubstantiation, and consecrated, debased, into the ground of all idolatry, the adoration of the mass; compared with the capital enormity of which, all image-worship, picture-worship, relic-worship, yea, and idol-worship, is but as a small offence; and finding it so, it was a great act of faith and discrimination in our fathers, or rather, I should say, a great work of God's Holy Spirit, that they were able to separate the holy substance from the most unholy intermixture, and preserve it free from all sensual interpretation. But in these times the state of things is wholly changed: the real presence is confounded with transubstantiation; the highest prerogative of faith, to feed upon the body of Christ always, and to discern the same in the bread and wine of the supper, is denied, or most imperfectly declared; and, in consequence thereof, the whole fruitfulness of faith, to dwell in Christ, and to bring Christ to dwell in us,—to suffer with Christ, to rise with Christ, to partake with Him in heavenly blessings, and sit with Him in heavenly places,—this, this, the true character, and, I may say, very definition of saving faith, is now lost, or imperfectly uttered in the Churches. And, therefore, it becometh necessary that we restore unto the sacrament what our fathers never took away from it, and assert that Christ's body and blood is really and truly present therein, and really and truly handled, partaken, and appropriated by every believer, so as that they dwell in Him, and He in them, even as the Father dwelleth in Christ, and Christ in the Father. And corresponding to these three spheres of faith,—the faith of sight, the faith of hearing, and the faith which incorporates, or, I may say, the faith of eating and drinking,—there are in the holy supper three acts done: first, The eye of faith looks upon the elements when they have been consecrated, and beholdeth in them Christ evidently set forth crucified in the midst of us, His body broken, His blood shed for us; secondly, Faith opens her ear, and hears the Son of God saying unto His disciples, "Take, eat; this is my body given for you." "This is the blood of the new covenant; drink ye all of it." "Whoso eateth my flesh, and drinketh my blood, hath eternal life; and I will raise him up at the last day.... He that eateth my flesh, and drinketh my blood, dwelleth in me, and I in him. As the living Father hath sent me, and I live by the Father; so he that eateth me, even he shall live by me." Hearing these words from the lips of the Lord, our faith no longer doubteth, but eagerly desireth this food, saying, "Lord, evermore give us this bread." But this is not all: there is a third and higher act of faith which layeth hold upon that body, and eateth and drinketh its flesh and blood, and incorporates with itself that which it had delighted to behold and receiveth into itself—that which the Lord had promised.

This is an essential part of saving faith—its appropriating act which constitutes the oneness between Christ and His members; and therefore it is not at one particular time, but at all times, to be done—seeing, I hold, that there is no saving faith without this incorporating and appropriating act; and to shew forth this, as an essential part of saving faith, is the very end of the supper,—and to maintain this doctrine for ever, that no faith on Christ is worthy of that name which doth not consubstantiate Him with us, and us with Him. This is the very end of that discourse which we have opened, to the attainment of which end the doctrine of the real presence of Christ's body and blood, in the sacrament of the supper, unto faith, is as necessary as the doctrine of the Spirit's presence, in the sacrament of baptism, is necessary to the doctrine of regeneration. And, therefore, because we would have you, dear brethren, to enter fully into the mystery of faith, have we been at pains to explain this doctrine of the real presence with so much care, and to defend it with equal diligence from the superstition of the Papists upon the one hand, and the derision of the intellectuals on the other. And now may the Lord bless what hath been said, and to His name be the praise and the glory.

It is not enough to say, in answer to the great doctrine of the real presence of Christ's body unto faith in the supper, that faith realiseth Christ as everywhere present; for, though it be true that in His divine nature He is omnipotent, yet is He not so in His human nature; or His body and blood with which, and with which only, this sacrament hath to do, and this human nature which was crucified for us, and which is now divided into parts, and delivered for the nourishment of His Church, is a substance which is nowhere present but in the consecrated elements of the Lord's Supper. His glorious body is, indeed, far removed in the heavens, at the right hand of God, but His humbled, bruised, and broken body abideth still with the Church, and is to the Church presented, and by the Church received, in the sacrament of the supper; so that by faith feeding thereon, and being incorporated therewith, we do perform the same offices in the world which, during His flesh, He performed. I mean to say, that it is not the glorious subsistence of Christ's body, now in the heavens, but it is the humiliated subsistence of His body, while on the earth, into the fellowship of which we eat and drink. And this, I say again, is not to sight subsisting anywhere, but to faith presented in the supper of the Lord; and nowhere but there only, where it is presented, can faith realise its presence.

Now, if any one refuse to acknowledge the real presence of the humbled humanity of Christ in the holy supper, I ask him, And what then is present? There can only remain bread and wine. And what to do with faith hath bread and wine? If it be said, Christ's words are also present; I answer, that the ear doth not incorporate sound, or the material of sound; and though Christ's words be truly spirit and life, yet is it not by the hearing of them, but by the believing of them, that they become so. And how shall you mark this most important distinction between a belief which incorporates, and a belief which doth but hear the outward voice? Besides, it is to the full as great a mystery that the Holy Spirit should inhabit a voice, as that He should inhabit bread and wine; and it is to the full as great a mystery that, by the sense of hearing, the Holy Ghost should make access to our souls, as by the sense of eating. But the truth is, there is no proportion whatever between the sensible and the spiritual, except inasmuch as the sensible doth, in its kind, symbolise the spiritual, in its kind; which kinds, however, are totally diverse from one another. Now, I say that the action of eating and drinking, which is the proper action of the supper, and not the action of hearing, which is not proper to it, but rather proper to the ordinance of preaching, is the only action of the senses which doth, or can, convey to the understanding of man the act of the Spirit; which, being endued by faith from God, doth receive the humanity of Christ, as it was heretofore sacrificed on Calvary, and incorporate it into the same substance with ourselves, to the end of our fulfilling the same functions of the Holy Spirit which He fulfilled during the days of His flesh.

The end, therefore, dear brethren, of the whole matter, and the object for which I have preached this discourse, is to instruct you that the act of faith, which you are this day to do or to witness done, is the constant and perpetual act of faith by which a Christian lives. The believer lives evermore upon the body and blood of Christ; and the believer is, therefore, ever ready to sit down at the table of the Lord, just as a hungry man is ever ready for food. The food also is ever present unto faith, whether the believer be at the table of the Lord or not. So that where the ordinance cannot be had, little loss is sustained to the true believer. But where the ordinance can be had, a true believer both denies the Lord, and denies himself, in abstaining from it. He denies the Lord, inasmuch as he neither obeys His commandment, nor commemorates His death, nor continues the mystery thereof for the profit of generations yet unborn, nor draws near to the open fountain of Divine life. He denies himself, inasmuch as having hungered, and food having been provided for him, he will not draw near to partake the same. There is no fasting ordinance for faith, which is never in repletion, but always in leanness. Faith hath a continual hunger and thirst, and seizeth with avidity upon every table which is spread for the children in the wilderness. Come, therefore, hither, O ye hungered people: come, therefore, hither, O ye thirsty people. The Spirit and the bride say, Come; and let every one that is athirst say, Come; and partake the waters of life freely. This is the only table on which the elements of eternal life are set forth. This table is the only assurance of food on this side the grave, as baptism is the only assurance of life. Come, then, and revive the pledge of life eternal, until ye are privileged to sit down at that table which shall never be drawn.

www.ingramcontent.com/pod-product-compliance
Lightning Source LLC
Chambersburg PA
CBHW070651300426
44111CB00013B/2368